THE
MARX–ENGELS
CYCLOPEDIA

SYMBOLS

→ The **arrow** refers to entries in Volume I (*Marx-Engels Chronicle*). It points to a specific **year and paragraph** in the chronology. In Volume I it points right (→) or left (←) depending on whether it refers ahead or behind. In Volumes II and III it points right only.

The "**number**" symbol refers to entries in Volume II (*Marx-Engels Register*), in conjunction with "ME," "M," or "E." For example, #ME74 = Marx and Engels' *Holy Family*; #M129 = Marx's *Capital*; #E23 = Engels' *Anti-Dühring*; etc.

* The **asterisk** refers only to the entries in Volume III (*Marx-Engels Glossary*). Marking a name (person, periodical, etc.), it means that there is an entry for this name in the *Glossary*; it is used only when there is special reason to signal the entry.

+ The **plus** symbol following a date means indefinite continuance; e.g., 1834+ means "From 1834 on. . . . "

/ The **solidus or slash mark** generally means "or," as in "M/E" (Marx or Engels). Similarly, "1834/35" means "1834 or 1835."

% The **percent sign,** used in Volume II (*Marx-Engels Register*), indicates a *partial* translation.

++ The **double plus sign,** used in Volume II (*Marx-Engels Register*), *indicates additional information or notes.*

DATE ABBREVIATIONS

Months: Months may be abbreviated with a three-letter form, without a period, except for June or July, which are spelled out; e.g., Jan, Feb, Mar, Apr, May, Aug, Sep, Oct, Nov, Dec.

Parts of the Month: In the absence of exact information, parts of the month may be indicated using the letters A, B, C, and D to stand for the four quarters of the month. For example,

Mar A = beginning of March
Mar AB = first half of March
Mar M = middle of March

Mar CD = last half of March
Mar D = end of March

"About" Dates: Before a date or its symbol, the word *about* may be represented by "c." (for "circa"). For example,

Mar c.7 = about Mar 7
c.1853 = about 1853
Mar c.A = about the beginning of March
Mar c.CD = about the last half of March

But the common abbreviation "ca." (also for "circa") may be used with the same meaning in other circumstances.

ABBREVIATIONS FOR MARX, ENGELS

The letters M and E (without periods) are often used for the names Marx and Engels, especially in concise presentations of information; ME = Marx and Engels (in *Register* titles), M–E = Marx and Engels (in certain other contexts), M/E = Marx or Engels.

For the full list of abbreviations, see page xv.

VOLUME III
of the Marx–Engels Cyclopedia

THE MARX–ENGELS GLOSSARY

Glossary to the Chronicle and Register, and Index to the Glossary

By HAL DRAPER

with the assistance of the Center for Socialist History

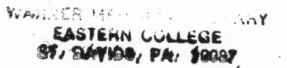

SCHOCKEN BOOKS • NEW YORK

This work is dedicated to the memory of

RICHARD BROADHEAD (1942–1985),

first (founding) Executive Director of the
Center for Socialist History.

*I have never known a more devoted champion
of socialist democracy. I have never known a better
person. We can fill his job but not his place in our
lives.*

H.D.

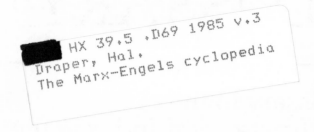

First published by Schocken Books 1986
10 9 8 7 6 5 4 3 2 1   86 87 88 89
Copyright © 1986 by Hal Draper

Library of Congress Cataloging-in-Publication Data
Draper, Hal.
      The Marx-Engels glossary.
      (The Marx-Engels cyclopedia ; v. 3)
      Includes index.
      1. Marx, Karl, 1818–1883—Language—Glossaries, etc.
2. Engels, Friedrich, 1820–1895—Language—Glossaries,
etc.   I. Center for Socialist History (Berkeley,
Calif.) II. Title. III. Series: Draper, Hal.
Marx-Engels cyclopedia ; v. 3.
HX39.5.D69   1985 vol. 3   335.4′014   85–25037

Designed by Nancy Dale Muldoon
Manufactured in the United States of America
ISBN 0-8052-4002-0

Contents

THE MARX–ENGELS GLOSSARY

General Introduction

The *Marx-Engels Cyclopedia* (*MEC*) comprises three reference works made one by interreference and interindexing:

Volume I: The *Marx-Engels Chronicle*. A day-to-day chronology of Marx and Engels' lives and activities.

Volume II: The *Marx-Engels Register*. A bibliography of Marx and Engels' individual writings.

Volume III: The *Marx-Engels Glossary*. A dictionary of all proper names mentioned in Volumes I and II: persons, periodicals, parties, organizations, etc.

Each volume can be used independently. At the same time, its usefulness is enhanced by the fact that the other volumes offer additional channels of access to its contents.

For example, Volume I, the *Marx-Engels Chronicle*, refers under the appropriate dates of composition and publication to the individual writings, by *Register* number if not title. Thus it offers a *chronological* mode of access to the entries in the *Marx-Engels Register* (Volume II), which are organized there alphabetically. Contrariwise, the entries in the *Register* are indexed to locations in the *Chronicle* (Volume I). The *Marx-Engels Glossary* (Volume III) indexes references to a given name occurring in Volume I or II.

In short, whether you start with a title, an event, or a name, you can work your way from the known fact to other sources of information. As additional aids, there are a number of special lists, particularly in Volume II, directed to the bibliographical control of Marx and Engels' contributions to certain periodicals, notably the *New York Daily Tribune*.

Not included in this *Cyclopedia* is another kind of work: a dictionary of ideas and terms, an exposition of Marx's thought in alphabetical format. This would be a laudable enterprise, but of a different sort altogether. Rather, this *Cyclopedia* is dedicated to hard facts. In an area as inevitably ideological as that of Marx studies, hard facts are not less but more important: they are moorings. True, one cannot hope to eliminate all ideological reflections from such a work; but at any rate the facts are here.

SOURCES

The main source of the information contained in this *Cyclopedia* is the scientific output of the Institute of Marxism–Leninism (IML) of Moscow, together with its predecessors and its collaborating institutions. Its most important predecessor was the original Marx–Engels–Lenin Institute founded by D. Ryazanov; its present main collaborator is the IML of East Germany.

These institutes, with their publishing affiliates and associates, have over the years accomplished a prodigious work. At the same time, like all scholarly work in the world of the Communist bureaucratic-collectivist states, this job has been done under well-known political constraints, which need not concern us except to explain that the IML output must be subjected to constant checking. In addition, the material quarried from IML sources must be compared with and supplemented by information available from other sources, as far as possible.

The principal IML sources, often referred to in the volumes of this *Cyclopedia*, are the following four editions of Marx and Engels' work:

1. The *Marx-Engels Werke* (*MEW*), published in East Germany. As this is written, it is still the only near-complete, or the nearest-complete, edition of Marx and Engels' works—in German only. Its notes and appendices are a mine of information.

2. The so-called *MEGA*—customary name for the old and original *Marx-Engels Gesamtausgabe* of 1927–1935—is still useful for some purposes; but of course it covered only up to 1848, and it has been largely superseded even for that period.

3. The *New Mega* (to use my own designation) got started in 1975, and as this is written, it has gone only about a seventh of the way toward its planned 100 volumes, which may not be completed until some time after the year 2001. Though it was given the old *Gesamtausgabe* name by the IML, it is really an independent project, not a continuation of the old *MEGA*.

4. The new English edition of Marx and Engels' *Collected Works* (*MECW*), likewise in process of publication, is little more than a quarter of the way to its final Volume 50, perhaps due also in the next century.

Smaller-scale publications have made some limited contributions as well; see the Sources and Translations ("ST") List in Volume II.

A definitive summing-up of the field covered by *MEC* is still some distance away. All I can do is give the state of information as of now—with many lacunae and a sprinkling of question marks.

A reference work of this sort is not by nature a one-man project, and there are bound to be errors of omission and commission. Alas, in the course of the present work I have found not a few mistakes even in the *Marx-Engels Werke*, which is usually a reliable source of raw facts; and the *New Mega* apparently suffers from even more. Alert users of this *Cyclopedia*, I am afraid, may find some here too; and I request that these be communicated to me through the publisher, with an eye to a revised edition.

TECHNICAL POINTS

Spelling. American spelling is used throughout, except in direct quotes from British sources and in British names. Thus there was a *Labor Standard* in New York and a *Labour Standard* in London; the group that met in Manchester called itself a Labour Parliament, but Marx's article on it in the *New York Daily Tribune* called it the Labor Parliament; and so on.

Good English. I am a militant proponent of using *contact, enthuse,* and *feature* as verbs, of splitting infinitives at will, of using *hopefully* like the best English writers, and of other practices condemned by certain misguided literati. I mention this only to absolve the publisher and its editors of any responsibility for these alleged deviations.

German Spelling. When using indexes and other alphabetized lists, readers should know that in German *Carl* and *Karl*, or *Conrad* and *Konrad*, are often interchangeable, and that therefore many names appear in both forms in different places. The same applies to some place names (Carlsbad, Coblenz, etc.). I have tended to give the right of way to the K. Also, there are some cases where the common English name of a place differs from the native name (for example, Hanover/Hannover); this text uses the English form, though alternative forms are explained in the *Glossary*.

Alphabetization. All alphabetization in this work follows the so-called Anglo-American rules, used in library catalogs. German alphabetization, which is different in several respects, has influenced some American publications (especially translations), creating some technical confusion. The following points should be noted: (1) Alphabetization is word by word, not letter by letter—except perforce in the "List of Abbreviations." (2) The German umlauted vowel is treated as if followed by an *e*: that is, ä = ae, ö = oe, ü = ue; just as "Mc" or "M' " is treated as if spelled out "Mac" no matter how a given name is written. (3) An initial definite or indefinite article is ignored for alphabetizing purposes, in English as in other languages. This pertains to the English *the, a, an*; the German *der, die, das, ein, eine*, etc.; the French *le, la, les, l'*, *un, une*; and so on, including the Portuguese article *O*.

Manuscripts. Information given here on a number of unpublished manuscripts by Marx or Engels is necessarily tentative, and probably defective, being based on incomplete descriptions. This cannot be fully remedied until, and unless, these manuscripts are published in the *New Mega*. Present information often comes from excerpts published in some collection by the IML. In some cases available references to some manuscripts are so fragmentary that I have preferred to include nothing at this time.

Number Interpolation. The *Register*, also the "ST" List (both in Volume II), is numbered from 1 on, in alphabetical order; but provision has had to be made for revisions, requiring the insertion of new numbers into the sequence. This has already proved necessary in the course of work on this *Cyclopedia*, and will no doubt continue to be necessary for future revisions. For this reason I have used a flexible decimal system. For example, between 150 and 151, the first interpolated number is 150.5; a future interpolation between 150 and 150.5 may be 150.3. Thus the revised list remains in numerical order.

THE CENTER FOR SOCIALIST HISTORY

The Center for Socialist History in Berkeley, California, has assisted this project in its later stages, since the Center itself was only recently established. Its help has been invaluable, and I am happy to acknowledge it. Steve Diamond, who has been associated with me throughout the work on the *Cyclopedia*, is also a director of the Center.

The Center's interest in this project will postdate publication too. This

Cyclopedia is published without a comprehensive subject index; still, some users may want to trace, say, Marx's views on party organization, war, anarchism, or some other theme. A "Selected Subjects Index" is planned by the Center, and possibly also other research aids. Inquiries should be directed to the Center for Socialist History, 2633 Etna, Berkeley, CA 94704.

H.D.

Preface to Volume III

Volume III of the *Marx–Engels Cyclopedia* is the *Marx–Engels Glossary*. It gives a brief account of each person, periodical, party, and organization, etc., mentioned in the *Marx–Engels Chronicle* (Volume I) and the *Marx–Engels Register* (Volume II). In fact, all proper names are covered. Each entry ends with an index to the *Chronicle* and the *Register*.

ENTRY INFORMATION

Most space is given to persons. The entries aim to provide the following information.

Names and Dates High priority has been given to establishing the full, accurate form of all names and accurate life dates. The reader will find that these are given variously in different reference works and histories; much of this variation is due to simple error.

Basic Biographical Information For famous personages, amply covered in general encyclopedias, only minimal information is given here. For example, Shelley is identified here with five words. These entries devote space to a different question: the person's relation to Marx and Engels in thought or action.

General encyclopedias tend to be defective in treating socialist figures—rather, in not treating them at all. Therefore many socialist figures are here given a somewhat longer account than would perhaps be justified by their importance. A conditioning fact is that no general encyclopedia (or "dictionary") of socialist history or biography exists in English, or has ever existed. (I expect that the Center for Socialist History will remedy this in a few years, but meanwhile it is a hard fact.) To some extent this *Glossary* has to be a partial substitute for the encyclopedia that isn't there.

Relation to Marx and Engels This information is, in principle, the main function of the *Glossary* entry. To be sure, part of this information is already given by the *Chronicle* or *Register* item that is being indexed; and the *Glossary* does not necessarily repeat this content. It may devote itself to a fuller account of the relation or to its background. This often explains why certain aspects are treated and not others. Where the relation is simply that Marx or Engels read a work by the subject person, attention is given to exact data on the book(s) concerned.

But an entry is not necessarily tied only to the specific references in the *Chronicle* or the *Register*. The person's general importance to and role in the socialist movement of the time may also be covered. There are cases, therefore, where persons who have perhaps only a single index reference at the end of the entry are given more space than this one mention might seem to justify.

Bibliographical References The entries do not include a bibliography of works about the subject person. But in the few cases where an outstanding work of this sort does exist (especially in English), it is mentioned. This reflects the realities of the extant literature: there are not many noteworthy achievements in socialist biography, even if one settled for less than, say, E. P. Thompson's *William Morris* or Yvonne Kapp's *Eleanor Marx*.

I have made extensive use of the multivolume *Dictionnaire biographique du mouvement ouvrier français (DBMOF)*, edited by J. Maitron, but it is mentioned only in connection with special problems. Let this stand for an enthusiastic acknowledgment of its contribution.

The preceding lines have sometimes sounded apologetic for making some entries too lengthy. In many cases the reader may be more impressed by the brevity and inadequacy of an entry. Of these I can say only that, as far as I know, more information is not available. Socialist history is full of characters who cross the stage briefly, transients who are, however, sometimes of considerable importance or interest. (The example that comes to mind first is Helen Macfarlane.) If any reader is aware of information that does not seem to have been used, I would appreciate hearing about it, via the publisher.

While the *Glossary* indexes the *Chronicle* and the *Register*, the Supplementary Index (at the end of this volume) indexes the *Glossary* itself.

FORM OF PRESENTATION

The reader should note the following points about the form of presentation.

1. The entry name is in boldface. In the case of persons, boldface is used *only* for the surname or family-name elements; given names are in lightface; titles and other non-name elements are in italics. This typographical pattern applies to all elements *preceding* the parenthesis containing the life dates.

2. The regrettable practice of entering a person under an "encyclopedia name" has been shunned. An "encyclopedia name" is one used only in encyclopedias and official birth certificates—like Jean Joseph Charles Louis Blanc, who was known to mortals as Louis Blanc. In these cases, the word *full* introduces the whole string, but the entry is under "Blanc, Louis." The same result is obtained in simpler cases by putting *dispensable* first names in parentheses, in particular if the dispensable name is *not* the first one. Thus, "Brousse, Paul (Louis Marie)" might also have been listed as "Brousse, Paul; *full* Paul Louis Marie." Also I have tried to pay special attention to the way an author signed his own books, since this may be the form of name looked for.

3. While M and E stand for Marx and Engels here as elsewhere in the *MEC*, the last initial of a subject person (with a period) may be used in the entry for that person—*but in that entry only.* Thus in the article on Bebel, the abbreviation "B." stands for the subject, Bebel. But this is not done for persons whose name begins with M or E.

4. Book titles are often given in short form, especially in the case of the many 18th- and 19th-century books with sesquipedalian names. This is *not* usually signaled by suspension points (. . .) after the title.

5. The asterisk is used, as elsewhere, for names entered in the *Glossary*, but this is done selectively; hence it constitutes a suggestion to look up the starred name.

6. Periodicals are entered with at least the following information, if available: place of publication, duration (dates), periodicity, publisher and/or editor(s). The language of the periodical is stated if it would otherwise be in doubt, and the periodical's status as an organ (of a party, etc.) is given if necessary; otherwise its political tendency, if possible. The name is entered, in principle, as it appeared on the masthead; that is, the *Times* (of London), but *New York Times; Allgemeine Zeitung* (Augsburg) and not *Augsburg(er) Allgemeine Zeitung.*

7. Names of parties and organizations are entered in English, followed by the original-language name where this information is at hand.

8. Initials are alphabetized as in library catalogs (see the explanation in the General Introduction), not letter by letter. See, for example, "E.T." in the *Glossary,* or "A.P.C." in the Supplementary Index.

H.D.

Abbreviations

This list covers all volumes of the *Marx–Engels Cyclopedia*. Alphabetization is letter-by-letter. Some standard abbreviations in general use may not be included.

Many of these abbreviations are used only in certain limited contexts, where their meanings are probably clear anyway. There is one extreme case, the letter E, which is used in three ways: for "Engels," throughout the *Cyclopedia*; for "English" *only* after the entry titles in the *Register*; and for "East" in common geographical names.

For symbols and the main date abbreviations, see the material facing the title page of this volume.

A	*In dates:* early part (first quarter) of month
AB	*In dates:* first half of month
Addr	*Esp in titles:* Address
AFL	American Federation of Labor
Angl.	Anglicized (form)
App.	Appendix
Apr	April
assoc(s)	association(s)
Aug	August
Aust.	Austria; Austrian
AZ	*Allgemeine Zeitung* (of Augsburg)
b.	born
Bd.	Band (Ger. = volume); or Board
Belg.	Belgium; Belgian
betw	between
bk	book
BM	British Museum (Library)
BM Cat.	British Museum Library catalog
BN	Bibliothèque Nationale (Paris)
BN Cat.	Bibliothèque Nationale catalog
Brit.	British
c.	*With dates:* circa, about
ca.	*In text:* circa, about
Can.	Canada; Canadian
CC	Central Committee
CC/CL	Central Committee of the Communist League
CCC	Communist Correspondence Committee (Brussels)
CC/NG	Central Committee of the National Guard (in Paris Commune)
CD	*In dates:* second half of month
cf.	compare
Ch.	Chapter
Chron.	*Marx–Engels Chronicle* (Vol. 1 of this *Cyclopedia*)
CL	Communist League
CL/CC	Same as CC/CL, q.v.
com	communist
comm	committee
commsn	commission
cont'd	continued
contribd	contributed

corr secy	corresponding secretary
CP	Communist party
CPC	Communist publishing complex. (See Preface to Vol. II.)
CPSFW	Cooperative Publishing Society of Foreign Workers in the USSR. (See Preface to Vol. II.)
Czech.	Czechoslovakia; Czechoslovakian
(D)	*In Register:* date; dateline
d.	dated
DB	See *DBMOF*
DBMOF	Jean Maitron, ed., *Dictionnaire biographique du mouvement ouvrier français*
DBZ	*Deutsche-Brüsseler-Zeitung* (Brussels)
DDR	Deutsche Demokratische Republic (East Germany)
Dec	December
Demo	Democratic
Demo Wochenblatt	*Demokratisches Wochenblatt.* (See *Glossary.*)
DFJ	*Deutsch-Französische Jahrbücher* (Paris)
do.	*In Register:* ditto (i.e., same translation title as the preceding)
D&A	Dubiosa and Apocrypha. (See Preface to Vol. II.)
E	Engels
E.	*In geog. names:* East; eastern
[E]	*In Register, after entry title:* English
ed	editor
ed bd	editorial board
ed by	edited by
ed note	editorial note
ed staff	editorial staff
edit	editorial
edn	edition
Eng.	England; English
erron.	erroneous(ly)
esp	especially
et al.	and others
Exec	Executive (Committee, Board)
Feb	February
fl.	*In dates:* flourished
Flem.	Flemish
FLPH	Foreign Languages Publishing House (Moscow)
FP	*Free Press* (London)
Fr.	France; French
GC	General Council (of the IWMA)
GC/IWMA	General Council of the IWMA
GCFI	The set titled *General Council of the First International.* (See ST/21.)
Gen.	General
gen secy	general secretary
Ger.	Germany; German
GGWA	General German Workers Association (Lassalleans). (See *Glossary.*)
Gr Brit	Great Britain
GWEA	German Workers Educational Association. (See *Glossary.*)
Hung.	Hungary; Hungarian
i.a.	inter alia, inter alii; among others, among other things
IISH	International Institute for Social History (Amsterdam)

ILP	Independent Labour party (Brit.)
IML	Institute of Marxism-Leninism (Moscow or E. Berlin). (See *Glossary* for name variation.)
incl	including
ind	independent (translation)
info	information
installs	installments
int'l	international
Int'l Pub	International Publishers (New York)
intro	introduction
intro note	introductory note
irreg.	irregular
It.	Italy; Italian
Ital.	Italian
IWMA	International Working Men's Association (the First International)
IWMA/GC	General Council of the IWMA
J.	*In titles:* Journal
Jan	January
Kerr	Charles H. Kerr, publishers (Chicago)
KMC	The book *Karl Marx, Chronik seines Lebens* (Moscow, 1934). (See Preface to Vol. I.)
KZ	*Kölnische Zeitung* (Cologne)
Labour Mo.	*Labour Monthly* (London)
L., Laura	Laura (Marx) Lafargue. (See "*Marx, Laura," in *Glossary*.)
Lib	Library
lib-lab	liberal-labor
Lon	*In imprints:* London
ltr	letter
L&W	Lawrence & Wishart, publishers (London)
M	Marx
M	*In dates:* middle of month
M&E	Marx and Engels
Mar	March
mar.	married
ME	Marx and Engels (as joint authors, etc.)
M–E	Marx–Engels
M/E	Marx or Engels
MEC	*Marx–Engels Cyclopedia*
MECW	Marx–Engels, *Collected Works.* (See the General Introduction.)
MEGA	*Marx–Engels Gesamtausgabe* (1927–35), the old *MEGA*. (For the new edition, see *New Mega*, below. See also the General Introduction.)
ME:SW	Marx–Engels, *Selected works in three volumes* (Moscow, 1969–70). (See ST/ME64.)
MEW	*Marx–Engels Werke* (Berlin, 1956–68). (See the General Introduction.)
MEW Daten	The Chronology section in *MEW*. (See the Preface to Vol. I.)
min	*In cabinet titles:* Minister
Mos	*In imprints:* Moscow
MP	Member of Parliament
ms	manuscript
mss	manuscripts
N.	North; northern
NAC	*New American Cyclopaedia* (New York)

N.B.	Nota bene
n.d.	no date
NDZ	*Neue Deutsche Zeitung* (Darmstadt, Frankfurt)
Neth.	Netherlands
New Mega	New edition, *Marx–Engels Gesamtausgabe* (Berlin, 1975+), in progress. (See the General Introduction.)
NG	National Guard (Paris)
NMW	*New Moral World* (London), Owenite organ
no.	number
Nov	November
NOZ	*Neue Oder-Zeitung* (Breslau)
NRZ	*Neue Rheinische Zeitung* (Cologne, 1848–49), ed by Marx
NRZ-Revue	*Neue Rheinische Zeitung politisch-ökonomische Revue* (London, 1850), magazine, ed by Marx
NS	*Northern Star* (Leeds, London)
n.s.	*In periodical dating:* new series
N/s	Not signed; no signature
N/t	No title
NUC	National Union Catalog
N.W.	Northwest; northwestern
NY	New York
NYC	New York City
NYDT	*New York Daily Tribune*
NYLNCo	New York Labor News Company (SLP publishers)
NYSWT	*New York Semi-Weekly Tribune* (edition of *NYDT*)
NYWT	*New York Weekly Tribune* (edition of *NYDT*)
NZ	*Neue Zeit* (Stuttgart)
N-Ztg	*National-Zeitung* (Berlin)
Oct	October
organizn	organization
orig	original; originally
(P)	*In Register:* published; publishing data
para	paragraph
PMG	*Pall Mall Gazette* (London)
Pol.	Poland; Polish
polit	political
polit eco	political economy
PP	*People's Paper* (London)
(P/P)	*In Register:* posthumously published
Pr	*In imprints:* Press
pres	president
prob	probably
prof	professor
Prog Pub	Progress Publishers (Moscow)
Prov Government	Provisional Government
pseud.	pseudonym
pubd	published
publ	publication
pub'r	publisher
pubs	publishes
q.v.	which see
re; in re	regarding; in regard to
(Re)	*In Register:* reprint, republication
rec'd	received
ref	reference

reorganizn	reorganization
repr	representative
repr'd	reprinted
repubd	republished
republ	republication
repubs	republishes
resp	respectively
retrans	retranslation
retransd	retranslated
retrotrans	retrotranslation
rev	revised (edition)
Rev	*In titles: Review*
Revol. Zent	Revolutionäre Zentralisation (group)
Russ.	Russia; Russian
RZ	*Rheinische Zeitung* (Cologne), ed by Marx
S.	South; southern
(S)	*In Register:* Source. (See Vol. II, "Guide to Register Entry.")
Scot.	Scotland; Scottish
S-D	Social-Democratic
SDF	Social Democratic Federation (Brit.)
SDWP	Social-Democratic Workers party. (See *Glossary.*)
S.E.	Southeast; southeastern
secy	secretary
Sep	September
SL	Socialist League (Brit.)
SLP	Socialist Labor party (U.S.)
SP	Socialist party
Sp.	Spain
[Sp.]	*In Register:* Spanish
Span.	Spanish
specif	specifically
SPGB	Socialist Party of Great Britain
S-R	Socialist-Revolutionary
ST	Sources & Translations: see the "ST" List in Vol. II.
Sub-Comm	Sub-Committee (of the IWMA/GC); see → 64:30, note, in the *Chronicle.*
subseq(ly)	subsequent(ly)
SUCR	Société Universelle des Communistes Révolutionnaires. (See #ME80 or *Glossary.*)
Switz.	Switzerland
S.W.	Southwest; southwestern
SWT	See *NYSWT.*
t.	tome (Fr. = volume)
TfD	*Telegraph für Deutschland* (Frankfurt, Hamburg)
t.p.	title page
(Tr)	*In Register:* translation(s) into English
trans	translation
transd	translated
TU	trade union
U.	University
UGWA	Union of German Workers Associations. (See *Glossary.*)
unanim	unanimously
Univ.	University
unpubd	unpublished
U.S.	United States

v.	volume
vice-pres	vice-president
VJ	*Volunteer Journal*
vol.	volume(s)
vs	versus
W.	West; western
W.S.W.	West-southwest
(W)	*In Register:* written; data on composition
WA	Workers Association
WEA	Workers Educational Association
WP	Workers party. (See "French Workers party" in *Glossary*.)
WT	See *NYWT*
W&P	*In Chronicle rubrics:* Writings and Publications
Ztg	Zeitung (in German newspaper titles)

THE
MARX–ENGELS
GLOSSARY

A

Aachen (Ger.); *Fr.* Aix-la-Chapelle City, near the Belgian border. → 44:35; 47:18; 61:18; 69:56.

Abarbanel Banker in the Paris area; friend of the M family from its Paris days; died in Jan 1863 (all this according to M's letters). Y. Kapp, in *E. Marx*, calls him "Arbabanel" (without explanation) in Vol. 1, but omits his name from the Vol. 2 index. *Note:* There was a European family, orig from Portugal, later in Spain and Italy, boasting Jewish scholars as well as financiers, since the 15th century, which spelled its name Abrabanel, Abravanel, or Abarbanel. → 62:20, 62.

Abd-el-Kader or **Abdu-l-Kadir** (c.1807 to 1883) Leader of Arab national-liberation struggles against French conquest (1832–1847). General Bugeaud defeated him and his Moroccan allies at Isly (1844). He surrendered in 1847, was imprisoned in France till 1852, then settled in Turkey, later Damascus. #E12, E261.

Aberdeen, *Earl of* George Hamilton **Gordon** (1784 to 1860) British statesman, b. Edinburgh, Scottish family. Tory leader; "Peelite" (1850+). Foreign min (1828–1830) under Wellington and (1841–1846) under Peel; prime min in the coalition cabinet of 1852–1855 which entered the Crimean War, whose mismanagement forced Aberdeen's resignation. → 55:6, 9, 10. #M310, M950.

About, Edmond; *full* Edmond François Valentin (1828 to 1885) French journalist and man of letters. After returning to France from Athens, he pubd a book on Greece, a few novels, political pamphlets, writings on polit eco, e.g., *L'ABC du travailleur* (1868). He edited the influential *XIXe Siècle* (1872–c.1877/78). A "liberal" Bonapartist, he later turned to republicanism. —His brochure *Napoléon III et la Prusse* (pubd June 1860) was soon retitled *La Prusse en 1860*. In the *NYDT*, M gave excerpts from another 1860 brochure of his, *La Syrie et l'alliance Russe.* → 60:35. #M275.

Abt A bourgeois-liberal German journalist who in the early 1850s became an émigré in Geneva. In 1860 M described him as the secy of the bishop of Fribourg, Switz.; *KMC* identifies him as editior of the *Freiburger Kirchenzeitung.* —Abt played a role in the invention of the slanderous tales about M and others that Karl *Vogt disseminated; for details, see #M454, M372 (Chap. 2 in the latter). The Geneva GWEA had publicly denounced him as dishonest, leading to his further furious polemics and then to his expulsion by the assoc; whereupon in autumn 1861 Abt pubd a new attack, "K. Vogt and K. Marx," in a Gotha monthly. → 61:46, 49, 57.

Adam French Blanquist; described as either a tanner or leather blocker or a woodworker (camberer). Little is known about him, incl his full name. He had been a member of revolutionary secret societies in the Louis Philippe era; in 1848, on the staff of the communist journal *La Fraternité*; in June, a socialist candidate in the election. In 1850, an émigré in London, he was one of the Blanquist signers of the S.U.C.R. agreement (cf. #ME80). There is no trace of him after 1856. → 50:15. #ME80, ME171.

Adam and Eve Biblical figures. → 91:23.

Adirondack Mts. (upper NY state) → 88:30.

Adler, Friedrich (1879 to 1960) A leader of the Austrian Social-Democratic party; son of Viktor *Adler. He produced the first book edn of E's *Notes on the war* in the original English (see #E531) while he was a leader of the Vienna Union, the so-called Two-and-a-Half International (1921–1923); he later became secy of the revived Socialist International. #E531.

Adler, Georg (1863 to 1908) German economics prof at various universities. Having early rejected his youthful socialism, he turned to writing anti-Marxist histories of the movement. E read his *Rodbertus, der Begründer des wissenschaftlichen Sozialismus* (1884) and his *Geschichte der ersten sozialpolitischen Arbeiterbewegung in Deutschland* (1885) soon after publ. Later Adler wrote his *Geschichte des Sozialismus und Kommunismus* (1899). He came out for structural social reforms in the Katheder-socialist sense. → 85:39.

Adler, Viktor (1852 to 1918) Austrian socialist leader; b. Prague; the main founder and longtime leader of the Austrian Social-Democratic party. Trained as a physician, he moved to Vienna (1855); started socialist activity by 1886, publishing *Gleichheit*; founded and edited the *Arbeiter-Zeitung* (Vienna). He corresponded with E (1889–1895). Deputy to the Reichsrat (1905+). One of the leaders of the Second International, he eventually moved to its reformist wing. He died just as the Hapsburg Empire was collapsing. → 89:37, 38; 91:34, 37, 41; 92:9, 26, 28; 93:42, 44, 49; 94:4, 14, 29, 48; 95:4–7, 20, 33. #E342, #E345.

Advertiser (London) *See* Morning Advertiser.

Afghanistan → 57:33. #M651; E7.

Africa → 89:21. *See also* individual countries.

Ahriman → 83:21. *See also* Ormuzd.

Aikin, John (1747 to 1822) English physician (till his 1798 retirement) and writer, mainly of biographical works and a popular series *Evenings at home* (family readings); editor of the *Monthly Magazine* (1796–1807) and *Athenaeum* (1807–1809). He stressed a radical devotion to liberty of conscience. M excerpted his book *A description of the country from thirty to forty miles round Manchester* (1795). → 45:52. #M575.

Airey, Gen. Richard (1803 to 1881) English Army officer (1821+). In 1854 he was made quartermaster general in the Crimean War; held responsible (by all except his military superiors) for the scandalous mismanagement of supplies, which killed more British soldiers than the enemy. E wrote that he was one of the officers under Raglan who "have been charged with destroying the English army by dint of routine, ostensible fulfillment of duty, and want of common sense and energy." Hence he was steadily promoted, to full general by 1871, and created a peer, Baron Airey, on his 1876 retirement. #E9.

Aitken, Lily G. #ME33.

L'Alba; Giornale politico-letterario Florence (It.), 1847–1849. Daily. Ed by G. La Farina (to Mar 1848; then A. Vannucci). Left-Democratic. → 48:34. #M912.

Albania #M319.

Albany (NY state) → 88:30.

Albert, *Prince; full:* Albert Francis Charles Augustus Emmanuel of Saxe-Coburg-Gotha (1819 to 1861) Royal consort of his first cousin Queen Victoria of England; married in 1840. Born a German princeling, he was created prince consort in 1857. #M211, M690.

Albuera; *properly* La Albuera (Spain) Town near Badajoz, in the S.W.; scene of a British victory (1811). #E10.

Aldershot (Eng.) Town near (S.W. of) London; site of a military camp 1855+. #E11.

Alembert, Jean **Le Rond d'** (1717 to 1783) French mathematician and philosopher; a coeditor of the *Encyclopédie* with Diderot, he wrote articles esp on these two subjects (1751–1757); a pioneer in scientific thought. Mathematics was his main interest; in mechanics he enunciated "D'Alembert's principle," and wrote a work on the theory of music, etc. He pubd much orig work on calculus; the *Chronicle* reference is in this connection. → 82:47.

Alexander II, Czar (1818 to 1881) Emperor of Russia, Mar 2, 1855, to Mar 13, 1881; he carried through the so-called emancipation of the serfs (1861). He was assassinated in St. Petersburg in a Nihilist bomb conspiracy. → 73:16; 81:13, 14, 17, 20.

Alexander III, Czar (1845 to 1894) Emperor of Russia, Mar 13, 1881, to Nov 1, 1894. He was regarded as more reactionary than his father, Alexander II; he carried through the entente with France (1891+). → 87:20.

Alexander, William (c.1730 to 1783) British physician, of Scottish descent; from 1769 he practiced medicine in London. In his professional field he was known for his research on the properties of various medicaments, and published a number of books on medicine. But M (1852) read his nonmedical work *The history of women*, 3d edn (1782; orig 1779). → 52:58.

Alexandria (library) → 94:31.

Algemeen Handelsblad Amsterdam, 1831+ (founded as the *Nieuwe Amsterdamsche Courant*). #M835.

Algeria; Algiers → 57:38; 82:14–16, 19. #M567; E12.

Alison, Sir Archibald (1792 to 1867) Scottish historian, b. England; lawyer and jurist. M was mainly interested in his economic work *The principles of population* (1840), written as an answer to Malthus. Alison was best known for his popular *History of Europe from 1789 to 1815* (1833–1842), which gloried in die-hard Toryism and defense of the oligarchic status quo on high moral principle—a book which E possessed in German trans. → 50:50, 68, 69; 55:5.

Alison, William Pulteney (1790 to 1859) Scottish physician; prof of medicine at Edinburgh. A Tory, he wrote (besides medical works) a number of tracts on the Poor Laws, incl *Observations on the management of the poor in Scotland* (1840). M also read his "Notes on the report of the Royal Commissioners on the operation of the poor laws in Scotland," in *J. of the Statistical Society of London*, 1844. → 51:68.

Alisov, Peter Fedoseyevich (1847 to 1928) Russian publicist. M (1881) read his brochure *Aleksandr II ozvoboditel*, perhaps in its French trans, *S. M. Alexandre II, le Libérateur*, par Pierre Alissoff (188?). → 81:13.

Allemane, Jean (1843 to 1935) French socialist leader; led a wing of the movement ("Allemanists") from 1890 to c.1905. A printshop compositor, he joined the movement in 1861; took part in the Paris Commune; was deported to New Caledonia until the 1880 amnesty; and returned to France to join the Possibilist (reformist) group under Brousse. In 1890 his tendency split, and (1891) formed the Parti Ouvrière Socialiste Révolutionnaire. The Allemanists were a tendency *sui generis:* they stressed TU action over parliamentary (electoral) work, supported the General Strike slogan and "direct action," yet were extremely sectist, and remained basically reform-minded. The group was esp strong in the Paris region, generally more energetic than the conventional reformists. (The *Chronicle* references are concerned with this split.) — Allemane's subseq history is a somewhat complex tale of splits and unities up to the

1905 socialist unification, after which Allemane tended to fade from the scene. After defeat in the 1914 election, he effectively retired from activity. He supported the prowar majority in 1914, but was a CP sympathizer in 1920 (without joining or accepting its Marxism). → 90:42; 91:8.

Allgemeine Deutsche Biographie Leipzig, Duncker & Humblot, 1875–1912. Ed by R. von Liliencron, assisted by F. X. von Wegele (till 1897). 56 vols, biographical encyclopedia. → 84:19.

Allgemeine Literatur-Zeitung Charlottenburg (Ger.), Dec 1843 to Oct 1844. Monthly. Ed by Bruno Bauer. → 44:19, 22.

Allgemeine Militär-Zeitung Darmstadt, Leipzig, 1826–1902. —A leading German, internationally circulated, military journal, organ of the Gesellschaft deutscher Offiziere und Militärbeamten. E contributed to it in 1860–1864. → 60:3, 44, 53; 62:1, 43, 58; 63:25, 35; 64:6, 18, 20. #E243, E244, E407, E442, E685, E686.

Allgemeine Volkszeitung Vienna, Mar 1868+. Ed by Wilhelm Angerstein. —Organ of the Arbeitervereine; socialistic views. → 68:15.

Allgemeine Zeitung Augsburg, 1810–1882; founded 1798, first pubd in Tübingen, Ulm, Stuttgart, then Augsburg, by J. F. Cotta. Ed by G. Kolb (in the 1840s–1850s). A leading daily in Germany, generally conservative-bourgeois, with leeway for moderate liberal views; oriented toward Austrian hegemony, not Prussian. → 40:13, 15, 16; 41:6; 42:26; 43:5; 44:12; 51:42; 59:8, 9, 44, 49, 53, 60, 65, 66, 71; 60:12, 13, 61; 61:21, 26. #M65, M165, M433, M460, M461, M592, M617, M667–M669, M701, M849, M851, M852, M869, M922.5, M923; E55, E184, E425, E506, E729, E780.

Alliance of the Socialist Democracy The Bakuninist group that functioned as Bakunin's instrument, semipublic and semisecret, to bore from within, and take over, the IWMA. Bakunin created it when, after failing to take over the congress of the League for Peace and Freedom (liberal) in Geneva, he turned, with his then small clique, to do the same to the International. It was first founded with the name Alliance Internationale de la Démocratie Socialiste, and its name wavered a bit as Bakunin adapted to the exigencies of conspiratorial tactics. In Bakunin's mind it was an "open" organization (front) which was to be controlled secretly by the "International Brothers" (the top Bakuninist dictators, with Bakunin at the apex—this in Bakunin's own conception). The Alliance applied (Dec 1868) to the GC for admission to the IWMA as a parallel international organization; when this modest proposal was rejected by the GC,

Bakunin pretended that the international organization of the Alliance would be dissolved, and the GC, on M's advice, agreed. The disruptive struggle ensued, helping to tear the organization apart. The Alliance was ousted, along with Bakunin and Guillaume, at the 1872 Hague Congress of the IWMA. → 68:1, 62, 68, 69; 69:12, 17, 18, 40, 70; 70:44; 71:3, 35, 47; 72:1, 15, 21, 36, 42, 49, 56; 73:1, 6, 23, 44; 74:4.

Allsop, Thomas (1795 to 1880) English stockbroker, with radical-democratic and anticlerical views. While best known to history as a friend and disciple of Coleridge, on whom he pubd a book of recollections, and a friend of other writers, he was far to their left: a supporter and member of the Chartist movement, trusted adviser to Feargus O'Connor; a friend of Robert Owen and his ideas; sympathetic to Comtism. In the 1870s he was active in aiding French Communard refugees, working on this with M; he also maintained friendly relations with the M family. → 71:28; 72:54; 75:48; 78:1, 21.

Alma River (Crimea) Scene of a Russian defeat, 1854. #E14, E70, E407.

Almanacco Repubblicano per l'anno [1874, etc.] Lodi. Annual. Ed by E. Bignami. → 72:39, 61; 73:9, 58. #M404; E538.

Almanach du Parti Ouvrier pour [1892, etc.] Lille, 1892–1894, 1896. Annual. Ed by J. Guesde and P. Lafargue. —Socialist yearbook; see *French Workers Party. #E757.

Alsace-Lorraine → 70:50, 52; 71:2; 91:33, 37; 93:40. #M813.

Altenmarkt (in Cologne, Ger.) → 48:65.

American Federation of Labor → 91:9; 92:7.

American Indians See Indians.

Amerikanische Arbeiterbund Eng. American Workers League. → 53:24.

Amsterdam (Neth.) → 38:9; 61:18; 64:7; 69:40; 70:44.

Amsterdamsche Courant Amsterdam, 1672?+. Daily. #M835.

Anabaptists. → 95:21, 31.

Anderson, Elizabeth Garrett (1836 to 1917) English physician and feminist pioneer; first woman in the country to qualify as an M.D. (1866); only woman in the British Medical Assoc, 1873–1892; first English woman mayor (Aldeburgh, 1908). She became Eleanor M's doctor in the early 1870s. Married J. G. S. Anderson (1871). → 75:48.

Anderson, James (1739 to 1808) Scottish economist, mainly on agricultural questions. After experience as a farmer and a writer on fisheries, he pubd the weekly *Bee* (Edinburgh, 1790–1794); retired from active work (1797); and devoted himself to writing on economics. He anticipated the Ricardian theory of rent in *An inquiry into the nature of the corn laws*

(1777). M (1845) studied his *A calm investigation of the circumstances that have led to the present scarcity of grain in Britain* (1801); M (1851) studied *An inquiry into the causes that . . . retarded the advancement of agriculture in Europe* (1779), and *Essays, relating to agricultural and rural affairs* (1775–1796). → 45:51; 51:67. #M575.

Andreä, Friedrich Wilhelm German heraldist. His book on heraldry *Das Wissenswürdigste der Heraldik und der Wappenkunde* (1842) was read by E soon after publ. #E262.

Anekdota zur neuesten deutschen Philosophie und Publicistik Zurich, Winterthur, 1843 (Mar). Ed by A. Ruge. —A two vol. collection (not a periodical) containing contributions by M, Ruge, B. Bauer, Feuerbach; pubd in Switzerland to escape the Prussian ban. → 42:8, 22; 43:6, 11. #M156, M204, M493, M566, M595, M613, M680.

Angerstein, Wilhelm (Emil) (1835 to 1893) Austrian journalist and writer. Editor-in-chief of the *Allgemeine Volkszeitung* of Vienna, which was launched in March 1868 as a socialistic organ of the Arbeitervereine. He also wrote a number of works in history and biography, incl a biography of Father Jahn and a book on the Mar 1848 revolution in Berlin. → 68:15.

Anglo-French War (i.e., *Crimean War) #ME9.

Anglo-Saxon language → 59:70.

Anneke, Friedrich, *called* Fritz; *full* Carl Friedrich Theodor (1818 to 1872) German communist. Orig, Prussian artillery officer; expelled (1846) for revolutionary activity. In 1848–1849, active in Cologne: member of the CL; a founder of the Cologne WA, and its secy; supported Gottschalk; an editor of the *Neue Kölnische Ztg*; member of the Rhenish District Comm of the Demo Assoc; jailed July-Dec 1848. In 1849, an officer in the Baden-Palatinate uprising, member of its Military Commsn. Emigrated first to Switzerland, then (1852) to the U.S., where he fought for the North in the Civil War, as a colonel. → 48:45, 60, 71, 84; 49:19; 62:26.

Anneke, Mathilde (Franziska); *née* **Giesler;** *also called* **Giesler-Anneke** (1817 to 1884) German radical and feminist; *see* Friedrich A., her second husband (mar. 1847). Writer and teacher; she early became a freethinker, social radical, and proponent of women's equal rights. In 1848–1849 she edited the *Neue Kölnische Ztg* when Friedrich was jailed; when the paper was banned, she tried to publish it as *Frauen-Zeitung* [Women's Gazzette] but the government quashed it. She fought in the Baden-Palatinate uprising as an ordnance officer. She then emigrated along with Friedrich; in the U.S. she founded a

women's journal, *Deutsche Frauenzeitung*; lectured on women's suffrage; directed a prominent girls' school in Milwaukee; and published some poetry and plays. → 48:66.

Annenkov, Pavel Vasilyevich; *Angl.* Paul (1813 or 1812 to 1887) Russian writer; a liberal landowner; as a "Westernizer," close to Belinsky, Herzen, later Turgenev, in the 1840s, when he often traveled in Western Europe (an "esthetical tourist," said Lavrov). He had no connection with the socialist movement; he broke off all connection with M in the post-1848 period. He is known mainly for his memoirs, as a source on the movement of the 1830s–1840s, *Literaturnye vospominaniya* (1880), translated as *The extraordinary decade* (1968). → 46:11, 14, 15, 39, 43, 48, 49; 47:50; 48:27; 80:2, 31.

Anrooy, A. van Dutch physician in Zaltbommel; his wife was Lion Philips' daughter, Henriette. Dr. van Anrooy treated M on one of the latter's visits to Philips. —Name also spelled Anrooij. → 63:41; 64:5.

Anseele, Edouard (1856 to 1938) Belgian socialist leader. After working as a notary clerk, typesetter, London docker, and journalist, he played a leading role in Ghent in founding the Voorhuit (co-op) movement, important also for the development of the socialist movement. He became a founder and leader of the Belgian Socialist party (1885), delegate to international socialist congresses, and a leader of the reformist wing of the Second International; deputy in 1894, 1898, 1900; author of socialist tracts. At E's funeral he spoke for the Belgian movement. → 91:28; 95:37.

Anti-Corn-Law League Formed (1839) to repeal the British corn laws of 1815, it favored free trade in grain, which would lower wages, and thus favor industry at the expense of agriculture. Led by *Cobden and *Bright, headquartered in Manchester. Repeal was won under *Peel (1846). → 45:52; 81:37.

Antipater of Thessalonica (c. 1st century B.C.) Greek poet; a minor epigrammatist. —*Caution:* The German form Antipatros is found by error in English edns of *Capital*. → 59:25.

Anti-Socialist Law (in Ger., usually called Socialist Law or Exceptional Law) Law, pushed through the Reichstag by Bismarck on Oct 19, 1878, outlawing the Social-Democratic party except for the continued legal operation of its Reichstag deputies. The pretexts were the attentats by *Hödel and *Nobiling. But by 1890 the S-D party had become the strongest party in the country; Wilhelm II had succeeded to the throne; Bismarck fell in Mar; and the law was not renewed.

Antwerp (Belg.) → 69:30; 70:24; 71:15, 21, 25.

Appian or Appianus (of Alexandria) (fl. 2nd century) Alexandria-born historian, writing in Greek, known for his history, *Romaika*, of Rome's conquests of various peoples up to Trajan's reign. → 61:13.

Applegarth, Robert (1834 to 1924) English trade-unionist. Son of a Yorkshire ship captain, he became a joiner-carpenter, and at first went to seek his fortune in the U.S. (1855–1858) where he worked at various jobs and supported the Abolitionists. Returning to Sheffield, he rose in his union, becoming gen secy of the Amalgamated Society of Carpenters and Joiners (1862–1871). During the 1860s and early 1870s he was a member of the London Trades Council and the so-called Junta (a TU leaders' group); active in reform movements, advocating political action; a leading member of the Reform League and the Labour Representation League (1869+); esp active in the struggle for the legal recognition of TUs. He joined the IWMA (Jan 1, 1865); his union affiliated in 1867; member of the GC (1865, 1868–1872); he broke after the Paris Commune. In 1871 he resigned from union leadership to accept appointment to a Royal Commsn (the one on the Contagious Diseases Act), the first worker to be consequently addressed by the king as "Our Trusty and Well-Beloved." Said trusty worker then disappeared from the TU scene. He subseqly made a living at various jobs (traveling salesman, etc.), becoming a small businessman by the end of the 1880s; retired from business in 1907. He remained, as earlier, a Liberal in politics. → 69:71; 70:49.

Aquila Town in central Italy. → 72:60.

Arabi Pasha, Achmed; or Ahmed **Arabi** (1839 or 1841? to 1911) Egyptian nationalist leader. Born of a fellah family, he became, as an army soldier, a prominent figure among the nationalists. The khedive Tewfik Pasha, under pressure, made him undersecy of war (1882); British pressure forced his dismissal for a while; but when Arabi began arming the Alexandrian forts, the British bombarded them and defeated the nationalist forces at Tell el-Kebir (Sep 1882). Arabi was exiled for life on Ceylon by the British; pardoned in 1901, he returned to Egypt. → 82:32.

Arabs → 82:15.

Arbeiter-Wochen-Chronik (with varying subtitles) Budapest, Jan 3, 1873, to Dec 28, 1890. Weekly. Ed by Leo Frankel. —German-language organ of the Hungarian Social-Democrats; for its continuation, see *Arbeiterpresse*; its Hungarian-language parallel (1873–1879) was *Munkás-Heti-Krónika.* → 76:29. #E832.

Arbeiter-Zeitung New York, Feb 8, 1873, to Mar 13, 1875. Weekly. Ed by K. Carl, R. Starke. —Organ of the IWMA founded after the transfer of the IWMA/GC to NY. So named to issue of Oct 17, 1874; then renamed *Neue Arbeiter-Zeitung.* → 73:9. #ME6.

Arbeiter-Zeitung Vienna, July 12, 1889+. First semimonthly, then weekly (through 1893), then semiweekly (1894), finally daily (Jan 1, 1895+); suspended 1934–1945. Ed by V. Adler, its founder (in the 1890s). —It was the central organ of the Austrian Social-Democracy, succeeding *Gleichheit;* one of the most important socialist organs in German. → 90:14, 25, 26; 91:40; 92:26; 93:19, 21, 24; 94:49; 95:4, 9, 37. #E2, E17, E166, E342, E345, E346, E385, E470, E473, E537, E613, E667, E764, E765, E813.5, E814, E824, E917.

Arbeiterinnen-Zeitung [Women Workers Gazette] Vienna, 1892 (or end of 1891) to at least 1899; one source has it continuing to 1934. Semimonthly. —Organ of the Austrian S-D women's movement; the ed bd included Louise Kautsky, and Eleanor and Laura M. → 91:47, 54; 92:3.

Arbeiterpresse Budapest, Jan 1891 to 1894. Weekly. —Continuation of the *Arbeiter-Wochen-Chronik* as the German-language organ of the Hungarian Social-Democrats. #E845.

Der **Arbeitgeber** [The employer] Frankfurt, 1856+. Pub'r: M. Wirth. → 61:56.

Archangel; *Russ.* Arkhangelsk (now USSR). Northern port, on the White Sea. #M323.

Archiv des Atheismus This was the name of a radical journal planned by the Young Hegelian tendency in 1841, incl M, but as far as I know it did not come into being. → 41:2.

Argenteuil (Fr.) Town on the Seine, close to Paris. → 81:24, 40, 43; 82:14, 23, 27, 30, 39; 83:2.

Ariosto, Lodovico (1474 to 1533) One of the greatest Italian poets of the Renaissance. His chief work, *Orlando Furioso,* an epic poem of chivalry (on the Roland story), was written for his patron, Cardinal d'Este (first pubd in 1516; final form, 1532). He also wrote lyric poems and comedies. → 83:36.

Aristotle (384 to 322 B.C.) The culminating thinker in ancient Greek philosophy; "the universal head" who "also already investigated the essential forms of dialectical thought" (Engels). —M's notebooks show i.a. notes on *De Anima* (read in Latin in 1840); *De republica . . . et oeconomica* in 1858; and his *Politics* in the early 1860s. → 37:8; 39:9; 40:1; 60:65. #M79.

Arkhiv K. Marksa i F. Engel'sa [Marx–Engels Archive] Moscow, Institute of Marxism–Leninism, 1924–1930; 5 vols. pubd. See ST/5. #ME72; M144, M145, M572, M573, M759, M872.5; E196, E352, E530.

Arlon Town in S.E. Belgium. → 46:9.

Armenia → 94:44.

Arndt, Ernst Moritz (1769 to 1860) German writer and publicist; prof of history at Greifswald (1806, 1810–1811) and Bonn (1818–1820, 1840–1860). After making an early reputation as a patriotic-nationalist champion of German unity and an opponent of Napoleon, he was persecuted by reaction after 1815. He played a role in firing the nationalist spirit with tracts and patriotic lyrics (*Was ist des Deutschen Vaterland?*), and regained his chair at Bonn in 1840. In 1848 he was a deputy to the Frankfurt National Assembly (right center). —E's essay on him portrays him as politically obsolete by 1840, and calls for a German nationalism infused with concern for political freedom. → 40:15, 18; 41:5. #E248.

Arnhem Town in E. Netherlands, on the Rhine. → 69:60.

Arrow (lorcha) **incident** The lorcha (small Chinese coasting vessel) was taken (Oct 8, 1856) for smuggling by Chinese authorities; whereupon the British envoy, pointing out that the smugglers were under the British flag, used this as pretext for launching the Second Opium War. #M32, M282.

Asia → 53:16, 18, 22; 58:45; 68:17. #M651, M977; E709, E902. *See also* individual countries.

Aspern (Aust.) Village near Vienna (now part of that city); scene of Austrian victory over Napoleon in 1809. #E43.

Assi, Adolphe Alphonse (1841 to 1886) French worker (factory mechanic); of an Italian father. Proudhonist in tendency; participated in Garibaldi's movement (early 1860s); active in strikes (Jan 1870); close to the IWMA. In 1870 a member of the CC/NG. In 1871 he was elected to the Paris Commune; member of the Commsn of Public Safety; commandant at City Hall; captured in the May fighting. He was hauled before the Versaillese tribunal in the first show trial of Communards, and in Sep sentenced to deportation to New Caledonia. He worked there, even after the 1880 amnesty, till his death. → 71:34.

Assing, Ludmilla (1821 to 1880) German writer; liberal in tendency; she pubd the correspondence and *Tagebücher* of Varnhagen von Ense, her uncle (1861–1870), and was prominent in the literary circles around Varnhagen and his wife's salon. Friend of Lassalle. → 61:15, 26.

L'Association; Bulletin international des sociétés coopératives Paris, Brussels, Nov 1864 to July 29 (or Aug 12?), 1866. Monthly (1864–1865); weekly (1866+). Ed by H. Lefort, Elie Reclus, J. E. Horn (A. Einhorn). —Organ of the French cooperative societies, left republican in outlook. Continued by *La Coopération.* → 65:7.

Association Démocratique (Brussels) I.e., *Democratic Assoc. #M57, M213.

Association for Administrative Reform #M58.

Association of Independent Socialists [Ger. Verein Unabhängiger Sozialisten] The organization formed (Nov 8, 1891) by the "Jungen" faction of the German S-D party after their expulsion from the party, publishing an organ called *Der Sozialist* (1891–1899). → 92:46, 53.

Association for the Advancement of Science (Brit.) → 61:38.

Assyria → 57:26.

Asturias Region of N.W. Spain. → 94:14.

Atabekjanc, Jos(s)if. In *MEW, etc., called* Jossif Nersessovich **Atabekjanz;** elsewhere **Atabekianc** (1870 to 1916) Armenian student of agronomy at a Stuttgart academy, in touch with K. Kautsky in that city; a socialist. He had pubd an Armenian trans of #E759 when he sent E the ms of his trans of the *Com Manifesto*, asking for a preface. It is not certain whether the latter trans was actually pubd. → 94:44.

L'Atelier Paris, Sep 1840 to Sep 1850. Monthly. Ed by A. Corbon. —Christian socialist in tendency, influenced by Buchez. → 47:42, 49. #E472.

L'Atelier Démocratique Brussels, July 26, 1846 to 1847. Weekly. Ed by L. Heilberg (1847). → 47:32.

Athenäum; Zeitschrift für das gebildete Deutschland Berlin, 1841 (under this title). Weekly. Ed by K. Riedel. —Young Hegelian organ; pubd for 18 numbers in 1838–1839 in Nuremburg, titled *Athenäum für Wissenschaft, Kunst und Leben*, with Feuerbach as one editor. → 41:2, 4. #M992; E897.

Atkinson, William (fl. 1830s–1840s) English writer on economics; member of the Statistical Society of London. He was an opponent of free trade, and advocated protectionism for agriculture. His writing operated much with religious arguments and was colored by a "feudal socialist" strain. M studied his The state of the *science of polit eco investigated* (1838) and *Principles of polit eco* (1840). Atkinson pubd other works in the period 1833–1858. → 45:52. #M575.

Atlantic Monthly Boston, Nov 1857 to present. Titled The *Atlantic*, 1960+. → 81:64.

Au, Juliusz (1842 to 1888) Polish economist. M (1874) read his *J. v. Liebig's Lehre* on agrochemistry. → 74:11.

Au Bois Sauvage (Brussels inn) → 46:21.

Aubry, Emile; *full* Hector Emile (1829 to 1900) French worker (lithographer). An organizer and leader of the IWMA in the Rouen area (1866+); delegate to IWMA congresses (1866–1869); Proudhonist in sympathy but supporter of land collectivization;

founded the local *Réforme Sociale* (1870). Coming to Paris just before the Commune, he participated with administrative work in the post office. He emigrated to Brussels (1871–1872), then settled there and opened his own shop. By 1873 he was pro-Bonapartist; later (1890s) pro-Boulanger, for a sort of caesarist socialism. → 69:4.

Auer, Ignaz (1846 to 1907) German Social-Democratic party leader. Orig a saddlemaker in Bavaria; active in the TU movement. He joined the Eisenacher party (1869); secy of the party Exec (1874). After the 1875 unity, he became one of the party secys, till 1877; editor of the *Berliner Freie Presse* (1877); after 1890, a member of the party Exec, in organizational leadership as party secy till his death. Reichstag deputy (1877–1907 with gaps). In the 1890s he moved to the reformist right wing, and is esp remembered for two bon mots: "General strike is general nonsense"; and his famous advice to E. Bernstein: "One doesn't say this sort of thing [revision of Marxism], one does it." → 74:32; 75:20; 95:3.

Augereau, Pierre François Charles; *Duke of Castiglione* (1757 to 1816) French military man, created marshal by Napoleon; went over to the Restoration in 1814. #E48.

Augsburg (Ger.) Chief city of Swabia; commercial center; part of Bavaria (1806+). #M701. *See also* Allgemeine Zeitung.

Augsburg Allgemeine Zeitung *See* Allgemeine Zeitung (Augsburg).

Augusti, Bertha (1827 to 1886) German writer; novelist. Sister of Lina *Schöler; acquainted with M since the 1840s. → 79:44.

Augustus, *Emperor.* Orig Gaius Octavius; *then* Gaius Julius Caesar Octavianus; *Angl.* Octavian (63 B.C. to 14 A.D.) First emperor of Rome (27+ B.C.). → 55:6. #M251.

Austerlitz Town in Moravia (now Czechoslovakia), near Brünn (Brno); scene of a decisive victory by Napoleon in 1805. #E49.

Australia → 80:51. #M121.

Austria; Austria-Hungary (the Hapsburg Empire), but *see* Hungary for all Hungarian refs —*See* *Vienna; following are references specif to Austria: —M&E's writings on: → 48:6, 11; 49:10; 50:10; 54:12, 19, 28; 55:19, 37; 56:41; 57:4; 59:45; 60:48, 52; 61:6. —Political questions about Austria: → 48:58; 59:4, 14, 17; 61:39; 64:29; 66:22, 26, 28, 30; 67:47; 80:6; 82:9; 93:53; 94:4, 29. —Socialist movement: → 89:37; 91:11, 47, 54, 59; 92:26, 44; 93:19, 21, 42, 44; 94:4, 29, 33; 95:33. —In IWMA affairs: → 67:47; 71:48; 73:6. —Miscellaneous: → 48:76; 60:12; 62:9, 35; 75:32; 87:49; 89:31; 90:22; 92:35, 51; 93:6, 40; 94:1. *See* *Haynau; *Ebner.

Austro-Prussian War (or Seven Weeks War) War fought June 15 to Aug 23, 1866, between Prussia (allied with Italy) versus Austria (allied with several southern German states); engineered by Bismarck to exclude Austria from German unification, ending in a crushing victory for Prussia. → 66:26.

Aveling, Edward (Bibbins) (1849 or 1851 to 1898) English socialist writer and publicist; of the Marxist circle around E in the 1890s. Son of a clergyman, he was trained as a physician, and his first career was as a lecturer and popular-science writer on botany and other scientific subjects. He was also active early as an atheist propagandist (Secularist, freethinker) (1879+); writer for Bradlaugh's *National Reformer*; vice-pres of the National Secular Society (1881); elected to the London School Board (1882); editor of *Progress* (1883). Also active as a playwright and dramatic critic (pen name: Alec Nelson), with participation in amateur theatricals and poetry recitals. He became interested in social questions of the late 1870s; joined the SDF, became a member of its Exec, then quit and helped found the Socialist League (1884), which he and others abandoned in 1889 as it was taken over by the anarchoid wing. In the late 1880s and early 1890s he was involved in the new TU organization of unskilled workers, with Eleanor M; attended international socialist congresses (1889–1893). He helped S. Moore translate M's *Capital*; also transd #E759; pubd his textbook *The student's Marx* (1891); and *see* Eleanor M for joint writings.
—Aveling and Eleanor M began to live openly as husband and wife in the summer of 1884. (He had married his first wife, Isabel, in 1872; separated in 1874.) He is usually blamed for Eleanor M's suicide; his alleged scoundrelism has had a wide press; but for a balanced account of these matters, see only Y. Kapp's biography of Eleanor M. → 73:47; 83:12; 84:6, 25, 39, 55, 59; 85:11, 33; 86:5, 11, 20, 23, 34, 35, 37, 50; 87:1, 2, 5, 14, 17, 23, 25–27, 30, 33, 47; 88:25, 28; 89:31; 91:2, 27, 55; 92:11, 14, 24, 39, 43, 61; 93:2, 13, 32, 52; 94:28; 95:33, 37. #M221; E759.

Avenel, Georges (1828 to 1876) French historian and publicist; leftist; author of works on the history of the French Revolution, esp its left wing. M&E warmly recommended the reading of his *Anacharsis Cloots* (1865) and his *Lundis révolutionnaires* (1871–1874). He was also the author of *Nouveaux éclaircissements sur la Révolution Française* (1875). → 78:42; 89:38.

L'Avenir Libéral Paris, June 21 to Sep 15, 1870; Versailles, Mar 22 to May 29, 1871; July 8 to Nov 18, 1871. Weekly. —Bonapartist organ; banned by the Paris Commune. → 71:49.

Avrial, Augustin (Germain) (1840 to 1904) French worker (mechanic); an organizer of the mechanics' union; Proudhonist.

He joined IWMA in 1867 or 1869; in 1870, was jailed as a leader; after Sep, active in the Paris Federal Council. Elected to the Paris Commune: member of the commsn on labor and on war; active in military work; voted with the minority on the Comm of Public Safety issue; prominent in the May fighting; escaped to London in Aug. His visit to M came soon after his arrival. In emigration, he was a founder of the "French Section of 1871," and its corr secy (Sep D). —He went to Alsace (1874–1876), having set up a factory there; then to La Chaux-de-Fonds (joining the Bakuninist IWMA) and to Geneva (1877–1878). After the 1880 amnesty he worked on the French railways (1881–1883), and tried business with some inventions. He briefly joined the Alliance Socialiste Républicaine (1880–1881), then the Allemanist group (1890+); in 1896 he ran as an independent left candidate in a local election, in Possibilist fashion. He

was buried in Père Lachaise cemetery with Communard honors. → 71:46.

Axelrod, Pavel Borisovich; *Angl*. Paul (1850 to 1928) Russian socialist; an early Marxist, later a Menshevik leader. Radicalized as a student at Kiev, he joined the Narodniks by 1872, at first sympathetic to Bakuninism; went to the Chernyi Peredel group (1879); became an émigré (1881). In 1883 he joined with Plekhanov in the first Marxist group, Emancipation of Labor; an editor of *Iskra* and *Zarya* (1883–1903). At the 1903 party congress, he went with the Mensheviks; after 1905, an advocate of so-called liquidationism (legal work only). In World War I he was pro-Allied but also Zimmerwaldist (social-patriotic center); after 1917, a right-wing Menshevik. → 93:40.

Ayacucho (Peru) Scene of the decisive battle (1824) that won Peruvian independence. #ME17.

B

Baake, Hans　Berlin pub'r; a Social-Democrat. → 95:25.

Babbage, Charles (1792 to 1871) English mathematician; inventor of a calculating machine and other mechanical devices; a founder of the Royal Astronomical Society and Statistical Society. Chief work: *On the economy of machinery and manufactures* (1832); M (1845, 1859–1862) read it in a French trans (1833). → 45:50; 58:17. #M575.

Babeuf, François Noël; *called* Gracchus **Babeuf** (1760 to 1797) First socialist/communist to organize a movement to realize the aim of a new antibourgeois social order. Son of a poor government official, he worked first as a clerk and servant; his communist views, adopted by 1785, came largely from Morelly and his interpretation of Rousseau. After gaining some prominence in his native Picardy as a social agitator, and being dismissed from minor office as too radical, he came to Paris (for the second time) in Feb 1793. In Paris he carried on agitation and pamphleteering in the sections, and founded (1794) the *Journal de la Liberté de la Presse*, using the name Camille B.: critical of the Jacobin dictatorship and sympathetic to the Thermidoreans from the democratic left (at first); then his paper became *Le Tribun du Peuple* (pubd by "Gracchus" B.) with a revolutionary platform for sans-culotte power, pointed against the Directory, rallying former Robespierrists and Hébertists, etc. In 1796, convinced that the revolution had been betrayed, he established an Insurrectional Comm with some links to the army, Paris

artisans, the provinces, and ex-Jacobins; Sylvain Maréchal drafted the Manifesto of the Equals as the platform of the movement (called the "Conspiracy of the Equals"). Denounced by an informer, the Comm was arrested in May, and tried from Oct to next May. Babeuf and another were sentenced to death; they committed suicide with a dagger, but were guillotined anyway. "Babouvism" gained European currency in the 1830s through the publ of a book by Babeuf's lieutenant Buonarroti, *La Conspiration pour l'égalité dite de Babeuf* (1828); transd into English by Bronterre O'Brien (1836). —N.B. The spelling *Baboeuf* and the term *Babeufism* are erroneous, though not infrequently seen. → 43:2, 33.

Bachmann, Karl Friedrich (1785 to 1855) German philosopher. Prof at Jena in ethics and polit eco. At the time of M's dissertation, Bachmann had pubd his main works, incl *System der Logik* (1828) and *Anti-Hegel* (1835). → 41:9. #M475.

Bacon, Francis. *Later Baron* **Verulam** (1561 to 1626) English philosopher, statesman, essayist. As statesman, he attained the eminence of lord chancellor in 1618, was created Baron Verulam, and then fell in disgrace (case of bribery); he retired from public life. His most popular writing is his aphoristic *Essays* (1597–1625). As a philosopher, he is noteworthy for developing the inductive method of modern science. M regarded him as the progenitor of scientific materialism (cf. #ME76, E762). M early read his *Advancement of learning* (1605). Other works: *Novum organum* (1620); *The new Atlantis* (1627). → 37:8.

Bad Ems See Ems.

Badajoz City in S.W. Spain; scene of much fighting in the Peninsular War, esp 1812. #E58.

Baden One of the former German states in S.W. Germany; capital, Karlsruhe. → 48:48, 63; 49:1, 27, 29, 30, 32; 50:10, 15; 53:11. #E226, E577.5, E701.

Bagnères-de-Luchon Resort town in the Pyrenees, S. France. → 71:32, 38, 43.

Bahr, Hermann (1863 to 1934) Austrian man of letters, best known as a dramatist representing *fin de siècle* symbolism; wrote art and literary criticism, also novels, at first mystic-chauvinist in content. Socialist acquaintances, incl Bebel and Liebknecht, influenced him to break with Pan-German circles and their anti-Semitic wing, and to move closer to socialistic views. For his correspondence with E in 1893, see *MEW* 39:79. —In 1890 Bahr had an article in the *Freie Bühne für modernes Leben* on the "woman question," directed against Paul Ernst's Marxism; hence Ernst's request to E. → 90:27.

Bailey, Samuel (1791 to 1870) English economist and philosopher. A Liberal capitalist, he first made a fortune as a Sheffield merchant and banker, then devoted himself to writing on a variety of subjects. His writings on polit eco include his *Critical dissertation on the nature, measure, and causes of value* (1825), attacking Ricardo's theory of value, excerpted by M in notebooks of 1859–1862; his *Money and its vicissitudes in value* (1837) was excerpted 1851. He also wrote *A defence of joint stock banks and country issues* (1840). → 51:61; 59:77.

Bailleul, Jacques Charles (1762 to 1843) French politician and writer. A Girondin member of the Convention, he took part in the Thermidorean reaction and subsequent governments; liberal journalist under the Restoration. A founder of the *J. de Commerce*, he wrote many works on finance, politics, and geography, up to an advanced age. M (1843) read one of his major works, *Examen critique de l'ouvrage posthume de Mme la B^{nne} de Staël* (1818). → 43:32.

Bakunin, Michael; *Russ.* Mikhail Alexandrovich (1814 to 1876) Russian revolutionist, founder of anarchism as an organized movement; he derived the ideology from Proudhon and Stirner, the organizational conceptions from Blanquist-Jacobin conspiratorialism. Son of a landowning noble, he became a Young Hegelian radical during a Berlin sojourn in the 1840s, and participated in the revolution of 1848–1849 with a message of messianic Pan-Slavism (cf. #E217). In 1849 his part in the Dresden uprising led to imprisonment in the Peter and Paul fortress for six years, during which we wrote for the czar his abject *Confes-*

sion, in which he early expressed that aspiration for an "invisible dictatorship" which remained his permanent aim while his rhetoric called for antiauthoritarian "libertarianism." From 1863, in Italy, he began his practice of founding conspiratorial Brotherhoods (sometimes with members), equipped with secret codes, etc., with himself as dictator. His first contact with M had been in 1844 in Paris (see → 44:9, 28, 35; cf. #M471); in 1847, in Brussels, he kept aloof, as always refusing to join any ongoing socialist or communist movement (→ 47:52). In 1864 his promise to M to work for the IWMA (→ 64:40) was not kept. Instead he tried to take over the liberal Peace and Freedom Congress in Geneva, and on failing, split together with his clique to form an "Alliance of the Socialist Democracy" (which existed under various names); he then turned his Alliance toward a capture-or-split adventure in the IWMA. It was around this point (1866–1868) that for the first time Bakunin adopted anarchism as his banner, in his drive to seize control of the International—using racist anti-Semitic and anti-German propaganda for this purpose to a much greater extent than anarchistic agitation. This helped to shake the organization apart; at the Hague Congress of 1872, Bakunin was expelled. By 1873 he started to disintegrate personally and politically. It is necessary to understand that Bakunin's anarchism occupied him only for a few years near the end of his life and more or less coincided with his takeover operation of the IWMA. —The standard and unsuperseded biography is E. H. Carr's *Michael Bakunin* (1961). On his ideas, a useful survey is E. Pyziur's *The doctrine of anarchism of M. A. Bakunin* (1955) (or A. P. Mendel's *Michael Bakunin* (1981). The essential documentation is largely contained in the new collected works in French, *Archives Bakounine,* pubd by the Amsterdam I.I.S.H., esp Vols. 1, 2, and 4. For the Nechayev episode, which was important for M in particular, but which in any case is vital for understanding Bakunin, see M. Confino, *Violence dans la violence* (1973), esp its text of B.'s letter to Nechayev of June 2, 1870.
→ 44:9, 28, 35; 47:52; 48:46, 50, 57; 49:10, 24; 53:32, 34; 54:20; 58:7; 63:31; 64:35, 40; 65:10, 19; 67:31, 37; 68:1, 62, 68, 69; 69:1, 5, 12, 17, 18, 40, 54, 57, 70; 70:1, 3, 4, 10, 18, 19, 25, 33, 44, 55, 56; 71:1, 3, 37, 56; 72:4, 15, 27, 36, 42, 49; 73:36, 42, 44, 51; 74:2, 4, 26; 75:4, 35; 76:21; 79:12; 83:20; 95:34. #ME6, ME33; M71, M178, M471, M510; E111.5. *See also* Alliance of the Socialist Democracy; Bakuninists.

Bakuninists Followers of *Bakunin, esp inside the IWMA. → 70:10, 18, 25, 36; 71:3, 35, 47, 51, 56, 58, 59, 62, 64; 72:1, 3, 4, 8–10, 15, 21, 24, 27, 30, 31, 35, 36, 42, 48, 49, 56, 60, 65, 66; 73:1, 6, 11, 12, 23, 33, 44, 49, 51; 76:21,

29, 36; *79:12; 82:40; 92:60, 68; 93:4; 94:5.*
#E59, E383, E834. See also *Alliance of the
Socialist Democracy.

Bałaszewicz-Potocki, Julian (Alexander); *in
KMC,* Julius Alexander **Balaševič** Polish
émigré in London; an agent of the Russian
secret police, using the name Count Albert
Potocki. → 71:56.

Baltic Sea; Ger. Ostsee #M939; E258.

Balzac, Honoré de (1799 to 1850) France's
great novelist and short-story writer, master of
the realistic novel and portraitist of *La
comédie humaine.* M&E admired him immensely, despite his royalist and conservative
viewpoint—which, to be sure, gave Balzac an
external slant on the world of the rising
bourgeoisie. According to Paul Lafargue, M
wanted to write an essay on B.'s *La comédie
humaine* when he finished *Capital,* since he
considered the novelist "the historian of his
time." → 67:9; *83:50; 85:31, 42.*

Bamberger, Ludwig; *also called* Louis
(1823 to 1899) German politician, and writer
and lecturer on economic affairs. A lawyer, he
became one of the bourgeois-democratic
leaders in the revolution of 1848 in his native
Mainz, and took part in the Baden-Palatinate
uprising in 1849, fleeing abroad before its end.
In the early 1850s he was an émigré in
London, editor of the *Deutsche Londoner Ztg.*
He later went to Paris, where he became a
bank manager. After the 1866 amnesty, he
returned to Germany, joined the National
Liberals, and sat in the Reichstag; in 1870 he
was Bismarck's adviser on French affairs. But
he later attacked Bismarck's "state socialism"
from the laissez-faire right, and joined the
1880 split from the National Liberals. →
51:31.

Banat A region (now divided among Yugoslavia, Roumania, and Hungary) which was
incorporated into Hungary (1779), then made
an Austrian crownland (1849), after which it
reverted to Hungary (1860). #E304.

Bancroft, Hubert Howe (1832 to 1918)
American historian; orig a book dealer and
pub'r; author of works on the history and
ethnography of the Americas, esp western
North America, Mexico, Central America. E
read his monumental *Native races of the
Pacific states* (1874–1876). → 82:51.

Banfield, Thomas Charles (1795 to 1880)
English economist. After a stint as tutor to
Ludwig II of Bavaria, he returned to England
and became prof of polit eco at Cambridge
(1844–1855). In 1846 Peel named him secy of
the Privy Council. M (1853) studied his chief
work, *The organisation of industry* (1845),
comprising his lectures on polit eco, liberal-
democratic in views, critical of Malthus.
Other works: *Industry of the Rhine* (1846,
1848, two series), and a series of works titled

Statistical companion (1848 to 1854). →
53:50, 52.

Bangya, János; Ger. Johann (1817 to 1868)
Hungarian officer and journalist; of a minor
aristocratic family; colonel in the Austrian
army. He took part in the revolution of 1848–
1849 in Hungary, and collaborated with Kossuth and Klapka. Afterward he became Kossuth's emissary abroad, and also an Austrian
police spy, active in émigré groups; in Paris,
vice-pres of an émigré comm. (*KMC* says: also
a secret agent for the Prussian and French
police.) In 1852–1853 he wormed his way
into M's confidence. Later in the 1850s he
entered Turkish military and police service,
under the name of Mehemed Bey. → 50:19;
*52:7, 9, 12, 15, 17, 18, 22, 24, 27, 29, 31, 33, 35,
41–43, 49, 51, 52; 53:7, 14; 57:12; 58:27, 38;
64:8.*

Bank of England → 68:64. #M135.

Banner, Robert Scottish socialist worker
(bookbinder); one of the first workers to
become an active socialist in Britain, influenced by Andreas Scheu; active first in Edinburgh, then London. In 1880–1881 he was a
young man trying to form a Scottish labor
party. He joined the SDF, became a member of
its Exec and an opponent of Hyndman; left
with the group forming the Socialist League;
worked mainly in the Woolwich area of
London, then in the Hammersmith Socialist
Society. He was a speaker at Eleanor M's
funeral; bitterly attacked Aveling as responsible for her death. → *80:2, 32; 81:35.*

Banquet of the Equals → 51:10, 14.
#ME81.

Barbès, Armand; *full* Sigismond Auguste
Armand (1809 to 1870) French revolutionary: radical republican, not really socialistic,
essentially a "man of action" without definite
ideas. Born in the French W. Indies, son of a
well-to-do physician, he came to Paris in
c.1831. At first, from 1834, he was an associate of Blanqui, in the Society of the Families, Society of the Seasons, etc., and one of
the triumvirate leadership in the May 1839
putsch, for which he was sentenced to life. In
the 1848 revolution he was a NG colonel and a
deputy to the Assembly, where he supported
Ledru-Rollin. He participated in the May 1848
invasion of the Palais Bourbon, and for this
was given a life sentence in 1849. Having
broken with Blanqui (against whom he supported the "Taschereau letter" smear) he
spent the next years in a feud; but his posture
as the purer revolutionist was damaged in Oct
1854 when Bonaparte granted him a pardon
for his patriotic support of the Crimean adventure. (As M wrote in the *NYDT,* this showed
who was the real revolutionist.) Barbès then
lived in emigration, first in Brussels, then The
Hague. → 54:42. #M535.

Barbeyrac, Jean (de) (1674 to 1744) French Calvinist jurist and legal scholar; prof of belles lettres in Berlin, prof of history and civil law at Lausanne, prof of public law at Groningen. As an opponent of church dogma he heralded the Enlightenment. His reputation rested notably on his French edn (preface and notes) of S. von Pufendorf's *De jure naturae et gentium.* In 1842 M's Bonn notebooks excerpted his *Traité de la morale des pères de l'église* (1728). #M93.

Barcelona (Sp.) → 71:21, 28.

Barclay de Tolly, Mikhail Andreyevich; *later (1815)* Mikhail, Prince **Bogdanovich** (1761 to 1818) Russian military leader, of Scottish descent; from 1814, field marshal. He served in wars against Turkey, Sweden, and Poland, and gained prominence in the war against Napoleon. War min (1810–1812), appointed despite antiforeigner prejudice; in 1812, commander-in-chief of Army of the West. M&E's article on him views him as the best Russian general of the period. #ME18.

Barmen (Ger.) E's birthplace. → 20:1; *29*:1; 34:3; 37:5.5, 12; 39:6; 41:8, 13, 17; 42:2, 27; 44:2, 35; 45:11, 13, 24; 46:24; 48:32–34, 67; 49:25; 60:21, 25, 33; 61:18, 48; 62:51; 69:19, 74; 93:39; 94:20; 95:37. #ME86; E183, E351.5. *See also* *Wuppertal.

Baron A book reviewer, so named in a letter by Kugelmann to M. (Source: *KMC.*) → 73:57.

Barry, Maltman (1842 to 1909) English journalist. He became active in the IWMA when in 1871 it established the British Federal Council, of which he was provisional chairman and a repr; member of the GC (1872); delegate to the Hague Congress, where he supported M's position. He also acted as a Tory agent in the labor movement; contributor to the Conservative paper *Standard.* In the mid-1870s M used Barry to get certain views into the London press, esp on the sins of England's Russian policy; but by the late 1870s their relations were cool. Barry was accused of causing dissension in the workers' movement. → 71:56, 62; 72:13, 35, 49; 74:5; 75:13, 35; 76:31; 77:6, 9, 33; 78:1, 23, 41; 88:38.

Bartels, Adolphe (1802 or 1803 to 1862) Belgian left-republican, later socialistic; publicist and journalist. A Calvinist convert to Catholicism, he was a leader against Dutch domination in the period leading to the 1830 revolution. In the 1830s he pubd the short-lived *Le Progressiste,* then *Le Patriote Belge;* jailed. With Jottrand et al., he founded (1844) *Le Débat Social* (Brussels), and was its editor till 1846; withdrew when the weekly adopted Fourierism; continued as editor of *J. de Charleroi.* Author of *Essai sur l'organisation du travail* (1842). → 47:55; 48:10. #M732.

Barth, Paul; *full* Ernst Emil Paul (1858 to 1922) German historian and sociological writer who set the aim of merging the two fields, also of overcoming the difference between Marx's and Ranke's approach to history—thus undercutting Marxism's appeal. His doctoral dissertation pointed in this direction: *Die Geschichtsphilosophie Hegel's und der Hegelianer bis auf Marx und Hartmann* (1890); likewise his book *Die Philosophie der Geschichte als Soziologie* (1897). → 91:35, 38.

Barthélemy, Emmanuel (b. c.1820, says *MEW/MECW;* c.1813, says Maitron/*DB;* for death, see below) French Blanquist worker (mechanic). Under Louis Philippe, active in secret societies; imprisoned for trying to kill a police agent. In 1848 he took part in the June uprising; sentenced to life in Jan 1849; escaped to London. In emigration he was a leader of the Blanquist group; but he turned hostile to Blanqui's 1851 "Warning to the People" (against Blanc et al.). In 1852 he fought a duel over a political difference with Frédéric Constant Cournet (father of F. E. *Cournet) and killed him; sentenced to two months, and shunned by the émigré community. According to *MEW/MECW* (but not Maitron/*DB,* which gives no death date) he was executed in London on a criminal charge in 1855. #ME171.

Barton, John (1789 to 1852) English economist. M (1851) studied his chief work, *Observations on the circumstances which influence the condition of the labouring classes of society* (1817); it criticized orthodox economic theories, which played down working-class misery, and advocated a public relief program; Ricardo and McCulloch sought to refute him. Other works: *Inquiry into the causes of the progressive depreciation of agricultural labour in modern times* (1820); *Consequences of the excess of population* (1830). → 51:66.

Basel; *formerly* Basle; *Fr.* Bâle Town and canton in Switzerland. → 41:11; 51:36; 53:5; 65:62; 69: 4, 10, 47, 53, 54, 62, 66, 70. #M747.

Basque region (Sp.) → 94:14.

Bassermann, Friedrich (Daniel) (1811 to 1855) German politician, moderate liberal; in the Baden Diet (1841+). A publisher in Mannheim, later Munich, he became a member of the Frankfurt National Assembly in 1848; till May 1849, undersecy of state in the Interior Ministry; in 1850, member of the united parliament in Erfur'. In the backwash of the revolution, illness and political despair brought about his suicide. → 48:71.

Bastian, Adolf (1826 to 1905) German anthropologist, esp ethnologist; traveler and explorer (to collect ethnographical material).

Prof at Berlin (1866+); founder (1866) and director of the Berlin Museum of Ethnology, also of the *Zeitschrift für Ethnologie*. His book *Der Mensch in der Geschichte* (1860)—studied by M on publ—was perhaps the first scientific description of an exotic society. Other works: *Die Völker des östlichen Asien* (1866–1871); *Die Culturländer des alten America* (1878–1889). M criticized his attempt at a psychological explanation of history. → 60:62.

Bastiat, Frédéric; *full* Claude Frédéric (1801 to 1850) French economist. Son of a merchant, he was a prominent defender of capitalism, free trade, and class harmony, and (esp after the 1848 revolution) a virulent opponent of socialism. M's 1851 notebooks excerpted his noted polemic with Proudhon, *Gratuité du crédit* by Bastiat and Proudhon (1850). Influenced by Cobden and the English anti–Corn Law agitation, Bastiat tried to organize a free-trade movement in France, in vain. The same 1851 notebooks by M excerpted his late-written exposition of economic theory, *Harmonies économiques* (2nd edn, 1851; pubd 1850), which tries to save Ricardian theory from its socialistic implications. M thought he was "the shallowest and hence most successful representative of vulgar-economic apologetics." → 51:52, 71; 64:13; 68:40. #M362, M534.

Batthyány, *Count* Lajoś; *Ger.* Ludwig, *Angl.* Louis (1806 to 1849) Hungarian political leader. Liberal aristocrat; before the 1848 revolution, a leader of the moderate nationalist opposition in the Upper House; supported Kossuth in 1847. In Mar 1848 he became the first constitutional prime min in Hungary; tried to stay in the Hapsburg Empire, but was overborne by Kossuth's influence. His policy of compromise was also rejected by the Austrians, who arrested and shot him in 1849. → 52:17.

Bauer, Bruno (1809 to 1882) German idealist philosopher, critic of theology, rationalist historian of Christianity. Son of a porcelain painter, he became a lecturer in theology at Berlin (1834+) as a right-wing Hegelian till c.1838. As he moved left to Young Hegelianism, he went to Bonn (1839), but was dismissed (1842) for his critique of the historical credibility of the Bible: in *Kritik der evangelischen Geschichte des Johannes* (1840) and *Kritik der evangelischen Synoptiker* (1840). His brief radical period as a leader of the Young Hegelians was ca. 1840–1843. In 1844, with his brother Edgar, he founded the *Allgemeine Literatur-Ztg*; see M's polemic in #ME76. His philosophical idealism merged into solipsism; in social theory, a Great Man view of history. After the 1848 revolution he lost all significant influence. After 1866 he

became a National Liberal; in later years, very conservative, an admirer of Bismarck, collaborator with Hermann Wagener. → 37:9; 39:1, 7, 9; 40:6, 12; 41:14–16, 19; 42:10, 24, 31; 44:1, 19, 22, 26, 30; 45:36, 43; 46:7; 55:50; 56:5, 10; 57:6; 82:17. #ME66, ME76, ME129; M204, M595, M609, M995; E105, E787.5, E872.

Bauer, Edgar (1820 to 1886) German writer; brother of Bruno B. (see him for their collaboration). In the early 1840s he was a Young Hegelian; generally communistic in viewpoint; member of the "Freie" group at Berlin, living by tutoring and proofreading. A pamphlet brought three years in jail (1846+). After the 1848 revoluton he lived variously in Altona, Flensburg, Hamburg; after 1849, an émigré in England; editor of the London *Neue Zeit* (1859). He changed his political view a number of times; eventually split with Bruno and returned to orthodox Christianity. He returned to Germany (1861) and became a Prussian government official. →37:9; 39:1; 42:18, 22; 54:21, 54; 55:50; 57:6, 32; 59:12. #E872.

Bauer, Heinrich; *full* Andreas Heinrich (b. c.1813) German communist worker (shoemaker) from Franconia. He became a leading member of the League of the Just in Paris (1838+); expelled from France (1842). In London emigration he was a founder and sometimes pres of the GWEA; member of the CC/CL (1847–1850); treasurer of the S-D Refugee Comm. after the revolution; emissary of the CL in Germany (Apr-May 1850). In 1851 he emigrated to Australia, and faded from view. For E's description of Bauer, see #E557. → 43:14; 48:19, 20, 22; 49:36, 40; 50:12, 19, 34, 45; 51:1. #ME47, ME52, ME87, ME164, ME179.

Bauer, Ludwig; *Angl.* Louis German physician, from Stolpe. In 1848 he was elected a deputy to the Berlin assembly (left wing); emigrated to England (1849). He was physician to the M family (Sep-Nov 1849), but at the end of 1849 he became a member (then chairman, 1850) of the refugee-aid comm formed by the right wing of the emigration; this produced a break with M. On emigrating to the U.S., Dr. Louis Bauer became a prominent surgeon in St. Louis and a founder of the College of Physicians and Surgeons. → 49:50; 50:16.

Bauer, Stephan; *Angl.* Stephen (1865 to 1934) Vienna-born economist and statistician. Editor of the *Zeitschrift für Social- und Wirthschaftsgeschichte*. In 1893–1899 he was a lecturer at a polytechnic college in Brünn (from where he wrote to E). He became a prof at Basel and the U. of Chicago, and head of the International Labor Bureau at Basel (1901+); known for advocacy of progressive labor legislation. → 95:26.

Bavaria; *Ger.* Bayern State, formerly a kingdom, in southeastern Germany. → 72:20; 94:39, 43, 48. #E74.

Bax, E. Belfort; *full* Ernest Belfort (1854 to 1926) English socialist writer, esp on history and philosophy. By occupation a barrister, he became one of the first English propagandists of a sort of Marxism, esp in historical interpretations. After studying in Germany (where he absorbed philosophical idealist ideas as his permanent influence), he became a founding member of the SDF, then (1884) part of the group which formed the Socialist League; editor of *Commonweal*. He was a friend of E, and part of E's social circle (1883+). When the anarchoids swamped the SL, he returned to the SDF and for a while edited *Justice*. In 1911 he was a founder and leader of the British SP, but broke in 1916 because of his prowar position. Author of *The religion of socialism* (1887); *The ethics of socialism* (1889); an autobiography (1918); *Handbook to a history of philosophy* (1886); etc. Probably his most interesting work, written with William Morris, was *Socialism, its growth and outcome* (1894). → 81:58, 60; 84:6, 55; 86:16, 36; 87:27, 39; 92:61; 94:15.

Bayer, Karl (1806 to 1883) German idealist philosopher. M wanted to review his book *Betrachtungen über den Begriff des sittlichen Geistes* (1839). → 42:6.

Bazancourt, *Baron* César (Lécat) de (1810 to 1865) French writer on military affairs, also of novels and histories; a Bonapartist. E worked on reviewing his book *L'expédition de Crimée jusqu'à la prise de Sébastopol* (1856). B. also wrote *La campagne d'Italie de 1859* (1859–1860). → 56:24, 34, 36. #E720.

Beachy Head (Eng.) Headland on the Channel; E. Sussex. → 95:37.

Bebel, August; *full* Ferdinand August (1840 to 1913) The outstanding founder and leader of the German socialist movement; prob the greatest all-around socialist (organizational) leader ever produced in the international movement. Son of a professional soldier, he lost his father as a child; became a wood turner (a master workman by 1864), settled in Leipzig (1860), and joined the labor movement (1861). He was converted to socialism (1865) by W. Liebknecht, who had been expelled from Berlin, and from the start was hostile to Lassalleanism and its sect, the GGWA. B. and Liebknecht founded the Saxon People's party, an alliance with anti-Prussian liberals, as a leftist political vehicle (an alliance which M worked to break up); both were elected (1867) to the N. German Reichstag. B. was a leading founder of the Verband Deutscher Arbeitervereine (Union of German Workers' Assocs), a step from liberal politics to Social-Democracy; it adopted the program

drafted by M for the IWMA, with which it collaborated, and encouraged the formation of trade unions independent of Lassallean control. This provided the basis for founding (1869) a new socialist party, alternative to the Lassalleans: the Social-Democratic Workers party, at Eisenach ("Eisenacher party"). Bebel was its political-organizational leader, with Liebknecht as ersatz theoretician (until Bebel developed as an independent Marxist thinker) and journalist. In the N. German Reichstag (1867–1870) B. and Liebknecht refused to vote money for the Franco-Prussian War, came out in defiant support of the Paris Commune, and against the annexation of Alsace-Lorraine. In 1871–1872 B. was one of the socialist leaders railroaded to jail for "treason"; up to 1875 he served a couple of jail terms. After the 1875 unity with the Lassalleans he emerged as the undisputed leader of the Social-Democratic movement, until his death. This self-educated worker became a masterly speaker, a brilliant practitioner of "revolutionary parliamentarism," an excellent writer and propagandist, and one of the most competent Marxists in the movement; a close friend, mainly by correspondence, with M&E; deputy in the Reichstag (1871–1881, 1883–1913). —Main political writings, besides collected speeches: *Unsere Ziele* (1870); *Für Volkswehr gegen Militarismus* (1898). Historical-political writings: *Die Frau und der Sozialismus* [Women and socialism] (1879); *Charles Fourier* (1887); *Der deutsche Bauernkrieg* (1876); *Christentum und Sozialismus* (1892); *Die mohammedanisch-arabische Kulturperiode* (1884); and an autobiography, *Aus meinem Leben* (1910–1914). → 68:2, 37, 39, 48–50, 56, 61, 64, 70; 69:2, 19, 25, 26, 41, 48; 70:1, 40, 45, 65; 71:3, 5, 6, 16, 17, 21, 22; 72:16, 20, 21, 34; 73:8, 18, 34; 74:13; 75:10, 12, 20, 36, 37, 48; 79:2, 27, 33, 38, 41, 45, 49; 80:18, 29, 44; 81:17, 19, 56; 82:20, 24, 34, 40, 50, 51; 83:10, 11, 16, 17, 19, 20, 23, 32, 33; 84:4, 33, 37, 49, 51, 52, 58; 85:13, 17, 22, 25, 27, 34, 35, 39, 45; 86:3, 7, 13, 16, 18, 32, 36, 40, 41, 43; 87:16, 39, 43; 88:7, 35, 36; 89:3; 90:6, 11, 25, 32, 47; 91:1, 6, 11, 13, 22, 26, 27, 33, 41, 45, 50, 52, 54, 56; 92:5, 8, 11, 12, 14, 18, 24, 26, 27, 29, 30, 32, 33, 35, 38, 39, 43, 44, 52, 55–57, 62, 65–67; 93:2, 6, 7, 9, 12, 20, 34, 40, 42, 44, 47; 94:43, 48; 95:5, 16, 37. #ME29, ME184; E341.5.

Bebel, Julie; *full* Johanna Caroline Julie (1843 to 1910) Wife of August Bebel; married 1866; an active socialist. → 71:5, 6; 83:11; 87:16; 93:40.

Beccaria, *Marchese* di. Cesare **Bonesana** (1738 to 1794) Italian jurist and economist; writer on criminology and penal reform; a man of the Enlightenment. Prof of law and economics at Milan (1768–1770); councillor of state and magistrate (1771+); perhaps best known for his work on criminal and penal law, *Tratto dei delitti e delle pene* (1764). His writings on polit eco, which anticipated Smith and Malthus to some extent, included *Elementi di economia pubblica* (1804), which M excerpted. His *Tentativo analitico sui contrabbandi* (1765) was a pioneering application of mathematics to economics. → 59:77.

Beck, Grigori Russian Narodnik publicist, active in the movement in the mid-1880s; emigrated (1886); withdrew from revolutionary activity (early 1890s). → 90:18.

Beck, Karl (Isidor) (1817 to 1879) Austrian poet, b. Hungary, of Jewish family. Trained as a physician, he pubd books of poetry (1838+); lived in Vienna (1848+) editing *Lloyd;* once well known for his novel in verse, *Janko* (1841). His poetry reflected his social concerns for justice, welfarism, etc., and "True Socialist" themes, influenced by Young Germany. E criticized his *Lieder vom armen Mann* (1846), with its foreword to the House of Rothschild. #E337, E404.

Beck, Wilhelmine (d. 1851) Austrian adventuress. She posed as a baroness and Kossuth's political intimate; agent of the Austrian and English police. → 51:15, 42, 45.

Becker, Bernhard (1826 to 1882) German socialist; he reached his zenith as pres of GGWA (1864–1865). First a writer, he contributed to *Meyer's Konversationslexikon*. In the revolution of 1848–1849 he fought in the Baden campaign; then emigrated to England, where he worked as a language teacher, returning to Germany in the early 1860s. He was the repr of the Frankfurt workers' assoc to the founding congress of the GGWA; then Lassalle appointed him its plenipotentiary for Frankfurt, and also designated him, in his political testament, as his successor to the GGWA presidency. He was unanim elected to this post (Nov 1864) but proved so hopelessly incompetent that he had to resign (1865). He then lived as a writer in Vienna, where he played a part in the Austrian workers' movement, and in Paris, till he was expelled from the country in 1870. In Dresden he joined the Eisenacher party; editor of the *Chemnitzer Freie Presse* (1871), *Braunschweiger Volksfreund* (1872); delegate to the Hague Congress (1872). Harassed by the government, he left for Switzerland. He pubd a worthless book on the Paris Commune, and his *Enthüllungen über das tragische Lebensende Ferdinand Lassalles* in 1879; abandoned socialist activity; and shot himself, partly under stress of poverty. → 64:27, 32, 38; 65:7, 24, 30; 74:8, 29; 76:27. #M688.

Becker, Hermann (Heinrich) (1820 to 1885) German politician, first a communist, then a liberal. Orig a lawyer and law official in Cologne, of liberal-democratic views, in 1848 he became active in the Cologne movement of the Democracy, i.e., the broad opposition to semifeudal absolutism, along with M and the NRZ group. He was a member of the Demo Assoc; elected to the Rhenish District Comm of this movement and to the Cologne Comm of Public Safety. He edited the *Westdeutsche Ztg* (1849–1850). In 1850 he joined the CL; in 1852 he was a defendant in the Cologne Communist trial (sentenced to five years). He later joined the Progressist party, became a member of the Prussian chamber of deputies (1862+), of the Upper House (1872+), of the N. German Reichstag and German Reichstag (1867–1874); mayor of Dortmund (1870) and of Cologne (1875–1885). His sobriquet was *der rote Becker* (red Becker). → 48:62, 65; 49:19, 35; 50:45, 46; 51:5, 6, 10, 11, 16, 20, 25, 27; 54:33. #M151.

Becker, Johann Philipp˙ (1809 to 1886) German communist publicist and organizer, chiefly active in Switzerland. As a young worker (brushmaker) in the Palatinate, he early adopted revolutionary-democratic views, and was jailed for them; emigrated to Bern (1838), became a Swiss citizen; gained Swiss militia training fighting against the Sonderbund; pubd a weekly *Die Evolution* (Biel), which was banned. In 1848 he formed a German legion to go to Germany to fight for the revolution; he withdrew to safety after its collapse. In the 1849 Baden uprising he commanded a Volkswehr (militia) detachment as a colonel, with unusual success (commended by E). After the revolution, he worked in Switzerland: to provide refugee aid, and organize German workers' education assocs, besides earning a living in various jobs, incl journalism. In 1856 he was a metalworker in Paris. In 1860 he went to Geneva to raise a German volunteer brigade to support Garibaldi (the project failed). He joined the IWMA near its inception; in Geneva he founded (1865) a Provisional German-language CC of Swiss sections of the International to organize in Germany and Austria; also founded *Vorbote* (1866–1871) as its organ; took part in all IWMA congresses; and kept in touch with M&E. In 1869 he participated in the founding of the Eisenacher party; and he remained active in the Swiss-German and international movements till his death. Essentially Becker was a man of action and an organizer rather than a thinker or theoretician, hence his contributions have been undervalued: see R. P. Morgan's *The German Social Democrats and the First International* (1965). The hardest thing to understand is how he managed to raise 22 children. → 60:13, 20, 24, 37; 61:30, 41; 62:12, 20; 65:7, 32, 51, 55, 56, 62; 66:2, 5, 6, 9, 36; 67:12, 32, 37; 68:62; 69:5,

41, 47; 70:44, 45; 71:29; 72:10, 48; 73:23; 75:48; 76:33, 36; 78:3; 79:12, 38, 49; 80:14, 29; 81:49, 53, 56; 82:10, 30, 34, 53; 83:11, 23, 24; 84:14, 42, 49, 50–52; 85:13, 22; 86:27, 30, 38, 41, 52. #E401.

Beckmann, Johann (1739 to 1811) German scholar known for his work on the history of technology. A history teacher in St. Petersburg till 1765, he became (1766) prof of philosophy at Göttingen, lecturing on economics. In 1851 M excerpted his *Beiträge zur Geschichte der Erfindungen* (1780–1805), a pioneering work on the development of scientific technology. → 51:71.

Bedorf, Engelbert German communist. A Cologne barber, B. became active in the workers' movement by the mid-1840s; member of the League of the Just before 1848; in 1848, an active member of the Cologne WA, in which he held various posts (branch secy, Exec member, treasurer). He was also a member of the CL, at least till 1850. → 49:11.

Bedouins Nomadic, Semitic, Islamic people of the Arabian and North African desert. #E73.

Bee-Hive or Bee-Hive Newspaper or *Penny Bee-Hive (with varying subtitles) London, 1861 to Dec 30, 1876. Weekly. Pub'r: G. Potter. Ed by G. Trupp, R. Hartwell, etc. —At first, a TU weekly, on the left side of the London labor movement, in collaboration with a group of Positivists (Comtists). From Nov 22, 1864, to Apr 26, 1870, official organ of the IWMA/GC, which finally broke relations as it went right. → 64:26, 35, 45; 65:19, 32, 33, 46; 67:31, 35, 40; 68:37, 42, 61; 69:11, 30, 65; 70:24, 31; 71:41. #M5, M7, M397, M590, M598, M599, M614, M707, M751; E673.

Beer, S. H. #ME33.

Beesly, Edward Spencer (1831 to 1915) Leading British Positivist (Comtist); prof of history; sympathizer with the IWMA; personal friend of M. Son of a clergyman and an Irish mother; he taught history at colleges, and became a prof (1859–1889) at University College, London. His Comtist tendency adopted a prolabor stance in 1861–1862 during a building workers' struggle, though it remained within the framework of bourgeois-radical ideas. In 1863 B. took part in agitation against supporting the southern states, and in favor of Polish independence; he also translated Odger's address to French workers— hence was chosen to chair the St. Martin's Hall meeting at which the IWMA was founded; but he refused to join. In the 1860s he took a series of radical positions: officer in the Reform League; for a workers' Defence Corps; for aid to TUs; for TU independence in politics; for defense of the Irish Fenian prisoners and for home rule, against coercion in Ireland; and in particular, defense of the Paris Commune against public hysteria. He was initially sympathetic with Bonaparte's regime but later lost confidence in it. From 1864 he became increasingly friendly with M. He never claimed to be a socialist, but his positions brought him into association with the organizers of the SDF. In 1893 he resigned his chair and founded the *Positivist Review*, which he edited till 1902. He pubd translations and a biography of Comte; his lectures on Roman history, *Catiline, Clodius, Tiberius* (1878), are still of interest. B. was the first university prof who became closely associated in the English public's eye with the labor movement. This combination of Comtism with a prolabor position was peculiar to England, and quite foreign to Comte himself or to French Positivism. (*See also* F. *Harrison.) 64:26; 67:31; 69:16, 22, 37; 70:49, 56; 71:2, 33, 36; 72:54; 73:52; 75:48; 77:12.

Beiträge zur Geschichte der deutschen Arbeiterbewegung Hamburg, Berlin, 1929 to 1931. #E676, E812, E843.

Belgium For most references to M&E's activity in this country, see *Brussels; following are references specific to Belgium. — Relations with Belgian leftists: → 45:3; 48:34; 55:7; 75:13; 91:28. —Other polit activity in Belgium: → 47:14, 39, 52; 48:14, 21. — Relations with Belgian government: → 45:13, 18; 48:16, 17, 19, 20; 52:47. —Belgium in IWMA affairs: → 65:29, 32; 66:5, 46; 68:26, 31, 37; 69:25, 30, 65, 70; 70:3, 39, 44, 49, 55, 62; 71:3, 24, 39; 72:3, 8, 21, 24, 27, 31, 36, 42, 56. —Socialist movement in: → 74:28; 75:5; 76:27; 90:37; 94:39. —M&E's writings on: → 48:21, 52, 59, 73. —Miscellaneous: → 62:51; 69:35; 70:5.

Bell, G. M. (*fl.* 1840–1842) British writer on economics. In 1841–1842 he pubd his views on the currency as given before a parliamentary comm; author of The *philosophy of joint stock banking* (1840). M (1851) read his economic writings. → 51:62.

Bellers, John (1654 to 1725) English social reformer; philanthropic Quaker landowner. He was best known for his *Proposals for raising a college of industry* (1695), i.e., a welfare institution using the labor of indigent workers, with labor-time notes for money; financed by the rich at a fair rate of interest; his answer to pauperism. M also excerpted his *Essay about the poor, manufacturers, trade* [etc.] (1699). As an economist, B. stressed labor's part in the creation of wealth; he influenced Owen. → 60:66.

Belletristische Journal und New-Yorker Criminal-Zeitung NY, Mar 18, 1853, to Mar 10, 1854, under this title; founded 1852 as *B. Journal;* cont'd with varying titles to at least Dec 1911. Weekly. —Established by German émigrés. The entry name above is my favorite periodical title of all time. → 53:43. #M374.

Belyayev, Ivan Dmitriyevich (1810 to 1873) Russian historian; Slavophile champion. Prof at Moscow (1852–1873); government archivist; editor of *Vremennik,* a historical journal (1848–1857). He pubd works on the Russian peasantry (1860) and Russian history (1861–1872). His polemic with Chicherin on the development of communal property in Russia went on in historical journals for some years (1856 +). → 73:21.

Bem, József (1795 to 1850) Polish gen. A military leader in the Polish uprising of 1830–1831, after which he fled to Paris. In 1848 he fought in the defense of revolutionary Vienna; in 1849, a brilliant leader of the Hungarian revolutionary army. He then took refuge in Turkey, still planning activity against Russia; became a Muslim; and was created Murad Pasha; in 1850, as military governor of Aleppo, he protected Christians against Muslim excesses. M&E's article on him emphasizes his hatred for Russia and analyzes his weaknesses. → 51:10. #ME19, M959.

Benary, Ferdinand; *full* Franz Simon Ferdinand (1805 to 1880) German Orientalist and theologian. Lecturer at Berlin (1829) on Oriental languages; later, prof for Old Testament exegesis. In 1842 E heard his lectures on the Revelation of St. John and took notes on his exposition of the mystic number 666. #E787.5.

Benedix, Roderich (Julius) (1811 to 1873) German playright and dramatic critic. Orig an actor, later a theater manager; in 1844–1845 he managed a theater in Elberfeld. His comedies of upper-middle-class life were popular. His posthumous book on Shakespeare, *Die Shakespearomanie; zur Abwehr* (1873), attacked excessive adoration. → 73:59.

Benevento Town in Italy, near Naples. → 83:29.

Bengal → 58:5.

Bennet, Richard M (1880) read three articles of his on Australia, in the *Victorian Review.* → 80:51.

Bennigsen, Rudolf von (1824 to 1902) German political leader. A founder and chairman (1859–1867) of the Nationalverein; chairman of the National Liberal party (1867–1883, 1887–1898). As a leading member of the Reichstag (1871–1883, 1887–1898) he advocated German unity under Prussian hegemony; later he opposed Bismarck's economic policy. He retired from politics 1897–1898. → 67:12.

Bennigsen, *Count* Levin August Theophil (1745 to 1826) German-born gen, in Russia's service (1773+). He was involved in the assassination plot against Czar Paul I (1801); saw service against Turks, Poles, and Per-

sians; fought in the Napoleonic wars (1806–1813); commander-in-chief (1807); chief of the gen staff (1812). In 1818 he retired from command, to his Hanover estate. #ME20.

Bentley, Thomas (*fl.* 1775–1819) British political pamphleteer. M (1859–1862) read his early brochure *Letters on the utility and policy of employing machines to shorten labour* (1780; pubd anon., also attributed to John Kay). B. also wrote *Reason and revelation* (1794), a reply to Tom Paine; *To the friends of truth and freedom* (1794); and a 1793 address to Parliament "in behalf of the poor and lower orders." —*Caution:* This is not the Thomas Bentley, porcelain manufacturer, who was a partner of J. Wedgwood; he is erroneously identified as such in *New Mega,* II, 3:1. → 59:78.

Der **Beobachter** Stuttgart, 1833+ (under this title). Daily. Ed by Karl Mayer. —In the 1860s, a liberal organ. → 64:39, 47; 67:31, 48. #M462, M900; E688.

Béranger, Pierre Jean de (1780 to 1857) French lyric poet and songwriter of revolutionary-republican tendency. His political songs, immensely popular among the masses, lashed royalist reaction, clericalism, and existing social conditions; fitted to popular melodies, they were spread more by singing than by publ. He took part in the 1830 revolution; later jailed for republican sentiments. His first collection was pubd in 1815. Some famous songs were: "Le roi d'Yvetot" (satire against Napoleon), "Le vieux drapeau," "Ce n'est plus Lisette," "Le Dieu des bonnes gens." One of the songs transd by Laura M was "Le sénateur." → 89:35.

Berends, Julius (b. 1817) Berlin printshop owner. In 1848, a radical-democrat, he was a leader of the city's Handwerkerverein (artisans' assoc), and deputy to the Prussian National Assembly (left wing); in 1849, deputy to the Second Chamber (left wing). In 1853 he emigrated to the U.S. → 48:58.

Beresford, William Carr. *Viscount* **Beresford** (1768 to 1854) British gen. He led military expeditions in the colonies; served in the Peninsular War (1808–1814); commanded Portuguese troops (1809–1823); was made baron (1814), viscount (1823), gen (1825); and after entering Parliament as a Tory, became master-gen of ordnance in Wellington's cabinet (1828–1830). M&E's article on him takes a moderately dim view of his ability. → 58:15, 19. #ME21.

Berg (Ger.) Former duchy on the Rhine, E. of Cologne; chief city Düsseldorf; part of Prussia (1815+). #M958.

Berg, *Colonel* Swiss army officer; in 1848, deputy from Zurich to the National Council. He was commander of the Zurich battalion stationed in Ticino; and according to E (see esp #E503) he was a reactionary martinet. #E232.

Bergamo Town in Italy, near Milan. → 90:24.

Bergen Seaport city in S.W. Norway. → 90:30.

Bergenroth, Gustav (Adolph) (1813 to 1869) German historian and publicist. An assessor in the Prussian judicial system (from which he was dismissed in 1848), he was active in Cologne (at least 1842+) as one of the RZ circle, a socialist by 1843, a founder of the Cologne WA; in 1845 he went to attend the Elberfeld communist meetings. He took part in the 1848 revolution as a radical Democrat. In 1850 he emigrated from Germany. → 50:6.

Berlin (Ger.) *Selected references; partial index.* M&E's moves to/from Berlin, trips, etc.: → 36:11; 37:6; 41:9, 14, 17, 18; 42:23, 25, 27; 61:14, 15, 17; 74:32; 92:43; 93:42. —In 1848–1849 revolution: → 48:23, 31, 57, 58, 60, 61, 72, 76; 49:14, 17, 33. And *see also* *Berlin Prussian Assembly. —Relations with Berlin leftists: → 42:20, 30. —Berlin events: → 50:20; 53:15; 62:61; 63:6. —Berlin police: → 52:13; 61:26. —Relations with Berlin press: → 56:34. —Relations with Berlin pub'rs: → 58:12; 59:10, 30, 43; 60:25. — *National-Ztg* lawsuit in Berlin: → 60:7, 13, 23, 34, 37. —Movement in Berlin: → 63:13, 39; 64:13, 39; 64:17, 38; 65:24, 42, 57, 64; 66:19; 68:50, 56; 69:49; 90:48; 91:13, 17, 27, 47, 54; 92:55, 56; 94:43; 95:24, 25. —In IWMA affairs: → 65:29; 68:37, 38, 61; 71:48, 56, 62, 64; 72:3, 9. —Miscellaneous → 59:72; 62:35; 63:16; 68:57.

Berlin Prussian Assembly → 48:37, 38, 51, 58, 62, 72, 76, 81–83. #M219, M245; E76, E207, E699.

Berlin, University of → 36:1, 11, 12, 15; 37:1, 3, 5, 6, 8–11, 14, 15; 38:1, 7, 12; 39:1, 7, 9; 40:17; 41:1, 7, 18; 42:23. See *also* Doctors Club.

Berliner Freie Presse Berlin, 1876 to 1878. Daily. Ed by J. Most (from mid-1876). — Social-Democratic. #M370.

Berliner Reform Berlin, 1861 to 1868. Daily. —Liberal paper. → 63:16; 65:24. #M688, M861, M924, M925; E21.

Berliner Volks-Tribüne Berlin, summer 1887 to 1892. Weekly. —Social-Democratic organ, founded by Max Schippel in his leftist days; sympathetic to the "Jungen" faction. → 92:60. #E2, E562, E834.

Berliner Volksblatt Berlin, Mar 1884 to 1890. Daily. Ed by W. Blos. Socialist; founded by F. Tutzauer; the first S-D paper to appear during the Anti-Socialist Law. The 1890 Halle party congress made it the party organ; in Oct 1890 it merged into *Vorwärts. → 90:24, 42, 48. #E272, E335, E473, E537, E666, E667, E832, E833, E858, E917.

Berliner Zeitungs-Halle Berlin, 1846+. Daily. Pub'r: Gustav Julius. —In 1848–1849 it became a leading voice of the oppositional Democratic camp. #ME47; E925.

Berlinische Nachrichten von Staats- und gelehrten Sachen; *also later called* Spenersche Zeitung Berlin, 1740 to 1874. Daily. Pub'r: J. C. Spener. —Semiofficial government organ, constitutional-monarchist. #E453.

Berlinische Zeitung See Königlich priv. Berl. Ztg.

Bermbach, Adolph (1822 to 1875) German lawyer and notary, in Cologne. In 1848 he was a radical Democratic deputy in the Frankfurt National Assembly; in 1849, member of the First Chamber in Prussia. In 1852 he acted as M's channel for getting materials to the defense in the Cologne Communist trial and for sending reports to M. (W. Blumenberg says he was never a CL member, but MEW states positively that he joined after the 1848–1849 revolution and was active as a Communist in 1851.) → 51:35, 45, 46; 52:3, 20, 31, 35, 39.

Bern; Fr. Berne Capital of Switzerland. → 48:75, 81, 82; 49:37, 43; 68:69; 76:29. #E79, E301, E583.5.

Bernadotte, Jean (Baptiste Jules) (1763–1764? to 1844) Marshal of France under Napoleon; from 1818, king of Sweden and Norway as Charles XIV John, founder of the present Swedish royal line. As a French soldier (1780+), he served under the Revolution, and in diplomatic service for Napoleon (1798–1799); became a marshal (1804); and was named Prince of Pontecorvo (1805). In 1810 he was named heir to the Swedish throne of Charles XIII; became king (1818–1844); and as such, made an alliance with Russia (1812), took part in the war against Napoleon (1813), and played an ultraconservative role. M&E's article on him is concerned with political interplay more than military affairs, and paints an unflattering portrait of "the Gascon." → 57:38, 41. #M81.

Bernard, M. Belgian worker (house painter). Member of the GC, corr secy for Belgium (Sep 1868 to Nov 1869). —MEW 32 gives his first name as Marie (apparently masculine); it seems he also signed himself P. Bernard (see ST/20); for a woman named Marie B., see ST/26. → 69:65.

Bernard, Simon (François) (1817 to 1862) French revolutionary republican; physician by profession. Before 1848 he was a navy surgeon, also editor of a paper in Perpignan. On the outbreak of the revolution, he went to Paris from Barcelona, and gained notoriety as a club agitator free with revolutionary language ("Bernard le Clubiste" to friends). Afterward he emigrated to England and dabbled in plots against European governments.

In 1857 he was charged with making the bomb for Orsini's attentat on Napoleon III, though he himself stayed in London; acquitted in the Old Bailey (Apr 1858). One deduces from M's approach to him that he must have been a Blanquist or a sympathizer (though I do not find this in the record). → 61:21. #M4, M945.

Bernays, Karl Ludwig; *Fr. and Angl.* Charles L.; *also used the given names* Ferdinand Coelestin (1815 to 1879) German radical journalist; lawyer by profession in his native Mainz. A contributor to the *Mannheimer Abendzeitung,* he fled under threat of arrest for his writings in 1843, and took refuge in Paris. (*New Mega* says he used the name Ferdinand Coelestin before 1844.) In Paris he was a member of the League of the Just; and helped found the émigré organ *Vorwärts!,* of which he became editor (July 1 to Sep 12, 1844); for articles in this paper he was sentenced in Dec to two months (Jan-Feb 1845). He was also a close collaborator on the *DFJ* with M and Ruge, and wrote two pieces for its one issue, incl a review of the press. In spring 1848 he was a member of the German Democratic Society in Paris. After the revolution he emigrated to Switzerland and then settled in the U.S. There he was editor of the St. Louis *Anzeiger des Westens;* colonel in the Civil War; appointed by Lincoln as consul in Zurich. He died in St. Louis. → 35:8; 44:9, 22.

Berner Zeitung Bern, Jan 1845 to Nov 1872 under this title; cont'd to 1894. Daily. Ed by N. Niggeler. —In the 1840s, an organ of the radical-democratic party. #ME11.

Bernese Oberland (Swiss Alps) → 93:40.

Bernier, François (1625 to 1688) French travel writer and man of letters; physician by profession, epicure by avocation. His most famous work was his *Voyages, contenant la déscription des états du Grand Mogol* [etc.] (1699; M studied the 1830 edn). He started his travels in Syria, then Egypt and India; in India he became physician to Emperor Aurangzeb, stayed 12 years, returned in 1668. He was a close friend of many great writers of the day. Among other works is his *Abrégé de la philosophie de Gassendi* (1678). → 53:18, 23, 53, 54.

Bernstein, Eduard (1850 to 1932) German Social-Democratic journalist; later, theoretician of reformist "Revisionism." Working as a bank clerk for about a decade, B. came to socialism through the influence of Lassalle and Dühring, joining the Eisenacher party (Berlin) in 1872. In 1878 he became private secy to *Höchberg, first in Lugano, then (1879) in Zurich; and as part of the Höchberg circle, he had a minor role in its diffusion of Schäffle's social-reform books on socialism and in its "Manifesto of the Three Zurichers" (see #ME29), which evoked a sharp attack by M&E. This was in fact the first programmatic statement of the essential viewpoint which would later be called Revisionism. In Dec 1880 Bebel took B. to see M&E, who were satisfied that he had developed away from Höchberg's views; and at the beginning of 1881 B. became editor of the party organ *Sozialdemokrat.* This inaugurated his leftist or Marxist period (till the 1890s), in between two collapses into reformism. For over a decade M&E—esp E—carried on political correspondence with B. which amounted to a correspondence school in revolutionary politics, supplemented by friendly personal association when the *Sozialdemokrat* staff moved to London in 1888. When the Anti-Socialist Law fell (1890) and *Sozialdemokrat* gave way to the Berlin-pubd *Vorwärts,* B. could not return to Germany (under indictment for sedition). Still living in London, he acted as correspondent for *Vorwärts* and a contributor to *NZ.* He also produced a couple of notable books: his excellent intro to Lassalle's works, which he edited for the party edn (1892–1893; pubd in English as a book, *Ferdinand Lassalle as a social reformer,* 1893); and a study exhuming the left wing of the Cromwellian revolution, the Levelers and Diggers (1895; pubd in English as *Cromwell and communism*). The former is still the best political study of Lassalle, written under E's keenly interested tutelage; the latter is a significant historical contribution, but its standpoint must be noted: vindication of the Cromwell dictatorship as against the revolution's left wing. Another transitional work was his preparation of a German edn of a history of the 1848 revolution by Louis Héritier (1897); B.'s notes and appended comments showed his "moulting" process: he justified the suppression of the June revolt on the basis of a liberal rationale about the impracticability of the revolution. (It was later repubd by B. as *Wie eine Revolution zugrunde ging,* 1921.) In these London years B.'s moulting (his and Bebel's term) took place esp under the influence of the Fabians, with whom he associated. E noticed his "Fabian-Schwärmerei," and recognized that something was happening to him, but put it down to a nervous ailment. Fabianism, however, was essentially the British analogue *mutatis mutandis* of the German *Katheder*-socialism (Schäffle redivivus) which also had an impact on his outlook. A year after E's death, B. shed the Marxist integument, moulting completed, and started "revising" all of Marx's views out of Marxism. The new Bernsteinism was first expressed in NZ articles ("Probleme des Sozialismus") of 1896–1898, then in a book *Die Voraussetzungen des Sozialismus und die Aufgaben der Sozialdemokratie* (1899; incompletely transd as *Evolutionary socialism*).

Thus the debate over "Revisionism" developed in the German and international movements. —In 1901 the German government decided that Bernstein could return to the country. He was a Reichstag member (1902–1906, 1912–1918, 1920–1928); in World War I he stood with the prowar Center (largely because of a pro-British attitude not shared by many cothinkers); joined the independents in 1916, and rejoined the Majority party 1919. In later years he effectually dropped the pretense, or illusion, that he had "revised" Marxism, recognizing (as do all competent historians) that the "revision" posture had been the practical (if not exactly intellectually honest) way to disembowel Marxism in Germany in a fashion which was not necessary for Fabianism in England. —B.'s theoretical works include: *Zur Geschichte und Theorie des Sozialismus* (1901); *Die heutige Sozialdemokratie in Theorie und Praxis* (1906); *Der Sozialismus einst und jetzt* (1922). His history of the Berlin labor movement (1907–1910) deserves mention. → 79:2, 26; 80:44; 81:1, 8, 15, 19, 44, 50, 56, 57; 82:4, 5, 9, 20, 22, 31, 32, 37, 39–41, 43, 44; 83:5–8, 10, 11, 17, 21, 22, 26, 27, 30, 32, 46, 47, 49; 84:5, 6, 11, 12, 16–18, 23, 26, 27, 33, 37, 40, 41, 45, 46, 54, 56, 57, 59; 85:5, 17, 34, 44; 86:3, 40–42; 87:26; 88:27; 89:12, 17, 19; 90:18; 91:1, 55, 61; 92:18, 32, 39, 47, 57, 61; 93:52; 94:11, 31; 95:21, 37. #ME35; E387, E388, E470, E613, E705.

Bernstein, Regina; *called* Gine; *née* Zadek Wife of Eduard B., her second husband; married 1886, but complications over her divorce from one Schattner delayed the legality of the marriage till June 1887. → 92:61; 93:52.

Berthier, Louis Alexandre. *Prince de Neuchatel; Duc de Valangin; Prince de Wagram* (1753 to 1815) Marshal of France. As a professional soldier, he served under Lafayette in America; in the wars of the French Revolution; in the Napoleonic wars in a number of countries; war min (1799–1808); made marshal (1804); Napoleon's chief of staff (1808–1814), after which he supported the restoration regime of Louis XVIII. When Napoleon emerged from Elba, he withdrew to Bavaria, and died there, perhaps by suicide, perhaps murdered. M&E's article paints him as a detail organizer of limited mentality, a reliable routinist, and a ready political turncoat. #M82.

Bessières, Jean Baptiste. *Duke of Istria* (1766 to 1813) Marshal of France. He served in the wars of the French Republic and under Napoleon; made marshal (1804), duke (1809); took command of all cavalry (1813) and was killed by a bullet while reconnoitering; very popular with the ranks. M&E's article is mainly noncommittal. #M83.

Besson, Alexandre French worker (locksmith). As an émigré in London, he belonged to the Commune Révolutionnaire group formed in 1852, then to the London French branch of the IWMA, under the influence of F. Pyat. He was a member of the GC (1866–1868), and for a while corr secy for Belgium. → 68:55.

Betham-Edwards, Maltilda (Barbara) (1836 to 1919) English novelist, writer esp on French life; author of *The white house by the sea* (1857), *Kitty* (1869), *The dream-Charlotte* (1896), etc. When M wrote to her in July he did not know her identity, but by Sep he identified her in a letter as a "trashy novelist." → 75:27.

Bettini, Pompeo (1862 to 1896) Italian poet; proofreader by trade, in Milan. An ardent socialist sympathizer, though not a party member, he contributed to *Critica Sociale*, and drafted the *Com Manifesto* trans pubd by Turati. His two volumes of poetry (1887, 1897) were later collected by B. Croce (1942). → 92:49. #ME33.

Bettziech, Heinrich; *pseud.:* H. **Beta** (1823 to 1876) German journalist. He was a contributor to the *Hallische Jahrbücher*, the *Deutsche Jahrbücher*, and a number of other radical-Democratic and "True Socialist" papers. After the 1848 revolution, he fled to England; in the London emigration, a supporter of Kinkel; returned to Germany 1868. → 51:36; 59:66; 67:37.

Beust, Anna (b. 1827) A cousin of E, living in Zurich in the 1890s. Y. Kapp refers to her also as Mrs. Friedrich von Beust; see next entry. → 93:40.

Beust, Friedrich (Karl Ludwig) von (1817 to 1899) German ex-army officer, radical-Democrat in the 1848 revolution in Cologne. His career in the Prussian army had ended because of his political convictions. In 1848 he was an Exec member of the Cologne WA, and its delegate to the second Demo Congress in Berlin (Oct 1848), where he supported revolutionary demands; an editor of the *Neue Kölnische Ztg* (Sept 1848 to Feb 1849); in 1849, a military leader in the Baden-Palatinate uprising. He took refuge in Switzerland, where he later became a well-known school reformer and head of a progressive-education institute à la Pestalozzi and Fröbel, in Zurich. Here, in 1867, he joined the IWMA; also took part in the Geneva Peace and Freedom Congress; after 1869 he withdrew from leftist connections. He was a distant relative of E. → 48:60, 71, 72, 80, 81.

Bianchi, Alphonse Alexandre (1816 to 1871) French socialist worker (plaster molder) and journalist, from Lille. His activity centered on the northern region, cooperatives, and republican secret societies; editor of local papers; political songwriter. In 1848, as leader of the Central Republican Club in Lille, he moved toward socialist views. After the Bonaparte coup of 1851 he fled to Brussels, then Jersey, finally London. In the London emigration, he joined Pyat's circle (Commune Révolutionnaire group); sympathetic to the Blanquists. Then he went to Geneva, till the 1859 amnesty permitted his return to France; back in Lille, he was active in radical journalism and a labor credit bank. He died soon after deploring the outbreak of the Paris Commune. → 52:7.

Bible #E872. *See also* New Testament.

Bibliothèque Nationale (Paris) → 85:3.

Bidassoa River Spanish stream near the French border; scene of fighting in the Peninsular War. #E80.

Bidaut, J. N. (*fl.* first half 19th century) French government official and publicist; writer on economic subjects. M (1859–1862 notes) studied his book *Du monopole qui s'établit dans les arts industriels et le commerce*, 2 vols. (1828). → 59:78.

Bielefeld City in western Germany, near Münster. → 45:21; 49:20, 21.

Bignami, Enrico (1846 to 1921) Italian journalist; socialist organizer. A radical republican and Mazzinian till 1871; participant in the Garibaldi movement (esp 1866–1867 campaigns); then a socialist, esp under the influence of B. Malon. He founded the IWMA section in Lodi; established *La Plebe* (1868), his main instrument of influence. From Oct 1871 he kept in touch with E, who had contacted him via Cafiero. B. was a consistent opponent of the Bakuninists and anarchists in the movement, an enemy of conspiratorial insurrectionism in general, and collaborated with the GC to this end; but politically he was by no means a Marxist; the common ground was that he looked to building a mass workers' party in Italy, and made an important contribution toward it, working also with O. Gnocchi-Viani (esp by 1875–1876) when he aided the organization of the Lombard Federation in N. Italy. → 71:63; 72:23, 35, 39, 56, 58, 61, 65, 67; 73:9, 19, 20, 58; 75:39, 48; 77:6; 78:4. #E381, E436, E538, E567, E751.

Bingen (Ger.) Town in the Rheinhessen district, on the Rhine. → 49:27, 28; 75:40; 76:26.

Birmingham Industrial city of west-central England. #M85, M444.

Biskamp, Elard; *also spelled* Biscamp German journalist. A radical Democrat in the 1848 revolution, B. worked for the *Hornisse*; afterward, emigrated to London. In 1859 he founded the weekly *Das Volk* as an émigré organ (later taken over by the GWEA and finally managed by M). → 59:8, 34, 35, 44, 46, 50; 68:54; #M342, M675.

Bismarck, Otto von; *full: Prince* Otto Eduard Leopold von **Bismarck-Schönhausen** (1815 to 1898) Leading German statesman of the century; beginning as a Prussian Junker, lawyer, parliamentary deputy, ambassador. From 1862, when he became Prussian prime min, his career coincided with the rise of the German state: its unification under Prussian hegemony, esp through a series of wars (Denmark, Austria, France), and its socioeconomic modernization under the class alliance of Junkerdom (as the political governing class) with the big bourgeoisie's economic domination. First chancellor of the Reich (1871–1890); his fall followed the accession (1888) of Wilhelm II and the abandonment (1890) of the Anti-Socialist Law. → 63:2, 24; 64:17, 39; 65:7, 8, 14, 15, 54; 66:22, 30; 67:12–14, 35; 70:45; 71:5, 20, 21, 40; 74:5, 8, 13, 28; 75:10, 17, 31; 76:30; 77:31; 78:13, 19, 32; 79:3, 16, 47; 80:6, 7, 9, 39; 81:19, 37, 44; 82:4, 20, 37, 42, 50; 83:7, 10, 23, 30; 84:14, 33, 58; 85:5, 38; 86:17; 87:48. #E40, E81, E758.

Bismarckism #E361.

Black Forest; *Ger.* Schwarzwald Region in S.W. Germany, along the Rhine. → 77:33, 34.

Black Sea Sea between Asia and E. Europe. #E258.

Black Sea Conference (London) → 71:14.

Blacks (U.S.) *See* Negroes.

Blake, William (*fl.*1810 to 1839) British writer on economics; Fellow of the Royal Society. M (1850–1851) read his *Observations on the effects produced by the expenditure of government during the restriction of cash payments* (1823). He also pubd a brochure on the "course of exchange" (1810), and a reply to Richard Jones on "the assessment of tithes to the poor's rate" (1839). Nothing else seems to be known about him. → 50:50; 51:66.

Blanc, Gaspard (Antoine) (1845 to after 1882) French Bakuninist. A railway track inspector by occupation, he was active in Lyons, where he helped build IWMA sections in 1868, and took part in the insurrectional movements of Sep 1870 and Mar 1871; contributor to *La Solidarité* (1871). After the Commune, in emigration, he became a pro-Bonapartist propagandist (*see* Albert *Richard for info). Thereafter isolated from the radical movement, he lived in Geneva till 1878 as a typographical worker; then in Belgium, and in Italy as a French tutor. → 72:8.

Blanc, Louis; *full* Jean Joseph Charles Louis (1811 to 1882) French socialist journalist and historian; born in Madrid, son of a functionary in Joseph Bonaparte's Spanish government. His *Histoire de dix ans* dealt with 1830–1840 (pubd 1841–1844); he was an editor of the *Revue Indépendante* (1841–1848) with Leroux and George Sand, and the editor of the *Revue du Progrès* (1839–1842), in which he pubd (1839) his first important socialist work, *Organisation du travail*, proposing workers' cooperative production financed by the state. A prominent member of the circle around *La Réforme* (left- Demo) and prominent in the "banquet" campaign leading up to the 1848 revolution, B. entered the Provisional Government, and, as its socialistic wing, was put in charge of the "national workshops" under the Luxembourg Commsn, which were set up to fail and thus discredit socialistic solutions. Although he was a mild pink who disapproved of all revolutionary militancy, B. was used as a scapegoat; he made a speech and then fled to London. In emigration (1848–1870), he finished his Robespierrist *Histoire de la Révolution Française* (1847–1862), edited *Le Nouveau Monde* (1849–1851), and pubd political pamphlets. Back in France, he was elected to the Feb 1871 Assembly, where he condemned the Paris Commune; but supported some radical-Democratic measures. Historically, B. represents an early formulation of reformist socialism quite alien to class struggle and with a strong state-socialistic cast. → 43:29; 44:9; 45:9; 47:42, 46; 51:10, 14; 54:43; 60:12; 64:45. #E455. *See also* *Flocon, F.; *La Réforme.

Blank, Emil; *full* Karl Emil (1817 to 1893) E's brother-in-law; married his sister Marie (1845). German merchant, in business in Barmen and London. Theoretically he held communistic views, which collapsed in 1848–1849; but even afterward he called himself "a communist in principle, bourgeois by interests," while using "we" about communistic affairs (so E reported, 1856). → 56:31.

Blanqui, Adolphe; *full* Jérôme Adolphe (1798 to 1854) French economist; liberal brother of L. A. *Blanqui. An Orleanist, disciple of Adam Smith and J. B. Say, he made contributions to the study of workers' conditions and slums; free-trader. History and economics teacher (1825+); prof of polit eco in Paris (1833+); first editor of the *J. des Economistes*. His chief work, *Histoire de l'économie politique en Europe* (1837), was the first gen treatment; M (1845) studied it. M (1859–1862) studied his *Cours d'économie industrielle* (1836–1839). Other works incl *Des classes ouvrières en France* (1848). → 45:50. #M575.

Blanqui, Auguste; *full* Louis Auguste (1805 to 1881) French revolutionist. A radical republican since youth, B. took part in the revolution of 1830, and was subseqly imprisoned a few times for secret-society activity. He was a leader of the Society of the Families (with Barbès) and of the Society of the Seasons, i.a., and made his reputation as the most

capable repr of the conspiratorial-Jacobin revolutionism of the period, amorphously combined with socialist/communist ideas. Even in his own lifetime his name tended to become a generic term ("Blanquism") for this type of left wing. However, his revolutionary activity in France was not extensive, for he spent thirty-odd years of his life in prison (hence the sobriquet L'Enfermé) and more years in exile. He took part in the May 1839 putsch in Paris, and was imprisoned till the 1848 revolution. In 1849 he was imprisoned again, till 1859; and again 1861 till 1865, when he escaped to Brussels. In 1870 he was forced into hiding after the putsch of Oct 31; arrested the next Mar, he was in jail during the Paris Commune; pardoned 1879, and died soon after. In the last two decades a Blanquist tendency, or "party," came into being, which took shape esp after the Commune under the leadership of Vaillant. His writings were posthumously collected in *Critique sociale* (1885); in 1870 he edited *La Patrie en Danger* in Paris; after the 1880 amnesty, the Blanquist organ *Ni Dieu Ni Maître.* —Blanqui stood for conspiratorial organization by a hierarchically led band, who aimed through the forcible seizure of power by an elite minority (a putsch) to impose their "revolutionary dictatorship" on society as a hothouse means of "educating" it toward some sort of socialist order. This was a conception of "educational dictatorship," but not of a "dictatorship of the proletariat"—a concept alien to Blanqui's thinking. Another widespread myth is the ascription to Blanqui of the theory of "permanent revolution"—a term he never used, and an idea that was incompatible with his strategy (which was to *forestall* the bourgeois-democratic revolution by his putsch). Essentially B. was not a theoretician or political thinker of any sort, but an activist interested in the art of insurrection (cf. his *Instructions for taking up arms*, 1868–1869); although I do not see why his record should inspire confidence in his expertise. His approach to social problems was not based on class struggle but on the cleavage of haves and have-nots, rich and poor, the "People" vs. the Aristos (in the language of 1792). There is a strong push to fuse Blanqui with M that comes from two opposite directions: those, like the historian M. Dommanget, who want to make Blanqui out to be a Marxist, and those, like E. Bernstein, who sought to make M out to be a Blanquist; hence the literature on this subject is packed with disingenuous argumentation.

—The view of B. held by M&E had two sides, both strongly held and quite steady through the years: (1) critical rejection of specific Blanquism as a political course, first expressed in #ME141, and most fully in #E621; and (2) admiration for B.'s revolutionary militancy and integrity, forcefully stated in letters. From M's viewpoint, Blanquists were good material for reeducation. The two men never met, though in late years (June 1879) Paul Lafargue invited B. to come to London; through most of the life of the IWMA, till the Commune, the French Blanquists refused to take part in the International, because of its Proudhonist domination. M&E's indirect points of contact with B. were primarily three: (1) the SUCR episode; → 50:15, 38; (2) the affair of Blanqui's toast (political message); → 51:10, 14; and cf. #ME81; (3) defense work, via Dr. L. *Watteau. → 51:10, 14; 61:15, 21, 26, 30, 41, 49; 62:61; 66:22; 69:14. #ME81.

Blanquism → 85:16.

Blanquists Followers of L. A. *Blanqui, or advocates of his conception of revolutionary policy, i.e., of "making" a revolution at will by a small band of elite activists. The best dissection of Blanquism is #E621. → 61:15; 66:22; 74:24; 92:13, 22. —In London: → 49:44; 50:5, 7, 15, 19, 38; 51:10; 71:56; 72:1, 60; 74:24. #E383, E621, E660. See also Boulangeo-Blanquists.

Bleibtreu, Georg (1828 to 1892) German painter of battle scenes, esp in Prussia's wars of the 19th century. → 61:15.

Blenheim; Ger. Blindheim Village on the Danube, in western Bavaria; scene of a British victory in 1704. #E83.

Blind, Ferdinand A stepson of Karl *Blind, he tried to assassinate Bismarck in 1886; then committed suicide in prison. → 86:17. See his mother, Friederike *Blind.

Blind, Friederike; née **Ettlinger** Wife of Karl *Blind. By her first husband, a manufacturer named Cohen, she had a daughter Mathilde (who became a writer as Mathilde Blind) and a son, Ferdinand *Blind, who made an attempt on the life of Bismarck. → 51:45; 54:54; 58:47.

Blind, Karl (1826 to 1907) German radical publicist. As a student in Mannheim and Heidelberg in the 1840s, he was active as a left republican. In 1848 he took part in the revolution in Baden; joined Hecker's republican rising; fled to Alsace, whence expelled by the French police; back in Baden, took a leading part in Struve's uprising of Sep 1848 and in the Baden revolutionary government of June 1849. In 1849–1850 he was a member of the CL, and collaborated with M on the NRZ-Revue, for which he wrote an article. In 1852, expelled from Belgium, he moved permanently to England (never naturalized); moved rightward to liberalism; by the 1870s, supported Bismarck. In England he devoted himself to support of nationalist-republican causes on the continent—Mazzini, Greece vs. Turkey, etc.; his Hampstead home became a rendezvous for political refugees. Besides

publishing a biography of Mazzini (1872) and political brochures, he also became known as a writer on German folklore and ethnology. → 49:27, 29, 33, 36, 40, 43; 50:10; 51:45; 52:48; 54:46, 54; 58:47; 59:6, 8, 9, 14, 35, 44, 49, 53, 56, 60, 65, 71; 60:12, 13; 64:39, 47; 65:24; 70:47; 71:22. #ME106.

Bloch, Joseph (1871 to 1936) In the 1890s, a student at the U. of Berlin, in math (till 1897). He later became a leading S-D Revisionist journalist; the Sozialistische Akademiker he founded in 1895 became the Sozialistische Monatshefte in 1897, main theoretical organ of Bernsteinism. B. himself wrote little. In World War I, prowar; in 1933, emigrated to Prague. → 90:38.

Bloomsbury Socialist Society In 1888 the Bloomsbury (London) branch of the Socialist League was ousted by the anarchoid leadership in control of the SL, and re-formed itself as the Bloomsbury Socialist Society. Eleanor M and Aveling were active members. → 93:13, 20.

Blos, Wilhelm (1849 to 1927) German Social-Democratic journalist, historical writer, and parliamentarian. Son of a Brunswick physician, he became a socialist in 1872, joining the Eisenacher party; an editor of Volksstaat (1872–1874); contributed to NZ and Neue Welt; he made M's acquaintance in 1874. From the late 1870s he was a leader of the right wing of the party's Reichstag Fraction (member 1877–1878, 1881–1887, 1890–1906, 1912–1918). In World War I, prowar; in 1918–1920, Württemberg state president. Author of Die Revolution zu Mainz 1792 und 1793 (1875); Die französische Revolution (1888–1889); Geschichte der deutschen Bewegung von 1848/49. → 74:22, 29, 32; 77:1, 38, 42; 81:8; 84:37; 90:17.

Blücher, Gebhart Leberecht von (1742 to 1819) German professional soldier: field marshal (1813); prince of Wahlstatt (1814). Starting out in Swedish service, his Prussian army career took off in 1787. He played a prominent military role in the Napoleonic wars, esp in 1813–1815, with a major role in aiding Wellington at Waterloo; occupied Paris (1815); after which he retired to his Silesian estate. B. was the most popular and populistic of the German commanders—plebeian in manner, coarse in character, passionately nationalistic, ill educated (could not read a map), competent only in tactical operations. M&E's article on him, one of the longest of their NAC biographies, concludes that he was "the model of a soldier" esp for the half-insurrectionary war operations of 1813–1815. → 57:38, 41. #ME23.

Blum, Babette; née Marx (c.1791 to 1865) M's aunt (his father's sister), resident in Frankfurt. → 63:41.

Blum, Robert (1807 to 1848) German journalist and bookdealer; political leader. A leading liberal Democrat in Leipzig, he was also a founder and leader of the German Catholic movement in 1845. In 1848 he organized the liberal party in Saxony; became vice-pres of the Pre-Parliament and the Frankfurt National Assembly (left wing). In Oct he went to Vienna in the midst of the uprising there, addressed the insurgents, and joined the student corps to defend the revolution. The victorious reaction under Windischgrätz had him court-martialed and shot, despite his parliamentary immunity. This act evoked a great outcry all over Germany. → 48:76, 79; 57:38; 68:64. #M87.

Blume, G. German Social-Democrat. He wrote to E as chairman for 1891 of the Berlin congress of workers' provident societies, *Kongress freier und auf Grund landesrechtlicher Vorschriften errichteter Hülfskassen.* Presumably he lived in Hamburg, since E replied to him there. → 90:48.

Blunt, Wilfrid Scawen (1840 to 1922) English poet: *Love sonnets of Proteus* (1880), etc. Although best known as such, he was also an anti-imperialist political writer, traveler in the Middle and Far East, critic of British policy, and champion of national independence for India, Ireland, etc. In particular, he defended the Egyptian nationalist party and *Arabi Pasha. → 82:39.

Bobczyński, Konstanty; Ger. Konstantin (b. 1817) Polish revolutionist. After taking part in the Polish uprising of 1863–1864, he emigrated to London, where he became a member of the GC/IWMA (1865–1868) and its corr secy for Poland (1866). In 1865 he took part in the London Conference as a delegate of the Polish National Society of the city; in 1866 he moved to Birmingham. → 65:50, 53; 66:23, 26, 30.

Bobzin, Friedrich Heinrich Karl (b. 1826) German worker (watchmaker's assistant) from Mecklenburg. In 1847 he was a member of the Brussels GWEA. In 1849 he took part in the Baden-Palatinate uprising; afterward, an émigré in London. There, with G. von Struve, he led the Demo Assoc and was treasurer of the liberal refugee group founded Apr 1850, rivaling the refugee aid comm supported by M. In 1851 he left England. → 50:16.

Bodelschwingh, Baron Ernst von (1794 to 1854) Prussian conservative politician, representative of reactionary Junkerdom. Chief state councillor in Cologne (1831), then in Trier; governor of the Rhine province (1834–1842); finance min (1842–1845); interior min (1845–1848); right-wing deputy to the Second Chamber (1849). #M710.

Böckh, August; *full* Philipp August (1785 to 1867) German historian of antiquity and philologist. Prof at Berlin (1811+); he pioneered the study of Greek epigraphics. In 1848 he was a signer of a servile address to the Prussian king. —M (1850) excerpted his book *Die Staatshaushaltung der Athener* (1817). Also author of: *Metrologische Untersuchingen* (1838), and a compendium of Greek inscriptions. → 50:51.

Böcking, Eduard (1802 to 1870) German law prof, at Bonn. By 1835 (when M was in his class) he had not yet made any important publ. → 35:5.

Boenigk, Baron Otto von (1867 to 1930) In 1889–1892, a student of economics at Breslau, prosocialist; took his degree at Heidelberg (1892) with a dissertation on insurance. Later he was a syndic of the Chamber of Commerce in Halle-Saale. → 90:33.

Börne, Ludwig; *full* Karl Ludwig (1786 to 1837) German writer, literary critic, and publicist; a leader of the Young Germany tendency. Son of a Frankfurt banker, in 1818 he converted from Judaism to Lutheranism, and changed his name from Löb Baruch. Politically, a radical Democrat and social reformer. He moved to Paris in 1830; in the 1840s there was a long polemic and feud between him and Heine. Late in life he became a supporter of Christian socialism. Editor of *Die Wage* (1818–1821, suppressed); author of *Briefe aus Paris* (1832–1834), *Menzel der Französenfresser* (1837). → 46:14.

Börnstein, Heinrich (1805 to 1892) Austrian radical journalist. In Vienna, an actor and theater manager, he also wrote plays and contributed to the press. In 1842 he settled in Paris; founded *Vorwärts!* (1844) and wrote for the German-American press. In 1848 he was pres of the German Demo Assoc in Paris, a leader in Herwegh's scheme for a "German legion." In 1849 he emigrated to the U.S.; in St. Louis he became a leading journalist (editor of *Anzeiger des Westens*), political leader in the Republican party, theater director, and businessman. In the Civil War he commanded a volunteer regiment for the Union, as a colonel. Lincoln appointed him consul in Bremen; he eventually returned to Vienna to write a colorful autobiography. → 44:22, 40.

Böttiger, Karl August (1760 to 1835) German philologist, art historian, archeologist. Chief inspector of museums of antiquity, Dresden (1814+). M (1842) excerpted his *Ideen zur Kunst-Mythologie* (1826–1836). #M93.

Bogdanovich, Ippolit Fedorovich (1744 new style/1743 old style to 1803) Russian poet, of Ukrainian gentry family. He wrote lyric and narrative poems, a collection of Russian proverbs (1785), comedies and dramas, and translations; pubd the journal *Ne-*

vinnoe *Uprazhneniye* (1763) and the newspaper *S. Petersburgskie Vedemosti* (1775–1782). → 51:49.

Bohemian (language) → 94:1.

Boisguillebert, Pierre (**Le Pesant,** Sieur de); also spelled **Boisgilbert** (1646–1714) Early French economist; a juridical official in Rouen. Forerunner of the Physiocrats in some respects, he stressed the importance of better consumption by the masses and the primacy of production of exchange rather than accumulation of money. M (1844–1845) excerpted essays by him in Daire's collection, incl *Le détail de la France* (1695) (*MEGA* I, 3), *Dissertation sur la nature des richesses.* → 44:48; 55:5. #M575.

Bolívar, Simón (1783 to 1830) South American national-liberation leader. Born of a wealthy family in Caracas, "El Libertador" headed the wars of independence against Spain in Venezuela, Colombia, Bolivia, Peru; pres of Colombia (1819–1830). M's article took a hostile view of his dictatorial and Bonapartist political course as an impediment to the mass liberation struggle. → 58:5, 10. #M88.

Bolte, Friedrich; *called* Fred German-born worker (cigarmaker) active in the German-American socialist movement by the 1870s, esp in the IWMA in the U.S.; corresponded with M&E. In 1872 he became gen secy of the Federal Council of American IWMA sections; member of the ed bd of the *Arbeiter-Zeitung* (NY); the Hague Congress elected him to the GC. In 1874, active in organizing the Assoc of United Workers of America. His rivalry with Sorge was disruptive as the International disintegrated; in 1874 he (with Konrad Carl) illegally seized control of its organ, the *Arbeiter-Zeitung*, and each side expelled the other. Nothing more seems to be known about him. → 70:59, 62; 71:41, 42, 59; 73:9, 11, 15, 33.

Bolton Abbey (Eng.) Village in the West Riding of Yorkshire, not far from Leeds. → 69:35.

Bomarsund (channel) Strait in the Gulf of Bothnia. → 54:40. #M774; E85, E120, E121.

Bomm, Carl German worker (metalworker). Business manager of the union which, first affiliated with the Lassalleans, then merged with the "International" union under Bebel's influence; an associate of J. *Hamann. → 69:65, 66.

Bonaparte, Louis Napoleon; *later as emperor,* Napoleon III (1808 to 1873) Nephew of Napoleon I; son of Louis Bonaparte, king of Holland. Exile (1815–1830) in Germany and Switzerland; took part in Romagna uprisings (1830–1831); on the death (1832) of Napoleon II, titular king of Rome, he became the French pretender. He plotted (1836) a revolt in Strasbourg; was briefly exiled in America, then Switzerland and England; organized a conspiracy in Boulogne (1840), was captured, imprisoned at Ham, and escaped (1846) to England. There, besides activity as a playboy and social lion, he also acted as a special constable in patriotic suppression of the Chartist movement. His career as a political adventurer took a rise as the revolution of 1848–1849 declined in general frustration. A member of the National Assembly, the Bonaparte name elected him (Dec 1848) to the presidency of the Second Republic; his forces organized a coup d'état (Dec 1851) which established his dictatorship; proclaimed (Nov 1852) the Second Empire as Napoleon III; confirmed by plebiscite (Dec). —The Second Empire was brought down after defeat in the Franco-Prussian War; Bonaparte was captured; the Third Republic was proclaimed (Sep 1870). The ex-emperor was first held a prisoner by the Germans, then lived as an exile in England. —Before 1848 Bonaparte pubd political pamphlets with a semi-pseudosocialist tinge: *Rêveries politiques* (1833); *Des idées napoléoniennes* (1839); *Extinction du paupérisme* (1844). —M and others used several sobriquets intended to express contempt. *Boustrapa* was a contraction of Boulogne-Strasbourg-Paris, three cities where he organized conspiracies (see above). *Badinguet* derives from his escape from Ham; one explanation is that it was the name of the workman in whose clothes he disguised himself. *Badingueux* means adherents of Badinguet. *Soulouque* comes from Faustin Soulouque, who proclaimed himself emperor of Haiti in 1849. *Crapulinski* (or variants) comes from a satirical poem by Heine, "Crapülinski und Waschlapski." *Napoleon the Little* (le Petit) was Victor Hugo's contemptuous contrast of the "nephew" with the "uncle" (Napoleon I). → 49:29; 50:14; 51:1, 3, 55, 56; 52:10, 15, 18, 43, 52; 54:8, 43; 55:17, 31; 56:6, 15, 40; 57:42; 58:8, 11, 16, 23, 27; 59:6, 8, 15, 22, 31, 35, 55, 57, 58, 66, 75; 60:7, 13, 24, 28, 31; 61:3, 21; 64:44; 65:14; 66:50; 68:37; 70:1, 32, 40, 45, 48; 71:22, 25; 82:15; 83:10. #M59, M63, M90–M92, M196, M221, M267, M275, M433, M435, M479, M489–M492, M500, M533, M535, M536, M632, M684; E197, E500–E502, E531, E607. *See also* next entry.

Bonaparte, Napoléon Joseph Charles Paul; *called* Prince Napoleon; *sobriquet* Plon-Plon (1822 to 1891) Nephew of Napoleon III; son of Napoleon I's brother Jérôme Bonaparte (Prince Jérôme). During the Second Empire he gave himself out to be the liberal, dissenting, or even semisocialistic wing of the regime, and associated with some Saint-Simonian elements. During the Second Republic he had been a deputy to the Constituent and National Assemblies. On the death of Bonaparte's heir (1879), Plon-Plon became the pretender to the throne and (1886) was exiled from France. → 59:35; 72:8.

Bonapartism, Bonapartists → 52:1; 53:40; 55:13; 56;6; 58:19; 59:4, 6–8, 34, 35, 41, 44; 60:23, 35; 64:31; 65:7, 9, 13, 14; 69:25; 70:31; 71:49, 62; 72:8, 11, 41; 88:21, 24; 89:8; 90:21. #M90. *See also* Bonaparte, L. N.

Bonhorst, Leonhard von (b. 1840) German socialist; mechanical engineer by profession. First, active in the Wiesbaden WEA (mid-1860s); then in the IWMA's Geneva CC (spring 1867+). He became a Lassallean repr (GGWA plenipotentiary) in Wiesbaden (autumn 1867), but quit the GGWA (1869), attended the Eisenach congress, and became secy of the SDWP's Brunswich Exec; a defendant in the Brunswick "treason trial" of 1871. He later withdrew from political activity. → 69:59, 62, 66.

Bonn (Ger.) In M's day, a smallish town known mainly for its university; on the Rhine south of Cologne. → 35:4; 40:12; 41:14; 42:8, 10, 19, 36; 45:16, 24; 69:56. #M93, #M436.

Bonn, University of → 35:1, 4; 36:1, 2, 4–9; 39:9; 41:14, 19; 42:10.

Bonnet, Victor; *full* Jacques Victor (1814 to 1885) French publicist and economist. Member of the Académie des Sciences Morales. M (1878–1879) read his *Questions économiques et financières à propos des crises* (1859) in an 1869 edn. Other works: *Le crédit et les finances* (1865); *Etudes sur la monnaie* (1870). → 78:51.

Bonnier, Charles (1863 to *after* 1905) French socialist writer and journalist; university lecturer. Son of a Lille white-collar employee, he joined the French Workers party as a youth (1880); delegate to international socialist congresses (1889–1893); took part in the 1905 unity congress in Paris; contributor to the Guesdist press in France, to NZ, etc. His best known book was *La question de la femme* (1897). For many years he was a lecturer at Oxford U., while remaining in close touch with his friend Guesde; and so E had to deal with him as a sort of repr of the French party. → 89:15, 17; 90:37; 91:37; 92:45, 52, 62. #E386, E443.

Boon, Martin James British "O'Brienite" radical; mechanic and owner of an ironmongery business. Member of the GC/IWMA (1869–1872); co-secy of the Land and Labour League; member of the British Federal Council (1873). He was also a supporter of the National Reform League and of Owen's "labor exchange" ideas; a prolific pamphleteer, esp on nationalization of land, credit schemes, and emigration. During the IWMA he pubd *Home colonization . . . how all the unem-*

ployed might have profitable work (1869) and other pamphlets. Later (early 1870s), he went into a publishing venture, failed, emigrated (1874) to South Africa, becoming a merchant in Bloemfontein. In the 1880s he issued a number of pamphlets on social reforms, exposure of abuses against the aborigines, and corruption in officialdom. → 69:10; 71:2, 39; 72:8.

Borchardt, Louis German-born physician in Manchester; a friendly acquaintance of E and W. Wolff in that city, politically sympathetic in a general way. → 53:29; 59:46.

Bordeaux (Fr.) → 67:25; 70:55, 59; 71:2, 27, 32, 59; 73:36; 88:38.

Borgius, Walt(h)er A law student at the U. of Breslau (1893–1895). E's letter of Jan 25, 1894, about historical materialism was long (till 1967) considered a letter to H. *Starkenburg, who pubd it, but it was actually sent to Borgius. → 94:7.

Boriani, Giuseppe Italian radical, active in the IWMA and workers' movement in the Romagna (1870s). He was one of the founders and leaders of the Associazione Internazionale degli Operai, and later of the Società dei Lavoratori Ferraresi (IWMA). #E190.

Borkheim, Sigismund (Ludwig) (1825 to 1885) German merchant; radical Democrat. He took part in the 1848 revolution (where he became acquainted with M&E); participated in the attack on the Berlin arsenal; in 1849 took part in the Baden uprising; then took refuge in Switzerland and France, finally (1851) in England, where he became a wine merchant. He entered (1860) into friendly relations with M&E; transd Russian writings for them on occasion. B. was an extreme Russophobe even in M's view, very anti-Pan-Slavist, hostile to Bakunin and eager to aid M against him. In 1867 at the Geneva Peace and Freedom Congress he made a speech against the czarist regime which he pubd as *Ma perle devant le Congrès de Genève.* → 60:12, 13, 14, 24, 35, 54; 61:4; 62:18, 44; 67:29, 37, 39, 42; 68:59; 69:32; 70:19, 32; 71:56; 79:37; 84:32; 86:33; 87:48; 88:2, 22. #E391.

Born, Stephan; *orig* Simon **Buttermilch** (1824 to 1898) German worker (typesetter); union organizer. He came to Berlin (1840) as a young printshop worker; went to Paris (1846) where, influenced by K. Grün, he joined the League of the Just, and traveled as its propagandist. In Paris in late 1846 he met E, joined the CL in 1847, met M in Brussels, where he was setting type for the DBZ, active in the WA. On the outbreak of the 1848 revolution he went to Berlin on behalf of the CL. There he became a leader of the printers' union and its Apr strike, and became the premier labor organizer: first of a workers' club, later of a more comprehensive *Arbeiterverbrüderung* (regarded as the first gen workers' union in Germany); also editor of *Das Volk*, which he set up. The expanded organization centered in Leipzig, where B. also put out the organ *Der Verbrüderung*. In the course of this organizational work, B. virtually dropped his communism in favor of a social-reform approach with strictly economic demands—quite different from the line of M's *NRZ* in Cologne (for which he wrote correspondence). In May 1849 he became involved semiaccidentally in the Dresden uprising, and had to flee Germany, first to Bohemia, then Switzerland. Thereafter he dropped not only the CL but also the workers' movement. In Basel he took up studies, became a teacher and journalist, and in his last year, a prof of German literature at the U. of Basel; pubd *Erinnerungen eines Achtundvierzigers* (1898). → 47:39, 45; 48:33; 49:6.

Bornstedt, Adalbert von (1808 to 1851) Prussian ex-army officer; from the late 1830s, a secret agent of the Prussian government operating in the Paris and Brussels emigration; an unstable adventurer, one historian calls him. In Paris (1844) he helped produce *Vorwärts!* with Börnstein; in 1847 he helped run the *DBZ* in Brussels. In 1848, in Paris, he was a leader in the German Demo Assoc and in the "German Legion" scheme (for which he was expelled from the CL, which he had joined). Later that year he took part in the Baden uprising, in his own way. → 47:29, 52; 48:19, 22, 27. #ME175.

Borodino (Russ.) Village near Moscow; scene of Napoleon's victory in 1812. #E95.

Borrosch (Czech. **Borroš**), Alois (1797 to 1869) Austrian-Czech liberal Democrat; bookseller of Prague. In the 1848 revolution in Austria he was a leader of the German-Bohemian group in the Imperial Diet. Later (1850+) he edited organs of the K.K. Patriotisch-ökonomische Gesellschaft im Königreiche Böhmen (Prague). → 48:58.

Bosanquet, Charles (1769 to 1850) English merchant capitalist; of a family of successful London merchants. He was governor (head) of the South Sea Co. (1838–1850). He pubd some brochures on economic subjects; they had some influence. His pamphlet *Thoughts on the value, to Gr Brit, of commerce in general* (1807) drew a reply by William Spence. M (1851) read his *Practical observations on the report of the Bullion-Committee* (1810); this pamphlet attacked the report, and was in turn refuted by Ricardo's reply → 51:63.

Bosanquet, James Whatman (1804 to 1877) English banker and writer. Sprung from a banking family, he became a partner in the house of B., Salt & Co. At first he wrote mainly on banking; M (1851) read his *Metal-*

lic, paper, and credit currency (1842), letters to the *Times* orig signed A. Lombard. Among B.'s other brochures was *Letter... on the Bank Charter Act of 1844* (1857). But later B. devoted his writing to biblical history and archeology, and financed the publ program of the Society of Biblical Archaeology. → 51:63.

Bosnia Now in central Yugoslavia; the province of Bosnia and Herzegovina was formerly part of the Austro-Hungarian Empire. → 82:9.

Bosost (Sp.) → 71:43.

Bosquet, Pierre; *full* Pierre Jean [*formerly given as* Joseph] François (1810 to 1861) French gen; a republican, later a Bonapartist. He served in the conquest of Algeria (1830s–1850s); commanded a corps (1854–1855) in the Crimean War, where he won the battle of the Alma and saved the British at Inkerman; created marshal of France and senator (1856). M&E's article presents him as a very able officer. #ME24.

Boston (Mass.) → 53:11, 19; 62:27; 81:17; 88:28, 30.

Der **Bote für Stadt und Land;** Pfälzisches Volksblatt Kaiserslautern (Ger.), May-June 1849. —During the 1849 uprising in the Palatinate, it was pubd as official organ of the Prov Government. #E701.

Botkin, Vasily Petrovich (1812 new style/ 1811 old style to 1869) Russian writer, critic, and publicist; liberal. During the 1830s–1840s he was close to radical Westernizers like Herzen; contributed to *Otechestvenniye Zapiski*, etc., esp on art, music, and literature. In the 1840s he toured Europe, meeting M inter alia; described impressions in articles in *Sovremennnik* [Letters on Spain]. After the 1848 revolution he became a rightish liberal, and after 1855, a defender of "pure art" and bourgeois regimes. → 44:9.

Botta, Carlo Giuseppe Guglielmo (1766 to 1837) Italian historian; b. in Piedmont; orig a physician. Rector of the U. of Rouen (1817–1822). His main historical work was his *Storia d'Italia dal 1789 al 1814* (1824); also wrote *Storia d'Italia in continuazione al Guicciardini* (1832), *Storia della guerra dell'-independenza d'America* (1809). #M141.

Boucharlat, Jean Louis (1775 to 1848) French mathematician; long a teacher at the Polytechnic, then prof at a military school; afterward he devoted himself to belles lettres and poetry. Chief math works: *Eléments du calcul différentiel* (1838); *Théories des courbes et des surfaces de second ordre* (1810). → 78:1.

Boulangeo-Blanquists This was a term used (by their opponents) for that section of the French Blanquist group, led by *Granger, which split off to support the would-be dictator *Boulanger (1889). → *89:25, 32;* *92:13, 22, 52.*

Boulanger, Georges (Ernest Jean Marie) (1837 to 1891) French gen; a would-be (and even could-be) Bonapartist dictator. After a successful military career in several French colonies and against the Paris Commune, he entered the Freycinet cabinet (1886–1887) as war min, with Clemenceau's support; popular enthusiasm for this "man on horseback" was whipped up by his platform of constitutional reform, anti-German revanchisme, jingo chauvinism, and by popular hopes for a new Bonaparte, the whole with a protofascist appeal. Mainly operated by reactionary royalists, his demagogic appeal also gained much plebeian and working-class support as an alternative to a corrupt bourgeois republic. By 1889 he seemed on the verge of a successful coup; but, threatened by prosecution, this political adventurer cracked up, fled abroad (Brussels, Jersey), and committed suicide on his mistress's grave. For a while, pro-Boulangism in the socialist movement (see E. *Granger for the "Boulangeo-Blanquists") was a serious problem. The worst case among the Guesdist leaders was Paul Lafargue; E's letters to him, denouncing "socialist" Boulangism, form one of the least known and most important contributions in the ME correspondence; see ST/E9 or E10; though many of these letters to Lafargue are not extant (perhaps destroyed). → *87:34;* *89:4, 8, 13, 25, 32; 90:11, 21.*

Boulogne (Fr.) Seaport city on the Channel. → *49:33.*

Bourbaki, Charles (Denis Sauter) (1816 to 1897) French gen. After a successful military career in Algeria, Italy, and the Crimea, he was in command of the Army of the East in the Franco-Prussian War (1870). Here he failed signally to raise the Prussian siege; his troops were interned in Switzerland (1871); he tried to commit suicide but failed this also; retired from the army by orthodox means in 1881. #E531.

Bourbon family Its descendants formed ruling dynasties in France, 1589–1792, 1814/15–1830; in Spain, 1701–1931; in Naples-Sicily (The Two Sicilies), 1735–1860; in Parma, 1748–1859. In France the first Bourbon king was Henri IV (1589–1610), followed by Louis XIII to XVI, and after the French Revolution, Charles X. Supporters of the main Bourbon line were called Legitimists, as distinct from other royalists (Orleanists and Bonapartists). #E424.

Bourne, Fox; *full* Henry Richard Fox (1837 to 1909) English journalist, author, social reformer. Born in Jamaica, he moved with his parents to London (1848); worked in the War Office; contributed to periodicals; finally made an impact with his biography of Sir Philip Sidney (1862); followed with many works on biographical and popular-historical subjects. Retiring from the War Office (1870), he purchased the London *Examiner,* but failed (1873); editor of the *Weekly Dispatch* (1876–1887); his journalistic standpoint was radical-liberal. Thereafter he focused his work on the Aborigines Protection Society, as its secy (1889+), undertaking many campaigns to defend the rights of natives in Africa and Asia, etc., in many books and brochures. → *71:20.*

Bourrienne, Louis (Antoine) Fauvelet de (1769 to 1834) French politician; he rose as private secy to Napoleon (1797–1802) and councillor of state. Having lined his own pockets, his corruption in danger of exposure, he went over to his friend's enemies; offered his services to Louis XVIII, supported the Restoration, and became an ultra-royalist spokesman; wrote *Mémoires sur Napoléon* (1829). → *57:38.* #M97.

Bouterwek, Friedrich (1766 or 1765 to 1828) German philosopher and literary historian. Prof of philosophy at Göttingen (1802+); at first a disciple of Kant, later a critic, also a disciple of F. H. Jacobi. M (1852) studied his chief work in literary history, *Geschichte der Poesie und Beredsamkeit* (1801–1819). B. also wrote mediocre poetry and novels. → *52:56, 57.*

Bovio, Giovanni (1841 to 1903) Italian academic (law prof at Naples), politician, writer. Orig influenced by Comtism, a left Mazzinist, he was a member of a workers' assoc in Trani during the IWMA period and a supporter of the Paris Commune. In 1876 he was elected a deputy from Bari, and became a leading figure in the Republican party. Works: *Sommario della storia del diritto in Italia* (1883); *Scritti filosofici e politici* (1883); also some bad plays. → *92:11.* #E669.

Bowring, Sir John (1792 to 1872) British writer and diplomatist. He was best known as a linguist, a prolific translator and anthologist of poetry from many languages, incl the Eastern European; his *Specimens of the Russian poets* (1821–1823) was his first such collection, read by E; he also wrote poems and hymns. Editor of the *Westminster Review* (1824–1825); Bentham's literary executor. His other career was as British diplomatic agent, a high official entrusted with many missions carrying out British colonial plans in the Far East; consul in Canton, governor of Hongkong for a while. On one mission he was involved in precipitating the Second Opium War with China. MP (1835–1837, 1841–1849). M's 1858–1861 notebooks treat his *Second report on the commercial relations between France and Gr Brit* (1835). → *51:49.*

Bracke, Wilhelm (1842 to 1880) German Social-Democratic leader. He began as a successful businessman (grain dealer) in Brunswick. There a founder of the Lassallean GGWA branch (1865); chief treasurer of the assoc (1867); and a leader of the opposition favoring the Bebel tendency. In 1869 he was one of the founders of the "Eisenacher" S-D party, a member of its "Brunswick Exec"; a reliable supporter of M&E, with whom he became personally friendly; a defendant in the Brunswick treason trial (1871), and spent some time in jail. In 1871 he established a printshop and publishing/bookdealer firm in Brunswick, which he then put at the service of his party; pub'r of *Braunschweiger Volksfreund* (1871–1878) and *Volks-Kalendar* (1876, 1877). Reichstag member (1877–1879). —He should not be confused with the French socialist A. M. Desrousseaux (1861–1955), who used the name Alexandre Bracke; also known as Bracke-Desrousseaux. → 68:43; 69:59; 70:3, 28, 31, 60; 71:58; 74:22; 75:12, 20, 36, 48; 76:16, 27; 77:1, 2, 13, 15, 22, 33, 37, 38; 78:13, 32; 79:47. #ME29; M928.

Bradford (Eng.) City in the West Riding of Yorkshire, near Leeds. → 52:42; 72:14; 93:2.

Bradlaugh, Charles (1833 to 1891) English social reformer and professional atheist. Son of a solicitor's clerk, he early became militantly antireligious; ousted Holyoake from the presidency of the National Secular Society (1858); founded and edited the *National Reformer* (1860+); became a popular Freethought lecturer, esp sought-after in the 1870s; tried for advocating birth control (1876); elected MP in 1880 but not allowed to sit till 1886. In politics, he was on the radical wing of liberalism, but virulently antisocialist, hostile to TUs, and firmly middle-class in sympathies. His influence faded as socialism grew in the 1880s. → 67:37; 71:62, 63; 72:5, 8; 81:4.

Brandenburg (Ger.) Town 37 miles W. of Berlin. → 48:76, 81, 83.

Brandenburg, Count Friedrich Wilhelm von (1792 to 1850) Prussian gen and political leader. He was head of the counterrevolutionary cabinet of Nov 1848 to Nov 1850. → 48:76, 78. #M611.

Brass, August (1818 to 1876) German journalist. After taking part in the 1848 revolution in Germany, he emigrated to Switzerland, becoming editor of the *Neue Schweizer Ztg* (1859–1860). Back in Germany, he pubd the *Norddeutsche Allgemeine Ztg*, for which Liebknecht was an editor. Later, a National Liberal supporter of Bismarck. → 48:58; 63:19, 36.

Bray, John Francis (1809 to 1895) American-born socialist writer, active in England for a period. Once thought to be an Englishman, he was actually born in Washington, D.C.; taken as a boy (1822) to Leeds, Eng. By 1835 he was a printing worker (compositor) in Leeds, beginning to publish his ideas in the local press; treasurer of the new (1837) Leeds Working Men's Assoc. His book, *Labour's wrongs and labour's remedy* (1839), is his claim to fame. In 1842 he returned to the U.S.; worked as a farmer, printer, journalist in the Detroit area; still active in the labor movement (American Labor Reform League, Knights of Labor). —His book makes him an important "Ricardian socialist," drawing Owenite socialist conclusions from Ricardo's theory; but it deprecates Chartist political aims and tradeunionism. It was much used in the Owenite movement, and highly regarded by M. → 46:52. #E886.

Bray, Vicar of Popular song prob of the early 18th century, about a timeserving vicar who cuts his cloth to whatever authority is in power: "And this is the law I will maintain/ Until my dying day, sir,/ That whatsoever king shall reign/ I'll still be the Vicar of Bray, sir." Bray is a parish in Berkshire, Eng., and the song may refer to a historical character. → 82:38.

Brazil See Porto Alegre; Rio de Janeiro.

Bremen Important commercial city of N. Germany, near the North Sea. Its port is Bremerhaven. → 38:2, 9–11; 39:2, 4–6; 40:12, 15; 41:1, 5, 8, 15; 49:20; 51:5; 64:8. #M256; E188.5, E233, E454, E456, E575, E651, E663, E674, E737, E774, E804.

Der **Bremer Stadtbote** Bremen, Jan 1839+. Weekly. Pub'r: Albertus Meyer. #E94, E816, E840.

Bremerhaven (Ger.) Port city on the North Sea. → 40:12; 41:15. #E575, E674. See Bremen.

Bremisches Conversationsblatt Bremen, May 3, 1838, to June 30, 1839. Ed by L. W. Heyse. —Moderate liberal literary journal pubd as a supplement to *Bremer Ztg.* #E73.

Bremisches Unterhaltungsblatt Bremen, 1823 to 1857. Ed by W. Fricke (1838–1840). —Literary paper. #E816, E840.

Brentano, Ludwig Joseph; *called* Lujo (1844 to 1931) German economist: of the late Historical School; a right-wing Katheder-socialist and a founder of the Verein für Sozialpolitik; social reformer. Prof of polit eco (1872–1914) at Breslau, Strassburg, Vienna, Leipzig, and (1891+) Munich. His chief work, based on his study of English trade-unionism, was *Die Arbeitergilden der Gegenwart* (1871–1872). → 72:30, 33, 39, 47; 90:40, 50; 91:12, 24; 93:30. #M737, M738; E374, E375.

Brescia City in N. Italy (Lombardy). #E96.

Breslau (Ger.); *now* Wroclaw in Poland → 48:33, 46; 49:3, 24; 54:1, 50; 55:1; 60:15; 62:47; 72:16, 41; 79:16; 94:7.

Breslau, University of → 76:24.

Breslauer Morgen-Zeitung Breslau, 1862 to 1873. Daily. Ed by M. Elsner. → 64:15.

Breslauer Zeitung Breslau, 1820+. Daily. —Liberal in the 1840s, conservative in the 1850s. → 60:13.

Bricourt, Jean Joseph (1805 to 1857) Belgian jurist and politician; in 1847–1848 a member of the Chamber of Deputies. Judge at Charleroi; in 1832–1842 he belonged to the Provincial Council of Hennegau; in 1846, took part in the first congress of the liberal party. He was elected deputy from Soignies in June 1847; stripped of his mandate (May 1848) by a new law. → 48:21.

Bridlington Quay (Yorkshire, Eng.) → 80:27; 81:41, 47.

Bright, John (1811 to 1889) English political leader on the radical wing of Liberalism; a founder and leader of the Anti-Corn-Law League, champion of free trade. Cotton mill owner, of a Quaker family, he gained prominence as an orator; entered Parliament in 1843 (till 1889 almost continuously); leader of the Liberal party from the 1860s; often a minister in Liberal cabinets (1868+); with Cobden, the foremost leader of left liberalism and the "Manchester School": his heart beat for Universal Freedom and he worked to beat prolabor legislation. → 53:26; 63:13; 65:25. #M227, M424.

Brighton (Eng.) Resort city on the Channel. → 64:25, 27; 71:45; 73:22; 76:23; 77:8, 20. #E99.

Brissot de Warville, Jacques Pierre (1754 to 1793) Political leader of the right wing of the French Revolution (Girondists or "Brissotins"). Son of an innkeeper (the "de Warville" was assumed later), he began as a lawyer; became a journalist, concerned with social reform, an admirer of the new American republic; author of works on the philosophy of law, incl Recherches philosophiques sur le propriété et le vol (1780)—source of the aphorism later publicized by Proudhon as "Property is theft." A Jacobin at the beginning of the revolution, he was a moderate in the Convention; guillotined with other Girondist leaders. #M575.

British Federation or **Federal Council** (of the IWMA) → 71:1, 46, 47, 52, 56, 62; 72:3, 24, 31, 37, 43, 53, 55, 60, 66; 73:7, 11, 23, 27. #M6, M110; E465, E664.

British Museum (Library) (London) "British Museum" is usually used here to refer to the library, not to the whole museum. → 45:31; 50:3, 24; 51:3; 52:25, 30, 34; 53:2, 23; 54:38; 55:26; 56:8, 13; 57:26; 58:5, 10; 59:76; 60:9, 65; 63:14, 20; 65:61; 66:8; 68:18; 73:38, 53. #E32.

Brittany Peninsular region of N.W. France. → 49:31.

Broadhouse, John Pseud. of H. M. *Hyndman. → 85:37. #E360.

Brocker-Everaerts, J. A.; for short **Brocker** The responsible pub'r and printer of the Cologne WA's organ, Freiheit, Brüderlichkeit, Arbeit and its successor in late 1848 and 1849; see this name. In Sep 1848 he became a member of the WA's leading committee. I have not found any other info on this man, not even his full name. → 48:71; 49:6.

Brockhaus, Heinrich (1804 to 1874) German pub'r, head of F. A. Brockhaus, a major publishing firm of Leipzig. The firm was founded by the merchant Friedrich Arnold B. (1772–1823) in Amsterdam in 1805; bought out (1808) the unfinished encyclopedia (Konversationslexikon) begun in 1796 by R. G. Löbel and C. W. Franke; moved (1811) to Altenburg, then (1817–1818) to Leipzig, where it established its own printshop. The sons Friedrich (1800–1865) and Heinrich first owned it together (1823–1849), then Heinrich became sole owner (1849–1874), moderate-liberal in policy. → 52:32; 61:17, 22, 31; 62:22.

Brockhaus Konversationslexikon; Allgemeine deutsche Real-Encyklopädie für die gebildeten Stände, 13th edn Leipzig, F. A. Brockhaus, 1882–1887. —Prob the leading German encyclopedia of the time. → 90:16.

Brooklyn A borough of NY City. → 83:12; 95:12.

Brooklyn Labor Lyceum → 83:12.

Brosses, Charles de (1709 to 1777) French scholar (historian, ethnographer, linguist, etc.); contributor to the Encyclopédie; a man of the Enlightenment. (KMC gives his name erron. as Debrosses.) He pubd an edn of Sallust; works on Australasia and Herculaneum; the book Formation mécanique des langues (1765). M (1842) excerpted Ueber den Dienst der Fetischgötter (1785), trans of his Du culte des dieux fétiches (1760). #M93.

Brougham, Henry Peter; Baron **Brougham and Vaux** [1830+] (1778 to 1868) British (Scottish-born) lawyer, politician, man of letters. As a lawyer, he first gained fame as counsel for Queen Caroline. In intellectual life, he made a mark as a founder of the Edinburgh Review and of London Univ.; author of a voluminous array of forgotten literary pieces. In politics: MP (1810–1812, 1816+ for decades); a noted Whig orator, his personal ambition ranged him against the Whig leadership, which at one point kicked him upstairs into the post of lord chancellor (1830–1835). He was a champion of free trade and parliamentary reform; opponent of the slave trade; advocate of certain progressive stands in foreign affairs, such as the cause of partitioned Poland. —M (1843) excerpted a German edn of his views on Poland, titled Polen (Brussels, 1831). M (1851) studied his Inquiry into the colonial policy of the European powers (1803). → 43:32; 51:69.

Brousse, Paul (Louis Marie) (1843–1844? to 1912) French socialist, first a Bakuninist, later leader of the reformist wing. Orig a physician, he served in the Paris Commune, then emigrated to Barcelona (1872), pubd *Solidarité Révolutionnaire* from an anarchist viewpoint, and in 1873 attended the Bakuninist IWMA congress in Geneva. For some years he was a leader in the Jurassian Federation, the Bakuninist center; later in the 1870s he belonged to the "extremist" wing of Kropotkin's Swiss group. He returned secretly to France (1877); pubd *L'Avant-Garde* (1877–1878); and began advocating some electoral action; then emigrated to Brussels and London, and around this time began to shed anarchism. The 1880 amnesty brought him back to Paris, from the beginning a reformist opponent of Guesde and Marx, having made an 180° swing. Editor of *Egalité* and *Prolétaire* (1882), he went with the Possibilist (right wing) split from the party, allied himself with Malon against Guesde, and became the leading figure among the reformist socialists ("Broussists")—uncontested after the Allemane split of 1890. "Broussism" in politics straddled the area between socialism and the bourgeois Radicals. The one view he never changed was bitter anti-Marxism: his pamphlet *Le marxisme dans l'International* (1882) pioneered the *-ism* term; and his obituary on M used the occasion to reveal that M "was not God" and that his theory was passé. Another brochure, *La propriété collective et les services publics* (1883), was a significant exposition of reformism as state-socialism. —There is a full-length study in English: David Stafford's *From anarchism to reformism* (1971). —Birth date: Stafford gives 1844; Maitron/*DB* says 1843; *MEW* etc. says 1854. → 80:11; 82:5, 24, 40, 55; 83:21; 90:42.

Brown, Sir George (1790 to 1865) British gen, b. Scotland. He served in the Peninsular War (1808–1814), and commanded a division in the Crimea (1854–1855), making full gen in 1856. Afterward, commander-in-chief in Ireland (1860–1865). #E104.

Brown, John (1800 to 1859) American revolutionary abolitionist. A farmer, he first became known ("Old Brown of Osawatomie") for making a stand in Kansas against proslavery raiders. In 1859 he led a band to seize Harpers Ferry (now in W. Va.) and its arsenal to establish a base for a slave stronghold and refuge, with a view to a general slave uprising. He was captured; hanged; and lived on in the song "John Brown's Body." → 60:8.

Brown, Willlard American journalist. A socialist, he was in touch with M by correspondence. NUC lists an anonymous pamphlet *Socialism in Germany* (1879?) under his name. → 81:23.

Browning, George A London writer who pubd *The domestic and financial condition of Gr Brit* (1834), apparently his only work; read by M (1845). → 45:51. #M575.

Brünn In M's day, the capital of the Austrian province of Moravia; today it is Brno (Czechoslovakia). → 91:59.

Bruges; *Flem.* Brugge City in W. Flanders, Belgium. → 69:56.

Bruhn, Karl von (b. 1803) German journalist; b. Schleswig-Holstein, later active in Hamburg. Orig an artillery officer, he became a member and propagandist of the League of Outcasts (1836+); later, member of the League of the Just and the CL. In the revolution of 1848–1849 he took part in the uprisings in Frankfurt and Baden. In 1850 he went over to the German émigré group in Switzerland called the Revolutionäre Zentralisation (Schurz, Techow, et al.), and was expelled from the CL (see the account in #ME3). He became a supporter of the Willich–Schapper group; later, a Lassallean, member of the GGWA, editor of *Nordstern* (Hamburg, 1861–1866). → 49:20; 50:45.

Brune, Guillaume (Marie Anne) (1763 to 1815) Marshal of France, prominent military leader during the French Revolution and in the Napoleonic war. When the Revolution started, he was a Paris printer-pubr; under Danton's wing he advanced quickly in the NG and army. He abandoned Danton fast enough to get through the Reign of Terror, and carried out various military commands under Napoleon; but he was not one of the great gens. He was murdered by a royalist mob during the White Terror at Avignon. #M117.

Bruno, Giordano (1548 to 1600) Italian philosopher, an ex-Dominican religious heretic, who—more from the standpoint of a Renaissance magus and mystic metaphysician than of scientific method—advocated the Copernican view, along with many pantheistic and magical ideas of less current respectability. His chief expositions were *De la causa, principio e uno* and *De l'infinito, universo e mondi* (both 1584); M (1852) excerpted these, at least the first, perhaps others. —On his returning to Venice from his European travels (1591) Bruno was seized by the Inquisition; in the course of two trials, he first recanted, then repudiated his recantation; and the Church Militant then criticized his philosophy by burning him alive in Rome. The late 18th century rediscovered his contributions; the 19th century esp emphasized that side of his ideas which objectively played a part in the development of scientific thought, and enshrined his name as a martyr to intellectual freedom and symbol of anticlericalism. → 52:56, 57.

Brunswick; *Ger.* Braunschweig City and former state in central Germany. → 41:17;

69:59, 62, 66; 70:3, 19, 28, 36, 44, 45, 48, 50; 71:58; 74:8; 77:46.

Brunswick, Duke of. Karl Friedrich August Wilhelm, Duke of **Brunswick and Lüneberg** (1804 to 1873) Having succeeded to the duchy in 1823, he was overthrown in 1830, went into exile, and schemed to recover his possessions. In the 1840s–1850s he maintained contact with the radical and liberal Demo movement, and in particular gave financial support to the Deutsche Londoner Ztg; hence he was looked on as a potential "angel" for various radical enterprises. → 48:25.

Brunswick Executive Committee See Social-Democratic Workers Party (Ger.).

Brussels Fr. Bruxelles Capital of Belgium —Selected references from the Chronicle: —M&E's residence, moves, personal affairs: → 45:1, 4, 13, 18, 23–26, 32, 39, 46; 47:5, 20, 26, 45, 50, 56; 48:1, 7, 68, 74. — Addresses: → 45:13, 26; 46:21, 44.5; 48:9. — M&E's polit activity in: → 45:3, 21, 37; 46:1, 8, 45; 47:1, 8, 11, 28, 39, 51, 52; 48:14–17, 21. —Brussels notebooks: → 45:14, 50, 52; 46:51, 52. —Lectures on polit eco: → 47:53; 49:18. —Free Trade Congress: → 47:3, 32. —Demo Assoc: → 47:44, 56; 48:10. — Correspondence with: → 49:12; 61:15; 67:16. —Leftists in: → 66:9; 69:30. — IWMA Congress (1868): → 68:26, 39, 42, 48, 49, 54, 55, 61. —IWMA in: → 70:4, 36, 55; 71:3, 25; 72:21, 24, 31, 33. —Int'l Socialist Congress: → 91:41, 44; 92:56. —Preconference: → 93:20. —Publ in: → 94:16. — Register index, used in titles only: #M118, M564, M584, M650, M887, M895; E106, E291, E439. See also Belgium; Communist Correspondence Comm; DBZ.

Brussels Democratic Association See Democratic Association (Brussels).

Brussels Workers Association See German Workers Association (Brussels).

Buchanan, David (1779 to 1848) British journalist and economist. A disciple of Adam Smith, he pubd an edn (1814) of Smith's work in three vols., plus a fourth vol. of his own commentary: Observations on the· subjects treated of in Dr. Smith's inquiry (2nd edn, 1817; excerpted by M, 1851). He was an opponent of the Physiocrats' theory of rent. Another work: An inquiry into the taxation and commercial policy of Gr Brit (1844). → 51:66.

Buchanan, James (1791 to 1868) The 15th president of the U.S.; a conservative, proslavery Democratic party man. → 58:49. #M375.

Bucher, Bruno (1826 to 1899) German art historian; brother of Lothar. His main writings on art, esp in connection with the Austrian Museum for Art and Industry in Vienna, came a couple of decades after his contact with M. → 48:74; 50:9.

Bucher, Lothar; full Adolph Lothar (1817 to 1892) German politician; a henchman of Lassalle, then of Bismarck. A Pomeranian lawyer, in 1848 he was elected to the Berlin National Assembly (left center); from 1850, an émigré, chiefly in London, where he acted as correspondent for the Berlin National-Ztg; pubd a critique of liberalism, Der Parlamentarismus wie er ist. He returned to Germany (1860) and became right-hand man to Lassalle, close political adviser during his GGWA campaign; named as Lassalle's literary executor. After Lassalle's death, Bismarck sought and acquired his services with a high post in the Prussian foreign office. Bucher made a complete break with his leftist past and, until his death, acted as Bismarck's private secy, confidant, collaborator, and intellectual serviceman. → 48:74; 62:31, 35; 65:54; 78:19. #M370, M739.

Buda (Hung.) #E107. See Budapest.

Budapest (Hung.) Formed in 1872–1873 by amalgamating Buda and Pest, each on one side of the Danube. → 76:6, 29; 93:4. #E832. See also Buda.

Budgen, F. C. #ME33.

Bücher, Karl (1847 to 1930) German economist and historian of economics; statistician. Prof of polit eco at Leipzig (1892–1917); founded and headed its Institute of Journalism (1917). Chief work: Die Entstehung der Volkswirtschaft (1893). M (1879) studied his Die Aufstände der unfreien Arbeiter 143–129 v. Chr. (1874). Other works incl Die Wirtschaft der Naturvölker (1898). → 79:54.

Büchner, Ludwig; full Friedrich Karl Christian Ludwig (1824 to 1899) German scientist (physiologist) and philosopher of science. A physician by training, he took part in the 1848 revolution as a left Democrat; later joined the IWMA, and was a delegate to its 1867 congress, though opposed to an independent workers' movement. A lecturer in medicine at Tübingen (1852), he was forced out because of his book Kraft und Stoff (1855), and was condemned as an antireligious materialist and Darwinist. He returned to medicine and writing: Natur und Geist (1857); Darwinismus und Socialismus (1894). The book M received in 1868 was his Sechs Vorlesungen über die Darwinische Theorie von der Verwandlung der Arten. B. became, with K. Vogt and Moleschott, a leading popular representative of propaganda counterposing science to religious metaphysicians; he called himself a "monist," not a materialist. To M&E, these three were outstanding examples of what they called "vulgar materialism"—mechanical materialism, unhistorical and undialectical. → 67:14. 68:64.

Bühring, Karl Johann (b. 1820) German

worker (joiner), émigré in London, acquaintance of M. In 1848 he had been active in the Hamburg WA; a CL member. → 61:14.

Bülow, Baron Friedrich Wilhelm von (1755 to 1816) Prussian gen. He served against Napoleonic France (1813–1815); was created Count Bülow von Dennewitz (1814); fought with Blücher in the Waterloo campaign. (Caution: There are a number of von Bülows around in the 19th century.) #M119.

Buenos Aires (Argentina) → 73:33.

Bürgers, Heinrich; full Johann Heinrich Georg (1820 to 1878) German radical journalist; communist for a while. Orig from Cologne, he made M's acquaintance in the Paris and Brussels emigration (1844); joined M's CCC and worked for it in Cologne (1846–1847); member of the CL (1847–1852). In the 1848 revolution he worked with M as a member of the ed bd of the NRZ (though he wrote little). In 1850–1851 he was on the CC/CL in Cologne, and thus became a leading defendant in the Cologne Communist trial (1852); sentenced to six years. In the 1860s he became a supporter of the Progressivist party, then a National Liberal; edited a Düsseldorf paper called the Rheinische Ztg. → 44:41; 45:13, 18; 46:9, 25, 29, 34, 42; 47:14, 16; 48:30, 62, 65, 68; 50:12; 51:20, 27; 52:39; 57:48; 60:46; 67:12. #M232.

Bürkli, Karl (1823 to 1901) Swiss socialist and cooperativist. Converted by Fourier's writings (1845), he took part as a youth in the 1848 revolution in Germany; elected to the Swiss cantonal council as a socialist (1851). A master tanner, he was a founder of the pioneering Zurich consumers' co-op society (1858); an active leader of the IWMA in Zurich (till 1869, when he dropped out); in 1893 he hosted the opening of the International Socialist Congress in Zurich. His writings expounded not only socialistic cooperativism but also Fourierism. → 82:4.

Büsch, Johann Georg (1728 to 1800) German economist, with mercantilist views; versatile scholar and linguist. After settling in Hamburg, he first became a prof of mathematics; then (1756) founded a commercial academy and managed it for nearly 30 years. His pubd works cover a wide variety of subjects, incl Encyclopädie der historischen, philosophischen und mathematischen Wissenschaften (1775); Grundriss einer Geschichte der merkwürdigsten Welthändel neuerer Zeit (1781). M (1850) studied his Sämtliche Schriften über Banken und Münzwesen (1801), Abhandlung von dem Geldumlauf (rev. edn, 1800; orig 1780). → 50:51.

Bugeaud de la Piconnerie, Thomas Robert (1784 to 1849) French gen. He commanded the suppression of the republican rising in Paris (1834); gained fame as suppressor of the national movements in Algeria and Morocco (1841–1847); in 1848, an Orleanist deputy; commander of the French Alpine army (1848–1849). Created marshal of France (1843), duc d'Isly (1844). —M's NAC article portrays him as a hated reactionary. → 57:46; 61:12. #M120; E563. See *Abd-el-Kader.

Bukovina or Bucovina Region of east-central Europe; part of Austrian Galicia, ruled by Austria till made a separate crownland (1849); joined Roumania (1918); part seized by the USSR (1940–1945). #E312.

Bulgaria → 79:17; 85:38; 93:32; 94:1. #E835.

Bulgarian language → 93:32.

Bulle, Konstantin (1844 to 1905) German historian, chiefly dealing with modern Europe. E (1888) excerpted his Geschichte der neuesten Zeit 1815–1885, Bd. 4 (1888; the work was orig pubd in 1876). → 88:4. #E705.5.

Bulletin de la Fédération Jurassienne (de l'Association Internationale des Travailleurs) Sonvilier, Le Locle, La Chaux-de-Fonds (Switz.), at various times, Feb 15, 1872, to Mar 25, 1878. Semimonthly, later weekly. Ed by J. Guillaume. —Organ of the Swiss Bakuninists; main Bakuninist organ of its period. #M346.

Bulwer-Lytton, Baron Edward. Orig. Edward George Earle Lytton **Bulwer.** Lord **Lytton** (1803 to 1873) English popular novelist and dramatist; also a politician. (He assumed the hyphenation Bulwer-Lytton in 1843 on inheriting the Lytton estate; created Baron Lytton of Knebworth in 1866.) —His novels were bestsellers, incl Eugene Aram (1832), The last days of Pompeii (1834), Rienzi (1835), The last of the barons (1843), The coming race (1871). —In politics, first a Whig, then (1852+) a Tory; MP (1831–1841, 1852–1866); colonial secy (1858–1859). #M391, M395. See next entry for his wife.

Bulwer-Lytton, Lady Rosina; née **Wheeler** (1802 to 1882) Wife of the novelist Bulwer-Lytton; mar. 1827; daughter of the socialist-feminist pioneer Anna Wheeler. Rosina Doyle Wheeler was famed as an Irish beauty, but was also a brilliant, strong-minded woman; the marriage was notoriously tempestuous, led to legal separation in 1836; in 1839 she pubd a novel, Cheveley, or the man of honour, pillorying Bulwer; denunciations flew about for years. In his NYDT comment M attacked the mistreatment of the wife and the use of psychiatric diagnoses of insanity for distorted ends. #M385.

Bunsen, Baron Karl von; full Christian Karl Josias (1791 to 1860) Prussian diplomat; also a scholarly writer. During 1842–1854 he served as Prussian ambassador in London; he had been the envoy to the Vatican (1837–1839) and to Bern (1839–1842). He stood close to the Prussian court, a friend of the king; pubd works on a variety of subjects incl theology; was named to the Prussian upper house and created baron (1857). He resigned the ambassadorship in 1854 because he favored a more pro-West policy on the Crimean War. → 50:20. #ME89.

Buret, Eugène; *full* Antoine Eugène (1811 to 1842) French journalist and writer on economics. Son of a shopkeeper, he began writing articles on this subject in the *Courrier Français* (1836). In 1840 he won an academy prize for his chief work, *De la misère des classes laborieuses en Angleterre et en France* (pubd 1841). He then made a research trip to Algeria but died before working up his material. B.'s viewpoint was that of an antisocialist liberal, favoring government-sponsored prolabor reforms in the spirit of Sismondi. → 44:48; 45:50. #M575.

Burgess, Joseph (1853 to 1924) English socialist journalist. A Lancashire cotton-mill worker as a boy, he went into journalism by 1884; edited local papers; then editor of the influential weekly *Workman's Times* (London), also its columnist (1890–1894). Pen name: Autolycus. He helped found the ILP (1893) and organized for it in Leeds and Glasgow. In World War I he followed Hyndman out of the British Socialist party to form the National Socialist party, which he quit when it affiliated to the Labour party. → 92:44; 93:49.

Burgundy; *Fr.* Bourgogne; *Ger.* Burgund Region of eastern France. #E301.

Burke, Richard (d. 1870) Irish-American Fenian revolutionary. A colonel in the U.S. Army, he was organizer of the Fenian attempt in 1867 to free their prisoners in Manchester; arrested, and died in prison. → 70:3.

Burma → 58:10, 15. #M977; E111.

Burns, John (1858 to 1943) English socialist and trade-unionist. A factory worker (machinist apprentice) from childhood, B. was self-educated; converted to socialism by reading. Soon active as a trade-unionist, he was arrested for speeches as early as 1877. In the 1880s he came to prominence as a militant and capable leader of unskilled workers; arrested in the 1886 Trafalgar Square demonstration; an organizer of the London dock strike of 1889; a leading figure in the "New Unionism" of the 1890s. He joined the SDF (1883) but was alienated by Hyndman's sectism and basic hostility to trade-unionism. Elected a MP (1892+), chairman of the TUC's Parliamentary Comm (1893), he went over in the 1890s to lib-lab politics, and became a Liberal party politician, abandoning socialism and the workers' movement; cabinet min

(1905–1914), pres of the Bd of Trade (1914), resigning from the government on the outbreak of World War I. He is remembered today only for what he repudiated. → 90:47; 91:28; 92:32; 93:9, 25; 94:8, 44.

Burns, Lydia; *called* Lizzy, Lizzie (1827–1878) E's second wife; younger sister of Mary Burns, his first. For her background, *see* the entry on Mary; virtually the same details apply. —During the 1850s she lived with Mary in E's household in Manchester. After Mary's death (1863) she became E's wife on the same terms. She became very ill by 1876–1877, and much worse in the summer of 1878. At her request, the day before her death, she was married to E in a legal ceremony. —In 1892 E wrote of Lydia in a letter as follows, in terms that apply equally to Mary: "My wife was of real Irish proletarian stock, and her passionate feeling for her class, which was inborn, was worth infinitely more to me and had stood by me in all critical moments more strongly than all the esthetic nicey-niceness and wiseacreism of the 'eddicated' and 'senty-mental' daughters of the bourgeoisie could have done." → 65:10; 69:58; 75:40; 76:17, 20, 23, 25; 77:8, 20, 29, 36; 78:35. #E533.

Burns, Mary (c.1823 to 1863) E's first wife; a Manchester workingwoman of Irish family. The relationship was not legalized, and was at first not definite. E met her in Manchester soon after his arrival in 1842 (no info on exactly when). Her father, Michael Burns, was a dyer; Mary worked in a cotton mill, perhaps Ermen & Engels (there are conflicting statements on this point in IML biographies). She and E became lovers but did not live together till much later. Mary has been described as a lively, sharp-witted young woman of great good nature, uneducated and largely illiterate. As a militant Irish nationalist, she introduced E to "Irishtown" ("Little Ireland" section of Manchester) and to Irish and working-class circles in the area; she and her sister Lydia brought Sinn Feiners to the house for aid or protection from police. Mary did not accompany E to the continent till M&E visited from Brussels in 1845; they renewed their relationship, and she returned with E to Brussels. She did not go to Germany with him in 1848; but they got together again in 1850 (still without living together at first). Later, in the 1850s, their relationship became similar to common-law marriage. Her death in 1863 was unexpected ("heart disease or stroke," said E). → 42:35; 56:22; 63:8.

Burns, Mary Ellen; *sobriquet* Pumps; *mar.* **Rosher** (b. c.1860) Niece of Mary and Lydia Burns. E took her into his household in the mid-1860s and brought her up virtually as her parent, incl provision for her education at a

Heidelberg boarding school. She has been generally described as a shallow-minded madcap type. She married Percy *Rosher in 1881. Her children—esp Lillian (or Lilian?), called Lily (b. 1882)—were also welcomed in E's household; were taken on vacation, etc.; and were provided for in E's will. → 75:40; 76:20, 25; 91:49; 95:37.

Burns, William; *called* Willie   Nephew of Lydia and Mary Burns. He lived in the Boston area, worked for a railway company, and was involved in the labor movement. E visited him on his American trip in 1888; Burns had emigrated many years before. → 95:12.

Burton, Robert (1577 to 1640) English writer; a clergyman. His chief work, *The anatomy of melancholy* (1621), by "Democritus Junior," is a treatise on melancholia which is a storehouse of miscellaneous learning, incl views on social reform and a sketch of utopia. → 94:8.

Butler-Johnstone, H. A. Munro; *full* Henry Alexander *etc.; listed by the NUC under* **Munro-Butler-Johnstone,** *elsewhere under* **Johnstone** (1837 to 1902) English politician. At first, a Conservative MP for Canterbury (1862–1878); author of a number of books on foreign policy and world imperialism; resigned over a difference with the party; then was defeated (1880) as an independent, and turned toward radicalism (left liberals). In 1881 he sought M's advice on the Eastern question; became interested in cooperating with J. Cowen and Hyndman to establish a new party representing labor; became a member of the Demo Federation, but soon dropped out as it moved toward socialism. It was he who in 1880 gave his friend Hyndman a copy of the French *Capital*. → 81:4.

Butt, Isaac (1813 to 1879) Irish nationalist leader. First a prof of polit eco (Dublin U., 1836+), then a lawyer; in the 1860s he was prominent as defense attorney for several nationalist defendants. Liberal MP (1852–1865, 1871); a leader of the Irish opposition group in Parliament. A founder (1870) of an Irish home-rule assoc—after 1873, the Irish Home Rule League. Author of *The Irish people and the Irish land* (1867). —*Note:* M erroneously calls him head of the Irish Workingmen's Assoc. → 69:70.

Butterworth, James (1771 to 1837) English local historian and topographer, concerned with Manchester and other Lancashire towns. Sprung of a family of weaving workers, he produced a long list of books and pamphlets in this field. E read him in connection with writing #E171. B. wrote: *The antiquities of the town, and a complete history of the trade of Manchester* (1822); *A complete history of the cotton trade* (1823), a revision of the preceding title. #M575.

Buttmann, Philipp (Karl) (1764 to 1829) Author of textbooks used by E as a schoolboy; German philologist; Berlin U. librarian; author of a Greek grammar and treatises on mythology and history. E studied his *Ausführliche Griechische Sprachlehre* (2nd edn, 1830), and made notes on his *Griechische Grammatik* (14th edn, 1833). #E528.5.

Buxton (Eng.) Resort town, near Manchester. → 73:32.

Buxton, Sir Thomas Powell (1786 to 1845) English philanthropist, social reformer, antislavery abolitionist. His wealth came from breweries. He advocated reform of criminal law and prison conditions (1816–1820), abolition of slavery in British dominions (1822–1833), suppression of the African slave trade (1839–1840); succeeded W. Wilberforce as leader of antislavery forces. MP (1818–1837). M (1851) read his *The African slave trade and its remedy* (1840). → 51:69.

C

Cabet, Etienne (1788 to 1856) French utopian socialist, writer, and movement organizer. His central contribution was his book *Voyage en Icarie* (1840), which—like *Looking Backward*—was a proposal for a detail-blueprinted utopia in the form of a novel; around it he organized a movement (or sect) whose followers were called Icarians, Icarian communists, communists, or of course, Cabetists. For a while in the 1840s Cabet had some influence in the London League of the Just. —Son of a cooper, Cabet was first a schoolteacher, then a lawyer. He took part in the revolution of 1830, and became attorney-gen in Corsica, dismissed in 1831 because of his social-reform aims. He pubd *Le Populaire* (1833–1834); was forced to emigrate because of his writings; in England (1834–1839) he was influenced by Owenism; and on his return to France, pubd *Le Populaire de 1841* (1841–1851), rallying an Icarian group. The Cabetists were active up to early 1848, but stood aside from the revolution, and then decided to flee the turmoil. Cabet sailed for America in Dec 1848, burying his movement in France; in the next years, tried to found an Icaria in the U.S., at Nauvoo, Ill.; Cabet himself became an American citizen (1854); but the colony collapsed after much dissension. —*Note:* The label "communist" used by the Cabetists meant only that they (unlike Fourierists and Saint-Simonians) favored completely communal ownership. —For a full-length study of the Cabetist movement in France, see C. H. Johnson, *Utopian communism in France* (1974). → 42:26; 43:2; 45:12; 46:36; 48:27. #ME87.

Cadettists Popular name for members of the Société des Droits de l'Homme et du Citoyen, formed in France (May 25, 1888) to fight the Boulangist movement from the standpoint of bourgeois liberal-republicanism; later joined by the *Possibilists. The society was headquartered in the Rue Cadet in Paris. → 89:4.

Caesar, Julius; *full* Gaius (*or* Caius) Julius **Caesar** (100–102? to 44 B.C.) Roman statesman, military commander, and ethnographer. In #E542 E was concerned with Caesar's report on the German tribes, esp vis-à-vis that of Tacitus. #E542.

Cafiero, Carlo (1846 to 1892) Italian socialist. Scion of a rich landowning family, he studied law and briefly entered the diplomatic service. He studied in Paris and London; made the acquaintance (1870) of M&E and of the IWMA; agreed to organize for it in Italy. He began in Florence (May 1871), then Naples; kept in correspondence with E, as corr secy for Italy. But he was persuaded by Bakunin to oppose the London Conference position for political action; by 1872 became a Bakuninist follower, and "betrayed" to Bakunin the letters E had sent him on trust. Cafiero then had a career of a few years as a Bakuninist organizer; first, he entrusted his fortune to Bakunin, who squandered it on a baronial villa (the fantastic episode is detailed in Carr's biography of Bakunin); also, Cafiero led the Italian anarchists in conspiratorial sallies and putsches disastrous enough to ruin several movements. Toward the end of 1881 Cafiero began to suffer from delusions of persecution. In early 1882 he made a turn toward accepting political action and abandoning anarchism; this turn completed by Oct. But by 1883 he was insane; died in some years in a "rest home." —Cafiero's condensation of *Capital* was called *Il Capitale di Carlo Marx* (Milan, 1879). → 71:28, 35, 37, 51; 72:21; 79:6, 29; 82:52.

Cagliostro, "Count" Alessandro di; *really* Giuseppe **Balsamo** (1743 to 1795) Italian adventurer-impostor, b. Sicily. He traveled through Europe posing as physician, magician, mesmerist, Grand Copt, potion dispenser, etc.—one of the great swindlers; died in the Inquisition's dungeon. #E111.5.

Cahan, Abraham; *pronounced* Kahn (1860 to 1951) Jewish-American socialist, editor, writer. He came to the U.S. in 1882; founded the *Jewish Daily Forward* (1897), editor-in-chief (1902+). Previously he had edited the monthly *Zukunft;* an opponent of De Leonism

in the SLP, he and the *Forward* group were expelled; helped found the S-D party, then the SP. Also wrote novels (*The rise of David Levinsky*). Influential in the Jewish TU movement of NY, he moved away from socialism in the 1920s and broke with the SP in 1936. → 90:4; 91:44. #E615.5.

Calabria Region of S. Italy, the "toe." #E320.

Calafat Town in Wallachia, now S. Roumania. #E682.

Calais (Fr.) Port city on the Channel. → 90:42.

Calberla, Georg Moritz German writer on agricultural economics. His book on M was *Karl Marx, "Das Kapital" und der heutige Socialismus* (1877), Heft 1 of the series *Socialwissenschaftliches.* → 77:14.

Calderón de la Barca, Pedro (1600 to 1681) Great Spanish dramatist and poet. Author of numerous comedias, many one-act religious plays, and smaller pieces; e.g., *La vida es sueño.* → 54:22; 83:36.

California (U.S.) → 80:37, 39; 88:30.

Callewaert A Brussels pub'r-printer. IML sources, incl *New Mega*, give no further info. Bertrand's history of Belgian socialism lists a P. Calewaert [*sic*] who was later a member of the Belgian council of IWMA, and who may or may not have been identical with a Louis Callewaert who was an Antwerp sculptor. → 48:8, 31.

Camberwell A southern borough of London. → 55:34, 38, 42.

Cambridge (Mass.) → 88:28.

Camélinat, Zéphirin (Rémy) (1840 to 1932) French socialist worker (bronze molder). A founder of the metal workers' union, strike leader (1867), a leader of the Paris IWMA, he took part in the Paris Commune (director of the mint); then emigrated to England. After the 1880 amnesty, he returned to socialist activity in France; elected deputy (1885–1889); active in Guesdist party; SP treasurer (1911); joined the CP on its inception. #M755.

Cameron, Andrew Carr (1834 to 1890) American labor leader; b. England; printing worker. Editor of the *Workingmen's Advocate* (1864–1877); pres, Chicago Trades Assembly; a founder and leader of the National Labor Union (1866+), which in 1869 elected him its delegate to the IWMA's Basel congress. He was an advocate of workers' political action; also of greenbackism. → 69:55.

Campbell, Sir George (1824 to 1892) British lawyer, b. Scotland; Liberal MP. He rose as an official in India (1842+): high court judge in Bengal (1862); chief commissioner, Central Provinces (1867); lieutenant governor of Bengal (1871–1874). His book *Modern India* (1852) was highly regarded by M; also pubd *Ethnology of India* (1865). → 53:54, 55.

Campe, Julius; *full* Johann Julius Wilhelm (1792 to 1867) Hamburg pub'r and book-dealer; owner (1823+) of the major firm Hoffmann und Campe, founded by a half-brother. It was an important force in publishing progressive and oppositional literature (in the 1830s, Heine, Gutzkow, Young Germany). Campe's politics was moderate-liberal but he was willing to court government harassment. → 45:40; 51:32; 52:40. *See also* Hoffmann & Campe.

Camphausen, Ludolf; *full* Gottfried Ludolf (1803 to 1890) Cologne merchant and banker; one of the biggest businessmen of the Rhineland; in politics, a leader of the bourgeois liberals. In 1842 he was a major shareholder in the company publishing the *RZ*; a member of the Rhenish Diet (1843) and the German Diet (1847). The 1848 revolution made him its first Prussian prime min (Mar-June); his role then faded into lesser posts; in 1849–1851, member of the Prussian Upper House. → 48:23, 29, 37, 38; 49:10. #ME51, ME57; M126–M28.

Campomanes, *Conde de.* Pedro **Rodriquez** (1723 to 1802 or 1803) Spanish statesman, advocate of economic reform under enlightened absolutism. Influenced by the Physiocrats, he aimed to end feudal restrictions (and the Jesuits), modernize the economy, promote trade and industry. Government career: finance min (1763–1788); pres of the Council (to 1793); state secy (to 1798); head of the Royal Academy of History (1764+).—M may have studied one of these works: *Tratado de la regalía de la amortización* (1765); *Discurso sobre el fomento de la industria popular* (1771); *Discurso sobre la educación popular de los artisanos* (1775). → 54:55.

Canada → 71:41.

Candelari, Romeo Italian journalist. → 82:52.

Canepa, Giuseppe (1865 to 1948) Italian socialist; lawyer and journalist. Besides working on *L'Era Nuova*, he also put out the collection *Biblioteca dell' Era Nuova* (brochures), incl the *Com Manifesto* (1895+). He was later a leading figure in the right wing of the SP, expelled in 1911 with Bissolati, and subseqly active in reformist politics; prowar in World War I, and so on. → 94:7.

Cannes (Fr.) Port and resort city on the Riviera, near Nice. → 82:23.

Canning, Charles John. *[1859+]* Earl Canning (1812 to 1862) British statesman, colonial administrator. Tory, then Peelite; postmaster-gen (1853–1855). He became governor-gen of India 1856, put down the Sepoy Mutiny of 1857, and followed it with a policy of liberal pacification. #M483.

Canossa An Italian village. "Going to Canossa" is a historical allusion meaning: submitting to a demand, "eating humble pie." → 80:44.

Cantillon, Richard (1680? to 1734) Irish-born merchant and banker active in France as well as London; his sole work on economics, *Essai sur la nature du commerce en général* (1755, purporting to be a trans from English), was a precursor of the Physiocrats and Adam Smith. In 1880 it was "rediscovered" by Jevons as a pioneering work; but M had studied it long before. → 44:49; 59:78.

Cape Town or **Capetown** (S. Africa) *See* Juta, J. C.; Zuid Afrikaan.

Caprivi, *Count* Leo von; *full* Georg Leo, *Graf* von **Caprivi de Caprara de Montecuculi** (1831 to 1899) Prussian military man who in 1890 was called to succeed Bismarck as imperial chancellor (till 1894) and Prussian prime min (till 1892). His army career (1849+) had made him chief of the admiralty (1883) and reorganizer of the German navy; then commander of an army corps. As a nonparty soldier without political background, Caprivi carried out the kaiser's orders, abrogated the Anti-Socialist Law, negotiated trade agreements, etc.; and then went into complete retirement. → 94:48.

Card, Joseph; *pseud. of* Józef **Cwierciakiewicz** (1822 to 1869) Polish radical journalist. After taking part in the Polish uprising of 1863, he became a refugee in Geneva, where he joined the IWMA; member of its Section Committee, delegate to the 1866 congress. → 68:5.

Cárdenas, Francisco de (1816 to 1898) Spanish lawyer and politician; writer and editor. First a liberal; harassed as a heretic, and recanted. He entered government (1850s), retired (c.1869) during the period of revolution; and came back after the restoration; min of justice, ambassador to Paris and the Vatican. His chief work, studied by M, was *Ensayo sobre la historia de la propriedad territorial en España* (1873–1875). Others: *Derecho moderno; Los partidos politicos en España durante la Edad Media.* → 76:40.

Carey, Henry Charles (1793 to 1879) First major American economist, with great influence in Europe. Orig a pub'r-bookdealer (1817–1835), he then turned to writing on polit eco. His combination of laissez-faire with protectionism (and reverence for class harmony) suited U.S. business conditions well; likewise his opposition to British control of the world market and to the British-invented notion of the class struggle, stemming from Ricardo. M read Carey extensively; his 1851 notebook excerpted *The credit system in France, Gr Brit and the U.S.* (1838); *The past, the present, and the future* (1848);

Essay on the rate of wages (1835); *Principles of polit eco*, Part I (1837); *Essays on polit eco.* In 1853 M read his new book *The slave trade, domestic and foreign;* prob later works too. → 51:61, 65, 66; 53:22–24, 36; 59:18; 68:40; 69:68. #M53.5, M362.

Carleton, William (1794 to 1869) Irish storyteller and novelist. Son of a tenant farmer, hostile to the Catholic church (eventually turned Protestant), he was highly critical of the dark side of Irish life. Best-known work: *Traits and stories of the Irish peasantry* (1830; second series, 1833). Other titles: *Fardorougha the miser* (1837); *The black prophet* (1847). → 79:31.

Carlo Alberto, King; *Angl.* Charles Albert (1798 to 1849) As prince of Savoy and Piedmont (since 1800), he succeeded in 1831 to the throne on the death of Carlo Felice (*Angl.* Charles Felix). Defeated by Austrian arms, he resigned in 1849 in favor of his son Victor Emmanuel II, and retired to a monastery. #E135.

Carlsbad or Karlsbad Watering place in Bohemia, Austria; now in Czechoslovakia as Karlovy Vary. → 74:18, 31, 32; 75:31, 32; 76:24, 26; 77:20; 93:42.

Carlyle, Thomas (1795 to 1881) Scottish-born writer active in England: essayist, historian, moral philosopher. Son of a stonemason; schoolteacher (1816–1819); then freelance journalist; finally a professional sage. In his early period (to c.1848–1850) his writings were edged with revulsion from bourgeois society from the standpoint of romantic idealization of the past; hence he had a certain radical reputation in workers' circles as a critic of the status quo. After the 1848 revolution he was more openly hostile to any radicalism, Chartism, the workers' movement, and democracy; moved to Toryism and a yearning for benevolent despotism. One of Carlyle's peculiarities was his steeping in German literature and history, which influenced him culturally; another was his increasingly crude hero cultism; a third was his virulent anti-Semitism, unusually strong even for the time. —E reviewed his essay collection *Past and present* (1843) and later *Latter day pamphlets* (1850). M's notebook (1845/1846) excerpted his *Chartism* (1840). Major works: *Sartor Resartus* (1833–1834); *The French Revolution* (1837); *Heroes and hero worship* (1840); *Oliver Cromwell's letters and speeches* (1845); *History of Frederick the Great* (1858–1865). → 44:5, 6; 45:52; 50:10. #ME139; M575; E169.

Carolingians Frankish dynasty, seventh to tenth centuries, at its peak under Charlemagne. #E289.

Caron, Charles Pres of a New Orleans club which M called the Club International et

Républicain, but which, according to the historian S. Bernstein, was the Club International Républicain et d'Assistance Mutuel; accepted as Section 15 of the IWMA, after Caron wrote to London (July 15) asking admittance. Its organ had been *L'Equité;* now it began issuing a monthly bulletin *La Commune* (June 1871 to end of 1873). —IML sources treat as a different person the Charles Caron who in 1890 asked for E's permission to put writings by M&E in his *Revue Politique et Littéraire* (Paris). Paul Lafargue warned E that this man had quit the workers' movement a long time ago. But I know no positive reason why he could not be the same man. → 71:35.

Carpenter, William Benjamin (1813 to 1885) English physiologist. Physician to begin with; prof at the Royal Institution, London. His work dealt with comparative neurology and marine zoology (hence deep-sea exploration); he wrote on microscopy as well; also argued in support of miracles. — M (1864) excerpted his *Principles of general and comparative physiology* (1839). → 64:48.

Carter, James British trade-unionist. A London leader of the Journeymen Hairdressers union, he was its representative on the GC/IWMA (1864–1867); the GC's corr secy for Italy (1866–1867). An anticlerical radical in politics, Carter was also active in the Reform League. → 66:26, 30, 43.

Caspari, Otto (1841 to 1917) German writer on philosophy. M (1878) read his work *Leibniz' Philosophie beleuchtet* [etc.] (1870). → 78:50.

Castelnau, H. French socialist. Editor of *L'Intransigeant.* (Source: MEW.) —NUC lists a H. de Castelnau as author of a brochure on the *Affaire Pierre Bonaparte* (1870), prob same man. → 77:10.

Castille, Hippolyte; *full* Charles Hippolyte (1820 to 1886) French writer: novelist and publicist. First a radical republican, and participant in the June Days of 1848; later a Bonapartist hostile to democratic ideas. His journalist work started with the *Musée des Familles* and *Esprit Public;* then he founded *Le Travail Intellectuel* (1847), *La République Française* (1848); editor of *La Révolution Démocratique et Sociale,* etc. He also pubd a number of early novels. His historical books include *Histoire de la seconde république française* (1854–1855); *Histoire de soixante ans* (1859). In 1869 M read his new book *Les massacres de juin 1848.* → 69:22.

Catholic Working Men's International Association (Belg.) → 71:40.

Caussidière, Marc; *full* Louis Marc (1808 to 1861) French socialistic radical of 1848. A commercial silk-factory employee in the Lyons area, he took part in the Lyons uprising of

1834, and was jailed till the 1839 amnesty. In Paris he was active in the workers' club movement and secret societies, and also associated with the Ledru-Rollin group around *La Réforme*. The 1848 revolution made him Paris police prefect (Feb-May) as well as an Assembly deputy; he formed a special "People's Guard" of freed political prisoners (Montagnards), and was said to prowl the city with a pair of pistols and a saber. The advancing reaction, esp after June, threatened to charge him with encouraging subversion, and in Aug he fled to London. There he became a successful wine importer; with Pyat, a founder of the Commune Révolutionnaire group (1853). After the 1859 amnesty, he returned to France, but died soon. —M reviewed his *Mémoires de M. Caussidière, ex-préfet de police et représentant du peuple* (1849). #ME141.

Cavagnari, Uriele Italian socialist; writer. In 1877 he planned to translate *Capital*. → 77:32.

Cavaignac, Louis Eugène (1802 to 1857) French gen and politician; right-wing republican and "democratic" dictator. A professional soldier (1824+), he served as army commander in Algeria (1832–1848), where he had a reputation for barbarous warfare. In May 1848 the Provisional Government called him to become war min. With the outbreak of the June uprising, the Assembly formally invested him with a "dictatorship" (the term derived from Rome)—i.e., with a free hand to carry out his bloody suppression of the movement, with the uninhibited slaughter characteristic of terror-stricken ruling classes. Then he was named chief executive (June-Dec). In the Dec presidential election he became the republican candidate, and was trounced by Bonaparte. Refusing to support Bonaparte's coup of 1851, he went into retirement, abandoned by the ungrateful wretches on whose behalf, in June, he had murdered 3000 workers *after* the fighting was over. → 48:40; 74:40. #M137; E478.

Cayenne Center of the French penal colony system in Guiana. → 61:30.

Cazenove, John (1788 to 1879) English economist; a follower of Malthus. M (1859–1862) studied his *Outlines of polit eco* (1832). Other writings: *Thoughts on a few subjects of polit eco* (1859); and an edition of Malthus. → 59:78.

Central America → 55:48. *See also* individual countries.

Central Committee of the European Democracy Tendency formed by the liberal-republican left after the 1848–1849 defeat, typified by the leadership of Mazzini, Ledru-Rollin, Ruge, et al. → 51:9, 10.

Central Democratic Club (London) → 89:16.

Central Labor Union (NY) → 83:12, 20.

Central Republican Association (Eng.) → 71:15, 16.

Cercle d'Etudes Sociales French émigré club in London. → 72:5, 11, 28.

Cervantes Saavedra, Miguel de; *commonly* **Cervantes** (1547 to 1616) Spanish novelist and man of letters, one of the great names of world literature. Author of *Don Quixote de la Mancha* (1605, 1615), a satire on romances of chivalry, introducing the peasant Sancho Panza. He wrote other novels, many plays and poems. → 54:22; 83:36.

Chalmers, Thomas (1780 to 1847) Scottish theologian and writer on the economics of Christian morality. A prof at St. Andrews and Edinburgh, leader of the split-off Free Church of Scotland, author of 34 vols. of published works, such as his *On the adaptation of external nature to the moral and intellectual constitution of man* (1833). The book excerpted by M (1851), *On polit eco in connexion with the moral state and moral prospects of society* (1832), preached that the masses' economic condition is dependent on their morals and denounced the poor laws. A "fanatical Malthusian," Chalmers was an opponent of coddling the poor. → 51:66.

Chalon-sur-Saône City in east-central France. The form Châlon is erroneous. #E723.

Chamberlain, Joseph (1836 to 1914) English statesman; Liberal party leader, on its bourgeois radical wing. Son of a screw manufacturer, he retired from business with a fortune; became a reform-minded mayor of Birmingham (1873–1875); MP (1876+); cabinet min (1880+). He joined the Liberal Unionists (1886), who opposed Irish home rule; became their leader in Parliament (1891). He stood i.a. for imperial expansionism, and for protectionism to counter German and U.S. competition. Ill health ended his public career (1906); sons Austen and Neville carried on for the empire. → 86:7; 94:9.

Chamborant, Count C. G. de (*fl.* 1st half of 19th century) Author of *Du paupérisme* (1842), which M studied (1845). BN lists another title by him, a report made in 1855; I have not been able to find any more info on this man. → 45:50. #M575.

Chamisso, Adelbert von; *orig* Louis Charles Adélaïde de **Chamisso de Boncourt** (1781 to 1838) German poet of the romantic, and liberal writer; b. in France of an aristocratic family fleeing the Revolution. A founder of the *Berliner Musenalmanach* (1803–1806); editor of the *Deutscher Musenalmanach* (1832+). Perhaps his best known verse was "Frauenliebe und -Leben" (set to music by Schumann); best known tale, "Peter Schlemihls wundersame Geschichte" (1814). He was also a serious naturalist and botanist. → 37:13; 83:9.

Chapman, John (1801 to 1854) English Radical publicist. He agitated for reforms in Indian administration, as in his *Principles of Indian reform* (1853). M cited his book *The cotton and commerce of India* (1851). → 53:55.

Charlemagne or Charles the Great or Charles I; Ger. Karl der Grosse (742 to 814) King of the Franks (768–814) and Emperor of the West (800–814). #M661.

Charleroi (Belg.) Coal and iron-mining region. → 67:16; 68:26.

Charles XII (1682 to 1718) King of Sweden (1697–1718). In connection with the locus, I should note that during much of his reign Charles was engaged in war with Russia. → 56:8.

Charlottenburg (Ger.) Town in the Berlin area, today a part of W. Berlin. → 39:1; 93:42.

Chartism; Chartist movement British working-class movement for democratic political reform organized around the 1838 drafting of the "People's Charter," centerpiece of which was universal suffrage. It reached its zenith in 1848 and petered out in the early 1850s. E first made contact with the Chartists in Manchester (1843), and soon started writing for the *Northern Star*. (See his passage in #E171, Ch. 8.) Later, M&E maintained relations with the left wing of the Chartist movement, the socialist wing, first with *Harney, then E. *Jones. The Chartists were "the first working men's party of modern times" (#E759; cf. also #E921). → 43:2; 45:32; 46:11, 13, 29; 47:42, 49, 50, 52; 48:5, 19, 25; 49:16; 50:5, 15; 51:9, 13; 52:12, 17, 20, 35; 53:7; 54:1, 43, 46; 56:4; 71:28; 84:17; 85:21; 86:26, 53; 87:32; 89:37; 93:11. #ME98; M58, M138, M302; E8, E136–E40, E148, E151.

Chateaubriand, René de; *full* François Auguste René, *vicomte* de (1768 to 1848) French writer and politician. As a writer, called the "father of French romanticism," his tales *Atala* and *René* are best known; also his journal *Mémoires d'outre-tombe*. He was an extreme royalist-reactionary, supporter of the Bourbon Restoration; French repr at the Congress of Verona (1823); foreign min (1822–1824) —M (1843) read his *De la restauration et de la monarchie élective* (1831) and *De la nouvelle proposition relative au banissement de Charles X et de sa famille* (1831), both in German trans. M (1854) read his work *Congrès de Vérone; Guerre d'Espagne* [etc.] (1838). → 54:44, 57; 73:54.

Chaux-de-Fonds, La *See* La Chaux-de-Fonds.

Chelsea A London borough. → 49:39.

Chemnitz (Ger.); *now called* Karl-Marx-Stadt (DDR). → 72:3; 76:12.

Chenu, Adolphe; *full* Jacques Etienne Adolphe (b. 1816 or 1817) French police agent; by trade, a self-employed shoemaker. After his own arrest for fraud and desertion in the 1830s, he worked for the secret police as an agent provocateur in the secret societies of the Louis Philippe era. In Feb 1848 he succeeded in making his way into the new police administration under Caussidière; after participating ambiguously in the June revolt, he betrayed participants to the police. Later he pubd various slanderous accounts of secret-society activities of the pre-1848 period, mainly unverifiable anecdotes. His book *Les conspirateurs* [etc.] (1850) was reviewed by M&E in #ME141. Other writings: *Les montagnards de 1848* (1850); *Les chevaliers de la république rouge en 1851* (1851). #ME141.

Cherbuliez, Antoine (Elisée) (1797 to 1869) Swiss and French economist; lawyer by profession. Swiss-born, prof at the U. of Geneva and a member of the Great Council (1846–1848); but after the fall of the Conservative party in 1848, he resigned everything and moved to Paris; naturalized French in 1850; then (1853) returned to Switzerland as prof at Lausanne and Zurich. In polit eco he was a follower of Sismondi, with elements of Ricardo, steadfastly conservative and antisocialist—as in his *Le socialisme c'est la barbarie* (1848). Major works: *Précis de la science économique* (1862); *Etudes sur les causes de la misère* (1853); and the book excerpted by M (notebooks of 1844–1847): *Riche ou pauvre* (1840), later retitled *Richesse ou pauvreté.* → 44:49.

Chernaya River (Russ.) In the Crimea; scene of a Russian defeat in 1855. #E71, E546.

Chernyshevsky, Nikolai Gavrilovich (1828 to 1889) Russian radical writer and publicist on social and philosophical issues. Son of a poor priest, starting as a schoolteacher, he went in for journalism and literary criticism; became editor of *Sovremennik*. Arrested (1862) and exiled (1864) to Siberia for life (till shortly before his death); his enduring influence was based on the high regard for his writings. His view of socialism was based on the peasant commune, heralding Narodnik peasant socialism; his influential novel *What Is To Be Done?* (1863) portrayed a socialist society. His critical standpoint—orig derived from reading in French socialism and from study of Feuerbach and the Young Hegelians—involved consistent advocacy of a materialism wedded to scientific method; in social affairs, it involved recognition of the importance of economic factors and class position. This is why M and later Marxists thought so highly of his work. In polit eco his main work

was a trans and exposition of J. S. Mill. →
69:64; 70:17, 42, 67; 71:6, 31; 72:22, 46, 68;
73:26, 41; 74:40; 76:10; 81:5; 84:35; 90:28.

Cherval, Julien; *pseud. of* Joseph **Crämer**
Around mid-century, a Prussian police spy in
émigré communist ranks, esp in the CL.
(*KMC,* but not *MEW,* describes him as a
lithographer by trade, turned adventurer.)
After the CL split of 1850, he led one of the
Paris branches of the Willich–Schapper
group, and became one of the defendants in
the trial of the so-called Franco-German
conspiracy in Paris, Feb 1852; after which he
escaped from prison with the help of the
police, and went to England. In 1853–1854
he acted as a spy-provocateur in Switzerland,
under the name Nugent. (According to the
KMC, he also used the name Frank.) →
52:27, 39; 60:1, 12, 20.

Chester (Eng.) Industrial city, near Liverpool. → 53:4.

Chiavenna (It.) Town, in Lombardy. →
41:11.

Chicago (Ill.) → 68:34; 83:12. —Chicago
Exposition:→ 93:15.

Chicago Daily Tribune Chicago, 1846+.
Daily. → 78:43; 79:10. #M415.

Chicago Workers Society → 60:24.

Chicherin, Boris Nikolayevich (1828 to
1904) Prominent Russian representative of
bourgeois liberalism in legal and social philosophy and politics. Prof at Moscow (resigned in 1868); mayor of Moscow (1881–
1883), precursor of the Kadet party. He based
his views on Hegelianism (law is derived from
Freedom and man's spiritual essence, etc.);
pubd works on philosophy and religion, on
history, on political theory. He was strongly
antisocialist and firmly opposed to social
legislation benefiting the lower classes, on the
highest moral grounds. → 73:21, 26.

Child, Sir Josiah (1630 to 1699) English
merchant capitalist and banker; he also wrote
books on economic subjects from a mercantilist viewpoint. He orig amassed a fortune as
victualler to the navy; as governor of the E.
India Co. for many years, he ran it despoti-
cally and unscrupulously (in the opinion of
many critics); said to be the "wealthiest
Englishman of his time," and a prominent
figure in the world of finance and foreign
trade. MP (1659, 1673–1678, 1685–1687). His
works included books on E. Indian trade; *Brief
observations concerning trade and interest of
money* (1668); *A new discourse of trade*
(1690). M (1844) studied a French collection
of his writings, *Traités sur le commerce* [etc.]
(1754). → 44:49.

China and Chinese affairs → 53:1, 22, 53;
57:4, 11, 15, 25; 58:35, 42, 49; 59:57, 61, 75;
94:35. #M32–M34, M140, M282, M512,
M542–M545, M640, M773, M803, M822,

M935; E508, E583. *See also* Sino-Japanese
War.

Chios (Greece) Island in the Aegean. →
81:20.

Christian Socialists → 47:42.

Christianity → 41:14, 18; 42:8. —Early
Christianity: → 82:17, 21; 90:34; 92:42; 94:26,
30, 36; 95:31. #ME26; M595; E105, E556,
E728, E872. *See also* Bible; New Testament.

Chur (Switz.) Town in the Graubünden
canton. → 41:11; 81:46, 49, 56.

Churchill, Lord Randolph (Henry Spence)
(1849 to 1895) English politician. As MP
(1874+), a maverick Tory trying to develop an
aggressive conservatism, then a "progressive"
form called "Tory democracy," challenging
Liberalism for leadership in necessary reforms. Secy of state for India (1885–1886);
chancellor of the exchequer and Parliament
leader (1886); later returned to Parliament
(1892) but his career had faded. Note that in
1881 he had just started to become prominent
as a leader of the "fourth party" of Tory
independents who were trying to move Toryism into the 19th century. → 81:20.

Ciccone, Antonio (1808 to 1893) Italian
politician and economist. A liberal, he was
persecuted by the police; elected deputy
(1861–1865, 1867–1870); gen secy to the
Ministry of Agriculture (1860s); senator
(1870+). He taught polit eco at Naples. His
chief work was *Principi di economia politica*
(2nd edn, 1874). → 78:38.

Cieszkowski, Count August von (1814 to
1894) Polish philosopher and political
leader. Of a rich landowning family in the
Posen region, he studied philosophy in Warsaw, Berlin (to 1835), and Paris (1836–1838),
and pubd an essay *Prolegomena zur Histori-
osophie* (1838), influential toward the development of Young Hegelianism; it advocated
replacing speculative philosophy with a philosophy of "praxis," action to change the
world. Though interested by Fourier's and
Saint-Simon's ideas, he was not a socialist; he
advocated various progressive reforms, and
his main economic work, *Du crédit et de la
circulation* (1839), proposed a new money
system. In 1848 he was a deputy to the
Prussian National Assembly in Berlin (left
wing), subseqly of the Prussian Diet, active in
its Polish deputies' group. → 44:9.

Cincinnati (Ohio) → 51:45; 70:36.

Circassia Region of southern Russia, N.E.
of the Black Sea. #M937.

Civil War (U.S.) → 61:1, 5, 25, 26, 30, 43,
49, 54, 55, 57, 58; 62:2, 9, 10, 11, 15, 16, 23, 25,
26, 32, 36, 37, 41, 42, 46, 48, 53, 54, 56, 58;
63:7, 13, 35; 64:40; 65:25; 78:39. #ME8,
ME156, ME563, ME812, ME872; E15.

Claessen, Heinrich Joseph (1813 to 1883)
Cologne physician, friend and confidant of L.

Camphausen, in 1842 an active official of the company publishing the *RZ*. After the 1848 revolution, one of the leaders of Cologne's liberals. → 44:9.

Clanricarde, Ulick John de Burgh, Marquis and Earl of (1802 to 1874) British diplomat and politician. A Whig, he was ambassador to St. Petersburg (1838–1841) and postmaster-gen (1846–1852). #M716.

Clausen, Johann Christoph (Heinrich) (1806 to 1877) German teacher; during E's schooldays in the Elberfeld *Gymnasium*, teacher of German, history, and geography; later, assistant master and professor. #E351.5.

Clausewitz, Karl von (1780 to 1831) Prussian gen and military theoretician. A professional soldier (1792+), he worked on reorganizing the Prussian army (1809–1812); served in the Russian army (1812–1814); headed, as major-gen, the Allgemeine Kriegsschule (1818–1830); chief of staff to Gen. Gneisenau (1831). His main work was *Vom Kriege* (1833, unfinished, posthumous), expounding a concept of total war and its relation to politics; other works dealt with military history, life of Scharnhorst, etc. → 52:2; 57:26, 31.

Clay, Sir William (1791 to 1869) English politician and writer on economics. Son of a leading merchant, he became chairman of a couple of water companies; MP (1832–1857); secy of the Bd of Control under Lord Melbourne (1839–1841). His writings on economic questions included: *Remarks on joint-stock companies* (1825); *Remarks on the expediency of restricting the issue of promissory notes* (1844); *Speech . . . on . . . the act permitting the establishment of joint-stock banks* (1836). → 51:61.

Cleanthes (b. c.300/331 B.C.; d. c.220/252 B.C.) Greek philosopher; second head of the Stoic school, succeeding Zeno (263 B.C.). He stressed a materialist side of the school's doctrine. —M's account of his wrestling with C. as the "starting point and necessary continuation of philosophy" is in #M455. #M149.

Cleveland (Ohio) → 83:12.

Cloots, Anacharsis; *really* Jean Baptiste (du Val-de-Grâce), Baron de Cloots (1755 to 1794) Born of a German family of the minor nobility, Cloots settled in Paris (1776), devoted his fortune to advancing the humanitarian ideals of the Encyclopedists, enthusiastically greeted the French Revolution, joined the Jacobin Club (1789), adopted French citizenship, and was elected (1792) to the Convention. His special concerns were internationalism (a universal republic) and de-Christianization; he styled himself "L'Orateur du genre humain," the title of his 1791 brochure; also pubd *La république universelle* (1792). "Anacharsis" was adopted from

a didactic romance by the abbé J. J. Barthélemy (1788). He was guillotined with Hébert's followers. → 89:38.

Club International et Républicain (New Orleans) → 71:35.

Club International Socialiste (London) → 71:33.

Cluseret, Gustave Paul (1823 to 1900) French military man and leftist adventurer. A graduate of Saint-Cyr, he led a battalion in repressing the June 1848 uprising in Paris; then served in the Crimean War, Algeria, Garibaldi's movement, the U.S. Civil War, and the Irish Fenian fight. Returned to France (1867), he contributed to Proudhonist (IWMA) papers, and, through Varlin, joined the IWMA (though he claimed to have joined in 1865 in NY, as a U.S. citizen). In 1870 he took part in the revolutionary outbreaks in Lyons and Marseilles; in 1871, elected to the Paris Commune. He briefly headed the Commune's war department; found suspiciously incompetent, jailed but released. Afterward he emigrated to Geneva and for a period associated with the Bakuninists. After the 1880 amnesty he eventually entered the growing socialist movement; was elected deputy as a socialist (1888–1898), and helped organize the International Socialist Congress in Paris (1885). Then in a final incarnation (1893) he became a violently antisocialist follower of Drumont's anti-Semitic movement. → 69:25.

Cluss, Adolf (1825 to 1905) German socialist, active in the U.S. An engineer by profession, he was first active in Mainz, where he joined the CL (1848) and was secy of the WEA during the revolution. He then emigrated to the U.S.; here, a close friend of Weydemeyer, he too became a regular collaborator with M&E by correspondence. He made his living as an engineer for the U.S. Navy Department in Washington, D.C.; wrote for the socialist press, esp German-American papers; and retired from socialist work in the latter 1860s, after Weydemeyer's death. → 51:45, 50, 51; 52:7, 9, 12, 17, 22, 27, 31, 43, 50, 52, 53; 53:1, 4, 5, 11, 14, 19, 20, 24, 36, 41–43, 45; 54:1, 5, 21, 25; 58:25. #M53.5, M212.5, M429, M762.

Cobbett, William (1763 or 1762 to 1835) English Radical journalist and political reformer. Son of a small farmer, autodidact, he adopted radical-democratic views in the period of about 1804–1807, esp concerned with conditions of rural workers. His *Political Register* (which started in 1802 with Tory views) was pubd intermittently throughout his life. In youth he fought in America as a soldier; on his return to England, he became the leading spirit among radical reformers hostile to the government; sentenced (1810) for a pamphlet against flogging in the army, and otherwise harassed. After another year in America (1817–1818) he returned, to devote himself to agriculture. He entered Parliament (1832); helped put through the poor law of 1834; advocated democratization of the political system. He was esp known for his superlative polemical style in pamphleteering, which was admired by M inter alia. Writings: *Rural rides* (1830); *Advice to young men* (1830). M (1845) studied his *Paper against gold* (1828 edn; orig, 1810–1815), and annotated excerpts from his *Cobbett's Weekly Political Register.* → 45:51; 69:75. #M141, M380, M575.

Cobden, Richard (1804 to 1865) Manchester manufacturer (wealthy calico printer), a Liberal leader, "apostle of free trade," a founder of the Anti-Corn-Law League; he and John Bright were the banner names of the "Manchester School." He was a special advocate of international peace schemes, peace congresses (1848–1851), etc.; he opposed the Crimean War and prolabor legislation. #ME60; M135, M227, M320.

Cobh Present name of *Queenstown, Ireland.

Coblenz, Peter Joseph (1808 to 1854) German lawyer, first in Trier, then in Bernkastel. In 1842 he was the *RZ's* Moselle correspondent; also contributed to the *Trier'sche Ztg.* In 1848 he became pres of the Bernkastel Demo Assoc. KMC says that in 1850 he got a half-year jail sentence, and in 1852 went insane. → 42:33. #M965.

Coburg (Ger.) Formerly a capital of the duchy of Saxe-Coburg-Gotha, today a part of northern Bavaria. → 52:36; 74:25.

Cochrane-Baillie, Alexander (Dundas Ross Wishart). Lord **Lamington** (1816 to 1890) English politician and writer. Son of Admiral Cochrane; he orig signed Cochrane or Baillie-Cochrane. —He was a Tory MP (1841–1880, with gaps), adhering to the Young English faction of Disraeli and Lord Manners; opponent of Palmerston; regarded as a defender of absolutism and despotism. As a littérateur, he dabbled in verse and history, and wrote bad novels. He was raised to the peerage (1880) as Baron Lamington. —In M's and the IWMA's documents, his name was written Baillie-Cochrane. → 71:51, 57; 72:20. #M856; E775.

Coehoorn, Baron Menno van; *also spelled* **Coehorn, Cohorn** (1641 to 1704) Dutch gen: military engineer, authority on fortifications. His career was mainly devoted to problems of defense in the Low Countries; invented the "coehorn," a light mortar. His chief work was *Nieuwe Vestingbouw op en natte of lage horizont* (1685). → 58:5, 10. #E147.

Cölln, Georg Friedrich (1766 to 1820) Prussian leftist publicist. A financial assessor in Berlin (1806), he refused allegiance to the French occupation; dismissed; fired pamphlets at the Prussian administration; fled to Austria; but was later pardoned and entered Hardenberg's service. He wrote on economic subjects i.a. —M (1863) excerpted his *Vertraute Briefe über die inneren Verhältnisse am preussischen Hofe seit dem Tode Friedrichs II* (1807). → 63:12.

Coenen, Philippe Belgian socialist worker (shoemaker). A leading figure in the IWMA: first active in the Volksverbond, which became the Antwerp section of the IWMA on affiliating; ed bd secy of *De Werker* (Antwerp); delegate to the Brussels Congress (1868) and London Conference (1871); at the Hague Congress, he supported the Bakuninists. Later, a founder of the Belgian Labor party, and active in its work. → 70:17; 71:15, 16, 21.

Colins, Baron Jean Hippolyte de; *full* Jean Guillaume César Alexandre Hippolyte (1783 to 1859) Belgian-born socialist theorist, mainly active in France; physician by profession. His "rational socialism" (or "Colinsian collectivism") constituted for a while a school with active disciples. Land and most capital was to be owned collectively but leased for private operation, with rent applied to social purposes; the new order was to be instituted by an enlightened autocrat (but Napoleon III declined the honor). Writings: *Le pacte social* (1835); *Qu'est-ce que la science sociale?* (1853–1854) *L'économie politique* (1856–1857); *La société nouvelle* (1857). His disciples pubd *La philosophie de l'avenir* (1875+). → 59:78.

Collected Essays of 1851 M's project for book publ of his earlier articles, to be issued by Hermann Becker in Cologne. Only one fascicule (physical vol) was pubd (see #M151 and ST/M44); the police crackdown on the Cologne movement forced abandonment of the enterprise. This fascicule (*Heft* 1) contained M's articles of 1842 on press freedom (#M156, M216), unfinished in this fascicule; few copies are extant today. —As the result of a discovery at the U. of Cologne library, it is now definitely known that this two-vol project was to include all, or the large majority, of M's RZ articles of 1842–1843, and more. M's own table of contents is not extant; but the Cologne library yielded M's marked-up file of RZ [→ 51:11] showing which articles were to be editorially modified. (For these editorial changes, all minor, see New Mega I, 1:976–979.) Another source of info is a prospectus issued by Becker on Apr 15, 1851. It describes a very inclusive collection, referring to "M's works . . . pubd partly in special pamphlets, partly in periodicals"—"works which cover exactly a decade" (1842–1851). The two vols., each comprising 25 printer's sheets, with M's portrait in Vol. 2, will comprise ten fascicules.

(Hence the pubd fascicule, or physical volume, is only one-fifth of Vol. 1.) The prospectus details Vol. 1: "The first volume will contain M's contributions to Ruge's *Anekdota*, to the (old) *Rheinische Zeitung* (in particular, the essays on freedom of the press, the wood-theft law, the situation of the Moselle peasants, etc.), to the *Deutsch-Französische Jahrbücher*, to the *Westfälische Dampfboot*, to the *Gesellschaftsspiegel*, etc., and a number of monographs which appeared before the March revolution [of 1848] but which still 'unfortunately' apply today." This already makes clear that the plan included much more than the *RZ* articles. The marked-up file shows that the following *RZ* articles were scheduled, besides the two actually pubd: #M164, M165, M188, M218, M233, M448, M601, M669, M741, M742, M781, M869, M965. Of the *RZ* articles not listed, *New Mega* remarks that M must have included at least two others: #M72 and M249. Now #M72 was the first of a group of seven articles on the banning of the *Leipziger AZ*; four others appear on the mark-up list; so it is hard to see why the remaining two (#M352 and M431) should be left out. In addition, there are six other *RZ* articles with at least as much claim: #M123, M473, M477, M655, M782, M866. We can perhaps put aside some brief items that were mere notes or comments: #M40, M43, M64, M667, M668. Becker's reference to other periodicals may mean inclusion of the following as well: #M205, M471, M609, M653, and #ME28. All this has to do with Vol. 1, according to the prospectus. Volume 2 may have covered M's articles from the Paris *Vorwärts!*, Brussels *DBZ*, perhaps even *NRZ*—in other words, articles of 1843–1850.

Collet, Charles Dobson   English radical journalist. Editor and pub'r of the London *Free Press* and (1866) of the *Diplomatic Review*—in both cases, as a follower of David Urquhart. As editor, he dealt with M's contributions to the Urquhartite press, and in the process became personally friendly with M. → 56:26, 30, 36; 57:12; 58:38; 59:56, 60; 60:12; 63:7; 64:13, 18; 66:44; 67:36; 68:64; 70:62; 72:54; 75:48; 76:33; 77:12; 80:2, 32.

Collmann   Nonexistent Berlin pub'r. → 52:49.

Cologne; *Ger.* Köln   City on the Rhine — M&E's residence, moves, personal affairs: → 36:9; 42:10, 27, 32; 44:35; 45:16. —Cologne church dispute: → 38:5; 42:20. —RZ affairs: → 41:16; 42:26; 43:4. —Correspondence with: → 45:21; 46:29, 34, 42; 47:16, 28; 54:1; 56:14; 60:63; 74:29. —Revolution of 1848–1849 in: → 48:1, 26, 28–85; 49:1–26 passim, 28, 30. —Cologne CL affairs: → 49:40; 50:12, 22, 34, 38, 40, 41, 45; 51:5, 10, 14, 19, 20, 23,

24. —M's visits: → 61:18; 62:46; 69:56; 75:31; 76:24. —E's visits: → 75:40; 76:25; 93:40. —Register index: #ME30, ME31, ME41, ME47, ME92, ME115, ME159, ME186; M51, M152, M217, M252, M453, M719, M943, M947; E22, E150, E259, E600, E670, E812. *See also* Cologne Communist trial; *RZ*; *NRZ*; index for #M947.

Cologne Communist trial → 51:1, 27, 35, 42, 45, 54, 55; 52:1, 3, 4, 7, 13, 20, 27, 31, 35, 36, 39, 45–47, 50, 53, 54; 53:1, 4, 5, 11, 15, 19, 20, 24, 29, 43; 55:50; 57:48; 59:72; 60:29; 61:18; 74:2, 37; 75:8; 85:24, 36. #ME2, ME58, ME163; M762, M836.5; E423, E557.

Combault, Amédée (Benjamin Alexandre) (1837 to *after* 1884)   French socialist; jewelry and goldsmith worker. A founding member of the IWMA in France, he was an émigré in England c.1866–1868; member of the GC (1866–1867). In 1868 he was back in Paris: active in the leading comm of the IWMA; arrested and jailed twice in 1870; reorganized the Paris section in May. Though he failed election to the Paris Commune, he was named its head of the Bd of Direct Taxes. Afterward, again an émigré in London; again active in IWMA work. It seems that he did not return to France after the amnesty; last heard from in 1884, still in London. → 75:48.

Committee for the Emancipation of the Working Classes (Parma) → 72:35. #E822.

Commonweal   London, Feb 2, 1885, to 1891; 1893 to May 12, 1894. Weekly. Ed by William Morris. —Organ of the Socialist League. → 84:59; 85:11, 40; 86:17, 24, 48; 89:35.

Commonwealth   London, Feb 10, 1866, to July 20, 1867. Weekly. Ed by J. G. Eccarius (to Apr 1866); G. Odger (Mar 1866+). —Continuing the *Workman's Advocate*, it was an official organ of the IWMA/GC; till June 1866, M belonged to the supervisory comm; under Odger, it turned toward liberalism. → 66:13, 17, 19, 24, 27, 31, 51.

Communards   *See* Paris Commune.

Communist Correspondence Committee   Committee, established by M&E in Brussels, early in 1846, as a political center to organize relations between socialists/communists internationally; it gained contacts, or "correspondents," in Paris, London, Germany, et al. This was the first structure for an international movement attempted by M. It was not established on the basis of a specific ideological program but was aimed at being inclusive within a general conception of its goal. It was superseded, in M's perspective, by the new relations established in the following year with the League of the Just (Communist League) in London. → 46:1, 8, 11, 13, 16, 20, 24, 29, 34, 36, 40, 42, 44, 45, 47; 47:14. #ME28, ME86; E439.

Communist International Leningrad, London, NY, May 1919 to 1924; n.s., 1924 to Dec 1940. —Organ of the C.I., pubd also in Russian, French, German, later in other languages. #E565. *See also* *Kommunistische Int.

Communist League (*Bund der Communisten*) Established by a congress (early June 1847, London) held by the *League of the Just after coming to an agreement with M&E. The change of name was accompanied by a democratization of its organizational structure and elimination of its conspiratorial nature, in general its "Marxification." E attended this first congress. The second congress was held Nov 29 to Dec 8 the same year, also in London, attended by M&E, who were charged with drafting a program, which appeared in a couple of months as the *Manifesto of the Communist Party* (#ME33). See esp #E557 for a historical sketch of the CL. —The CL was shelved by M&E during the period of the NRZ (Cologne) in the course of the revolution of 1848–1849; revived after M's arrival in London (Aug 1849); dissolved (Nov 1852) after the Cologne Communist trial. → 47:1, 20, 26, 28, 39, 42, 43, 45, 46, 50; 48:2, 15, 19, 20, 22, 25–29, 33, 36; 49:1, 11, 35, 36, 39–41, 44; 50:1–3, 5, 7, 12, 15, 19, 22, 25, 30, 34, 38, 40, 41, 45; 51:1, 5, 10, 14, 19, 24, 31; 52:3, 7, 13, 17, 25, 31, 35, 39, 40, 46; 77:42; 85:36, 39, 40. #ME2, ME3, ME45, ME47; M474.5, M564, M836.5; E229, E557, E582. —Re: ex-CL members: → 53:45; 54:33; 55:33, 34; 56:6; 57:48; 59:62; 61:18; 93:48. See also Cologne Communist trial.

Communist Workers Educational Association See German Workers Educational Association.

Communist Workingmen's Club (London) → 93:13.

Como Town in N. Italy, on the lake. → 65:49.

Comte, Auguste; *full* Isidore Auguste Marie François (1798 to 1857) French founder of a "Positivist" school and movement, advocating a would-be scientific doctrine of social evolution and a program of social reorganization on the basis of an authoritarian "religion of humanity." He coined the word *sociology*. His Positivism should not be identified with other uses of that protean term in one sense or another, usually undefined; Comtism was a specific creed. French Comtism was antisocialist and antilabor (for the exceptional position of the British wing, *see* Beesly), but it had considerable influence inside the socialist movement, usually unacknowledged. Comte, a mathematician, was early a disciple of and secy to Saint-Simon (1818–1824), ending with a violent break. Chief work: *Cours de philosophie positive* (1830–1842). —For M,

Comte was "the prophet in politics of Imperialism [Bonapartism] (of personal *Dictatorship*), of capitalist rule in political economy, of hierarchy in all spheres of human action, even in the sphere of science, . . . the author of a new catechism with a new pope and new saints in place of the old ones." → 66:34; 69:35; 95:6.

Comtists Followers of A. *Comte; their own term was Positivists. —In England: → 66:34; 67:3; 68:27; 69:35; 71: 2; 74:4. —In France: → 66:34; 70:17.

Concord (Mass.) → 88:28.

Concordia; Zeitschrift für die Arbeiterfrage Berlin, Oct 1, 1871, to June 24, 1876. —Spokesman of big industry; influenced by Katheder-socialists. → 72:30, 39.

La **Concordia** Turin, 1848 to 1849. Daily. —Liberal paper. #ME188.

Concordia Festsälen (Berlin) → 93:42.

Confederacy (U.S.) *See* Civil War (U.S.).

"Confessions" game In this game, popular in England in the 1860s, one answered a list of set questions: often jocularly, frivolously, flirtatiously, as well as seriously. There are three extant forms filled out by M, for which see #M170; for E's "Confessions," see #E178. For an informative comment on one of M's versions, see Ryazanov (ed.), *KM, man, thinker, and revolutionist*, p. 261. A "Confessions" form filled out by Mrs. M is reproduced in facsimile in ST/36.5, p. 181. The same book, p. 208, shows a facsimile of "Confessions" by daughter Jenny. For the text of "Confessions" by Eleanor M (aged 10), see ST/35.5 (Kapp) 60–61. → 65:28; 68:25.

Conradi, Johann Jakob (1821 to 1892) M's brother-in-law; married M's sister Emilie (1859). Waterworks engineer in a Trier suburb. → 65:60.

Conservatives (Eng.) *See* Tories.

Considérant, Victor; *full* Prosper Victor (1808 to 1893) French socialist (Fourierist) leader. An Ecole Polytechnique student, then a printer, he early became the leading disciple of Fourier, whose ideas he expounded in *Destinée sociale* (1834–1844). Head of a Fourierist tendency (1837+), he founded and edited the daily *Démocratie Pacifique* (1843–1851), breaking away from those Fourierists who were interested only in utopian colonies ("phalansteries"); he pointed toward a broader goal, looking to political action, with a liberal-progressive appeal—i.e., a reformist S-D type of movement rather than a communist-colonizing sect only; exalting class harmony, deploring revolutionary struggles, not appealing primarily to workers. This tendency came to shipwreck after the 1848 revolution. C. emigrated (1849) to Brussels; then went to Texas (1852) to establish a Fourierist phalanstery (1854–1869) near Dallas, winding up broke and discouraged. Returning to Paris (1869), he joined the IWMA; supported the Paris Commune; and ended up a Latin Quarter "character" in a quaint costume. —Other writings: *Principes du socialisme* (1847); *Le socialisme devant le vieux monde* (1848); *Manifeste de l'école sociétaire* (1841); *Exposition abrégée du système phalanstérien* (1845). → 42:26.

Constant, Benjamin; *full* Henri Benjamin **Constant de Rebecque** (1767 to 1830) French (Swiss-born) liberal writer and politician. After serving under Napoleon, then supporting the Restoration, he came out for a constitutional monarchy with a measure of civil liberties, and gained a reputation as a liberal publicist, an admirer of British parliamentarism like his lover Mme de Staël. He knew whom he wanted liberty for: liberty is "the triumph of individuality, not only over authority which would like to govern through despotism, but also over the masses who demand the right to subject the minority to the majority." —M (1842) excerpted his *De la religion* (1826). #M93.

Constantinople (Turkey); *now* Istanbul → 58:38. #ME60; M783, M977.

Die **Constitution** Vienna, Mar 20 to Oct 1848. Daily. Ed by L. Häfner. —Liberal paper. #M449, M831.

Contemporanul Iaşy (Jassy) Roumania, July 1881 to Dec 1890 (under this title). Semimonthly, then monthly. —Socialist journal, on literature and politics. It pubd some M&E writings. → 88:1.

Contemporary Review London, 1866+. Monthly. —Liberal views. → 81:52; 82:39.

Convention of London Conference held Oct 13, 1861, at which France, England, and Spain decided for the intervention in Mexico. → 61:49.

Conway, Moncure Daniel (1832 to 1907) American radical preacher and militant abolitionist; writer. In the 1850s–1860s, a Unitarian pastor (converted from Methodism) in Cincinnati; editor of the *Dial* and *Commonwealth*. He went to London (1862) to lecture on behalf of the North; remained (1863–1884) as a minister and writer for the English press; in 1870 a correspondent for the *NY World*. He later converted to Freethought. Pubd *The Wandering Jew* (1881); *Life of Thomas Paine* (1892); an edn of Paine's writings (1894–1896); *Autobiography* (1904). —M's contact with Conway came when Conway wrote to ask permission to attend the next GC meeting. → 71:41.

Cooper, Thomas (1759 to 1839) American physician, educator, and scholar. He pubd works on a number of technical subjects, incl polit eco. Prof of chemistry at Carlisle College, Penna. (1812); later pres of the S. Carolina College. He was tried in 1798 under the Sedition Act for "libel" against the U.S. pres. He pubd books on chemistry, the slave trade, tariffs, Calvinism, law, etc. M (1845) studied his *Lectures on the elements of polit eco* (2nd edn, 1829; orig, 1826). Other writings: *A manual of polit eco* (1833); *Political arithmetic* (1798). → 45:51. #M575.

Cooper, Thomas (1805 to 1892) English journalist and poet; Chartist leader and apostate. (Not to be confused with the preceding Thomas Cooper.) A self-educated shoemaker, he became a schoolmaster; went to London (1839), became active in radical journalism; editor of the *Midland Counties Illuminator*. At first a leader of the extreme-militant wing of Chartism, he was imprisoned for two years urging the strike of 1842; in jail he wrote the epic poem *The purgatory of suicides*. On getting out of jail, he turned his coat, became a very dove of peace, advocating love and nonresistance. Expelled from the National Charter Assoc (1846), he was taken up by literary society as a reformed workingman. He later became a Methodist preacher. He was the prototype of Kingsley's *Alton Locke*. → 46:11.

Cooper Union (NY City) A unique educational institution in Manhattan, founded 1857–1859 by Peter Cooper; often used as a meeting place. → 83:12, 20.

Copenhagen (Denmark) → 71:48; 72:24; 76:15; 89:37.

Coppel, Carl Young banker from Hanover, in London on business, referred to M by Dr. Kugelmann. All we know of him is that M thought him a "lively fellow." → 68:11, 20.

Coquelin, Charles (1803 to 1853) French writer on economics; lawyer by profession in Dunkirk. He started devoting himself to economics (1830/1832+); contributed to major periodicals, incl the *J. des Economistes* (1846+); secy of the Free Trade assoc; pubd an antisocialist tract, *Jacques Bonhomme* (1848); and, with Guillaumin, pubd the *Dictionnaire d'économie politique* (1853+), which he did not live to complete. —M (1851) excerpted his *Du crédit et des banques* (for U.S.-style liberty of banking) from the *Revue des Deux Mondes*, 1842 (pubd as a book in 1848). → 51:71.

Corbet, Thomas English writer on economics; author of *Inquiry into the causes and modes of the wealth of individuals* (1841), excerpted by M (1851). IML indexes describe him as a Ricardian who contributed to the theory of crises. Other than this one book, I have found no information on him. → 51:71.

Corinth (Miss.) Site of Civil War battles. → 62:23, 26.

Cork Second- or third-largest city of Ireland. → 69:58; 72:14.

Le **Corsaire** Paris, 1871 [+?]. Daily. Republican paper. → 72:51. #M901.

Cosmopolitan Conference (NY) → 71:49.

Cossa, Luigi (1831 to 1896) Italian economist. Prof of polit eco at Pavia (1858+), which he made the national center for economic studies. He had been much influenced by German training in Vienna and Leipzig, esp by L. von Stein and Roscher. Chief work: *Primi elementi di scienza delle finanze* (1876); also: *Guida allo studio dell' economia politica* (1876); *Saggi di economia politica* (1878). → 78:38.

Cotta, Johann Georg. *Baron* **Cotta von Cottendorf** (1796 to 1863) German pub'r-bookdealer of Augsburg; owner of the J. G. Cotta firm, one of the largest, i.a. pub'r of the *Allgemeine Ztg*. The original J. G. (1631–1692), of Italian descent, had established it in Tübingen; his grandson, Johann Friedrich (1764–1832), a moderate liberal, had moved to Augsburg (1810), built the enterprise to a new literary eminence, and was created baron. His son, the contemporary J. G., had expanded still more, and had the distinction of refusing to publish *Capital*. → 51:22, 33.

Coullery, Pierre (1819 to 1903) Swiss social reformer in the IWMA. A physician by profession ("doctor to the poor") in La Chaux-de-Fonds; influenced by Buchez and Proudhon, C. was not so much a socialist as an advocate of agrarian reforms, welfarism, and cooperatives; active locally since the 1850s. He took part in founding the local IWMA section; editor of *La Voix de l'Avenir*; delegate to the IWMA congresses of 1866–1867; dropped out of the International after the Brussels Congress of 1868 voted for land collectivization, and subseqly withdrew from political activity. In French-speaking Switzerland, his tendency energetically fought the Bakuninists, who pointed to his reformism as the ineffectual alternative to their own ineffectual revolutionism. → 65:56.

Courcelle-Seneuil, Jean Gustave (1813 to 1892) French economist. Orig a lawyer in Seneuil (which he added to his family name), he became manager of an ironworks; studied economic questions; in 1848, became director of the public domains, in the Finance Ministry. After the Bonaparte coup, he went to Chile, as finance advisor to the government, and prof of polit eco in Santiago (1853–1863). After his return to France, he became councillor of state (1879). —He was of the liberal school in economics; an authority on banking. Chief work: *Traité théorique et pratique d'économie politique* (1858). M (1859–1862) studied his *Traité théorique et pratique des entreprises industrielles, commerciales et agricoles* (2nd edn, 1857; orig, 1855). He also

pubd *Liberté et socialisme* (1868), and transd J. S. Mill. → 59:78.

Cournet, Frédéric (Etienne) (1839 to 1885) French Blanquist and Communard. Orig a commercial clerk, active as a radical journalist, he edited Delescluze's *Le Réveil* (1868) in the course of oppositional activity against the Bonaparte regime. With the fall of the Empire, a NG commandant (1870); elected to the Paris Commune (Commsn of Gen. Security, Exec). Afterward he emigrated to London: member of the GC (Nov 1871+), delegate to the Hague Congress (1872+); a loyal Blanquist, he supported their protests against moving the GC, and signed their manifestos. After the 1880 amnesty, he returned to France; wrote for Rochefort's *L'Intransigeant* and Blanqui's *Ni Dieu Ni Maître*, and helped found the Blanquist Comité Révolutionnaire Central, in which he was active to the end. —Re his father, *see* Barthélemy. → 71:51; 72:24.

Le **Courrier Français** Paris, Sep 1864 to June 1868 (see note). Weekly; then daily (June 1867+). Ed by A. Vermorel (1866–1868); L. de Schryver (1868). —Left republican; organ of IWMA in France (May 20, 1866+). —Note: Dating above is after BN Newspaper Catalog; four other sources give four different accounts, no two agreeing. → 67:29, 33. #M313, M498.5.

Le **Courrier International** London, Nov 1864 to July 20, 1867. Weekly. Pub'r: Jos. Collet. —French-language edn of the *International Courier*. → 67:13. #M406, M787.

Cowen, Joseph (1831 to 1900) English liberal politician. Successful businessman, son of a rich pipe-casting manufacturer (J. C. Sr.), he was a radical-liberal who began with special sympathy for continental national movements (Mazzini, Garibaldi, Kossuth, anti-Bonapartists); editor of the *Northern Tribune* (1854–1855); an early friend of Harney, whom he aided in the early 1850s. In 1857 he took part in forming the Northern Reform Union (electoral reform). MP (1874–1885) for Newcastle; his radicalism involved him (1880–1881) in the first stages of organizing Hyndman's Democratic Federation, but he did not come in. It also turned out that he was an early Limp (Liberal Imperialist), which is what M was complaining about in 1883. When he dropped out of politics (1886+) he devoted himself to publishing his *Newcastle Daily Chronicle*, to his business, and to denouncing "doctrinaire Radicalism." → 81:4; 83:4.

Cracow; *Pol.* Kraków City in southern Poland. → 48:10; 71:64; 72:3; 92:24. #M825; E769.

Crawfurd, John (1783 to 1868) Scottish Orientalist; E. India army physician. Author of *History of the India archipelago* (1820). He pubd numerous works on India and on the China trade, Java, the Malay language, Siam, etc. M (1859–1862) read his article "On the cotton supply," in the *J. of the Society of Arts,* Apr 19, 1861. → 59:78.

Crédit Mobilier French bank, founded 1852 by the Pereire brothers with Bonaparte's support, acting as a sort of holding company to promote the development of industrial and public-utility enterprises, etc. → 56:24, 28, 36, 41; 57:20, 25, 39. #M194, M195, M263, M332, M333.

Creizenach, Theodor (Adolf) (1818 or 1819 to 1877) German poet, also literary critic and historian. A liberal, associated with Young Germany, he pubd *Dichtungen* (1839), *Gedichte* (1848). Jewish by birth, he converted to Christianity (1854). → 35:8.

Cremazy M (1876) read his work *Le droit français et lois hindous comparés*—so according to *MEW Daten* (*MEW* 19) but I have been unable to verify the author's name or his book. → 76:40.

Cremer, William Randal (1838 to 1908) English trade-unionist and pacifist. Son of a coach painter, he came to London as a carpenter (1852); a founder of the carpenters' union (1860). A participant in the founding meeting of the IWMA, he was a member of its GC, also the GC gen secy (1864–1866); also on the Exec of the Reform League (moderate wing). In 1871, after working for British neutrality in the Franco-Prussian War, he led in founding the Workmen's Peace Assoc; in 1889, in founding the Inter-Parliamentary Union; he was secy of both till his death. Liberal MP (1885–1895, 1900–1908); also longtime secy of the International Arbitration League; editor of its organ *The Arbitrator.* His pacifist work won him the Nobel Peace Prize (1903) and a knighthood (1907). Sir William was the very model of the reform-pacifist who, while the wheels of war ground on, supplied the squeak. To the last he was a staunch opponent of the Labor party. — Note: The frequent spelling Randall is erroneous. → 64:26, 31; 65:23, 32, 36; 66:17, 36, 43.

Crémieux, Adolphe; *orig* Isaac Moïse (1796 to 1880) French liberal politician and lawyer; of a prominent rich French-Jewish family, later pres of the Alliance Israélite Universelle. Under Louis Philippe, an opponent of Guizot; the 1848 revolution made him its first min of justice (Feb-May) as well as deputy to the Assembly (1848–1851). He first supported, then broke with, Bonaparte; after the coup, withdrew to private life till 1869; reentered the government on the fall of the Empire (1870–Feb 1871); appointed lifetime senator (1875). → 72:11.

Crete (Greece) Mediterranean island. → 67:29.

Le **Cri du Peuple** Paris, Feb 22 to May 23, 1871; revived Oct 28, 1883, to Feb 10, 1889. Daily. —Founded by Jules Vallès in 1871, and revived by him in 1883, after which it had a checkered history: at first, nonpartisan socialist, then Guesdist-dominated, Possibilist, and Blanquist in turn. → 85:4.

Crimean War (1853–1856) Predecessor of the later world wars, with Russia ranged against Turkey, England, France, and Sardinia, this war was fought to decide who would inherit the declining Ottoman Empire and, in general, to set the relations of international domination in E. Europe and the Middle East. It began with Russia's occupation of the Danubian Principalities in July 1853, and ended with the Treaty of Paris in Mar 1856. For M's position on the war as a whole, see → 54:28. → 50:3, 36; 53:1, 37; 54 and 55: all year, passim; 56:2, 7, 12, 15, 24, 34; 57:6; 63:25; 77:5; 92:29. #ME1, ME9, ME40, ME105, ME108, ME110, ME147, ME187; M331, M387, M388, M761; E102, E116, E117, E141, E191–E194, E305, E340, E372, E510, E522, E553, E566, E681, E787.

Criminalistische Zeitung für die Preussischen Staaten Berlin, 1841 to 1842. Weekly. —Moderate-liberal. #E240.

The **Crisis.** *Later* **The Crisis and National Co-operative Trade Union Gazette** (also variations in title and subtitle) London, Apr 14, 1832, to Aug 23, 1834. Ed by Robt. Owen (and R. D. Owen), later J. E. Smith. —Organ of the Owenite movement. → 77:30.

Critica Sociale Milan, Jan 15, 1891, to 1926; revived 1945+. Suspended May 1898 to July 1899. Fortnightly. Ed by F. Turati. —Most important socialist theoretical journal in Italy. Superseded *Cuore e Critica.* → 91:19; 92:5, 11; 94:4, 12, 41, 45, 48; 95:32. #E290, E319, E346, E385, E395, E669, E757.

"Croat" troops → 48:72. #E199.

Croatia Region of S.E. Europe: once a S. Slav kingdom, now a province of Yugoslavia; in-between, a vicissitudinous part of the Hapsburg Empire. Chief city, Zagreb. #E507.

Cromwell, Oliver (1599 to 1658) English political leader in the bourgeois revolution. Lord protector (1653–1658). —The locus is to E. Bernstein's book on the Cromwellian revolution; *see* Bernstein. → 95:21.

Crystal Palace (London) → 94:28.

Cuba → 58:35.

Cunninghame(-)Graham, Robert Bontine (1852 to 1936) British socialist and writer, of an aristocratic Scottish family. He entered politics as a Radical MP and Scottish nationalist; joined the socialist movement (1887) before the Bloody Sunday demonstration in Trafalgar Square in which he was a prominent participant. MP (1886–1892, 1918); first socialist sitting in the House of Commons; strong advocate of the eight-hour day; a founder of the Scottish Labour party (1888) and its pres (with Hardie as secy); delegate to the International Socialist Congress (1889) as repr of the Electoral Labour Assoc. —Also an extensive traveler (e.g., cattle rancher in Argentina), and writer on travel and historical subjects, of tales, South American sketches, etc. → 89:16; 90:47; 92:24 (his wife).

Cuno, Theodor (Friedrich) (1847 to 1934) German socialist. Engineer by occupation, he was active (1870) in the Vienna WEA; moved to Italy (1871) where he founded and led the Milan section of IWMA, as an opponent of Bakuninism, and corresponded with E. After Italy, he worked in Belgium; delegate to the Hague Congress (1872), where he was on the Comm of Inquiry on the Bakuninist Alliance. Afterward he emigrated to the U.S.; active in the IWMA there for a while, and in the Knights of Labor; later, on the staff of the *New Yorker Volkszeitung*. In later years he settled in Louisiana. → 71:59; 72:4, 20, 27, 42, 48, 49, 51, 55; 79:43; 82:12; 83:14; 88:30, 37. #E389, E564.

Cuore e Critica Milan, Savona, 1887 to 1890. —This title was continued by *Critica Sociale*. → 90:24. #E572.5.

Curran, John Philpot (1750 to 1817) Irish lawyer; Radical defender of civil liberties and Irish revolutionaries. First known as a trial lawyer in Dublin (1775+), he gained fame as defense lawyer for Wolfe Tone, Napper Tandy, leaders of the 1798 insurrection and the United Irishmen society. Although a Protestant, he fought for Catholic emancipation and against British repression. Member of the Irish Parliament (1783+); later sat in U.K. Privy Council (1806+) under Fox. —M read Curran's *Speeches* (ed by T. Davis, 1855 edn), and circulated it to GC members. "I consider Curran the only great lawyer (people's advocate) of the 18th century and the noblest personality," he wrote. → 69:75.

Custodi, Pietro (1771 to 1842) Italian journalist, economist, and politician; lawyer by profession. Under Napoleon I he became gen secy of the Milan finance department, later state councillor, created baron. His main achievement was his edn of Italian writings in polit eco up to the early 19th century, in 50 vols., *Scrittori classici italiani di economia politica* (1803–1816), with biographical and critical notices. Also pubd a life of Beccaria (1811), and a history of Milan (1824–1825); a founder of the economic journal *Cui Noli Universali di Economia Publica* (1824–1871). → 59:77.

Cyples, William (1831 to 1882) English journalist and writer. Self-educated, he took to journalism and edited a number of provincial newspapers, contributing to others. He became a follower of Urquhart's views; in 1856 he was a contributor to the Urquhartite *Sheffield Free Press* and secy of the Sheffield Comm for Foreign Affairs, an Urquhartite front. In 1877 he moved to London and devoted himself to writing on philosophy, producing i.a. *Inquiry into the process of human experience* (1880). → 56:21, 26.

Czechoslovakia;   Czechoslovakians → 48:38, 43, 58; 93:19, 21, 24, 44; 95:32. #E699, E824.

Czobel, A. #M574.

D

"Dâ-Dâ Vogt," i.e. Karl Vogt M orig intended to use this as the title for the book pubd as *Herr Vogt*, Chap. 8 of which is indeed headed "Dâ-Dâ Vogt and His Studies." There M explains that Dâ-Dâ (M's spelling) was an Arab journalist in Algeria who in the 1850s had transd Bonapartist propaganda pamphlets into Arabic. Perhaps the title also appealed to M because *dada*, in French, means a hobbyhorse one keeps on riding (origin of the later Dadaist movement). → 60:45, 51, 54.

Dagblad van Zuid-Holland en 'S Gravenhage The Hague, 1853 to 1922? Daily. —Newspaper covering S. Holland and The Hague. #M835.

Daily Chronicle London, 1877 to 1930 under this title; founded 1856, daily 1866+; in 1930, merged into the *News Chronicle*. Daily. Pub'r: Edw. Lloyd (1876+). —Liberal paper. → 91:59; 92:24; 93:32, 37. #E290, E421.

Daily News London, Jan 1, 1846, to 1930 under this title; in 1930, merged into *News Chronicle*. Daily. Ed by H. J. Lincoln (early 1850s); John Robinson (1868–1901). —Liberal-bourgeois organ. → 48:85; 51:27; 52:3; 54:10, 18, 23; 71:5, 30; 72:52; 78:19, 32; 81:14, 20. #ME176, ME180, ME330; M370, M902, M903; E440, E710.5, E776, E777.

Daily Telegraph London, 1855 to 1937 under this title; founded in 1853. Daily. Ed by E. L. Lawson (1850s). —Liberal up to 1880s; then Conservative. → 60:12, 13; 71:28, 33. #M222, M904.

Daire, Eugène; *full* Louis Francois Eugène (1798 to 1847) French writer, journalist, and editor. Originally a tax collector, he turned to a literary career in 1839; contributed to the *J.*

du Peuple, Le National, and (1842+) *J. des Economistes.* He is best known as gen editor of the multivolume collective work *Collection des principaux économistes* (1840–1848; Vol. 1, 1843); he annotated and edited in particular Vols. 1–2, 14–15. M (1844, 1860) studied esp Vol. 1 (*Economistes financiers du XVIIIe siècle*). → 44:48; 60:66.

Dakyns, John Roche (1836 to 1910) English geologist. He joined the International in 1869, and became a friend of M, whose reading in 1878 was of Dakyns' contribution to the *Geological Magazine* on "The antiquity of man" (1877). → 69:35; 70:12; 78:47.

Dalmatia Region comprising most of the Yugoslav coast; held by Austria as a crownland till 1918. #E507.

Dalrymple, Sir John (1726 to 1810) Scottish historian and publicist; lawyer by profession (1748+). Baron of the exchequer (1776–1807). M (1851–1852) studied his chief work in economic history, *Essay towards a general history of feudal property in Gr Brit* (1757) in its 1759 edn. Other works: *Address of the people of Gr Brit to the inhabitants of America* (1775); *Memoirs of Gr Brit and Ireland* (1771). → 51:70; 52:56.

D'Alton, Eduard; *full* Joseph Wilhelm Eduard (1772 to 1840) German art historian; prof at Bonn. M took his lectures on the history of modern art. → 35:5.

Dana, Charles Anderson (1819 to 1897) American journalist. Largely self-educated, a Harvard dropout, he was a leading spirit in the Brook Farm utopian colony (1841–1846); adopted Fourierist views; with G. Ripley, edited *Harbinger* (1845–1849). Horace Greeley appointed him (1847) city editor of the influential *NYDT,* then a mildly radical organ of social reform; later (1849) managing editor. In 1848 D. toured the European revolution in progress; met M in Cologne, and admired him ("the leader of the people's movement"); and acquired Proudhonist views, on which he pubd a series of articles in the *NYDT.* Under D.'s sponsorship, the *NYDT* hired M to send regular correspondence; also to contribute to the NAC. But D. became increasingly disillusioned (1855+) with Fourierist colonization schemes and with social reform; in the Civil War, he became a bitter-ender, broke with Greeley, and left the *NYDT* (1862); became asst secy of war (1863–1864). Always hostile to TUs and any militant labor movement, D. turned right, became more pro-imperialistic, and involved with Tammany politics; an admirer of "captains of industry." In later years his fame rested on his long editorship of the NY *Sun* (1868–1897), a forerunner of Hearstian yellow journalism. → 48:81; 50:27; 51:35, 38, 45, 57; 52:18, 22, 44; 53:22, 26, 44, 46, 47; 54:4, 5, 12, 19, 45; 55:1, 7, 20, 26, 41, 46, 49; 56:34;

57:4, 8, 11, 14, 19, 24, 28, 33, 38, 41, 42; 58:5, 10, 15; 59:13, 18, 20, 27, 55; 60:20, 49; 61:6, 9, 41; 62:14; 68:5; 71:36, 39, 43; 79:34. #M467.

Daniels, Amalie; *née* **Müller** (1820 to 1895) Wife of Roland Daniels; mar. 1848; daughter of a Cologne lawyer. She corresponded with M while Dr. Daniels was on trial in Cologne. → 51:45; 52:13; 55:41; 61:18.

Daniels, Roland (1819 to 1855) German communist; physician in Cologne. On a trip to Paris (1844) he met M and other radicals, and in a sojourn of some months, adopted communist views; returned to Cologne in Jan 1845, and thereafter followed M's political course and remained in correspondence with him: into the Brussels CCC, the CL on its formation, etc. There is no info on his participation in the 1848–1849 revolution except that he was active as "physician to the poor." Afterward he played a leading role (1850–1851) in the CC/CL in reorganizing the League and in aiding the NRZ-Revue. He was arrested (1852) in the government's preparation of the Cologne Communist trial, but acquitted. — M&E considered D. the best brain in the Cologne group. In 1850–1851 he wrote a long ms titled *Mikrokosmos, Entwurf einer physiologischen Anthropologie,* orig (in first draft of 1849) a critique of medicine, now a broader attempt to apply materialist analysis to the natural sciences; M read it on request and was highly critical. → 44:13; 46:25; 47:14, 16; 48:26; 49:31; 50:39; 51:16, 19–23, 25, 27; 54:33; 55:41; 61:18.

Danielson, Nikolai Frantsevich (1844 to 1918) Russian economist and Narodnik writer; pen name Nikolai—on and other pseudonyms. He worked (from the late 1860s) for a banking institution as bookkeeper, rising to chief comptroller. In the 1860s–1870s he was associated with a circle of young radicals of the intelligentsia; by the 1880s–1890s he was a prominent ideologist of the populist view of Russian economic development, on which he pubd a book in 1893. He corresponded with M for years (1868+), supplying much material on Russia, and continued with E; but by the 1890s E was severely critical of his views. D. completed Lopatin's trans of *Capital,* Vol. 1, and transd Vols. 2–3, but believed that its analysis did not apply to Russia. → 68:52, 59; 69:64; 71:26, 28, 31, 54, 60; 72:22, 24, 27, 29, 42, 45, 46, 54, 63, 65, 68; 73:16, 21, 26, 30, 40, 41; 75:42, 44, 48; 77:9, 40; 78:39; 79:14, 19, 28, 39; 80:26, 31, 35; 81:5, 10, 60; 85:6, 14, 23, 29, 30, 40, 41; 86:5, 6, 50; 87:12, 21; 88:33; 90:7, 28; 91:4; 92:16, 29, 48; 93:10, 46; 94:10, 17, 25, 44; 95:12, 20. #M464.

Danilo Petrovich of Nyegosh (or **Danilo Petrovič** of Njegoš), *called* Prince Daniel (1826 to 1860) Prince of Montenegro

(1852+); prince-bishop of Montenegro (1851+). He established Montenegrin independence after warring with Turkey (1852–1853, 1856–1858); assassinated by a Montenegrin exile. —In reference works, this ruler is called either Danilo I or II, depending on whether a previous Danilo is numbered. #M89.

Danish language → 57:22.

Dante; *full* **Dante Alighieri** (1265 to 1321) The great Italian poet of the *Divina commedia* and *La vita nuova*. M quotes him most conspicuously at the end of his preface to #M181. → 83:36; 94:7.

Danube River; *Ger.* Donau Great river of central Europe, now dirty gray in color. #M323, M651; E910, E911.

Danubian principalities; *i.e.,* *Moldavia and *Wallachia. → 56:2, 34. #M153, M212, M302.

Darimon, Alfred (Louis) (1819 to 1902) French journalist and politician. He started as a disciple of Proudhon and as his secy (1848); editor of Proudhonist organs; then (1852) an editor of Girardin's *La Presse*, reflecting the new patron's views, esp in writing on financial affairs. His book *De la réforme des banques* (1856) had an intro by Girardin; studied by M (1857). D. was elected to the Legislative Corps (1857, 1863); there, became Emile Ollivier's mouthpiece on economic and labor affairs; also a friend of Plon-Plon, he collaborated with conservative republicans; then (1864) he went over to the Bonapartist camp, named secy of the Legislative Corps (1865–1867); and became a target for contemptuous satire. On the fall of the Empire, he retired to private life and wrote self-justificatory books. → 57:5.

Darmstadt (Ger.) Hessian city, near Frankfurt. → 45:14; 49:27; 60:3; 62:1; 84:62. #E442.

Daru, Pierre Antoine (Noël Mathieu) **Bruno,** Count (1767 to 1829) French governmental administrator and writer. He rose as an army administrator in the Revolution, then under Napoleon, who created him count, also ministerial secy of state (1811). Under the Restoration he was eclipsed till 1819, when he became a member of the Chamber of Peers. —Chief work: *Histoire de la république de Venise* (1819), excerpted by M (1843), Vol. 4; he also wrote a *Histoire de Bretagne* (1826). → 43:32.

Darwin, Charles (Robert) (1809 to 1882) Great English natural scientist, a founder of evolutionary theory. Author of *On the origin of species by means of natural selection* (1859), *The variation of animals and plants under domestication* (1868); *The descent of man* (1871). —M was a great admirer of his work, but not an uncritical one. E saw Darwin's discovery of the "law of development of

organic nature" as coordinate with M's of the "law of development of human history" (#E317). But the basis that Darwin provided for the theory of evolution, i.e., "struggle for life, natural selection," is "only a first, provisional, imperfect expression of a newly discovered fact" (ltr, Nov 1875). → 59:74; 60:5, 62; 61:8; 62:31; 68:60, 64; 73:45, 48; 80:37; 82:45; 94:37.

Darwinism → 84:28.

Daumer, Georg Friedrich (1800 to 1875) German writer. A student of Schelling, he devoted himself to the study of philosophy, esp religion. His first standpoint was anti-Christian, radical-atheist in tendency; e.g., *Geheimnisse des christlichen Altertums* (1847); next he turned to a sort of Christian pantheism; then turned Catholic (*Meine Konversion*, 1859) and moved further right. M&E's review of his 1850 book *Die Religion des neuen Weltalters* was mainly concerned with his reactionary social views. → 50:4. #ME137.

Davenant (or **D'Avenant**), Charles (1656 to 1714) English economist and statistician; lawyer by profession. Son of the poet William Davenant. Tory MP (1685, 1698, 1700); author of *The true picture of a modern Whig* (1701). Excise commissioner (1683–1689); later, secy of the commsn on union with Scotland; inspector-gen for imports and exports (1705+). As an economist he was a strong mercantilist. M (1845) studied his writings: *Essay upon the probable methods of making a people gainers in the ballance of trade* (1699); *Discourses on the publick revenues, and on the trade of England* (1698); *Essay upon ways and means of supplying the war* (1695); *Essays upon peace at home and war abroad* (1704). Later M studied his *Essay on the East-India trade* (1692) in 1697 edn. → 45:51; 55:5. #M575.

Davies, Edward (1756 to 1831) Welsh antiquary; self-educated schoolmaster and curate. His special avocation was Celtic antiquarian studies, the subject of his chief work, *Celtic researches on the origin, traditions and language of the ancient Britons* (1804), studied by M (1869). He also wrote *The mythology and rites of the British Druids* (1809) and a work which attacked Macpherson ("Ossian") (1825). → 69:75.

Davisson, A. N. Sec of the Schiller Institute in Manchester in the late 1860s, when E was an active member. → 68:60.

Davydovsky, Ivan Mikhailovich Russian revolutionary; husband of E. L. *Tomanovskaya. He was sentenced in the trial of the so-called *Chervonnye valety*, and sent to Siberia. → 77:3.

Dawkins, Sir William Boyd (1837 to 1929) British (Welsh-born) geologist, specialist in research on fossil mammals and the antiquity of man; investigated prehistoric cave dwellers; author of *Cave hunting* (1874); a coauthor of *British Pleistocene mammalia* (1866–1912). M (1881) excerpted his *Early man in Britain and his place in the Tertiary Period* (1880). → 81:64.

Daxbeek, Gommaire M. (b. c.1803) Belgian police officer; assistant commissioner of police in Brussels. His older brother was the police commissioner; other brothers were in the force; his eldest son became a police inspector. —In 1848 he was dismissed by the city council because of his illegal treatment of the M family; there is no info on his later career. —His name appears with various spellings: Daxbeék, Daxbeck, Daxbek. → 48:21.

Deák, M. A Hungarian socialist. (His name appears in *MEW Daten;* I have not been able to find further identification.) → 94:25.

Le **Débat Social;** Organe de la Démocratie Brussels, 1844 to 1849. Weekly. —Organ of left-republican tendency, associated with A. Bartels. → 47:39; 48:10. #M213, M888, M892.

Decazeville (Fr.) Mining and industrial town. → 86:8.

Defoe, Daniel (1659–61? to 1731) Now famous as a novelist, he turned to fiction in his later years, producing *Robinson Crusoe, Moll Flanders,* et al. Before this he had a variegated career in political journalism. M read his pamphlet *Giving alms no charity* (1704) in 1845–46; also his *Memoirs of a cavalier* (1720), praising it in an 1869 letter. Besides his famous novels, M also may have read his *Everybody's business is nobody's business* (1725). → 45:52. # M575.

Delachaux, Dr. Swiss physician; surgeon in Interlaken. M met this doctor in Monte Carlo. → 82:19.

Delahaye, Pierre Louis (b. 1820) See the note appended to Victor (Alfred) *Delahaye.

Delahaye, Victor (Alfred) (1838 to 1897) French socialist worker (mechanic); IWMA activist and Communard. A collaborator with Tolain and Lefort already by 1863, he became prominent in the Paris ranks of the new IWMA; pres of the mechanics' union. During the Commune he did administrative work; afterward, emigrated to London. There he entered the GC (1871–1872); as delegate to the London Conference (1871) he made a proposal for an international federation of TUs which evoked much discussion. He then (1872) became a founder and leader of a new group, Comité Révolutionnaire du Prolétariat, which in 1874 issued a programmatic pamphlet, *A la classe ouvrière,* advocating a workers' party. In 1879 he returned to France; became a Radical councillor in a Paris suburb (1883–1889), and a government repr to labor

conferences, and was rewarded with the Legion of Honor. —*Note:* The preceding is based on Maitron *DBMOF;* recently confirmed in *New Mega* I, 22. Previously all IML publications, esp *MEW* and *GCFI,* had listed the Delahaye of the GC/IWMA as Pierre Louis, b. 1820; and most secondary studies used this name. *DBMOF* lists no Pierre Louis at all. → 71:47.

Delcluze, Alfred; *full* Marc Louis Alfred (1857 to 1923) French socialist. First a commercial employee, then tavern keeper, he was a founder of the WP branch in Calais, also some TUs; municipal councillor (1888–1904); mayor (1898–1900). Gen secy of the national TU federation (1890–1892); delegate to most WP congresses (1890–1900) and international socialist congresses. After 1900 a Millerandist; though he briefly joined the united party in 1905, he soon quit and faded away as an unsuccessful independent; joined the SP after World War I. → 94:24.

Delescluze, Charles; *full* Louis Charles (1809 to 1871) French journalist; radical republican and Communard. —After taking part in the 1830 revolution, he opposed Louis Philippe's regime; joined republican societies; emigrated to Belgium (1836–1840); then editor of *L'Impartial du Nord* (1841–1848). In the 1848 revolution, he was first a leader in the north, then founded *La Révolution Démocratique et Sociale* in Paris; after June, disillusioned with his friend Ledru-Rollin's government. Afterward (1850–1853) he took refuge in England, and was a bitter opponent of Bonaparte's regime. Arrested in Paris (1853), he remained in prison till the 1859 amnesty. He founded *Le Réveil,* but was steadily harassed by the government; on the fall of the Empire (Sep 1870) he returned from a Brussels exile; and on the outbreak of the Paris Commune, was elected a member. In the Commune, he was outstanding as one of the prominent "old Jacobins"; in the last days he became military head, and died on the barricades in a suicidal gesture of despair. #M54.

Delhi (India); *now called* Old Delhi Ancient city of northern India, former Mogul capital; *not* the capital of British India in M's day. #E122.

Dell, William British radical. An interior decorator, Dell was active in the working-class and Democratic movements of the mid-century; member of the British National League for the Independence of Poland and of the Universal League for the Welfare of the Industrious Classes. He took part in the founding meeting of the IWMA; member of the GC (1864–1869); its treasurer (1865, 1866–1867); also a leading member of the Reform League. → 65:50.

Dell'Avalle, Carlo Italian socialist. In 1894

he was a leader (secy of the Exec) of the Partito Socialista dei Lavoratori Italiani in Milan; also an editor of *Lotta di Classe* and contributor to *Italia del Popolo*. → 94:36. #E868.

Dembiński, Henryk (1791 to 1864) Polish military man and national-revolutionary; of the minor gentry. An officer under Napoleon (1809–1813), he took part in the Polish uprising of 1830–1831: first, commander of a detachment; then, as commander-in-chief, he repressed popular discontent with the conservative leadership. Afterward, in emigration in Saxony and France. In 1849 he held a command in the Hungarian revolutionary army; after the eventual defeat by the Russians, he fled to Turkey, later settled in France. #E752.

Demelić, Fedor (1832 to 1900) Yugoslav author. M (1876) studied his work *Le droit coutumier des Slaves méridionaux* (1876). → 76:40.

Democratic Association In the movement leading up to 1848, and in the 1848–1849 revolution, "Democratic" was a political term (not to be confused with our contemporary meaning of the term) which designated the Left of the political spectrum in a general way, as a movement of The People against absolutism and feudal leftovers. The right wing of "The Democracy" (name of a general movement) was liberal-constitutional; the left wing was socialist or communistic; hence the term covered a wide spectrum, more or less the various camps supporting the 1848 revolution. M&E themselves, however, did *not* count the main body of the liberal bourgeoisie as a part of The Democracy, considering this therefore as basically an antibourgeois force. However, in the aftermath of the revolution, "Democratic" perforce came to have a pejorative content, designating the pinkish liberals whom the revolutionary Left henceforth considered simple enemies. *Caution:* This term was, is, and has always been protean, and must always be considered in its specific context to determine what it is really intended to denote, esp in the 19th century. See the references for this term in the index to ST/14 (KMTR). —Before and during the 1848–1849 revolution, M&E systematically sought to organize on two parallel levels: a communist political center of some sort and a Democratic club or assoc; and M&E, like many of their associates, belonged to and supported *both* at the same time, quite publicly. —The next three entries are on the most important Democratic Associations with which M&E were affiliated. For other Demo Assoc mentioned, see → 48:48, 57, 71, 72, 78; 49:12, 14. #M46, M232, M832; E226.

Democratic Association, Brussels M&E were instrumental in establishing this assoc in 1847, as a sort of united front of avowed communists with left liberals of an antibourgeois cast; M was vice-pres. → 47:1, 36, 39, 44, 46, 52, 56; 48:3, 4, 10, 14, 16, 17. #M57, M213, M825, M888, M892, M895; E769.

Democratic Association, Cologne and Rhineland During the 1848–1849 revolution, M was a leader (member of the Exec) of the Rhenish organization of Democrats, while at the same time a member of the Workers Assoc. → 48:33, 36, 39, 49, 53, 55, 60–81 passim; 49:8, 19, 22. #M40, M47–M49, M748, M854, M947; E670.

Democratic Association, Paris In the period between the Feb revolution in Paris (1848) and the Mar revolution in Berlin, while M was in Paris, a Demo Assoc had already been organized in Paris by a group of German émigrés who made it esp the vehicle for an adventuristic plan to organize a "German Legion" to invade the home country with French financing. M fought this scheme, and stayed hostile to this Paris group. → 48:19. #ME87, ME175.

Democratic Communists of Brussels M seems to have used this as a name for the *Communist Correspondence Committee. → 46:29. #ME4.

Democratic Federation (Eng.) See Social Democratic Federation.

Democratic Party (U.S.) → 62:56.

The **Democratic Review** of British and foreign politics, history and literature. London, June 1849 to Sep 1850. Monthly. Pub'r/editor: G. J. Harney. —Left-wing Chartist organ. → 50:7, 11. #M148; E433, E434, E800, E882.

Democratic Socialist Committee for German Political Refugees See Social-Democratic Aid Committee for German Refugees.

Democratic Society See Democratic Association.

La **Démocratie Pacifique** Paris, Aug 1, 1843, to Nov 30, 1851, with summer suspensions in 1849, 1850. Daily. Ed by V. Considérant. —Superseded *La Phalange.* Organ of the Fourierist movement; reform-socialistic. → 43:28. #M459.

Democritean philosophy See Democritus.

Democritus (c.460 to c.370 B.C.) Greek philosopher. Disciple of Leucippus, he developed a theory of the physical world as an assemblage of atoms. For M's dissertation, *see* Epicurus. #M235.

Demokratisches Wochenblatt (with varying subtitles) Leipzig, Jan 4, 1868, to Sep 29, 1869. Weekly. Ed by W. Liebknecht. —Organ of the Bebel–Liebknecht tendency. At first it called itself "Organ of the German People's Party," then added also "Organ of the *UGWA," and last, organ of the SDWP, after which it was superseded by the

Volksstaat. → 67:45; 68:10, 13, 22, 35, 44, 50, 54, 56; 69:41. #M7, M75, M177, M325, M747, M929; E405, E552, E673, E689.

De Morgan, John Irish socialist, from Cork; active in the English republican movement. He was also active in the IWMA, in particular in its British Federation, where he supported the GC against the lib-lab wing. In later years (c.1877) he did organizing work in Yorkshire. → 72:55; 73:14.

Demuth, Frederick; *full* Henry Frederick; *later* Frederick Lewis Demuth; *called* Freddy (1851 to 1929) Illegitimate son of Helene Demuth. It is generally believed nowadays that M was the father; at the time E assumed responsibility. The child was given into foster care soon after birth, and was brought up in a London working-class environment (prob by a family named Lewis, to judge by the middle name Frederick used in adult life). He was trained as an engineering worker; later, a tool maker; joined the Amalgamated Society of Engineers in 1888; was an active member of the Labour party and a staunch socialist. Eleanor M and other family members came to know him as a family friend, prob after 1883. —The main reason for some continued questioning of M's paternity is the unreliability of the main source of the information, Louise Kautsky. For a negative view of the conclusion, see Heinz Monz, *Karl Marx; Grundlagen der Entwicklung zu Leben und Werk* (1973). The main documentary source is a letter by Louise Kautsky to Bebel, dated Sep 2–4, 1898, first pubd in W. Blumenberg, *Karl Marx* (1962). For an explanation of the indubitable misstatements in this letter, and of the gen unreliability of its writer, see the biographies of Eleanor M by Y. Kapp and by C. Tsuzuki, which also explain Louise Kautsky's dark role in the E household and the reasons for Eleanor M's hatred of her. The information about M's paternity is said to have had Samuel Moore's confirmation, however; but this does not exist in documented form. → 51:23, 30; 95:37.

Demuth, Helene; *sometimes* Helena; *called* Lenchen, Nim, Nym, Nimmy (1820 to 1890; her gravestone bears the birth date 1823) The M family's longtime housekeeper, household manager, and friend. She came to the M household in Brussels in Apr 1845, sent as a servant by Mrs. Jenny M's mother, whose maid she had been. After M's death she became E's household manager and gen factotum, until her death, when E remarked in a letter: "I shall also sadly miss her wonderfully tactful advice on party matters...." → 45:23, 30; 49:31; 51:23, 30; 52:38; 54:31; 62:24; 63:32; 82:23; 83:15; 89:11; 90:46. See also her son, Frederick *Demuth.

Denmark and the Danes → 48:35, 43, 52, 60, 61, 64; 53:23, 30, 37, 55; 54:29; 65:8; 67:26; 71:62, 63; 72:15, 20, 21, 24; 75:5; 76:15; 87:19; 89:37; 92:1, 40; 93:35. #ME60; M9, M12, M54, M85, M265D, M302, M396, M651; E34, E35, E201–E203; E265, E349, E596, E922. See also Danish language.

Dentraygues, Emile (Jean Philippe) (b. c.1836–1837) French railway clerk, draftsman. A member of the IWMA section in Toulouse, delegate to the Hague Congress (1872) under the name Swarm, he was put on trial (1873) in a Toulouse trial of IWMA members. During this trial he was denounced as a government provocateur, and admitted that he had given the police info on the IWMA; in 1874 his penalty was reduced to six months; on his release, he offered his further services to the government for a career as a stoolpigeon. #E529.

De Paepe, César; *full* César Aimé Désiré (1842 to 1890) Belgian socialist; typesetter, later (1871) a physician. Early influenced by Colins and Proudhon, he began (1859–1860) with Demo Assoc activity. A founder of the IWMA in Belgium, he was the leading ideologist of the Belgian sections; delegate to IWMA congresses, where he made some important reports, esp on "The public services in future society" (1869) and on land collectivization, which he supported against the Proudhonists. After the Hague Congress, he stayed briefly with the Bakuninist rump organization. In 1885 he was a founder of the Belgian Labor party; and subseqly led the Belgian delegation at the 1889 International Socialist Congress. His political career showed a typical pattern in its evolution from anarchoid rhetoric to parliamentary socialism. —His name (Paepe) is pronounced much like *poppa.* → 65:55; 66:5; 68:69; 69:15, 36, 40, 65, 70; 70:4, 5, 11; 72:24; 73:57; 75:48. #M287.

Deprez, Marcel (1843 to 1918) French electrical engineer and pioneer in physicist technology. In 1882 at the Munich Exposition, he demonstrated a device for transmitting electrical energy over several kilometers, a step toward the development of long-distance lines. He also worked on the theory of friction, magnetic fields, etc. → 81:62; 82:47.

De Quincey, Thomas (1785 to 1859) English writer; most famous for *Confessions of an English opium eater* (1821–1822). His writings on polit eco deal with Ricardo's system. Son of a Manchester merchant, he had studied German literature and metaphysics i.a. —M (1851) excerpted his book *The logic of polit eco* (1844), also his article "Dialogues of three templars on polit eco" in *London Magazine* (1824). → 51:65.

Derby, *Earl of.* Edward George Geoffrey Smith **Stanley** (1799 to 1869) English statesman; Whig till 1835; thereafter Tory leader.

MP (1820+). Prime min (1852, 1858–1859, 1866–1868). His protectionist cabinet of 1852 was short-lived; he opposed Palmerston's foreign policy (1855–1858). #M234, M484, M485.

Derzhavin, Gavriil Romanovich (1743 to 1816) Russian poet; poet laureate under Catherine II; often called the greatest Russian poet before Pushkin. Known for his patriotic odes, "Ode to God" (1784), *The death of Prince Meshchersky* (1779–1783), *The waterfall* (1791–1794). → 51:49.

Descartes, René (1596 to 1650) French philosopher. A mathematician by training, his aim was to make philosophical analysis scientific; his system was dualistic (separating the worlds of mind and matter). He is perhaps best known for his circular *Cogito ergo sum* and for his injunction to doubt everything. → 78:45, 50.

Desmoulins, Camille; *full* Lucie Simplice Camille Benoist (1760 to 1794) French journalist; orig a lawyer. He was very prominent in the early stage of the French Revolution; his agitation led to the storming of the Bastille; his paper *Révolutions de France et de Brabant* (1789–1791) was very popular. A friend of Mirabeau, he later (1790+) drew closer to Danton's moderation, and was guillotined with him. Writings: *La France libre* (1789); *Discours de la lanterne aux Parisiens* (1789); *Histoire des Brissotins* (1793). —M (1843) made notes on his reading of *Révolutions de France et de Brabant.* → 43:33.

Dessau (Ger.) City in the former state of Saxony-Anhalt, now DDR. → 51:47.

d'Ester (or **D'Ester**), Karl; *full* Karl Ludwig Johann (1811 to 1859); *New Mega* now gives the birth date 1813) German radical Democrat and communist. A "physician to the poor" in Cologne, he was active in the RZ circle in 1842, as contributor, shareholder, and member of its discussion group; prominent in radical Democratic circles in Cologne. He joined the local CL in the summer of 1847. In the 1848 revolution he was elected a deputy to the Prussian National Assembly (Berlin), played a role in its left wing and (1849) in the Prussian Second Chamber; also (1848–1849) a member of the CC of the Demo Assoc; supported the Palatinate provisional government in the uprising. Afterward he emigrated to Switzerland, where he seems to have faded out as a radical. → 46:42; 47:52; 48:57, 72, 74, 78; 49:12, 27, 29; 50:25.

Destutt de Tracy, Count Antoine (Louis Claude) (1754 to 1836) French philosopher. A member of the States General in 1789, he lasted through the Directory and Consulate, and was appointed a peer of France under the Restoration. Napoleon, under whom he produced his chief work, regarded him as the head of the "Ideologues." His magnum opus was his *Elémen(t)s d'idéologie* (1800–1815), which aimed to reform all political, moral, and physical sciences. —M (1844) was concerned with the section of this work on polit eco (*MEGA* I, 3) called *Traité de la volonté et de ses effets* (1815), pubd 1823 as *Traité de l'économie politique.* → 44:48. #M575.

Deutsch, Simon (1822 to 1877) Austrian radical journalist; a bibliographer of Jewish literature. In 1848 he wrote for *Der Radikale* (Vienna); then emigrated to Paris, where he associated with Proudhon and his circle, and also went into business. In 1852 M was very hostile, in fact thought him an agent of the French police; but later D. sought him out on a visit to Carlsbad and must have smoothed out relations. → 74:31; 75:48.

Deutsch-Französische Jahrbücher Paris, Feb 1844. Ed by A. Ruge and Karl Marx. One double-number was pubd. —German-language magazine, intended to serve as a bridge between German and French leftists; in fact, no Frenchman accepted to contribute. For Ruge, the magazine was a continuation of his **Deutsche Jahrbücher.* → 43:1, 11, 12, 18, 20–22, 25, 26, 28; 44:1–8, 12, 19, 27. #M205, M254, M256, M471; E167–E169, E576.

Der **Deutsche Bote aus der Schweiz** Zurich, Winterthur (Switz.), Jan 5 to Oct 1, 1842. Semiweekly. Pub'r/editor: Karl and Julius Fröbel. —Radical in tendency, with good relations with the RZ. Herwegh did not succeed in turning it into a monthly magazine; the articles gathered were pubd in the **Einundzwanzig Bogen.* → 43:7.

Deutsche-Brüsseler-Zeitung Brussels, Jan 3, 1847, to Feb 27, 1848. Semiweekly. Founder/pub'r/editor: A. von Bornstedt. — Founded by German émigrés in Brussels, its orig political character reflected Bornstedt's vague radicalism and the support funds he got from French Legitimist and Belgian Catholic sources. But radicalization during 1847 pushed it to left-democratic views and close ties with the **Deutsche Londoner Ztg* (then influenced by the League of the Just in London) and with the German WA in Brussels. From Sep 1847, M and his Brussels circle were regular contributors, and by the end of 1847, dominated it editorially, using it to build the Demo Assoc and CL. → 47:5, 16, 19, 23, 29, 31, 32, 41, 48, 49, 54, 55, 57; 48:5, 6, 10, 11, 14. #M167, M213, M441, M531, M732, M820; E75, E144, E152, E234, E275, E337, E455, E497, E638, E659, E807, E920.

Deutsche Gerichts-Zeitung Berlin, 1857 to 1866; n.s., 1866 to 1867; first 3 vols. called *Preussische Gerichts-Ztg.* → 62:27.

Deutsche Jahrbücher für Wissenschaft und Kunst Leipzig (and Dresden?), July 1841 to

Jan 1843 under this title; preceded by *Hallische Jahrbücher* (1838–1841). Pub'r: A. Ruge, T. Echtermeyer. —Young Hegelian literary-philosophical organ. → 42:6, 21, 31; 43:7. #M156, M995; E684.

Deutsche Londoner Zeitung London, Apr 1845 to Feb 14, 1851. Weekly. Founded by David Cahn and the ex-duke of Brunswick, Karl von Braunschweig. Ed (with the ex-duke) by L. Bamberger; then (from June 1846) by J. Schabelitz. —This literary-political weekly for German émigrés in England was subsidized by the ex-duke. In 1847–1851 Freiligrath (then close to M&E) was a member of its ed bd; it pubd liberal anticommunists and also ran the first reprint of the *Com Manifesto* in its columns, some reprinting from M's *NRZ-Revue* of 1850, and some signed M&E statements. → 47:54; 48:18; 51:5. #ME33, ME136, ME157C, ME157E; M148, M163D, M226, M833; E768.

Deutsche Zeitung; *also called* Gervinus-Zeitung Heidelberg, July 1, 1847, to Sep D, 1848; Frankfurt, Oct 1848 to Dec 1850. Daily. Ed by G. G. Gervinus (in Heidelberg period). —Liberal; for a constitutional monarchy and Prussian hegemony; chief voice of the Frankfurt Assembly majority. #ME170.

Deutscher Courier Stuttgart, 1834 to 1842. Weekly —Subtitled a "European" journal, dealing with political affairs. → 41:5. #E524.

Deutscher Musenalmanach für das Jahr... Leipzig, 1830 to 1839; Berlin, 1840. Pub'r: A. von Chamisso and G. Schwab (for the Leipzig edns); T. Echtermeyer and A. Ruge (for the Berlin edn). → 37:13.

Deutsches Bürgerbuch für 1845 Darmstadt, Dec 1844. Pub'r: Hermann Püttmann. —Contributions by "True Socialist" writers and some communists (W. Wolff, G. Weerth, and E). #E218.

Deutsches Bürgerbuch für 1846 Mannheim, summer 1846. Pub'r: Hermann Püttmann. —Similar combination. #E288.

Deutsches Wochenblatt Berlin, Apr 1888 to Sep 1900. Weekly. —Merged into *Deutsche Zeitschrift* (Berlin, 1898–1903). → 90:50.

Le **Devenir Social** Paris, Apr 1895 to Dec 1898. Monthly. —Contributions mainly by Guesdists (Marxists). According to its subtitle, it dealt with "economics, history, and philosophy." #E556.

Deville, Gabriel (Pierre) (1854 to 1940) French socialist. Orig a lawyer; joined the Paris IWMA (1872), collaborated with *L'Egalité* (1877+) and became an active Guesdist for two score years: one of the top leaders of the Guesdist party, known esp for popular propaganda brochures, notably his abridgment of *Capital* (1883). His views

shifted right by 1896–1899; he joined (1902) the Possibilist–Jaurès–Millerand party. Refusing to enter the united party in 1905, he began a new career as a diplomatic repr of France abroad, ending as French min to Athens (1909–1915), after which he lived in retirement. —Guesdist brochures: *Cours d'économie sociale* (1884); *L'anarchisme* (1885); *Philosophie du socialisme* (1886); *G. Babeuf et la Conjuration des Egaux* (1887). → 82:14, 30; 83:34, 38, 42; 84:3, 11, 28; 85:3; 93:31.

Devy, Thomas English Chartist who emigrated to the U.S. (This name does not appear in the GC minutes; it is given in the notes to ST/21 [GCFI], Vol. 5. Does it perhaps stand for the American socialist Thomas Devyr?) → 72:8.

Dézamy, Théodore; *full* Alexandre Théodore (1808 to 1850) French socialist/communist pioneer. Orig a schoolteacher, he settled in Paris (c.1835+); was influenced by the writings of Owen, Buonarroti, Fourier; and became secy to Cabet. He was active in publishing Cabetist-communist (Icarian) propaganda; but broke with Cabet (1842) over the latter's religiosity and orientation toward bourgeois aid; D. favored a more revolutionary approach. He was one of the first socialist writers whom M read when he started studying the subject in 1842–1843. In #ME76, M came out wholly for Dézamy against Cabet as one of "the more scientific French communists," devoted to materialism as "real humanism and the logical basis of communism." D. joined secret societies of the time, pubd brochures and edited papers; and took part in the 1848 revolution; his *Les droits de l'homme* advocated universal suffrage and democratic freedoms. He died soon after; perhaps this is why he has remained an unjustly neglected figure among M's predecessors. —Alternative spellings: Dezamy, Dezami. → 42:26.

Dick, Alexander British trade-unionist; baker, active in the Amalgamated Bakers. He was a member of the IWMA/GC (1864–65); on Jan 31, 1865, he was appointed the IWMA's corr secy to New Zealand in connection with his preparations to move to that country. → 64:37.

Dickinson, John (1815 to 1876) English critic of the British India administration. Instead of entering the family business, he studied languages, art, and politics; only in 1850 did he begin his lifelong career as a reformer of British policy in India, writing on its deficiencies from the standpoint of empire. He took the lead in forming the India Reform Society (1853), of which he became honorary secy. In 1852 he had pubd a book, *India, its government under a bureaucracy* (repr'd 1853 in the India Reform Tracts series, no. 6), and he continued to produce critiques along these lines. → 53:55.

Diderot, Denis (1713 to 1784) French *philosophe* of the Enlightenment; editor and leading spirit of the great *Encyclopédie*. Philosophically, a militant rationalist and materialist who evolved from deism to atheism; politically, an enemy to all absolutist or benevolent despotism; one of the great pioneers of the scientific and democratic spirit of inquiry. M&E were great admirers of his *Le neveu de Rameau*, a satire; his *Supplément au voyage de Bougainville* was a portrayal of a free society (both works posthumously pubd). → 69:28.

Didier, Heinrich In 1849 D. was on the Defense Comm of the Palatinate uprising and became its embassy secy in Paris; expelled from France, he emigrated to Switzerland, then to the U.S., where he became an editor of the *Deutsche Schnellpost* (NY) in 1850. He has been rescued from oblivion by the *NRZ-Revue*'s note denying, for the record, D.'s claim to have been on the *NRZ* staff in Cologne. → 50:14. #ME54C.

Diest-Daber, Otto (Karl E. H.) von (1821 to 1901) German politician. Trained as a lawyer, he became a judge (1850), and district governor in Elberfeld (1851). Having exposed the bribery system whereby rich scions evaded military service, he was dismissed (1858) by the government. He bought an estate in Pomerania (1861); entered the Prussian Chamber of Deputies as a conservative; anti-Semite; repr of the old landed class. But he fought corruption in the Bismarck regime. — M (1878–1879) read his *Geldmarkt und Sozialismus* (1874) and *Der sittliche Boden im Staatsleben* (1876). → 78:51.

Diet See Rhineland Diet.

Dietz, Johann Heinrich Wilhelm (1843 to 1922) German Social-Democrat; pub'r. Beginning as a typesetter, he established a printshop in Hamburg, then went into publishing. He founded the firm J. H. W. Dietz Verlag in Stuttgart (1881), at first as a private enterprise; Bebel and Singer for the party Exec became partners (1897) in the firm, which was named J. H. W. Dietz Nachfolger GmbH; the firm was officially taken over (1904) by the S-D party as its party press, called Verlag von J. H. W. Dietz Nachf. (1905+); later (1921) merged with the Vorwärts-Verlagsbuchhandlung Berlin; liquidated by the Nazis (1933); reestablished postwar in both Germanies, in the DDR as a state publishing house. —Dietz himself was long a Reichstag deputy (1881–1918); in later years, a supporter of the Social-Democratic right wing. → 84:37, 38; 87:48; 90:17; 91:37; 92:9, 11, 23; 93:19; 94:27. #E341.5.

Dietzgen, Joseph (1828 to 1888) German philosopher and socialist. Self-educated, he worked out a system of materialist and dialectical philosophy often compared with that of M, who, however, was quite critical of D.'s views. A tanner by trade, D. became a master by the early 1850s; set up as a shopkeeper; in the early 1860s, took charge of a family tannery. He then went to Russia (1864) to manage a large government tannery; returned (1869) to his native Rhineland to run a tannery inherited from an uncle. In Russia he wrote his first book *Das Wesen des menschlichen kopfarbeit* (1869). D. also contributed articles to the S-D press; organized an IWMA section, and was a delegate to the Hague Congress (1872). In 1884 he settled in the U.S. for good (having emigrated there twice before); editor of *Der Sozialist* (NY); moved to Chicago (1886); in 1887 wrote *The positive outcome of philosophy* (1906). Throughout he remained active in the socialist movement. → 67:37, 42; 68:29, 44, 58, 63, 71; 69:56; 72:48, 54; 75:47, 48; 82:7; 84:15; 86:36.

Dijon City in E. France, wine center of Burgundy. #E455, E658.

Dilke, Sir Charles Wentworth (1843 to 1911) English radical politician, a leader of the Liberal party. He combined strongly imperialistic politics with progressive prolabor measures; entered the cabinet (1882) but his brilliant parliamentary career was torpedoed by a divorce scandal. He later rested a political comeback on the aim of combining the Radical wing of Liberalism with the lib-lab politicians, as alternative to the rise of an independent labor party. Pub'r, *Fortnightly Review*; author of *Greater Britain* (1886–1867); *The British Empire* (1899). → 71:56, 57; 75:13.

Diplomatic Review London, June 1866 to 1877. Monthly till July 1870; then quarterly. Ed by D. Urquhart. —In numbering, it continued Urquhart's *Free Press*. Subject: foreign policy from the Urquhartite standpoint. → 56:26; 69:32; 76:33. #M381.

Disraeli, Benjamin (1804 to 1881) English political leader. He first made his mark as a novelist; *Sybil, or the two nations* (1845) is of sociological interest. He joined the Young England group as a MP (1837+); working his way up to the leadership of the Tory party (prime min 1868, 1874–1880), he revived and modernized it by adapting it to parliamentary democracy and modern imperialism. Created Earl of Beaconsfield (1876). —The spelling D'Israeli (used by his father, who converted to Christianity and had his son baptized) was occasionally used by M and others. M's view of Disraeli was both hostile and appreciative: "He is the best evidence of how great talent without conviction makes scoundrels..."; "...the man, who is said to despise the aristocracy, to hate the bourgeoisie, and not to like the people" is however the ablest man in Parliament. #ME25; M59, M244, M392, M519, M635, M939.

Dmitriev, Fedor (Mikhailovich) (1829 to 1894) Russian law historian. With *Samarin, he wrote the Slavophile brochure *Revolutsionni konservatizm* (1875). → 75:37.

Dobrolyubov, Nikolai Alexandrovich (1836 to 1861) Russian revolutionary Democrat; socialist writer, materialist philosopher. As literary critic and contributor to the periodical press (esp *Sovremennik*), D. became an influential spokesman of the radical intelligentsia. Son of a priest, influenced by the writings of Feuerbach and Belinsky, he was skeptical of liberalism and looked to peasants and workingpeople to change society; a forerunner of Narodism. E thought highly of his historical writings. → 84:35.

Dobrovský, Josef (1753 to 1829) Czech scholar; of Bohemian family, active in Hungary, he became the father of modern Czech philology and literature, a founder of modern Slavistic studies, esp as writer of the first scientific grammar of Old Slav. M seems to have been interested mainly in his historical writings, e.g., *Slavin; Bothschaft aus Böhmen an alle Slawischen Völker* (1834). → 56:8.

Doctors Club (U. of Berlin) → 37:9; 38:1; 40:1; 41:2.

Dombasle, Christophe Joseph Alexandre Mathieu de (1777 to 1843) French agriculturist; inventor of a plow, founder of an agricultural school near Nancy (1822). M (1851) studied his *Annales agricoles de Roville*, Livr. 4 (1825); also his *De l'étendue des exploitations rurales.* → 51:67.

Dombrowska (or **Dąbrowska**), Pelagia; née **Pyotrovska** (1843 to 1909) Wife of Jaroslaw *Dombrowski. In 1872 she left France to become a teacher in Galicia. → 71:33.

Dombrowski (or **Dabrowski**), Jaroslaw (1838 to 1871; IML books give the birth date as 1836) Polish military man; revolutionary Democrat. Trained in the St. Petersburg cadet corps, he took part as an officer in the Polish uprising of 1863; sentenced to prison, he escaped and came to Paris (1865). At Bonaparte's fall (Sep 1870) he was on the war council of the CC/NG; in the Paris Commune, he was named gen, and in May became commander-in-chief of the armed forces. He fell during the barricade fighting in Montmartre. → 71:33.

Dombrowski (or **Dąbrowski**), Teofil; Fr. Théophile; Ger. Theophil (1841 to 1890) Brother of Jaroslaw Dombrowski. A Polish revolutionist, Teofil commanded a detachment during the Paris Commune; afterward he fled to England. → 71:33.

Donkin, Horatio (Bryan) English physician; the last doctor in attendance on M. He treated the M family in 1881–1883. Still a young man at this time, he had been an M.D. since 1873. → 83:11.

Dornemann, Luise References to Dornemann in the *Chronicle* are to her book *Jenny Marx* (Berlin, DDR: Dietz, 1969). Unfortunately, even apart from its expected hagiographic tone, it is by no means satisfactory in detail, and may be usefully supplemented with L. von Schwerin-Krosigk's biography *Jenny Marx* (Wuppertal: Staats-Verlag, 1976, 2. Auflage). → 49:27, 28.

Douai, Adolph; *full* Karl Daniel Adolph (1819 to 1888) German-American socialist. Born in Altenburg, he spent time as a private tutor in Russia; then founded a private school in his native town. After taking part in the 1848 revolution, he emigrated to the U.S. (1852), first to San Antonio, Tex., where he ran an abolitionist paper, the *S.A. Zeitung*. He then settled in NY; editor of the *Arbeiter Union* (1868–1870), a radical and TU organ. On the formation of the Working Men's party (1876), which became the SLP the next year, he took the editorship of its English and German publications; editor of the *New Yorker Volkszeitung* (1878–1888). First a Greenbacker, member of the NLU, he became an ardent Marxist after publ of *Capital*, and was one of the first to propagandize for Marxism in the U.S. Besides his socialist activity, he played a role in launching the Froebel kindergarten movement in America. → 77:39; 83:12.

Doubleday, Thomas (1790 to 1870) English politician and writer. He early became a follower of Cobbett; advocated the Reform Bill of 1832; joined the Northern Reform Union; author of a life of Sir Robert Peel (1856). His writings on economics include: *Essay on mundane moral government* (1832); *Financial, statistical and monetary history of England from 1688* (1847). M (1851) excerpted his *The true law of population* (1842), which attacked Malthus. → 51:68, 69.

Dourlens Paris police commissioner in the Faubourg St. Germain, 1849. → 49:33.

Dover (Eng.) Channel port. → 47:20, 30, 45.

Dragomanov, Mikhail Petrovich (1841 to 1895) Ukrainian historian and nationalist. Prof at Kiev (1873–1876); then exiled; prof at Sofia (1888+). He was a leader of the Federalists' tendency of Ukrainian moderate nationalists; a founder and editor of the journal *Hromada*. Author of books on Ukrainian ethnography, his publicist works incl *La Pologne historique et la démocratie Moscovite* (1881). M (1881) read his brochure *Tiranoubiystvo v Rossii* (French edn, *Tyrannicide en Russie*). —His name has also been spelled Drohomanov; NUC gives Mykhailo Petrovych Drahomaniv. → 81:13.

Dresden (Ger.) Former capital of Saxony;

now DDR. → 43:12; 48:58; 49:24; 51:27; 74:32.

Dresdner Journal und Anzeiger Dresden, 1848 to 1904. Daily. —At first, liberal; from Oct 1, 1848, official organ of the Saxon government; taken over by the state Apr 1, 1849. #ME2.

Dreyfus Affair (Fr.) → 93:5.

Drigalski, General von Prussian lieutenant-gen, commanding a division in Düsseldorf in 1848; reactionary. → 48:81, 84. #M241, M255.

Dronke, Ernst (1822 to 1891) German writer and radical. A "True Socialist" in the mid-1840s, he wrote stories and songs with a socialistic content; also a novel, Berlin (1846). Sentenced to prison for lèse majesté (late 1846), he escaped (Mar 1848) and came to Brussels. At or before this time he joined the CL. With E, he went to Paris to meet M; after Apr organizational travels in Germany on behalf of the CL, he worked in Cologne as an editor of M's NRZ. Afterward he emigrated to France; later to Switzerland as a CL emissary (July 1850–1851). In the CL split (Sep 1850) he supported M. In England, where he went into business, he helped M&E prepare defense materials for the Cologne Communist trial (1852). After the dissolution of the CL (Nov) he withdrew from political activity, but did not change his views, remaining on friendly terms with M&E. → 48:28–30, 33, 45, 54, 60, 62, 65, 68, 75; 49:4, 28, 29; 50:6, 15, 25, 34; 51:10, 42, 45; 52:17, 22, 24, 39; 53:1, 42, 43; 54:9, 33, 53; 55:18; 61:59; 63:15; 64:15; 73:32; 91:60.

Drouyn de Lhuys, Edouard (1805 to 1881) French diplomat and politician. Under Louis Philippe, a moderate monarchist and Orleanist; after 1851, a Bonapartist; he was foreign min in 1848–1849 and at various times till 1866; in 1849–1850, ambassador to London. He served at Napoleon III's elbow during the Crimean and Austro-Prussian Wars. #M810.

Droysen, Johann Gustav (1808 to 1884) German historian. As prof at Kiel (1840+), he worked for unification of Schleswig-Holstein with Prussia; member of the Frankfurt Assembly (1848); coauthor, with K. Samwer, of a work M (1853) studied, Die Herzogtümer Schleswig-Holstein und das Königreich Dänemark seit dem Jahre 1806 (1850). His earlier work was on classical Greek history; his later work, on Prussian history. Prof at Jena (1851+), Berlin (1859+). He was an ardent Prussian patriot who thought the historian should be a willing handmaiden of the Machtstaat. → 53:55.

Drucker, Louis German liberal journalist. Pub'r of the London humorous weekly How Do You Do? (This info is from MEW 27; but this publication does not appear in reference catalogs.) → 51:36.

Drumann, Wilhelm Karl August (1786 to 1861) German historian. Prof at Halle (1810–1817), thereafter Königsberg. His chief work was the Geschichte Roms (1834–1844); in latter years, wrote Die Arbeiter und Communisten in Griechenland und Rom (1860). M (1852) studied his Grundriss der Culturgeschichte (1847). → 52:58.

Dublin (Ireland) → 56:22; 69:58; 72:14.

Du Bois-Reymond, Emil (Heinrich) (1818 to 1896) German physiologist, Berlin-born of French descent. Prof at Royal Institution (London) under Faraday; named to Academy of Sciences, Berlin (1851), and succeeded to its chair of physiology (1856). He was a pioneer in the investigation of animal electricity, muscles and nerves, and metabolism. M (1878) read his lecture "Leibnizische Gedanken in der neueren Naturwissenschaft" (pubd 1870 orig). Also author of Über die Grenzen des Naturkennens (1872). → 78:50.

Duchiński, Franciszek Henryk; Fr. François Henri; Ger. Franz (1817 to 1893) Polish ethnographer and historian; émigré in Paris and Italy after the 1830–1831 Polish uprising. His view, that Great Russians were not Slavs and were entirely distinct from Poles ethnographically, was popular in nationalist Polish circles all over Europe. During 1848–1849 he wrote for the Corriere Mercantile (Genoa). Author of: La Moscovie et la Pologne (1855); Les origines slaves; Pologne et Ruthénie (1861). → 65:39.

Dühring, Eugen (Karl) (1833 to 1921) German philosopher and economist; famed as the target of E's Anti-Dühring. Orig a lawyer, an eye ailment (which later led to blindness) turned him to scholarship; he became a lecturer in philosophy and economics (1864) at Berlin; pubd Kapital und Arbeit (1865) and Die Verkleinerer Carey's und die Krisis der Nationalökonomie (1867); in 1877 was forced out because of his radicalism in Kritische Geschichte der Nationalökonomie und des Socialismus (1871); later pubd Kursus der National- und Specialökonomie (1873). These writings, which attacked Marxism, gave him a following as a socialist theoretician by the mid-1870s esp among a number of Berlin Social-Democrats, notably Johann Most. M&E warned the German party leaders to combat his influence; and they, esp Liebknecht, urged E to undertake a refutation of Dühringism. A special characteristic of D.'s works was his virulent anti-Semitism on a racial basis, in which D. claimed to be a pioneer. He entered this field with Die Judenfrage als Racen-, Sitten-, und Kulturfrage (1880) and Die Ueberschätzung Lessing's und dessen Anwaltschaft für die Juden (1881): these being clear forerunners of Hitlerite-type racism. Although D. taught that not private property and capital but only their misuse must be eliminated, he was regarded as anticapitalistic; his future order stressed national self-sufficiency in a controlled economy. → 68:5, 10, 13; 74:13, 22; 75:10, 16; 76:1, 13, 28; 77:10, 26. #E23.

Düsseldorf (Ger.) River port city in the northern Rhineland. → 45:24; 48:31, 70, 78, 84; 49:10, 12, 24; 50:14; 53:45; 56:6, 14; 64:46. #M805; E883.

Düsseldorfer Zeitung Düsseldorf, 1826 to 1926 under this title; founded 1745. Daily. —Moderate-liberal in the 1840s–1860s. → 67:43. #ME11, ME47; E690.

Duff, Sir Mountstuart Elphinstone Grant (1829 to 1906) Scottish man of letters; British administrator in India. Undersecy of state for India (1868–1874); for colonies (1880); governor of Madras (1881–1886). He is known for the 14 unnumbered vols. of his journal running from *Notes from a diary 1851–1872* (pubd 1897) to *Notes . . . 1896 to . . . 1901* (pubd 1905). NUC et al. enter his name under Grant Duff; his family name was Duff. → 79:8, 13. #M184.

Duisburg (Ger.) City in N. Rhineland. → 65:25.

Dulce (y Garay), Domingo. Marqués de Castellflorite (1808 to 1869) Spanish gen. He fought in the first Carlist war under Espartero; in the second Carlist war, winning victories near Castellflorite. He initiated an uprising which led to the revolution of 1854–1856. He became captain-gen of Catalonia (1858–1862); ditto of Cuba (1862–1866, 1869), where he was eventually ousted from power. → 54:32. #M962.

Duncker, Franz (Gustav) (1822 to 1888) German pub'r and politician. Founder of the Berlin *Volkszeitung* (1853) as a liberal oppositionist organ; a founder of the Nationalverein (1859), later of the Progressivist party; entered the Prussian Diet (1861), the N. German Reichstag (1867), and the Reichstag (1871–1877); advocate of social reform and labor legislation; supporter of Schulze-Delitzsch and cooperatives. In the late 1860s, with Max *Hirsch, he became a mentor of the so-called Hirsch–Duncker trade unions, i.e., secular alternative to the S-D unions, based on class harmony. He was a friend of Lassalle till the latter broke with the liberals. His firm pubd #M181 among other progressive works. → 52:42; 58:17, 22, 24, 36, 39, 50; 59:10, 13, 18, 22, 33, 36, 43, 51; 61:17.

Dundee (Scot.) Industrial city, on the Firth of Tay, east coast. → 56:20; 57:37; 59:46, 48; 75:35.

Dundee Advertiser Dundee (Scot.), 1801 to 1926. Daily (1861+). —Liberal. → 75:35.

Dupont, Eugène (c.1837 or perhaps 1831 to 1881) French worker (musical instrument maker) in England; IWMA activist. He took part in the delegation of French workers sent to the 1862 Exposition in England, found a job in a London factory, and stayed. He was active in the organization of the IWMA from the beginning; member of the GC (1864–1872); corr secy for France (1865–1871); attended most congresses; long active also in the London French section. In 1870, fired for political reasons, he went to Manchester for a new job; there organized a French section; became a member of the British Federal Council (1872–1873). Contributor (1866–1868) to the IWMA organ *Courrier Français*. Throughout his IWMA activity, he worked very closely with M, who had a high opinion of his ability and reliability. In 1874 he emigrated to the U.S., where he was active in the labor movement. —Note: He is sometimes erroneously identified with a Communard named Clovis Dupont. —Maitron's *DBMOF* knows nothing of his earlier life. *New Mega,* which gives his birth as c.1837, states that he participated in the Paris June uprising of 1848 (i.e., at age 11); ditto *MEW,* which, however, gives his birth as 1831. → 65:29; 68:42, 48, 69; 70:24, 50, 59, 65; 71:20; 72:17, 28, 33, 37; 73:27; 75:21. #M537.

Durand, Gustave French member of the IWMA expelled as a police spy by the GC in Oct 1871. According to Maitron's *DBMOF,* this Durand was confused with another man, whose full name was Gustave Paul Emile Durand; the GC itself made this confusion, and it is still reflected in *MEW* and other sources. —Little is known about the police spy named Gustave Durand. A co-op activist and member of the Lyons IWMA in 1870, he emigrated to London after the Commune and became secy, or temporary secy, of the so-called French Section of 1871, which fought the GC. Soon afterward his police role came to light; he was repudiated by all. —The innocent Durand (b. 1835) was a Paris jewelry worker or goldsmith, active cooperator and trade-unionist, a Proudhonist delegate to the 1868–1869 congresses. He filled a Treasury post for the Commune; was in hiding in Paris in Oct 1871; captured 1873, deported, and amnestied in 1879. → 71:51.

Dureau de La Malle, Adolphe Jules César Auguste (1777 to 1857) French scholar and poet. His works of scholarship on a variety of subjects won membership in the Académie des Inscriptions. M (1851) excerpted his *Economie politique des Romains* (1840). Other writings: *L'Algérie, histoire des guerres des Romains* (1852); *Mélanges d'histoires* (1858). → 51:33, 40.

Dutch In gen, see Netherlands. —Dutch language: → 64:14; 69:24; 80:19.

E

E.T. Unidentified correspondent to *Commonweal.* #E665.5.

East End (London) → 85:33; 87:2, 5, 17, 23, 26; 88:9.

East India Company (Brit.) (1600 to 1874) Chartered trade monopoly, operating mainly for the exploitation of India. After the Sepoy Rebellion (1857–1858) the British government assumed control. → 53:18, 22, 26, 53, 54. #ME150; M257, M399, M579.

East Indies *See* India.

Eastbourne (Eng.) Resort town on the Channel. → 79:32, 33; 81:36, 40; 83:34, 37; 86:28, 35, 38; 87:35, 39; 89:27; 93:20, 38; 94:13, 34, 38; 95:33, 36, 37.

Eastern Post London, Oct 18, 1868, to Dec 29, 1873; cont'd with title changes till 1938. Weekly. —Pubd as a workers' paper in the East End of London; organ of the IWMA/GC (Feb 1871 to June 1872); pubd leftist contributions. → 71:3, 9, 30, 34, 57, 62, 63; 72:5, 13, 20, 31. #ME48, ME85; M222, M466, M521, M755, M856, M857, M859, M902, M905–M907; E564, E596, E664, E678, E722, E749, E775, E776, E777.

"Eastern question" Popular 19th-century term for the imperial rivalries swirling around the declining Ottoman Empire; the question was who would take over what in Eastern Europe and the Near East. Central to the situation was Russia's drive toward Constantinople versus West European expansionism. → 53:9; 54:7, 17, 24; 77:5, 6, 13; 78:6. #M223, M258, M259, M355, M621, M626, M795.

Eberle, Carl Chairman of the Social-Democratic Assoc in Barmen, in the mid-1890s. → 94:20.

Ebner, Hermann (Georg Friedrich) German journalist from Frankfurt; friend of Freiligrath (who put him in touch with M) and Young Germany writers. From 1833 on, Ebner worked for the Austrian police as a secret agent, reporting on radicals in Europe; he began reporting on M with the founding of the RZ (1842). —KMC gives his dates as 1805–1855, but MEW and other IML works give no life dates. → 51:22, 33, 47, 52; 52:21, 28, 33, 36, 39.

Eccarius, Johann Georg; *Angl.* John George (1818 to 1889) German worker (tailor) active in England as communist and IWMA militant. He emigrated to London from Thuringia as a young man; joined the League of the Just, then the CL; member of the CC/CL; a GWEA leader. During the 1850s he became active in the English TU movement; and from 1849–1850 on, developed his journalist talent, beginning

with Harney's publ and M's *NRZ-Revue,* despite intense poverty and personal troubles, sustained by close relations with the M family. With the founding of IWMA, E became the leading German repr in its work, after M: member of the GC (1864–1872); gen secy (1867–1871), as well as lesser posts; also through M's influence, he was for a while secy of the National Reform League, and editor of the *Workman's Advocate;* later, employed as an IWMA correspondent by the *Times.* By 1871, as the IWMA bogged down, he went over to an alliance with M's enemies, esp the reformist TU leaders who looked to lib-lab politics, and in 1872 he sharply broke with M. But the *Times* let him go by 1877, and his new career got nowhere. —For sketches, see Collins and Abramsky, *KM and the British Labour Movement,* p. 305+; and, for relations with M, see ST/14, v. 2 (p. 644+). → 50:7, 34, 39, 41; 51:1, 8, 56; 53:1; 59:14; 60:24, 38; 62:57; 63:13; 64:26, 31, 36; 65:18, 41; 66:13, 17, 26, 51; 67:3, 22, 32, 35; 68:39, 42, 48, 49, 54, 61; 69:18, 30, 67; 70:45, 62; 71:3, 9, 21, 23, 24, 56; 72:3, 8, 13, 20, 25, 26. #ME53, ME54; M325, M599, M743, M744, M859; E433, E882.

L'Echo de Verviers Verviers (Belg.), 1864 to 1866. Daily. —Liberal-reform standpoint; it lent its pages to the people in the London French section of IWMA. → 65:62; 66:5, 21.

L'Eclair Paris, Mar 15, 1889, to Jan 28, 1926; previously titled *Le Peuple* (1888–1889). Daily. Ed by Dénécheau. —The editorial staff included two Guesdists, A. Duc-Quercy, E. Massard. → 92:22. #E390.

The **Economist** (with varying subtitles) London, Sep 2, 1843, to present. Weekly. *Investor's Monthly Manual* was issued in connection with it, Oct 1864 to Dec 1870. —Capitalist spokesman; liberal. M made excerpts from its files at various times, incl 1844, 1847, 1850, 1851, 1853, 1855, 1858, 1868–1869. → 50:28, 50; 51:22, 61, 64; 53:52; 55:5; 69:7.

Eden, Sir Frederick Morton (1766 to 1809) English economics writer and businessman. Founder and head of the Globe Insurance Co. In economics a disciple of Adam Smith, advocate of ruthless laissez-faire, he wrote the valuable repository of information *The state of the poor* (1797), which M (1845–1846) studied. → 45:52. #M575.

Edinburgh (Scot.) → 66:23, 77:36; 79:37.

Edinburgh Review. Edinburgh, London, Oct 10, 1802, to Oct 1929. Ed by Sydney Smith; then Francis Jeffrey (1803–1829); next Macvey Napier. —Liberal; organ of the

Whigs (1820s–1830s); perhaps the most prestigious literary review. → 51:67.

Edmonds, Thomas Rowe (1803 to 1889) English social reformer. After Cambridge graduation, he pubd *Practical moral and political economy* (1828), a Ricardian-socialist analysis and proposal for an Owenite-type society, with an original treatment of social psychology; he advocated gradual change from above. M studied this book (1845). In *Enquiry into the principles of population* (1832) Edmonds proposed welfare and reform plans to counteract subversion. He then became actuary of a life insurance co. and devoted his life to vital statistics. → 45:51. #M575.

Edmonton (Eng.) Suburb of London; now part of Greater London. → 54:31.

L'Egalité; Journal de l'Association Internationale des Travailleurs de la Suisse Romande Geneva, Dec 1868 (special no., before no. 1) to Dec 18, 1872. Weekly till Sep 3, 1870; suspended Oct 4, 1870, to Jan 14, 1871; then fortnightly and irreg. —Organ of the IWMA Swiss federation. At first, Bakuninist; in Jan 1870 the Federal Council changed the ed bd, Utin became editor, policy became pro-GC. → 68:62, 69; 69:70; 70:3.

L'Egalité (with varying subtitles) Paris, Nov 18, 1877, to Oct 1891 with gaps, as follows. —Usually Guesdist. —*First series:* Subtitled "Republican socialist journal." Nov 18, 1877, to July 14, 1878. Weekly. Ed by J. Guesde. —*Second series:* Subtitled "Revolutionary collectivist organ." Jan 21, 1880, to Aug 25, 1880. Weekly. —*Third series:* Subtitled "Organ of the Workers Party." Dec 11, 1881, to Nov 5, 1882. Weekly. Ed by J. Guesde. —*Fourth series:* Oct 24 to Dec 8, 1882. Daily, as continuation of *Le Citoyen.* Ed bd: Guesde, Deville, P. Lafargue, and other Guesdists. —*Fifth series:* For a period prob till Dec 8, 1883. Weekly. —*Sixth series:* Subtitled "Organe de concentration socialiste" (till Oct 12, 1889). Feb 8, 1889, to Oct 1891. Daily. → 78:7, 17; 80:7, 9, 13, 15, 20; 81:50, 59. #M224, M682, M752.5, M754, M857; E564, E679, E758, E766.

Ehmann, Paul American socialist; a leader of the Chicago SLP in the 1880s. → 83:12.

Ehrenfreund, Isidor Austrian bank clerk; in the 1890s, member of the Klub der Wiener Bank- und Kreditinstitut. #E537.

Ehrhart, Franz Josef (1853 to 1908) German Social-Democrat. A joiner/carpenter in the Palatinate, he became an active socialist at age 19; supporter of J. Most, whom he followed into London emigration in 1878. He assisted Most in publishing *Freiheit*; secy of the London GWEA (1878–1879). He later broke with Most's anarchism (by the 1880s), returned to the Palatinate, where he became a leader of the S-D party; member of the Reichstag (1898–1908). —MEW states he was a paperhanger by trade. → 79:10.

Eichhoff, Wilhelm; *full* Karl Wilhelm (1833 to 1895) German journalist and editor; also, businessman. He was jailed (1860) for publishing revelations on Prussian police corruption; emigrated to England (1861–1866), and became acquainted with M, who had helped his case. He then worked (1868+) in the Berlin workers' movement; member and correspondent of the IWMA; later (1869+) a member of the SDWP, and contributor to the German socialist press. —In 1868, with M's active help, he wrote a brochure on the history of the IWMA: *Die Internationale Arbeiterassociation; Ihre Gründung, Organisation, politisch-sociale Thätigkeit und Ausbreitung* (pubd Aug); still a useful source. → 56:13; 59:72; 60:29; 61:41, 54; 62:12, 18, 47, 63; 64:15; 68:13, 32, 38, 42; 69:32; 93:11.

Eichhorn, Johann Gottfried (1752 to 1827) German historian; prof at Jena and Göttingen. M (1852) excerpted his *Allgemeine Geschichte der Cultur und Literatur des neueren Europa* (1796–1799); and he wrote other works on general history, such as his *Geschichte der drei letzten Jahrhunderte* (1817–1818); but he was best known as an Orientalist and for his historical treatment of biblical writings; Protestant theologian. → 52:56, 58.

Eichmann, Franz August (1793 to 1879) Prussian government official; a cog in the reactionary aristo-bureaucracy. Governor of the Rhineland province (1845–1850); interior min (1848); deputy to the Prussian First Chamber (1849). → 49:8, 14. #M225.

Eilau, N. German merchant. A regular commercial traveler between London and Paris, he acted as a go-between for M in relation to contacts in the Paris Commune (like Frankel et al.). → 71:20, 23.

Einundzwanzig Bogen aus der Schweiz Zurich, Winterthur, July 1843. Ed by G. Herwegh. —For genesis, see *Deutsche Bote aus der Schweiz.* Not a periodical, but a collection of articles in book form; the title (Twenty-one printer's sheets from Switzerland) refers to the fact that books over 20 were exempt from the German precensorship; pubd by Fröbel's press. Seized by the Zurich government, but many copies got to Germany and created a stir (articles by E, M. Hess, B. Bauer et al.). → 43:19.

Eisenach (Ger.) Industrial city in Thuringia, near Erfurt. → 69:41, 47, 48.

Eisenachers; Eisenacher party Popular name for the *Social-Democratic Workers party of Germany,* founded at Eisenach.

Eisengarten, Oskar Social-Democratic writer; émigré in London. E hired him as secy (1884–1885) esp for the transcription of M's manuscripts. → 84:36.

Eisenmann Nonexistent Berlin bookdealer-pub'r. → 52:42.

Elastic Web-Weavers Union (Eng.) → 70:62.

Elberfeld (Ger.) Former city; see Wuppertal. → 21:1; 34:3; 35:6; 36:10; 39:6, 8; 45:16, 25, 34; 46:24; 48:33; 49:24, 25; 50:15, 19; 56:6, 11; 61:18; 69:19, 26. #ME86; E236, E300, E472.5, E745, E747, E770, E883.

Elberfelder Zeitung Elberfeld (Ger.), 1834 to 1904 under this title; founded 1789/1790. Daily. Ed by Martin Runkel (for many years). —In the 1830s–1840s, Evangelical-orthodox and conservative; in the 1860s, liberal. → 62:47; 67:38, 43. #E572, E691.

Elkemann According to E's article on the Prussian Second Chamber session (Apr 1849), this "Pastor Elkemann from Worringen, deputy of the rural constituency of Cologne and Mülheim" belonged to the Left Center wing. MECW provides no further info. #E239.

Elsner, Moritz; full Karl Friedrich Moritz (1809 to 1894) German (Silesian) radical-Democratic publicist and politican. He became editor (1842) of the Schlesische Chronik. In the 1848 revolution he was elected to the Prussian National Assembly, where he supported the left wing; tried after the May 1849 uprising, he was sentenced (May 1850) to two years, but fled to London, where he may have met M. The sentence was revised; he returned to Breslau, went back to journalism; edited the NOZ till 1855; cofounded the Breslauer Morgen-Ztg, with which he was associated till 1890. → 54:50, 54; 55:16, 21, 27, 39, 43, 47; 64:15.

Elster, Ludwig (Hermann Alexander) (1856 to 1935) German polit economist; official in the Prussian university system and Ministry of Culture and Religion. He was esp active as an editor of Jahrbücher für Nationalökonomie und Statistik and in the publ of the Handwörterbuch der Staatswissenschaften by the Jena pub'r Gustav Fischer. → 91:29. #E470.

La **Emancipación** Madrid, June 19, 1871, to Apr 12, 1873. Weekly. Ed by J. Mesa, A. Lorenzo, P. Iglesias, et al. —Orig pro-Bakuninist, it became pro-M and pro-GC; organ of the IWMA Madrid section, Sep 1871 to Apr 1872; from July 1872, organ of the New Madrid Federation; from Feb 1873, of the Spanish Federal Council. → 71:62; 72:23, 27, 42, 58, 61; 73:6, 20. #ME132, ME173, ME177, ME745, ME756, ME857; E325, E369, E679, E820, E863.

L'**Emancipation**. Lyons, Oct 3 to Nov 24, 1880. Daily. Ed by B. Malon, J. Guesde. — Organ of the French Workers party (Guesdist); issued during a period of suppression of Egalité. → 80:30.

L'**Emancipazione del Proletario** Socialist group in Turin. #E839. —Also, the group's organ, in Turin. → 72:53.

Ems or **Bad Ems** Town and watering place in western Germany (Hesse). → 37:10.

Encyclopaedia Britannica (London, NY, 1910–1911), 11th edn, vol. 17: Article "Marx, Heinrich Karl," by E. Bernstein. #E470.

Endemann, Wolfgang #M499.

Enfield rifle Type of rifle manufactured by the Royal Small Arms plant in Enfield, near London. #E704.

Engel, János Keresztély; Ger. Johann Christian (von) (1770 to 1814) Hungarian historian; author of works on Hungarian and Slavic history. In one letter (1856) M cited his Geschichte von Dalmatien, Croatien, Slavonien (1798)—which was actually part of a work called Geschichte des Ungrischen [sic] Reichs und seiner Nebenländer, in turn part of a set called Allgemeine Welthistorie. Engel also authored Geschichte des Königreichs Ungarn (1814–1815); Monumenta Ungarica (1809). → 54:52.

Engelhardt (or **Engelgardt**), Alexander Nikolayevich (1832 to 1893) Russian chemist and Narodnik publicist. Prof of chemistry at St. Petersburg Agrarian Institute; author of Khimicheskiye oznovy zemledeliya, which M read (1875) in connection with his study of agrochemistry. He also wrote Ocherk krestyanskago khozyaistva (1892) on the peasantry. M (1882) read his new book Iz derevny, 11 pisem 1872–1882. → 75:42; 82:55.

Engelmann, Paul; Hung. Pál Gábor (1854 to 1916) Hungarian socialist; tinsmith by trade. Editor of the Arbeiter-Wochen-Chronik (Budapest), and a founder of the Hungarian S-D party (1890). He became the leader of the party's left wing, which was undemocratically expelled by the right wing (1892); and thereafter founded the Social-Democratic Workers party (1892–1894). E's criticism of Engelmann's expulsion was suppressed by the party leadership. → 93:4.

Engels, Caspar; full Johann Caspar (1753 to 1821) Friedrich E's grandfather; a godparent at his baptism. (The name Johann Caspar comes from the index to the IML biography by Gemkow et al.) —Note: Friedrich E also had an uncle named Caspar E. (1792–1863), sole owner (1849+) of the firm Caspar Engels & Sons. → 21:1.

Engels, Charlotte; née **Bredt** (1833 to 1912) Friedrich E's sister-in-law; wife of his brother, Emil. → 84:62.

Engels, Elisabeth; full Elisabeth Franziska (or Francisca) Mauritia (or Mauritzia); called Elise; née **van Haar** (1797 to 1873) Friedrich E's mother. → 46:31; 53:29; 56:33; 59:59; 64:29; 68:53; 73:50.

Engels, Emil (1828 to 1884) Friedrich E's brother; a partner in the Engelskirchen firm of

Ermen & Engels. Note that the name Emil was also conferred on this Emil's son and grandson. → 84:62.

Engels, Friedrich [Sr.] (1796 to 1860) Friedrich E's father. Cotton manufacturer; a cofounder (1837) of the cotton mill of Ermen & Engels in Manchester; then of the E&E branch in Engelskirchen (1841). → 37:2; 38:8; 41:11, 13; 49:25; 59:59; 60:21, 33.

Engels, Friedrich The name occurs in titles, in the *Register*, as follows: #M322, M765, M867; E185, E290, E389, E432, E453.5, E471, E533, E572.5, E583.5, E596, E664, E670, E769, E871, E886. For E's pseudonyms, see *Oswald, *Hildebrand(t).

Engels, *Colonel* Friedrich; *full* Karl Friedrich Gottfried Ludwig (1790 to 1855) Prussian army officer; as colonel, from 1847 on, the junior commandant in the Cologne fortress garrison; created gen in 1851. During the 1848–1849 revolution, Colonel Engels confronted the NRZ group of M&E as the representative of the army's police power. No relation to E. #M453; E22.

Engels, Hermann (1822 to 1905) Friedrich E's brother. He was active in the father's firm up to the latter's death; then (1860/1861–1873) business manager for the mother; then chief manager and partner in the firm Friedr. Engels & Co. of Barmen and Ermen & Engels of Engelskirchen. → 42:27; 76:36; 88:30; 93:40; 95:37.

Engels, Marie; *mar.* **Blank** (1824 to 1901) Friedrich E's favorite sister. She married Emil *Blank in 1846. → 42:23; 46:31. #E94, E231, E590.

Engelskirchen (Ger.) Small town east of Cologne. → 44:35; 60:25; 62:51; 66:42; 69:52; 73:50.

Enghien-les-Baines (Fr.) Watering place near Paris. → 82:23.

English language → 86:9.

Enschut, Cornelis Adrianus van (1778 to 1835) Dutch legal historian; lawyer by profession. Prof at Groningen (1822+). M (1878) read his work *Over de bevoegdheid der markgenootschappen . . .* (1818). → 78:49.

Ensor, George (1796 to 1843) English publicist. Critic of English rule in Ireland, as in his *Anti-union* (1831); *Observations on the present state of Ireland* (1814); *Defects of the English laws and tribunals* (1812). Opponent of Malthus' economics, as in *An inquiry concerning the population of nations* (1818), which M cited in *Capital;* also cf. his *The poor and their relief* (1823). → 69:75.

Epicurus (341/342 B.C. to 270/271 B.C.) and **Epicureanism** The views of this Greek philosopher, extant only in fragments, were expanded by Lucretius' *On the nature of things.* M preferred Epicurus' development of Democritus' atomic theory, since Epicurus

introduced the factor of alternatives in history, rather than a mechanistic sort of determinism, and therefore allowed for the effects of human activity. This emerges in M's doctoral dissertation. —Note that Epicurus' views were the very opposite of the vulgar meaning of "epicureanism": a fate which he shares with M. → 39:1, 9; 40:1; 64:14. #M235, M239, M576.

Epirus Region of N.W. Greece → 54:26.

L'Era Nuova Geneva, Mar 4, 1894, to ?. —Italian émigré weekly. → 94:7.

Erbslöh, Karl August (1819 to 1894) A friend and schoolmate of E in Barmen, who became a Barmen manufacturer. (His son, Karl Alexander, married E's niece Elisabeth, i.e., brother Emil's daughter.) → 42:32.

L'Ere Nouvelle Paris, July 1, 1893, to Nov 1894. Monthly. Founder/editor: Georges Diamandy. Manager: Leo Frankel. —Socialist; largely Marxist in outlook, with international contributors. → 93:45; 94:36, 45. #ME33; E856.

Erfurt (Ger.) City, in the former state of Thuringia; now DDR. → 91:33, 46, 50. #M296; E198.

Eritrea Autonomous state formerly federated with Ethiopia. Italy established its colony there in 1890. → 90:15.

Ermen & Engels Cotton mill firm, founded in 1837 in Manchester by Friedrich Engels (Sr.) together with a number of Ermen brothers; in 1841 the firm established another mill in Engelskirchen (east of Cologne). — E's first post with the firm was as corresponding clerk and gen assistant to the managing director, G. Ermen. In Sep 1862 a new contract gave him 10% of the profits plus a £100 annual salary. In 1864 he became a partner, with a 20% share, the other partners at this point being Gottfried (Godfrey) and Anton Ermen; he was now responsible for the entire office administration. In autumn 1868 G. Ermen made an offer to buy E out, and in Aug 1869 they signed the contract of dissolution. For more info, see the two Ermen brothers below, to whom we may add Anton Ermen (1807–1866) and Franz Ermen, also brothers and partners in the Manchester E&E. → 38:9; 42:35; 43:2; 50:1, 44; 51:4; 52:23; 60:25, 33; 62:51; 64:19.5; 68:67; 69:45; 70:2, 53.

Ermen, Gottfried; *Angl.* Godfrey; *full* Peter Jakob Gottfried (1812 to 1899) A founding partner in the Ermen & Engels mills in Manchester and Engelskirchen. After his brother Peter's retirement in 1852, he became the chief partner in the Manchester enterprise and managed it till its dissolution. In 1874–1875 he founded, together with Henry John Roby, the firm of Ermen & Roby, Manchester. —It was therefore Gottfried/Godfrey who was E's principal in the period 1851–1864, thereafter his partner till the buy-out. Though German-born, he was considerably anglicized by long residence in England. → 62:51; 64:19.5; 68:67; 69:3.

Ermen, Peter (Albert); *Angl.* Pitt (1802 to 1889) Oldest of the Ermen brothers; according to the IML biography by Gemkow et al., a Dutchman by birth; one of the founding partners of Ermen & Engels (which see, for the background). Peter had founded the Manchester mill—on the outskirts of the city; making cotton cloth and knitting yarns as well as thread—in 1820 with his brothers Gottfried and Anton; it took the name Ermen & Engels when the Ermens merged their business with Engels Sr. Peter retired from the business in 1852; after renegotiations with Engels Sr., Gottfried became the managing director in Manchester. → 38:9; 42:27.

Ernst, Paul (1866 to 1933) German writer and critic; as a man of letters he produced a variety of writings—plays, tales, translations, narrative poems, novels. But he is of interest here for his Social-Democratic interlude: in the late 1880s he joined the S-D party, became a prominent journalist in its ranks, a leader of the faction called the "Jungen" (youth), which appeared to criticize the leadership from the left. After an internal struggle, he was expelled in 1891, despite E's advice to Bebel against such measures. While most of the Jungen evolved to the right, Ernst went further than most: to the extreme nationalist right wing of German politics, defense of Hitler, and an intellectual position close to fascism. → 90:27, 42. #E666.

Erpel (Ger.) Town, on the Rhine S. of Bonn. #M731.

Espartero, Baldomero; *full* Joaquin Baldomero Fernandez. *Conde de* **Luchana.** *Duque de* **la Victoria** (1793 to 1879) Spanish gen and politician of the Progressive party. He rose as a soldier in service against the French in the Peninsular War (1808–1814) and later against the liberation movement in S. America. In Spain, in support of Isabella II he defeated the Carlist revolt (1834–1840)—his outstanding achievement. The Cortes made him (1841) regent, or virtual dictator, to suppress the threatening revolutionary movements, esp in Barcelona. But a general uprising drove him abroad, to England (1843). He later came back to office as prime min (1854–1856) to shore up the weak throne. Finally, after adhering to the republic, he wound up recognizing Alfonso XII (1875). → 54:37. #M297.

Esser, Christian Joseph (b. c.1809) German radical worker (cooper and/or towboat worker) in Cologne. In 1848–1849 he was an active member of the Cologne WA, pres of a branch; a supporter of Gottschalk, with whom

he was arrested (July 1848) and tried on charges of subversion; acquitted. In 1849 he was editor of *Freiheit, Brüderlichkeit, Arbeit* for a time, and a member of the provisional District Comm of Rhenish Workers Assocs. → 48:84; 49:6, 9, 11, 19.

Esser, J. P. At the time of his proposal to M in 1843, he was a counselor to the Rhenish Court of Appeals in Berlin; previously, an officer of the Prussian judiciary in Trier, involved in the trial of M's father in 1832–1833, and a friend of M's father, whom M used to visit during his stay at Berlin U. Later (1848) he became a liberal deputy to the Prussian National Assembly, and (1849) to the Prussian Second Chamber. In these assemblies he was called "Esser III" because of the plethora of Essers. (For the three Essers in the 1848 assemblies, see the index to *MEW* 6 or *MECW* 8; for other Essers, see D. Dowe, *Aktion und Organisation*.) In some works, this J. P. Esser has been erroneously identified with C. J. Esser (above). → 43:16.

Estonia Baltic country; ceded by the Swedes to Russia (1721); independent republic (1918); annexed by the USSR (1940). #M319.

Les Etats-Unis d'Europe Bern, Geneva (1870+), Bern (1896+), 1868 to 1870, 1872 to 1919. Variable periodicity. In German and French, or simultaneous edns in German, French, Italian. —Pubd by Ligue Internationale de la Paix et de la Liberté (see *Peace and Freedom Congress). → 67:42.

Eteocles In Greek mythology, a son of Oedipus, who usurped power in Thebes; character in Aeschylus' tragedy *Seven Against Thebes*. #E745.

L'Etudiant Socialiste Brussels, Liège. — No info on duration. #E856.

Euler, Leonhard (1707 to 1783) Swiss-born mathematician (one of the greatest) and physicist, who was called to St. Petersburg by Catherine I (1727–1741), to Berlin by Frederick the Great, and again to St. Petersburg (1766+). He was a pioneer in the calculus of variations and analytical mathematics and in various fields of physics. → 78:1; 82:47.

Euripedes (c.480–485 B.C. to c.406 B.C.) One of the three great Greek dramatists of antiquity, author of *Medea, Iphigenia in Tauris, The Trojan women, Electra,* et al. → 40:17.

Europe The following indexes its use in titles only: #ME60, ME191; M9, M55, M55.5, M75, M136, M200, M201, M208, M299, M300, M355, M524, M525, M539, M647, M671, M673, M676, M773, M819, M838, M844, M963; E106, E118, E250–255, E418, E567, E593, E913, E914, E916, E922.

Evening Post NY, 1801 to 1934 under this title; subseqly *The Post.* Daily. —In 1856 it

became an organ of the Republican party. →
62:43.

The **Evening Standard** London, June 11,
1860, to Mar 13, 1905, under this title, as the
evening edn of the *Standard. Founder:
Charles Baldwin. —Conservative paper. →
71:46. #M908.

Ewerbeck, Hermann; *full* August Hermann
(1816 to 1860) German radical journalist,
orig from Danzig; physician by profession. An
émigré in Paris in the 1840s, he was on the
Exec of the League of the Just (1841–1846);
contributor to *Vorwärts!* (1844); an editor of
its successor, *Blätter der Zukunft* (Paris,
1845–1846), in touch with M's CCC in
Brussels; and translator of Cabet's *Voyage en
Icarie* into German (1847). In 1848 he was
secy of the German Demo Assoc in Paris, and
correspondent for the *NRZ*; a member of the
CL—which he left in 1850. In 1851 he pubd
L'Allemagne et les Allemands for the enlightenment of the French. → 44:13; 45:33; 46:8,
15, 29; 48:30, 33, 34, 46, 74, 79, 85; 49:4, 29;
51:45; 52:7.

Examiner London, 1808 to 1881.
Weekly. —Liberal. In 1871, it defended the
Paris Communards. → 71:20, 30; 74:5.
#ME31; E826.

Exeter Hall (London) → 69:37.

F

Fabian, Heinrich Wilhelm German Social-
Democratic émigré in the U.S. → 80:43.

Fabian Society; Fabians English socialist
group founded (out of part of the Fellowship
of the New Life) in 1884 under Frank Podmore
and E. R. *Pease; its dominant leaders soon
became Sidney and Beatrice *Webb and G. B.
*Shaw. Esp after publ of the *Fabian essays*
(1889), it grew in influence as a type of
social-reformism, aggressively middle-class in
tone, elitist in approach. Although at first
oriented to the Liberal party, it attached itself
to the Labour party once the latter became
important, and sought to act as labor's political brain trust. —E's attitude to the Fabians
was marked as much by contempt as hostility
to its political character: "a clique of bourgeois 'socialists' . . . united only by their fear
of the threatening rule of the workers. . . ."
And again: "stuck-up bourgeois, who would
graciously condescend to emancipate the
proletariat from above if it will only be
sensible enough to realize that such a raw and
uneducated mass cannot free itself . . ." (letters of 1892–1893). → 86:4; 90:5, 12, 20;
92:35, 39, 44, 47, 57; 93:2, 13, 49; 95:18.
#E841.

Fabrice Berlin judiciary official (*Intenda-
tur-Rat*). → 58:28.

Faedrelandet Copenhagen, 1834+.
Weekly, 1834–1839; later, daily —In 1848,
semiofficial organ of the Danish government;
in the second half of the 19th century, a conservative organ. —Note: The NRZ articles gave
the name as *Faedreland,* followed by *MEW* and
MECW except in indexes. #E264, E265.

Faerber, Salo Breslau Social-Democrat;
businessman by occupation, corresponding
with E about an article for the party press. →
85:38.

Famin, César; *full* Stanislas Marie César
(1799 to 1853) French diplomat and writer.
As diplomat, he served France in various
foreign posts, finally (1853+) consul at San
Sebastián, Spain. As a writer, his works were
also various: *Histoires des amazones* (1834);
*Peintures, bronzes et statues érotiques for-
mant la collection du Cabinet secret du musée
de Naples* (1832); etc. M (1854) studied his
*Histoire de la rivalité et du protectorat des
églises chrétiennes en Orient* (1853), which
dealt with the causes of the Crimean War. →
54:19.

Fantuzzi, Romualdo Brother and associate
of the anarchoid Italian pub'r Flaminio Fan-
tuzzi (Milan), who pubd an unauthorized
Italian edn of the *Com Manifesto* (1891) which
E considered poor. In 1892 Romualdo pubd an
Italian trans of #E759. → 91:19.

Far East → 53:1, 18; 62:10. #E718. See
also China, India.

Fasci movement (Sicily) → 93:44.

Faubourg de Namur (Brussels) → 46:44.5.
Faubourg d'Ixelles (Brussels) → 46:44.5.
Faubourg Saint-Antoine (Paris) → 48:40.
Faubourg St. Germain (Paris) → 43:23.

Faucher, Julius (1820 to 1878) German
publicist and economist. At first a Young
Hegelian, free-trader, with anarchoid tendencies; editor of the Berlin *Abend-Post* (1850);
émigré in England (1850–1861), contributor
to *Morning Star*. He returned to Germany
(1861); became a Progressivist supporter; after
1866, National Liberal; member of Prussian
Chamber of Deputies. In 1868 he edited the
*Vierteljahrschrift für Volkswirthschaft und
Kulturgeschichte* (Berlin), which pubd an
unusually ignorant review of *Capital,* drawing
M's ire. → 51:68; 59:34; 60:7.

Favre, Jules (Claude Gabriel) (1809 to
1880) French politician; a leader of moderate bourgeois republicanism. Lawyer by profession, he acquired a liberal reputation by
defending Lyons workers arrested in the 1834
revolt; settled in Paris (1836). At first a
supporter of Louis Philippe, he joined the

republican opposition; in 1848, became a leader of the Provisional Government; supported Cavaignac. Under Bonaparte, as a deputy (1858–1870), he supported the liberal constitutional opposition; acted as lawyer for Orsini (1858). With the fall of the Empire (Sep 1870) he became foreign min, negotiated the armistice of Jan 1871, signed the Frankfurt treaty of May 10; then took an active part in suppressing the Paris Commune and in the subseq campaign to destroy the International in Europe. Senator (1876–1880), mostly retired from politics. —Various reference works give his three first names in every possible order, but Jules alone was his common appellation. → 71:2, 9, 20, 28, 30. #ME85.

Fawkes, Guy (1570–1606) English conspirator, leader of the famous Gunpowder Plot (1604–1605) to blow up Parliament in revenge for anti-Catholic laws. The plot discovered, Fawkes and others were executed. Nov 5 is Guy Fawkes Day, when effigies of the conspirator (the "guy") are burned. → 49:42.

La Fédération London, Aug 24, 1872, to Sep 28, 1872 (six weekly issues); Jan 1873 (two irreg. issues); Mar 18, 1875 (special Commune no.). Ed by Vésinier, Landeck, et al. —Organ of the Universal Federalist Council (French émigrés hostile to the IWMA/GC); pubd in French and English. → 72:53.

Fédération Socialiste Révolutionnaire du Centre (Paris) A section of the Guesdist party. #E848.

Felix Character in "Scorpion and Felix." #M811.

Felleisen Zurich, Geneva (1867–1869). July 1862 to Dec 1874. Monthly, weekly, sometimes semimonthly. —Organ of the German Workers Assocs in Switzerland, which had nominally joined the IWMA before the Franco-Prussian War, never paid dues, and distanced themselves from the movement under the impress of the Prussian victory. → 71:2.

Feller, Friedrich Ernst (1800 or 1802 to 1859) German philologist and lexicographer; myriad edns of his pocket dictionaries in various languages were in print in mid–19th century. In Capital M cited Das Ganze der kaufmännischen Arithmetik by Feller and C. G. Odermann (7th edn, 1859), on commercial arithmetic. M (1869) read his economic writings, perhaps such titles as: Die Staatspapier- und Actien-Börse (1846); Einige Worte über Zettel-Banken (1856). → 69:13.

Fenians; Fenian Brotherhood, also called Irish Republican Brotherhood, and variants. Revolutionary secret society for Irish independence from England, organized c.1856–1858 in Ireland (by James Stephens) and the U.S. (by John O'Mahony). M was a critical supporter of the Fenian movement, critical of its terrorism, conspiratorialism, and vague ideas, but active in involving the IWMA in support of its independence struggle; the rest of the M family was said to be fanatically pro-Fenian. → 67:2, 18, 41, 45; 69:1, 60, 61, 65, 70; 70:1, 3, 11, 20; 72:61. #M287, M313.

Fermé, A. French lawyer, republican, exiled to Algeria by the Bonaparte Empire; later judge in the Algiers state tribunal; acquaintance of Longuet and Paul Lafargue. (KMC, but not MEW, gives his first name as Albert. Maitron's DBMOF lists an A. Fermé: a Blanquist student who attended the IWMA congress 1866; not otherwise connected up.) → 82:15.

Fernando Po Island of Spanish Guinea, W. Africa, in the Gulf of Guinea; briefly occupied by the British (1827–1844). #M265A.

Ferrara City in Emilia, N. Italy. → 72:13, 21, 24, 42. #E869.

Ferré section (of the IWMA), Paris → 72:35.

Ferri, Enrico (1856 to 1929) Italian criminologist; socialist turned fascist. —Prof of law (1883–1885); a disciple of Lombroso, advocating "Positive Criminology"; author of Socialismo e criminalità (1883). He entered political life (1886), and joined (1893) the SP, where for a while he was a leader of the left; editor of Avanti (1898+). He soon moved to the center, and then to the party's right wing; virtual SP leader (1904–1908). He then deserted this career, and went to the U.S. as a sociologist. After Mussolini's victory, he returned (1922), became a Fascist supporter and encomiast of Mussolini; appointed senator (1929). —His best-known socialist work was Socialismo e scienza positiva (1894); E thought that it was "terribly confused," and that he was a "driveler." → 94:37.

Ferrier, François Louis Auguste (1777 to 1861) French economist. A customs inspector (1804+), he rose to director-gen of the department under Napoleon, and eventually rehabilitated himself under the monarchy. Champion of protectionism and late mercantilism. M (1845) excerpted his Du gouvernement considéré dans ses rapports avec le commerce (1805). Other works: De l'impôt (1833); De l'enquête commerciale (1829); Mémoire sur le crédit (1817). → 45:50. #M575.

Ferry, Jules (François Camille) (1832 to 1893) French politician. Orig a lawyer and journalist, he entered politics under Bonaparte as a moderate republican. After the fall of the Bonaparte Empire (1870), he became secy of the "Government of National Defense"; mayor of Paris (1870–1871); a strong opponent of the socialist movement. After political vicissitudes, he rose to premier (1880–1881, 1883–

1885), and became known for his expansionist colonial policy, with an aggressive philosophy of imperialism, till his political downfall in 1885. → 89:32.

Feuerbach, Ludwig (Andreas) (von) (1804 to 1872) German philosopher. His early influence on M represented for him an essential bridge between Hegelianism and materialism, best described in #E457. F. was the leading inspirer of Young Hegelianism in the 1840s; a champion of humanistic atheism and (after the late 1840s) materialism in an early form. —Son of an eminent lawyer, Anselm von F., he was a student of Hegel at Berlin. At Erlangen he pubd his unorthodox *Gedanken über Tod und Unsterblichkeit* (1830). His marriage (1837) enabled him to be an independent writer without an academic post (till 1860). M tried (1845) to involve F. in political radicalism, unsuccessfully. F. might call himself a "communist at heart but not in form," meaning a believer in a sort of communality, but not in political communism. However, in his last years F. joined the SDWP. —F.'s importance lies in the impact of his writings, esp in the early 1840s: above all, *Das Wesen des Christenthums* (1841); also his "Vorläufige Thesen zur Reform der Philosophie" (pubd 1843), and *Grundsätze der Philosophie der Zukunft* (1843). → 37:8; 41:14, 18; 43:11, 22; 44:26, 27; 46:44; 51:21; 85:24; 86:4, 15, 24. #ME66, ME129; M368, M471, M493, M565, M878; E278, E457.

Fickler, Joseph (1808 to 1865) German journalist and politician; a liberal émigré in London in 1851. —Orig a businessman in Constance, he pubd (1830+) liberal opposition papers; agitated for a republic in 1848, and (1849) took part in the Baden revolutionary government. Afterward he fled to Switzerland; then emigrated to London; then to the U.S. where he turned into a partisan of slavery; after the Civil War, returned to Constance. → 51:31.

Fielden, John (1784 to 1849) English Radical-liberal mill owner. Son of a small cotton spinner, he (with brothers) built a large cotton manufacturing concern; but having adopted Radical and Unitarian views, he became an early advocate of ten-hour-day legislation, limitation of child labor, and parliamentary reform. MP (1833–1847); follower of Cobbett. His chief pamphlet was *The curse of the factory* system (1836); read by M (1851). He also wrote *The mischiefs and iniquities of paper money* (1832). → 51:67.

Le **Figaro** Paris, Apr 20, 1854+. Daily (1866+). Ed by J. H. Cartier (till 1879). — Conservative; in the 1850s, linked to Bonapartist circles. → 72:51; 93:25, 28. #E185.

First International *See* International Working Men's Association.

Fischel, Eduard (1826 to 1863) German lawyer and publicist; an assessor in the Berlin municipal court (1858+). As editor of the *Neue Portfolio* (1859–1860), he supported Urquhart's views; called himself an independent liberal; sharply criticized Palmerston's and Louis Bonaparte's foreign policy. Several of his writings were also translated into English, incl *Die Verfassung Englands* (1862, *Die Despoten als Revolutionäre* (1859), *Der entlarvte Palmerston* (1860). → 60:7, 12, 13, 29.

Fischer, Inka Daughter of Richard *Fischer. → 92:61.

Fischer, Karl Philipp (1807 to 1885) German philosopher; prof at Tübingen (1834+), Erlangen (1841+). Opponent of Hegelianism, follower of Schelling, his *Die Idee der Gottheit* (1839)—which young M attacked—was praised by *Trendelenburg. F.'s later major work was *Grundzüge des Systems der Philosophie* (1848–1855). → 40:4.

Fischer, Richard (1855 to 1926) German Social-Democratic party administrator. Orig a typesetter, he joined the German Social-Democracy in Swiss emigration (1873), and became a compositor on its publ, to which he also contributed; edited S-D papers in Augsburg and Berlin (1876–1878). With the establishment of the *Sozialdemokrat* because of the Anti-Socialist Law, he went to work on it in Zurich as compositor (1880–1888) and, with it, to London (1888–1890). The law abrogated, he returned to Berlin, and became secy to the party Exec, also a member of it; then business manager of the *Vorwärts* press, which he developed into the biggest socialist printing enterprise in Europe (his best-known achievement). He entered the Reichstag (1893), became a leading party repr, and around the turn of the century went over to Revisionism. He went through World War I as a social-patriot, and through the postwar years as a regular S-D official. → 90:42; 91:12, 17, 24, 27, 33; 92:61; 95:3, 8, 11, 16, 25, 29, 33.

Fitzgerald, Charles L. English socialist; retired army officer. In 1884–1885 he was assistant secy of the SDF; an editor of its organ *Justice.* In 1885 he resigned over the so-called Tory gold scandal, and helped form the short-lived Socialist Union. In 1905 he was a leader of the split-off forming the SP of Gr Brit. → 84:6.

Fix, Théodore (1800 to 1846) Swiss-born economist and journalist, active in France. Son of refugee French Protestants, he was orig a land surveyor in Bern; settled in France (1829); founded the *Revue Mensuelle d'Economie Politique* (1833–1836); contributed to many publ, incl the *J. des Economistes.* M (1845) excerpted F.'s work in his journal for 1842. Ultraconservative and antisocialist, his last work was *Observations sur l'état des classes ouvrières* (1846), which argued that workers' conditions are due only to their own thriftlessness. → 45:50. #M575.

Flanders   Roughly, the Flemish-speaking sector of Belgium. → 70:24, 62.

Fleckles, Ferdinand (1836 to 1894) Vienna physician, resident doctor in the Gen Hospital till 1864; then spa physician in Carlsbad (1864–1886). Also pub'r of *Der Sprudel.* At first hostile to M, he became a personal friend; M sought his medical advice even by mail. → 75:48; 76:24; 77:2; 80:35.

Flemish (people, etc.)   See Flanders.

Flerovsky, N.; *pseud. of* Vasily Vasilyevich **Bervi** (1829 to 1918) Russian Narodnik socialist, known for his economic work *Polozheniye rabochevo klassa v Rossii* [Condition of the working class in Russia] (1869), the first extensive study on the subject. Orig an official in the Ministry of Justice, his antigovernment protests cost him exile; released in 1870. He pubd another book, on "the ABC of the social sciences" (1871); arrested again, and exiled to Siberia (1874); escaped to London (1893). → 69:64; 70:15, 17; 71:6.

Fleury   According to *MEW Daten,* author of *Elections aux états généraux 1789,* read by M (1881). However, this title has not been found in NUC, BM, or BN catalogs; it is not listed among the works of Edouard Husson Fleury, who pubd many historical studies of the period. → 81:43.

Fleury, Charles; *pseud. of* Carl Friedrich August **Krause** (b. 1824) German businessman in London, where he was active as a Prussian police agent. He was responsible for forging documents for use in the Cologne Communist trial of 1852. Also known as Schmidt. → 52:45.

Flocon, Ferdinand (1800 to 1866) French left republican politician and journalist; member of the Provisional Government after the "Feb Revolution" of 1848. Early a political contributor to *Courrier Français* (1825+), he became (1845) editor of *La Réforme,* leading leftist journal in Paris. As a cabinet min in 1848, he was of aid to M&E (*see* the *Chronicle*), but played an increasingly rightwing role in government. After the June uprising, which he denounced, he joined the Cavaignac cabinet of repression. A squeezed lemon, he was defeated in the May 1849 elections; moved to Strasbourg; edited *Le Démocrate du Rhin.* He opposed Bonaparte's coup (1851); fled to Switzerland, where he lived in poverty under police surveillance, and died, blind, in Lausanne. → 47:42; 48:16, 22, 27. #E723.

Florence; *Ital.* Firenze (It.)   Chief city of Tuscany. → 72:10, 35; 94:33.

Florez, José Segundo (b. 1789) Spanish historian and publicist. A liberal, he pubd a biography, *Espartero,* in 1843; emigrated to France (1848); in Paris, edited *El Eco Hispano-Americano,* which became (1854) *El Eco de Ambos Mundos;* acted as correspondent for Madrid papers; wrote on Comte, pubd a Spanish grammar in French, *Almanachs Hispano-américains,* etc. M (1854) prob read his book on Espartero. → 54:56.

Florida (U.S.)   #E281.

Flourens, Gustave (Paul) (1838 to 1871) French revolutionist (Blanquist). By profession a naturalist and biologist, prof at the Collège de France, author of *Histoire de l'homme* (1863), *Ce qui est possible* (1864), *Science de l'homme* (1865), he was dismissed (1864) for his radical and materialist views. After some travels, incl participation in the Cretan uprising of 1866 and popular struggles in Naples, he returned to France; took a prominent part in the revolutionary events of 1870–1871. Elected to the Paris Commune, active in its armed forces, he was captured by the Versaillese and shot out of hand (Apr 1871). His book *Paris livré* was pubd at this time. —On visits to London, F. was friendly with the M family, who all admired him as a sterling revolutionist of ardor and integrity without being a poseur of the Pyat type. → 70:27.

Flushing (Neth.)   See Vlissingen.

Förster, Friedrich Christoph (1791 to 1868) German historian, man of letters, writer of war songs celebrating Prussian glory. Curator, Royal Museum, Berlin (1829+). When M met him, he had recently finished his seven volumes on *Preussen Helden in Krieg und Frieden* (1849–1860). → 61:15.

Folkestone (Eng.)   Port/resort on the Channel near Dover. → 90:36.

Fontaine, Léon   Belgian leftist journalist, from Charleroi. Sympathetic to Proudhonism, he acted as director of the French-language edn (*La Cloche*) of Herzen's *Kolokol* (1862–1865); also pubd *Uylenspiegel.* Active in IWMA: GC's corr secy for Belgium (briefly, 1865); delegate to the 1868 congress. → 65:29, 41.

Forbonnais, François (or Francis) Vérons Duverger de (1722 to 1800) French economist and financial authority. Gen inspector of currency (1756+). After travels in Europe, he pubd *Considérations sur les finances de l'Espagne* (1753), *Elémens du commerce* (1754); best known for *Recherches et considérations sur les finances de France* (1758), which M (1852) excerpted. Champion of neomercantilism and opponent of the Physiocrats, his writings are esp valuable for info on French finances of the 16th and 17th centuries. → 52:57.

Forcade   The entry "Forcade (London)" is

given by KMC from M's address book; possibly a French émigré (though Maitron's DBMOF does not know him). Note that Eugène Forcade (next entry) died before 1875. → 75:48.

Forcade, Eugène (1820 to 1869) French political-financial journalist. A bank employee in Marseilles, he founded Le Sémaphore (1837–1840); came to Paris as Guizot's protégé, and became best known as political editor of and longtime columnist for Revue des Deux Mondes; M (1851) excerpted his article of 1848, "La guerre du socialisme." He also founded and edited other publ during the 1840s–1860s, but it was his regular articles in the Revue des Deux Mondes that gave him European influence (till he was stricken with insanity). → 51:71.

Forster, Charles (1790? to 1871) English clergyman; rector of Stifsted. He pubd books of sermons and on biblical history and interpretation, Mohammedanism, etc. In 1853 E read his work The historical geography of Arabia; or, patriarchal evidences of revealed religion (1844); M read his then-recent book The one primeval language traced experimentally, vol. 1 (1851). → 53:18.

Forstmann Rhenish merchant; in 1848 a right-wing deputy to the Prussian National Assembly. No other info available. #ME75.

Fortin, Edouard French socialist (Guesdist). He translated M's Eighteenth Brumaire (1891) and other writings. Orig active in Beauvais, F. became a national leader of the WP (Guesdist party), esp in administrative posts (1895+); one of Guesde's executors. → 80:48; 85:26; 87:19; 90:49; 93:45.

Fortnightly Review London, May 1865 to July 1934 under this title; subseqly The Fortnightly. Founder: G. H. Lewes. Ed by Lewes (1865–1866); John Morley (1867–1883). —Left liberal. → 68:27, 33, 40, 44; 69:27; 70:49; 71:11; 75:13; 77:12; 80:42; 81:64. #E692.

Foster, John Leslie (c.1780? to 1842) Irish lawyer, judge, politician. Tory MP (1807–1812, 1816–1820, 1824+); he acquired various minor governmental posts, and was appointed baron of the Court of the Exchequer in Ireland (1830). In younger years he wrote An essay on the principles of commercial exchanges (1804); this is the title M must have found while reading up on credit and banking. → 69:13.

Fould, Achille (1800 to 1867) French banker and politician, first Orleanist, then Bonapartist. Finance min (1849–1852, 1861–1867); a leading backer of Bonaparte's coup d'état. Next to Rothschild, the best-known name among the rich Jews of the French Establishment. #M489, M529.

Fourier, Charles; full François Charles Marie; the family name was orig spelled **Fourrier** (1772 to 1837) With Saint-Simon, the greatest of the early French utopian socialists; his writings exerted enormous influence up to 1848–1850, even apart from the circle of disciples around *Considérant. —Son of a well-to-do Besançon shopkeeper, F. conceived an early hatred of the chicanery and inefficiency of business and the bourgeoisie. He settled in Lyons (1800+), and pubd his first writings there; moved to Paris (1828); worked as a traveling salesman and bookkeeper. His first disciples came around 1816; then Considérant; in 1834 Jules Lechevalier opened his Revue du Progrès Social to his ideas. The first organ of the école sociétaire (Fourierist school), La Phalange, appeared in 1836 under Considérant. —His social order, the "phalanx," was based on a model community, the phalanstère (phalanstery); the movement generally used the term association(ism) rather than socialism. F.'s leading American disciple was Albert Brisbane; the best-known phalanstery, Brook Farm (see C. A. *Dana). Aside from his proposed social order (which was not actually fully socialist from a modern standpoint), F. was noteworthy for his advanced views on women's equal rights and sexual liberation (played down by his disciples, but esp admired by M&E). Notable writings (short titles): Théorie des quatre mouvements (1808); Traité de l'association domestique et agricole (1822); Le nouveau monde industriel et sociétaire (1829); La fausse industrie morcelée (1835–1836). — M&E on Fourier and other utopian socialists: Disciples apart, Fourier, Saint-Simon, and Owen have had few more appreciative admirers than M&E. E's Socialism: Utopian and Scientific (#E759) offers a veritable panegyric of Fourier. Yet there are a myriad books and articles which, after diligent research into E's title, report that he expressed only contempt for the great utopians. To be sure, E discussed Fourier in his historical context, and did not carry his enthusiasm over to Fourier's disciples and epigones. The same is true mutatis mutandis for Saint-Simon and Owen. → 42:26; 43:2; 45:5. #E288.

Fox, Peter; orig Peter **Fox** André (d. 1869) British radical journalist and anticlerical propagandist. In the period before his association with the IWMA and M, he was a pub'r of the Secularist National Reformer; a leader of the Brit National League for the Independence of Poland; and a Positivist (Comtist). Fox took part in the 1864 founding meeting of the IWMA and became active in its organization: member of the GC (1864–1869), and its press repr (1865+); briefly, gen secy of the GC (Sep-Nov 1866). During this period he was also an Exec member of the Reform League

and (1866) an editor of *Commonwealth*. →
64:44; *65*:5, 23, 36, 43; *66*:23, 43; *67*:31, 32, 35,
40, 41; *68*:37; *69*:35.

Fraas, Karl Nikolaus (1810 to 1875) German botanist and agriculturist. Prof of botany
at Athens (1836–1842); of agriculture at Munich (1847+). M studied his scientific works
in connection with agricultural economics; he
(1868) excerpted his *Klima und Pflanzenwelt
in der Zeit* (1847), and *Die Natur der Landwirthschaft* (1857); also read *Historisch-
encyklopädischer Grundriss der Landwirth-
schaftslehre* (1848); *Geschichte der Landwirthschaft* (1852); *Die Ackerbaukrisen und
ihre Heilmittel* (1866). → *68*:72.

Francis, John (1810 to 1886) English bank
accountant; writer on business affairs. He
entered the service of the Bank of England
(1833), rose to chief accountant (1870), retired
(1875). M (1851) read his *History of the Bank
of England* (1848; orig 1847), which began
with a sketch of the history of interest and
banking. F. also wrote: *History of the English
railway* (1851); *Chronicles and characters of
the Stock Exchange* (1849). His history writing tends to be anecdotal. → *51*:62.

Franckenberg, H. German Social-Democratic émigré in Brazil. When he wrote to M
in 1877, he was the founding pres of the
Deutsche Handwerkerverein in Porto Allegre. → *77*:37.

Franco-Prussian War (1870–1871) Engineered by Bismarck to achieve German unity
under Prussian hegemony, the war ended
rather quickly with Prussia (supported by the
S. German states) crushing the French army.
Key events: (1870) France declares war, July
19; battle of Sedan, Sep 1–2; proclamation of
the Third Republic in Paris, Sep 4; Prussians
begin siege of Paris, Sep 19. (1871) Prussian
king proclaimed German emperor at Versailles, Jan 18; capitulation of Paris, Jan 28;
preliminary peace treaty signed, Feb 26. →
70:1, 40, 41, 44, 45, 48, 50, 52, 57, 59, 61, 66;
71:2, 7, 9, 13, 14, 17, 19; *91*:56. #ME88;
M318, M813; E531.

Frankel, Leo; *Hung.* Leó; *Fr.* Léo; *often
spelled* **Fränkel,** *sometimes* **Franckel,** *but the
Magyar Lexikon authorizes only* Leó **Frankel**
(1844 to 1896) Hungarian-born pioneer socialist: Paris Communard, friend of M, and a
founder of the Hungarian S-D movement. —
Son of a doctor, of Jewish family, he lived in
Germany in the early 1860s; there as a Prussian soldier he met the prisoner Bebel and was
converted to socialism; became a goldsmith
and jewelry worker by trade. He went to
Lyons (1867), where he built the IWMA
section; then to Paris, where he entered the
Paris Federal Council of the IWMA, and was
jailed as such (1870); in the late 1860s he had
made the acquaintance of M in London.

Elected to the Paris Commune (foreigners
being welcomed), he was head of its Labor
and Exchange Commsn, for which he wrote to
M about taking socialist steps; he did in fact
initiate a number of measures looking to
socialist change. Wounded in the May fighting, he fled to Geneva, then emigrated to
London. A member of the GC (1871–1872)
and a corr secy, he supported M at The Hague.
In 1875 he left England for work in Germany,
which expelled him, and in Vienna, which
jailed him (1875–1876). Back in Hungary
(1876+), he became an editor of the German-
language socialist organ *Arbeiter-Wochen-
Chronik* and its Hungarian-language twin, and
worked to help found a Hungarian workers'
party (by 1880), of which he became the
political-intellectual mentor. Threatened with
jail because of his Communard past, F. left
Hungary (1883) for Vienna, then Paris, where
he edited and contributed to the socialist
press, and participated in the international
socialist congresses of 1889–1893 as a Hungarian repr. He died in Paris and was buried in
the Père Lachaise cemetery. → *71*:15, 20, 23,
48; *74*:3; *75*:4; *76*:6, 12, 14, 29; *90*:51.

Frankenplatz (in Cologne, Ger.) → *48*:62.

Frankfurt (Ger.) Here, always Frankfurt
am Main (Frankfurt a.M.) → *41*:9; *42*:27;
45:15; *48*:33, 39, 61, 63, 64; *49*:16, 27; *50*:18;
51:45; *52*:18; *63*:41; *65*:60; *74*:31; *78*:12; *85*:13;
94:39, 43. #ME46, ME190; E843, E884.

Frankfurt National Assembly → *48*:35,
38, 44, 52, 55, 60, 61, 63, 71, 76, 81; *49*:17, 24,
27, 28; *52*:10; *59*:6. #ME117 ME130; M327,
M553, M679, M736; E44, E205, E280, E643,
E699.

Frankfurter Journal Frankfurt, 1684 to
1903 under this title; founded ca. 1665.
Daily. —In the 1840s, liberal. #M463,
M853.

Frankfurter Oberpostamts-Zeitung Frankfurt, 1617/1619 to 1866. —Owned by the
princes of Thurn and Taxis; during the 1848–
1849 revolution, an organ of the imperial
government. #M329.

Frankfurter Zeitung und Handelsblatt
Frankfurt, 1866 to 1943 under this title;
founded 1859. Daily. Founder/editor: L. Sonnemann. —Liberal. → *71*:57; *75*:31.
#M739, M858.

Frankish epoch The age, fifth to ninth
centuries, dominated by the Frankish empire
of the Merovingian and Carolingian dynasties,
founded by Clovis I and peaking with Charlemagne. #E289.

Franscini, Stefano (1796 to 1857) Swiss
economist-statistician and radical politician.
He was a leader in the Ticino revolutionary
movement (1838–1839) and an Italian Swiss
political leader; in 1848, deputy to the Federal
Council. As economist, his chief books on

statistics (specially praised by E) were: *Statistica della Svizzera* (1827); *Nuova statistica della Svizzera* (Vol. 1, 1847). #E79.

Franz Joseph (I); *Angl.* Francis Joseph (1830 to 1916) Emperor (Kaiser) of Austria (1848+); king of Hungary (1867+) with the establishment of the "dual monarchy" of the Austro-Hungarian Empire. #M59.

Fraser's Magazine London, Feb 1830 to Dec 1869; n.s., Jan 1870 to Oct 1882. Monthly. Superseded by *Longman's Magazine.* —Liberal; dealt with literature, science, politics. → 75:27, 35.

Fraternal Democrats "The first international organization of any permanence in England" (Schoyen), organized under the leadership of *Harney, in concert with a number of foreign émigré groups in London (French, German, Polish in particular, plus some Swiss, Hungarian, and Scandinavian contacts). It was set up at a banquet in London (Sep 22, 1845) held to celebrate the French 1792 constitution; generally socialistic in its platform, "for international proletarian unity," with loose organizational forms. M&E in Brussels and the Germans of the League of the Just in London were close supporters; the Chartist right wing and Mazzinians, i.a., stood apart from it. Banned by government action in 1848, it continued to exist, and in 1849 Harney reorganized it as an alliance of the Chartist radicals and the socialists (the "Red Republicans"), against F. O'Connor. In 1850 it still had over 20 chapters in England; it petered out in the course of 1852. → 45:32; 47:46, 52; 48:10, 14; 49:44; 50:15; 50:35, 49. #M57, M888; E140.

Frauenzeitung [Women's Gazette] While this paper was banned by the Cologne government and did not come into existence, a publ of this name was later pubd in Leipzig in 1849 by Luise Otto. → 48:66.

"The Free" [*Die Freien*] Berlin club, successor to the *Doctors Club around the U. of Berlin, characterized by a bohemian lifestyle and a tone of *je-m'en-fichisme*, incl Max Stirner, Edgar Bauer, E. Meyen, with E on its periphery. M (editing the *RZ*) was hostile. → 42:20, 30, 32. #M64.

The **Free Press**; Journal of the Foreign Affairs Committees London, Oct 13, 1855, to May 1866. Weekly (till Apr 1858); then monthly. Pub'r: D. Urquhart. —Succeeded by Urquhart's *Diplomatic Review. See also* *Sheffield Free Press. → 55:49; 56:4, 9, 21, 30; 57:12, 16; 59:50, 55, 56, 58, 60; 60:12; 64:13, 18. #M308, M321, M426, M433, M474, M701, M764, M802.5, M908.5, M937; E709.

Free Thought movement, or Secularism Both terms are minced British forms of atheism (a "dirty word"); this usually, though "Freethinkers" or Secularists might also be agnostics or even Deists. The organized movement was launched by the former Owenite, G. J. *Holyoake; its chief organizational form was the National Secular Society, with its organ, the *National Reformer.* In the 19th century there was an important overlap between socialism and radical Secularism, esp through Holyoake and Annie Besant, though *Bradlaugh was virulently antisocialist. → 67:37.

Freiberg (Ger.) City in the Dresden district. On Aug 4, 1886, the Freiberg provincial court sentenced nine S-D leaders, incl Bebel, to prison terms on a trumped-up charge of conspiratorial organization. → 86:32.

Freiburg (Switz.) This is the German name of Fribourg (Fr. and Eng.); see Fribourg.

Freie, Die See The *Free.

Freiheit London (1879–1882), Switzerland (1882), NY (1882+). 1879 to Aug 13, 1910. Weekly. Founder/editor: J. Most. — When founded in London, it was not at first clearly anarchist, but rather left-socialist, opposed to the German S-D leadership; but it became the leading German-language anarchist organ. → 79:3, 10, 24, 26; 80:12, 14, 29; 82:14, 20, 28. #E395.

Freiheit, Arbeit Cologne, Jan 14 to June 17, 1849. Ed by W. Prinz. —Pubd by Gottschalk's supporters in the Cologne WA, at first in the guise of the WA organ; but the WA Exec repudiated it and pressed publ of their own organ (see next entry). → 49:6, 9. #M830.

Freiheit, Brüderlichkeit, Arbeit Cologne, Oct 26, 1848, to Dec D, 1848; Feb 8, 1849 to June 1849. Weekly at first, then semiweekly. —This was orig the subtitle of the Cologne WA's organ, *Zeitung des Arbeiter-Vereines zu Köln* (Apr–Oct 1848); after the government's ban on the left press, the name was changed to this extent. → 48:71; 49:6, 9. *See also* *Freiheit, Arbeit.

Freiligrath, Ferdinand (1810 to 1876) German revolutionary poet; long a friend of M. Orig engaged in business and banking (1831–1839), his successful *Gedichte* (1838) turned him to a career as a poet of social and humanist aspirations. Then he repudiated his political poetry, and the Prussian king gave him a pension. His *Ein Glaubensbekenntnis* (1844) and *Ça ira!* (1846) repudiated his repudiation; and the tide of revolution took him into emigration; then to collaboration with M as an editor of the Cologne *NRZ* (1848–1849), also membership in the CL. He pubd *Die Toten an die Lebenden* (1848); *Neuere politische und soziale Gedichte* (1850); then had to flee Germany (1851), and emigrated to London. In the course of the 1850s he drifted rightward, toward the liberals and away from M, became a naturalized British subject, and manager of a bank which failed (1867). He returned to Germany (1868) and devoted himself largely to translations and, during the Franco-Prussian War, patriotic poems. → 45:13, 18; 48:70, 81, 85; 49:26, 31; 50:5, 27; 51:1, 22, 31, 33, 36, 38, 43, 45, 53, 56, 59; 52:3, 6, 22, 25, 38, 39, 47; 53:4, 31; 55:41; 56:34; 58:7, 13, 28, 37, 51; 59:4, 12, 14, 25, 31, 46, 49, 50, 63, 66, 71; 60:14; 62:57, 61; 64:27; 67:24, 31; 68:20. #ME31, ME58.

Der **Freischütz** Hamburg, 1825 to 1878. Weekly. —On literature, theater, art. In 1849–1850 it supported the fundraising of the S-D Refugee Aid Comm in London. → 59:35, 65; 60:13, 20. #M163B, M863.

Frémont, John Charles; *pronounced Free' mont* (1813 to 1890) American explorer, military man, and politician (left-wing Republican party). His explorations (1842–1845) were important in opening the West; unsuccessful Republican candidate for pres (1856). M's article concerned his dismissal (Nov 1861) as Union commander in Missouri because of his radical antislavery policies. #M242.

French Revolution (of 1789+) → 43:3, 29, 32; 44:4; 47:46; 48:38; 78:42; 81:43; 84:16; 87:15; 89:9, 38.

"French Section of 1871" (IWMA, London) → 71:51, 56, 59. #M604, M753.

French Workers Party (Parti Ouvrier de France, "Guesdists") The P.O.F. was founded (1879) at a Marseilles congress, but it was the split of the *Possibilists (Broussists) in 1881–1882 that left it clearly "Guesdist," that is, politically led by *Guesde, flanked by Paul *Lafargue and *Deville; regarded as the more or less Marxist party of the country. → 80:2, 15, 20, 30, 39; 82:24, 34, 40, 43; 83:12; 84:24, 28; 85:3, 28; 87:19; 88:38, 39; 89:3, 12, 15, 17, 25, 32; 90:42, 48, 51; 91:8, 23, 27, 45, 52, 56, 62; 92:13, 45, 62; 93:5, 8, 28, 44, 53; 94:16, 24, 35. #ME33; M683; E848, E858, E859.

Freund, Dr. Physician to the M family in the 1850s; not the same as the next entry. → 54:31; 55:42.

Freund, Wilhelm Alexander (1833 to 1918) Physician; gynecologist in Breslau, and a lecturer in the university there and Dresden, also doing research in medicine. Kugelmann first brought him to M's attention (1868) as a possible disciple; M then met him in Carlsbad, at least by 1876. → 76:24; 77:2.

Freundschaft [singing society] → 68:6.

Freyberger, Ludwig (1865 to 1934) Austrian physician. He married Louise Kautsky (Feb 1894) and, with her, established himself in E's household. —In Vienna he had qualified as a physician (1889); held a minor post at the university for a few years; prob met Louise Kautsky in Vienna; came to England (Nov 1892); qualified as an M.D. there (1893–1894). F. was an Austrian National Liberal, never a

socialist. E admired his medical ability; Eleanor M detested him. → 94:13, 34; 95:15, 23, 36, 37.

Freytag, Gustav (1816 to 1895) German liberal writer: playwright, novelist, critic. An editor of *Die Grenzboten* (Leipzig). *Die Journalisten* (1854), which M saw in 1861, was his most successful play; his realistic novel *Soll und Haben* (1855) was well known at the time. → 61:15.

Fribourg; Ger. Freiburg (Switz.) [not to be confused with Freiburg in Germany] City, mainly French-speaking, S.W. of Bern. #E499.

Fribourg, E. E.; *full* Ernest Edouard French worker (engraver, later a businessman in the trade); a founding leader of the Proudhonist tendency in the Paris IWMA, as Tolain's lieutenant. He was esp active as an editor of IWMA papers, i.a. *Tribune Ouvrière* (1865), *La Fédéraliste* (1868). He later dropped out of IWMA work because of business difficulties; in 1871, with Tolain, he denounced the Paris Commune ("bloody maniacs" and other pleasantries). His "history" of the IWMA, *L'Association Internationale des Travailleurs* (1871), was an apologia for the Proudhonist wing and a violent attack on the Commune. —A French Archives document later indicated that he might have been a paid police agent linked with Girardin and Plon-Plon; *DBMOF* gives the facts with a cautionary question mark. → 65:13, 23, 51.

Friedberg, Hermann (1817 to 1884) German physician; prof at Breslau (1866+). M met him in Carlsbad. → 76:24.

Friedländer, Julius German lawyer, Berlin assessor. Brother of Max *Friedländer. → 61:17, 25.

Friedländer, Ludwig (1824 to 1909) German historian; prof at Königsberg (1847–1892). At first a specialist in Homer studies, his life work was his history of Rome till Commodus, *Darstellungen aus der Sittengeschichte Roms* (1862–1871), which M (1879) studied and excerpted. → 79:54.

Friedländer, Max (1829 to 1872) Austrian journalist; a leading liberal publicist. In the 1850s he was in Germany as an editor of the NOZ; in the 1860s he was an editor of the Vienna *Presse*; M contributed to both of these papers. In 1864 he was a founder of the *Neue Freie Presse* (Vienna), which fought for constitutional liberties; he became its editor (1870–1871). F. was a cousin of Lassalle, who introduced him to M. → 54:50; 57:53; 59:21, 28, 40; 61:17, 25, 43; 62:9, 23; 69:50; 71:30.

Friedrich Wilhelm IV; *Angl.* Frederick William (1795 to 1861) King of Prussia, June 7, 1840, to Jan 2, 1861. —Background info related to M&E's writings: He began his reign by reneging on the promises of constitutional reforms made to spur the war against Napoleon; he confronted the 1848 revolution, and came out of it with an effort to restore semifeudal reaction; and he ended his reign insane. → 47:19; 48:23, 76; 49:26; 50:20. #M383, M427, M428, M735, M736; E299.

The **Friend of the People** London, Dec 1850 to July 26, 1851; n.s., Feb 7 to Apr 24, 1852. Pub'r/editor: G. J. Harney. —This superseded Harney's *Red Republican*, and was superseded by his *Star of Freedom* (Aug 14 to Nov 27, 1852). → 50:49; 51:9, 14; 52:3.

Friends of Light (Ger.) A movement in the Protestant church directed against Pietism. → 69:36.

Frisch, *Herr* von → 49:21.

Frisian language Germanic language of the Frisian Islands (Neth.), close to English. → 69:24; 73:3.

Fritzsche, Friedrich Wilhelm (1825 to 1905) German socialist trade-unionist and pioneer organizer. He took part (1848) in the Schleswig-Holstein revolt, and (May 1849) the Dresden uprising. By the 1860s he was active in the Leipzig labor movement; helped Lassalle found the GGWA (1863); built the national cigarmakers' union (1865+) and was its pres till 1878; editor of its organ *Der Botschafter* (1866–1878). He broke with the Lassalleans and their party-controlled TU system, and was a founder of the Eisenacher party (SDWP, 1869). Member of the N. German Reichstag (1868–1871); orig elected as a Lassallean, but in 1870, though an Eisenacher then, he voted for the war credits (unlike Bebel and Liebknecht); in fact he retained many Lassallean views. Member of the Reichstag (1877–1881). The 1880 party congress sent him on a fundraising tour of America. In late 1881, discouraged by the situation under the Anti-Socialist Law, he emigrated to the U.S.; there he exchanged the workers' movement for saloon-keeping in Philadelphia. → 69:25, 40; 79:41; 81:4, 17.

Fröbel, Julius (1805 to 1893) In the 1840s (when M dealt with him) he was a German pub'r, esp of progressive literature. He took part in the 1848 revolution (deputy to the Frankfurt assembly, CC of the Demo Assocs); and after it, emigrated to the U.S.; pubd a paper in San Francisco after the gold rush. He returned to Europe (1857), engaged in journalism, and later entered the Prussian diplomatic service. Autobiography: *Ein Lebenslauf* (1890–1891). → 43:25; 44:40.

Frohme, Karl (Franz Egon) (1850 to 1933) German Social-Democratic leader; orig a mechanical engineer. He early became a Lassallean propagandist-organizer; jailed several times; took part (1873–1874) in building a S-D movement in Belgium and Holland. In the united German party after the 1875 Gotha unity, he became a right-wing leader and parliamentarian; editor (1876–1878) of *Volksfreund* (Frankfurt); editor (1890+) of the *Hamburger Echo.* Reichstag deputy (1881–1924). → 93:7.

Füster, Anton (1808 to 1881) Austrian radical. Orig a prof of philosophy and theology at Vienna, he took part in the 1848 revolution as a so-called field chaplain of the Student Legion; went (1849) to Leipzig and Hamburg, then (1852) emigrated to London, where he was active in refugee-aid comm work; later moved to the U.S., where he taught school; perhaps returned to Austria later. → 49:36, 40.

Fullarton, John (1780 to 1849) English writer on economics. Orig (1802–1813) a physician of the E. India Co. in Bengal and part-owner of a newspaper; then (1813+) partner in a Calcutta banking house, where he made a fortune. In the ensuing years, partly in England, partly traveling, he supported the Tories on parliamentary reform, and did diplomatic missions in China. Later (1838), bad speculations shaved his fortune. During the conflict over Peel's Bank Charter Act, he pubd his one important work, *On the regulation of currencies* (1844; 2nd edn, 1845), which M studied in 1850–1851 and after. → 50:50; 54:51.

Furnivall, Frederick James (1825 to 1910) English philologist, best known as the initiator of the *Oxford English Dictionary,* on behalf of the Philological Society, of which he was the longtime secy. He was also a founder of a number of literary societies. —F., a Huxley-type agnostic, had strong leanings toward Christian socialism and social reform; helped Ruskin found the Working Men's College (London); he was acquainted with M, and Eleanor M did some work for him. → 78:23.

G

Gabler, Georg Andreas (1786 to 1853) German prof of philosophy; a Hegelian, and Hegel's successor at Berlin (1835+). Author of *Die Hegel'sche Philosophie* (1843). → 38:7.

Gaelic language → 69:61.

Galiani, Ferdinando (or Fernando) (1728 to 1787) Italian political economist and scholar. Besides his activity as a writer, G. also spent many years in Paris as a diplomatic repr, also in London; and (1769+) served in various high posts in Naples. His early work *Della moneta* (1750) criticized mercantilist and Physiocrat views; M (1853, 1859) studied it in the Custodi collection. G's *Dialogues sur* *le commerce des blés* (1770) gained him a bigger reputation. → *53*:51; *59*:76.

Galicia Region of N.W. Spain. → *94*:14.

Gallatin, Albert (Abraham Alphonse) (1761 to 1849) American statesman and financier; b. Geneva; came to the U.S. in 1780. He began (1789+) a steady ascent in the U.S. government, from Congress (1793+) to Treasury secy (1801–1814) and diplomat, esp involved in international economic negotiations. He became pres, National (later Gallatin) Bank of NY (1831–1839). His avocation was historical and ethnological studies; his best known scientific writings are in the latter field; pres, N-Y Historical Society (1843+). He also pubd much on financial questions. M (1851) studied his *Considerations on the currency and banking system of the U.S.* (1831). → *51*:63.

Galway (Ireland) West-coast port city. → *56*:22.

Ganilh, Charles (1758 to 1836) French economist and politician. A lawyer by profession, he was a deputy to the National Assembly during the French Revolution; an oppositionist in the Tribunate (to 1802); liberal in the Chamber of Deputies (1815–1823). As an economist, he was known as the liveliest defender of the Mercantilist school; the "economist of the Empire" (M). Author of *Dictionnaire analytique de l'économie politique* (1826). M (1845–1846) studied his *Des systèmes d'économie politique* (1809). → *45*:50. #M575.

Gans, Eduard (1797 or 1798 to 1839) German law prof and historian of jurisprudence; a pupil, disciple, editor, and expounder of Hegel, and opponent of Savigny's "Historical School" of law. Jewish by birth, a founder of the first society for Jewish studies, he converted (1825) in order to be appointed prof at Berlin (1826), after beginning publ of his chief work *Das Erbrecht in weltgeschichtliche Entwicklung* (1824–1835). Visiting Paris (1830, 1835), he became acquainted with Saint-Simonianism and other left currents; in Berlin (1833–1834) his lectures on "the last 50 years" were banned. → *36*:12; *38*:7.

Gans, Jr., Dr. Physician in Prague; M met him in Carlsbad, and sent him a copy of *Capital* and #M267. → *74*:31.

Garcia, Charles J. London correspondent of the *Sozialdemokrat*; a supporter of Hyndman's SDF; hostile to M&E. (This info appears from E's correspondence.) → *82*:41.

Gare de Lyon (Paris) → *87*:34.

Garibaldi, Giuseppe (1807 to 1882) Italian (b. Nice) national-revolutionary partisan leader and radical Democrat. Son of a fisherman, supporter of Young Italy, refugee in S. America for a while, in 1848 he fought with the Piedmontese against Austria, and organized defense of the Roman Republic (1849). Through the 1850–1860s he became the national hero of the Italian liberation struggle, with exploits esp in S. Italy and Sicily; marches on Rome (1862, 1867). He fought for France against Prussia (1870–1871). Among the noncommunist revolutionaries of the European left, he was notable for his sympathy with and support of both the IWMA and the Paris Commune. → *60*:36, 43, 48; *61*:30, 41; *62*:35, 49, 54; *64*:13, 35; *70*:62; *71*:56, 64; *73*:14; *94*:33. #M341, M409, M505; E320–E323, E749.

Garibaldi, Ricciotti (1847 to 1924) Son of Giuseppe Garibaldi, b. Montevideo (in emigration). He fought alongside his father in the Italian liberation movement of the 1860s; distinguished himself as a French commander in the 1870 war and as a Greek commander against the Turks (1897). After World War I, in which he fought for France, he became a supporter of Mussolini. → *71*:56.

Garnier, Count Germain (1754 to 1821) French politician and economist. Lawyer by profession, he was a royalist émigré (1792–1795), then a follower of Napoleon, finally a peer under the Restoration. As the "economist of the Directory and the Consulate" (M), he was a late follower of the Physiocrats, straddling Quesnay and Adam Smith (whose work he transd, 1802). M (1850) studied his *Histoire de la monnaie* (1819). → *50*:50.

Garnier-Pagès, Louis Antoine; orig **Pagès** (1803 to 1878) French politician; moderate republican. Orig a lawyer and commercial broker, he was during 1848 a member of the Provisional Government, mayor of Paris, finance min. Later (after 1864) he was in opposition to Bonaparte; member of the Government of National Defense (1870–1871), retiring from politics after parliamentary defeat. Author of *Histoire de la révolution de 1848* (1860+). #E723.

Die Gartenlaube; Illustriertes Familienblatt Leipzig (till 1903); then Berlin, 1853 to 1937 (or 1943). Weekly. —A literary paper. → *59*:66; *68*:41, 57. #E405.

Gas Workers and General Labourers Union (Eng.) → *89*:36. #E841.

Gaskell, Peter (*fl.* 1830s) English physician; Liberal publicist; active in Manchester. His book *The manufacturing population of England* (1833) was much used by E in writing #E171; see E's critique of Gaskell (*MECW* 4:366 fn). G.'s *Artisans and machinery* (1836) was a reprint, with some additions, of the 1833 book; he deals mainly with the physical and social conditions of cotton factory workers. Inter alia, G. prophesied that the time when machinery would displace human labor was rapidly approaching. —M read both edns of G.'s book in 1851. → *51*:67.

Gassiot, John Peter (1797 to 1877) English wine merchant, who turned to scientific research, mainly on electricity; pubd a number of scientific papers; also financed science projects. However, what M (1878) read was his publications on financial questions, viz., *Address to the shareholders of the London and Westminster Bank* (1876); *Monetary panics and their remedy* (1869; orig, 1867), a pamphlet. G. also pubd *Monetary panic of 1866* (1875); *The present crisis in administrative reform* (1856). → 78:48, 51.

Gathorne-Hardy, Gathorne; *orig* Gathorne **Hardy**; *later Earl of* **Cranbrook** (1814 to 1906) British Tory politician; MP (1856+). As Home secy (1867–1868) he took government measures against the Fenians. He later filled the posts of secy for war, secy for India, lord pres of the Council, and retired (1892) with his earldom. #M313.

Le **Gaulois** Paris, 1867 to 1929. Daily. Founder: E. Tarlé. Ed by Arthur Meyer (1879–1882). —Founded as an opposition journal; suppressed by Thiers (1872); subseqly conservative-monarchist, Bonapartist after the Franco-Prussian War; in 1882 it absorbed *Paris-Journal* and became anti-Bonapartist. → 71:42. #M897.

Gazette des Tribunaux Paris, 1825 to 1935. Daily. —Conservative. → 71:41.

Il **Gazzettino Rosa** (with varying subtitles) Milan, Jan 23, 1868, to Nov 15, 1873. Daily. Ed by Achille Bizzoni (Fortunio). —First, left-Mazzinist organ; defending the Paris Commune, it oriented toward the IWMA, against Mazzini; IWMA organ in Italy, 1871–1873; in 1872 it came under Bakuninist domination. → 71:52; 72:10, 21, 27. #M224, M616; E475, E564, E810, E821, E829, E836.

Die **Gegenwart** Berlin, Jan 1872 to Sep 1931. Pub'r/editor: Paul Lindau. → 72:16, 30.

Die **Gegenwart**; Eine encyclopädische Darstellung der neuesten Zeitgeschichte für alle Stände Leipzig, 1848 to 1856. Pub'r: Brockhaus. —Superseded by *Unsere Zeit.* → 52:32.

Geib, August; *full* Wilhelm Leopold August (1842 to 1879) German Social-Democrat. A Hamburg bookdealer, he first joined the Lassallean GGWA, but went over (with Bracke) to Bebel's tendency and helped found the Eisenacher party (1869), of which he became a leader (secy of the Control Commsn). In the united party (1875+) he was treasurer; member of the Reichstag (1874–1876). → 74:32, 38; 75:20.

Geibel, Emanuel (1815 to 1884) German poet; a leading lyricist of the midcentury. A revolutionary Democrat before 1848, he later became a conservative pensioner of the Prussian king; at the U. of Munich (1851+), center of an important poetry circle; by 1871, a Bismarck admirer. → 35:8.

Geiger, Wilhelm Arnold   Prussian police official; in 1848, examining magistrate, then police director, in Cologne. → 48:53, 60; 49:17. #ME63; M889.

Geijer, Erik Gustaf (1783 to 1847)   Swedish historian and man of letters. Prof at Uppsala (1817–1846); a leader in the Swedish cultural revival. His history of Sweden, *Svenska folkets historia* (1832–1836), was a pioneering work; M (1843) excerpted a German trans of it. A longtime conservative, G. declared for liberalism in 1838. → 43:32.

Geiser, Bruno (1846 to 1898) German Social-Democrat; journalist. He joined the SDWP (1869); active in Silesia; a member of the IWMA (1872); editor of the Munich *Zeitgeist* (1873). In 1875 he became a coeditor, with Liebknecht, of *Volksstaat*; editor of the Breslau *Die neue Welt* (1877–1886). Reichstag deputy (1881–1887). —Although Liebknecht's son-in-law, he was by the early 1880s an extreme right-winger in the party; part of the right-wing cabal to dump the *Sozialdemokrat* for a paper controlled by the parliamentary faction. In 1887, for overt acts, the St. Gall party congress removed him from all party posts; he had esp enraged Bebel by flaunting a luxurious lifestyle. → 72:16; 84:37.

General Council See International Working Men's Association.

General German Workers Association (Lassalleans); *Ger.* Allgemeiner Deutscher Arbeiterverein, *abbrev.* ADAV   The first German socialist organization established legally in Germany, under the leadership of *Lassalle; at a congress in Leipzig (May 22, 1863) with delegates from ten German states. Lassalle was elected pres, with a constitution emphasizing extreme centralization ("presidential dictatorship"). Claiming 1000 members at the end of a year, and 8000 in 1868, it rose to 21,000 (claimed) in 1872, and then declined to 15,000 at the time of its merger (1875) with the "Eisenachers" (Bebel, Liebknecht, etc.) to form the mass S-D party. After Lassalle's death, its most influential pres was *Schweitzer, who had been preceded by B. *Becker and *Tölcke, and was succeeded by *Hasenclever. → 63:23, 24, 39; 64:17, 27, 32, 38, 46; 65:5–8, 14, 24, 30, 57, 63; 67:47; 68:2, 35, 37, 39, 42, 43, 48, 50, 56; 69:19, 25, 26, 31, 48; 74:38, 39; 75:2. #M929; E552. *See also* *Lassalleans.

Geneva (Switz.)   *Selected references; partial index.* —M&E's moves to/from Geneva, trips, etc. → 48:68, 75; 49:35; 82:30, 34. —Possibility of M's moving there: → 68:4, 18. —Siebel's mission to: → 60:13, 23. —In IWMA affairs: → 65:32, 51, 62; 66:21, 31, 36,

43, 46, 47, 50; 67:28; 68:42, 62; 69:25, 65; 70:4,
17, 36, 39, 44, 64; 71:6, 56, 62; 72:8–10, 27, 31,
49; 73:23, 36, 39, 43. —Movement in: →
68:20, 69:41; 73:7; 80:39; 84:20; 93:16, 24, 55.

Geneva Peace Congress See Peace Congress.

Geneva Society of Free Thinkers See Society of Free Thinkers.

Genoa (It.) → 49:38; 92:40.

Geological Institute (London) → 63:5.

George, Henry (1839 to 1897) American social reformer, founder of the Single Tax school; author of *Progress and poverty* (1879). A San Francisco newspaperman, he developed his theory (entire tax burden on land, freeing industry from taxes) while studying California economics. He moved to NY (1880); pubd *The Irish land question* (1881); devoted 1881–1884 to publicist work in Gr Brit. He ran for NYC mayor, with a working-class appeal, on a social-reform platform (1886); again lectured in Britain (1888–1889); ran a second NYC mayoralty campaign (1897) in which he died of apoplexy. → 80:37; 81:23, 27, 33, 61; 83:12, 19, 27; 86:47, 51; 87:40. #E174.

Geppert, Karl Eduard (1811 to 1881) German classical philologist; prof at Berlin (1836+). His chief early work was *Über den Ursprung der Homerischen Gesänge* (1840), later pubd works on the dramatic poets. → 40:17.

German language → 86:16.

German Legion → 48:19, 22, 26–28.

German Workers Club (Paris) → 48:20, 26, 27. #ME87.

German Workers (Educational) Association (Brussels) → 47:28, 45, 46, 52, 53.

German Workers Educational Association (London); *Ger.* Deutscher Arbeiter-Bildungs-Verein (DABV); *see note below re name* Organization of German communist émigré workers and artisans, established in London (Feb 7, 1840) on the initiative of Karl *Schapper and a half dozen members. In the early days it was allied with, indeed modeled after, the already-existing society of French leftist refugees, the Société Démocratique Française; and directed against the existing Deutsche Gesellschaft (liberal). Although based on the German emigration, it was international in approach, and had members and collaborators among other foreign émigrés as well as Chartists like *Harney. It was "the first international association"—so it claimed in 1859. It had about 500 members in 1845. In the pre-1848 period, leaders like Schapper looked on the GWEA as the "above-ground" arm of the then-conspiratorial *League of the Just, and later (1847+) as the broader "front" organization of the nonconspiratorial Communist League, with which it closely cooperated. For a considerable period after the 1850

split in the CL, the GWEA was controlled by elements hostile to M&E, who resigned from it. Their subsequent on/off relations with it are partly reflected in the *Chronicle*. In 1865 the GWEA affiliated with the IWMA. The organization continued to exist until 1917, when Germans were interned in London. —*Warning:* The name of the organization used above is mainly a convenience; in fact, its name seems to have been protean; at least by 1871, if not before, the final form of its name became Communistischer Arbeiter-Bildungs-Verein (CABV). In-between, its variant names would take half a page to list; this is one for the record book. Hence, although I use GWEA throughout to avoid confusion, its actual name in any given context may be different if the sources are consulted. → 46:20; 47:28, 46, 50, 52; 49:36, 40, 41, 44; 50:1, 12, 19, 20, 24, 30, 34; 51:36, 54; 52:3; 59:3, 12, 34; 60:12, 15; 61:49, 56; 63:10, 34, 37, 39; 64:13, 31; 65:2, 18, 30; 67:8, 31, 46; 68:27, 42, 64; 69:71; 72:37; 74:3, 5; 76:3; 78:41; 79:23, 24; 80:12; 81:46; 83:12; 84:16; 90 :47; 91:59; 92:61; 93:6, 13, 20, 56; 94:29, 51; 95:22. #ME52, ME163; M163C, M600.5, M625, M695, M743, M748, M826, M864; E430, E818, E842, E853, E854. —GWEA Choral Society: → 91:59. —The name Communist Workers Educational Assoc: → 79:23, 24; 80:12. #E818, E853.

Der Gesellschafts-Spiegel; Organ für Vertretung der besitzlosen Volksklassen . . . Elberfeld (Ger.), July 1845 to June 1846. Monthly. Ed by M. Hess. —E took part in establishing this, but did not enter the ed staff. It largely pubd "True Socialist" material. → 45:11. #ME129; M653; E862.

Gewerbeblatt aus Württemberg Stuttgart, 1849 to 1921. Weekly. Supplement to *Staats-Anzeiger für Württemberg*, commercial-industrial organ. → 67:48. #E693.

Ghent; *Flem.* Gent; *Fr.* Gand (Belg.) Chief city of east Flanders. → 48:4; 77:33.

Gibson, Thomas Milner; *also called* **Milner-Gibson** (1806 to 1884) English Liberal politician. One of Cobden's chief allies of the "Manchester school." MP (1837–1839 as a Tory, then 1841–1868); pres, Bd of Trade (1859–1866). M's article comments on the electoral defeat of the Manchesterites in 1857. #M227.

Gigot, Philippe (Charles) (1819 or 1820 to 1860) Belgian (French-born) communist in the 1840s. At first attached to the paleographic division of the Interior Ministry, he lost his post in the police crackdown on the CL in 1848; later he had the post of archivist in the Brussels library system. A member of the CL, he was close to M&E in the 1840s; a member of the CL District Comm for Brussels (1847–1848). → 46:11; 47:28; 48:47, 74. #ME4, ME28.

Gilbart, James William (1794 to 1863)
British banker and writer on bank economics.
He rose from a bank clerk (1813) to manager of
the London and Westminster Bank (1834+);
active in developing the legal basis of joint-
stock banking. He also pubd (c.1827+) writings on banking affairs. M (1845, 1850) excerpted his *History and principles of banking*
(1834). Other works: *History of banking in
America* (1837); *Logic of banking* (1857). →
45:51; 50:50; 54:51.   #M575.

Giraldus Cambrensis, pen name of **Giraldus**
(or **Gerald) de Barri** (1146? to 1220?) Welsh
cleric, scholar, and man of letters; historian and
geographer; of Norman descent. His election as
bishop being vetoed by the authorities, he was
compelled to devote his life to higher pursuits.
After taking part in an expedition into Ireland
(1185), he described its natural history and
people in his *Topographia Hibernica*; also
wrote *Expugnatio Hibernica* on Ireland; described Wales in his *Itinerarium Cambriae*
(1198); wrote an autobiography, Latin poems,
churchmen's lives, etc. M (1869) browsed in his
Opera, vols. 1–7 (1861+).   → 69:75.

Girardin, Emile de (1806 to 1881) French
newspaper pub'r and publicist; also politician; best known as creator of the cheap, mass
daily paper; somewhat the Hearst of his
day. —After some court posts and business
ventures incl papers, he revolutionized journalism with *La Presse* (1836–1856, 1862–
1866), using advertisements, feuilletons,
varied matter, social demagogy, etc. After
selling it off, he later also pubd *La Liberté, La
France, Le Petit Journal*, et al.; authored a
number of books and tracts on current issues.
His political views were flexible (i.e., unprincipled) and mercurial but independent. In
1848 he supported the Republic, opposed
Cavaignac; in 1849–1850, claimed to be socialistic; soon after Bonaparte's coup, came to
support him. Chamber of Deputies (1834–
1851, 1877–1881). → 45:50; 50:14; 52:36;
92:63.   #ME140; M575.

Giraud-Teulon, Alexis (1839 to 1916)
Geneva prof of history, specializing in the
development of primitive society. He pubd
Les origines de la famille (1874), revised as
Les origines du mariage et de la famille
(1884), which E (1891) read. → 91:30.

Girondins or **Girondists** The so-called
moderate wing of the Great French Revolution, to the right of the Jacobins; led by
*Brissot de Warville. #M338.

Gisborne, Thomas, *called* The elder (1758
to 1846) English clergyman, who preferred
to live as a country cleric while writing
books on absolute ethics. Besides sermons
and theological essays, he pubd *An enquiry
into the duties of men in the higher and
middle classes of society in Gr Brit* (1795;

orig 1794), read by M (1845–1846). →
45:52. #M575.

La **Giustizia** Agrigento (Sicily), Feb 9,
1873, to July 19, 1874. Irreg. Pub'r: A. Riggio.
Ed by C. Palamenghi, V. Di Benedetto. —
Pubd by the IWMA section in the city;
continuation of *L'Eguaglianza*. #E272.

La **Giustizia Sociale** Palermo (Sicily). →
94:36. #E346.

Gladbach, Anton (d. 1873) German left
Democrat; teacher in Odenthal (Rhineland). In
1848 he was a deputy to the Prussian Constituent Assembly, sitting with the left wing;
pres of the Democratic Clubs in Berlin. →
49:9.

Gladstone, William Ewart (1809 to 1898)
English political leader. He entered politics as
a Tory protégé of Peel, and followed Peel in
the Tory split; MP (1832+); pres, Bd of Trade
(1843–1845); chancellor of the Exchequer
(1852–1855, 1859–1866). Then going over to
the Liberal party, he assumed its leadership
(1867); prime min (1868–1874, 1880–1885,
1886, 1892–1894). He also wrote books about
politics and Homer. —G. incarnated British
Liberalism for most of the second half of the
century. Pro-Gladstone politics was a problem
for M in the GC/IWMA in the person of labor
leaders like Odger. In his journalistic writings
M had special occasion to attack G.'s Irish
policy and his foreign policy on France,
Russia, etc. → 53:15, 19, 26; 54:24; 69:65;
70:20, 49, 55; 72:13, 30; 76:33; 77:6, 9; 81:21;
82:22; 90:50; 92:64. #M323, M381, M394,
M547, M798.

Glaser de Willebrord, E. Belgian socialist.
A businessman, he pubd #M143 in Belgium;
as a member of the Brussels IWMA, he
corresponded with M&E. No further info. →
71:33; 72:23, 30; 75:13, 48; 76:27.

Glasgow (Scot.) → 92:44.

Glennie, J. S.; *full* John Stuart **Stuart-Glen-
nie** English writer, folklorist, traveler;
trained as a lawyer. He accompanied H. T.
Buckle on his journey through Palestine
(1862); pubd works on Buckle's travels and
theory of history (1875–1876); also pubd
works on the Arthurian legend (1867–1880).
He consulted M for his book *Europe and
Asia: Discussions of the Eastern Question
and travels through . . . Illyria* (1879). →
78:23.

The **Globe and Traveller** London, Dec 30,
1822, to Feb 5, 1921, under this title; founded
as *The Globe* (1803+). —Whig organ till
1866; later, Conservative. → 50:22. #M909.

Głos Wolny London. —No info on its
dates. An organ of the revolutionary-democratic Polish emigration. #M828.

Gneisenau, *Count* August **Neithardt von**;
full August Wilhelm Anton (1760 to 1831)
Prussian gen and military theoretician;

created field marshal (1825). He served with British mercenaries in America (1782+) and in Poland as well as Prussia. He made his mark as reorganizer of the Prussian army (1806–1809) under Scharnhorst, and in the Napoleonic war (1813–1815) as chief of staff to Blücher, his strategic brain. He died leading a force against the Polish uprising. → 70:58.

Gnocchi-Viani, Osvaldo (1837 to 1917) Italian socialist. Orig a nationalist-republican supporter of Garibaldi and Mazzini, he turned socialist by the late 1860s and became active in the workers' movement. An ally of *Bignami, he looked to TU action, not revolution; though active in the IWMA in Italy (1872–1873), he was opposed to both the Bakuninists and the Marx/GC line. He helped to found associations for pure-and-simple trade-unionism, antipolitical from a reformist standpoint. Author of Le tre internazionali (1875), L'Internazionale nella Comune de Parigi (1893). → 72:41.

Godwin, William (1756 to 1836) English social-political theorist; herald of anarchist thought. Orig a dissenting minister, he turned atheist (for a while) and devoted himself to writing. His chief work, Enquiry concerning political justice (1793), is an exercise in deducing the extreme consequences of bourgeois liberalism's antistate aspects, to the point of repudiating "authority" on principle. It exercised considerable influence on left-wing thought, but not a specif anarchist one; in fact, M—like others—did not think of Godwin as an anarchist but rather as an extreme Benthamite who carried "philosophical radicalism" to more leftist conclusions. —G. himself was never a consistent anarchist or even radical, and later retreated to more conventional opinions. His forgotten works include novels (Caleb Williams), a history of England, children's books, etc. His first wife was Mary Wollstonecraft (mar. 1797). #M575.

Goegg (or **Gögg**), Amand (1820 to 1897) German radical. A Baden customs official in 1848, he took part in the revolution, and became finance min in the Baden Provisional Government of 1849. Afterward he emigrated via Switzerland and Paris to London; then (1852) to the U.S.; later to Australia and S. America. In 1867 he was an initiator of the League for Peace and Freedom and its Geneva congress; also active (1869) in the German WA of Geneva. In c.1872 he returned to Germany; joined the Social-Democracy. → 49:27, 43; 50:25, 40; 51:31; 52:7, 12; 59:65; 90:48.

Göhringer (or **Göringer**), Karl (b. c.1808) German radical. A Baden tavernkeeper, he took part in the 1848 revolution there; afterward, emigrated to England; joined the CL. In the CL split of 1850 he went with Willich–Schapper. His London pub was a German

émigré hangout. He later settled in the U.S. and became an affluent hotel operator and restaurant manager. → 51:53.

Görgey, Arthur; Hung. Artúr (1818 to 1916) Hungarian gen. Commander-in-chief of the army in 1849, he surrendered to the Russians (who had come to the aid of Austria), thus undercutting Kossuth's position. Spared by the Russians, he was eventually pardoned and allowed back to Hungary; hence widely regarded as a traitor. He wrote Mein Leben und Wirken in Ungarn 1848–1849 (1852). — The spellings Gorgey and Görgei are also met. → 52:2, 17, 30.

Görtz, Franz Damian (1788 to 1865) Prussian government official. District governor and chief burgomaster of Trier, 1841 to Apr 1848. #M885, M886.

Goes, Franc (or Frank) van der (1859 to 1939) Dutch socialist. A pioneer Marxist in the Netherlands and exponent of left-wing socialist views. Aveling and Eleanor M corresponded with him (1895–1896). —The spelling Goës is erroneous. → 95:37.

Goethe, Johann Wolfgang von (1749 to 1832) The greatest figure in German literature; in particular, the greatest German poet, author of Faust and a body of lyrical poetry; often associated with Weimar, where he settled (1775). Some other landmark writings: the tragedy Götz von Berlichingen (1773); the sentimental novel Die Leiden des jungen Werthers (1774); a late novel Die Wahlverwandtschaften (1809), etc. → 83:36. #M171; E337.

Göttingen (Ger.) City in Lower Saxony. → 35:8; 57:21.

Götz (or **Goetz**), Theodor German communist; friend of M. He took part in the Baden-Palatinate uprising (1849); emigrated to England (1850) where he was a CL member; jailed in Mainz (1850–1851); afterward, lived in London. → 55:11.

Götze, Peter Otto von (1793 to 1880) Russian government official and writer; translated Serbian and Russian folk songs into German. M (1856) read his Stimmen des russischen Volkes in Liedern (1828), but erroneously attributed to Götze the anonymous work Fürst Wladimir und seine Tafelrunde (1819). → 56:13.

Gogarten, E. Rhineland radical; no further info available. → 69:31.

Goldheim Prussian police official, operating as a secret agent in London in the early 1850s. → 53:14.

Golochvastav, Pavel Dmitriyevich (1839 to 1892) Russian historian and publicist; a collaborator on the reactionary-aristocratic organ Grazhdanin (St. Petersburg, 1872–1878). → 76:30.

Golovachov, Alexei Adrianovich (1819 to

1903) Russian liberal publicist and politician. Of a gentry family, he took an active part in preparing the "emancipation of the serfs" in 1861; a sympathizer of right-wing Narodism and liberal bourgeois reforms. His chief works were *Desyat let reform 1861–1871* (1872), *Istoriya zhelezno-dorozhnovo dyela v Rossii* (1881). → 73:16; 81:5.

Golovin, Ivan Gavrilovich (1816 to c.1886/1890) Russian liberal landowner who semiaccidentally became an oppositionist. He emigrated (1844); pubd the first oppositional literature abroad (Paris, 1849); later, an émigré in England. Friend of Herzen and Bakunin. → 53:32, 34.

Gompers, Samuel (1850 to 1924) American labor leader; founding pres, AFL (1886+). Born in London of a Dutch-Jewish family, he came to NY in 1863. Cigarmaker; pres of his TU local (1877); a leader of the AFL's predecessor federation. In his early years he was a socialistic sympathizer; associated with some U.S. followers of M, and corresponded with European socialists; indeed, in a letter to E, he called himself a "student" of M&E's writings. He developed in the direction of his procapitalist ideology of class harmony not only under the pressure of American social forces but in the context of his initial reaction of justified revulsion against the sectarianism of American socialists, esp the SLP. → 91:9; 92:7.

Gorbunova, Minna Karlovna; *later mar. name* **Kablukova,** *also called* **Gorbunova-Kablukova** (1840 to 1931) Russian economic statistician, said to be the first Russian woman in this field; also a trade-school educator. She wrote from a Narodnik viewpoint for *Otechestvenniye Zapiski*; investigated women in Moscow industry for the local government (1880s); studied vocational education systems in Europe. —Kablukova was her married name after a second marriage (*see* N. A. *Kablukov) but not at the time of her correspondence with E. She and Kablukov later helped M collect materials for his Russian library. → 80:22, 26.

Gori, Pietro (1869 to 1911) Italian anarchist; lawyer by profession. He did an unauthorized trans of the *Com Manifesto* for *Fantuzzi. He emigrated (1894) and spent some time anarchizing the Argentinian TU movement. —Note: NUC lists a Pietro Gori (1854–1911) who was an Italian anarchist writer and poet; the same? → 91:19.

Gotha (Ger.) City in Thuringia, near Erfurt. → 61:46; 75:2, 12, 16, 20, 36; 90:51; 91:23. #M207; E285.

Gothic languages → 59:70.

Gottraux, Jules Swiss-born émigré in London, naturalized British; member of the IWMA. For the French government's seizure of the IWMA documents he carried, see #ST/21, 2:43, 271+. → 66:46.

Gottschalk, Andreas (1815 to 1849) Physician ("doctor to the poor") in Cologne; workers' assoc organizer. He was a leading founder of the Cologne CL in summer 1847; on the outbreak of revolution, a founder and first pres of the Cologne WA (Apr-June 1848). With a group of supporters he entered into bitter opposition to the NRZ group around M; resigned from the CL (May). He was arrested by the government (July), tried and acquitted (Dec). His anti-M campaign having failed to regain WA leadership, he went into voluntary exile (first near Bonn, then Brussels) to await the people's summons, which did not come. He returned to medical practice, and soon succumbed to disease. —G. was usually for a constitutional monarchy (the "Social Monarchy" line) rather than the Democratic and Social Republic which was the general platform of the alliance called the Democracy; hence he advocated boycotting the elections instead of making an electoral alliance with left Democrats; this has given rise to the frequent erroneous statement that he was an ultraleftist of some sort. → 47:39; 48:29, 33, 45, 54, 71, 84; 49:6, 9, 19; 89:33. #ME50; M698, M944.

Gouge, William M. (1796 to 1863) American publicist and writer on economics and finance. Part owner of the *Philadelphia Gazette* (1823), but soon left it for journalism; official of the Treasury Dept. (1834–1841); pub'r of the *J. of Banking* (1841); special officer in the Treasury Dept. for revision of bookkeeping (1854+). —M (1851) read his work *A short history of paper money and banking in the U.S.* (1833). → 51:64.

Gradaus Philadelphia. —No info on its dates. An organ of the German-American workers assocs in Philadelphia in the 1850s. → 53:31.

Graeber, Friedrich (Christian Ludwig) (1822 to 1895) The Graeber brothers, whose father was a pastor in Elberfeld, were young E's closest friends in boyhood. There was a copious correspondence between them, autumn 1838 through 1839, petering out in the next two years. Friedrich, the younger, studied theology in Berlin (1838–1839) and Bonn (1839–1841) and later became a pastor in Issum, Ger. (1846–1885). #E73, E211, E281, E332, E357, E590A.

Graeber, Wilhelm (Heinrich) (1820 to 1895) Boyhood friend of E; *see* preceding entry. Wilhelm studied theology in Berlin (1838–1840) and Bonn (1840–1841) and later became a pastor in Elberfeld, Eickel, and Essen. #E73, E816.

Gräfrath arsenal (Ger.) Formerly an independent Rhineland town, Gräfrath is now part of Solingen. → 49:25.

Graetz (or **Grätz**), Heinrich (1817 to 1891) German-Jewish historian; author of the pioneering history of the Jews, *Geschichte der Juden von den ältesten Zeiten* (1853–1875); a moderate liberal. He was on the staff of the Breslau Seminary (1853+); prof at Breslau (1869+). → 76:24; 77:7.

Graham, Sir James Robert George (1792 to 1861) English politician. MP as a Whig (1818–1821); then as a Liberal (1826+) interested in financial reforms; went over to the Tories (1830s), then became a Peelite; Home secy in the Peel cabinet (1841–1846), first lord of the Admiralty (1852–1855). — During a period when the voters retired him to his border estate, he studied polit eco and produced a pamphlet *Corn and currency* (1826) in favor of free trade and free banking. It was doubtless this that was read by M (1850). → 50:50.

Granger, Ernest Henri (1844 to *after* 1911) Franch Blanquist; journalist. Orig trained in law, he joined the Blanquist group as a student and remained one of its leading activists. He took part in the Paris Commune; emigrated to London till after the 1880 amnesty; then resumed his Blanquist journalism and organization work. After the death of Eudes (1883) he became the leading figure of the traditional (unreconstructed) Blanquists as counterposed to *Vaillant: essentially an untheoretical agitator, exclusively political-oriented, and without organic ties to the working-class movement. In the 1880s his wing of Blanquism chose to support the protofascist Bonapartist challenger *Boulanger; there was a split (Aug 1889); G.'s "Boulangeo-Blanquists" called themselves Comité Central Socialiste Révolutionnaire. G. was elected deputy (1889) as a Boulangist, but faded out by 1893, and withdrew from political activity. → 92:13.

Graubünden; *Fr.* Grisons Largest Swiss canton; Alpine, eastern part of country. → 93:40.

Gray, John (1798 or 1799 *to* 1850) British radical economist; a "Ricardian socialist" disciple of Owen. Influenced by Sismondi as well as Owen, he first leaned to an Owenite-type reorganization of society but later favored mainly monetary-reform nostrums (labor money, cheap credit, etc.). M discusses his views esp in #M181. Chief works: *A lecture on human happiness* (1825); *The social system* (1831); *Lectures on the nature and use of money* (1848). M (1851) excerpted at least the last two. → 51:62, 68, 70.

Great Yarmouth (Eng.) Port on the North Sea. → 82:33.

Greece, Ancient, and the Greek language, etc. → 57:26. #E728.5, E745.

Greece, Modern, and Greek affairs → 54:2, 12, 26; 67:29; 68:68. #M89, M319, M358–M360, M512, M824.

Green, John Richard (1837 to 1883) English historian; Anglican clergyman and Lambeth Palace librarian. His *Short history of the English people* (1874) was a standard work, later expanded into *History of the English people* (1877–1880); also pubd *The making of England* (1881); *The conquest of England* (1883). #M872.5.

Greenback–Labor Party (U.S.) In 1877–1878 the Greenback party (which advocated the issuance of paper currency as an economic nostrum) united with labor elements, adding labor and reform planks; polled over a million votes in 1878; elected 14 congressmen. It nominated J. B. Weaver for pres (1880), gaining a small vote. → 79:43.

Greenwich (Eng.) London borough; 0° longitude. → 68:64.

Greenwood, Frederick (1830 to 1909) English journalist. He succeeded Thackeray as editor of the *Cornhill Magazine* (1862–1868); a founder of the *Pall Mall Gazette*. As its editor (1865–1880) he wielded much influence; orig a "philosophical liberal," he moved to conservatism, though not a party man; supported Disraeli, admired Bismarck. By 1880, when the *PMG* was "the most thoroughgoing of Jingo newspapers" (L. Stephen), a new owner forced G. out. He founded and edited *St. James's Gazette* (1880–1888); his weekly *Anti-Jacobin* (1891–1892) failed; he continued to write for magazines. → 71:30. #M465, M466.

Greg, William Rathbone (1809 to 1881) English essayist; orig mill manager and businessman; Free-trader. In 1842 he won the Anti-Corn-Law League's prize for best essay on "Agriculture and the Corn Laws." He gave up business for writing (1850); pubd volumes on political and social philosophy, and was rewarded with government posts; but he was not mainly an economist like his brother Robert Hyde G. → 45:52. #M575.

Greiff or **Greif** Prussian police agent, attached to Prussia's London embassy in the early 1850s. He recruited *Fleury and W. *Hirsch as spies. → 52:45.

Greifswald (Ger.) City in Pomerania. → 42:10.

Gretchen German girl from Barbeln, a wet nurse sent to the M family by Mrs. M's mother, to care for their first child, Jenny: her family name seems to be unrecorded. She stayed in the M household in Paris from Sep 1844 till (prob) M's expulsion from France in Jan 1845. → 44:34.

Greulich, Hermann (1842 to 1925) Swiss Social-Democrat; German (Silesian) by birth; bookbinder. Brought to socialism by Bürkli and J. P. Becker, he went to Switzerland

(1865), helped found an IWMA section in Zurich (1867), took part in the Eisenach congress of the SDWP (1869); pubd *Tag-wacht* as the organ of the German Swiss IWMA sections; founded a Swiss S-D party (1870) and the Schweizerische Arbeiterbund (1873). He became a right-wing leader in the country and in the Second International. → 81:4.

Griboyedov, Alexander Sergeyevich (1795 to 1829) Russian writer, whose fame rests on one play in verse, *Gore ot uma* (transd as *Woe from wit* or *Misfortune from intelligence*), completed in 1823, stopped from publ till 1833; a satire on Russian official society and its type. G. was killed by an anti-Russian mob when acting as min plenipotentiary in Teheran. → 51:49.

Griesheim, Gustav von; *full* Carl Gustav Julius (1798 to 1854) Prussian general; writer on military subjects. M (1863) read his book *Über den Krieg mit Russland* (1848). In 1848 Griesheim also pubd *Die deutsche Centralgewalt und die preussiche Armee*, which the Democratic movement attacked; and he was also perhaps the author of the pamphlet *Gegen Demokraten helfen nur Soldaten.* → 63:12.

Grillenberger, Karl (1848 to 1897) German Social-Democrat. Orig a locksmith, he joined the SDWP (1869); engaged in S-D journalism (1874+) as a writer and editor; member of the Reichstag (1881–1897). He became prominent as a right-wing spokesman in the party's Reichstag Fraction. → 91:11.

Grimaldi family Ruling family of Monaco; orig Genoese (1419+). The male line becoming extinct (1731), the daughter married an undistinguished French count who took the Grimaldi name. In 1882 when M visited, the sovereign was Prince Charles III, the entrepreneur who had introduced gambling as the local industry. M's reference to piracy goes back to the 14th century, when the extortion of tolls from vessels passing the port began (till the late 18th century). → 82:23.

Grimm, Jacob (Ludwig Karl) (1785 to 1863) Great German philologist; pioneer in Germanistic studies, with his brother-collaborator Wilhelm (Karl) (1786–1859). The Grimm brothers are world-famous for their fairy-tale collection. Jacob—who in 1848–1849 was a member of the Frankfurt assembly, and in 1837 took part in a famous liberal protest against Hanover's monarch—was the author of *Deutsche Grammatik* (1819–1837) and *Geschichte der deutschen Sprache* (1848); M (1856) excerpted the latter book's 2nd edn in 1853. The brothers collaborated on *Kinder- und Hausmärchen* (1812, 1815), *Deutsche Sagen* (1816–1818), *Deutsches Wörterbuch* (1854+). → 56:22.

Grohmann, W. Baillie Author of *Cattle*

ranches in the Far West (1880)—read by M (1881). → 81:64.

Grolmann, Karl (Ludwig Wilhelm) von (1775 to 1829) German law prof and statesman. His influential works covered civil and criminal law; known for sympathy with the French legal system; in 1819 became min of state at Darmstadt for Hesse-Darmstadt. His chief work was *Grundsätze der Criminalrechtswissenschaft* (1798), which M read at Berlin (1837). → 37:8.

Gronlund, Laurence (1846 to 1899) American socialist, Danish-born; came to the U.S. in 1867. Orig a lawyer, he became a socialist (c.1875) and turned to lecturing and writing; active in the Bellamy movement and numerous other socialistic campaigns and circles. His chief book was *The co-operative commonwealth* (1884), the most popular socialist work before Bellamy. —G. identified socialism with statification and trustification; was a violent enemy of class struggle; and eventually supported McKinley against Bryan. The myth that he was a "Marxist" is due to his books' use of shards of M's *Capital.* → 84:45.

Gross, Gustav (1856 to 1935) Vienna economist; privatdocent at the university there during the 1880s, also pubd a number of economic works. His book *Karl Marx. Eine Studie* was pubd 1885. → 84:19.

Grove, Sir William Robert (1811 to 1896) British (Welsh-born) physicist, also lawyer and judge. The career as jurist came first and last: he rose to high court justice (1875–1887) and privy councillor (1887+). In a period of ill health he took up scientific studies, became prof of physics at London Institution (1840–1847); inventor of the "Grove cell"; author of *Correlation of physical forces* (1846), on the theory of mutual convertibility of forces. It was this work that M (1864) read, in its 3rd edn of 1855. → 64:24.

Grübel, Friedrich Ludwig Hamburg communist in the 1840s. → 49:20.

Grün, Karl; *full* Karl Theodor Ferdinand (1817 to 1887) German writer, radical philosopher, publicist. During the 1840s he was a leading repr of "True Socialism," and a popularizer of Proudhon's views. His *Mannheimer Abendzeitung* (1842) got him expelled from Baden—a radicalizing experience; he associated with Hess in Cologne; emigrated to Paris (1844); and in 1845 pubd his book *Die sociale Bewegung in Frankreich und Belgien* (one of the earliest accounts of the movement). In the 1848 revolution he was a deputy in the Prussian National Assembly and (1849) the Prussian Second Chamber. He later wound up as a teacher first in Frankfurt, then in Vienna; never took part in the workers' or socialist movement. → 35:8; 44:41; 45:33;

46:15, 17, 20, 40; 47:16, 25, 29, 34; 50:33. #M220; E337.

Grund, Johann Jakob (Norbert) (1755 to c.1812/1815) German miniature painter, also musician and poet. After art studies in Italy, he was a prof at Florence. His chief work in art history was his *Die Malerey* [*sic*] *der Griechen* (1810–1811). #M93.

Grunzig, Julius (b. 1855) In 1876 G. was still a student at Berlin, Social-Democratic. Later, a journalist, he was expelled from Berlin under the Anti-Socialist Law; emigrated to America and went into socialist journalism. M (1890) had a poor opinion of his work as a "*belletriste, more triste than belle.*" → 76:27, 33.

Gruppe, Otto Friedrich (1804 to 1876) German conservative philosopher; writer and politician. Entering the Ministry of Religion (1842), he pubd (1842–1843) two pamphlets to justify Prussian government measures against B. Bauer, incl *Bruno Bauer und die akademische Lehrfreiheit*; prof at Berlin (1844+); permanent secy of the Academy of Fine Arts (1863+). #M995.

Gülich, Gustav von (1791 to 1847) German merchant, and writer on economics and economic history. A leader of the protectionist school, opponent of F. List's views, his chief works were his *Geschichtliche Darstellung des Handels, der Gewerbe und des Ackerbaus* (1830–1845), which M read (prob 1847), and *Über die gegenwärtige Lage des englischen und des deutschen Handels* (1834). Also an inventor, practical farmer, philanthropist. → 47:58; 73:4, 49; 89:2. #E181.

Gümpel, Johann Heinrich German communist worker. In the early 1850s he was an émigré in London; member of GWEA and CL. → 51:1.

Gürzenich Hall (in Cologne) → 48:71; 49:14.

Guesde, Jules; *orig* Mathieu Jules **Basile** (1845 to 1922) French Marxist socialist leader. His adopted name (mother's maiden name) is pronounced *ghedd*. —Son of a schoolteacher, he was early exiled for praising the Commune in journalistic writing (1871). In Geneva he became a Bakunin follower in the IWMA; later in the 1870s, esp in Italy, he moved away from anarchism. He returned to France (1876), wrote for various papers, and launched *L'Egalité* (1877); association with Paul Lafargue, Deville, et al., aided his adoption of Marxism. In 1880 he went with Lafargue to consult M on the program of the French WP. In 1882 the Possibilist right-wing split made the WP the "Guesdist" or "Marxist" party. At various times he was associated with the journals *Droits de l'Homme, Cri du Peuple, Le Socialiste, Le Socialisme,* etc.

Elected deputy (1893+). In the united SP of 1905, he represented French Marxism such as it was, with a rigid-sectarian side which in 1914 turned into its opposite: prowar Union Sacrée and postwar unity with the reformists. —Prob his best-known brochure is *Collectivisme et révolution* (1879); M read it on publ, prob also his *Services publics et socialisme* (1884). → 78:2; 79:6, 12, 18, 53; 80:2, 10, 15, 30; 82:5, 14, 30, 43; 85:4; 86:44; 88:39; 89:17, 32; 91:37; 92:45, 62; 93:28, 41; 94:14. #E529.

Guesdists *See* French Workers Party.

Gugenheim, J. German émigré in London; from Apr 1879, secy of the London GWEA, at this time called Communist Workers Educational Assoc. → 79:23, 24.

Guillaume, James (1844 to 1916) Swiss Bakuninist; by profession, trade-school teacher in Le Locle. —Born in London of a father (of French origin) who was a liberal Swiss politician, and of a French mother, he was naturalized as French in 1889. —Active in the Jura artisans' movement (1869–1878), he came under Bakunin's influence, and became the chief organizer of Bakunin's Swiss base in the IWMA; leader of the Bakuninist drive to take over or split the International; expelled in 1872. Editor of the *Bulletin de la Fédération Jurassienne* (1872–1878). In 1878 he abandoned leftist activity, settled in Paris, and became active in the field of pedagogy. A couple of decades later he was reactivated as an exponent of syndicalism; contributed to French syndicalist journals. In 1914 he became a violent social-patriotic supporter of France in the war; his *Karl Marx, Pangermaniste* (1915) was a virulently anti-Semitic and racist diatribe combined with glorification of the war. His still important writing is *L'Internationale: Documents et souvenirs* (1905–1910), combining some documentary material with a factional-Bakuninist version of IWMA history. → 72:49; 79:12.

Guillaume-Schack, Gertrud (1845 to 1903/1905?) German feminist, socialist-anarchist; active also in England. Born Countess Schack von Wittenau, she married a Swiss artist, Eduard Guillaume; later separated. In the 1880s she moved from the German feminists to the socialist women's movement, where she played a leading role in Berlin for a while. In 1886 her paper *Die Staatsbürgerin* was closed by the Berlin police; she went to England (July); briefly stayed at E's house; soon moved to the anarchists; E said, in effect, good riddance. — A couple of sources give her husband's name, hence her own, as Guilleaume. → 85:28; 91:47, 54.

Guinard French Communard refugee in London, visitor to M. —Maitron's *DBMOF* lists two Communards named Guinard—A.

Guinard and Jean Baptiste Alexandre Guinard—but neither could have been an émigré
in London at this time. → 71:51.

Guizot, François; *full* François Pierre Guillaume (1787 to 1874) French politician and
historian. Of a Huguenot family, orig a lawyer,
he became prof of modern history at Paris, and
went into politics as one of the so-called
Doctrinaires (middle-of-the-road royalists)
(1816–1830). Deputy (1830+). He took part in
the 1830 revolution which installed Louis
Philippe, and prospered as an Orleanist champion in the July Monarchy; entered the cabinet (1832). Moving closer to conservatism, as
a repr of finance-capitalist interests in the
state, he became the leading figure in government (foreign min, 1840–1848), and finally
premier (1847), thrown out of power by the
1848 revolution. He devoted the rest of his life
to writing history. Early works had been:
Histoire de la civilisation en Europe (1828)
and [Ditto] *en France* (1830). Also: *De la
démocratie en France* (1849); *Discours sur
l'histoire de la révolution d'Angleterre* (1850);
Histoire parlementaire de France (1863). →
45:8; 47:23; 48:13, 16; 50:6. #ME138; E212,
E261, E723.

Gumpert, Eduard (1855 to 1893) German-
born physician in Manchester; doctor to and
good friend of E, also M. Though in London,
M often sought his medical advice. → 59:34,
46; 73:32, 38, 55, 60; 74:18, 31; 75:48; 80:25;
93:22.

Gumplowicz, Ludwig; *Polish* Ludwik (1838
to 1909) Polist sociologist, of Jewish birth,
active in Austria as prof at Graz. His works
were pubd mainly in German, incl *Der Ras-*

senkampf (1883); *Rasse* (or *Raçe*) *und Staat*
(first pubd 1875); *Grundriss der Sociologie*
(1885). M (1881) read his *Rechtsstaat und
Sozialismus* (1881). → 81:64.

Gurowski, Count Adam (1805 to 1866)
Polish publicist. After studies in Germany, he
took part in revolutionary club activity in
Warsaw in the 1830 period, after which he
fled to France; organized a Polish Democratic
Society, with which he later broke. Making
peace with the Russians, his apostasy obtained him only a minor provincial post. After
the 1848–1849 revolution, he moved to America, where i.a. he contributed to the *NYDT*
with Pan-Slavist views (1850s). → 56:34;
57:8. #E57.

Gutenberg, Johann (1397–1400? to 1468)
German inventor, perhaps the first European
to print with cast-metal movable type; little is
known about him. The first printed book (a
Bible) was produced in Mainz (perhaps in
Strassburg), perhaps in 1456. Gutenberg was
his mother's family name or perhaps her place
of origin; his father's name was Gensfleisch,
perhaps Ganzfleisch. #E559.

Gutenbergs-Album Brunswick, Ger. —
No info on dates. #E559.

Gutsmann Breslau worker; no further
info. → 69:72.

Gutzkow, Karl (Ferdinand) (1811 to 1878)
German writer and literary critic; a leader of
the Young Germany tendency in the 1830–
1840s. Editor of the *Telegraph für Deutschland* (1837–1848); playwright at the Dresden
theater (1847–1850); his best known literary
work was the novel *Wally, die Zweiflerin*
(1835). #E491.

H

H. A correspondent of the *Chicago Daily
Tribune*, not further identified. → 78:43;
79:10. #M415.

Haar, Franziska (or Franciska) C(h)ristina
van; *née* **Snethlage** (b. 1758) E's grandmother; his mother's mother. She acted as
godparent at his baptism. → 21:1.

Häfner, Leopold (b. 1820) Austrian journalist; a left Democrat in the revolution of
1848–1849; editor of the Vienna daily *Die
Constitution.* He emigrated to Paris. KMC says
flatly that he became a police spy, but this is
not repeated by MEW et al. → 52:35, 41.

Hafiz; *pen name of* Shams ud-din **Mohammed** (c.1326? to 1388–1390?) Persian
lyric poet, famed for love songs, drinking
songs, etc.; chief work: the Dīwān (or Divan),
made up of short odes (ghazels). He was a
teacher of the Koran, learned in the mystic
philosophy of the dervishes. → 53:18.

Hagen (Ger.) Industrial city, N. Rhineland. → 45:11; 49:24.

Hagen, Theodor (1823 to 1871) German
businessman, journalist, pub'r in the 1840s, in
Cologne and Hamburg. A CL member in
Hamburg, he helped M (1849) get a printer
and pub'r for the NRZ, and acted as his agent
(1850) for the NRZ-Revue. Later, as an émigré
in England and NY, he became a prominent
music critic. → 49:20, 40; 50:4.

The Hague (Neth.) → 70:62; 71:18; 72:1,
31, 35, 36, 39, 41, 42, 48, 52, 53, 55, 56, 65–67;
73:7, 17, 23; 75:25; 89:7. —For the Hague
Congress, see IWMA.

Hain, August German émigré in London;
member of the CL; supported M in the 1850
split. → 51:1.

Hales, John (b. 1839) English weaving
worker; labor leader. By the 1860s he was a
prominent leader in the London TU move-

ment, pres of the Elastic Web Weavers union when he joined the GC of the IWMA (1866–1872); secy of the GC (May 1871 to July 1872); also on the Exec of the Reform League and the Land and Labour League. At first a supporter of M in the GC, by 1872 he began, at first underhandedly, to undermine the GC while still its secy, as he began moving over to the reformist wing coalescing around the British Federal Council of the International. His aim was to initiate lib-lab politics, but, unfortunately for him, the Liberals were not yet ready to play; H. faded into oblivion. → 67:32; 68:31; 70:39; 71:1, 3, 30, 39, 48, 62; 72:1, 3, 8, 13, 20, 24, 26, 31, 35, 37, 43, 49, 53, 66; 73:7. #ME85; E775–E777.

Hallam, Henry (1777 to 1859) English historian. Orig a lawyer; fervent Whig; resigned from a sinecure post as commissioner of stamps to devote himself to historical studies. M (1851) studied his chief work in an 1846 edn, *A view of the state of Europe during the Middle Ages* (1818). M (1852) read other writings, perhaps his *Constitutional history of England* (1827); *Intro to the literature of Europe* (1837–1839). → 51:70; 52:56.

Halle (Ger.) City in the former Saxony; now DDR. → 90:32, 37, 42; 91:6.

Hamacher, Adolph Cologne communist. → 56:14.

Hamann, J.; *full (prob)* Johannes German metal worker and trade-unionist, of Hanover. In 1869 he was treasurer of the GGWA-affiliated metal workers' union, whose leadership (incl H.) opposed Lassallean party control. In Nov this union merged with the Bebel-type union in the same field, recently founded at Nuremberg; H. became treasurer of the new union (Internationale Metallarbeiterschaft). —For further info on H.'s conversation with M on Sep 30, 1869, and its background, see ST/14 (Vol. 2, p. 580+); this also discusses his first name, since he signed himself only J. Hamann. → 69:56, 65, 66.

Hamburg (Ger.) → 45:21; 49:20, 21; 50:4, 6, 10, 14, 18, 34, 41, 45; 60:45; 64:11; 66:8; 67:12, 14, 31; 68:35, 37, 42, 48; 69:43, 59, 72; 72:9; 73:35; 74:32; 83:32; 84:11; 86:24; 94:46.

Hamilton, Robert (1743 to 1829) Scottish economist; also teacher and writer in mathematics. Beginning as a partner in a paper mill, he became rector of Perth Academy, then prof at Aberdeen. His chief work was *Inquiry concerning the rise and progress... and management of the national debt* (1813)— which was prob what M (1851) read. He also pubd *The progress of society* (1830); an early work was *Introduction to merchandise* (1777). → 51:62.

Hamilton, Thomas (1789 to 1842) Scottish writer. Orig a military man (1810+), he retired from the army as a captain, pubd articles and a

novel (1827) in *Blackwood's Magazine,* and a book, *Annals of the Peninsular Campaign* (1829). His only other book was the widely reprinted and translated book *Men and manners in America* (1833), based on a trip to the U.S. in 1830. M (1843) read it with great interest, in German translation. → 43:32.

Hamm (Ger.) City in N. Rhine-Westphalia, near Dortmund. → 47:25; 49:20.

Hammer-Purgstall, Baron Joseph von (1774 to 1856) Austrian historian; Orientalist. He served as a diplomat (1796–1835), esp in Constantinople (1799+). His chief historical work was *Geschichte des osmanischen Reichs* (1827–1832), which M studied in 1854, dealing with Turkey. His over-100 volumes also covered Persian and Arabic history and literature. → 54:17.

Handel, George Frederick; *orig Ger.* Georg Friedrich **Händel** (1685 to 1759) German-born composer of oratorios, operas, etc.; settled in England (1712); naturalized British (1726); musical director of various institutions. His oratorio *Messiah* (1742), which E went to hear, is doubtless his best-known work. → 9428.

Handwörterbuch der Staatswissenschaften [Dictionary of the political sciences] Ed by J. Conrad, L. Elster, et al. 1st edn, Jena, 1890–1894. 6 vols. —E's sketch appeared in Vol. 4 (1892). #E470.

Hangö Seaport, at the southern tip of Finland. #M39.

Hanover; *Ger.* Hannover City in north-central Germany. → 62:61; 63:2; 67:8, 12, 14, 26; 68:11; 69:56, 58, 59; 70:3, 41. #M187, M473, M594.

Hansemann, David (Justus Ludwig) (1790 to 1864) German (Rhinelander) merchant and banker; a political leader in 1848. First an Aachen wool merchant, H. built a pioneer fire insurance firm, promoted railways, and founded banks, esp the big Diskonto-Gesellschaft; and thus became a leading capitalist and a leader of the Rhenish liberal bourgeoisie, as an advocate of a limited constitutional monarchy with representation for the propertied. In 1847 he was a member of the United Diet. In the first (Camphausen) cabinet, inaugurated Mar 29, 1848, H. served as finance min, and remained so in the next cabinet ("Government of Action") formally headed by Rudolf von Auerswald (June 26 to Sep 21); but M's NRZ and others called this the "Hansemann government" because they considered H. to be its actual leader. → 48:38, 61. #ME73, ME74; E202.

Hanssen, George (1809 to 1894) German agrarian historian and economist. Prof at various universities; distinguished as a teacher and statistician. M (1876) studied his work *Die Gehöferschaften (Erbgenossenschaften) im Regierungsbezirk Trier* (1863); and

(1878) excerpted *Die Aufhebung der Leibeigenschaft* (1861). A later work: *Agrarhistorische Abhandlungen* (1880–1884). → 68:57; 76:40; 78:49.

Harburg (Ger.) Seaport near Hamburg, today incorporated into that city. → 49:21.

Hardanger Fjord On the S.W. coast of Norway. → 90:30.

Hardcastle, Daniel, Jr.; *pseud. of* Richard **Page** (1773 to 1841) English publicist. His main work was read by M (1851): *Banks and bankers* (1843; orig 1842—posthumous). Earlier the same man had pubd two collections of his letters to the *Times* on various subjects (1819, 1826). → 51:68, 71.

Hardie, Keir; *full* James Keir (1856 to 1915) Scottish socialist and TU leader in the British working-class movement. A coal miner at age 8, a worker in the mines till 1878, he was an organizer of the miners' union; secy of the Scottish Miners' Federation (1886); founder and editor of *The Miner* (1887), which became the *Labour Leader* (1889). He fought (1887+) for the establishment of a labor party as speaker and journalist as well as organizer; was an initiator of the Scottish Labour party (1888), of the Independent Labour party (1893), and later of the British Labour party; the first independent labor MP (1892–1895, 1900–1915); antiwar from a pacifist standpoint in 1914. Writings: *From serfdom to socialism* (1907); *After twenty years* (1913). —For reasons not altogether clear (perhaps Aveling's influence), E often viewed him with suspicion as overly inclined to personal ambition and demagogy. — While H.'s politics were essentially reformist, his monument was the creation of an independent party of the working class on the basis of an alliance between trade-unionism and socialism. → 89:18; 92:32, 39, 44; 93:2, 9; 94:44. #E490.

Harkness, Margaret (Elise) (1825 to 1897) English novelist; socialist writer. Daughter of a clergyman, she used the name John Law for tales of working-class lives, incl *A city girl* (1887), which E commented on; also *Out of work* (1888), *In darkest London* (1889), *A Manchester shirtmaker* (1890). In the 1880s she was a member of the SDF, and contributed to *Justice*; in 1891 Hyndman listed her as one of the "Marxist clique" around that disrupter Engels—which, however, prob meant only that she frequented E's at-homes. → 88:14.

Harney, George Julian; *for short* Julian (1817 to 1897) English Chartist; for many years a leader of Chartism's revolutionary socialist left wing. —Of a working-class family, he joined an early workers' group as a youth (1833); entered the unstamped-press struggle as shop boy for the Owenite H. Hetherington; formed the East London Demo Assoc (1837) as a more radical alternative to the London Working Men's Assoc; became editor (1843) of O'Connor's *Northern Star*. From early on, he was a leader of the so-called physical force wing of the Chartist movement (a tag which overstates the issue of violence abstracted from revolutionary policy). Harney was also distinctive in being strongly international minded in policy and interests; he joined the GWEA; joined M's CCC of Brussels as part of his alliance with the German émigré communists around the League of the Just and the CL (of which in fact he was a member); and above all he took the lead in launching the Society of Fraternal Democrats (1845–1853), a forerunner of the International. Eventually breaking with O'Connor, he founded the *Democratic Review* (June 1849 to May 1850), *Red Republican* (June-Dec 1850), *Friend of the People* (Dec 1850 to Apr 1852). As the decline of Chartism intensified, H. drifted rightward and lost heart; he left London (Dec 1853) and for two years worked in Newcastle for Joseph Cowen's radical-liberal *Northern Tribune* (1854–1855); then moved to Jersey (summer 1855), where he stagnated. Finally (May 1863) he moved to the U.S.; became a clerk in the Massachusetts State House, detached from politics and the labor movement (though maintaining membership in the IWMA), with occasional visits to England. In 1888 he returned to England: to Newcastle and Cowen's paper *Newcastle Weekly Chronicle*, to which he contributed regularly. Though his socialism was now dimmed out with despair, he remained to the last a champion of social justice. —H. first met E in autumn 1843, soon after the latter's arrival in England, and they became very good friends. (M maintained that it was E's influence that made a good revolutionist out of H. for so many years.) Close relations, personal and political, with both E and M continued till 1851, when the aforementioned decline of the movement began to affect H.'s politics drastically. A symptomatic episode (→ 51:10 and on) opened a rift between him and M&E; this hardened into estrangement, esp as E. Jones took over effective leadership of the Chartist left wing, and the disheartened H. faded out of politics and out of England, to a sterile exile in America. Friendly correspondence resumed by at least 1858, but H. was now out of the movement. —There is an outstanding biography by A. R. Schoyen, *The Chartist challenge* (1958). → 43:24; 45:32; 46:8, 11, 13, 29; 47:50, 52; 48:19; 49:16, 38, 44; 50:7, 15, 38–40, 49; 51:1, 8–10, 13, 14, 19; 52:3, 17; 57:45; 58:9; 69:32, 33; 71:3, 4; 79:31; 86:35; 87:28; 88:28; 89:11; 91:36; 92:6; 93:11; 94:8. #ME33, ME80, ME171; M888; E139, E433.

Harris, George E. English follower of Bronterre O'Brien; a London bookseller. A former Chartist, he was active in the International Assoc and on the management of the *Working Man*, before becoming a member of the GC/IWMA (1869–1872); financial secy of the GC (1870–1871). Also a member of the Reform League; contributor to Bradlaugh's *National Reformer.* → 70:31; 72:20.

Harris, James (1709 to 1780) English politician and scholar. MP (1761–1780); a lord of the Treasury (1763–1765); secy to the queen (1774); in politics, a follower of George Grenville; in Dr. Johnson's eyes, a prig. His 1751 work *Hermes* on "universal grammar" was once renowned. M (1859–1862) annotated his treatise on happiness in his *Three treatises* (1772 edn; orig, 1744). → 59:78.

Harrison, Frederic (1831 to 1923) English publicist and historian, a leader of the Comtist-Positivist school in Britain. By profession a lawyer (1858–c.1873); his law career was impeded by his pro-TU attitude and activities in gaining legal rights for labor in the 1860s–1870s; member of the TU parliamentary commission of 1867–1869, for which he wrote a prolabor minority report. For more on British Comtism, *see* E. S. Beesly. —A Comtist since c.1856. H. became a key figure in the British movement: for 25 years, pres of the English Positivist Comm; with Beesly and J. H. Bridges, a leader of the Positivists who split off in conflict with Richard Congreve. In national politics, H. was a Radical; in London city politics, a Progressive; not a socialist in any sense, in fact antisocialist, but favorable to extending public ownership. Like Beesly, a courageous defender of the Paris Commune in the face of contumely, and a contributor to refugee aid. —He was one of the founders of the *Positivist Review* (1893); author of *The meaning of history, order and progress* (1874); *Social statics* (1875); *Oliver Cromwell* (1888); *The positive evolution of religion.* → 67:3; 74:4.

Harrogate (Eng.) Resort in Yorkshire. → 73:55, 60.

Hartmann bindery (in Cologne) → 51:25.

Hartmann, Leo; Russ. Lev Nikolayevich (1850 to 1908) Russian Narodnik revolutionist. Son of a German emigrant in Russia; member of the Exec of Narodnaya Volya. In 1879 he took part in the N.V. attentat on Alexander II; in Oct 1880 the Exec made him ambassador to the West to plead the party's cause. H. went to Paris; expelled by the police. In London he frequented the M&E households in particular (incidentally proposing marriage to Mary Ellen Burns), and made vast plans (on paper only) for raising funds and publishing periodicals. In danger of extradition, he left for NY (June 1881); there he became the storm center of a dispute on extradition; in Aug he announced his intention to become a U.S. citizen; in 1882 he showed up again in London; but then returned to the U.S. for good. It is said that he worked in a machine shop and started a business. → 80:2, 11, 26, 40; 81:13, 32, 33, 49, 51.

Hasenclever, Wilhelm (1837 to 1889) German socialist; orig a tanner. Joining the Lassallean GGWA (1863–1864), he became secy (1866), treasurer (1870), and pres, succeeding Schweitzer (1871+), also a coeditor of its organ (1870+). After the Gotha unification (1875), he was one of the two chairmen of the united party (1875–1876) and, with Liebknecht, an editor of *Vorwärts* (1876–1878). N. Ger. Reichstag deputy (1869–1871), Reichstag deputy (1874–1888, with a brief gap), supporting the non-Marxist wing. He fell ill of a nervous ailment in 1887. → 77:23.

Hasse, Friedrich Rudolf (1808 to 1862) German Protestant theologian. Prof at Greifswald (1836–1842) and Bonn (1842+). He was named consistorial councillor (1853). His main works on religious history were written after 1842. → 42:10.

Hasselmann, Wilhelm (b. 1844) German socialist, transmogrified from Lassallean to anarchist. Orig a chemist, H. was converted by Lassalle's writings; under Schweitzer he rose to become editor of the party organ *Neue Social-Demokrat* (1871–1875); member of the Reichstag (1874–1876, 1878–1881). But he remained unreconciled to the 1875 party unity; went into opposition to the leadership, with his own organ *Die rote Fahne* (Elberfeld, 1876–1878) and *Die deutsche Zeitung*; he was esp intent on championing the traditional Lassallean rejection of equal rights for women; made an alliance with the anarchist dissident J. Most for joint denunciation of Bebel, parliamentarism, etc. At the 1880 party congress, he was expelled (with Most) for disruption and slander. H. then emigrated to the U.S. where he tried to publish a paper, ran a NY café for a while, and (unlike Most) faded from view. → 91:11.

Hastings (Eng.) Town on the Channel. → 63:32; 79:37; 84:32.

Hatzfeldt, Countess Sophie von (1805 to 1881) German friend and supporter of *Lassalle. —Daughter of Prince Franz Ludwig von Hatzfeldt, she was unhappily married (1822) by family arrangement to a cousin, Count Edmund von Hatzfeldt-Kinsweiler. A woman of spirit and intelligence, she brought about a separation, and decided (1846) to fight for her legal property rights. The young lawyer Lassalle took up her case, and occupied himself with it fully for the next eight years, using legal and other weapons, through a series of lawsuits and public scandals, finally forcing the count, by virtual blackmail, to make a heavy financial settlement (1854), which gave the countess a fortune and gave Lassalle affluence for life. Lassalle lived in the countess's Düsseldorf household (1848–1855), perhaps as her lover; they later moved to Berlin. She remained a close friend of Lassalle till his death, also a supporter of his socialist views. Indeed, when she believed (1867) that the GGWA was departing from the true-Lassallean principles, she organized a split and formed her own Pure Lassallean sect, which later remerged. → 50:6; 55:8; 60:54; 61:15, 21, 26, 30; 62:35; 64:27, 32, 39, 46, 47; 65:7.

Haude German Communist worker (tailor); member of the CL in Cologne, where in 1848 he was active as one of the NRZ group; in the fall, became a member of the WA Exec. Afterward he emigrated to London; in the 1850 CL split he went with the Willich–Schapper group, and made a swing through Germany (Nov) in its behalf. (Somehow his first name has been unrecorded by history.) → 49:11.

Haupt, Hermann Wilhelm (b. c.1831) German CL member; shop assistant from Hamburg. He took part in the 1849 revolutionary campaign in Germany; then emigrated to Switzerland and on to London, where he became a member of GWEA and CL. In Sep 1850 he went to Cologne, to give the CC/CL there, on M's behalf, oral info about the CL split; then went on to Hamburg (Oct) to stay. He was arrested in Hamburg the next year (May 1851) as the police were preparing the Cologne Communist trial. In the hands of the police, he turned state's evidence, betrayed his CL comrades in Germany, was released in Aug, and fled to Brazil. → 50:34, 38, 39, 41, 45; 51:6, 11. #M836.5.

"Haussmannization" of Paris   Baron Georges Eugène Haussmann (1809 to 1891) was Napoleon III's prefect for Paris, responsible for a thoroughgoing facelifting of Paris, esp much new construction and the layout of boulevards to hamper revolutionary barricade fighting—"those long, straight avenues which H. had expressly opened to artillery fire" (#M143). → 69:46.

Havana (Cuba) → 56:33.

Haxthausen, Baron August von; full August Franz Ludwig Maria (1792 to 1866) German agrarian historian and economist; Prussian state official. On behalf of the Prussian government, he made an extensive study of agrarian conditions in Prussia and adjacent provinces, pubd as Die ländliche Verfassung in der Provinz Preussen (1839). In 1843 the czarist government subsidized him to make a like study of institutions in European Russia, the result pubd as Studien über die innern

Zustände, das Volksleben und insbesondere die ländlichen Einrichtungen Russlands (1847–1852). H. presented much material on the obshchina, the Russian village community, which was thus "discovered" to be the peculiarly Russian base for a noncapitalist road to socialism, and stimulated much Narodnik theorizing. H.'s own views were reactionary and proserfdom. → 54:52; 75:22.

Haymarket Affair (Chicago, May 4, 1886) At a labor demonstration for the eight-hour day held in Haymarket Square, a bomb (of still uncertain origin) was exploded, killing and wounding many. A lynch-court tried and convicted eight anarchist workers for "inciting" to violence. → 86:36.

Haynau, Baron Julius (Jakob) von (1786 to 1853) Austrian reactionary gen notorious for bloody suppression of revolution in Italy (1848) and Hungary (1849), for reprisals against civilians, flogging of women, and other demonstrations of ruling-class morality. He resigned his command in 1850 after a quarrel, and went traveling abroad: in London he was beaten up by brewery draymen, and was barely rescued from a similar attack in Brussels. → 50:35.

Heaton Park Area on the north side of Manchester (Eng.). → 62:43, 58.

Hecker Prussian judiciary official; in 1848, public prosecutor (state procurator) in Cologne. (It seems that his given name has baffled historical research.) → 48:45, 65, 68, 69, 79. #ME124; M718.

Hecker, Friedrich (Franz Karl) (1811 to 1881) German republican, a leader of the Baden uprising of Apr 1848. Orig a lawyer in Mannheim, he entered the Baden Diet (1842) as an oppositionist and became a popular figure of republican dissent; with G. von Struve, he led the protest movement of 1847. In 1848 he was a member of the Frankfurt Pre-Parliament; after taking part in the first Baden uprising, he emigrated to Switzerland, then to the U.S.; in 1849 he sailed back, but arrived after the new uprising had collapsed; thereupon returned to America. In Illinois he became a leader of German-Americans, a Lincoln Republican, and a colonel in the Civil War (1861–1864). As the result of a popular song and a special hat, his name became for a while a byword for republican militancy, with a minimum of aid from Hecker himself. → 48:69.

Heckscher, Martin German-born physician in Manchester, in contact with E. → 59:46.

Heeren, Arnold (Hermann Ludwig) (1760 to 1842) German historian. Prof of philosophy (1787+) and history (1801+) at Göttingen. His works emphasized economic and technological elements in ancient history, and the importance of colonies and trade for politics. M (1851) read his *Ideen über die Politik, den Verkehr und den Handel der alten Völker* (1824; first pubd, 1793–1796) and *Handbuch der Geschichte des europäischen Staatensystems und seiner Colonien* (3rd edn, 1819). → 51:69.

Heffter, August Wilhelm (1796 to 1880) German law prof, at Berlin (1833+), previously at Bonn and Halle. His chief work was on international law, *Das europäische Völkerrecht der Gegenwart* (1844). Member of the First Prussian Chamber (1849–1852), supporting the right wing. → 37:8, 14.

Heffter, Moritz Wilhelm (1792 to 1873) German historian and philologist; brother of the preceding. Prof at the College of Brandenburg (1839+). M (1856) read his *Der Weltkampf der Deutschen und Slaven* (1847) and *Das Slawenthum* (1852). H. had previously pubd *Die Religion der Griechen und Römer* (1845). → 56:8.

Hegel, G. W. F.; *full* George Wilhelm Friedrich (1770 to 1831) German philosopher: the culmination of German classical philosophy of the 19th century, the repr of objective idealism, the founder of modern dialectics (albeit in idealist form); M&E's starting point in philosophy. The *Chronicle* traces the high points in M&E's encounter with Hegel and Hegelianism. Besides the literature on Hegelianism itself, there is a massive literature dealing with M&E's relationship to Hegel, which is not the province of this *Glossary.* Following is some useful info. • *Career outline:* At the U. of Jena, lecturer (1801); prof (1805). At Bamberg: editor of the *Bamberger Zeitung* (1807–1808). At Nuremberg: rector of a Gymnasium (1808–1816). At Heidelberg: prof (1816–1818). At Berlin: prof (1818–1831). • *Major works:* Dates refer to first edn only. *Die Phänomenologie des Geistes* [Phenomenology of the mind] (1807); *Wissenschaft der Logik* [Science of logic] (1813–1816); *Enzyklopädie der philosophischen Wissenschaften im Grundrisse* [Encyclopedia of the philosophical sciences in outline] (1817); *Grundlinien der Philosophie des Rechts* [or] *Naturrecht und Staatswissenschaft im Grundrisse* [Basic lines of the philosophy of right (or) Natural law and political science in outline] (1821)—this work usually called *Philosophy of right* for short. • *Posthumous collections of lectures:* The following selection omits early writings. *Vorlesungen über die Philosophie der Geschichte* [Lectures on the philosophy of history] (1837), subseqly revised as *Die Vernunft in der Geschichte* [Reason in history] (1917–1920); *Vorlesungen über die Aesthetik* [Lectures on esthetics] (1835–1838); *Vorlesungen über die Philosophie der Religion* [Lectures on the

philosophy of religion] (1901); *Vorlesungen über die Geschichte der Philosophie* [Lectures on the history of philosophy] (1908). —Most of these titles have been translated into English in whole or part and for good or ill. → 37:3, 6; 38:2; 39:1; 40:6; 41:15, 16, 20, 21; 42:8; 43:18, 20, 28; 44:4, 6, 24, 26, 27, 40; 45:7; 58:7, 33; 59:55; 62:31; 66:34; 67:17; 68:13, 29, 63; 70:38; 82:7; 90:33; 91:38, 57; 92:10; 93:45; 94:22. #M93, M204–M206, M261, M368, M575, M595, M658; E727. See also Hegelianism (*the distinction here is sometimes merely verbal*).

Hegelianism; Hegelian school → 37:6, 11, 15; 44:22; 52:7; 58:13; 86:10; 90:49. See also Hegel; Young Hegelians.

Heide (pseud. of W. *Wolff) #E229.

Heidelberg (Ger.) University city in Baden. → 48:48; 75:40; 76:20, 25. #E793.

Heidfeld, Oscar German businessman in Liverpool; a friend of Ernst Dronke in the latter's last years. → 91:60.

Heilberg, Louis (1818 to 1852) German journalist; as an émigré in Brussels in 1846, he was codirector of the journal *L'Atelier Démocratique;* also a member (with M) of the Brussels CCC; writer for the *DBZ* in 1847–1848; later, a CL member. He took part in the 1848–1849 revolution in Germany; worked as journalist in Berlin and Breslau, editor of the *Schlesische Volkszeitung,* secy of the Arbeiter-Verbrüderung in Silesia, persecuted by police; after which he emigrated to London (end of 1850). → 46:11. #ME28.

Heine, Heinrich (1797 to 1856) German poet and man of letters (essayist, journalist, critic)—the second name in German literature after Goethe. Born in the Rhineland, of a Jewish family, Harry Heine was baptized (1825) to avoid the professional disabilities visited on Jews, taking the name Heinrich. He was early a spokesman for the politico-literary current of moderate liberal dissent called Young Germany; gained fame with *Reisebilder* (Vol. 1, 1826), then *Buch der Lieder* (1827); moved to Paris (1831). There, strongly influenced by Saint-Simonism, the high point of his radicalism came in his association (1844) with the German left-wingers around the Paris émigré organ *Vorwärts!* in which H. pubd some of his most outspoken political verse. This period ended with M's expulsion from France (→ 45:8). In 1848 H.'s progressive disease laid him up in bed permanently. The defeat of the revolution turned him to disillusionment with radical aspirations, back to a promonarchist elitism; his terrible personal situation on his "mattress-grave" turned him back to religion and protestations of belief in Christianity. He still produced great poetry, in two collections: *Romanzero* (1851) and "Poems of 1853–54" in his *Vermischte Schriften*

(1854); also volumes of collected essays and articles. —H. met M in Paris by the end of 1843, and they were close friends for over a year, associating constantly and intimately, with H. often visiting the M family to go over his poems. M (related Eleanor M later) "would even make all sorts of excuses for H.'s political vagaries. Poets, Mohr [Marx] maintained, were queer kittle-cattle, not to be judged by the ordinary, or even the extraordinary standards of conduct." But in their letters to each other, M&E sometimes lamented H.'s backsliding in his late years, esp when it came out that he was getting a pension from the Bonaparte government. But M&E's writings were peppered with quotes and phrases from H.'s works, to a greater extent than ed notes ever show. → 43:30; 44:32; 45:8; 46:14; 48:30, 34; 49:29; 51:48; 52:41; 56:11, 34; 89:35. #E649.

Heinrich, Christoph Gottlob (or Gottlieb) (1748 to 1810) German historian; prof at Jena (1782+) for 28 years. Author of *Handbuch der teutschen Reichsgeschichte* (1800), *Geschichte von England* (1806–1810). M (1843) studied his *Geschichte von Frankreich* (1802–1804). → 43:32.

Heinzen, Karl (Peter) (1809 to 1880) German, later German-American, liberal publicist. In the early 1840s he collaborated on the *RZ* and *Leipziger Allgemeine Ztg*; friendly with M. His book *Die preussische Bureaukratie* (1845) enraged the Prussian authorities; he emigrated to Brussels, where at first he had relations with M's circle. In 1847 he began publishing attacks on both the communist and "True Socialist" tendencies, leading i.a. to a polemic with M&E; he remained antisocialist (and also anti-Prussian) throughout his career. After brief participation in the Baden-Palatinate uprising of 1849, he emigrated to Switzerland, later to England, finally (1850) to the U.S., where he was editor of *Der Pionier* (NY/Boston, 1854–1879). → 42:26; 45:13, 18; 47:37, 41, 48; 49:40, 44; 51:46; 52:7, 9, 12, 22, 43; 62:27; 72:26. #M531, M966; E152.

Heise, Heinrich (1820 to 1859 or 1860) S. German publicist; left Democrat. Editor of *Hornisse* (1848–1850); took part in the revolution of 1848–1849 in Germany; emigrated to England (1853) and settled in Manchester (1854), where he was E's frequent visitor. In 1859 he collaborated on *Das Volk* with M&E. —*Caution: KMC* gives his name erron. as Hermann. → 53:31; 54:11, 21; 59:46; 60:8.

Heller Czech socialist; no further info. (This item is from *MEW Daten*.) → 95:32.

Hember Member of the London Dialectical Society. → 78:31.

Hemming, George Wirgman (1821 to 1905) English lawyer and writer on mathematics. He became a barrister (1850), counsel to Cambridge Univ. (1875), and author of

books on law. But M (1878) read him as part of his math studies: H. pubd an *Elementary treatise on the differential and integral calculus* (1848) and one on plane trigonometry (1851). → 78:1.

Henning, Leopold (Dorotheus) von (1791 to 1866) German philosopher; prof at Berlin. A pupil of Hegel's, and known as an Old Hegelian, he was an editor of the Jubilee Edition of Hegel's works, and author of *Principien der Ethik in historischer Entwickelung* (1824). #E224.

Hentze, A. German army lieutenant, member of the CL who in the 1850 split went with the Willich–Schapper group. At the Cologne Communist trial (1852) he testified for the prosecution; it is not clear whether he was a police spy to begin with, or a case like H. W. *Haupt. → 52:39.

Hepner, Adolf (1846 to 1923) German Social-Democrat; first a bookdealer and journalist. In 1869 he was a member of the Demokratische Arbeiterverein in Berlin, with Paul Singer et al., and helped to found the SDWP at Eisenach that year. Coeditor of the *Volksstaat* (1869–1873); delegate to the Hague Congress (1872). He was a defendant, with Bebel and Liebknecht, in the Leipzig treason trial (1872); sentenced to two years. He later (1882) moved to the U.S., where i.a. he edited the *St. Louis Tageblatt*; returned to Germany (1908). In World War I he was a prowar Majority Social-Democrat. → 70:65; 71:17; 72:42, 48, 52; 73:12, 23, 27, 39; 74:22; 75:17, 48; 82:5, 25, 29; 83:3, 14. #ME96D; #E543, E555.

Heraclitus of Ephesus (c.535–540 B.C. to c.475–480 B.C.) Greek philosopher: a herald of naturalistic materialism, with a dialectical view of change as the constant in nature and of the process of becoming as the basic reality. Lassalle's book *Die Philosophie Herakleitos des Dunklen von Ephesos* (1858) gave a Hegelian-idealist treatment of Heraclitus as a forerunner of the dialectic method. → 57:53; 58:8, 13, 25.

Herbert, Sidney; **Baron Herbert of Lea** (1810 to 1861) English politician. He became MP as a Tory (1832+); subseqly a Peelite; war secy under Peel (1845–1846); also during the Crimean War (1852–1855); and under Palmerston (1859–1860), when he presided over some army reforms. #M369.

Héritier, Louis (1863 to 1898) Swiss socialist; publicist and writer; party delegate (1893) to the International Socialist Congress at Zurich. —Besides his pro-Bakunin material, H. authored a book *Geschichte der französische Revolution von 1848 und der zweiten Republik* (189?) which was edited by W. Eichhoff and E. Bernstein, with supplementary material by Bernstein of importance to the origins of the latter's Revisionism. → 92:60, 68; 93:4. #E834.

Herman, Alfred (1843 to 1890) Belgian socialist, a sculptor by profession, from the Liège area. An organizer of IWMA sections in Belgium, he became a member of the GC and corr secy for Belgium (1871–1872); delegate to IWMA congresses of 1868 and 1871, and to the Hague Congress (1872). A Proudhonist in viewpoint, he supported the Bakunin wing at The Hague. For vignettes on him, see ST/27 (HCFI), pp. 400, 548. —Note: The spelling Hermann in KMC is erroneous. → 71:39; 72:36.

Hermann; Deutsches Wochenblatt aus London Jan 8, 1859, to Dec 24, 1869. Pub'r/editor: G. Kinkel (Jan-July 1859). — Continued as Londoner Zeitung; Hermann (Jan 1, 1870, to Aug 22, 1914). → 59:12, 44, 46, 50, 72; 60:7; 62:12; 65:24; 68:42.

Hermann, Ludimar (1838 to 1914) German physiologist; prof at Zurich (1868+), at Königsberg (1884+). His main field was neuromuscular physiology, esp bioelectric reactions. M (1876) may well have read his Grundriss der Physiologie des Menschen (1863), also in English as Elements of human physiology (1875), or his Lehrbuch der Physiologie (1863). → 76:9.

Hermes, Georg (1775 to 1831) German Catholic theologian. Prof at Münster (1807+) and Bonn (1819+), he pubd Einleitung in die christkatholische Theologie (1819, 1829), influenced by Kant and Fichte. The followers of "Hermesianism," which sought to ground Christian theology on reason alone, forced Pope Gregory XVI to issue a bull condemning the doctrines (1835); but they did not die (as M's interest in 1840 indicates). F. X. Werner pubd a work refuting Der Hermesianismus (1845), and in 1847 Pope Pius IX confirmed the earlier condemnation. → 40:12.

Hermes, Karl Heinrich (1800 to 1856) German journalist and historian. In 1841 he began publishing his Geschichte der letzten fündundzwanzig Jahre. He was editor of the Cologne KZ (1842–1843), rival to M's RZ. He later collaborated on the Allgemeine Preussische Ztg and other conservative papers. MEW 27 says he was a "secret agent of the Prussian government," but this was not repeated by New Mega I, 1. → 42:17, 20, 22.

Herwegh, Georg (Friedrich) (1817 to 1875) German left-wing poet. A journalist in Stuttgart in the late 1830s, he was forced to flee to Switzerland (1839), where he pubd his best-known work Gedichte eines Lebendigen (1841, part 2 in 1844); also lived in Paris and (1847) Brussels. In 1842 he had made the friendly acquaintance of M; one of the papers he contributed to was the RZ of Cologne. At the outbreak of the 1848 revolution he was a

leader of the German Demo Assoc in Paris, an organizer of the adventuristic "German Legion" of émigrés, which sallied into Baden and was scattered at a blow (Apr). H. fled to Zurich; retired into study and writing; revived politically with the founding of the GGWA by Lassalle, who named him a "plenipotentiary" of the assoc (1863). H. broke with the Lassalleans (1865) and joined the new Eisenacher party (1869). → 42:30; 43:4, 7; 44:8; 47:21, 39; 48:19, 27; 52:55. #M64.

Herzegovina See Bosnia for info. → 82:9.

Herzen, Alexander; full Alexander Ivanovich (1812 to 1870) Russian revolutionary émigré; populist-socialist writer. —Illegitimate son of a rich Moscow aristocrat, I. A. Yakovlev (who conferred the name Herzen on his son). H. was first turned to socialism by Saint-Simon's writings. He moved to France (1847); took initial part in the June demonstration of 1849, but, leaving as soon as troops appeared, he went home to write letters about the left's cowardice; then moved to Geneva. He returned to Paris (1850), and with Baron James Rothschild's help, got his paternal fortune out of Russia and safely invested, adopting Swiss citizenship for this purpose—thus becoming the wealthiest émigré operating in Europe in the century. For a while (1850–1852) he lived in Nice (then Italian) in contact with Mazzini and Proudhon; moved to London in 1852. There (1852–1853) he established the Free Russian Press, first uncensored Russian-language pub'r; it pubd his organ Kolokol (1857–1865 in London) and his books, e.g., My past and thoughts (1855), aided by his close collaborator N. P. Ogarev. —H.'s "Russian socialism" was based on hopes for the peasant obshchina (village community), derived from *Haxthausen and due to become the Narodnik socialism of the second half of the century. In H.'s Slavophile conception, "young" Russia would regenerate old, decayed Europe, because Russians are "born revolutionaries" and can bypass capitalism (via the obshchina); this revolution would be brought about from above, mainly by the radical gentry. —There is a full-length study in English: Martin Malia, Alexander H. and the birth of Russian socialism (1961). → 50:19; 53:16, 28, 32, 34; 54:52; 55:11, 20; 68:69; 69:64; 70:6.

Hess, Moses (1812 to 1875) German socialist writer. Son of a well-to-do Rhineland merchant, H. early became a journalist; got acquainted with socialism in Paris (late 1830s); became one of the first socialists (or communists) in Germany; pubd Die heilige Geschichte der Menschheit (1837); Die europäische Triarchie (1841). Indeed, in a letter H. claimed to have converted young E to communism in 1842. H. was an initiator of and editorial contributor to *RZ* (1842) and, during the rest of the 1840s, to *DFJ* (1843), Paris *Vorwärts!* (1844), Herwegh's collection *Einundzwanzig Bogen;* pubd *Gesellschafts-spiegel* (Elberfeld, 1845–1846), initially planned with E. After its failure, he went to Brussels. During this period H. represented the views of so-called "True Socialism." In the more heated period of around 1847–1850 he moved closest to M; joined the League of the Just, then the CL; in the 1850 CL split, he went with the Willich–Schapper group, for which he worked in Germany (1852–1854). There then ensued, in Paris, a period in which he devoted himself to natural-science studies. In 1863 he joined up with Lassalle to build GGWA and state-socialism, as the plenipoten-tiary in Cologne; while Lassalle looked to Bismarck, H. looked to Bonaparte. In IWMA congresses (1868–1869) H. was a clear voice for reformism, very hostile to both the Baku-ninists and Proudhonists. This period coin-cides with his emergence as a pioneer of Zionism, with his book *Rom and Jerusalem* (1862). In 1877 his widow pubd a posthumous work, *Dynamische Stofflehre.* —The most thorough study of H. is by Edmund Silberner, *MH, Geschichte seines Lebens* (1966), marred by its devil-theory of M; there is no reliable book on H. in English. —H. also used the given names Moritz and Maurice. → 41:16; 42:14, 27; 43:26; 45:9, 11, 19; 46:20; 47:28, 43; 48:74; 56:11; 57:9; 64:27, 32; 65:7, 9, 14; 68:48; 77:43. #ME66; M722; E862.

Hess, Sibylle; née **Pesch** (1820 to 1903) Wife of Moses Hess. Daughter of a Catholic day laborer, she worked as embroiderer-mil-liner; may have become a prostitute when Hess met her—in any case, this was widely believed. She went to live with him in 1843–1844; married in late 1851 or early 1852, after Hess's father died. She remained with Hess till his death; became an enthusiastic social-ist. → 77:43.

Hessian Adjectival form of Hesse (Ger. Hessen), region and former state of S.W. Germany. → 49:27.

Highgate Cemetery Highgate is a northern suburb of London. → 81:59; 83:12; 84:19; 92:21.

Hilberg, Arnold Austrian journalist. Pub'r and editor of the Vienna *Internationale Revue* (1866–1868). → 66:9, 16.

Hildebrand, Max Teacher in a Berlin *Volksschul;* engaged in research on Max Stirner. → 89:33.

Hildebrand or **Hildebrandt,** Theodor (pseud.) Pen name used by E in 1839, for three poems pubd in the Bremen press; actu-ally written three different ways: Theodor H., Th. Hildebrandt, Theodor Hildebrand. —It

happens that a German painter of historical scenes, Theodor Hildebrand(t) (1804–1874), had recently gained fame in 1836 with a notable picture; his *t* was likewise optional. There is no indication in E's letters that there was a connection in E's mind at the time. → 39:5, 6. #E94, E816, E840.

Hilditch, Richard (fl. mid-19th century) English writer on economics. M (1845) anno-tated his *Aristocratic taxation* (1842). → 45:52. #M575.

Hillmann, Hugo (1823 to 1898) German Social-Democrat. A brewer and pubkeeper in Elberfeld, H. took part in the 1848–1849 revolution there; afterward, emigrated to Lon-don, where he was a member of the GWEA. In 1863, back in Germany, he joined Lassalle's GGWA and became its plenipotentiary for Elberfeld, but he became an opponent of the Lassalleans, joined Bebel's tendency (Verband Deutscher Arbeitervereine) in 1868, and in 1869 was a delegate to the founding congress of the Eisenacher party. → 69:26.

Hind, John (1796 to 1866) English math-ematician; teacher at Sidney Sussex College. M's math studies may well have been on one of his works on calculus, *Principles of the differential calculus* (2nd edn, 1831) or *Prin-ciples of the differential and integral calculus* (1827). → 78:1.

Hins, Eugène (Marie); *also called* Eugen (1839 to 1923) Belgian IWMA activist; first Proudhonist, later supporter of Bakunin. A teacher and journalist, brother-in-law of *De Paepe, H. was a founder of the IWMA in the country; delegate to the congresses of 1868–1869, where he was a swing vote on the issue of land collectivization: in 1868 he voted against, as a Proudhonist; in 1869 he voted for, on the basis of a sort of syndicalist line. In early 1869 the Belgian IWMA established a Gen Council of its own, with H. as gen secy (also repr of the Verviers area). H. was also on the ed staff of *La Liberté* (Brussels). —In an 1872 letter, E described H. as "a blockhead but shrewd, intriguing, ambitious and active" and "in contact with Bakunin through his [Hins'] Russian wife." → 69:25; 71:37.

Hirsch, Karl (1841 to 1900) German Social-Democratic journalist. An active so-cialist journalist already in youth, he joined the GGWA, but quit it (1868) in favor of the Bebel–Liebknecht tendency; helped to found the Demokratische Arbeiterverein (Berlin); delegate to the founding congress of the Eisenacher party (1869). He had worked (1868) with Liebknecht on the staff of the *Demokratisches Wochenblatt* (Leipzig); now (1869–1871) he took over the pioneer S-D daily of Crimmitschau (Saxony), *Bürger- und Bauernfreund.* When Liebknecht and Bebel were jailed in the Franco-Prussian War, he temporarily took over running *Volksstaat* (Dec 1870 to Mar 1871), for which he was awarded four months in jail. Then, from Paris, H. worked as a correspondent for German S-D papers. With the banning of this press by the Anti-Socialist Law (1878), H. launched (Dec) his *Laterne* (Brussels) as an illegal paper to be smuggled into Germany; suspended (end 1879) in favor of the S-D party's own organ. H. then went to live in London, visiting M on occasion; went to France again; and (1896) returned to Germany and withdrew from political activity. He was briefly editor of the nonsocialist papers *Frankfurter Ztg* and Cologne's *RZ*. → 75:35; 76:33; 77:10, 23, 24; 78:7; 79:2, 24, 27, 33, 38; 80:24, 30, 50; 81:43; 82:28; 95:21. #ME29.

Hirsch, Max (1832 to 1905) German writer on economics; a founder of the so-called Hirsch–Duncker trade unions. (See Franz *Duncker.) With TU legalization in Prussia, H. pubd a series of articles (1868) urging the English unions as models: TUs based on class harmony, hostile to strikes, politically attached to liberals rather than to socialists. A conference laid the foundation of the Gewerkvereine (H-D unions), characterized by great centralization. To stress the joys of democracy, H. demanded (1876) that new members sign a yellow-dog statement rejecting Social-Democracy. By the end of the century the weak H-D movement tended to turn into benefit societies. —H. was a Reichstag deputy (1869–1893) of the Progressivist party, later the Freisinnige liberals. —Writings: *Die hauptsächlichsten Streitfragen der Arbeiterbewegung* (1886); *Die Arbeiterfrage und die deutschen Gewerkvereine* (1893). → 68:54.

Hirsch, Wilhelm   Shop assistant from Hamburg; an agent of the Prussian police in London (early 1850s). He joined the London CL (Dec 1851), but was soon suspected and expelled. He earned his pay by forging CL records for use by the prosecution in the Cologne Communist trial. → 51:1; 52:7, 13, 39, 45; 53:14, 19; 59:72. #M374.

Hirschfeld, Rudolf Printshop owner in London. Besides M's *Herr Vogt,* H. also printed *Die Neue Zeit* (not the later magazine) and the weekly *Hermann.* He also printed the so-called Hirschfeld edn of the *Com Manifesto* in the first half of the 1860s; see #ME33. → 60:45, 54. #ME33.

Hitchens, C. #M143.

Hlubeck, F. X.; *full* Franz Xaver Wilhelm von (1802 to 1880) Austrian authority on agriculture. Prof of rural economy at Vienna (1830+), he also held posts in various agricultural societies. M (1878) studied his chief work, *Die Landwirtschaftslehre* (1851–1853; first pubd, 1846). → 78:18.

Hobbes, Thomas (1588 to 1679) English philosopher of the Enlightenment; advocate of an early mechanical-materialist theory of natural law and of a political rationale for absolutism. Most of modern political philosophy is refutation, confirmation, or obfuscation of Hobbesianism. Chief work: *Leviathan* (1651). Others: *De corpore politico* (1650); *De homine* (1658); *De cive* (1642). → 60:65.

Hoboken (New Jersey) City on the Hudson opposite NY City. → 67:22; 88:28.

Hodde, Lucien de la; *or* Lucien **Delahodde**; *also spelled* **De la Hodde,** L. (1808 to 1865) French writer and journalist—publicist, poet, and policeman. As a young soldier, he joined secret societies in the army. Come to Paris, he lived the lit'ry life and pubd some books of poetry (1831, 1844); as a good republican, he became a leader in secret societies, incl the Society of the Seasons. He then entered the secret police and—allegedly to preserve society for Law and Order—betrayed his associates for 300 francs per month, for seven or eight years. After the 1848 revolution he inserted himself into the police under *Caussidière, becoming gen secy of the department. In Mar he was unmasked and imprisoned; but when Caussidière was ousted, he was able to flee to London (Aug), where he pubd a satiric journal, *Le Bossu,* denouncing the revolution as immoral. He also pubd works of dubious revelations: *La naissance de la république en février 1848* (1850) and *Histoire des sociétés secrètes et du parti républicain de 1830 à 1848* (1850). #ME141.

Hodgskin, Thomas (1787 to 1869) English journalist, expounder of "Ricardian socialist" views. Having run afoul of authority with his pamphlet *Essay on naval discipline* (1813), H. was influenced by Francis Place to study European economic conditions; as a result, pubd *Travels in the north of Germany* (1820). He became copublisher of *Mechanics Magazine* (1823), which pubd his *Popular political economy* (book, 1827). In 1825 he became associated with the London Mechanics' Institute, and that year (signing "A Labourer") pubd *Labour defended against the claims of capital.* M had a high opinion of H., but about his next work—*On the British African colonisation society* (1834)—he commented: "Rubbish. Effusive enthusiasm for Liberia." This, plus *Enquiry into the merits of the American "Colonisation Society"* (1835), were read by M in 1851, in addition to the 1827 and 1825 books listed above. —H. had a strong antistate side, being in favor of minimal government involvement with the individual—sometimes called his anarchist tendency. It was this laissez-faire side which blossomed when H. later abandoned his radicalism and spent his later years writing for the *Economist.* → 51:66–69.

Höchberg, Karl (1853 to 1885) German Social-Democratic writer; pioneer of reformism in the party. H. inherited a fortune and used it to finance S-D literature and periodicals, after joining the SDWP (1876). He pubd and edited Zukunft (1877–1878); Staatswissenschaftliche Abhandlungen (1879–1882) under the pseud. Dr. R. F. Seyffert; Jahrbuch für Sozialwissenschaft und Sozialpolitik (1879–1881) under the pseud. Dr. Ludwig Richter; also helped finance the party's Sozialdemokrat, to found the NZ, and establish the J. H. W. Dietz publishing firm. In 1879 he distributed from Brussels 10,000 copies of Schäffle's Katheder-socialist book Die Quintessenz des Socialismus (1877), to professionals and intellectuals. —In 1878, for health reasons, H. moved to Switzerland (first Lugano; in 1879, Zurich), with E. Bernstein as private secy, to carry on the afore-listed activities. The Jahrbuch, in its first issue, carried an article "Rückblicke auf die sozialistische Bewegung in Deutschland," written by a trio (signed with three stars: ***)—the first systematic statement of the reformist theory later developed by Bernstein as "Revisionism." M&E launched a campaign (see #ME29) against the tendency represented by this article, esp since the party leadership was thinking of entrusting the planned party organ to the Zurich Höchbergites, with an eye to Höchberg's financial support. The campaign was successful. In any case, H.'s chest ailment soon carried him off. → 77:26, 37; 79:2, 3, 33, 38, 41, 49, 53; 80:44.

Hödel, Max; full Emil Heinrich Max (1857 to 1878) German tinsmith or plumbing worker, from Leipzig. This unemployed artisan, half-witted or half-sane, made an assassination attempt on Wilhelm I (May 11, 1878); executed Aug. 16. H. had distributed papers for the Social-Democrats, but had been expelled as a member in April, after which he worked for the National Liberals and Christian Socials. Bismarck used H. as part of his pretext to impose the *Anti-Socialist Law. → 78:15, 19.

Hörner, Lothar   Düsseldorf innkeeper; a contributor to the RZ (Cologne) in 1842. #M187.

Hoffmann & Campe   For info, see *Campe, J. → 51:37.

Hoffstetter, Gustav von (1818 to 1874) Swiss army officer and military writer. He took part in the war against the Sonderbund (1847); on Garibaldi's staff (1849) in the siege of Rome, on which he wrote Tagebuch aus Italien, 1849 (1851. → 52:2.

Hofmann, August Wilhelm von (1818 to 1892) German organic chemist; known esp for discoveries in coal-tar products and aniline dyes; a student of Liebig's. Prof at London (1845–1864), Bonn (1864–1865), Berlin (1865+); founder of the German Chemical Society (1868). —E (1867) studied his Intro to modern chemistry (1865). → 67:21.

Hofstetten, Johann Baptist von (d. 1887) German journalist; Lassallean. Orig a Bavarian army lieutenant, with independent wealth, he was persuaded by Schweitzer to join him in founding and editing the Social-Demokrat (Berlin) as the GGWA organ; hence copublisher and co-owner of the paper (1864–1867). But he quit Lassalleanism and was a delegate at the founding congress of the Eisenacher party (1869); subseqly withdrew from the working-class movement. —Note: Like Schweitzer, who (it happened) had the same given names, he seems to have used Jean for Johann, at least in part. → 66:7.

Hohenzollern family   The ruling family of Brandenburg from the early 15th century, of Prussia from the beginning of the 18th, and of the German empire from 1871—up to 1918. → 49:26; 56:42; 57:4; 63:12. #M226, M247, M378, M379.

Holland   See Netherlands.

Hollinger, Fidelio   German émigré in London; printshop owner. Das Volk was printed in his shop. → 59:8, 44, 49, 56, 59, 64, 65; 60:12.

Holstein   See Schleswig-Holstein.

Holy Alliance   The united front of Russia, Prussia, and Austria against revolutionary change, 1815+. #E177, E434.

Holyoake, George Jacob (1817 to 1906) English Owenite, cooperator, Secularist. An Owenite lecturer and Chartist at an early age (1830s–1840s); a minister to Owenites at Worcester (1840); Owenite social "missionary" (organizer) (1841–1846). He then abandoned socialism, and moved to favor a lib-lab alliance in politics. He moved to London (1843); founded the weekly Reasoner (1846), and pioneered the "Secularist" movement (his invented term for rationalism, atheism); a founder of the National Secular Society; founded the Leader (1850). In later years he supported the Liberal party against the developing Labour party, and was valuable to the Liberals as a workingman who could be brandished against socialism. He pubd a History of co-operation in England (1875–1877), covering Owenism; also a couple of autobiographical volumes, which need to be used with caution as sources. M&E considered him outstandingly dishonest. → 52:35; 71:28, 30. #E776, E777.

Homer (eighth century B.C. or earlier)   The name that tradition has conferred on the epic poet(s) of ancient Greece to whom are ascribed the Iliad and the Odyssey. → 35:5. #E590A, E728.5.

Hontheim, Richard von (d. 1857)   German

lawyer in Cologne; a defense counsel in the Cologne Communist trial of 1852. → 52:39.

Hook of Holland Cape, S.W. Netherlands, near Rotterdam and The Hague. → 93:40.

Hope, George (1811 to 1876) Scottish agriculturist; a tenant farmer. Opponent of the Corn Laws; friend of Cobden and Bright; his prize essay (see the *Chronicle*) netted £30. He later pubd "Hindrances to agriculture from a tenant farmer's point of view" in *Recess studies*, ed by A. Grant (1870). In 1875 his landlord arbitrarily kicked him off his internationally famous model farm held by the Hope family for three generations. → 45:52.

Hopkins, Thomas (d. 1864?) English writer on economics; also author of a couple of works on weather (perhaps related to his profession?). —M (1851) read four works by H., excerpting the last three: *Bank notes the cause of the disappearance of guineas* (1811); *Economical enquiries relative to the laws which regulate rent, profit, wages and the value of money* (1822); *On rent of land and its influence on subsistence and population* (1828); *Gr Brit for the last forty years* (1834). H. also pubd a pamphlet, *Wages: or, Masters and workmen* (1831). → 51:67; 59:77.

Horner, Leonard (1785 to 1864) Although M's encomiums on H.'s incorruptible work as a factory inspector has given him a niche in social history, H. was primarily a geologist and educator. Scottish-born, orig partner in the family linen factory, he settled in London at age 21; became a Fellow of the Geological Society (1808), its secy (1810), vice-pres (1828), and pres (1846, 1860); after his retirement as inspector, he again concentrated on this field. In his second career as educator, he was a founder of the pioneering trade-education institution, the Edinburgh School of Arts; took an active part in founding the Univ. of London, becoming a warden (1827); studied and wrote on educational reform; in particular, published on Dutch workers' education. Finally, career no. 3: he was appointed (1833) one of the commissioners to inquire into child factory labor, and subseqly became one of the factory inspectors under the law. He published *On the employment of children in factories* (1840); wrote his last factory report in 1859. M often quotes his reports in *Capital*, and added: "He rendered undying service to the English working class. He carried on a lifelong contest, not only with the embittered manufacturers, but also with the Cabinet. . . ." The Francis Horner who is also quoted in *Capital* was H.'s older brother, lawyer, and MP, a parliamentary specialist in economic affairs. → 60:9.

Die Hornisse Cassel (Ger.), 1848 to 1850. Pub'r: H. Heise, G. Kellner. —Left liberal. → 54:11. #ME68, ME157A.

Hospitalier, Edouard (1852 to 1907)

French physicist. M (1882) studied his *Principales applications de l'électricité* (2nd edn, 1882), and *La physique moderne* (1881). *Caution:* MEW calls him L. Hospitalier. → 82:47.

Hôtel de Saxe (Brussels) → 45:13.

The Hour London, Mar 24, 1873, to Aug 4, 1876. → 75:13.

Hourwich, Isaac A.; orig **Gurvich,** Izaak Adolfovich (1860 to 1924) Russian-born economist active in the U.S. After escaping from Siberia, he emigrated to the U.S. (1891); became a lawyer; lectured at the Univ. of Chicago (1893–1894). He became an active member of the American socialist movement; one of the earliest Marxist economists in the country; in later years, pro-Revisionist in outlook; contributor to the Yiddish press. His chief works were *Immigration and labor* (1912), *Economics of the Russian village* (1892). → 93:26.

House, Edward Howard (1836 to 1901) American journalist. After acting as war correspondent for the *NYDT* through the Civil War, he became prof of English in Tokyo (1871); editor of the *Tokyo Times* (1875–1877). Author of a number of books on Japanese affairs. M (1881) read his article "The Martyrdom of an empire" (*Atlantic Monthly*, May 1881). → 81:64.

How Do You Do? London. Weekly. Pub'r: Louis Drucker. Ed by H. Bettziech. —Apparently a German-language periodical; the preceding info is from MEW; but no info on this periodical has been found in periodical catalogs. → 51:36.

Howell, George (1833 to 1910) English labor leader, prototypical lib-lab. He joined a Chartist group (1848); settled in London (1855) as a bricklayer; took part in the bricklayers' union and strike movement of 1859–1862, and rose in the union leadership. He was also active in the London Trades Council Exec till 1867; its secy (1861–1862); secy of the Reform League (1865–1869). —His relations with M arose from his participation in the founding meeting of the IWMA (1864) and subseq membership in the GC (1864–1869). However, the IWMA was never important to his perspectives, and he began fading out of it by 1866. Later, as he grew increasingly anxious for liberal respectability, he attacked the International in a slanderous article (see #M520). —His subseq career passed through a number of political-action bodies before he achieved his ruling ambition, Parliament; his stint as a Liberal MP (1885–1895) was unmarked by any delusion about acting as a tribune of labor. Life was unfair to him: his virtual abandonment of workers' interests for the sake of a parliamentary career was negated by the class consciousness of the

Liberals, who refused to let their lib-lab tail even wag itself, let alone them. He turned to the compensations of literature, but his book *The conflicts of capital and labour* (1878) was largely a plagiarism from *Brentano (misunderstood at that); his *Trade unionism new and old* (1891), which denounced the New Unionism, disgusted good trade-unionists without convincing the Liberals that he deserved a political handout; and his last book, *Labour legislation, labour movements and labour leaders* (1902) simply had nothing to say. A tragic life. → 66:17; 78:25, 29; 83:18. #M520.

Howitt, William (1792 to 1879) English writer on a variety of subjects: *Book of the seasons* (1831); *Popular history of priestcraft* (1833), esp well received; *Rural life of England* (1838); *Student life of Germany* (1841), etc. In several books, esp for young people, he collaborated with his wife, Mary Howitt. — In 1846 he wrote "Letters on labour" for the *People's J.* (London), which Harney praised to M&E. The book studied by M (1851) was his *Colonisation and Christianity: A history of the treatment of natives by Europeans* (1838). → 51:69.

Hubbard, John Gellibrand (1805 to 1889) English financier and politician. He entered the family business, the Russia trade (1821); by 1838, was a director of the Bank of England. MP (1859–1868, 1874–1887) as Tory; member of the Privy Council (1874+); raised to the peerage as Baron Addington (1887). In Parliament he was an authority on financial questions, esp the income tax, on which he wrote several pamphlets; also on the coinage. The work annotated by M (1851) was *The currency and the country* (1843). → 51:63; 54:51.

Hubert, Adolphe (Antoine) (b. 1827) French Communard leftist. During the Paris Commune, he was member of an arrondissement council; as émigré in London, he worked as a journalist; joined the IWMA; active in its defense and refugee work. → 71:33, 41; 72:11.

Hudson River (NY state) From the Adirondacks to NY Bay. → 88:30.

Hübner, Otto (1818 to 1877) German economist and statistician. He established (1849) the Central Statistical Archives of Prussia, and became its longtime director; editor of the *Jahrbuch für Volkswirthschaft und Statistik* (1851+); founder/chairman of the Prussian Hypothekenversicherungs-Gesellschaft (1862+). → 67:33.

Hüllmann, Karl Dietrich (1765 to 1846) German historian; authority on medieval economic history. Prof at Frankfurt (1797+), Königsberg, Bonn (1818–1841). At Bonn, M audited his lectures (1835–1836) without signing up for the course. Later (1851–1852, 1878) M studied his chief works: *Deutsche Finanz-Geschichte des Mittelalters* (1805); *Städtewesen des Mittelalters* (1826–1829); *Geschichte der Ursprungs der Stände in Deutschland* (1830; first pubd, 1817); *Geschichte des byzantinischen Handels* (1808); *Handelsgeschichte der Griechen* (1839). → 51:70; 52:56; 78:38, 48.

Hülstett, George Karl Anton (fl. first half 19th century) German philologist; assistant master in a Düsseldorf school. He edited school readers; one of E's textbooks was Dr. H.'s *Sammlung ausgewählter Stücke aus den Werken deutscher Prosaiker und Dichter* (1831), which went through eight edns by 1855. #E528.5.

Hünermund, Eduard German police official; a police inspector in Cologne, keeping surveillance on subversives in 1848. → 48:29.

Hüser, (Johann) Hans Gustav Heinrich von (1782 to 1857) Prussian gen; supporter of reactionary military circles. Commandant in Mainz (1844–1849). #E362.

Hughes, Terence McMahon (1812 to 1849) English writer. He pubd poetry and literary criticism; but what M (1854) read was his *Revelations of Spain in 1845, by an English resident*, Vol. 1 (1845). MEW says that H. lived in Spain for many years. He next brought out *Revelations of Portugal* (1847) and *Portuguese perfidy exposed* (1848). H. must have lived in Paris too, for he had pubd a guide to the city (1839). → 54:55.

Hugo, Victor (Marie) (1802 to 1885) French writer: eminent as poet, novelist, dramatist; a leader of the Romantic movement in Europe. Best-known novels: *Les misérables* (1862); *Notre Dame de Paris* (1831). —A republican in politics, H. was elected to the Constituent Assembly (1848–1851). After brief support to Bonaparte, he went into opposition; was exiled; emigrated to Brussels, then Jersey, finally (1855+) Guernsey; refused Bonaparte's amnesty, and returned to Paris in triumph after his downfall (1870). H. made the greatest impression on the left with his steadfast opposition to "Napoléon le Petit." Besides, in 1871, after being elected to the National Assembly, he resigned on the outbreak of the Paris Commune, and moved to Brussels and Luxemburg. In Brussels he publicly welcomed communard exiles. → 54:43.

Hull English Yorkshire seaport. → 56:25; 61:20.

Humboldt Publishing Co. (NY) → 91:32.

Hume, David (1711 to 1776) Scottish philosopher and historian; a founder of philosophical skepticism, one of the basic alternatives to materialism. —Trained as a lawyer, he lived in France for a period (1734–1737), during which he wrote his chief work, *Treatise on human nature* (1739), which M (1841) read in German. He later saw service on the staff of the British embassy in Paris (1765) and as undersecy of state (1767–1768). During his lifetime his *History of England* (1754+) was extremely popular. —Although H. is most important as a philosopher—primarily for the *Treatise* and his *Enquiry concerning human understanding*—his writings on economic and sociopolitical questions were not inconsiderable, incl *Essays moral and political* (1741–1742); *Political discourses* (1752); *Essays and treatises on several subjects* (1750–1753), the last two read by M in 1851. —For E on Hume (treated together with Kant), see #E457, ch. 2. → 41:4; 51:62, 68. #M79.

Hume, Joseph (1777 to 1855) English Radical politician; i.e., left liberal. Physician by profession; in medical service in India (1797–1807). MP (1812–1855, with gaps). A former Chartist, H. became "the classical repr of the so-called 'independent' opposition, which Cobbett aptly and exhaustively described as the 'safety valve' of the old system" (M in his obit sketch). #M382.

Hume, Robert (William) American socialist. A leading member of the National Labor Union, he was also a member of the IWMA; acted as its correspondent with the GC (1870). An advocate of women's rights, he collaborated with Victoria Woodhull for a while until he found out (1875) that she was shedding her radical phase. → 70:3, 24, 51.

Humpty Dumpty Nursery rhyme. → 93:53.

Hungarian émigrés → 50:7, 19; 51:15; 52:7, 12, 31, 41; 58:28; 59:58; 62:25.

Hungary In M's day, a part of the Hapsburg Empire; its dominant ethnic component was the Magyar people. → 48:75; 49:5, 9, 26; 51:20; 52:2, 9, 30; 53:48; 54:3, 30; 64:8; 71:48; 76:12, 14; 90:48, 51; 94:25. #M25; E199, E306, E309, E363–E366, E411, E426, E427, E459–E464, E488, E495, E516, E748, E786, E844, E845, E855, E903–E906, E922. See *also* *Austria-Hungary.

Hutten, Ulrich von (1488 to 1523) German partisan of the Reformation; a noble of the free imperial knights; the most important spokesman of this class's grievances against the papacy and its support of Luther, not, however, as a theologian but as a humanist and nationalist; both a soldier and a writer-intellectual. He joined *Sickingen in the struggle against the princes. —His fame as a satiric poet was launched by his participation in the *Epistolae obscurorum virorum* (1515); crowned poet laureate (1517) by Emperor Maximilian I; also pubd satires against the papacy, and engaged in a noted polemic with Erasmus. → 92:21.

Huxley, Thomas Henry (1825 to 1895) English biologist; great popularizer of evolutionary theory. Orig a navy medico; lecturer, naturalist to the Geological Survey, prof at the Royal College of Surgeons (1863–1869); Royal Society secy (1871–1880), pres (1881–1885). —Converted by Darwin's 1859 book, H. gave up his own research for an influential career as the premier scientific publicist for the theory of evolution and as an agnostic champion of the scientific spirit against religious dogmatism. Among his books: *Zoological evidences as to man's place in nature* (1863)—which E read on publ; *Evolution and ethics* (1893); *Science and culture* (1881). → 63:17; 66:9.

Hyde Park In west-central London; the Marble Arch area is the famous free-speech enclave. → 55:25, 33; 69:61; 72:61, 67. #M44; E450, E451.

Hyndman, Henry Mayers (1842 to 1921) English socialist; founder of the first Marxist organization in Britain. Of a wealthy family, hence his own "angel"; orig a lawyer; converted by *Capital* (French edn) in 1880. He founded the not-yet-socialist Democratic Federation (1881), which became the Social Democratic Federation (1884). His first propaganda book was *England for all* (1881); also pubd *The historical basis of socialism* (1883); *The economics of socialism* (1896); *The awakening of Asia* (1919); *The evolution of revolution* (1920); and autobiographical volumes. —The immediate reason for his quick falling-out with M was his suppression of M's name and contribution in his first (1881) book; but the continuing and basic reason was the Hyndman–SDF type of combination of sectist and sectarian rigidity (incl hostility to trade-unionism) with political opportunism and reformism—a combination seen also among his American cousins of the SLP. Added to this was H.'s deep-going John Bull chauvinism and pro-imperialism, plus his pattern of manipulative demagogy and inner-organizational dictatorship. It should be noted that while H. struck the pose of a disciple with respect to M, his attitude toward E was one of rather slanderous abusiveness. —Hyndman's overt political collapse came after E's time: in 1911 the SDF became the British Socialist party, still under H.; but in 1916 the prowar Hyndman wing had to split from the BSP and form a new organization, the National Socialist party, which got nowhere. —That British Marxism was nursed in the cradle by a Hyndman was one of the historical disasters that Marxism suffered. It has been well said that H. was in the tradition of the Tory Radical (the Oastler type), interested in re-forming an effective ruling oligarchy, and willing to take from M what was needed to beat the backside of the bourgeoisie, provided that all Krauts and Heinies knew their places like wogs, fuzzies, etc. → *80*:2, 24, 36, 47; *81*:4, 35, 38, 60; *82*:22, 41; *83*:33; *84*:1, 6, 46, 55, 59; *85*:11, 37, 44; *86*:7, 13, 46; *87*:1; *89*:7, 12, 17; *91*:11; *93*:13. #E360, E387, E388. *See also* H.'s *pseud.* John *Broadhouse.

I

Ibsen, Henrik (1828 to 1906) Norwegian dramatist and poet, renowned for plays with sociopsychological themes, esp women's rights; also, defiance to society by the lone strong individual. —Director and dramatist at Ole Bull's National Theater, Bergen (1851–1857); director of the Norwegian Theater, Oslo. Political disaffection led him to live abroad (esp Italy and Germany) from 1863–1864 to 1981. —Major plays: *Pillars of society* (1877); *Doll's house* (1879); *Ghosts* (1881); *An enemy of the people* (1882); *The wild duck* (1884); *Hedda Gabler* (1890); *The master builder* (1892). Dramatic poems: *Brand* (1866); *Peer Gynt* (1867). Eleanor M. was the first English translator of some of his plays. →*90*:27.

L'Idée Nouvelle Paris, Jan 5, 1890, to 1892. Monthly. —Socialist journal on societal and literary affairs; Guesde, Paul Lafargue, and Vaillant were among the contributors. #E284.

Iglesias, Pablo; *full* **Iglesias Posse** (1850 to 1925) Spanish socialist. Printshop worker by trade, he was under age 20 when he joined the IWMA, soon becoming the corr secy of the Madrid Federal Council (1871–1872). Editor of *La Emancipación* (1871–1873); leader in the fight against Bakuninism. Often jailed for TU and political activity, he was instrumental in founding the Unión General de Trabajadores as well as of the SP (becoming its president) and launching its organ, *El Socialista*; first socialist deputy in the Cortes (1910+); later a leader of the reformist wing; not a writer or theoretician →*93*:21, 24; *94*:4, 14, 29, 31, 39; *95*:16. #E841.

Illustrirte Zeitung (with varying subtitles) Leipzig, July 1843 to Sep 1944. Weekly. —Moderate-liberal, in mid-19th century. → *68*:8.

Im neuen Reich Leipzig, 1871 to 1881. Weekly. —On "politics, science, art." → *73*:57.

Imandt, Peter (b. c.1824) German communist. Before the 1848 revolution he was a teacher in Krefeld (Rhineland), active in the local WA (along with his brother Kaspar, who died in 1849). Peter took part in the revolution in Cologne and Trier; in 1849 he was in Trier, which he represented at the Rhenish congress of Democrats. By this time he was a member of CL, a supporter of M. He took part in the Baden uprising of 1849, a leader in the storming of the Prüm arsenal, for which he was sentenced to death in absentia. Afterward he emigrated to Switzerland, then to England; settled in Dundee (Scot.) to earn a living as a language teacher. In the 1860s he was a member of IWMA; in correspondence with M till 1875. → *48*:55, 65; *52*:31; *55*:34; *56*:20; *57*:37, 48; *58*:13; *59*:12, 14, 34, 46; *60*:8, 12; *61*:49, 57; *62*:44; *70*:12; *72*:54; *75*:35, 48.

Imbert, Jacques (1793 to 1851) French republican-socialistic journalist. He took part in the 1830 revolution in Paris. In his native Marseilles, he launched the organ *Le Peuple Souverain* (1832–1833); in the aftermath of the Lyons uprising he fled to Belgium. In Brussels (1835–1838, 1844–1848, with an interlude of return to Paris) he collaborated with M&E as vice-pres of the Demo Assoc; wrote for *L'Atelier Démocratique* (1846–1847). In 1848 he returned to Paris; for a time, held an administrative post; in 1849 he was arrested in Avignon, and died of disease in a Lyons prison. → *47*:44.

Immermann, Karl (Leberecht) (1796 to 1840) German writer: novelist, poet, dramatist, critic, theater director. After studying law, he began as a Prussian district judge in Düsseldorf; then theater director there (1835–1837). His many plays were mostly historical tragedies (*Merlin*, 1831; *Trauerspiel in Tirol*, 1827 etc.); he wrote poetic satire (e.g., *Tulifäntchen*, 1830); his novels were his most popular productions (e.g., *Die Epigonen*, 1836; *Münchhausen*, 1838–1839) → *40*:18; *41*:10. #E368, E550.

Imola (It.) Town near Bologna. → *72*:35; *94*:36.

Independent Labour Party (Brit.) The first socialist organization in Britain not organized as a sect, whether a rightist one like the Fabians or a leftist one like the SDF. It was established (Jan 1893) at a conference in Bradford, esp through the efforts of Keir *Hardie. It was instrumental in creating the Labour party, and became an affiliated organization. —Eleanor M attended the Bradford conference as a sympathetic visitor; Aveling was a delegate, elected to the Exec. The *Workman's Times* for Mar 25, 1893, reported a Paris Commune anniversary meeting at which E praised the ILP as follows: "Engels spoke, reviewing the progress of socialism since the Commune. He recalled that in 1871 the London Conference of the International adopted a resolution for an independent labour party 'distinct and separate from all other political parties.' But nothing happened till 1888, when the New Unionism sprang up—'and from that sprang up the movement which ultimately developed in the formation of the Independent Labour Party at Bradford in January of this year. This new party was the very party which the old members of the International desired to see formed, and he urged all Socialists to join it, believing that, if wisely led, it would eventually absorb every other Socialist organisation." This indicates that E actually joined the ILP; but he did not subseqly believe that it was "wisely led," esp by Hardie, being much too reformist in its operation, even though it was the type of organization he favored as against the sects. → 92:44; 93:2, 9, 13; 94:31, 44; 95:4, 18, 27, 36. #E823, E841.

India, i.e., British India, incl areas now independent, and Indian affairs → 53:1, 18, 22, 23, 26, 30, 51, 53–55; 57:1, 25, 29, 34, 39, 42, 47, 51; 58:5, 6, 11, 19, 23, 27, 32, 42; 59:26; 62:29; 79:5, 42; 80:1, 36, 38; 81:4, 10; 82:20. #M8, M12, M53, M100, M113, M115, M294, M340, M357, M369, M399–M403, M421, M483, M536, M554, M557, M567, M579, M638, M660, M766–M772, M798, M846, M876, M954, M984, M990; E100, E376, E697, E698, E709. *See also* Asia, Bengal, Burma, Mogul Empire.

India Reform Association → 53:54.
Indians (American) → 39:3.
Indies *See* India.
Industrial Exhibition (London, 1862) The second great world's fair held in England, following the International Exhibition of 1851. → 62:23, 34, 42.

Ingram, John Kells (1823 to 1907) British (Irish-born) man of letters, scholar, and economist. Prof of oratory, of Greek, librarian, vice-provost (successively) at Trinity College, Dublin (1852–1899); pubd writings on a remarkable variety of subjects, esp economics and sociology, from the Comtist-Postivist viewpoint. Author of: *Present position and prospects of polit eco* (1878), his address to the British Assoc in that year—annotated by M the same year; and *History of polit eco* (1888), a book reprint of his article in the 9th edn, *Encyclopaedia Britannica* of 1885, the first comprehensive history in English. → 78:47.

Inkerman (Russ.) Village in the Crimea; scene of a Russian defeat in 1854. #E67.

Institute of Marxism-Leninism *See* the *Register*, Appendix IV. #ME66, ME92.

L'International London, Jan 30, 1863, to Nov 15, 1871. Daily. —French-language paper, unofficially the spokesman of the Bonaparte government. → 71:41. #M898.

International Alliance of the Socialist Democracy *See* Alliance of the Socialist Democracy.

International Congress of Economists (Brussels, 1847) → 47:32. #M705.

International Congress of Socialist Students (Geneva, 1893) → 93:55; 94:12, 16 #E856.

International Courier London, Nov. 1864 to July 1867. Weekly. —Its French edn was *Le Courrier International*, which issued more numbers than the English in 1867, when both were organs of the IWMA. #M406, M787.

International Democratic Association → 71:28.

International Exhibition (Eng.) → 65:32.

The **International Herald** London, Mar 2, 1872, to Oct 18, 1873. Weekly. Pub'r/editor: William Riley. Ed by J. Mitchell, T. Mottershead, J. De Morgan, J. G. Eccarius, et al. —Subtitled "Official organ of the British section of the IWMA" (May 11 to Nov 30, 1872); after the split in the British Federal Council (Nov-Dec 1872) it remained with the GC; from June 1873, as a result of Riley's break with the movement, M&E ceased collaboration. → 72:8, 33, 65–67; 73:6, 7, 14, 24; #ME132, ME177; M110, M537, M745, M755, M857; E675, E679.

International Review of Social History Leiden, 1956+. Pubd by the International Institute for Social History, Amsterdam. — Note that previously (1936+), this organ of the Amsterdam institute had been titled *International Review for Social History*. #ME66; M170Z, M836.5.

International socialist congresses 1889: Int'l Working Men's Congress. #E387, E388. —1891: Int'l Workers Congress. #E386. — 1983: Int'l Socialist Workers Congress. #E166. *See* *IWMA *for that organization's congresses*.

International Socialist Workers Congress (Zurich, 1893) #E166.

International Society of Revolutionary Communists *See* Société Universelle des Communistes Révolutionnaires.

International Working Men's Association (the "First International"). Although it had been preceded by more short-lived or smaller-scale efforts toward international organization, this is generally considered the first substantial int'l organization of the working-class movement. Established at a meeting (Sep 28, 1864) in St. Martin's Hall, London, sponsored by a combination of English trade-unionists and visiting French workers' reprs, mainly Proudhonists. M, invited to attend but by choice silent on the platform, was elected to the first Gen Council, and soon established his intellectual sway over the Council members. He had no post other than being one of the several corr secys (in his case, for Germany, sometimes for another country). E became a GC member only after moving to London (Sep 1870). —It is important to note that the IWMA was not established as a socialist organization, but as an assembly of workers' organizations regardless of program; and it adopted mildly socialistic positions (as on the collectivization of land) only in the course of its existence, as it became possible to do so without crises. —List of congresses and conferences: London Conference, Sep 25–29, 1865; Geneva Congress, Sep 3–8,1866; Lausanne Congress, Sep 2–8, 1867; Brussels Congress, Sep 6–13,1868; Basel Congress, Sep 6–11,1869; London Conference, Sep 17–23, 1871; Hague Congress, Sep 2–8, 1872. At the Hague Congress, on M&E's proposal, the seat of the GC was transferred to NY. The NY GC, under Sorge's secyship, called a congress for Geneva, Sep 1873, which was a "fiasco" (as M said); the organization was formally dissolved at a Philadelphia conference July 1876. The Bakuninist rump-International held a series of its own congresses—Geneva (1873), Brussels (1874), Bern (1876), Verviers (1877)—and gradually disintegrated. Subseq international congresses are properly part of the history of the Second International. —Name: The organization at first sometimes used the name Workingmen's Int'l Assoc, but this soon disappeared. Its name was sometimes written as Int'l Workingmen's Assoc, abbreviated IWA; in French, Association Internationale des Travailleurs (AIT), rarely "des Ouvriers"; in German, Internationale Arbeiterassoziation. —*See also* British Federation (of the IWMA). → 64:1, 2, 26, 30, 31, 35, 36, 40, 44–46; 65:1, 2, 5–10, 12, 13, 15, 19, 20, 22, 24, 25, 27, 29, 30, 32–34, 37, 38, 41, 43–47, 50, 51, 53, 56, 62, 63; 66:1, 5–7, 17, 21–23, 26, 31, 32, 36, 43, 44, 46, 47, 50, 53; 67:1, 4, 7, 16, 19, 22, 28, 32, 35, 40, 41, 45, 46; 68:1, 4, 7, 12, 14, 18, 21, 26, 31, 32, 37–39, 42, 43, 47–49, 54, 55, 61, 62, 68, 69; 69:1, 4, 5, 10–12, 17, 18, 23, 25, 26, 30, 31, 35, 36, 40, 41, 47, 48, 53–55, 60, 65, 70; 70:1, 3, 4, 9, 10, 17–19, 24, 25, 31, 36, 39, 40, 44, 45, 49–52, 55, 59, 60, 62; 71:1–3, 5, 9, 10, 14–17, 20, 21, 23, 24, 28–30, 33–37, 39–41, 46–49, 51–53, 55–59, 62–64; 72:1, 3, 4, 8–10, 13–16, 20, 21, 24–27, 30, 31, 35–37, 39, 41–43, 48–53, 55, 56, 60, 65–68; 73:1, 6, 7, 9, 11, 14, 17, 23, 27, 33, 36, 39, 43, 51; 74:4, 23, 28, 33; 75:7, 21–25, 27, 28, 35; 76:21; 78:25; 82:10; 83:24, 27; 87:4; 91:37; 92:60, 68; 93:11, 27; 94:1, 2, 45; 95:21, 31 #ME5–ME7, ME48, ME56, ME173; M5, M30, M110, M143, M173, M175–177, M222, M224, M251.5, M306, M313, M318, M325, M343, M344, M345, M346, M347, M348, M397, M406, M412, M416, M467, M478, M520, M521, M537, M566.5, M590, M598, M599, M604, M610, M614, M616, M665, M696, M707, M744, M745, M747, M751, M752, M752.5, M753, M754, M756, M786, M787, M813, M829, M834, M856–59, M915, M931; E179, E190, E307, E324, E380–382, E445, E451, E465, E475, E480, E545, E555, E564, E567, E596, E664, E671, E672, E673, E675, E678, E679, E722, E749, E775–777, E789, E790, E809, E810, E813, E817, E819, E821, E826, E829, E846, E847, E850, E851, E863, E864–866. —New York GC: → 73:1, 6, 7, 11, 17, 23, 33, 36, 43; 74:28, 33; 75:25, 28. —The Hague Congress (in the M-E *Register* only): #ME6, ME7, ME96, ME132; M306, M346, M347, M348, M518, M745, M835; E369, E381, E449, E451, E555, E672, E679, E789 —London Conference of 1871 (in the M–E *Register* only): #ME56, ME119, ME120, ME133; M347, M596, M754; E565.

International Workers Congress (1891) #386.

International Working Men's Congress (1889) #E387, E388.

Die Internationale Berlin, Apr 1915; 1919 to 1932. —Founded by Mehring and Luxemburg in 1919, it was revived later as a German CP weekly. #E588.

L'Internationale Brussels, Jan 17, 1869, to Dec 28, 1873. Weekly. Ed by D. Brismée, R. Splingard, E. Steens (Sep 1870+). —Organ of the Belgian IWMA, as such successor to *La Tribune du Peuple*. After the Hague Congress (1872), it was taken over by the Bakuninists and merged into *Le Mirabeau* (Jan 1874). → 70:11, 18, 62; 71:33; 73:57; #M75, M143, M287, M587, M745, M747, M752.5, M896; E678, E864.

Internationale Revue Vienna, 1866 to Mar 1868. Monthly. —Liberal. → 66:9, 16.

L'Intransigeant Paris, July 14, 1880, to 1948. Daily. Founder/pub'r: Henri Rochefort (till 1910). —Radical-republican agitational organ in the 1880s–1890s, with a large circulation; pro-Boulangist in that affair. → 88:11.

Invalides, Hôtel des; or Les Invalides (Paris) Orig a veterans' hospital, later a military museum; behind it a church and a notable dome, under which are famous tombs, esp Napoleon's. #E370.

Ionian Islands Greek islands in the Ionian Sea, incl Corfu, Ithaca. → 59:11. #M724.

Iran *See* Persia.

Ireland and the Irish → 53:30; 54:28; 55:13; 56:20, 22; 59:11; 67:2, 18, 41, 46; 68:3, 6, 31; 69:1, 43, 58, 60, 61, 65, 70, 75; 70:1, 3, 8, 11, 20, 26, 35, 41; 71:16, 47, 51; 72:14, 20, 24, 55, 61; 77:9; 80:39, 42; 81:4, 9, 15, 21, 61; 82:22; 83:19; 91:49; 92:64. #M86, M304, M314, M391, M402, M422, M577, M610, M625, M743, M834;

E140, E148, E151, E275, E352, E353, E450, E528, E664. —Irish movement: → 48:5. — Irish home-rule movement: → 69:70. See also Fenians.

The **Irish World** NY, 1870+. Weekly. — Nationalist organ. → 81:17.

The **Irishman** Belfast, then Dublin, 1858 to 1885. Weekly. —Nationalist organ; pro-Fenian. → 70:20.

Ironside, Isaac (1808 to 1870) English radical journalist and publicist, active in Sheffield. Having prospered with his father's accountancy and estate agency business, first as partner (1833), then owner (1840s), he was able to devote much time to agitation for his left-liberal views, esp for parliamentary reform and universal suffrage; also to building the Sheffield Mechanics' Institute and Sheffield Political Union. He came out for Chartism (1838); for Owenism (1839), and helped Owen build a local Hall of Science; but he began drawing away from both movements in the 1840s. Then, influenced by the ideas of Joshua Toulmin Smith (who pubd Local self government and centralization in 1851), he took his Sheffield followers into experiments with "direct legislation" on a local scale, which failed. Breaking with Smith in the 1850s, he became a follower of David *Urquhart. Having gained financial control of the Sheffield Free Press (1855), he made it an organ of Urquhartite views in foreign policy, implemented by the Sheffield Foreign Affairs Comm. —Ironside was an agitator, not a writer; he did, however, turn out two pamphlets on Urquhartite policy (1856, 1866), also Trades' unions: An address (1867). — See the article on I.I. in Dictionary of Labour Biography, which, however, is mistaken in describing his political views as anarchist → 56:23, 26.

Irwin, Henry Crossley English writer; a member of the Bengal civil service. His book The garden of India (1880) dealt with Oudh. He also pubd poetry. → 80:51.

Isaiah; Ger. Jesaias (eighth century B.C.)

Bible figure, in the book of that name; major Hebrew prophet, outstanding for his denunciation of the corruption of society. → 39:7.

Isayev, Andrei Alexeyevich (1851 to 1924) Russian Narodnik economist, statistician, sociologist. Lecturer at St. Petersburg U. (1879–1893); prof in Yaroslavl (1884+); did statistical work for the Moscow government (1875+). Sympathetic to socialist reform ideas, advocate of cooperativism, he wrote over 20 books on econ and sociological subjects, plus articles. For M's reading of his work in 1882, prob the most likely candidate is his Arteli v Rossii (1881), or his statistical publ on Moscow in 1876–1877. → 82:55.

Iserlohn (Ger.) City in N. Rhine-Westphalia, near Dortmund. → 49:24; 53:45; 56:6.

Islam Religion of the Muslims, Mohammed its prophet. → 53:10.

Isle of Wight See Wight.

Italian language → 41:2; 83:36.

Italy and Italian affairs Selected references —E's travels in and visits to: → 41:11–13; 49:38; 65:49; 82:14. —M&E's writings on: → 48:43, 59, 73; 49:10, 15, 17; 55:19; 59:11; 77:10; 93:4, 12, 55; 94:4, 12. — Trans of M&E: → 72:45, 58; 73:20; 77:32; 79:6; 83:29, 31; 84:52; 85:15, 19; 86:15, 24; 91:3, 19, 42; 92:5, 11, 49; 93:4, 12, 19, 31; 94:36; 95:7, 24, 32, 34. —Studies on: → 52:2. —The Italian War of 1859: → 59:4, 14, 17, 22, 31, 34, 36, 38, 41, 50, 58, 66; 60:18, 46. —In IWMA affairs: → 66:31; 71:1, 39, 47, 48, 51, 52, 56, 57, 64; 72:3, 10, 13, 15, 20, 21, 24, 27, 35, 41, 42, 60, 65; 73:6, 27, 33. — The left movement in: → 61:30; 64:35, 40; 74:28; 91:3, 42; 92:1, 17, 24, 40; 93:44; 94:1, 4, 12, 31, 32, 36, 41; 95:34. —Italian émigrés: → 66:18. Italian bookkeeping: → 62:30. —Italian liberation: → 48:11, 35, 52; 49:9; 54:26; 59:22; 60:18; 61:41. See also *Rome and other cities. See *Bovio, *Garibaldi, *Labriola, *Martignetti, *Mazzini, *Turati, for many references to Italy.

Ixelles, Faubourg d' (Brussels) See Faubourg d' Ixelles.

J

Jacini, Count Stefano (1827 to 1891) Italian economist and administrator. A moderate liberal, he was public works min (1860s); elected deputy (1860–1870). Created count (1880), he headed an important inquiry into agricultural conditions (1881–1886). During the 1850s (the Austrian restoration in Lombardy), he devoted himself to studies. M (1878) studied his La proprietà fondiaria e le popolazione agricole in Lombardia (1847 edn; 1st edn, 1854). → 78:49.

Jaclard, Victor; full Charles Victor (1840 to

1903) French Blanquist; Communard. Math teacher and M.D. by profession. He came to Paris (1864) as a medical student, and joined the Blanquist group; took part in the Int'l Student Congress in Liège (1865); expelled from school; jailed (1866). He began moving away from Blanquism (1869); with the fall of the empire (Sep 1870), in Paris, he was elected a commander in a NG battalion; supported the Commune (1871), fought in Bloody Week, escaped after capture—to Switzerland, where he worked for the IWMA. In 1874 he went to

Russia with his Russian wife (see A. V. *Korvin-Krukovskaya) till after the 1880 amnesty. After collaboration with Clemenceau and involvement in municipal politics (1880s), he was a delegate to the Int'l Socialist Congress in Brussels (1891) and secy of the union of socialist journalists (1890s); active in co-op work. → 72:58; 77:46; 81:43.

Jacob, William (c.1762 to 1851) English traveler, writer on economic matters, merchant in the S. America trade. MP (1808–1812); comptroller of corn returns to the Bd of Trade (1822–1842). Besides articles on agriculture and economics in the *Encyclopaedia Britannica* (7th edn) and reports on the condition of agriculture in northern Europe, he pubd a highly regarded *Historical inquiry into the production and consumption of the precious metals* (1831). M (1850–1851) excerpted this work, also his *Considerations on the protection required by British agriculture* (1814) and *A letter to Samuel Whitbread* (1815). → 50:50, 51; 51:61.

Jacobi, Abraham (1830 to 1919) German physician, later a leader of the medical profession in the U.S. —Born of a poor Jewish family in Westphalia, active in the student movement at Bonn, he joined the CL as a young doctor; became a defendant in the Cologne communist trial of 1852, was acquitted, but jailed for lèse majesté. He emigrated (1853) to England, then to the U.S., where he propagated socialist ideas in the press till the mid-1850s, after which he ceased political activity. Becoming a pediatrics specialist in NY, he entered on a long, distinguished career for which any encyclopedia may be consulted; he was also an early advocate of birth control. → 53:29, 43; 64:17.

Jacobins In the French Revolution, members and followers of the Jacobin Club, esp followers of Robespierre. → 89:9. See also Montagnards.

Jacoby, Joel; *full* Franz Karl Joel (1810 to 1863) German publicist and poet. A convert to Catholicism, anti-Hegelian, he was considered an advocate of religious intolerance— e.g., by E, discussing his book *Kampf und Sieg* (1840). In 1837 he pubd poems and *Religiöse Rhapsodien.* #E400.

Jacoby, Johann (1805 to 1877) German liberal politician, eventually a Social-Democrat. Son of a German-Jewish merchant, J. became a physician in Königsberg, and practiced medicine throughout his political career. He gained a reputation (1830+) as a liberal in politics, with militant demands for a Prussian constitution, etc.; tried for lèse majesté, acquitted. His 1841 *Vier Fragen* made his name widely known as a Democratic oppositionist; likewise his *Preussen im Jahre 1845,* etc. In 1848 he was a leader of the left wing in the Prussian National Assem-

bly; in 1849, ditto in the Prussian Second Chamber and Frankfurt National Assembly. After the revolution he returned to medicine, but continued to fight for constitutional democracy; he became alienated from the Progressivist party by coupling social reform with political reform, in ever more socialistic speeches. In 1870 he came out against annexing Alsace-Lorraine; and as German liberalism turned to Bismarck, J. turned to the socialists; he publicly came out for the S-D party in 1872, after Bebel and Liebknecht's condemnation in the Leipzig treason trial; elected as a S-D deputy (1874). → 71:11, 14. #E206.

Jaeger (or **Jäger**), Eugen (1842 to 1926) German social historian. As a result of his 1873 researches, he produced the book *Der moderne Sozialismus; Karl M, die Internationale Arbeiter-Association, Lassalle und die deutschen Socialistes* [sic] (1873). He later also pubd *Geschichte der socialen Bewegung und des Socialismus in Frankreich* (1876–1890), *Die Agrarfrage der Gegenwart* (1882–1893), et al. → 73:47.

Jahrbuch für Sozialwissenschaft und Sozialpolitik Zurich, 1879 to 1881. Pub'r: Ludwig Richter (pseud. of K. Höchberg). — Höchberg's reform-socialist views were expounded here. → 79:38, 41.

Das **Jahrhundert** Hamburg, 1856 to 1859. Weekly. —Liberal-reform magazine of politics and literature. → 57:9.

James, William (d. 1827) English naval historian. Author of the standard work, *Naval history of Gr Brit* (1822–1824), a compendium of facts with little analysis. James began his career (1801) as a proctor in the Jamaica admiralty court. → 56:41.

Janus NY, 1851 to 1852. Pub'r: K. Heinzen. —German-language paper, organ of German-American liberal-reform circles. → 52:7.

Japan See Sino-Japanese War.

Jarrold, Thomas (1770 to 1853) English physician; in practice mainly in Manchester, where he was an ornament of the Manchester Literary and Philosophical Society. His notable publ was *Dissertations on man . . . in answer to Mr. Malthus's essay* (1806), excerpted by M (1845), who may also have read his *Letter to Samuel Whitbread . . . on the Poor's Laws* (1807). → 45:51.

Jaurès, Jean (Léon) (1859 to 1914) French socialist; leader of the reformist wing of the pre-1914 movement. Orig a prof of philosophy; elected from the Tarn to the Chamber of Deputies as a moderate republican (1885–1889). After joining the Socialists, he went back to the Chamber (1893–1898, 1902–1914), soon parliamentary leader of the SP. Founder/editor of *L'Humanité* (1904+); esp active as pacifist antimilitarist. Still important are his *Histoire socialiste de la Révolution française* (1901–1909) and *L'armée nouvelle* (1911). He was assassinated by "patriots" on the eve of World War I. → 94:14, 18, 25.

Java Island in what used to be called the E. Indies, now part of Indonesia; controlled by the Dutch from the early 17th century, briefly by the British (1811–1815/1816), then again by the Dutch till World War II. → 81:45, 64; 84:14.

Jena (Ger) City in Thuringia. → 91:29

Jena, University of → 41:9. #M235, M475.

Jersey, Isle of (Eng.) Largest of the Channel Islands. → 57:32, 45; 74:30, 34; 79:31; 85:31.

Jesus of Nazareth or **Jesus Christ** → 64:5. #M956; E728.

Jevons, William Stanley (1835 to 1882) English economist; a pioneer of marginal-utility theory. Son of an iron merchant; an assayer at the Australian mint; prof of polit eco at Manchester (1866–1879), at Univ. College, London (1876–1880). His theory based on utility first appeared in an 1862 paper, then fully in his *Theory of polit eco* (1871)—about the same time as in Karl Menger and Léon Walras—and was to influence the Fabians via P. H. Wicksteed. Other works: *The state in relation to labour* (1882); *Methods of social reform.* → 92:35, 47.

Jewish question; Jews; Judaism → 42:22; 43:21, 22; 44:6; 90:22; 91:44; 93:11. #M609; E919. *See also* Yiddish language.

Jhering (or **Ihering**), Rudolf von (1818 to 1892) German legal scholar, historian of law; a founder of the later, modern "historical school," and one of the most influential and encyclopedic authorities on Roman law. Prof at a number of universities, lastly Göttingen (1872+). His chief works were *Geist des römischen Rechts* (read by M in the 1871–1877 edn; first pubd, 1852–1858); *Der Zweck im Recht* (1877–1883); *Der Kampf um's Recht* (1872); and many others. → 79:54.

Johann, Archduke of Austria; *full* Johann Baptist Joseph Fabian Sebastian; *Angl.* John (1782–1859) Younger son of Emperor Leopold II. Gen; commanded the Austrian army in Bavaria (1800) and Italy (1809); after 1815 retired to private life, till named imperial regent of Germany by the Frankfurt National Assembly (June 1848 to Dec 1849). #ME109.

Johannard, Jules (Paul) (1843 to 1892) French Blanquist. By occupation, an artificial-flower salesman. He went to London as a refugee (1867); active in the IWMA; member of the GC (1868–1869); corr secy for Italy (1868, 1869). He returned to France after the 1869 amnesty; founded (1870) an IWMA section in Saint-Denis; member of the Paris Federal Council; arrested (Apr) and involved in the third trial of IWMA leaders. On the fall of Bonaparte, he was active in the revolutionary events of 1870–1871; elected to the Commune, where he served on the External Relations and War Commsns. Afterward he emigrated to London; again on the GC (1871–1872) and delegate to the Hague Congress (1872), where he generally supported the GC. In 1879 he was still involved in the socialist movement, but there is no further record; he became a salesman for a Manchester firm until his death; and did not return to France after the 1880 amnesty. → 71:52.

John Swinton's Paper NY, Oct 14, 1883, to Aug 21, 1887. Weekly. Founder/editor: John Swinton. —Socialistic journal → 85:41. See *Swinton.

Johnson, Andrew (1808 to 1875) 17th pres of the U.S., succeeding on the death of Lincoln → 65:32; 67:29. #M5.

Johnson, Reverdy (1796 to 1876) American lawyer and politician; ambassador to London in 1868–1869. One of the country's best-known constitutional lawyers, J. was first a Whig, then (1856+) a conservative Democrat; sympathetic to the South but opposed to secession; opposed to stringent Reconstruction measures. U.S. senator (1845–1849); attorney-gen (1849–1850); senator (1863–1868). He was recalled from the London embassy because, after he had negotiated the *Alabama* claims, the Senate scuttled the treaty. → 68:68.

Johnston, James Finlay Weir (1796 to 1855) Scottish agricultural chemist. Prof at Durham (1833–1855); chemist to the Agricultural Society of Scotland (1843+); his specialty was applying recent scientific discoveries to agriculture and manufactures. His most popular book was *Catechism of agricultural chemistry and geology* (1844). M's notebooks excerpted his *Lectures on agricultural chemistry and geology* (1847; orig, 1841–1844), and *Notes on N. America, agricultural, economical, and social* (1851). → 51:68, 69, 71; 69:68; 78:18.

Jomini, Baron Henri; *full* Antoine Henri (1779 to 1869) Swiss-born gen in the French army, also in Swiss and Russian service; writer on military arts and history. Orig a bank clerk, he rose in the Swiss army to command a battalion, and organized the militia. In the French army (1804+), aide-de-camp to Marshal Ney; created baron after the Peace of Tilsit. In Russia, aide-de-camp to the czar and (1837) military instructor to the czarevich (later Alexander II). When these three loyalties conflicted, he skated around on thin ice. Major works: *Traité des grandes opérations militaires* (1804–1805); *Histoire critique et militaire des campagnes de la Révolution* (1806); *Vie politique et militaire de Napoléon*

(1827); Précis de l'art de la guerre (1836). → 52:2; 57:31.

Jonas, Alexander (d. 1912) German-American socialist; born in Berlin, active in the U.S., a leader of the early Socialist Labor party. Orig a bookdealer and journalist, by the 1870s he was already prominent in the American socialist movement as a speaker and Marxist analyst; associated with the *New Yorker Volkszeitung* (1878+), one of its two editors (1880s). In 1888 he ran for NYC mayor on the socialist ticket; low vote. → 87:22.

Jones, Ernest (Charles) (1819 to 1869) English left Chartist leader. His mother (and wife) from the landed gentry, father an army officer who had bought an estate in Holstein, J. was born in Berlin and educated in Germany; resettled in England (1838); called to the bar (1844). A disastrous venture lost him his fortune; he joined the Chartists (winter 1845), publicly espoused the movement (1846), became a Chartist leader (by early 1847), by then prob acquainted with M&E; prominent as an orator and journalist; jailed (1848) for two years. He then belonged to the prosocialist wing of Chartism. His journals *Notes to the People* (1851–1852) and the *People's Paper* (1852–1858) were organs of left Chartism-in-decline, edited in close assoc with M. They also carried J.'s poems and stories of working-class life. Near the close of this period (c.1857) he moved away from independent working-class politics and toward a middle-class alliance, leading to a break (1859) with M&E. Personal relations resumed by mid-1864; besides, Jones joined the IWMA. When J. died, E commented that "he was the only *educated* Englishman among the politicians who at bottom stood entirely on our side." —See the sketch in John Saville, *Ernest Jones, Chartist* (1952). → 47:50; 48:19; 50:48; 51:2, 9, 10, 19, 25, 28, 39; 52:3, 9, 12, 15, 17, 18, 20, 31, 35, 47, 54; 53:1, 7, 41; 54:1, 13, 15, 41, 43; 55:11, 13; 56:12, 16; 57:48, 53; 58:8, 40, 41; 59:14; 60:12; 61:12; 64:15; 65:6, 19, 25, 36, 50; 68:45, 64; 69:6, 10, 20. #M180, M566.5, M590.5; E139.

Jones, Richard (1790 to 1855) English political economist; clergyman. Prof at King's College, London (1833–1835); succeeded Malthus (1835) at E. India College, Haileybury; commissioner of tithes (1836–1851). His chief work was *Essay on the distribution of wealth and on the sources of taxation* (1831)—excerpted by M (1851), who also studied his *Introductory lecture on polit eco* (1833) and *Text book of lectures on the polit eco of nations* (1852). Other writings are in *Literary remains,* ed by Whewell (1859). A critic of Ricardo, Jones pubd no comprehensive exposition of his views; but M valued J.'s greater stress on historical method and the effect of social institutions. → 51:66; 59:77.

Joplin, Thomas (c.1790 to 1847) English economist and banking specialist. As early as 1822, in his *Essay on the general principles and present practices of banking in England and Scotland,* he explained the Scottish bank system and suggested a joint-stock bank; this attracted notice but was not then carried out. He was active in managing, directing, and establishing various banks in the next decade. He published *Outlines of a system of polit eco* (1823) and treatises on the Corn Laws and currency questions. → 51:61.

Joshua; *Ger.* Josua Israelite captain who led the invasion and seizure of Palestine (Book of Joshua, Old Testament). The sun stood still in Josh. 10:12–14. #E263.

Jottrand, Lucien (Léopold) (1804 to 1877) Belgian leftist democrat; lawyer by profession (Brussels, 1825+). A leader of the movement leading to the 1830 revolution, he sat in the National Assembly (1830–1831) and subseqly in the Chamber of Deputies; wrote for the liberal press; declared for republicanism (1834), and his *Courrier Belge* proposed semisocialistic reforms. In 1847–1848 he was pres of the Demo Assoc, with M as vice-pres. In May 1848 he greeted the establishment of the Cologne NRZ by M, even though (as M wrote in #M372) J. belonged to "the so-called American school of republicans, hence is of a tendency alien to me." → 47:39; 48:10, 34.

Jouffroy, C. G. Author of the work *Das Princip der Erblichkeit und die französische und englische Pairie* (1832), read by M (1843). However, this title has not been confirmed, nor the author further identified; the book may be a translation. → 43:32.

Journal de Bruxelles Brussels, 1820+. —Conservative-Catholic organ. → 47:52.

Journal des Economistes Paris, Dec 15, 1841, to 1940 (in six series). Monthly. — Liberal; pubd by the Société d'Economie Politique. → 45:50; 84:40.

Jovellanos (y Ramírez), Gaspar Melchor de (1744 to 1811) Spanish progressive politician, man of letters, writer on economics. To begin with, a lawyer and judge (Seville, Madrid); rose to be min of justice (1797–1798); then, after exile and jail, became (1808–1810) the leading Progressive in the Central Junta. As a writer, successor to the Encyclopedists and Enlighteners of the French 18th century; wrote plays and poems. As an economist, inclined to mercantilism; author of *Informe sobre un proyecto de ley agraria* (1787); *Informe ... en el expediente de la ley agraria* (1795). —M (1854) studied his writings in his *Obras,* nueva ed., t. 1–8 (1839–1840). → 54:55, 57.

Joynes, James Leigh (1853 to 1893) English socialist writer. Dismissed as a master at Eton after touring Ireland with Henry George, he went over to socialism; in 1882 he pubd *Adventures of a tourist in Ireland;* formed part of the group around Thomas Davidson (from which the Fabian Society emerged). In 1883 he joined the SDF. He was a founder and editor of *To-Day;* contributed to *Justice* and *Commonweal;* pubd socialist songs, *The Socialist catechism,* translations of Freiligrath et al.; also transd #M968 (1891); ill, in retirement, in his last years. → 84:6.

Jozewicz, Ferdinand German Social-Democrat. In 1871 and till mid-Mar 1872, he was corr secy of the Berlin section of the IWMA, also a member of the SDWP and the Arbeiterverein in Berlin, which supported the IWMA. → 71:56, 62, 64; 72:8, 9.

Juch, Ernst German journalist émigré, active in London. A liberal supporter of Kinkel, he was editor of the weekly *Hermann* (1859+); pub'r of the *Londoner Deutsche Post* (1869+); founder of the *Londoner Journal* (1878). → 59:72; 60:7, 12; 67:37; 69:71.

Judaism See Jewish question.

Jukes, Joseph Beete (1811 to 1869) English geologist. Surveyor in Canada, Britain, and Ireland; prof of geology in Dublin institutions. —M (1878) studied his popular textbook, *Students manual of geology* (1857), in an 1862 edn. Other books: *Excursions in and about Newfoundland* (1842); *School manual of geology* (1863). → 78:18, 22.

Julius, Gustav (1810 to 1851) German leftist publicist. Editor of the *Leipziger Allgemeine Ztg* (1842–1843); pub'r (1846–1849) of the daily *Berliner Zeitungs-Halle;* after the revolution he emigrated to London, where he was friendly with M. *New Mega* says his views were "True Socialist." He authored *Bankwesen* (1846), which M studied in 1851, and other writings on banking. → 48:57; 51:31, 71.

July Days (of 1830) #E332.

June Revolution, or "June Days" (of 1848) #M137, M425, M730; E219, E403, E410, E875, E876, E879.

Jung, Alexander; *full* Jakob Friedrich Alexander (1799 to 1884) German literary critic and publicist; sympathetic to Young Germany (attacked as wishy-washy by E). The review #E684 is on J.'s *Vorlesungen über die moderne Literatur der Deutschen* (1842), also mentioning J.'s *Briefe über die neueste Literatur* (1837) and *Königsberg in Preussen und die Extreme des dortigen Pietismus* (1840). Editor of the *Königsberger Literatur-Blatt* (1841–1845). → 42:18, 21. #E684.

Jung, Georg (Gottlob) (1814 to 1886) German publicist; lawyer by profession, in 1841 an assessor in the Cologne provincial court. A Young Hegelian left Democrat in this period, J.

was a founder and responsible *Gerant* of the Cologne *RZ* in 1842; friendly with M and Ruge. In 1848 he was a deputy to the Prussian Assembly, a leader of its left wing. He later (1866–1876) became a National Liberal, member of the Prussian chamber of deputies. — NUC (which lists him only as "Jung, Georg, of Berlin" for identification) contains only one work by him aside from 1848–1849 pamphlets, viz., his *Geschichte der Frauen* (1850), Part I (no more pubd) on women's suppression and emancipation up to the coming of Christianity; M annotated it in 1852. → 41:16; 42:22; 44:9, 19, 22, 26; 45:21, 44; 48:57; 49:27; 52:56, 58.

Jung, Hermann (1830 to 1901) Swiss watchmaker. After taking part in the 1848–1849 revolution in Germany, he emigrated to London. Soon after the IWMA's founding he became a member of its GC and corr secy for Swizerland (Nov 1864 to 1872); GC treasurer (1871–1872). He presided as chairman over several congresses (1865–1871). A supporter and close coworker of M in the GC up to this point, he went over (autumn 1872) to the reform wing of the British Federal Council and its lib-lab TU leaders; then quit the labor movement (1877). → 65:23, 25, 29, 36, 55, 56; 66:5, 17, 21, 26, 36, 50; 68:31, 54, 55, 68, 69; 69:47, 65, 70; 70:3, 4, 31, 39, 44; 71:15, 23, 45, 46, 51, 56; 72:8, 36, 41; 73:7. #ME48; M185, M346, M508, M566.5, M696, M752.

Junge or **Jungen,** Adolph (Friedrich) German worker (joiner/carpenter) from the Rhineland. Member of the League of the Just in Paris; from 1847; member of the CL. In Brussels, member of the CL District Comm and a founder of the local GWEA. He emigrated to the U.S. at the beginning of 1848. → 46:25; 47:28.

Jungen, Die (faction in the German S-D party) → 90:32, 39, 42; 92:46, 53.

Jura Federation of the IWMA (Switz.) This organization was the Bakuninist base for the takeover operation in the IWMA; led by *Guillaume. → 71:56; 72:36, 60, 66; 73:11, 17; 79:12. #M346. *See also* Bulletin de la Fédération Jurassienne.

Justice London, Jan 1884 to Jan 22, 1925. Weekly. Founder: H. M. Hyndman. Ed by Harry Quelch (1884–1912). —Organ of the SDF. It was superseded by *Social-Democrat / incorporating Justice* (1925–1933). → 84:6; 89:12, 15, 17, 19; 91:10; 94:18.

La Justice Paris, Jan 16, 1880, to at least 1931. Director: Georges Clemenceau. —Clemenceau's organ of left Radicalism, i.e., the extreme bourgeois left, till 1897. Charles Longuet joined its staff after his return to France following the 1880 amnesty. → 81:4. #E230.

Justitia (*pseud.*) → 71:41. #E828.

Juta, Henry (1857 to 1930) M's nephew; son of his sister Louise and J. C. *Juta. Lawyer; later, a presiding judge in Cape Town. → 76:39; 79:11.

Juta, Jaan Carel; *Dutch* Johan Karel; *Ger.*

Johann Karl (1824 to 1886) M's brother-in-law, married to his sister Louise (1853). Then a *Notariatskandidat* in Zaltbommel, Neth.; later, a bookdealer and pub'r in Cape Town. → 53:25, 47; 54:5; 59:16; 61:9; 65:21; 76:39.

K

Kablukov, Nikolai Alexeyevich (1849 to 1919) Russian economist and statistician; Narodnik. He was in touch with M, helped him acquire Russian books, and visited him (1881) while traveling abroad (1879–1881). Statistics chief of the Moscow zemstvo (1885–1907); prof at Moscow (1893+). In 1918, executive head of the Soviet statistical organization. → 80:26; 81:5.

Kahn, C. #M574.

Kaiserslautern (Ger.) Industrial city in the (Rhenish) Palatinate. → 49:29, 30.

Kalachov, Nikolai Vasilyevich (1819 to 1885) Russian historian, archivist, and archeographist. Prof at Moscow (1848–1852); head of Moscow archives of Justice Ministry (1865–1885); founder of the monthly *Iuridichestii Vestnik,* its editor (1860–1864, 1867–1870). His works dealt largely with archival theory and practice, also document collections. → 73:37.

Kalafat *See* Calafat.

Kamm, Friedrich (d. 1867) German worker (brushmaker) from Bonn, where he was active in the 1848 revolution, working with Carl Schurz in the Demo Assoc, which K. represented at the Demo Congress in Frankfurt (June 1848). In 1849 he took part in the Baden-Palatinate uprising. Afterward he emigrated to Switzerland, where he was a member of the German WA in Geneva; and in 1852, to the U.S. In 1857 he played a leading role in forming the NY Communist Club, becoming its first pres (1857–1859). → 58:13, 31.

Kant, Immanuel (1724 to 1804) German philosopher: landmark in the development of critical idealism. Prof at Königsberg (1770+). His best-known works are *Kritik der reinen Vernunft* [Critique of pure reason] (1781, rev. 1787); *Kritik der praktischen Vernunft* [Critique of practical reason] (1788); and one of his last works was *Religion innerhalb der Grenzen der blossen Vernunft* (1793). —E accorded special praise to K.'s early scientific work, e.g., *Allgemeine Naturgeschichte und Theorie des Himmels* (1755), the source of the "Kant–Laplace theory" of the solar system. → 41:7; 54:5. #M79.

Kapp, Friedrich (1824 to 1884) German lawyer, for a time active in America; left Democratic political publicist and historical writer. —A Rhinelander, friend of Herwegh, he took part in the revolution of 1848–1849,

during which time he wrote i.a. for M's *NRZ.* He emigrated to the U.S. (1850); became active in NY as lawyer and editor: member of the NY Immigration Commsn; member of the important German-American law firm of Kapp, Zitz & Fröbel; author of a number of books, esp on German immigration to America, history of slavery, biographies, etc. In 1862–1863 he returned to Germany temporarily or on visit; then returned permanently in 1870, to Berlin. Here he quickly became a Bismarckian, denounced by his friend Herzen; a National Liberal deputy in the Reichstag (1871–1878, 1881–1884); author of the autobiographical *Aus und über Amerika* (1876). —His son Wolfgang was leader of the 1920 "Kapp putsch." → 49:4; 62:46.

Kapper, Siegfried (1821 to 1879) Czech writer, poet, and historian; translator of Slavic songs and legends into German, e.g., *Die Gesänge der Serben* (1852), *Slavische Melodien* (1844), *Südslavische Wanderungen im Sommer 1850* (1851)—these titles mentioned by M&E. Other works dealt with Slavic customs and literature. → 56:13.

Karadžić, Vuk Stefanović; *also written* Vuk Stefanovich **Karajich** (1787 to 1864) Serbian scholar, founder of modern Serbian linguistics and folkloric studies; author of a dictionary (1818) and the first grammar (1814), and of works on Serbian ethnology and history. E (1863) read his great collection of folk songs, *Narodne serpske pyesme* (1823–1833). → 63:22.

Karamzin, Nikolai Mikhailovich (1766 to 1826) Russian historian and man of letters. He wrote novels; introduced reforms in the language affecting literary styles. As a historian, he early moved from liberalism to conservatism; his works are pro-autocracy. E (1851) prob read K.'s work *Istoriya gosudarstva rossiskago* [History of the Russian state] (1818–1824). → 51:49. #M141.

Kareyev, Nikolai Ivanovich (1850 to 1931) Russian historian and sociologist. His liberal views got him dismissed from St. Petersburg U. (1899) but he was restored (1907) and finally retired on a government pension. Before 1905 he was a Cadet party supporter; sympathetic to the Narodnik view of peasant problem. His field was modern European history, esp the French Revolution, incl the peasantry; his method: subjective and idealist. —The book which M (1879) criticized was his *Krestyane i krestyansky vopros Frantsii v posledney chetverti XVIII veka* [The peasants and the peasant question in the last quarter of the 18th century] (1879). Also wrote on: Chief questions of the philosophy of history (1883–1890); Essay on the history of the revolution in Poland (1886). → 79:20.

Karlsruhe (Ger.) City on the Rhine, capital of the former state of Baden. → 49:27.

Kars Town in N.E. Turkey (Armenia). → 56:12, 13, 15–17, 21. #M308, M309, M426.

Kaub, Karl German worker; an émigré in London when the IWMA started, a member of the GWEA (now called the Communist WEA), he was a member of the GC (Nov 1864–1865); delegate to the London Conference (1865). After this conference he settled in Paris. M's acquaintance with K. resumed in 1875 when, accompanied by Karl Hirsch (now his brother-in-law), K. visited London; friendly correspondence followed, at least till 1881. — Note: The IML (in *MEW* and *GCFI*) decided, for unexplained reasons, to identify Kaub with a man named Kolb who was a GC member in 1870–1871; but this seems to me erroneous, at the least very dubious. → 64:36; 65:55; 67:31; 75:35.

Kaufman, Illarion Ignatyevich (1848 to 1916) Russian economist; prof at St. Petersburg (1893–1916). Author of many works on money circulation and credit, history of Russian finance. —In 1872 K. pubd one of the first reviews of *Capital* in *Vestnik Yevropy*, "Tochka zryeniya politiko-ekonomoicheskoi kritiki y Karla Marksa." Later he was one of those who helped M collect books for his Russian library. —M (1877–1878) studied K.'s *Teoriya kolebaniya tsyen* (1867) and *Teoriya i praktika bankovago dyela. I. Kredit, banki i denezhnoe obrashchenie* (1873). → 77:28; 78:12.

Kaufmann, Moritz (1839 to 1920) English (German-born) clergyman and writer. First a lecturer in Dublin, he entered the Church of England, ordained (1865); chaplain abroad; curate of Blickling (1884+). Besides sermons and tracts on theological matters, he pubd a number of books on socialism. His *Socialism: Its nature, its dangers* [etc.] (1874) was based on Schäffle; next was his *Utopias . . . From Sir Thomas More to Karl Marx* (1879). He also wrote on Christian socialism, *Socialism and modern thought* (1895), et al. → 78:33, 36, 44.

Kaulfuss, Roman St. Historian; no other info found. M (1853) read his *Die Slawen in den ältesten Zeiten bis Samo, 623* (1842). → 53:51.

Kautsky, Johann; *called* Hans (b. 1864) Austrian theatrical scene painter; brother of Karl *Kautsky. → 88:36.

Kautsky, Karl (Johann) (1854 to 1938) Son of a Czech scene-painter and a German mother (*see* Minna Kautsky); b. Prague; came to Vienna at age 9. Student of history and science at U. of Vienna; became a socialist (c.1874), joined the still-weak Austrian Social-Democracy (1875), and began writing for the *Volksstaat* and other S-D papers. At the time he wanted to be a painter or actor, and tried to write novels and plays. His first book, heavily influenced by Darwin, was *Der Einfluss der Volksvermehrung auf den Fortschritt der Gesellschaft* (1899), pubd with the financial aid of *Höchberg, who also made him his "literary adviser" in Zurich. In Zurich K. became acquainted with the S-D circle around the *Sozialdemokrat*; Bernstein became his friend. He went to London (Mar 1881); met the M family (July); E befriended him, somewhat quizzically, and led him to study M's *Capital*. Höchberg's money failing, K. returned to Vienna, where he came to know V. Adler and Heinrich Braun; did his doctoral dissertation on marriage and the family: *Die Entstehung der Ehe und Familie*. In summer 1882 he proposed to the Dietz publishing firm a scientific Marxist journal; *Die Neue Zeit* apppeared in Jan 1883, edited by K. for 35 years. From 1885 to 1890 he lived in London, in close assoc with E; wrote *Marx' ökonomische Lehren* (The economic doctrines of KM); pubd *Thomas More und seine Utopie* (1888); *Die Klassengegensätze von 1789* (1889). After the fall of the Anti-Socialist Law (1890), the NZ became a weekly; K. went to Stuttgart where it was pubd by Dietz. For the Erfurt party congress of 1891, the program which he had put into revised form was adopted; on the program he wrote a commentary, *Das Erfurter Programm* (1892); and coauthored *Grundsätze und Forderungen der Sozialdemocratie* (1893); in these Stuttgart years he also wrote *Parlamentarismus und Demokratie* (1893) and *Vorläufer des neueren Sozialismus* (1894). In 1897 he moved to Berlin, the party center, and, E gone, became the mentor ("pope") of the international movement; pubd *Die Agrarfrage* (1899). With the outbreak of the debate on "Revisionism," K. became the chief defender of "orthodox" Marxism against Bernstein; his main polemic was *Bernstein und das sozialdemokratische Programm* (1899). Also: *Handelspolitik und Sozialdemokratie* (1901), against Schippel's tariff policy; *Sozialdemokratie und Kolonialpolitik* (1907); *Ethik und materialistische Geschichtsauffassung* (1906), against Kantianism; *Die soziale Revolution* (1902); *Der politische Massenstreik* (1905–1906); the first edn of M's *Theorien über den Mehrwert* [Theories of surplus value], edited by K.; *Der Ursprung des Christentums* (1908); *Rasse und Judentum* (1914); and *Der Weg zur Macht* [The road to

power] (1909)—this last being the high point of K.'s radicalism as a revolutionary Marxist. With the outbreak of World War I, at first K. took a middle-of-the-road position and went with the Independent Social-Democrats as long as this group existed; in argumentation, however, he justified the legitimacy of the prowar position. After the Russian Revolution of 1917 he went rapidly to the right in his political views (as well as in his hostility to the new Soviet government) until his position was indistinguishable from the Bernsteinian Revisionism he had once fought. Besides a number of anti-Bolshevik polemics, he pubd *Die materialistische Geschichtsauffassung* (1927) and *Sozialisten und Krieg* (1937). In 1924 he had returned to Vienna to live; with the Nazi threat to Austria, he emigrated to Amsterdam. —*Note:* The nickname Baron, used for K. by E and Eleanor M, possibly came (according to Y. Kapp) from the putative gentility of his first wife's family; *see* Louise *Kautsky.
→ 81:9, 15, 16, 19, 34, 42, 44, 45; 82:9, 20, 36, 45; 83:8, 10, 38–40, 48, 49; 84:3, 8, 11–14, 21, 22, 26, 33, 37, 38, 40, 41, 46, 47, 54; 85:9, 17, 27, 31, 39; 86:24, 31, 33, 39, 45, 49; 87:15, 31, 37; 88:25, 36; 89:5, 9, 28; 90:17, 19, 23, 39, 40, 46, 49, 50; 91:4, 6, 11–13, 23, 24, 33, 46, 50, 55, 61; 92:4, 12, 14, 28, 30–32, 39, 44, 45, 51, 65, 67; 93:6, 13, 18, 19, 30, 50, 53, 56; 94:6, 11, 27, 29, 30, 35, 37, 43; 95:16, 20, 21, 24, 30, 31. #M365, M877; E341.5, E429, E699.

Kautsky, Louise; *née* **Strasser;** *second mar. name* **Freyberger** (1860 to 1950) Austrian socialist. First wife of Karl Kautsky; married in 1883; separated in 1889; divorced in 1890. By occupation, midwife. After Helene Demuth's death she became E's household major-domo (from Dec 1890 to his death). In 1894 she suddenly married an Austrian physician, *Freyberger. —Under E's tutelage and as his protégé, she began to play a role in the Austrian party; became a contributor to the socialist press; member of the ed bd of the Vienna *Arbeiterinnen-Zeitung* in the 1890s. —Eleanor M came to distrust her, indeed despise her; both of Eleanor's biographers, Kapp and Tsuzuki, paint Louise K. as an intriguer and clever schemer; their books should be consulted for further info. — Louise Kautsky (she continued to use this name in the movement despite Karl K.'s objection) should not be confused with Karl's second wife, Luise, née Ronsperger (1864–1944). → 88:36; 90:46; 91:21, 47, 49, 54; 92:3, 22, 28, 38, 39, 43, 51, 61; 93:32, 40; 94:13, 28, 34; 95:37. #M318, M813.

Kautsky, Minna; *née* **Jaich** (1837 to 1912) Mother of Karl Kautsky; Austrian novelist. Daughter of a theatrical artist, she was an actress till 1862. She wrote popular novels in good part based on the life of the working poor, e.g., *Stefan vom Grillenhof* (of which M spoke favorably), *Die Alten und die Neuen, Herrschen oder Dienen.* —She had become a socialist under her son's influence; joined the Austrian party; acquainted with E. → 85:31, 42.

Kavelin, Konstantin Dmitriyevich (1818 to 1885) Russian historian and publicist. Prof of legal history at Moscow (1844–1848), of civil law at St. Petersburg (1857–1861); at Military Law Academy (1878–1885). A Westernizer in the 1840s; liberal in the 1850s; later, a conservative-monarchist close to the Slavophiles. His works advocated transforming the peasantry into a conservative small-property-holding class topped by a "social monarchy." → 75:34.

Kaye, Sir John William (1814 to 1876) English military historian and colonial official (secy of the India Office, 1858–1874). His works include: *History of the war in Afghanistan* (1851); *Administration of the East India Co.* (1853); later work, *History of the Sepoy War in India* (1864–1876). → 57:31.

Kayser, Max (1853 to 1888) German Social-Democratic parliamentarian, a leader of the right wing of the party's Reichstag Fraction. Son of a Breslau businessman, he went into business, but early joined the S-D party. He edited party organs in Mainz and Dresden (1873–1874), became known as a speaker; was elected to the Reichstag (1878), and harassed by government prosecution under the new Anti-Socialist Law. He died at an early age after illness. —K. was sympathetic not only to Bismarck's tariff program but also to his nationalization program ("Bismarckian state-socialism"). → 79:3, 41.

Keay, John Seymour (1839 to 1909) British (Scottish-born) administrator and bank official in India; Liberal MP (1889–1895). He went to India (1862) as a bank branch manager; then served in the Hyderabad government; founded a spinning-weaving firm; returned to Britain in 1882, when he pubd *Spoiling the Egyptians; a tale of shame* (read by M the same year). This was not on Egypt but on the government of India; Keay, an "advanced liberal," member of the British committee of the Indian National Congress, sympathized with Indian home-rule aspirations. He later pubd *The great imperial danger: An impossible war in the near future* (1887), which deprecated fear of war with Russia; and *The fraud of the protection cry* (1906). → 82:56.

Keen, Charles English radical. Business manager of the *Eastern Post.* He was a member of the GC/IWMA (1871–1872), also of the British Federal Council of the International, succeeding Hales as its secy. → 72:31.

Keene English journalist; correspondent

of the London *Daily News* in the 1840s–1850s. No further info. → 48:85; 51:27.

Kegan Paul & Co. British pubrs. → 83:26; 86:14.

Keil, Ernst (1816 to 1878) German pubr and bookdealer; publicist. A left Democrat, he was editor of *Die Gartenlaube* (1853+). → 68:41.

Keller, Charles (1843 to 1913) French anarchoid socialist. Orig a civil engineer and mill manager, he moved to Paris (1868), associated with the Reclus brothers i.a., and sought to live by translating. In 1868 he took part in Bakunin's caucus in the Peace and Freedom Congress, joined Bakunin's Alliance, and became active in the Paris IWMA. He began working on a trans of M's *Capital* (1869–1870), but quit. In 1871 he was wounded in the May fighting for the Paris Commune, and emigrated to Switzerland. After the 1880 amnesty he was active in the socialist movement in Belfort and Nancy. Though anarchoid in tendency, he did not join any group; later pubd poems under the name Jacques Turbin. → 69:63, 73; 72:54.

Kelly, Walter Keating (*fl.* mid-19th century) The reference in #M141 is no doubt to this voluminous author's *History of Russia* (1854–1855; repubd in many edns to 1902)—not an orig work but called by Kelly "compiled" from various historians. As a writer Kelly was a jack-of-all-trades, his productions covering French history, folklore, an anthology of translated erotica, Cervantes, a *Handbook of homeopathic practice*, the Middle East, translations from Ranke and L. Blanc, and more. #M141.

Kennan, George (1845 to 1924) American journalist and travel writer. An official of the Associated Press (1877–1885), K. became known as an authority on Siberia after a trip there (1885–1886) written up in a series of articles "Siberia and the exile system," *Century Illustrated Monthly Magazine* (1888–1890); this was the exposé that E referred to. It was pubd as a book (1891), widely translated, and had a big world impact. K. later hailed the Russian Revolution of 1917 and opposed Allied intervention.   —K. also wrote up travels to Cuba, Japan in the Russo-Japanese War, and Mt. Pelée. → 90:17.

Kentish Town London district. → 56:35.

Kerdijk, Arnold (1846 to 1905) Dutch school inspector. Editor of the *Sociaal Weekblad* (1887–1911) and of *Vragen des tijds* (1875+). In 1879 he pubd the work *Karl Marx* as Vol. 10 of the series *Mannen van beteekenis in onze dagen.* → 79:9.

Kern, Johann Konrad (1808 to 1888) Swiss politician. He was Switzerland's ambassador to France during 1857–1883, i.e., during the Paris Commune. He had previously been a member of the Swiss Diet (1833–1848), active in drawing up a new federal constitution (1848), pres of the federal court (1850). → 71:23.

Kertbény, Karl Maria; *real name* Benkert (1824 to 1882) Hungarian writer and historian. A liberal, he had ties with leading figures in the 1848–1849 revolution. → 64:8; 68:8, 41. #M70.

Keussler, Ivan Avgustovich; *Ger.* Johannes **von Keussler** (1843 to 1896) Russian economist. E read his German-language book *Zur Geschichte und Kritik des bäuerlichen Gemeindebesitzes in Russland* (1876–1882). → 88:4.

Kheraskov, Mikhail Matveyevich (1733 to 1807) Russian poet, the "dean of Russian literature" of his time. Besides tragedies and novels, he wrote two well-known epic poems: *Rossiade* [The Russiad] (1779); and *Vladimir vozrozhdennye* [Vladimir reborn] (1785; revised as *Vladimir,* 1809). → 51:49.

Kiel (Ger.) Baltic port, in Schleswig-Holstein. → 44:22; 74:23.

Killarney Town (and lakes) in S.W. Ireland. → 69:58.

Kinglake, Alexander William (1809 to 1891) English historian of the Crimean War. Son of a banker, trained as a lawyer, he adopted military history as his central interest. Before finding his vocation he traveled in the East (1835) and wrote *Eothen, or Traces of travel* (1844). In 1854 he followed the British army to the Crimea; met Lord Raglan; was invited (1856) to write the history of the campaign; and then devoted the rest of his life to doing so, in *The invasion of the Crimea*—in more detail than anyone wanted to know and with amusing glorification of the British. Eight volumes were issued in 1863–1887 (read by E on publ). K. was also a Liberal MP (1857–1868) of no consequence. → 63:25. #E407.

Kingston (Can.) City on Lake Ontario, at head of the St. Lawrence River. → 88:30.

Kinkel, Gottfried (Johann) (1815 to 1882) German man of letters and political publicist. At first a lecturer in theology and a preacher in Cologne, he shifted focus to the history of art, becoming a prof at Bonn (1846). He took part in the Baden-Palatinate uprising (1849); was sentenced to life; escaped with the aid of Carl Schurz (Nov 1850); and fled to England, then to the U.S. (Sep 1851). In America he carried out a campaign to raise money by selling bonds for a new German revolution; when his group convened a congress in Cincinnati to underwrite the national loan, there were eight delegates; the fund netted a small amount only. He returned to London (1853) as a lecturer on German literature; founded *Hermann* (Jan 1859; K. was pub'r and editor only the first six months). In the course of the 1860s he became a pro-Bismarck supporter of German unity under Prussian hegemony; prof at Zurich (1866). —Young K. had pubd poems (*Gedichte*, 1843), verse romances and tragedies, and a history of art, *Geschichte der bildenden Künste bei den christlichen Völkern* (1845) → 48:55; 49:4, 10; 50:14; 51:20, 36, 45; 52:3, 4, 7, 12, 17, 27, 31, 43; 58:32, 51; 59:12, 14, 34, 44, 46, 63; 62:12, 18; 66:30. #ME69; M342.

Kinkel, Johanna; *née* **Mockel;** *later mar. name* **Matthieux** (1810 to 1858) First wife of Gottfried Kinkel. She was a writer, esp on musical subjects. An autobiographical novel *Hans Ibeles in London* was pubd posthumously. → 49:4; 58:51.

Kinnear, John Gardiner Glasgow writer. The book of his that M (1851) read must have been *The crisis and the currency* (1847; 2nd edn, 1848). In 1840 K. had pubd *Cairo, Petra, and Damascus in 1839,* after traveling there. → 51:62.

Kirkwood, Daniel (1814 to 1895) American astronomer. M read his work *Meteoric astronomy* (1865). → 65:45.

Klapka, György; Ger. Georg (1820 to 1892) Hungarian gen; national-revolutionary. He entered the Austrian army (1838); rose in the Hungarian revolutionary army (1848–1849) esp as defending commandant of Kormárno fortress; then emigrated to England, then Switzerland et al. In the 1850s he was connected with Bonapartist circles; in 1859, organized a Hungarian legion to fight with Kossuth in Italy; in 1866, as a Prussian major-gen, organized a Hungarian corps in Silesia to take part in the Austro-Prussian War; in 1867, after an amnesty, returned to Hungary where he was elected to the Hungarian chamber as a member of Deák's party. Later (1877) he worked for Turkey to reorganize its army for service against Russia. Author of: *Der Nationalkrieg in Ungarn* (1851); *Der Krieg im Orient* (1855), on the Crimean War; and memoirs. → 52:22; 58:28; 64 :27. #M346.5.

Klein, Carl (Wilhelm) German worker (knife-grinder) from Solingen. He took part (1849) in the Elberfeld and Solingen uprisings as a CL member. Afterward he emigrated to the U.S. (1852); then, after an amnesty, returned to Prussia. He joined the GGWA (1863), and was active in the German working-class movement in the 1860s–1870s; one of the founders of the Solingen ironwares co-op, and of the IWMA in Solingen, which he represented at the congresses of 1867–1868. → 50:22; 53:31; 61:18; 66:32. 67:42; 71:17.

Klein, Johann Jacob (c.1818 to c.1895–1897) Cologne physician; CL member (at least in 1848–1849), and defendant in the Cologne Communist trial of 1852, in which he

was acquitted (for, though he had been a member of the Cologne WA in 1848, he had not been esp active). Through the 1860s he was still giving E occasional help (e.g., in distributing #E644), but by 1870 he had become "cool" and bourgeoisified, according to E. → 61:18.

Klemm, E. English trade-union leader. → 91:28.

Klemm, Gustav (Friedrich) (1802 to 1867) German cultural historian; a pioneer in the analytical history of civilizations. Prof at Dresden (1825+), Nuremberg (1830+), Dresden again (1831+). —M (1853) read his *Allgemeine Cultur-Geschichte der Menschheit* (1847–1849; all pubd during 1843–1852), and (1869) read his work *Die Werkzeuge und Waffen* (1858). → 53:53; 69:44.

Klings, Carl (c.1825 to *after* 1874) German socialist worker (cutlery worker) from Solingen. A member of the CL, he maintained relations among CL members in the Rhineland even after the league was dissolved in 1852; active through the 1850s in the Rhineland, esp in organizing strikes of the Wuppertal dye workers. He was founding member of the GGWA (1863) and its Exec; was named (1864) plenipotentiary for Solingen; but became a leader of the internal opposition to Lassalle. He corresponded with M&E (1864–1865); and his opposition to B. Becker and Hatzfeldt as GGWA leaders got him expelled. He emigrated to the U.S. (1865); there, was active in the Chicago workers' movement; attended the first congress (1872) of the N. American Federation of IWMA; later (1873), active in organizing Chicago unemployed. → 64:17, 27, 32, 33, 46; 65:7, 25.

Klose, Gottfried German communist. Orig a soldier, he took part in the 1848–1849 revolution in Breslau; emigrated to London (1850), where he joined the London GWEA and the CL. He went with M in the 1850 split. → 51:1; 52:27.

Knies, Karl; *full* Karl Gustav Adolf (1821 to 1898) German economist; a leader of the older Historical School of polit eco in Germany. Prof at Freiburg i. Br. and (1865–1896) Heidelberg. He was a prominent liberal in the Baden Diet (1861–1865). —M (1877) read his *Das Geld* (1873), which was Part I of his work *Geld und Credit* (1873–1879). Other writings: *Die politische Ökonomie vom Standpunkt der geschichtlichen Methode* (1853); *Weltgeld und Weltmünzen* (1874). → 77:28.

Knights of Labor American labor organization, nationwide and all-inclusive, founded (1869) orig as a secret society, under Uriah S. Stephens; later led (till 1893) by Terence V. Powderly; declined after the formation of the AFL. → 82:12; 86:47, 51; 91:15. #E174.

Knille, Otto (1832 to 1898) German painter of historical subjects. After residence in Paris, Munich, and Rome, he came to Berlin (1866). A year after his encountering M in Carlsbad, he went on the faculty of the Berlin Academy. → 74:31.

Knowles, Sir James (Thomas) (1831 to 1908) English architect and editor pub'r. He practiced as an architect for 30 years, but we are interested in his other career. He edited *Contemporary Review* (1870–1877); founded and edited the *Nineteenth Century* (1877–1908). This career was aided by his contacts in the Metaphysical Society, which he founded (1869–1880), without (admittedly) ever discovering what metaphysics was. → 78:25; 83:18.

Koch, Eduard Ignaz (b. 1820) German Catholic priest who took part in the 1848 revolution; he may have been the same as the Ignaz Koch who represented the Volksverein of Dortmund; also participated in the Baden-Palatinate uprising (1849). He then went to the U.S. (1850); as a journalist, became a contributor to the *New Yorker Staatszeitung;* and after 1851 was a spokesman for the "Free Community" in NY. K. distributed Blanqui's writings too, not only M's. → 51:16.

Köhler, J. E. M. German printshop owner in Hamburg; a book printer mainly. He printed the first number of M's *NRZ-Revue.* → 49:40.

Kölliker, Albert (von); *full* Rudolph Albert (1817 to 1905) Swiss-born biologist active in Germany; known esp for research in zoological histology and embryology, the use of the microscope, spontaneous variation in evolution, etc. Prof at Würzburg (1847+). M (1864) studied his *Handbuch der Gewebelehre des Menschen,* 4th edn (1863). → 64:48.

Kölnische Zeitung [Cologne Gazette] Cologne, 1802 to present (under this title); founded 1762. Daily. —A leading voice of the Rhineland bourgeoisie; Catholic; liberal esp in the 1840s after the demise of the RZ; in the 1870s it became pro-Bismarckian. It was counterposed both ideologically and journalistically to the dailies that M edited in Cologne, the RZ and NRZ. → 48:61, 85; 52:13, 39; 61:54; 79:44. #ME2, ME82; M164, M188, M233, M248, M430–432, M448, M617, M849, M850, M960, M964; E408–411, E460, E489, E888.

Königgrätz City in Bohemia, Aust. (now in Czechoslovakia as Hradec Králové), scene of a decisive battle in the Prussian-Austrian War (July 3, 1866), also called battle of Sadowa. → 66:30.

Königlich Preussischer Staats-Anzeiger *See* Preussischer Staats-Anzeiger.

Königlich privilegirte Berlinische Zeitung von Staats- und gelehrten Sachen; *also called*

Vossische Zeitung Berlin, 1785 to 1911 under the long title; founded earlier; assumed name V.Z. (1911–1934). Daily. Founder: C. F. Voss. —In the 1840s, moderate-liberal. #M739.

Königsberg Baltic seaport, formerly capital of E. Prussia; now in the USSR as Kaliningrad. #E467.

Köppen, Karl Friedrich (1808 to 1863) German teacher of history in a Berlin secondary school. In the 1840s, as a Young Hegelian, he met M in the Berlin "Doctors' Club" and became a very close friend, remaining a friend throughout life. He dedicated his 1840 book *Friedrich der Grosse und seine Widersacher* to M; contributed to the *Hallische Jahrbücher* (1841) and RZ (Cologne, 1842); in 1848–1849, was active in the Demo movement. He later became best known for his book *Die Religion des Buddha und ihre Entstehung* (1857–1859); an early book was *Literarische Einleitung in die nordische Mythologie* (1837). → 37:9; 39:9; 40:1, 7; 48:57; 61:15, 17.

Köslin (Ger.) Pomeranian town, now in Poland as Koszalin. → 50:9.

Köttgen (or **Koettgen**), Gustav Adolph (1805 to 1882) German painter and poet from the Rhineland (Barmen). In the early 1840s he held views close to "True Socialism"; by 1845, participated in the Elberfeld communist meetings with E and Hess, and in 1845–1846 collaborated with M&E to build a communist organization in Germany; corresponded with the Brussels CCC. During the 1848–1849 revolution he was active in Bremen, esp the workers' assoc; pubd *Vereinigung. Ztg für sämtliche Arbeiter* (Apr-June 1849) till it was banned and he was banished from Bremen. → 46:24; 67:24. #ME86.

Kokosky, Samuel (1838 to 1899) German left journalist. Orig trained in law, he became a supporter of the left-liberal deomocrat J. *Jacoby; editor (1871) of the *Demokratische Blätter* (Königsberg). In 1872 he joined the Social-Democracy with Jacoby; editor of the *Braunschweiger Volksfreund.* During the Anti-Socialist Law period, he pubd the *Braunschweigische Unterhaltungsblatt;* later (1890s) became editor of the *Neue Welt* (Berlin). → 73:51; 74:4. #ME6.

Koller A partner in the publishing firm of Petsch & Co. in London. → 62:27.

Kommunistische Internationale Berlin, Hamburg, Basel, Leningrad, Aug 1919 to Aug 1939. —German-language edn of the organ of the Com International; *see also* *Communist International. #ME29.

Komp, Albrecht; *Angl.* Albert German-American socialist; friend of *Weydemeyer. Based in NY, where he represented a German firm, he became secy of the Int'l Association (which preceded the IWMA in America), and also a founder (1857) and vice-pres of the Communist Club of NY. → 58:25, 31; 59:14, 36.

Koppe, Johann Gottlieb (1782 to 1863) German agronomist and economist. After experience as a farm manager, he became a teacher at a Möglin agricultural academy (1811); also served in a number of government posts in his field. His chief work was *Unterricht im Ackerbau und in der Viehzucht* (1836), of which M (1878) studied the 10th edn of 1872. → 78:18.

Koran Islam's holy book. → 94:31.

Korff, Hermann Prussian ex-officer, dismissed from the army for his political views; member of the Cologne CL before 1848. He became a company commander in the militia in 1848 and, more important, the business manager and *Gérant* (responsible pub'r) of M's NRZ in Cologne (June 1848 to Apr 1849). He was out of the CL by 1850. Afterward he emigrated to the U.S. In 1859 M heard that he had been sentenced to prison in New Orleans for forgery. → 48:45, 84; 49:8, 28.

Korvin-Krukovskaya, Anna Vasilievna; *mar. name* Anna **Jaclard** (1843 or 1844 to 1887) Russian revolutionary, writer, and Communard; wife of Victor *Jaclard. Daughter of a landowner-gen, she went to Paris to study; frequented Blanquist circles (meeting Jaclard). In the Paris Commune, she took part in the Comité des Femmes and other activities, incl agitation for women's rights. Afterward she and Jaclard went to Switzerland, then to Russia (where she devoted herself to writing); and after the 1880 amnesty, returned to France; she died in Paris after an illness. —In the 1860s she had had stories and a novel pubd with the help of Dostoyevsky; her writings of her last years reflected Narodnik belletristic literature. For more info, see Maitron's *DBMOF* and E. Thomas, *Women Incendiaries.* → 72:58.

Kościelski, Wladyslaw (1818 to 1895) Polish émigré revolutionary; in 1848, a friend (but apparently not a political follower) of Bakunin. Later, in the 1850s, a gen in the Turkish army fighting Russia. → 48:50, 58.

Kosel, Esther; née **Marx** (c.1786 to 1865) M's aunt; his father's sister. (The birth date given is from *MEW*; M thought it was c.1792.) → 63:41; 65:60; 66:41.

Koshelyev, Alexander Ivanovich (1806 to 1883) Russian publicist; Slavophile; advocate of a repr consultative assembly. Of a gentry family, he took part in the execution of many reforms incl the "emancipation of the serfs" of 1861. Publisher/editor of Slavophile journals *Russkaia Beseda* (1856–1860) and *Selskoye Blagoustroistvo* (1858–1859). M (1875) read his just-pubd *Nashe tsolzhoyenye.* → 75:34, 37.

Der **Kosmos** Leipzig, later Stuttgart, 1877 to 1886. Monthly. —Scientific journal, esp devoted to evolutionary theory. → 83:8.

Kossuth, Lajos; *Angl.* Louis; *Ger.* Ludwig (1802 to 1894) Hungarian revolutionary leader. Orig a lawyer, he was a political prisoner in Austria (1837–1840); editor of *Pesti Hirlap* (Budapest), a reform organ (1840–1844); member of the Hungarian Diet (1847–1849). In the 1848 revolution he headed the uprising and the National Assembly which declared independence, and was named dictatorial governor of Hungary. The revolution defeated, he resigned and fled to Turkey; imprisoned there (1849–1851). In the 1850s he lived as an émigré, talking about another revolution, esp in England and the U.S. During the Austro-Sardinian War (1859) he formed a Hungarian Legion in Italy; afterward, resided in Turin, refusing amnesty offers. → 49:9; 51:15; 52:7, 12, 17, 27, 31, 43, 52; 53:5, 11; 56:20; 59:57, 58; 62:25; #M320, M433–M435, M533, M740; E412, E646.

Kostomarov, Nikolai Ivanovoch (1817 to 1885) Russian-Ukrainian historian and writer. His father a Russian landowner, his mother a Ukrainian serf, he became a Ukrainian nationalist. After becoming a prof at Kiev (1846), he was exiled to Saratov (1847–1854) for joining a Ukrainian secret society. A prof at St. Petersburg (1859–1862); resigned on political grounds; then moved rightward toward a less radical nationalism. —His work stressed ethnography; he was well known for books on Stenka Razin and other popular movements. Besides his work as a historian, he was a leader in Ukrainian life and culture (1858–1880); wrote poetry, drama, criticism. —M (1879–1880) excerpted his *Bunt Stenki Razina. Istoricheskye monografyi* (1872). → 77:48; 79:51.

Kothes, D. German businessman, in Cologne; the postal go-between for M's correspondence with the defense of the Communists on trial in 1852. → 52:35, 39.

Kovalevsky, Maxim Maximovich (1851 to 1916) Russian sociological historian. Trained as a lawyer, he became a prof of law and institutional history at Moscow (1877+); was dismissd for liberal views (1887), and settled in France, lecturing and publishing in W. Europe in four languages. During the 1905 revolution he returned to Russia; organized a rightish liberal party; entered the First Duma, and served in legislatures (1906–1916); editor of *Vestnik Yevropy* (1909+). His viewpoint was sympathetic to Comtism and social-Darwinism. Author of: *Die ökonomische Entwicklung Europas bis zum Beginn der kapitalistischen Wirtschaftsform* (1901–1914); *Proiskhozhdeniye sovremennoy demokratii* (1895–1897); *Tableau des origines et de l'évolution de la famille et de la* propriété (1890); *Modern customs and ancient laws of Russia* (1891). For the work which M excerpted, see ST/37. → 75:32, 48; 76:36; 77:3; 78:15, 33, 39; 79:5, 17, 20, 38, 39, 42; 83:49; 90:26; 92:48. #M567.

Kräcker, Julius (1839? to 1888) German Social-Democratic worker (saddler) from Breslau. After journeyman travels, he founded the Breslau Arbeiterverein (1867), and joined the Eisenacher party (1869). He was one of the first worker-editors in the party, collaborating on the *Breslauer Tageblatt, Schlesische Courier* et al., till the Anti-Socialist Law suppressed the S-D press. Member of the Reichstag (1881–1888). → 80:17.

Krapka, Josef Czech socialist. Editor of the party organ *Sociální Demokrat* (Prague) in the 1890s. → 93:21.

Kraus, Bernhard (1828 to 1887) Austrian physician. Founder and pub'r of the *Allgemeine Wiener medizinische Zeitung* (1856–1887). M orig met him in Carlsbad (1874). — *Note:* KMC gives his name erron. as Felix K. → 74:31; 80:11.

Kravchinsky, Sergei Mikhailovich; *known by pen name* Stepniak (1852 to 1895) Russian revolutionist; writer and propagandist in emigration. Of a gentry family, he was active in the student and populist movement in the 1870s; left Russia (1874) for activity in Europe. In 1878, back in Russia illegally, editor of the Zemlya i Volya organ, he assassinated the St. Petersburg police chief N. V. Mezentsov, and later fled abroad; in London (1884+). In England he was the leader of the Free Russia group, active as lecturer and writer; by the 1890s he came out against terrorism as a method of struggle. His circle of friends in the left movement was wide, incl close relations with E and Eleanor M. Author of: *Underground Russia* (1881); *Sketches and profiles* (1883), which Eleanor reviewed; *Russia under the tsars* (1885); *The career of a nihilist* (1889); etc. → 84:39; 86:18; 90:9, 17; 92:24, 48, 61; 95:37.

Kreuz-Zeitung See Neue Preussische Zeitung.

Kreuznach or Bad Kreuznach (Ger.) Town near Coblenz. M and his wife spent most of their honeymoon here because Jenny's mother had a house in town. → 42:34; 43:1, 3, 13, 15, 18, 20, 22, 23; 76:26. #M436.

Kriege, Hermann (Rudolph) (1820 to 1850) German socialistic radical, from Lienen (Westphalia). By 1844, having been expelled from a Münster school and the U. of Berlin for radical activity, he was known as a leading socialist agitator; sympathetic to "True Socialism" and Weitling. In 1845 he met E in Barmen and M in Brussels, on Julius Meyer's recommendation, and in May was accepted into the London branch of the

League of the Just. Supposedly on behalf of the League, he went to NY (Sep 1845), where he founded a weekly, *Der Volks-Tribun* (pubd during 1846). Here he advocated the Free Soil reform program (160 acres of free land for all, to create smallholding farmers) plus effusions about Supernal Love, communion with the infinite, etc. Since he represented this to be communism, M's CCC group in Brussels issued a repudiation (#ME28). K. allied himself with Tammany Hall, appealed to the rich to put his reform program through, and opposed the abolition of slavery. In the 1848 revolution he returned to Germany, was active as a liberal Democrat, then returned to the U.S. Insane thereafter, he died soon and was buried wrapped in an American flag by his instructions. → 45:13; 46:1, 15, 20, 24, 29, 42. #ME28.

Kronstadt (Russ.) Town and fortress on Kotlin Island, near St. Petersburg, founded in 1703. → 54:10. #E287.

Krummacher, Friedrich Wilhelm (1796 to 1868) German preacher; Reformed Church pastor; leader of the Pietists in the Wuppertal; promoter of the Evangelical Alliance. He was a pastor near Barmen (1825+); Elberfeld (1834+); appointed to the Trinity Church, Berlin (1847); court chaplain at Potsdam (1853+). Author of: *Salomo und Sulamith* (1827); *Elias der Thisbiter* (1828); *Elisa* (1837); *Das Passionsbuch* (1854); and an autobiography (1869). → 39:8; 40:14. #E263, E881.

Krylov (or **Kriloff**), Ivan Andreyevich (1768 to 1844) Great Russian fabulist. He pubd several collected volumes of his fables (1809–1841); also translated La Fontaine; chief librarian in St. Petersburg imperial library. His fables are in idiomatic verse and colloquial language. → 51:49.

Kryński, Jan (1811 to 1890) Polish revolutionist. An organizer of the Lud Polski group in the 1840s (disbanded after the 1846 Cracow uprising), he was one of those who revived it in 1853–1856, and again in 1872–1876, together with Wróblewski, Dombrowski, et al. The group maintained contact with the Russian Narodniks and with M&E. → 74:19.

Krzywicki, Ludwik (Joachim Franciszek) (1859 to 1941) Polish sociologist and publicist; an early exponent of Marxism and translator of *Capital*. He was active in the student movement (1878–1884); then in emigration chiefly in the U.S. and France; editor of *Przedświt* and *Walka Klas* (Paris), organs of the "Proletariat" group. He returned to Poland (mid-1980s); worked in the Statistical Office; after 1918, prof at Warsaw. → 84:3; 90:44.

Kühlwetter, Friedrich Christian Hubert von (1809 to 1882) Prussian politician and bureaucrat. Min of the Interior (June-Sep 1848); later, governor (*Regierungspräsident*) in Düsseldorf, and *Oberpräsident* in Westphalia province. → 48:53, 60. #M174.

Kuentzel, *Captain* H. Author of *Die taktischen Elemente der neuen Fortificationen* (1851). I presume this is the work that figured in E's notebook. → 52:2.

Küpper, Johann Abraham (1779 to 1850) German pastor. The religious instructor at the Trier Gymnasium, he confirmed M. He became consistory counsellor. → 34:2.

Kugelmann, Gertrud; *née* Oppenheim (1839 to *after* 1902) Wife of Dr. L. *Kugelmann; married ca. end of 1857. Sister of Max *Oppenheim. M's nickname for her was Frau Gräfin (Madam Countess). → 68:70; 74:31, 32.

Kugelmann, Louis, *sometimes* Ludwig (1828 to 1902) Physician (gynecologist) in Hanover. Son of a Jewish businessmann, K. was brought up in Westphalia and the Rhineland; read early socialistic literature; took part in the 1848 revolution; was a member of the CL till 1852 (according to Hundt). He was introduced to M, via letters, by Freiligrath in 1862; and correspondence ensued till 1874 (and later, with E). K. was active for the IWMA in Germany; delegate to its congresses 1867 and 1872; he helped publicize *Capital,* and tried to be helpful to M as much as possible. He joined the Eisenacher party (1869) and remained a member of the S-D party till his death. —M's personal break, or cooling off, with K. took place in Carlsbad, where M and daughter Eleanor were visiting (→ 74:32), and it was occasioned by both Marxes' revulsion at the domineering way in which K. treated his own wife. See letters, M to E, Sep 1 and 18, 1874, and Eleanor M to her sister Jenny, Sep 5, 1874. The account of this episode in Payne's biography of M is fictional. —There is a full-length biography by Martin Hundt, *Louis K.* (1874). *Note:* Hundt says that K. virtually always used the name Louis, not Ludwig. → 62:57, 61, 62; 63:2, 13, 14; 64:35, 41; 65:15; 66:2, 6, 8, 36, 39–41, 44, 46, 48, 49; 67:2, 12, 14, 15, 26, 31, 37, 38, 41, 48; 68:8, 11, 13, 18, 20, 22, 35, 40–42, 57, 59,

70, 71; 69:13, 56; 70:18, 38, 41, 64; 71:9, 20–23, 35, 64; 72:31, 36, 48; 73:38, 56, 57; 74:5, 6, 21, 31, 32; 76:32; 92:50; 93:42; 95:8, 25. #M70, M172.

Kuliscioff, Anna; *née* Rosenstein; *Russ.* Anna Mikhailovna **Kulishova** (1854 to 1925) Kuliscioff or Kulisciov is the Italian spelling; it is under this name that she figures in most books. —Russian revolutionary, at first Narodnik-anarchist-nihilist in tendency; active in the Russian émigré movement in Zurich (1870s), and with the Emancipation of Labor group in the mid-1880s. On a return to Russia, she married Kulishov (who was imprisoned during 1876–1883), was active in Odessa and Kiev, and emigrated permanently in 1877. With Andrea Costa, she worked in Lugano and Paris for the anarchists; was expelled (1878) to Switzerland, where she met Malon. Most of the rest of her life she was active in the Italian socialist movement, as a leading figure and prominent Marxist. From 1885 she was Turati's companion; with him, a founder of *Critica Sociale* (1891). → 93:19; 94:4. #ME33.

Kulturkampf Bismarck's campaign to undermine the power of the Catholic church in Germany (1871–c.1887). → 75:31.

Kunemann, *Dr.* (b. c.1828) German physician in Monte Carlo; Alsatian in origin. M was under his care in Monte Carlo in 1882. (In politics, a "republican philistine," thought M). → 82:19.

Kurz, Isolde (1853 to 1944) German writer of poetry and fiction. Her best-known works were pubd a good deal after her dealings with M on the trans of Lissagaray. Author of: books of poems (1888, 1903); short stories in *Florentiner Novellen* (1890), *Italienische Erzählungen* (1895). → 76:33; 77:1, 38.

Kwasniewski, Gustav (1833 to 1902) German Social-Democrat; teacher, writer, editor. A founder of the Demo Workers Assoc in Berlin, he was active in the Berlin section of IWMA, and in the Eisenacher party (1869+). Editor of the *Crimmitschauer Bürger- und Bauernfreund* (1871–1875). Later on, he withdrew from the socialist and workers' movement. → 71:48.

L

La Albuera (Sp.) *See* Albuera.

Labor *See also* Labour (for British references).

Labor Reform Association. (U.S.) Organization founded by Osborne Ward (1865). → 68:31.

The **Labor Standard** NY, Paterson (NJ), Fall River (Mass.), Apr 12, 1876, to 1900. Weekly. Ed by J. P. McDonnell, A. Douai, et

al. —Socialist paper; it continued the numbering of *The Socialist* (which appeared as Vol. I nos. 1–17). Official organ of the Workingmen's party of the U.S.; connected with the IWMA till its dissolution, then became organ of the International Labor Union. —Not to be confused with the *Labour Standard* (London). → 76:24, 37; 77:47; 78:10; 88:29; #E394, E922.

Laborde, Count Alexandre (Louis Joseph) de (1773 or 1774 to 1842) French archeologist, politician, travel writer. Serving (1800+) on a diplomatic mission to Spain, he worked on a descriptive survey of the Iberian Peninsula, producing Voyage pittoresque et historique de l'Espagne (1806–1820) and other works. —M (1845) read his De l'esprit d'association dans tous les intérêts de la communauté (1818). #M575.

The **Labour Elector;** The organ of practical socialism London, June 1888 to July 1894. Weekly. Ed by H. H. Champion. —Socialist journal. → 89:15, 17, 19, 24, 26, 31. #E2, E388, E443, E562, E598.

The **Labour Leader** London, Oct. 10, 1891, to Sep 28, 1922, under this title. First, monthly; then (1894+) weekly. Ed by Keir Hardie (till 1904). —Founded 1887 as The Miner (Edinburgh), it became the organ of the Scottish Labour party with its new name; later (1893+), organ of the ILP; superseded by the New Leader (1922). → 89:18, 20. #E490.

Labour Parliament (Manchester, Mar 6–18, 1854) A Chartist group headed by E. *Jones inaugurated (1853) a broad workers' organization, called the Mass Movement, to coordinate the burgeoning strike movment, under a delegated assembly of TU and other workers' reprs. This "Parliament" met only once before the movement petered out. → 54:7, 12, 13, 15. #M86, M439, M468, M494, M619.

The **Labour Standard** London, May 7, 1881, to July 4, 1885. Weekly. Ed by George Shipton. —Trade-union periodical. E collaborated with it May 7 to Aug 6, 1881. — Not to confuse with the Labor Standard (NY, etc.). → 81:3, 25, 31, 37, 42. #E16, E40, E81, 187, E266, E295, E753, E870, E880, E894, E895, E921.

Labriola, Antonio (1843 to 1904) Italian academic Marxist; one of the first university profs to expound M. Prof at Rome (1874+), he was at first a Hegelian; began lecturing on historical materialism in 1891. Delegate to the International Socialist Congress of 1893; he later opposed Bernstein's Revisionism in his own abstract way. Works: His In memoria del Manifesto dei Comunisti (1895) and Del materialismo storico (1896) were transd, together, as Essays on the materialistic conception of history (1904); his Discorrendo di socialismo e di filosophia (1898) was transd as Socialism and philosophy (1907). —Note: He is often confused with the Italian syndicalist writer Arturo Labriola (1873–1959). → 90:15; 91:12, 15, 42; 92:17, 24, 40; 93:4, 44, 55; 94:30, 32; 95:7, 24, 34.

Labusquière, John (Delille) (1852 to 1939) French socialist; born in Louisiana (U.S.) of well-off émigré parents; educated in medicine in France. There he early joined IWMA (1870); wrote for L'Egalité (1877–1878) and other left papers; opposed Boulanger in the 1880s; became a Possibilist (1882), active in the group's work. He sat in the Paris city council (1896–1902) as an independent socialist. He later played a role in the consolidation of socialist unity. Author of a volume in the Histoire Socialiste ed by Jaurès; also of fiction under the name Jean Maubourg. → 78:17.

Lacambre, Antoine Louis Cyrille (1815 to 1894) French Blanquist; physician; Blanqui's nephew. He was a member of secret societies during the July monarchy; in 1848, vice-pres of the Central Republican Society; arrested, but escaped to Spain (1849), where he became a prominent physician. From there, he continued to aid Blanqui and finance Blanquist organs. Returning to France in Sep 1870, he later retired to a provincial estate, where Blanqui was arrested in Mar 1871. — Caution: L.'s given names are subject to much variation; above I use the NUC form. → 61:30, 41.

La Cécilia, Napoléon; full Napoléon François Paul Thomas (1835 to 1878) French revolutionist; French-born of a Neapolitan father and Corsican mother. After studying in Corsica, Paris, Leipzig, he joined Garibaldi's forces (1860); taught school in Naples; became prof of math at Ulm (Ger.); fought in the French army (1870). In the Paris Commune he became Gen. Eudes's chief of staff, then a gen; afterward, escaped to England; émigré (1871–1877), in assoc with Vermersch, living by teaching (under the name Paul Lacombe). Maitron's DBMOF says he did not join the IWMA though he was in contact with M. After moving to Egypt (1877) he died of TB. —The info in IML sources (MEW, GCFI, also KMC) on his name and nationality is erroneous. → 71:46; 72:45, 54, 58; 75:48.

Lachâtre (or **La Châtre**), Maurice (1814 to 1900) French pub'r and leftist writer; his firm pubd the French edn of Capital, I (1872–1875). —Early converted by reading Saint-Simon, Fourier, and Cabet (1835+), he first set up a "model commune" on a Gironde family estate; authored a Histoire des papes (1842–1843) and Dictionnaire universel (1853–1854), which drew government persecution along with his publishing activities; fled to Barcelona (1858); returned to Paris (1864), and resumed his publishing business. As a supporter and officer of the Paris Commune, he was a refugee in various countries till the 1879 amnesty. The publishing firm of Maurice Lachâtre et Cie had been established in 1870 and was put in trust, by government order, under Just Vernouillet, managed by L.'s son-in-law Henri *Oriol, who was in actual charge of producing Capital. —Note: Maitron's

DBMOF (alone) states that he was born Claude Maurice, Baron de Lachastre, called Maurice La Châtre and Marius Lebrenn or Lebrein. All this it leaves unexplained, but I presume Lebrenn or Lebrein were refugee pseudonyms. → 71:65; 72:7, 12, 18, 29, 58; 73:57; 74:2, 20; 85:3. #M131.

La Chaux-de-Fonds (Switz.) Industrial town in the Jura Mts. → 70:36.

Lachmann, Karl; *full* Karl Konrad Friedrich Wilhelm (1793 to 1851) German philological scholar; a pioneer in modern methods of textual criticism. His academic career included posts at Königsberg and, finally, Berlin; his works comprise laborious investigations into a number of German and Latin authors, the principles of Middle High German, etc. #E528.5.

Lacretelle, Charles de; *full* Jean Charles Dominique de (1766 to 1855) French historian and journalist; *orig* a lawyer; called Lacretelle [le] jeune to distinguish him from brother Pierre Louis. A royalist sympathizer during the French Revolution, he became under the Empire a prof of history at Paris (1809). His rather pedestrian works include *Précis historique de la Révolution française* (1801–1809), *Histoire de France pendant le XVIIIe siècle* (1808–1812). M (1843) read his *Histoire de France depuis la Restauration,* t. 3 (1831–1832). → 43:32.

Lacroix, Silvestre François (1765 to 1843) French mathematician; prof at the Ecole Polytechnique and College de France. His chief works were *Traité du calcul différentiel et du calcul intégral* (1797–1800); *Traité élémentaire du calcul des probabilités* (1816). → 78:1.

Lafargue, Charles Etienne; *called* Schnapps, Schnappy, Fouchtra (1869 to 1872) First child born to Paul and Laura Lafargue; M's grandson. Note that the Lafargues had a second son who did not live long: Marc Laurent (1871–1872). → 69:9; 72:40.

Lafargue, François (1806 to 1870 or 1871) Father of Paul Lafargue. —He was the son of a French father living in San Domingo (orig from the Bordeaux area) and a mulatto woman of San Domingo. His father disappeared (prob killed) during revolutionary upheavals on the island. His mother fled to Cuba, later to New Orleans (or perhaps New Caledonia) with her son François, earning her living as a street seller. François eventually became a successful planter around Santiago de Cuba; then (1851) moved to Bordeaux, where he became a prosperous wine merchant. → 67:25.

Lafargue, Laura   *See* Marx, Laura.

Lafargue, Paul (1842 to 1911) French Marxist organizer and writer. Born in Cuba, he was brought to France (1851) by his father (q.v.); studied at Bordeaux and Toulouse, then started medical studies at Paris. Involved in the republican and socialist student movement, he began writing for the left press, esp *Rive Gauche,* and was an organizer of the first international student congress at Liège (1865), for which he was expelled from school; emigrated to England to finish medical studies. In London he came to know M, and joined the IWMA; member of the GC and corr secy for Spain (1866–1868). Admitted to medical practice in England, he returned to Paris, then Bordeaux; married Laura M (1868). He was active for the IWMA in Bordeaux, where he gave support to the Paris Commune in the provincial movement. After its fall, he fled to Spain for a year; worked with *Iglesias in building the IWMA, fought the Bakuninist operation and contributed to *La Emancipación,* the socialist organ. He took part in the Hague Congress (1872); then settled in London; contributed to Guesde's *Egalité* and Malon's *Revue Socialiste.* After the amnesty, he returned (1882) to France and joined up with Guesde to build a socialist party, the French Workers party. In the ensuing years (until committing suicide in the face of old age) he was a prominent spokesman and writer of the "Guesdist" party; occasionally a member of the Chamber of Deputies; recognized as a leading Marxist; later, a leader of the united SP after 1905. He remained for years in close correspondence with E, who used him (as well as Laura) as a channel for advice to the French movement, though often with misgivings about Paul's inadequacies as a socialist thinker and political guide—above all, during the Boulanger crisis, when Paul tended to a line of left-Boulangism against E's strenuous dissuasion. —Lafargue was a facile writer, and his articles and brochures ran in a vein of Marxist popularization: *Le droit à la paresse* (1880); *Le religion du capital* (1887); *Idéalisme et matérialisme dans l'histoire* (1895); *Propriété, origine et évolution* (1895); *Socialisme et les intellectuels* (1900); *Question de la femme* (1904); etc. —The ethnic mixture in L.'s ancestry has often been noted, esp since L. liked to boast that "in [his] veins ran the blood of three oppressed races" (see the entry for François L., his father). As for Paul's mother: her father was Abraham Armagnac, who was (prob) a French Jew, whose parents resided in Santo Domingo and sent him to France to be educated. Her mother was a Carib Indian (not formally married). → 65:19; 66:22, 31, 41, 42, 47, 50, 53; 67:13, 22, 25, 34, 37; 68:24, 31; 69:14, 23, 35, 46, 47, 55, 63; 70:18, 20, 24, 25, 40, 42, 55, 59; 71:2, 9, 27, 32, 38, 39, 43, 59, 64, 65; 72:3, 15, 21, 27, 31, 35, 40, 41, 49, 68; 73:1, 20, 23, 44; 74:4; 75:35; 80:2, 4, 8, 15, 16, 23, 27, 35, 39; 81:50, 51, 57; 82:5, 30, 40, 43; 83:2, 12; 84:9, 11, 12, 16, 19, 24, 25, 28, 40, 61; 85:4, 13, 17, 18, 34, 40, 44; 86:8, 22, 38, 40, 44, 48, 55; 87:5, 11, 13, 34, 45,

49; 88:6, 11, 12, 16, 21, 32, 38, 39; 89:3, 4, 8, 12, 13, 15, 17, 25, 32; 90:7, 32, 37; 91:7, 8, 11, 12, 14, 18, 23, 30, 44, 51, 56; 92:13, 25, 52, 56, 58, 59, 62; 93:5, 8, 9, 20, 28, 29, 44; 94:4, 8, 28, 31, 43; 95:10, 11, 21, 24, 37. #ME6, ME88, ME185; M322, M348, M406, M786; E106, E326, E435, E446, E474, E593, E759.

La Farina, Giuseppe (1815 to 1863) Italian politician; b. Sicily. He took part in the revolutionary events of 1848–1849 in Tuscany and Sicily, as a moderate liberal; pubd *Storia della Rivoluzione Italiana 1821–48* (1849) and other historical writings. From 1855 he was linked to Cavour; founded (1856) *Piccolo Corriere d'Italia*, organ of the Società Nazionale Italiana, of which he became pres. In 1860 he acted as Cavour's emissary in Sicily (to dish Garibaldi, M thought); councillor of state in Sicily (1860–1861). #M409.

Lagrange, Joseph Louis (1736 to 1813) Great French mathematician, also astronomer; b. Turin of a French-Italian family. Prof at Turin at age 19; helped develop the calculus of variations; succeeded Euler (1766) as director of the Berlin Academy of Sciences for two decades. In Paris (1787+), became prof at the university; created senator and count by Napoleon I. Author of: *Leçons sur le calcul des fonctions* (1806); *Théorie des fonctions analytiques* (1797); *Mécanique analytique* (1787). → 82:47.

Lahure, Louis (c.1850 to 1878) French printer, in Paris. It was in his shop that the *Lachâtre firm had the French edn of *Capital* printed. → 75:41.

Laing, Samuel, *called The younger* (1812 to 1897) British (Scottish-born) lawyer, railway administrator, and politician. Starting as private secy (1837) to the pres of the Bd of Trade, he rose as secy of its Railway Dep (1842–1847) and a member of the parliamentary Railway Commsn (1845), finally becoming head of the London, Brighton & S. Coast Railway (1848–1855, 1867–1894); also chairman of the Crystal Palace Co. (1852–1855). He was a Liberal Limp (i.e., lib-imperialist) MP (1852–1885, with gaps), and held financial posts in government (1859–1865). —M (1851) excerpted his first pubd work, a prize essay: *National distress, its causes and remedies* (1844). L. later pubd books on popular science. → 51:67.

Lake Champlain Long lake between upper NY state and Vermont. → 88:30.

Lake George Lake in NY state, south of Lake Champlain. → 88:30.

Lake Ontario Easternmost of the Great Lakes, between the U.S. and Canada. → 88:30.

Lake Placid Lake and resort town in the Adirondack Mts., NY state. → 88:30.

Lallerstedt, Sven Gustaf (1816 to 1864) Swedish historian and publicist. M (1857) studied his *La Scandinavie, ses craintes et ses espérances* (1856). → 57:6.

Lalor, John (1814 to 1856) Irish-born journalist and writer, active in England; trained as a lawyer. Of a Catholic merchant family, he settled in London (1836), rose as a reporter, became senior editor of the *Morning Chronicle*, specializing on social and domestic questions. He joined the Unitarians; edited this church's weekly, and contributed articles on the Factory Bill, Ireland, and education. His last work was *Money and morals: A book for the times* (1852), which M excerpted. → 59:78.

Lamartine, Alphonse de; *full* Alphonse Marie Louis **de Prat de Lamartine** (1790 to 1869) French writer, politician, and poet, first known for his *Méditations poétiques* (1820). Orig a Legitimist royalist, diplomat under the Bourbons, he stood aside in the revolution of 1830; gradually turned liberal. His *Histoire des Girondins* (1847) glorified the right wing of the French Revolution; in the Chamber he gained renown as an orator. In the 1848 revolution he joined the Provisional Government as foreign min and de facto head. His attempt at a middle-of-the-road course failed, since sentimental elocution about Truth and Justice solved nothing about truth and justice; the Cavaignac massacre of the June uprising wrecked his government; L. deflated till the presidential election of Jan 1849 gave him few votes. He wisely devoted the rest of his life to literary pursuits. → 43:28; 47:49, 55. #M441; E466.

Lamplugh, George William (1859 to 1926) English geologist; on friendly terms with E; friend of *Dakyns. He worked for the Geological Survey; his publications are technical reports. → 93:23; 94:8.

Lancashire (Eng.) Industrial county in the north country, incl *Manchester and *Liverpool. → 71:62; 92:38.

Lancaster rifle Rifle with slightly oval bore, named for its inventor. #E704.

Lancizolle, Karl Wilhelm von (Deleuze de) (1796 to 1871) German historian, of French (Languedoc) family. He completed his law training in Berlin and Göttingen; became a prof at Berlin (1820+). His main field was the history of German law; appointed (1852) director of the Prussian state archives. → 43:32.

Land and Freedom *See* Zemlya i Volya.

Land and Labour League (Eng.) Organization, founded (Oct 27, 1869) at a conference in London to work for a land-nationalization program. Its leadership overlapped with the membership of the GC/IWMA, with *Eccarius and *Boon as joint secys and *Weston as treasurer. → 65:2, 58; 69:1, 67.

Land Tenure Reform Association English organization founded in mid-1869, under the leadership of J. S. Mill, to advocate abolition of primogeniture and entailment ("free trade in land," i.e., complete bourgeoisifcation). → 71:10.

Landolphe, Pierre François (1809 to 1889) French socialist. He took part in the June 1849 demonstration in Paris, then emigrated to London. Friend of L. Blanc, member of Louis Greppo's Comité Central de Résistance, he supported the Willich–Schapper group of the CL. He later moved to Guernsey, and returned to France in 1871, but stayed out of political activity. → 51:5, 10.

Landor, R. American journalist; in 1871, a correspondent in London for the NY *World*. (This much emerges from his interview with M; otherwise nothing is known about him.) → 71:36. #M417.

Lange, Friedrich Albert (1828 to 1875) German neo-Kantian philosopher and social reformer. After teaching philosophy at Bonn and Duisberg (1855+), he was forced out by political harassment; became coeditor of the *Rhein- und Ruhr-Zeitung* (1862); secy, Chamber of Commerce in Duisberg (till 1864). Oriented toward the labor movement, he became a member of the Exec of the UGWA (1864–1866) as a left progressive; pubd a book advocating social reform, *Die Arbeiterfrage* (1865); member of the IWMA, and delegate to its 1867 congress. Feeling isolated in Germany, he moved (1866) to Switzerland, and worked on various papers; prof at Zurich (1870+) and at Marburg (1872+). Perhaps best known for his *Geschichte des Materialismus* (1866). → 65:25; 70:38.

Lange, Ludwig (1825 to 1885) German classical scholar and philologist. Prof at Prague (1855+), Giessen (1859+), Leipzig (1871+). His chief work was *Handbuch der römischen Altertümer* (1856–1871); he also authored a history of Roman military institutions, in Latin (1846). M (1879) studied his first-named work. → 79:54.

Langethal, Christian Eduard (1806 to 1878) German botanist. Prof of natural history at Eldena (1834+), Jena (1839+), with focus on the study of rural economy. His chief works were a *Handbuch der landwirthschaftlichen Pflanzenkunde* in many edns, and his *Geschichte der teutschen Landwirthschaft* (1847–1856), which E (1873) made notes on. → 73:49.

Lankester, Sir Edwin Ray; *called* Ray (1847 to 1929) English zoologist and naturalist. Prof at London (1874+), Oxford (1891+); director, Natural History Dept., BM (1898–1907); knighted (1907); founder, Marine Biological Assoc (1884). Author of: *Science from an easy chair* (1910–1912); *Great and small*

things (1923). —L. became a friend of M at some point, and attended his funeral. In 1880 M made inquiries about a possible Russian trans of L.'s new *Degeneration. A chapter in Darwinism.* → 80:32; 83:12.

Łapinski, Teofil (1826 to 1886) Polish national-revolutionary officer. He took part in the Polish liberation movement; in the revolution of 1848–1849, a colonel in the Hungarian revolutionary forces; also (under the name Teffik Bey) in the Crimean War on the side of Turkey against Russia; in Circassia, against Russia (1857–1858). Later, as an émigré in London, he was active in forming a Polish Committee to support a new Polish uprising; provided M with info on Poland. → 63:31, 33.

Laplanders or Lapps Inhabitants of Lapland, the arctic region in the N. of Scandinavia. → 90:30. #M319.

Lappenberg, Johann Martin (1794 to 1865) German historian. Archivist to the Hamburg Senate (1823–1863); many of his works deal with Hamburg history. Collaborator on *Monumenta Germaniae Historica*. Prob his chief work was *Geschichte von England* (1834–1837), which M (1843) excerpted. → 43:32.

Larroque, Edouard; *real name* Charles (b. 1829) Bookkeeper in a Bordeaux candle factory, he joined the IWMA in this city and (at least by 1870) was active in the local leadership, including during the Paris Commune period, when he helped to mobilize Bordeaux support for the Commune. After the Hague Congress (1872) L. acted as the GC's repr in Bordeaux, keeping in touch via E. Soon fleeing arrest, he crossed the Spanish border to San Sebastián, from where he vainly tried to maintain links with the IWMA in southern France, using the name Latraque.
—This account follows Maitron's *DBMOF*, which says that the MEW info on him is erroneous. MEW, but not DBMOF, gives variant spellings of his name, Larocque, Lorocque. → 73:36.

Lasker, Eduard (1829 to 1884) German liberal politician; lawyer by profession. Son of a Jewish businessman, he took part in the 1848 revolution in Vienna; entered Prussian government service (1856); member of the Prussian Diet (1865–1870), and of the Reichstag (1867+), first as a Progressivist party man, then as a founding leader of the National Liberals, till he broke with Bismarck's tariff policy (1878) and left the Liberals (1880), losing influence. —M (1876) discussed L.'s book *Erlebnisse einer Mannes-Seele* (1873). → 76:24.

Laski, Harold J. #ME33.

Lassalle, Ferdinand (1825 to 1864) Son of an affluent Jewish merchant named Lassal, young L., then a law student, was engaged by the Countess Sophie von *Hatzfeldt to defend her interests (financial) in a fight with her husband: a contest which lasted ten years, and which L. brought to a successful end by dint of a noted robbery and less noted blackmail. As a result of the financial settlement, L. became a man of independent wealth for the rest of his life. —During the 1848 revolution in Düsseldorf, L. took part in the movement; came to know and admire M as editor of the Cologne NRZ. Afterward, in emigration, M tried to get L. admitted to the CL in the Rhineland, but the local group refused to take him in. During the 1850s L. (in correspondence with M) performed services for him with pub'rs, etc. In 1859 L. moved to Berlin, where he led the life of a wealthy man in society, and made an attempt to gain the leadership of the liberals, who, however, fought shy of him. In 1862 a Leipzig workers' group which wanted to initiate an independent working-class political movement asked him to head it, which he consented to do. Reshaping the initiative in his own image, he led in founding the *General German Workers Assoc by spring 1863, with himself as permanent pres and, literally, dictator by statute. For about two years in all, L. conducted a campaign of agitation, with limited success, which discouraged him mightily. Then came his final affair with Helene von Dönniges: L (always a womanizer) wanted to marry her, but her aristocratic father betrothed her to the Wallachian Count von Racowitza. Lassalle challenged the count to a duel; on Aug 28, 1864, L. was wounded, and died three days later. —L. founded the GGWA on the basis of a specific state-socialist platform. State-socialism looks to the existing state to institute socialism; for L. the existing state was that of Bismarck, with whom he tried to make a secret deal (known in gen at the time, later documented): i.e., L. proposed to trade working-class support (mobilized by his GGWA under its presidential dictatorship) for a dictatorship by a "social monarchy" which would introduce the basic reform advocated by Lassalleanism. This basic reform was a demand for state aid to producers' cooperative assocs. The role of universal suffrage was to be to mobilize a working-class vote to counterbalance that of bourgeois liberalism, which was recognized as the joint enemy. Behind this platform was L.'s "cult of the state," his glorification of the state as such as "the immemorial vestal fire of all civilization." L. was hostile to trade-unionism both in practice and in theory; he argued that the so-called "iron law of wages" (which M rejected) made it impossible for workers to improve their conditions under capitalism. Though the

documents in the case were not published till 1927, M was informed at the time on L.'s real politics; on a number of occasions he expressed his strong rejection of L.'s notion of a state-socialism based on a deal with the Junker-absolutist state. "Politically," he told L. himself, "we agree in nothing except some far distant ultimate ends"; L., he charged, was "the future workers' dictator" in aspiration; his theory was that of Hegelian idealism, not of a materialist view of society. In this connection, it is worth stressing that the myth that M's hostility to L. was simply a matter of personal hostility is utterly contrary to the facts of their relationship. The best account of M's view of Lassalle and Lassalleanism was written, under E's direct tutelage, by E. Bernstein in London and is available in English under the title *Ferdinand Lassalle as a social reformer* (1893), transd by Eleanor M. For general background, there is a biography by David Footman, *FL, romantic revolutionary* (1947). —L.'s first works purported to be theoretical and scholarly; none survives as a work of significance: *Die Philosophie Herakleitos des Dunklen von Ephesus* (1858); *Franz von Sickingen, ein historische Tragödie* (verse drama, 1859); *Der italienische Krieg und die Aufgabe Preussens* (1859); *Das System der erwobenen Rechte* (1861); *Die Philosophie Fichte's und die Bedeutung des deutshcen Volksgeistes* (1862). For the political agitation of the last couple of years, the chief pamphlets were the following, all dated 1863, except the last: *Offnes Antwortschreiben an das Central-Comite zur Berufung eines Allgemeinen Deutschen Arbeitercongresses; Arbeiterlesebuch, Rede Lassalle's zu Frankfurt am Main am 17. und 19. Mai 1863; Arbeiterprogramm: Ueber den besondern Zusammenhang der gegenwärtigen Geschichtsperiode mit der Idee des Arbeiterstandes; Das Criminal-Urtheil wider mich mit kritischen Randnoten zum Zweck der Appellationsrechtfertigung; Die indirecte Steuer und die Lage der arbeitenden Klassen; Was nun? Zweiter Vortrag über Verfassungswesen; Die Wissenschaft und die Arbeiter*. And an economic polemic: *Herr Bastiat-Schulze von Delitzsch, der ökonomische Julian, oder Capital und Arbeit* (1864). → 48:78; 49:3, 10, 12, 13, 17, 23, 31, 43; 50:6, 14, 16, 22; 51:19, 26, 28, 31, 58; 52:7, 8, 16, 33, 36, 55; 53:14, 24; 54:1, 8, 16, 20, 29, 50; 55:5, 8, 11, 22, 33; 56:6; 57:17, 52, 53; 58:8, 12, 13, 17, 24, 25, 28, 41, 46; 59:4, 10, 13, 14, 17, 18, 21, 23, 25, 29, 30, 33, 36–38, 40, 47, 62, 65, 66, 68; 60:7, 13, 15, 21, 23, 24, 29, 35, 45–47, 51, 54; 61:1, 3, 5, 8, 10, 11, 14, 15, 17, 21–23, 28, 30, 31, 41, 49; 62:3, 20–22, 29–31, 34, 35, 44, 61; 63:2, 3, 6, 16, 24, 36, 39; 64:1, 13, 17, 22, 27, 32, 38, 39, 46; 65:2, 7, 8, 24; 66:22; 68:56; 69:27; 74:8, 29;

77:42; 91:11, 55, 61; 92:39; 94:2; 95:11, 13.
—*Lassalle "cult"*: 64:46; 65:15; 7019.
#M52, M361, M442, M443, M694; E415–417.

Lassalleans Followers of *Lassalle; specif, members of the *German General Workers Assoc. → 65:8, 15, 18, 24, 54; 66:14; 67:47; 68:2, 50, 56, 64, 70; 69:2, 41, 48, 66, 70; 70:36, 40; 71:59, 62; 72:62; 73:1, 12, 23, 27; 74:3, 25, 29, 36, 38, 39; 75:2, 12; 77:37; 82:37; 83:7, 30; 87:49; 89:37; 90:6, 51; 91:8, 11, 23, 50. #M688; E380, E552, E644. *See also* *Schweitzer, J. B.

Latvia Baltic country; incorporated into the USSR (1940); capital, Riga; ethnically Lettish. #M319.

Lauderdale, Earl of. James **Maitland** (1759 to 1839) British politician and economist; lawyer by profession. MP (1780–1789); a Scottish peer (1789+) in the House of Lords, where he headed the Whig opposition; later, a British peer (Baron Lauderdale of Thirlestane); lord high keeper of the Great Seal of Scotland. He shifted to the Tories (1821) and voted against the reform bills. In economics, he was a critic of Adam Smith from a bourgeois standpoint. Author of *The depreciation of the paper-currency of Gr Brit proved* (1812). M (1844–1845) excerpted a French trans (1808) of his *Inquiry into the nature and origin of public wealth* (1804; rev, 1819). → 44:48.

Lausanne (Switz.) City on the N. shore of Lake Geneva. → 48:75, 82; 49:33, 35; 67:22, 28, 32, 37.

Laveleye, Baron Emile de; *full* Emile Louis Victor (1822 to 1892) Belgian liberal economist. Prof of polit eco at Liège (1864+); disciple of the left Catholic François Huet; a sort of Belgian Katheder-socialist, as evidenced in his *De la propriété et de ses formes primitives* (1874); *Eléments d'économie politique* (1882); best known for his much-reprinted *Le socialisme contemporain* (1881). E, however, was contemptuous: L. spread only "lies and legends" about IWMA history, for example. → 76:32.

Lavrov, Peter (*Russ.* Pyotr) Lavrovich (1823 to 1900) Russian socialist; a leading theoretician of the Narodnik revolutionary tendency. Son of a well-to-do noble, he had a military education, but, influenced by radical writers like Chernyshevsky, he entered revolutionary activity (1862). He was arrested (1866), exiled (1868), helped to escape by Lopatin, and fled to Paris (1870); took part in the Paris Commune. In emigration in Zurich he edited *Vperyod!* (1873–1876); also *Vestnik Narodnoi Voli* (1883–1887). A longtime friend and correspondent of M&E, he was recognized as one of the most representative leaders of Russian socialism; a vice-chairman at the International Socialist Congress of 1889. His writings were influential in the Russian movement. There is a full-length study: P. Pomper, *Peter L. and the Russian revolutionary movement* (1972). → 71:23, 33, 41; 74:14, 26, 37; 75:5, 11, 21, 26, 35, 38, 43, 44, 46, 48; 76:24, 30, 32; 77:7, 9, 12, 13, 16; 81:43; 82:6, 8, 17, 25, 29; 83:12, 17; 84:3, 7, 11, 12, 16, 52; 87:42; 90:48; 93:26, 32, 46; 94:6; 95:7. #E767.

Law, Harriet (Teresa); *née* Frost (1831 to 1897) English radical secularist/freethinker (atheist). After her father, a contractor, lost his money, she ran a school; was converted in arguments with freethinkers; married Edward Law (1855). By 1859 she was a lecturer on freethought and radical issues; toured the provinces; known for courage in the face of hostile mobs, and blunt honesty; hostile to physicians as bunco artists. Though a leader of the movement, she never joined Bradlaugh's National Secular Society. She also championed women's suffrage, women's rights, republicanism, the Reform League; member of the GC/IWMA (1867–1872), though not active. She took over the *Secular Chronicle* (1876–1879) as her organ, losing money; in genl, she was financed by her husband's business (property dealing). → 68:42, 70; 78:29.

Law, John; *called* John **Law of Lauriston** (1671 to 1729) Scottish finance speculator, operating in France. He parlayed government support into his "Mississippi Scheme," using a royal bank issuing credit and paper money; a frenzy of speculation swept France; the bubble burst in 1720. L. died a poor gambler in Venice. Author of *Money and trade considered* (1705). M (1844) excerpted his *Considérations sur le numéraire et le commerce* in Daire's collection. → 44:48.

Lawrence, Matthew British trade-unionist. Secy of the Glasgow Trades Council; then pres of the Operative Tailors' Protective Assoc in London. Member of the GC/IWMA (1866–1868); delegate to its Geneva congress (1866). → 66:43.

Layard, Sir Austen Henry (1817 to 1894) English politician; also an archeologist. In politics, L. was a radical liberal, esp in the 1850s; MP (1852+); later, undersecy in the Foreign Office and a diplomat at Madrid and Constantinople. —In 1855 he was on the commsn of inquiry into army conditions in the Crimea; he attacked the practice of appointing upper-class nonentities to government posts. M's mentions were of occasions (1853, 1855) when L. disclosed the way the government oligarchy operated. #ME1; M446, M447.

Leach, James English Chartist worker (weaver, spinner); a leader of the movement in Lancashire in the 1840s; in 1840, first pres of the Chartist Exec. —E became acquainted with him in Manchester, and through him with other Chartist workers. → 43:24.

The **Leader** London, Mar 30, 1850, to Dec 31, 1859, under this title. Weekly. —Liberal. Continued as *The Leader and Saturday Analyst* (1860). #ME31.

League of Peace and Freedom See Peace Congress.

League of the Just; Ger. Bund der Gerechten (1836 to 1847) Immediate predecessor of the *Communist League, this organization had developed out of the radical German artisan émigrés in Paris, where they had first (1832) formed a Deutscher Volksverein (German People's Assoc), which the French government broke, then a secret society, the League of the Outcasts (or Outlaws) (Bund der Geächteten) under the leadership of *Venedey and T. *Schuster. Venedey quit in the face of the group's movement toward a communistic program (community of goods), and more radical émigrés like *Schapper came in; these more leftist workers formed the League of the Just in Paris, still as a secret society. After its participation in the Blanquist putsch of May 1839, Schapper and other leaders were expelled from France, and re-formed the League in England. It was here that the League leaders moved close to M (then in Brussels, but acquainted with the League from Paris 1844 days); until in 1847 the League and the M circle merged to form the Communist League. → 43:14; 44:1, 13; 45:3, 32; 46:1, 20, 36, 40, 44, 45; 47:1, 8, 11, 20. See also K. *Schapper.

Leatham, William (b. end of the 18th century) English banker; author of a couple of pamphlets addressed to an 1840 comm of Parliament, *Letters on the currency* (1840) and *Letters to William Rayner Wood . . . on the currency* (1841). These must have been the writings studied by M (1851). → 51:63.

Le Creusot (Fr.) Town in east-central France, site of the Schneider ironworks. → 70:24.

Ledru-Rollin, Alexandre (Auguste) (1807 to 1874) French politician; lawyer by profession. (Family name was Ledru; he added Rollin.) —Elected deputy (1841), he became the leading figure in the left wing of republican liberalism, allied with L. Blanc's socialism in *La Réforme*. In the 1848 revolution, he became interior min in the Provisional Government and a member of its Exec Commsn. As a moderate, he supported *Lamartine in the May 15 crisis, thus losing mass support without becoming palatable to the Right. After the bungled semiputsch of June 1849, he fled to England, where for two decades he played the role of impotent Demo leader in exile. Returning to France (1869), he stood aside from the Paris Commune and other events,

and faded out of history as a ghost of yesterday's radicalism. With *Flocon he was one of history's lessons in the futility of riding two horses in different directions in time of revolution. → 49:29; 51:9, 10,. #E656, E723.

Lee & Shepard Boston pub'r. → 88:41; 89:6.

Lee, Henry William (1865 to 1932) English socialist; SDF functionary. He joined the SDF (1883) after reading a book by Hyndman; in 1885 this "colorless clerk" became full-time asst secy of the SDF under Champion; some months later, gen secy, for many years, till he handed the post to Albert Inkpin and became editor of *Justice*. Always a reliable follower of Hyndman, he went with him in the splits to the British SP and, later, to the National Socialist party, and finally spoke at Hyndman's funeral. Author of *The Social-Democratic party (S.D.F.) and socialist unity* (1910) → 94:18.

Leeds (Eng.) Industrial city in Yorkshire. → 43:24.

Lefèvre Presumably a French émigré in London; the entry "Lefèvre (London)" comes from M's address book. Even Maitron's *DBMOF* suggests no good identification; allowing for variant spellings, possibilities are an E. M. Lefebvre, H. A. Lefebvre, P. F. Lefebvre-Roncier, Louis Lefeuvre. → 75:48.

Lefort, Henri (1835 to 1917) French leftist journalist; a founder of the IWMA. A law student (without finishing his studies), he resisted Bonaparte's 1851 coup, and was exiled to Jersey; during the 1850s, arrested several times for subversive activity; after the 1859 amnesty, became editor of *L'Avenir National*. With Tolain, he drafted the then-famous Manifesto of the Sixty (labor's challenge to capital). His views were left-republican, vaguely socialistic, influenced by Proudhon; he was active in cooperative work. In 1863 he went to London with a worker-student group to explore possibilities for an international assoc, with the aid of his friend *Le Lubez, and played a substantial role in the subseq founding of the IWMA. M had high regard for his work; but the Proudhonist-controlled Paris section, on narrow sect grounds, strenuously objected to his being given any posts, since he was not their man. The GC (and M) reluctantly yielded to their ultimatum, and L. was forced out. In the ensuing years, he edited French provincial papers. → 65:7, 13, 23.

Lefrançais, Gustave (Adolphe) (1826 to 1901) French leftist; a teacher. A left Proudhonist, he took part in the 1848 revolution; after Bonaparte's 1851 coup, emigrated to London; returned to Paris (1853). In 1870 he was active in the club movement, and then in the Paris Commune. As a refugee in Geneva, he joined the IWMA; became a supporter of the Bakuninists and a contributor to their press. After the 1880 amnesty, he remained on the fringes of the French socialist movement, sympathetic to the anarchists. Author of *Etude sur le mouvement communaliste à Paris en 1871* (1871); *La Commune et la révolution* (1896); *Souvenirs d'un révolutionnaire* (1902). → 72:14.

Legal Eight Hours and International Labour League Group of English socialists formed (July 1890) with the support of E and Eleanor M and their friends, to implement demands raised by the recent Int'l Socialist Congress. → 92:14; 93:24. #E841.

Leghorn; *Ital.* Livorno Tuscan west-coast seaport. → 49:4.

Le Havre (Fr.) On the Channel, port for Paris. → 80:15.

Leibniz, *Baron* Gottfried Wilhelm von; *also spelled* **Leibnitz** (1646 to 1716) German mathematician and philosopher. In the 1670s he developed the infinitesimal calculus (pubd 1684, before Newton's). As a philosopher, he was best known for his work in logic and metaphysics, interpreting the world as consisting of "monads." L. was also active in politics and diplomacy; he never took an academic post, but became pres of the Academy of Sciences in Berlin. —M read such works of his as *La monadologie* (1714); *Essais de théodicée sur la bonté de Dieu* (1710); *Nouveaux essais sur l'entendement humain* (1703). → 41:4; 78:45, 50; 82:47. #M79.

Leicester Square (London) → 50:17.

Leipzig (Ger.) Industrial city, Saxony (now DDR). → 45:27; 49:17; 63:2, 16; 65:29; 66:5, 7, 23, 37; 67:12, 45; 68:40, 50, 56; 69:26, 31, 36, 48, 60; 70:65; 71:48; 72:16, 20, 21, 33, 34, 41; 74:32; 77:27; 78:24; 79:2, 33; 84:3; 90:1. #ME33, ME184; E420, E744.

Leipziger Allgemeine Zeitung Leipzig, 1837 to Apr 1, 1843. Daily. Pub'r: Brockhaus. Ed by Gustav Julius. —Spokesman for the liberal opposition; banned by Prussia from Jan 1, 1843; when Brockhaus changed the editorship, also the name to *Deutsche Allgemeine Ztg* (beginning June D, 1843), the Prussian ban was lifted. → 42:33; 43:4. #M72, M431.

Leipziger Zeitung Leipzig, 1810+ (under this title). —Conservative paper. #ME3.

The **Leisure Hour** London, 1852 to Oct 1905 under this title; then *Leisure Hour Monthly Library.* → 78:44.

Lelewel, Joachim (1786 to 1861) Polish historian; revolutionary democrat. Prof at Warsaw (1818–1821); at Vilna (1821–1824), dismissed for political activity; elected to the Polish Diet (1828). In the 1830–1831 uprising he was a member of the Provisional Government; fled to France, then (1833) to Brussels, where he continued to be a leader of the Polish democratic emigration, and to carry on his scholarly work as the outstanding Polish historian of his time, author of a long list of important works. —In Brussels he became a good friend of M&E, and helped found the Demo Assoc, becoming a member of its Exec; but he was not a communist. → 49:12; 56:38; 60:12.

Le Locle (Switz.) Watchmaking center in the Jura Mts., on the French border. → 69:70.

Le Lubez, Victor (Paul); *erron. called* **Lubez** (b. 1834) French-born radical, active in the IWMA for a while. Little more is known of his background than this summary in M's letter (1864): "a young Frenchman, i.e., in his thirties, who however has grown up in Jersey and London, speaks English excellently, and makes a very good intermediary between the French and English workers. Music teacher and lessons in French." (Though *DBMOF* and other sources call him a "French émigré in London," none seems to know how he became an émigré.) Perhaps because of friendship with *Lefort, he was involved in the preliminaries to the founding of the IWMA, and was elected to the initial GC (member, 1864–1866); corr secy for France (1864–1865). The GC sent him (Feb 1865) to Paris to resolve the fight over Lefort, but, finding himself opposed to the Paris people, he resigned as corr secy. Subseqly he discredited himself by allying himself with Vésinier and the group of French émigrés involved in anti-GC intrigue, and was repudiated by the London French section; the Paris section pressured the Geneva congress of 1866 into voting for his expulsion as a slanderer of the French IWMA. He was also heard from in 1870 as a member of the so-called French section which was in fact outside the IWMA. → 64:26, 31; 65:13, 29, 62; 66:5, 9, 17, 46; 68:55.

Lemaître, Frédéric French émigré in London; owner of a small printshop. He was proposed for the GC/IWMA (1866), but five of his workers objected and the nomination was dropped. He returned to France (1868–1869) where, according to the French IWMA leaders, he constantly intrigued against the GC à la Felix Pyat. In July 1870 he visited London and appeared before the GC with statements in the same vein. In Paris he took part in the Commune (probably); afterward, returned to London, joined the so-called French Section of 1871, which fought the GC. —Note: The GC minutes followed by *GCFI,* spell his name Le Maître; I here follow *DBMOF.* → 66:31; 70:39.

Lemke, Gottlieb (c.1844 to 1885) German émigré in London. A member (according to *KMC,* secy) of the London GWEA, which was now called the Communist WEA, he represented this assoc at M's funeral, also the staff of the *Sozialdemokrat*. → 83:12.

Le Moussu, Benjamin Constant (b. 1846) French Communard émigré in London. Arrived in Paris from his native Morbihan, he worked as a draftsman and, before the Commune, was involved with Blanquists in a local Vigilance Comm. In the Commune, he served as a police official and then as a judicial commissioner. Afterward, a refugee in London, he entered the GC; was corr secy for French-American branches (1871–1872), then corr secy for all of the U.S. for a while; took part in the London Conference (1871) and was a delegate to the Hague Congress (1872) where he supported M's position. By 1874, as the IWMA broke up, he broke with M, but there is no further info on this or on his later life. — There is confusion about his given name: *MEW* gives A. Le Moussu; Freymond also gives C. Le Moussu. I here follow *DBMOF*. → 72:24; 73:4; 74:4, 17.

Leo, Heinrich (1799 to 1878) German historian and publicist. Prof at Halle (1826–1868). By 1838, influenced by "Father" Jahn, he became a leading ideologist of Prussian Junkerdom, a polemicist for extreme reaction, anti-Semitism, patriarchal order, hostility to bourgeois modernization; friend of King Friedrich Wilhelm IV. Author of *Geschichte der italienische Staaten* (1829–1832); *Lehrbuch der Universalgeschichte* (1835–1844). #E591.

Leopold I, King (1790 to 1865) King of the Belgians (1831+), the first in an independent Belgium. #M887.

Lepelletier, Edmond; *full* Edmond Adolphe **Lepelletier de Bouhelier** (1846 to 1913) French socialist; writer; lawyer by profession. Socialistic in sympathy, under the Paris Commune he acted as curator for the archives of the Palais du Conseil d'Etat; but generally he was on the margin of the socialist movement. His notable contribution was his *Histoire de la Commune de 1871* (1911–1913). An opponent of Boulangism, he became a Paris city councillor (1900) and a deputy (1902). → 71:33.

Lépine, Jules French socialist. At the time of M's death, he was secy of the Paris section of the French Workers party (Guesdists). Later (1890) he cofounded the monthly *L'Idée Nouvelle*; shortly thereafter, joined the Blanquist group. —For an interesting letter about personal "rottenness" in the movement, involving Lépine, see Laura Marx Lafargue to E, Nov A, 1887. → 83:12.

Leroux, Pierre (1797 to 1871) French socialist pioneer. He was influential, esp before 1848, in promoting an eclectic socialism alongside the isms of the utopian sects, but since he established no ism of his own, his name faded into the background. —Artisan and printshop worker, L. quit the Saint-Simonian group (1831) when Enfantin took it over; and propagated his eclectic, rather sentimental-reformist, socialism through a number of periodicals and many tracts, esp the *Revue Indépendante* (1841–1848) in collaboration with George Sand. His mystical approach to religion was an element in the development of Christian Socialism. In 1848–1849 he was a deputy in the Constituent and Legislative Assemblies. An opponent of Bonaparte, he was exiled for several years. When he died in April 1871, the Paris Commune took time off to honor him. → 42:26; 44:9; 66:26.

Leroy-Beaulieu, Paul; *full* Pierre Paul (1843 to 1916) French economist. An editor of the *J. des Débats* (1871+), founder and editor of the *Economiste Français* (1873+); prof of finance in a Paris school (1872+), of polit eco at the Collège de France. He was the author of a number of works on polit eco (e.g., *Nouveau traité d'économie politique*, 1895), on finance (e.g., *Science des finances*, 1899), and became esp known as an enemy of collectivism: his book *Le collectivisme, examen critique du nouveau socialisme* (1884) was much praised. An enemy of state intervention in gen (cf. *L'état moderne et ses fonctions*, 1900), he advocated state encouragement of large families and of colonial expansion, undeterred by his ownership of large land tracts in the colonies as well as France. → 84:40.

Leske, Karl Friedrich Julius (1821 to 1886) German pub'r; a liberal Democrat. He was head of the C. W. Leske publishing firm in Darmstadt; often confused (as by *KMC*) with his father, Carl Wilhelm (1784–1837), who had founded the firm, esp since L. often used "C. W. Leske" to sign formal papers for the firm. The firm was first run by C.W.L. (1827–1842), then by his son, K.F.J.L., who gave it up (1867) for financial reasons and set up the Buchdruckerei Leske in Darmstadt. In the 1860s he was a Progressist party supporter; editor/pub'r of the Progressist organ *Hessische Landeszeitung* (1862–1864). → 45:9, 10, 12, 14, 19, 29, 47; 46:12, 28, 33; 47:12.

Leslie, Thomas Edward Cliffe (1827 to 1882) British economist; Irish-born of Scottish-Irish descent; lawyer by profession. Prof of law and polit eco in Belfast (1853+) but resident in London. He pioneered historical methods in polit eco. Author of *Essays in political and moral philosophy* (1879); *Land systems and industrial economy of Ireland, England and continental countries* (1870). E (1881) read his article "Polit eco in the U.S." (*Fortnightly Review*, 1879). → 81:64.

Lessing, Gotthold Ephraim (1729 to 1781) German man of letters, one of the most influential figures of the Enlightenment in

Germany; dramatist, critic, literary historian. Connected with the Berlin and Hamburg theaters, he produced many plays; the best known is *Nathan der Weise* (1779), famed as a Deist philo-Semitic study in toleration; also *Emilia Galotti* (1772); *Minna von Barnhelm* (1763); *Die Juden* (1749). Critical work: *Zur Geschichte und Literatur* (1773–1777); *Laokoon* (1766). He helped to introduce Shakespeare into German literature. → 92:18; 93:34.

Lessing Theater (Berlin)   → 93:42.

Lessner, Friedrich (Carl Eduard); *Angl.* Frederick (1825 to 1910) German artisan (tailor), early communist activist, esp active in England. —Son of a poor petty officer in the Weimar area, he worked as a tailor's apprentice in several cities; adopted communist ideas from the League of the Just group in Hamburg (1846–1847) and Weitling's writings; active in the WA. In Apr 1847 he emigrated to England; became active in the London GWEA and League of the Just, which was turning into the CL under M&E's influence. It was L. who took the ms of the *Com Manifesto* to the printer when it arrived from Brussels. By Aug 1848 he went to Cologne to work with M's NRZ group during the revolution; was an activist in the WA and a member of its Exec (under the name Friedrich Wilhelm Carstens), also a member of the militia. After the revolution (Feb 1850) he moved to Wiesbaden, and was active in the WA there till expelled by the police; then built a WA in Mainz, becoming its pres; went back to Cologne (Aug 1850), and continued CL organizing work in Mainz, Frankfurt, Nuremberg. He was arrested in Mainz (June 1851) in the police drive leading to the Communist trial in Cologne of 1852, and was sentenced to three years. In 1856 he went to England, where he worked uninterruptedly with M&E, in the GWEA and elsewhere. From 1864 he became active in the IWMA: took part in most of its congresses; member of the GC (1864–1872); member of the British Federal Council (1872–1874). Throughout, he was one of M's closest and oldest friends, later also Eleanor M's. With the development of the German movement, he registered his membership (from abroad) with the SDWP and its successor parties; he was founding member of the ILP (1893). His autobiographical memoir was *Sixty years in the Social-Democratic movement; Before 1848 and after; Recollections of an old communist* (1907). → 49:40; 59:50; 64:36; 66:23, 31; 67:8, 13, 32; 68:42, 48; 69:30, 54; 73:7, 11; 78:41; 80:39; 83:11, 12, 42; 91:41; 93:16; 95:24, 37. #ME185; M826.

Letourneau, Charles (Jean Marie) (1831 to 1902) French anthropologist; orig a physician by profession. Prof at the Ecole

d'Anthropologie, Paris (1885–1902). A strong evolutionist and exponent of a scientific materialism, he wrote *L'évolution de la propriété* (1889), *La condition de la femme* (1903), et al. M (1880) read his *La sociologie d'après l'ethnographie* (1880), which advocated basing the former science on the latter. → 80:51.

Leupold, Heinrich (d. 1865) German businessman. Young E worked (1838–1841) as a learner in his commercial firm in Bremen, in the export business. L. also acted as consul in Bremen for the Kingdom of Saxony. → 38:10.

Levasseur, René; *called* René **Levasseur de la Sarthe** (1747 to 1834) French physician, born in the Sarthe district; active participant in the French Revolution as a Jacobin-Robespierrist member of the Convention (1792+). After Thermidor, he was in exile in Louvain till 1830. —M made extensive notes on the *Mémoires de R. Levasseur (de la Sarthe) ex-conventionnel . . .* (1829–1831). → 43:3; 44:4. #M338.

Levelers (in the English Revolution) → 50:15.

Lewis, Sir George Cornewall (1806 to 1863) English politician, also historical writer. Besides authoring a number of books on varied subjects (nonfiction), L. was editor of the *Edinburgh Review* (1852–1855). M's article of 1857 was concerned with him as politician; Whig MP (1847+); undersecy for the Home Office (1848); financial secy to the Treasury (1850–1852); chancellor of the Exchequer (1855–1858); home secy under Palmerston (1859–1861); secy for war (1861–1863). #M546.

Lewis, Leon American journalist. Resident in London in 1865, he was elected to the GC/IWMA and as corr secy for America; in June he made a proposal for a newspaper organ; but by Oct he had attended no meetings and done nothing; another corr secy was elected in May 1866. → 65:37.

Lewy, Gustav German communist activist in the Rhineland, later a Lassallean socialist. He was a member of the CL in Düsseldorf; a businessman (or, according to Dowe, a clerk or sales clerk); and remained active with the remnants of the CL in the Rhineland even after its dissolution. He visited M in 1853 and 1856 as a spokesman for the ex-CL friends in the area. Although in 1856 he warned M strongly against Lassalle, in 1861 he was converted into an enthusiastic supporter by Lassalle's speeches, and with the founding of the GGWA he became a leading organizer of this movement. —M's letters call him Levy, and *MEW, MECW*, etc., follow this spelling without discussion; but all other sources make it Lewy. → 53:45; 56:6, 11, 14.

Liberal Party and Liberals (Brit.)   → 53:15; 65:63; 68:54; 74:9; 90:17; 92:32, 39, 44, 57;

93:2, 9, 49; 94:9, 14, 22; 95:18. *See also* Whigs.

Il Libero Pensiero Milan, Florence, 1866 to 1876. Weekly. Ed by L. Stefanoni. — Organ of left republicans and Rationalists; hostile to the IWMA/GC. → 72:10, 27. #E475, E810.

La Liberté Brussels, Mar 12, 1865, to June 29, 1873. Weekly; daily, Apr 18 to Nov A, 1871. Ed by E. Picard, P. Janson, L. L. Jottrand, E. Hins, et al. —Orig Proudhonist-influenced; from 1867, an organ of the IWMA in Belgium; after the Hague Congress, leaned to Bakuninism. → 71:37; 72:8, 14, 27, 50, 52, 56. #M521, M696, M745, M755, M835, M893; E679, E820.

La Libre Pensée Paris, Jan–July 1870. Weekly. —Founded by a group of Blanquists (Tridon, Flourens, Rigault, Verlet); Paul Lafargue contributed too. → 70:24.

Liebers, Bruno (1836 to 1905) Dutch IWMA activist. A pub'r-printer in The Hague, he produced IWMA literature, and also some writings by M. He took an active part in preparing the Hague Congress (1872); opponent of Bakuninism. —*Note:* The forms *Lieberse* and *Lieber* are erroneous. → 72:65.

Liebig, *Baron* Justus von (1803 to 1873) German chemist; a founder of agricultural chemistry. Prof at Giessen (1824+) and Munich (1852+). L. was a pioneer in theoretical chemistry as a whole, esp organic and analytical chemistry. —M studied his writings on agricultural chemistry in connection with agrarian economics, had an extremely high opinion of his work, and often expressed it. M (1851) excerpted L.'s *Die organische Chemie in ihrer Anwendung auf Agricultur und Physiologie* (4th edn, 1842; 1st edn, 1840). → 51:67, 68; 65:61; 66:12; 74:11.

Liebknecht, Natalie; *née* **Reh** (1835 to 1909) Second wife of Wilhelm Liebknecht; married 1868. → 70:65; 71:3, 5, 6, 17; 73:18; 86:55; 93:39, 56.

Liebknecht, Wilhelm; *full* Wilhelm Philipp Martin Christian Ludwig (1826 to 1900) German Social-Democratic party leader. Son of a Hessian civil servant, he studied philosophy at three universities; was converted to socialism mainly by reading the French utopians. In the 1848 revolution he took part in the activity of the German Demo Assoc in Paris and its German Legion fiasco (cf. → 48:19); landed in jail; eventually fought in the Baden-Palatinate uprising (May–July 1849); also met his first wife, Ernestine Landolt. Afterward he took refuge in France, then Switzerland (from which he was expelled), finally in London (1850–1862). Here he joined the CL (or perhaps was already a member); was active in the GWEA; lived by tutoring and journalism, incl (1851+) correspondence for the Augsburg

Allgemeine Ztg. Here too he came to know M and his family on a very personal, friendly basis. After an amnesty he returned to Germany (1862). In Berlin he was an editor of the *Norddeutsche Allgemeine Ztg.* From 1863 to early 1865 he was a member of the Lassallean GGWA, but as a dissident, reporting to M on developments. In 1865, banished from Prussian territory, he went to Leipzig, where his association with Bebel was crucial in determining his career (as well as providing Bebel with his initial elements of education). This base in Saxony also enforced his anti-Prussian attitudes. During the war of 1866 he was editor of the *Mitteldeutsche Volkszeitung,* which was suppressed in Aug; spent three months in jail because of an illegal trip to Berlin. In 1867 he was elected to the N. German Reichstag (where he sat till 1870); from 1868 he was editor of the *Demokratisches Wochenblatt,* organ not only of the Verband Deutscher Arbeitervereine (the workers' movment already led by Bebel) but also of the Saxon People's party. This alliance with the (non-Prussian) bourgeois liberals represented the compromising political line that L. was now following, despite M's epistolary pressure to strike out on the path of independent working-class political organization—a line that L. finally ditched with the organization of the "Eisenacher party." This development was further complicated by the pressure, esp from M, to organize IWMA sections in Germany—about which L. did little—and by the growth of an anti-Schweitzer opposition inside the Lassalleans, which was going to lead to a split. These events combined to bring about the rupture with the People's party that M had pushed for; and so L. became a founder of the SDWP at Eisenach in 1869. In 1870 Bebel and L, as N. German Reichstag deputies, alone refused to vote for war credits—in part on class grounds, on pacifist anti-militarist grounds, on anti-Prussian grounds. As a result, L. was one of the defendants in the 1870–1872 Leipzig treason trial (an early show-trial) and got two years in prison. —In the ensuing years, as the party grew, it was Bebel who emerged as the political and organizational leader of the movement, with his early mentor Liebknecht relegated to the secondary role of parliamentarian, agitator, journalist, and (in the often-expressed opinion of M&E) leading confusionist. As parliamentarian, L. was an active leader of the party Reichstag Fraction (1874+); also a member of the Saxon Diet (1879–1886, 1889+). After the Anti-Socialist Law ended, he moved back to Berlin and was editor of the party organ *Vorwärts* (1890+). Esp in the last period, he transformed himself into a sort of party monument titled "Soldier of the Revolution," and played a prominent role at the International Socialist Congresses of 1889,

1891, 1893. —Among his writings (none of
theoretical importance, essentially agit-prop
even when historical) were: *Robert Blum und
seine Zeit* (1892); *Geschichte der französische
Revolution* (1890); *Die Emser Depesche* (1899);
Robert Owen (1892); *Über die politische Stel-
lung der Sozialdemokratie* (1869); and his
best-known work available in English: *No
compromises, no political trading* (or *election
deals*) (1899). M helped him with his brochure
*Zur orientalischen Frage oder Soll Europa
kosakisch werden?* (2nd edn, 1878). —M&E's
letters to each other are chock-full of private
laments over L.'s political muddleheadedness,
inability to think a question through, theoretical and organizational incompetence, even
journalistic incapacity. All these passages
were suppressed when the M–E correspondence was first pubd by Bernstein, in order to
preserve the party legend of Liebknecht the
Soldier of the Revolution and Anointed of
Marx. (For a note on this bowdlerization—
more bluntly, falsification—see R. P. Morgan,
*The German Social Democrats and the First
International*, 1965.) L.'s influence in the
movement was in good part a triumph of
personal style. It should be stressed that M&E
were personally quite fond of L. (as was M's
whole family) and were quick to forgive him or
palliate his sins; not only was no personal
hostility involved in M&E's sad appraisal of L.
but the case was quite the opposite. Incidentally, M's daughters' nickname for L. was
"Library"—prob a garbling of his name (so
Kapp thinks). → 49:35; 50:19; 51:1, 8, 36, 45;
52:39; 55:25; 58:32; 59:8, 34, 35, 44, 49, 53, 56,
60; 60:24, 60; 62:35, 52; 63:2, 3, 13, 16, 19, 36,
39; 64:17, 27, 32, 38, 46; 65:2, 7, 8, 14, 15, 18,
24, 29, 30, 42, 47, 50, 56; 66:5–8, 14, 23, 26, 30,
37; 67:2, 12, 33, 35, 36, 45, 47; 68:2, 10, 16, 22,
35, 39, 48–50, 68, 70; 69:2, 5, 19, 21, 26, 40, 41,
48, 62, 66, 70; 70:14, 19, 31, 33, 36, 40, 45, 65;
71:5, 6, 14, 17, 20–22, 25, 29, 35, 43, 44, 48, 58;
72:3, 4, 6, 10, 12, 16, 20, 21, 23–25, 27, 30, 34,
42, 44, 51, 62; 73:9, 12, 18; 74:5, 7, 10, 22, 25,
32, 36, 38; 75:10, 12, 16, 20, 29, 48; 76:13, 21,
29, 30; 77:4, 15, 23, 26; 78:6, 13, 37, 41; 79:2, 16,
33, 41; 80:6, 29; 81:59; 82:31; 83:7, 11, 12, 19,
23, 24; 84:58; 85:5, 8, 13, 17, 43; 86:3, 13, 16, 22,
35, 37, 38, 55; 87:1, 16; 88:15, 38; 89:15, 17, 24,
29, 32, 33; 90:10, 32, 42, 47, 49 50; 91:1, 6, 11,
22, 26, 33; 92:29, 52, 62, 63; 93:7, 39, 42, 55;
94:28, 43, 48; 95:16, 24, 37. #ME29, ME33,
ME184; M251.5, M318, M675, M836.5; E393.

Liège or Liége City in eastern Belgium.
→ 45:13; 69:56; 72:42; 76:26.

Liguria Region of N.W. Italy; its coastal
strip is the "Italian Riviera." → 72:49.

Lille Industrial city of N. France. →
90:42; 91:51, 56. #E656.

Limerick City of S.W. Ireland, on the
Shannon. → 56:22.

Lincoln, Abraham (1809 to 1865) Pres of
the U.S. (1861+); assassinated Apr 14,
1865. → 62:53; 64:37, 45; 65:32. #M884.

Lincoln, Henry John English journalist.
Editor of the London *Daily News* (early
1850s). → 54:23. #E440.

Lindau, Paul (1839 to 1919) German novelist and dramatist; theater critic and theater
manager. Early on he was a journalist in Paris
and (1863+) the Rhineland; founded *Das
Neue Blatt* (Leipzig, 1869–1870); editor of the
weekly *Die Gegenwart* (Berlin, 1872–1881);
founder/editor of the monthly *Nord und Sud*
(1878–1904); managed theaters (1899–1905).
He was a voluminous writer in many fields,
much transd into English; edited the 1891 publ
of Lassalle's youthful diary. → 72:16, 30.

Lingard, John (1771 to 1851) English historian. Catholic priest; prof of philosophy at
Douai College; but (1811+) devoted himself
only to writing; created doctor of divinity by
the pope (1821). Author of: *The history and
antiquities of the Anglo-Saxon church* (1845).
M (1843) excerpted a German trans (1827–
1828) of his *History of England from the first
invasion by the Romans* (1819–1830). →
43:32.

Lingenau, Johann Karl Ferdinand (d.
1877) German-American socialist. After taking part in the 1848–1849 revolution in
Germany, he emigrated to the U.S., where he
became wealthy. In his will, he left a fortune
to the socialist movement, esp the SDWP
(Eisenachers) of Germany; but, after long legal
machinations, the Bismarck government pre-
vented the execution of the will. → 77:31;
79:47; 81:34.

Linguet, Simon Nicolas Henri (1736 to
1794) French publicist and social critic;
lawyer by profession. Editor of *Annales Politiques* (1777–1792); pubd *Mémoires sur la
Bastille* (1783) after a stay there; fled to
Brussels from the Revolution but returned;
guillotined. He was noted for his attacks on
comtemporaries—the rich, the church, the
philosophes, all liberals and democrats, all
notions of equality, etc.—from the standpoint
of defending absolutism and the right of an
elite to exploit the masses without bourgeois
subterfuges; hence he openly criticized bourgeois society from the reactionary right. M
(1859–1862) excerpted his *Théorie des lois
civiles* (1767), a defense of despotism, an
attack on Montesquieu and bourgeois-liberal
economics. → 59:78. #M575.

Lisbon; Port. Lisboa Capital of Portugal.
→ 72:53, 55.

Lissagaray, Hippolyte Prosper Olivier
(1838 to 1901) French revolutionary journalist, now remembered as author of a basic
history of the Paris Commune. L. (who was
always called by surname alone, sometimes

shortened to Lissa) came from a middle-class Basque family; finished his education with a trip to the U.S.; then settled in Paris (1860). In politics he was a revolutionary republican in the neo-Jacobin tradition, with amorphous social views; never a socialist. Under the Bonaparte regime, he carried on a journalistic guerrilla war with the government (editor of *L'Avenir*, 1868+); took refuge in Brussels (1870); on Bonaparte's fall, returned as a henchman of Gambetta. In the Paris Commune, he gave it stout journalistic defense—in *Action* and *Tribun du Peuple*—and fought on the barricades to the last. Afterward he emigrated (via Belgium) to England. L. joined no group, not even the IWMA, neither now nor later, though he moved somewhat toward socialistic views. After publishing preliminary studies on Commune history—*Les huit journées de mai derrière les barricades* (1871); *La vision de Versailles* (1873)—he finished his *Histoire de la Commune de 1871* (pubd 1876). It was widely transd (into English by Eleanor M, pubd 1886); M worked hard to ensure its translation and circulation. After the 1880 amnesty, L. returned to France; resumed his free-lance radical journalism (editor of *La Bataille*, etc.). Unsuccessful in elections, he remained unattached organizationally; hostile to the Guesdist party. He issued a final edn of his history in 1898. —In person, L. was known as a hot-headed Lone Ranger type of operator, who never collaborated long with anyone else. —During his stay in England, Eleanor M fell in love with him; they were secretly engaged in 1872; but her parents strongly opposed the marriage with L. Eleanor formally broke off the engagement in early 1882. → 72:5, 11; 74:3; 75:4, 7; 76:27, 33; 77:1, 6, 38, 46; 81:43. #E527.

List, Friedrich; *full* Georg Friedrich (1789 to 1846) German economist, active also in the U.S. He began as a liberal prof of eco at Tübingen, with ties to business and proposals for reforming modernization; forced into exile by Reaction, emigrated to the U.S. (1825). Here he developed as a champion of protectionism; pubd *Outlines of American polit eco* (1827); as U.S. consul in various German cities (1832+) he became a leading advocate of the Zollverein and a national railway system, and a prominent spokesman of the economics of German industrialism on the rise. His best-known work, *Das nationale System der politischen Ökonomie* (1841), was studied and annotated by M (1844–1845). → 44:48; 45:10, 19. #M591.

Littlehampton (Eng.) Watering place on the Channel, near Brighton. → 78:35.

Liverpool (Eng.) West-coast seaport city in Lancashire. → 52:16; 57:32; 62:12, 18, 63; 63:35; 66:25; 86:35; 88:28; 90:40; 91:60.

Lloyd, Henry Demarest (1847 to 1903) American social reformer and journalist. Orig a lawyer; then on the staff of the Chicago *Tribune* (1872–1885). He became a pioneering muckraker with his *Story of a great monopoly* (1881) on Standard Oil and the railways (which M read in magazine publ); also pubd *Wealth against commonwealth* (1894) on monopoly. He resigned (1885) from the newspaper to fight for social reforms: against Tammany, the Tweed Ring, monopoly, and child labor; for labor rights, public ownership, the eight-hour day, Pullman strike, etc. He latterly became socialistic in his views, but did not join the SP. → 81:64; 93:15.

Lochner, Georg (b. c.1824) German communist worker (joiner/carpenter); long an émigré in London. He took part in the 1848–1849 revolution in Germany; moved to England; was a member of the CL and the London GWEA; longtime friend and coworker of M&E. He was esp useful to M as an activist in the IWMA: member of the GC (1864–1867, 1871–1872). → 59:34; 64:36; 71: 35; 83:12.

Locke, John (1632 to 1704) English philosopher and sociopolitical theorist of the Enlightenment; champion of empiricist sensualism, liberal toleration, scientific progress, and bourgeois property rights. His main works were: *Essay concerning human understanding* (1690); *Two treatises on civil government* (1690); *On the reasonableness of Christianity* (1696); *Essay concerning toleration* (1667). —M (1851) read another essay, *Some considerations of the consequences of the lowering of interest, and raising the value of money* (1692). → 51:62; 55:5; 60:65.

Lodi (It.) Industrial city near Milan. → 72:60; 73:6. #E813.

Löwenthal, Zacharias; *later* Carl Friedrich **Loening** (1810 to 1884) German pub'r and bookdealer; a liberal. Owner of the firm C. Löwenthals Verlagsbuchhandlung in Mannheim (1835–1836); penalized for publishing the literature of Young Germany (1836). In 1857 he converted to Protestantism and changed his name. His firm merged with the Literarische Anstalt J. Rütten to form (1858+) the Literarische Anstalt Rütten & Loening, Frankfurt. → 51:43, 52; 52:21.

Lohbauer, Rudolf A Württemberg officer, he became editor of the Stuttgart *Hochwächter*; oppositionist in 1830; fled to Strassburg; then became prof of military science at Bern (1835+). He returned to Berlin (1845+), where he contributed to the government press and rightist periodicals. E's article discusses his career. #E348.

Loire River Great river of central France, flowing into the Bay of Biscay. #E301.

Lombardy Region of N. Italy. → 41:12. #E813, E897.

Lommel, Georg   German publicist. A left Democrat, he took part in the Baden uprising of Apr 1848, then emigrated to Switzerland. He helped M collect material for *Herr Vogt.* → *60*:13, 23, 24, 37.

Lomonosov, Mikhail Vasilyevich (1711 to 1765)   Russian scientist and man of letters. Besides his great achievements in science (in physics and chemistry, nature of heat and gases, and many modern scientific concepts), he was also one of the great cultural influences in 18th-century Russia—in reforming the language (he pubd a Russian grammar, 1755), in establishing its prosody and orthography, in writing history (he pubd a history of Russia, 1766), etc. Besides, he wrote poetry, plays, essays, and so on. → *51*:49.

London (Eng.)   *Chronicle* index for M&E's sojourns before their final settlement in England:→ *38*:9; *42*:32; *45*:30–32; *47*:20, 45, 46, 50, 51; *49*:1, 2, 33, 34, 36, 40. —Register index for use in titles only: #ME68, ME123, ME157A, ME163; M55, M77, M337, M479, M494, M625, M631, M695, M743, M749, M752.5, M815, M826, M829, M864, M888; E188, E277, E430, E447–E451, E473, E562, E768, E842, E853–E855.

London Conference (IWMA, 1871)   *See* International Working Men's Association.

London County Council → *95*:18.

London Dialectical Society → *78*:31.

Londoner Deutsche Poste   London, Jan 1 to Sep 6, 1870. Weekly. Ed by E. Juch. — German-language organ for émigrés. → *69*:71.

Longuet, Charles; *full* Charles Félix César (1839 to 1903)   French socialistic radical; best known as M's son-in-law. Of a clerical-monarchist family, L. came to Paris as a law student (1860) and was quickly radicalized; launched *La Rive Gauche* (1864) as an anti-Bonapartist left-republican paper. In this period he was more or less sympathetic to Blanquism (later, more influenced by Proudhonism). In 1865 he had to flee to Belgium (1865), then to England. Here he became a member of the GC/IWMA (1866–1867) and corr secy for Belgium (1866); delegate to a number of congresses. Back in France after Bonaparte's fall, he headed a NG battalion, and later was elected to the Paris Commune: he edited the Commune's *Journal Officiel* for three months, worked on the Labor Commsn and other posts, as well as military service; supported the minority against the Comm of Public Safety. Afterward, a refugee in London, he rejoined the GC (1871–1872) and supported M against the Bakunin operation. In 1872 he married M's daughter Jenny; became (1873) a lecturer at Oxford on French language and literature; prof at King's College, U. of London (1874+). After the 1880 amnesty, he

returned to France: he was an editor of Clemenceau's paper *La Justice*; as always, hostile to the revolutionary socialist tendency, specif to the Guesdist party ("Marxists"); as M quipped in 1882, "the last Proudhonist." After Jenny's death (1883), he did not keep in touch with the M family. Active in electoral politics, he succeeded in getting on the Paris city council as a "radical socialist," i.e., left republican (1886–1893); he also took part in some socialist congresses on the right wing. In 1894 he was named inspector of modern language teaching for Paris. → *65*:29; *66*:5, 46; *70*:48; *71*:39; *72*:7, 59, 64, 68; *73*:46; *80*:23, 27, 35, 48; *81*:4, 21, 43, 62; *82*:14, 15, 23, 27, 30, 34, 39, 47; *83*:11, 12. #M143.

Longuet, Charles Félicien (1873 to 1874)   Charles and Jenny Longuet's first, but short-lived, son; M's grandson. → *73*:46; *74*:27.

Longuet, Edgar (Marcel); *called* Wolf (1879 to 1950)   M's second surviving grandson; son of Jenny and Charles Longuet. A physician by profession, he joined the socialist movement by at least 1900, and was active in the SP's Paris region, which he represented at party congresses (1908–1914). In World War I he supported the prowar majority, unlike his brother Jean. He quit the SP in 1937 and joined the CP (1938). → *79*:36; *80*:27; *81*:30.

Longuet, Henri; *Angl.* Henry; *full* Henri Michel; *called* Harry, Harra (1878 to 1883)   Son of Jenny and Charles Longuet, M's grandson; died in childhood. → *78*:27; *80*:27; *81*:30; *83*:13.

Longuet, Jean; *full* Jean Frédéric Laurent; *also called* Johnny (1876 to 1938)   Son of Jenny and Charles Longuet, M's grandson; b. London but active in France as a leader of the SP. He was early (1894) involved in forming a socialist study group at school in Caen; then active in socialist student groups in Paris (1895–1896). Admitted to the bar, he practiced little as a lawyer; turned to socialist journalism, e.g., *Le Devenir Social* and other organs. Though at first a Guesdist, he turned away from this tendency, toward Jaurès' type of reformism. —He has been called a "left Jaurèsist"; in gen, his political career was as the left shading of the right wing; a classic "centrist." —In the united SP of 1905, he was elected to the National Exec; also active in the International. He was elected a deputy in 1914. In World War I he took a centrist position: pacifist critique without opposing the Union Sacrée or entering on revolutionary opposition; led a party minority on this position (1915+), founded its organ *Le Populaire* and the Reconstructeur group to rehabilitate the old party. At the 1920 Tours congress, he opposed affiliation to the Communist Int'l, and became a leader of the Vienna Union (2½

Int'l) until it collapsed back into the Socialist Int'l. → 76:17; 80:27; 81:30; 82:39; 95:37.

Longuet, Jenny, *called* Mémé (1882 to 1952) Daughter of Jenny and Charles Longuet; M's granddaughter. → 82:35.

Lopatin, German Alexandrovich; *first name also spelled* Herman, *Ger.* Hermann (1845 to 1918) Russian revolutionist. Of a noble family; went to Italy (1867) to fight with Garibaldi. Back in Russia, he was arrested (1868) and exiled to Stavropol, where he studied socialist writings incl M's; fled (1870) to St. Petersburg, organized the escape of *Lavrov, and went into emigration. In Paris he joined the IWMA; then (still 1870) moved to London, where he became very friendly with M; joined the GC/IWMA. At the end of this busy year, he set out to rescue *Chernyshevsky from Siberia; unsuccessful. For a number of years he shuttled between Russia and the West, esp Paris; arrested in Russia (1879) and escaped (1883). In 1887 he was sentenced to life; freed by the Revolution of 1905, but broken in health. —Lopatin did a large part of the Russian translation of *Capital*; politically, however, he was like Danielson, who translated the rest—never a Marxist but a revolutionary Narodnik. → 70:42, 51, 63; 72:22, 68; 73:52; 74:1, 4, 37; 75:11, 48; 78:40; 83:40; 87:42; 93:26.

Lord, Percival Barton (1808 to 1840) British (Irish-born) physician and diplomatic agent. After taking an E. India Co. medical post in Bombay, he traveled around the Middle East; then, through turning his regional medical work to use for intelligence reports, he shifted into formal service as a British government agent; killed in a local military expedition. —But as a matter of fact the book of his that M studied (1864) was not, e.g., his *Algiers* (1835) but his *Popular physiology* (1855 edn; orig, 1834). *Note: MEW* gives Perceval as his first name. → 64:48.

Lorenzo, Anselmo (1841 to 1914 or 1915) Spanish anarchosyndicalist leader; printer by trade. Joining the IWMA (1869), he became active in organizing sections in Spain; member of the Spanish Federal Council (1870–1872), and its secy (1872); delegate to the London Conference (1871). At first a Bakunin follower, by 1872, critical of Bakunin's disorganizing practice; anarchist in ideology, active in developing the anarchosyndicalist movement in Spain, esp as a leader in Catalonia (1874–1896). He wrote a number of propaganda pamphlets. → 71:46; 72:31.

Loria, Achille (1857 to 1943) Italian sociologist and economist. Prof at Siena, Padua, finally Turin (1903–1932); senator (1919+). Sometimes erroneously called a Marxist, L. was not even a socialist, looking for reform of capitalism through the diffusion of property. His books on "economic determinism" put forward a view quite different from M's historical materialism. Loria's writings transformed what he was able to get out of M into a theory heavily influenced by Henry George. His chief works were transd into English: *The economic foundations of society* (1899); *The economic synthesis* (1913); *Karl Marx* (1920). → 79:46, 50; 80:5, 33, 41; 81:22; 82:27, 30, 39; 83:17; 94:32; 95:7. #E551.

Lotta di Classe Milan, 1892 to 1898. Weekly. —Organ of the *Socialist Party of Italian Workingmen. → 92:49; 93:4; 94:36. #ME33; E868.

Loudon, Charles (1801 to 1844) Scottish physician and medical writer; practiced in Leamington, Eng. (1826+). He was appointed to the royal commsn on child factory labor (1830) and took part in drafting its report (1833). Through this he was led to concern himself with the conditions of the working class; wrote an anti-Malthus book *The equilibrium of population and sustenance demonstrated* (1836) with a theory of birth control via prolonged breast-feeding. → 51:68.

Louis XV (1710 to 1774) King of France, 1715–1774. → 64:44.

Louis XVI (1754 to 1793) King of France, 1774–1792. He was condemned to death by the National Convention on Jan 16, 1793, and guillotined on Jan 21. → 48:38.

Louis Philippe (1773 to 1850) King of the French, 1830–1848; previously, Duke of Orléans. Some terminological points: His reign was called the "July Monarchy," having been inaugurated by the "July Revolution" of 1830. His followers were known as Orleanists, since he belonged to the Orleans branch of the Bourbon line, as distinct from the Legitimists, i.e., royalists who favored the restoration of the main Bourbon line. His appellation "Citizen King" (*roi citoyen*) is related to the common characterization of his reign as a "bourgeois monarchy," stressing the shift in class basis as compared with the Bourbons. → 48:13.

Louvain, Porte de See Porte de Louvain.

Louvet de Couvrai, Jean Baptiste (1760 to 1797) French writer, publicist, and politician. Member of the Convention in 1792, he switched from the Jacobins to the Girondists; fled Paris (1793–1795); returned after Thermidor and, under the Directory, became secy of the Council of 500. His account *Quelques notices pour l'histoire* [etc.] (1795) was later pubd with his *Mémoires* (1821), studied by M (1843). → 43:33.

Lubbock, Sir John; *later* Baron **Avebury** (1834 to 1913) English popular-science writer; by trade a banker (partner in his father's bank by 1856); also a Liberal MP active in bank reform, and an officer of

London U., London Chamber of Commerce. He became best known for his works of popularization (not original research work) in the field of archeology, ethnology, entomology; e.g., *Prehistoric times* (1865). M (1882) studied his book *The origin of civilisation and the primitive condition of man* (1870). → 82:39. #M568.

Lucas German worker; in 1849, a member of the WA in Mülheim. → 49:9.

Luciani, Giuseppe Italian journalist. A member of the IWMA, he was in correspondence with M&E (1871–1872; active in Rome workers' organizations; contributor to the left press. → 71:64.

Lucknow City in N. India; capital of Uttar Pradesh. #E220, E665, E739, E782.

Lucraft, Benjamin (1809 to 1897) English trade-unionist; a leader of the British TU movement. A cabinetmaker and joiner, he took part in the Chartist movement; secy of the N. London Political Union (1859), active in the National Reform Assoc. He was a member of the GC/IWMA (1864–1871); on the Exec of the Reform League. In 1871 he succumbed to the public pressure of hostility to the Paris Commune and resigned after #M143. Subseqly he ran for Parliament as a Liberal, unsuccessfully, and was briefly elected to the London School Board. → 67:41; 69:60; 71:28, 30. #E377.

Ludlow, John Malcolm (Forbes) (1821 to 1911) English Christian socialist leader. Born in India, educated in Paris, he came to London (1838), became a lawyer (1843), began (1848) his association with J. F. D. Maurice and Charles Kingsley, with whom he launched the Christian socialist organ *Politics for the People*. He studied (1849) Buchez's movement and took up cooperativism; founder-editor of the *Christian Socialist* (1850+). He was active in helping the Working Men's College (1854+), the Christian Social Union, the Friendly Societies. His type of Christian socialism was largely elitist, paternalistic, antidemocratic, hostile to trade-unionism. → 69:27.

Ludwig, Carl Friedrich Ernst (1773 to 1846) German governmental administrator, later journalist and writer. First a tutor and private secy for notables, he entered government service in Altenburg (1799). Moving to Dresden (1820), he devoted himself to writing; edited a Bremen periodical; journalist in Hamburg, finally on the *Börsenhalle*. His book *Geschichte der letzten funfzig Jahre* (1832–1834) got him a Ph.D. from Jena; M (1843) read its Part II, "Geschichte der französischen Revolution" (1833). → 43:32.

Ludwigshafen (Ger.) City in the S.E. Rhineland, on the Rhine opposite Mannheim. → 49:27.

Lüneburg City of N. Germany, near Hamburg. → 69:65, 66.

Lüning, Otto; *full* Heinrich Otto (1818 to 1868) German socialistic journalist; physician by profession. Politically a "True Socialist" (1844+), he pubd *Weserdampfboot*, then *Westphälische Dampfboot* (1845–1848) and *Neue Deutsche Ztg* (1848–1850), latterly in association with M's follower Weydemeyer (who married L.'s sister in 1847). *New Mega* I, 10 says that L. was briefly a member of the CL. He wrote M (July 1847) that his viewpoint was "close" to M's—this mainly indicates his good will. L. later joined the Nationalverein (1859) and, after 1866, the National Liberals. → 47:40; 50:22. #ME165.

Lützelberger, Ernst Carl Julius (1802 to *after* 1874) German Protestant theologian, unorthodox independent scholar. He ceased being a clergyman (1838) on personal grounds. Later, Nuremberg city librarian (1856+); also pubd a history of German literature. Young E's notes covered his book *Die kirchliche Tradition über den Apostel Johannes und seine Schriften* (1840). #E787.5.

Lugau (Ger.) Industrial city in Saxony (now DDR). → 69:10.

Luther, Martin (1483 to 1546) German leader of the Protestant Reformation. — Luther's own economic views were hostile to usury and commercialism (merchant capital), looking backward to the natural economy of an older agrarian society. Allied with the princes, he foamed over against the peasants' revolt: "Crush them, strangle them and pierce them . . . he who can, even as one would strike dead a mad dog." —M (1856 excerpted his *Von Kauffshandlung und Wucher* (1589); in notebooks of 1859–1862, excerpted his *An die Pfarrherrn wider den Wucher zu predigen* (1540) and *Eyn Sermon auff das Evangelion von dem Reychen man und armen Lasaro* (1555). → 59:78. #M493.

Luvini, Giacomo (1795 to 1862) Swiss military man (colonel) and radical politician; lawyer by profession; of Italian descent. He fought in the war against the Sonderbund (1847); deputy from Ticino to the National Council (1848+). #E232.

Luxemburg or **Luxembourg** Grand Duchy, wedged into Germany, Belgium, France. → 62:51; 67:35.

Lvov; *Pol.* Lwów; *Ger.* Lemberg In M's day, capital of the Austrian province of Galicia (after the first partition of Poland). Orig Ukrainian, it was successively taken by Poles, Austrians, Ukrainians, Poles; now annexed to the USSR. → 92:24.

Lyell, Sir Charles (1797 to 1875) British geologist, Scottish-born; "father of modern geology." He advocated the theory of uniform development as against catastrophism; his work facilitated the acceptance of Darwinism. Besides his *Principles of geology* (1830–1833) and *Elements of geology* (1838), he pubd *Travels in N. America* (1845), and esp the book which E read on its publ: *The geological evidences of the antiquity of man* (1863). → 63:17; 66:9.

Lyon Socialiste Lyons, Sep 14, 1884, to 1885. Weekly. —Guesdist organ, for the eastern region of France; the first 11 numbers lithographed. → 84:61.

Lyons; *Fr.* Lyon Second-largest industrial center of France. → 69:47; 70:10, 18, 55, 56; 86:24. #E570.

Lyubavin, Nikolai Nikolayevich (1845 to 1918) Russian Naronik revolutionary; later, prof of chemistry at Moscow and author of works on the science. At the time we are concerned with, he was located in Berlin, where he had a depot for socialist literature, kept in touch with revolutionary student circles in Russia. A member of the IWMA, friend of Lopatin and Danielson, he acted (1868) as go-between for M's letters to Danielson in St. Petersburg. It was L. who, meeting Bakunin in Geneva and desiring to help him financially, had arranged for him to get an order to trans *Capital* from a St. Petersburg pub'r. → 68:52; 72:42, 49, 65, 68.

M

Maastrict City, south end of the Netherlands, near Belgium. → 42:19; 47:38.

NOTE ON ALPHABETIZATION OF "Mc," "MAC," ETC.

I here follow the library catalog practice of treating all names beginning *Mc, Mac, M'*, etc., as if spelled "Mac . . ." regardless of whether the next letter is capitalized. *Caution:* Misspellings of this prefix are common in French and German, hence misspellings of names so prefixed; and these misspellings sometimes show up in English as a rebound, especially in translations; for example, the economist McCulloch. In foreign-language indexes (e.g., *MEW*) this prefix is often alphabetized letter by letter.

McClellan, Gen George Brinton (1826 to 1885) U.S. Army officer. He left the army (1857) to become a railway official, then pres of a line. In the Civil War, he became commander-in-chief (Nov 1861), then commander of the Army of the Potomac (Mar 1862+); dismissed by Lincoln (Nov). McC. had opposed the Emancipation Proclamation and favored compromise with the South. The Democratic party ran him against Lincoln (1864). After the war, he was a NY docks engineer; governor of New Jersey. #M243.

McCulloch, John Ramsay (1789 to 1864) Scottish economist and statistician. Prof of polit eco in London (1828–1832); comptroller of the Stationery Office (1838–1864); the Peel government eventually gave him a government pension. He was a Whig in politics. His early reputation was as an expounder of Ricardo. M, who studied his writings closely, saw him as a deteriorated version of Ricardo and esp as a systematic apologist for capitalism. M read and annotated his works at various periods, incl the following (the parentheses give the date of M's work): (1844–1846) a French edn of his work, *Discours sur l'origine, les progrès, les objets particuliers et l'importance de l'économie politique*, 1825 (*MEGA*, I, 3); (1845–1846) *Principles of polit eco*, 1830; (1851) his edn of Adam Smith on money theory, 1836; also *The literature of polit eco*, 1845; *Definitions in polit eco*, 1827; *Dictionary, practical, theoretical, and historical, of commerce and commercial navigation*, 1847; (1853) *The literature of polit eco*, 1845. —Note: The name may also be written *M'Culloch*; but the misspelling *MacCulloch* or *Mac Culloch*, common in non-English publications incl the IML's, has sometimes been taken over into English books. → 43:2; 44:48; 45:50, 52; 51:63, 66, 68; 53:53. #M575.

McDonnell, J(oseph) Patrick (1847 to 1906) Irish socialist, active in England and America. A Fenian leader (1850s+) he was a member of the GC/IWMA, its corr secy for Ireland, and delegate to its conference (1871–1872); member of its British Federal Council (1872). He started to form IWMA Irish branches in England and Ireland, with M's support; but in Dec 1872 he emigrated to the U.S. Here he became active as an American socialist in the labor movement and as an Irish nationalist; editor of the *Labor Standard*; member of the Workingmen's party, then of the SLP. In 1883 he organized the N.J. State Federation of Trades and Labor Unions, and was its chairman till 1898. —Caution: His name is often misspelled in foreign-language accounts. → 71:28, 35, 51; 72:14, 20, 55; 75:13; 76:37.

McEnnis, J. T. American journalist. Correspondent of the *Missouri Republican* of St. Louis. → 86:18, 29, 33. #E778.

Macerata (It.) City in the east-central region called the Marches. → 71:64.

Macfarlane, Helen British socialist. An active contributor to Harney's *Democratic Review* and *Red Republican* in 1850, she was also prob the author of pieces signed Howard Morton. Her trans of the *Com Manifesto* (1850) was the first in English. Resident near Manchester (in Burnley) she knew M&E, who thought highly of her ability. She was "an ardent feminist, thoroughly emancipated and advanced in her expression; well-read in philosophy and an admirer of Hegel; and evidently a traveled woman as well, having witnessed the Vienna revolution in 1848" (Schoyen). Harney's narrow-minded wife forced him into a personal break, which ended her writing; M deplored Harney's "very discreditable way of breaking with the only contributor . . . who really had ideas. A *rara avis* in his sheet." To be sure, her writing shows her approach to history to be strongly idealist; but it must be remembered that she appeared on the scene for one year only: what happened before or after is not known. → 50:40; 51:46; 71:66. #ME33.

McGuire, Peter J. (1852 to *after* 1900) American trade-unionist and socialist. Orig a Lassallean-type socialist hostile to trade unions, he entered the TU movement (1872); organized the Brotherhood of Carpenters and Joiners (1881); active in the formation of the AFL, and became its secy (1886), later vice-pres (by 1890). —For a time he remained active as a socialist; an officer of the S-D Workingmen's party (1874); organizer of an English-speaking branch of the SLP (1876); briefly a member of the Bellamyite club (1880s); delegate to the Int'l Socialist Congress of 1881. —By 1894 he was an ex-socialist, opposed to labor political action, and finally even joined the National Civic Federation with Gompers. → 83:12.

Machiavelli, Niccolò (1469 to 1527) Italian political theorist of the Renaissance period; best known for his work *Il principe* (*The prince*) (1532). Of an impoverished noble family, he became secy to the exec council of Florence; took part in diplomatic missions; and was exiled after the restoration of the Medicis. His writings pioneered a more scientific approach to politics and history, critical of feudal conditions and practices, likewise hostile to the "rabble," looking for progress to commercial and artisan (proto-bourgeois) elements in society. M (1843) studied a German trans (1832) of his *Discorsi sopra la prima deca di Tito Livio* (1521). Other writings: *Dell'arte della guerra* (1521), which was highly regarded by E; *Istorie fiorentine* (1532); also plays and poems. → 43:32; 52:56.

Mackay, John Henry (1864 to 1933) Scottish-born writer who adopted German as his literary language. A wealthy Scot, Mackay became a naturalized German, in fact; pubd poetry and other belletristic writings, incl a novel *The anarchists* (1891). But chiefly he became known as a devotee of Max *Stirner; anarchist in viewpoint. He pubd a biography, *Max Stirner, sein Leben und sein Werke* (1898) and an edn of *Max Stirners kleinere Schriften* (1898). In 1891 Mackay, who was then living in Rome, no doubt wanted to see the ms of *The German ideology* because he had heard of its section on Stirner. → 91:12.

Mackinnon, William Alexander (1789 to 1870) British (Scottish-born) politician and writer. MP (1830–1865); for many years a Tory, but (c.1852) became a Liberal, as exponent of commercial liberty. M (1851) studied his chief work *History of civilisation* (1846), based on his book *On public opinion in Gr Brit and other parts of the world* (1828). → 51:65.

Maclaren, James British writer on economics; barrister by profession. His chief economic work, which M read on publ, was his *Sketch of the history of the currency* (1858). He published shorter tracts in this field in the 1850s and 1870s. → 58:36.

Maclaurin, Colin (1698 to 1746) Scottish mathematician. Prof at Aberdeen, then Edinburgh; authority on fluxional calculus, also did work on mechanics. Author of: *A treatise of algebra* (1748); *A treatise of fluxions* (1742); *Geometrica organica* (1720). → 78:1.

Macleod, Henry Dunning (1821 to 1902) British economist; Scottish-born, a lawyer in England. Director of the Royal Bank till 1858. M (1857) studied his *Theory and practice of banking* (1855). His chief work was *The theory of credit* (1889–1891); also wrote *Principles of economist philosophy* (1873); *Elements of polit eco* (1858); *A dictionary of polit eco* (1859). M thought he had the mentality of a narrow-minded bank clerk. → 57:10.

MacMahon, *Marshal* Patrice de; *full* Marie Edmé Patrice Maurice; *Duke of* **Magenta** (1808 to 1893) French military man; descended from an exiled Irish family. (The name is written Mac-Mahon in French.) A Bonapartist, he served in the Crimea, Algeria, Austrian war; created marshal and duke (1859); governor-gen of Algeria (1864–1870). In the Franco-Prussian War he surrendered at Sedan; then victoriously commanded the Versaillese army that suppressed the Paris Commune. In politics, a dyed-in-the-wool reactionary monarchist, hence pres of the Third Republic (1873–1879). → 73:28; 77:23.

Macnab, Henry Grey (1761 to 1823) Author of *The new views of Mr. Owen of Lanark* (1819). This book title, read by M, is given by *KMC*, p. 363, which, however, prints the author's name as "Marcual"—evidently a misreading of handwritten notes. → 77:30.

Macpherson, David (1746 to 1816) Scottish historian. After a successful career as a land surveyor in Britian and America, he settled in London (c.1790) as a man of letters; also deputy keeper of the public records. Besides editing some scholarly works, he pubd *Geographical illustrations of Scottish history* (1796); *The history of European commerce with India* (1812). M (1847) studied his *Annals of commerce, manufactures, fisheries and navigation* (1805). → 47:58.

M'Pherson, James New Zealand agricultural worker, a supporter of the IWMA, in Christchurch, Canterbury. His Nov 1871 report said that "a year ago" he had launched the Canterbury Working Men's Mutual Protection Society. → 72:13.

MacVey An American socialist, delegate to the 1891 International Socialist Congress; no further info. → 91:44.

Madier French émigré. Besides visits to M and E, he wrote E in 1853 about an invention; perhaps for this reason *MEW* says he was a "mechanic" (without apparently knowing anything about him). *KMC* identified him as Edouard Anatole Madier de Monjau, a republican; but *MEW*, ignoring this, presumably rejected this identification. Maitron's *DBMOF* lists two men named Madier de Monjau, of whom one (no given name) was not known to have emigrated. Noël François Alfred Madier de Monjau (1814–1892), a lawyer, did emigrate after the Dec 1851 coup d'état, but to Belgium. Of course, he may have visited London first; but this is all conjecture. → 52:3.

Madrid (Spain) → 54:32; 56:28; 71:21, 59, 64; 72:3, 15. #M259, M407, M561; E325, E847.

Magenta City in N. Italy, near Milan; scene of Austrian defeat in 1859. #E134.

Magyars See Hungary.

Mahon, John Lincoln (1865 to 1933) British socialist. A mechanic in Edinburgh as a young man, he early became a socialist propagandist in Scotland; at age 19, the youngest on the SDF Exec (1884). With William Morris, he quit the SDF to form the Socialist League, becoming its first secy. He was later active in forming and organizing the Scottish Land and Labour League, the North of England Socialist Federation, the Scottish Labour party, and the ILP; also active as a militant TU organizer. He early made E's acquaintance; a friend of Eleanor M. → 84:55; 87:26, 27, 33; 88:3, 20; 89:16. #E788.

Maine, Sir Henry; *full* Henry James Sumner; *often* H. S. Maine (1822 to 1888) British (Scottish-born) lawyer and historian of law and primitive society. Prof at Cambridge and Oxford; in India (1863–1869), member of the Council to the governor-gen, vice-chancellor of the U. of Calcutta. His methological approach was comparative-historical in investigating early social institutions among Indo-European peoples; he partly adopted *Maurer's views. Chief work: *Ancient law* (1861). M filled a notebook (see #M569) on his *Lectures of the early history of institutions* (1875). Other writings: *Early law and custom* (1883); *Village communities in the east and west* (1871); *Popular government* (1885). → 80:3; 81:26. #M569.

Mainz; *sometimes (Fr.)* Mayence (Ger.) City on the Rhine and Main Rivers. → 48:27–29, 33; 69:56; 70:31, 36; 71:33; 93:40. #M696.

Majer, Adolph (b. c.1819) German communist; member of the CL, he followed Willich and Schapper in the 1850 split, and was bookkeeper of their Refugee Aid Comm. In 1850–1851 he acted as an emissary and repr of the Willich–Schapper group in France and Switzerland; also working for the Central Comm of the European Democracy (the Mazzini–Ledru–Ruge group), which Willich–Schapper collaborated with. In Feb 1852 Majer was defendant in a conspiracy trial in Paris. (*KMC* gives his name as Adolf Maier.) → 51:10.

Málaga (Spain) Port city, on the S. coast. → 94:39.

Malines; *Flem.* Mechelen; *sometimes (Eng.)* Mecheln City in N. Belgium, near Antwerp. → 47:14; 71:40.

Malmö City at the south end of Sweden, opposite Copenhagen. → 48:52.

Malon, Benoît (1841 to 1893) French socialist writer. Orig a dye worker, he was active in the French IWMA from early on; worked in his TU and its 1866 strike; joined the ed bd of *La Marseillaise*. Elected a deputy to the National Assembly (1871), he resigned to become an elected member of the Paris Commune, in which he was on the Labor Commsn. Afterward he took refuge in Switzerland; helped to found the (Bakuninist) Jura Federation, and became an active proponent of Bakunin's Alliance and its war against the GC inside the IWMA. During part of the 1870s he lived in various Italian cities. From ca. 1876–1877 he started moving away from anarchism, toward reformism (in a pattern like *Brousse's). Returning to France after the 1880 amnesty, he joined the French WP; but broke with the Guesdists (ca. 1882), at first went with Brousse, then struck out on his own account (1883) using the *Revue Socialiste* (which he edited, founded in 1880) as his political instrument. Malon invented a school of socialism which he called "integral socialism"—actually simply a variety of Possibilism or an early model of Bernsteinian "Revisionism." His influence was largely based on his books: *Précis historique, théorique et pratique du socialisme* (1892); *Le socialisme intégral* (1890–1891); *Histoire du socialisme* (1878, 1882–1884); *Le socialisme réformiste* (1885); *Le parti ouvrier en France* (1882); *Exposé des écoles socialistes françaises* (1872). → 80:13, 30; 81:57; 82:5, 24, 40, 43, 52; 90:49.

Malthus, Thomas Robert (1766 to 1834) English political economist. He took orders as a clergyman (1798), and pubd his *Essay on the principle of population;* traveled on the continent three years, and pubd a revised *Essay* (1803); became prof of history and polit eco at the new College of Haileybury. —M studied his works at great length. In 1851: *Definitions in polit eco* (1827); *Principles of polit eco* (2nd edn, 1836; orig edn, 1820); *The measure of value stated and illustrated* (1823); rereading of *Essay on the principle of population* (rev edn). In 1859–1862 notebooks: *Inquiry into the nature and progress of rent* (1815); *Definitions in polit eco* (new edn of 1853). —M saw Malthus as an unscientific apologist for capitalism deserving little respect, even apart from disagreement over economic theory; there were few economists of whom M had a lower opinion. → 51:65–69; 59:76, 77; 60:65; 62:31.

Malvern Resort town in west-central England (Worcestershire). → 78:35.

Manchester (Eng.) —E in Manchester and the family business: → 42:2, 27, 32, 35; 43:2, 31; 44:2, 29; 50:1, 44; 51:4, 9, 13, 23, 41, 49; 52:2, 16, 23, 38; 53:3, 13, 29; 54:3, 6; 57:50; 58:4; 60:6, 25, 33; 61:20; 62:4, 43; 63:31; 64:4, 15, 34; 66:42; 67:30; 69:45; 70:2, 8, 53. —E visits Manchester: → 77:29; 92:28, 30, 34; 93:22. M&E's trip to: → 45:30–32, 51. M's visits to: → 51:23, 53; 52:22, 24; 53:17, 21; 55:15, 18, 42, 43, 48; 56:24, 25; 58:24, 26; 59:46, 48–50; 60:13, 17, 20; 61:36, 38, 39; 62:18, 19, 62, 63; 64:12; 65:6, 55; 67:15, 34; 68:30, 31; 69:35, 39; 70:34, 37, 45–47; 73:32, 55, 60; 80:25. — Mrs. M's visits to E in: → 78:9; 80:25. —Other vistors to E in: → 53:31; 54:11; 59:16. —W. Wolff in: → 61:26; 64:15. —S. Moore in: → 73:31, 32. —Studies on: → 57:43; 58:20; 59:11; 65:59; 66:25; 67:5; 69:31. Labor and left in: → 55:51; 58:41; 59:34, 46; 66:43; 68:46; 71:21; 72:17, 28, 33. —Labour Parliament: → 54:13. —In IWMA affairs: → 65:12; 70:59; 72:17, 28, 33, 37, 55, 60, 66; 73:23, 27. See also *Schiller Institute, *Ermen family.

Manchester Guardian Manchester, 1821+. Daily. —Organ of the Free Traders; in mid-19th century, of the Liberals. → 61:4; 64:9, 40; 66:28. #E532, E784.

Mancini Italian radical in Macerata, central Italy. → 71:64.

Manis, G. The reference to this Manis and his book *Java* is in the *Daten* of MEW 19:620; but I have been unable to confirm this author's name or title in any bibliography. incl NUC, BM and BN. → 81:45.

Mann, Charles A. Author of *Paper money, the root of evil* (1872), read by M (1878). Since it was pubd in NY, perhaps he was American; no other info available. → 78:38, 48.

Mannheim (Ger.) City in the former state of Baden; at the Rhine–Neckar confluence. → 49:27.

Mannheimer Abendzeitung Mannheim (Ger.), 1841 to 1849. Evening daily. — Founded by Moritz Brühl; turned to Democratic left under Karl Grün and Bernays. In 1842–1843 it defended the *RZ* from government harassment. → 43:6. #M156.

Manteuffel, *Baron* Otto von; *full* Otto Theodor (1805 to 1882) Prussian politician, from Pomerania. Interior min (1848–1850); prime min and foreign min (1850–1858). He presided over the reaction following 1848–1849 and then faded from national scene. → 49:14, 17. #ME92, ME109; M89, M494, M611, M642.

Mantua; *Ital.* Mantova (It.) City in Lombardy. → 79:46.

Marble Hall (Mainz) → 70:36.

March Association; *Ger.* Märzverein Organized in various cities, founded in Frankfurt (Nov 1848) by left-liberal members of the *Frankfurt National Assembly; named after the "March revolution" in Berlin. #M328, M496; E843.

Marheineke, Philipp (Konrad) (1780 to 1846) German Protestant theologian and religious historian. Prof at Erlangen, Heidelberg, then (1811+) Berlin; later, member of the Supreme Consistorial Council. He was regarded as a leading right-wing Hegelian, i.e., defender of orthodoxy in Hegelian terms. Chief works: *Christliche Symbolik* (1810–1814); *Geschichte der deutsche Reformation* (1816). E's article concerned his *Einleitung in die öffentlichen Vorlesungen über die Bedeutung der Hegelschen Philosophie in der christlichen Theologie* (1842), and *Zur Kritik der Schellingschen Offenbarungsphilosophie* (1843). #E224.

Markheim, Bertha; *née* **Levy** A close friend of the M family (1854–1865); sister of the German writer Julius *Rodenberg (name orig Levy); in the early 1850s, fiancée of J. Miquel. She was a CL sympathizer; helped the M family financially on occasion. (MEW spells the family name Levi) → 54:27; 62:52, 57; 64:35

Marliani, Manuel (de) (d. 1873) Italian-Spanish politician, writer, and historian. Of Spanish origin, he was a liberal senator in Spain, supporter of Espartero. Then he moved to Italy; was elected to the Emilia assembly (1859), where he advocated union with Piedmont; later, a senator. His chief work was *Historia politica de la España moderna* (1840)—read by M (1854). → 54:55, 57.

Marr, Wilhelm; *full* Heinrich Wilhelm (1819 to 1904) German journalist, from Hamburg. In youth he decided for communism on reading Weitling; became a leader of the Young Germany tendency in Switzerland; was influenced by Proudhon's writings toward anarchist ideas; pubd a monthly *Blätter der Gegenwart für sociales Leben* (1844); pubd a brochure, *Das junge Deutschland in der Schweiz* (1846), *Anarchie oder Autorität?* (1852). His first anti-Semitic production, *Der Judenspiegel* (1863), attracted little attention; ten years later, *Der Sieg des Judentums über das Germanentum* (12 edns, 1873–1879) made something of a sensation; it introduced anti-Semitism on racial (not religious) grounds. He is believed to be the inventor of the term anti-Semitism for *Judenhass* (Jewhatred). (*MEW* states that he was a Prussian police spy in the 1860s.) → 67:14.

Marrast, Armand; *full* Marie François Pascal Armand (1801 to 1852) French politician and publicist; right-wing republican. A liberal émigré in England (1834–1836), he returned to Paris, joined the staff of *Le National*, became its director (1841) and a leading figure in the opposition to Louis Philippe's regime. In the 1848 revolution he entered the Provisional Government (Feb-Apr); mayor of Paris (Mar +); established the Garde Mobile; became pres of the Assembly (1848–1849). Disappointed in the elections (1849), he retired from public life. → 48:42. #ME93.

La Marseillaise Paris, Dec 19, 1869, to May 1870; July D to Sep 9, 1870. Daily. Ed by H. de Rochefort. —Left republican in outlook, with participation of Blanquists; open to IWMA materials and to contributions by French Marxists. → 70:11. #M752.5.

Marseilles; *Fr.* Marseille Mediterranean seaport, southern coast of France. → 70:50; *82*:14, 19; *92*:45, 52.

Martello, Tullio (1841 to 1918) Italian economist. Orig trained in civil engineering, he transferred to economic studies. Prof at Bologna (1884–1916); a disciple of Francesco Ferrara. His writings propagated economic liberalism and antisocialism in i.a. *Storia della Internazionale dalla origine al congresso dell'Aja* (1873); *L'economia politica antimalthusiana e il socialismo* (1894). In 1883, then teaching in a Venice school, he sent M his new book *La moneta e gli errori che corrono intorno ad essa*. → *83*:4.

Martignetti, Pasquale (1844 to 1920) Italian socialist; a government official by trade. He corresponded with E, and transd M&E

writings, incl the *Com Manifesto*; pubd the first Italian edn of #E759 (1883). → 83:29, 31, 36; *84*:52; *85*:15, 19; *86*:15, 24; *87*:8; *90*:15, 24; *91*:3, 19; *92*:19; *94*:36; *95*:24. # E572.5, E573.5.

Marx, Caroline (1824 to 1847) M's sister.
—*Note:* Another Caroline Marx was M's cousin (1844 to after 1865), daughter of his aunt Michle. → 24:1; 47:10.

Marx, Edgar; *full* Henry Edgar; *called* Musch (*Fr.* Mouche) (1846 or 1847 to 1855) M's firstborn son. Uncertainty over his date of birth is a matter of a few days, end of Dec 1846 or beginning of Jan 1847. → 46:50; 47:10; 55:2, 12, 15, 18, 22, 33, 34.

Marx, Eduard (1826 to 1837) M's brother; died early. → 26:1; 37:17.

Marx, Eleanor; *full* Jenny Julia Eleanor; *nicknamed* Tussy (rhymes. with *pussy*); *later called* **Marx-Aveling** or **Marx Aveling** (1855 to 1898) M's youngest daughter; born in England. At first she worked as a private tutor, sometime actor and journalist. She joined the SDF (1884), helped to found the Socialist League; later, a founder of the ILP (1893). In the late 1880s and early 1890s she was one of the leading TU organizers of the so-called New Unionism, organizing the unskilled, esp the London dock workers and gas workers. She did considerable writing, editing, and translating, on socialism, the women's movement, etc. —In 1884 she entered into an unlegalized marriage with E. Aveling, who allegedly could not get a divorce from his wife; this disastrous relationship led to her suicide. Eleanor and her friends used the name Mrs. (Marx-) Aveling, the name itself being an assertion about the validity of the relationship, which some were reluctant to recognize on "moral" grounds. —Y. Kapp's two-volume biography *Eleanor M* (1972–1976) is far superior to C. Tsuzuki's biography (1967). → 55:8, 12; 56:22, 33, 35; 58:30; 62:44; 64:14; 67:25; 68:30, 36, 45; 69:23, 35, 45, 58, 61; 70:34, 37, 46; 71:27, 32, 38, 39, 43, 49; 72:48, 51; 73:25, 55; 74:3, 31, 32, 35; 76:24, 26; 77:33, 34; 79:31; 81:39, 43, 59; 82:3, 14, 27, 39; *83*:3, 4, 12, 16, 28; *84*:7, 10, 16, 25, 39, 55, 59; *85*:11, 33; *86*:17, 20, 35, 37; *87*:1, 2, 5, 17, 23, 26, 27, 47; *88*:20, 25, 28; *89*:26, 31, 36; *90*:20, 28, 42, 47; *91*:2, 27, 41, 47, 54, 55; *92*:14, 21, 24, 39, 43, 61; *93*:32, 52; *94*:28, 33, 47; *95*:20, 25, 33, 36, 37. #M221, M455, M764, M971; E375, E562, E615.5, E699.

Marx, Emilie (1822 to 1888) M's sister; married (1859) to J. J. *Conradi. → 24:1.

Marx, Eva Moses Lvov (1737 to 1823) M's grandmother; his father's mother. The name Eva was apparently used as a German cognate for Chaya (also spelled Chaje—the *ch* as in the German *ach*). Her family name was Moses Lvov (or Lwow). She married Rabbi Marx-

Levy, who, however, at some point shortened the name to Marx; the variations Marx-Halevy and Mordechai Halevy have been suggested as previous forms of that surname. At any rate, their son Heinrich (M's father) used the surname Marx. (The preceding info is not completely certain.) → 23:1.

Marx, Francis (Joseph Peter) (1816 to 1876) English publicist; a landowner. Friend and supporter of David Urquhart. → 53:32; 54:20.

Marx, Franziska (1851 to 1852) M's daughter; died as a baby. Kapp gives her full name as Jenny Eveline Frances, *called* Franziska. → 51:18; 52:19.

Marx, Guido or Heinrich Guido; *registered as* Henry Edward Guy; *nicknamed* Föxchen (1849 to 1850) M's second son, likewise short-lived. Named in part after Guy Fawkes. → 49:42; 50:43.

Marx, Heinrich (1777 to 1838) M's father; senior member of the bar in Trier. Born in Saarlouis; for his parents, *see* *Marx, Eva Moses Lvov. In 1818 (when M was born) he was a lawyer in the upper Appeals Court in Trier; in 1820, became a counsellor in the newly founded Trier provincial court. —His Jewish (given) name was Heschel, Herschel, or Hirschel. → 19:1; 24:1; 34:1, 2; 35:7; 36:4, 7, 14; 37:1, 4–7, 10, 11, 15, 16; 38:1, 3, 5, 6; 40:9; 42:16; 43:16; 47:4, 38; 48:9; #M61, M149, M252, M455, M663, M967.

Marx, Henriette; *née* **Pres(s)burg** or **Pres(s)borck** (1788 to 1863) M's mother; born in Nijmegen, Neth., of a Dutch Jewish family; daughter of a well-to-do businessman. Married in 1814. → 25:1; 38:4; 40:9; 42:16; 43:10; 44:20; 47:38; 48:9; 51:18; 59:24; 61:15, 18, 53; 62:46; 63:40, 41; 64:12; 68:24.

Marx, Henriette; *mar* **Simons;** *nicknamed* Jettchen (1820 to 1845) M's sister; married (1844) Theodor Simons (1813–1863), an architect. —The death date above is given by *New Mega; MECW* gives the date c.1856. → 24:1.

Marx, Hermann (1819 to 1842) M's brother. → 24:1; 42:13.

Marx, Jenny; *née* **von Westphalen;** *full* Johanna Bertha Julie Jenny (1814 to 1881) M's wife; mar. in 1843. The full name as given above appeared on her baptismal certificate and marriage certificate. For the family background, *see* her parents, Caroline and Ludwig von *Westphalen. Born in Salzwedel, which she left at age 2; raised in Trier. A firm and well-read communist/socialist, she helped M as secy, copyist, business manager; often described as a charming, witty woman; her letters show her to be an excellent writer. There are two full-length biographical studies: Luise Dornemann, *Jenny M, Der Lebensweg einer Sozialistin* (1969); Lutz Graf Schwerin

von Krosigk, *Jenny M, Liebe und Leid im Schatten von KM* (1975; 2nd edn, 1976). → 36:9, 13, 14; 37:1; 39:1; 42:34; 43:1, 10, 13, 15; 44:20, 34; 45:23, 30, 35; 46:9; 48:17, 19, 21; 49:4, 27–29, 31–33, 36, 42; 50:39, 48, 49; 51:44; 52:4, 9, 24, 38; 53:14, 17, 19; 54:31, 36, 39, 50; 55:15, 18, 22, 33, 34, 38, 42, 48; 56:22, 29, 33, 35; 57:13, 32, 52; 58:22, 25, 30, 37, 46, 50; 59:73; 60:54, 59, 60, 62, 63; 61:53; 62:33, 44, 61, 62; 63:15, 32; 64:25, 27; 66:9, 16, 42; 67:37; 68:45; 69:35, 51, 61; 70:46; 71:23, 50; 72:25, 48, 51; 75:43.5; 76:23, 37; 77:5.5, 8.5, 20.5, 33, 34; 78:9, 27, 35; 79:15, 48; 80:21, 25, 27, 35; 81:12, 30, 36, 40, 43, 55, 58, 59; 83:12. #ME35; M313, M319, M325, M346.5, M662; E399, E421, E766.

Marx, Jenny; *mar.* **Longuet** (1844 to 1883) M's eldest daughter; married Charles Longuet (1872). She did some journalistic writing, particularly on the Irish Fenian movement; active in Communard refugee work in London; helped M on the French trans of *Capital.* → 44:1, 16, 20, 34; 45:30; 49:31, 36; 52:38; 56:22, 33, 35; 62:13, 44; 63:15, 23; 64:14; 65:36; 67:25; 68:25, 36, 45, 66; 69:23, 56, 61; 70:11, 20, 41, 46; 71:27, 32, 38, 39, 43, 49, 53, 64; 72:31, 59, 64; 73:46; 74:27, 30, 34; 76:17; 78:27, 35; 79:31, 36; 80:23, 27, 35; 81:9, 19–21, 24, 30, 36, 40, 43, 59; 82:14, 23, 27, 30, 34, 35, 39; 83:2, 3, 6. #M170; E178, E398.

Marx, Karl (Heinrich) (1818 to 1883) *The name:* M's name appeared on his birth certificate as *Carl,* though he almost never used this spelling. He signed his middle name to his doctoral dissertation, but in general did not use it as an author. The erroneous form "Heinrich Karl Marx" appeared as entry for the article contributed by Eduard Bernstein in the *Encyclopaedia Britannica,* 11th edn, and has traveled somewhat from that source. — *Indexed here for appearance in titles only:* #M151, M174, M415, M6ʋ2, M748, M825, M860, M862, M946, M947; E230, E285, E317, E360, E374, E375, E392–E395, E405, E406, E437, E469–E471, E551, E600–E609, E616, E687–E696, E799, E806.

Marx, Laura; *mar.* **Lafargue** (1845 to 1911) M's second daughter; married (1868) Paul *Lafargue. Besides being closely involved with Paul's party work on returning to France, she undertook translations and some journalism; aided strikes and TU organization in France; delegate to the French WP congress in 1900. Both Lafargues committed suicide instead of facing old age. —The extant body of her correspondence with E (*see* ST/E9 or ST/E10) shows to what extent, and how justifiably, E had more confidence in her political judgment than in Paul's. → 45:35; 49:31, 36; 56:22, 33, 35; 62:44; 64:14, 66:41, 42; 67:25; 68:24, 25, 45; 69:9, 23, 35, 46; 70:6, 16, 20, 23, 25, 40; 71:12, 27, 32, 38, 39, 43, 49,

65; 72:40; 74:27; 80:23, 27, 35; 82:30, 34; 83:2, 6, 9, 11, 16, 19, 24, 26–28, 38, 41, 42, 49, 50; 84:11, 12, 16, 22–25, 30, 31, 39; 85:10, 30, 32, 36, 40; 86:2, 7, 13, 16, 17, 20, 45–47, 49, 55; 87:10, 17, 19, 27; 88:21, 24, 36, 38, 39; 90:7, 8, 10, 21, 25, 42; 91:18, 27, 31, 34, 37, 41, 45, 47, 54, 56; 92:3, 14, 21, 22, 24, 25, 30, 32, 52, 62; 93:8, 18, 20, 28, 40–42, 44, 45, 53–56; 94:1, 18, 35, 36, 43, 45, 47, 50; 95:2, 3, 13, 16, 18–20, 23, 25, 33, 36, 37. #ME33; M170, M361, M828; E290, E390, E443, E556, E699.

Marx, Louise; *mar.* Juta (1821 to 1893) M's sister. In 1853 she married J. C. *Juta and went with him to Cape Town. → 24:1; 53:25; 61:9.

Marx, Samuel (1781 to 1829) M's uncle; his father's older brother. Rabbi in Trier. → 27:1.

Marx, Sophie; *mar.* Schmalhausen (1816 to 1886) M's sister, the one to whom he was closest. In 1842 she married W. R. *Schmalhausen of Maastricht. (The above death date is from *New Mega*; *MECW* gives 1883.) → 24:1; 33:1; 35:1; 36:2, 14; 42:19.   #M661, M664.

Massachusetts (U.S.) → 79:35.

Massard, Emile; *full* Nicolas Emile (1857 to 1932) French (Belgian-born) journalist. He worked for various papers after the Paris Commune, in which he took part as a youth; an editor of Guesde's *Egalité* (1877); later supported the Boulangist movement; became an officer of *La Presse*; Paris city councillor (1904–1932) on a nationalist republican platform. In the 1890s he devoted himself esp to military studies and articles. → 92:22.   #E390.

Massman, W. Member of the GC/IWMA from July 1866; reelected (according to the *GFCI* Index) at the Geneva Congress in Sep; but the GC Minutes record only one definite attendance at a GC meeting. In Nov the GC was told that he was leaving for Germany; he was "authorized to act" for the IWMA in that country. This may indicate that he was a German; but his name has only one final *n* in the GC records. → 66:31.

Massol, Alexandre; *full* Marie Alexandre (1805 or 1806 to 1875) French radical journalist. Orig an officer in the army engineers, he became a republican (1830) and a Saint-Simonian "missionary" under the influence of Enfantin; edited *L'Observateur Français* as an antigovernment organ. In 1848 he came to Paris; worked on the staff of *La Réforme*; as a friend of Proudhon, contributed to his *Voix du Peuple*. He did not follow other Saint-Simonians in becoming a Bonapartist. In 1867 he supported the Peace Congress in Lausanne; contributed to the *Almanachs de la Coopération*, and to the 1868 *Encyclopédie de la Révolution*. → 52:7; 62:62.

Maughan English Owenite and Freethinker. → 67:37.

Maujean, E. French Communard refugee in London; piano worker. He was associated with V. *Delahaye in the Comité Révolutionnaire du Prolétariat, and in 1874 signed its program as a member of its Exec Comm. → 71:51.

Maurer, Georg Ludwig von (1790 to 1872) German historian of law and early social institutions in Germany; prof at Munich. According to his researches, the Mark community was a voluntary assoc of free men, holding lands communally, governed by an elected chief; i.e., he saw the roots of German society in institutions of primitive democracy and communality. This theory was violently attacked, esp from the political right. M&E greatly admired his work and set great store by it (e.g., #E573, E468). The continuing dispute over Maurer's views is, in part involved with controversy over Marxist views of history.
—Maurer's chief works: *Einleitung zur Geschichte der Mark-, Hof-, Dorf- und Stadtverfassung und der öffentlichen Gewalt* (1854); *Geschichte der Markenverfassung in Deutschland* (1856); *Geschichte der Fronhöfe, der Bauernhöfe und der Hofverfassung in Deutschland* (1862–1863); *Geschichte der Dorfverfassung in Deutschland* (1865–1866); *Geschichte der Stadtverfassung in Deutschland* (1869–1871). → 68:17; 76:14, 18; 82:38, 51.

Mayall A London photographer. Since M sent him the French trans of *Capital*, perhaps he was French in origin. After M's death, E had photos of M made up in quantity by Mayall; E thought he was the best in London; besides, Mayall's maxim was: "We do not take money from eminent people." → 75:48.

Mayer, Gustav #E337.5.

Mayer, Milton #ME33.

Mazas prison (Paris) → 61:21.

Mazzini, Giuseppe; *Angl.* Joseph (1805 to 1872) Italian nationalist-republican revolutionary. Orig a lawyer in Genoa, he joined the Carbonari (c.1830), fled Italy to Marseilles, formed (1832) the secret society called Young Italy (slogan: God and the People). Expelled by France, he operated mostly from London till 1848, when he returned to Italy; one of the founders of the Roman Republic. After the French crushed it, he returned to emigration in Switzerland and London. During the 1850s he worked at inciting various uprisings against Austrian rule in Italy (Milan, Piedmont, Sicily, Naples), and continued to plan republican putsches up to his death. — Mazzini was virulently antisocialist; one of the first skirmishes in the IWMA was over the attempt of Mazzinists to take over the new assoc. Later, Mazzini bitterly attacked the Paris Commune. From M's view, often expressed, Mazzini was the very model of the

bourgeois political revolutionary bereft of a social program who was therefore incapable of mobilizing the mass of the Italian people behind his rather empty elocution about (in the words of his slogan) "Unity, Independence, Liberty, Equality, Humanity." →
50:46; 51:9; 52:7, 15, 52; 54:43; 58:23, 42; 59:41, 45; 61:30; 64:31; 66:17; 68:61; 71:28, 34, 35, 37, 41, 56, 63, 64; 72:16.   #ME25; M77, M320, M434, M435, M494, M500–M503, M533, M788; E475, E749, E829.

Mazzinists Supporters of *Mazzini. →
61:30; 66:17, 21; 71:34, 56.

Mechelen or **Mecheln** See Malines.

Mehring, Franz (1846 to 1919) German historian and journalist, eventually a socialist. Of a semifeudal Pomeranian family, he studied philosophy and history in youth; and joined the bourgeois-democratic left wing around J. *Jacoby; collaborator of liberal papers, esp the *Frankfurter Ztg.* In the 1870s, as an admirer of the good nationalist Lassalle against the bad internationalist Marx, he pubd a couple of works in which he sharply attacked the Marxist Social-Democrats: *Herr v. Treitschke, der Sozialistentöter und die Endziele des Liberalismus* (1875) and esp *Die deutsche Sozialdemokratie, ihre Geschichte und ihre Lehre* (1877). The latter work was also excerpted in the widely read *Gartenlaube* (1879–1880). The S-D party, then fighting for its life against Bismarck's Anti-Socialist Law, regarded this liberal as one of its worst enemies. In the period 1876–1882 Mehring pubd a number of writings attacking M very violently. It came as a surprise when later Mehring, indignant (it is said) over the administration of the Anti-Socialist Law, came to the defense of the Social-Democrats in the *Berliner Volkszeitung* (of which he was editor, 1885+) and the *Weserzeitung,* and finally, at an advanced age, joined the S-D party in about 1900–1901. He quickly became a leading editorial staff writer on the NZ, Kautsky's chief associate, and (1901–1908) editor of the important left-socialist *Leipziger Volkszeitung.* In two decades he produced an edn of M&E's journalistic writings in the first three vols. of *Aus dem literarischen Nachlass von Marx, Engels und Lassalle* (1902)—the fourth vol. of which was devoted to Lassalle in order to present the latter as of coordinate importance with M&E; a well-known biography of M (1918), now thoroughly superseded, in any case extremely weak on M's political thought, and incompetent in its handling of Lassalle and Bakunin; a number of writings on German history; a history of the German party, *Geschichte der deutschen Sozialdemocratie* (1909); a much-acclaimed work on Prussian history and literature, *Die Lessinglegende* (1906); and other books. Although he became

a strong opponent of Bernstein's "Revisionism" on its appearance, in 1913 in the NZ Mehring launched his own war against Marx with an attack on him for criticizing Lassalle; followed this up by provoking a polemic with Kautsky in which he more and more glorified Lassalle and began to rehabilitate even Bakunin against M. This new stage in Mehring's history of twists and turns was aborted by the outbreak of World War I, which activated Mehring's anti-Prussian, antimilitarist side, and threw him together with Luxemburg and K. Liebknecht, first in founding the Spartacus League and then the CP in 1918.   —When the Revisionists once launched a specially prepared attack on Mehring (and his peculiar past) at the Dresden party congress, Bebel, who defended Mehring, called him a "psychological riddle." This riddle has not been plumbed, and indeed the vicissitudes of Mehring's politics have been regularly suppressed in biographical sketches of the man.
—See Thomas Höhle, *Franz Mehring* (Berlin, 1956). → 77:28; 82:28; 85:27; 92:18, 47; 93:34; 95:25, 29.   #ME28.

Meiners, Christoph (1747 to 1810) German cultural historian. Prof of philosophy at Göttingen (1772+); he helped reorganize the Russian university system at the czar's invitation. His scholarly works, characterized by immense erudition, chiefly treated antiquity and the Middle Ages, with eclectic views. M (1842) studied his *Allgemeine kritische Geschichte der Religionen* (1806–1807); M (1852) studied his *Geschichte des weiblichen Geschlechts* (1788–1800) → 52:56, 58. #M93.

Meissner, Alfred (1822 to 1885) Austrian-Bohemian-born writer, best known for his poetry, novels, and plays. Orig a physician (1846+), he lived in Paris till returning to Germany in 1848; friend of Heine. A "True Socialist" in the 1840s, his *Revolutionäre Studien aus Paris* (1849) described the French leftist scene. He moved to Prague (1850), esp writing poetry; later a liberal. His autobiographical work was *Geschichte meines Lebens* (1884). → 48:85; 49:4.

Meissner, Otto (Karl) (1819 to 1902) German pub'r; owner of the Hamburg firm usually called Verlag von Otto Meissner (1848+). In the late 1840s he was close to the CL; later a left liberal. He pubd *Capital* and other writings by M&E. → 60:45; 65:11, 20, 24, 26; 66:8, 12, 48, 52, 54; 67:1, 11, 12, 14, 17, 23; 68:13; 69:8, 13, 21, 58, 59; 71:60; 72:7, 18, 22, 32, 38; 73:9, 10, 15, 25, 29, 48; 74:32; 75:48; 81:54, 60; 84:22; 94:6, 21, 27, 46.

Melchior, Julius German socialist worker, from Solingen; member of the GGWA. In 1864 he emigrated to the U.S. → 64:17.

Ménard, Louis (Nicolas) (1822 to 1901)

French man of letters—poet, philosopher, historian, essayist, political pamphleteer, art critic, landscape painter—and chemist (discoverer of collodion). A Democratic opponent of the Louis Philippe regime, he hailed the February Revolution of 1848, and was indignant over the bloody repression of the June Days in Paris. He thereupon wrote his *Prologue d'une révolution. Février–juin 1848*, which appeared in feuilleton in Proudhon's *Le Peuple* and finally as a book (1849). Ménard fled arrest, took refuge in London, where he came to know M&E. Thus he became the contributor of a poem (also recently pubd in *Le Peuple*) to M's *NRZ-Revue*, the only non-German piece there: "Jambes" (Legs), a cry of revenge for the government's June slaughter. (Freiligrath was supposed to do a German trans but never did.) Ménard also contributed to Harney's *Red Republican* (1850). He returned to Paris after the 1859 amnesty. At the time of the Paris Commune, he wrote in its defense. His later books cover a wide range, as indicated above. → 50:18. #ME115.5.

Mendelson, Stanislaw (1857 to 1913) Polish socialist; publicist and journalist. A delegate to the International Socialist Congress of 1889 and 1891, he was founder of the Polish SP in 1892. He left the movement in the mid-1890s. → 80:46; 91:10, 15; 92:11, 24; 93:40; 95:37. #ME33; E615.

Mendelsonowa, Maria (or Marja); née **Zaleska** (1850 to 1909) Polish writer and socialist; wife of Stanislaw *Mendelson (mar. 1889). She was active in the Polish workers' movement; member of the IWMA; delegate to the International Socialist Congresses (1889–1893); participant in the founding of the Polish SP (1892). *Note on names:* Born Maria Zaleska, she became Maria Jankowska by her first marriage; later she also used Jankowska-Mendelsonowa. Three pen names complicate the picture: Stefan Leonowicz, Maria Schopar, Sofia Schopar. → 84:40; 91:10; 93:4.

Menger, Anton (1841 to 1906) Austrian prof of law (U. of Vienna); brother of the economist Karl *Menger. Best known for his work *Das Recht auf den vollen Arbeitstag* (1886), transd as *The right to the whole produce of labor;* very popular with the Social-Democracy as a presentation of socialistic views. Menger also pubd *Neue Staatslehre* (1903). He advocated state-socialistic control of economic life with the negation of democratic control. → 86:45, 49; 87:15. #E429.

Menger, Karl (1840 to 1921) Austrian economist; prof at Vienna (1873–19(3). A leading theorist of the Austrian school of polit eco; one of the founders of the marginal-utility

theory; opponent of historical method in economics. Chief work: *Grundsätze der Volkswirthschaftslehre* (1871). → 92:47.

Menke, Theodor Heinrich A friend of Dr. Kugelmann and an IWMA member, whom M tried to get to contribute money to a Solingen cooperative. *MEW* 32 Index identifies him as "Statistician; manufacturer, . . ." *MEW* 31 Index leaves out "manufacturer." —*Caution:* I think there is a mixup of more than one person involved in *MEW*'s descriptions; also see → 67:12 for a Hanover statistician whom M called "Merkel," and whose name may have been confused with this Hamburg money man; this problem cannot be resolved here. Into the bargain, there is a Heinrich Theodor von Menke who is unrelated to this problem; see *MEW* 18 Index. → 69:72.

Merivale, Herman (1806 to 1874) English economist; lawyer by profession; Liberal politician. Not successful as a lawyer, he succeeded Senior as prof of polit eco at Oxford (1837–1842). From 1847 he filled cabinet posts dealing with the colonies; undersecy of state for India (1859+). He pubd *Lectures on colonization and colonies* (1841), which M studied (1851). Also author of *Historical studies* (1865), biographies, etc. → 51:69.

Merovingians #E289. *See* Frankish epoch.

Mesa, José; *full* **Mesa y Leompart** (1840 to 1904) Spanish socialist pioneer; printing worker. He joined the Republican Federalists in Spain; took part in the revolutionary activity of 1866; then moved to Paris (till 1868); joined the IWMA (1870) and helped to found sections; member of the Spanish Federal Council (1871–1872), of the ed bd of *La Emancipación* (1871–1873); a founder of the New Madrid Federation (1872–1873); active opponent of the Bakuninists. Then he again had to emigrate to Paris (1873); settled there as a journalist; close to Guesde, he transmitted Guesdist material to Iglesias in Spain, thus becoming a link in propagating Marxism in Spain. He also transd a number of M&E writings. In 1879 he was active in founding the Spanish SP. → 72:13, 21, 42, 61; 73:6, 13; 74:14; 75:48; 82:14, 30; 83:12, 87:20; 91:20, 40. #M681; E437.

Meshchersky, Prince Vladimir Petrovich (1839 to 1914) Russian leader of reactionary court circles. Editor of *Grazhdanin* (St. Petersburg weekly), spokesman of absolutism, anti-Semitism, and feudal privilege, subsidized by the czars he served. → 76:30.

Metz (Fr.) Chief city of Lorraine, on the Moselle. #E531.

Metzner, Theodor (1830 to 1902) German socialist worker (shoemaker); a founding member of the GGWA, member of its Exec, plenipotentiary in Berlin. He belonged to the anti-Lassallean opposition in the organization; in 1866 he helped found the Berlin section of the IWMA. He left the GGWA (1868), helped found the Demokratische Arbeiterverein in Berlin; and was a delegate (1869) to the Eisenach Congress founding the SDWP. → 65:57, 63.

Mexico → 54:48; 61:49; 62:2, 11, 14. #M413, M414, M509, M871.

Meyen, Eduard (1812 to 1870) German journalist and publicist. In the early 1840s he was a Young Hegelian leftist; member of the group called "The Free"; collaborator with the *Hallische Jahrbücher* and *Deutsche Jahrbücher* (1839+); a copublisher of the weekly *Athenäum* (1841); contributor to the *RZ* (1842–1843). After the 1848–1849 defeat, he emigrated to England; later a National Liberal; editor of the *Berliner Reform* (1861–1863). → 41:4; 42:30; 49:27; 51:36; 57:9; 59:35, 65; 60:13, 20.

Meyer, Gottfried Christian Ernst German pub'r, in Brunswick. —N.B.: *MEW* and *MECW* give his name as G. C. A. Meyer, erron. according to *New Mega* III, 1:185. → 41:17.

Meyer, H. A member of the London GWEA, then called the Communist WEA. No further identification is available. → 80:12.

Meyer, Hermann (1821 to 1875) German socialist, esp active in America. A merchant by occupation, he took part in the 1848–1849 revolution in Germany; then (1852) emigrated to the U.S., where he worked closely with his friend Weydemeyer; also a friend of Sorge. In the 1850s he was secy of the Communist Club of NY; in the 1850s–1860s he played a leading part in struggles to liberate Alabama blacks. He became active in organizing IWMA sections in St. Louis; also active in Milwaukee; attended the first congress of the N. American Federation (1873). → 67:15, 37; 68:5; 76:7, 11.

Meyer, Julius (1817 to 1863) German "True Socialist"; an ironworks owner in Westphalia. → 45:13.

Meyer, Rudolph (Hermann) (1839 to 1899) German publicist. He was best known for his pioneering study of the labor movement, *Der Emanzipationskampf der vierten Standes* (1874–1875); editor of the *Berliner Revue*. His book *Politische Gründer und die Korruption in Deutschland* (1877), an exposé, made it necessary for him to take refuge in London, where he became acquainted with M&E, whom he occasionally visited. He wrote for the *NZ* on agriculture, as a scholar, but he was not a Social-Democrat; rather a socialistic theorist à la Rodbertus, plus a leaven of Christian cooperativism, "social monarchy" theory, and anti-Semitism. In the 1870s he was a leader of the anti-Bismarck Antikanzlerliga. → 79:22, 25, 34, 37; 93:34, 42, 51.

Meyer, Sigfrid; *sometimes* Siegfried (1840 to 1872) German socialist, later active in America. A mining engineer by profession, he was a supporter of M in the Berlin branch of the GGWA, where he belonged to the anti-Lassallean opposition; corresponded with M. He helped to found the Berlin section of the IWMA; in 1866, pubd an edn of the *Com Manifesto* at his own expense, then (same year) emigrated to the U.S. There he became a member of the Communist Club of NY; also an active organizer of IWMA sections. He and his friend August *Vogt were hostile to Sorge, without visible political grounds, apparently as rivals for control of the organization, and this contributed to its disruption. → 65:57; 66:9, 16, 19; 67:12, 13, 27; 68:34, 37, 40, 49; 69:17, 32; 70:26; 71:2, 3, 6. #ME33.

Meyers Konversations-Lexikon; Eine Encyklopädie des allegemeinen Wissenschaft Leipzig, Bibliographisches Insitut, 1874–1884. 3rd edn. 21 vols. → 68:57.

Middle Ages → 92:62.

Middle East → 53:9, 18. See also individual countries.

Midlands A number of counties in central England, collectively. → 93:44.

Mieroslawski, Ludwik (von); Fr. Louis (1814 to 1878) Polish revolutionist; writer on military questions and history. He took part in the Polish uprisings of 1830–1831 and 1846; military leader of uprisings in Posen, later in Sicily (1848); commander of the Baden-Palatinate forces (1849); thereafter an émigré in France. In the 1850s–1860s he was associated with Bonapartist circles, and represented the right wing of the Polish emigration. In the 1863–1864 Polish uprising he was named dictator; after the defeat, retired to France. —M (1856) prob read two new works by him: *Histoire de la commune polonaise du dixième au dix-huitième siècle;* and *De la nationalité polonaise dans l'équilibre européen.* → 56:38.

Mikhailovsky, Nikolai Konstantinovich (1842 to 1904) Russian publicist and sociological critic, a spokesman for liberal Narodniks. He wrote for *Otechestvenniye Zapiski* (1869–1884), first as contributor, then as editor; contributor to *Narodnaya Volya* (1879–1883); editor of *Russkoye Bogatstvo* (1892+). His viewpoint was far from M's: subjective in its sociology, denying objective truth in history; uninterested in political democracy; related to Katheder-socialism. To be sure, he defended M's *Capital* against *Zhukovsky in his 1877 article titled "Karl Marks pered sudom g. Yu Zhukovskago," but later he attacked the Russian Marxists who criticized his theory of peasant socialism. → 77:40, 41.

Milan Chief city of N. Italy. → 41:11;

53:8, 11; 71:52, 59; 72:3, 10, 20, 24, 42; 77:6; 79:6; 91:24, 42; 92:17. #M59; E481, E836, E861.

Mill, James (1773 to 1836) British (Scottish-born) economist, historian, philosopher, and publicist; father of J. S. Mill. In philosophy, a follower of Bentham's utilitarianism; in economics, of Ricardo. Son of a shoemaker, he first studied theology; became a preacher; then moved to London as publicist (1802). Pub'r, *Literary Journal* (1803+); editor of the *St. James's Chronicle* (1805–1808); collaborator, *Edinburgh Review* (1808–1813). After he pubd his chief work, *History of India* (1806–1818), he was hired by the E. India Co., and ended as its administrative head. Other works: *Elements of polit eco* (1821)—which M studied in French trans in 1843 (*MEGA* I, 3), also in 1859–1862 notebooks; *Analysis of the mind* (1829). M (1853) annotated his India history. → 43:2; 44:1, 3, 10. #M303, M575.

Mill, John Stuart (1806 to 1873) English philosopher and economist. He followed his father, James Mill, in critically developing the principles of utilitarianism and Ricardian economics, and also in working for the E. India Co. (1823+), becoming head of India House. He subseqly became the outstanding contemporary authority on polit eco, but is best known today for his writings on democratic theory (*On liberty,* 1859; *Representative government,* (1861), on feminism (*The subjection of women,* 1869, with Harriet Taylor); also his autobiography (1873). —In 1845–1846 M studied his *Essays on some unsettled questions of polit eco* (1844) and his *On combination of trades* (new edn, 1834); in 1850, his *Principles of polit eco* (1848); and other writings. M's comments on Mill are often contemptuous; he considered him a very shallow thinker: "On the level plain, simple mounds look like hills; and the imbecile flatnesss of the present bourgeoisie is to be measured by the altitude of its great intellects." → 45:52; 50:50; 54:51; 59:76; 66:51; 67:3. #M575.

Millar, John (1735 to 1801) Scottish law prof and liberal publicist. A lawyer (1760+), he became a prof at Glasgow (1761). A Whig in politics, he favored parliamentary reform, American independence, and abolition of the slave trade. M (1852) studied his *Observations concerning the distinction of ranks in society* (1771), later titled *The origin of the distinction* [etc.] (3rd edn, 1779). His other well-known work was *Historical view of the English government* (1787). → 52:56, 58; 53:55.

Milner, George Irish-born radical, active in the English working-class movement, esp the IWMA. He was first a Chartist, follower of Bronterre O'Brien; secy of the National Re-

form League; Exec member, Land and Labour League. He was an active member of the GC/IWMA (1868–1872); member of the British Federal Council (1872–1873), opposed to Hales' reformist tendency. → 72:37. #M755.

Milwaukee Chief city in Wisconsin. → 58:25.

Mincio River River of N. Italy, from Lake Garda to the Po. #M837; E56.

The **Miner and Workman's Advocate** London, June 13, 1863, to Sep 2, 1865. Weekly. Director: W. Whitehorn. Ed by J. Towers; J. B. Leno. —Continuation of the *British Miner;* continued by the *Workman's Advocate;* organ of the Miners union; served as IWMA organ in England. → 65:46.

Mineyko, Gerhard (1832 to 1888) Russian statistician. M (1882) read his just-pubd *Sel'skaya pozemel'naya obshchina.* → 82:55.

Miquel, Johannes (1828 to 1901) German politician; lawyer by profession. Radical in his youth, he took part in the 1848–1849 revolution, and joined the CL in the late 1840s. During the 1850s, practicing law in Göttingen, he moved rightward; helped found the Nationalverein (1859); mayor of Osnabrück (1865 to 1870, 1876–1880); a leader of the National Liberals (1867+); a director of the Discontogesellschaft banking enterprise (1870–1873); mayor of Frankfurt (1879). He entered the Reichstag (1887); helped to reorganize the National Liberals; became min of finance (1890–1900), putting through the Prussian tax reform of 1891–1893; was ennobled ("von Miquel") in 1897. —Miquel continued to supply political info to M for some years after more or less abandoning his left politics, apparently under duress (fear of exposure). In his later period he moved well to the right of the liberals, toward Bismarckian conservatism. The standard biography, in German, is Wilhelm Mommsen's *JM* (1928). → 50:27; 51:5, 27, 31, 50; 54:27, 39; 56:14, 27, 31; 57:9, 21, 53; 60:46; 62:52, 57; 64:35; 67:14; 71:2, 20, 21; 73:56; 90:19.

Le **Mirabeau** Verviers (Belg.), Dec 1, 1867, to May 8, 1880. At times monthly, semimonthly, weekly. —It incorporated *L'Internationale* (Brussels) in Jan 1874. #M752.

Mirbach, Otto von Prussian military man. An artillery officer, he took part in the 1848–1849 revolution as a leftist liberal; commandant in the Elberfeld uprising of May 1849. He emigrated after the defeat. → 49:25.

Mirès, Jules Isaac (1809 to 1871) French banker and stock speculator. After buying up a number of Paris papers (1848+) and setting up profitable operations in stockjobbery, he launched several financial operations by 1854, based on his takeover of the Caisse

Général des Chemins de Fer. He was arrested, sentenced to prison, but finally acquitted on appeal in 1862. #M411.

Mirkhond; Persian **Mirkhvand;** properly Muhammed ibn-Khavand Shah ibn-Mahmud (1433 to 1498) Persian historian; author of a great work of early Persian scholarship, Garden of Purity. . . , a universal history and biography from ancient times onward, begun c.1474. → 53:18.

Misselden, Edward (fl. 1608+; d. 1654) English merchant and writer on economics. He was deputy governor (1623–1633) of the Merchant Adventurers' Co. in Delft, then active for it in Amsterdam and Hamburg. His writings were defenses of mercantilism on behalf of the company: Free trade (1622), studied by M 1845; The circle of commerce (1623). → 45:51. # M575.

Missouri (state, U.S.) → 60:8.

Missouri Republican St. Louis (Mo.). 1822 to 1888 under this title; then till 1919 as St. Louis Republic. Daily. —Democratic party organ. → 86:18.

Mitteldeutsche Volks-Zeitung Leipzig, 1862 to 1866. —Liberal paper; W. Liebknecht took over as editor when it faced bankruptcy in 1866, but, banned in Prussia, it failed. → 66:37.

Mitternachtzeitung für gebildete Leser Brunswick, 1830 to at least 1840 under this title. Ed by E. Brinckmeier (1835+). —Liberal. —Previously (1826–1829) titled Mitternachtblatt für gebildete Stände, pubd by Adolph Müllner; other permutations of this name are found too, and the sequence of names is unclear. → 40:2. #E491.

Modern Thought London, 1879 to 1884. Monthly. —Liberal magazine, dealing with "religion, politics, ethics, science and literature." → 81:58.

Möser, Justus (1720 to 1794) German historian and publicist of the Enlightenment; lawyer by profession, rising to chief justice and privy councillor of Osnabrück, of which he wrote a history. His influential Patriotische phantasien (1774–1786) advocated a modernized state constitution, but he was hostile to the French Revolution; M (1843) studied this book (1820 edn). → 43:32.

Mogul Empire Muslim empire in India (1526–1857). → 53:18, 23.

Mohr M's nickname, used by family and intimate friends: meaning Moor, which at the time had much of the connotation of the later "nigger." It referred to M's swarthy complexion, and stemmed from very early in his life. In his letters to E, his signature Mohr had variations: Der Mohr; Old Mohr; Moro; El Moro; Il Moro; K. Moro; K. Mohr. → 57:18; 63:11; 83:14.

Moldavia One of the "Danubian princi-palities"; now part of Roumania. → 56:2. #M301, M407.

Molesworth, William Nassau (1816 to 1890) English clergyman and writer on history. He was vicar in the Rochdale district (ordained 1839), and became an early supporter of the Cooperative movement; politically radical, a friend of Bright and Cobden. As a historian, he produced a history of England covering 1830+ (1871–1873), of the reform bill of 1832 (1864), and of the Anglican church (1882). However, M's correspondence with him dealt with astronomy, apparently because Molesworth had pubd a book Plain lectures on astronomy (1862). —Note: Not to be confused with Sir William Molesworth (1810–1855), a Radical politician. → 65:45.

Molinari, Gustave de (1819 to 1912) Belgian economist. Prof at Brussels, then Antwerp; moved to Paris as editor of the J. des Débats (1871–1876) and the J. des Economistes (1881–1909). He advocated extreme economic liberalism: free trade, "free enterprise," corporate capitalism; against state intervention. Chief works: Etudes économiques (1846), which M studied (1859); also Cours d'économie politique (1855); Esquisse de l'organisation politique et économique de la société future (1899). → 59:76.

Moll, Friedrich (Wilhelm); called Fritz (c.1835 to 1871) German socialist worker (metal worker), from Solingen. In 1863 he was a member of the Exec of the GGWA; in 1864, emigrated to U.S., where he helped to found the GGWA organization in NY; then returned to Germany. He became active in a Solingen iron and steel wares cooperative (about which he corresponded with E), but esp active in the IWMA local section; delegate to the Geneva Congress (1866); corresponded (1869–1871) with J. P. Becker who was organizing IWMA work from Switzerland. → 64:17; 69:26, 31; 71:17.

Moll, Joseph (1813 to 1849) German communist worker (watchmaker); a leading founder of the Communist League. Cologne-born, he became active in revolutionary secret societies as a traveling artisan in France, Belgium, and England; first joined the Mazzinian secret society Young Germany in Switzerland; then joined the League of the Just in Paris. After participating in the Blanquist putsch of May 1839, he emigrated to London, where (with Schapper et al.) he built the League of the Just and also the GWEA (1840+); later into the CL when it was formed. In 1846 the League sent him to Brussels to invite M&E to join. After the February Revolution of 1848 in Paris, he moved to the CL branch there, and thence to Cologne, where he was active in the WA (April+) as a part of M's NRZ group. He became pres of the WA (July to Sep, after Gottschalk's arrest); also a member of the overall Exec of the Cologne Demo Assocs. In the Sep crisis in Cologne, the government's attempt to arrest him was foiled by mass intervention; he fled to London, and there helped to reestablish a CC/CL. During the winter this CC sent him to Germany to reorganize the CL on the basis of new statutes, a mission that was discussed in Cologne with M&E. In May 1849—after a trip to Brussels and its German WA—he threw himself into the Baden-Palatinate uprising; fatally wounded at the battle of Murgtal. —Moll was known as a practical-revolutionary type, not a theoretician but an activist; bold and ready for action, and as such highly praised by E. → 43:14; 45:32; 47:8, 11; 48:19, 22, 39, 49, 65, 71; 49:11. #ME15, ME47, ME87.

Moltke, Count Helmuth (Karl Bernhard) von (1800 to 1891) Prussian gen and military theoretician. After serving in and reorganizing the Turkish army (1835–1839), he rose to chief of the Prussian gen staff (1858–1888), reorganizing the Prussian forces; strategic leader in wars against Denmark, Austria, and France (1864–1871); field marshal and head of the Imperial gen staff (1871–1888). Often regarded as a creator of modern military strategy in the field, he also wrote considerably on military history and theory. → 74:13. #E744.

Momberger, August German Social-Democrat, from Wiesbaden. No further info. → 94:15.

Money, James William B. British barrister. His book *Java* (1861) was appreciatively studied by M&E; no other info available. → 81:64; 84:14.

The **Money Market Review** London, June 9, 1860, to 1895 under this title; then *Investors' Chronicle* and other changes. Weekly. → 69:7.

Mongin, Alphonse French Communard refugee—member of the Exec of the Société des Refugiés de la Commune—in London. — *Note:* KMC lists "Mongin" among the people to whom M sent the French edn of *Capital,* but its index makes it "Mougin." In any case, the above entry is the likeliest, based on Maitron's *DBMOF.* → 72:54.

Le **Moniteur Parisien** Paris, 1830 to Feb 1848. Daily. Semiofficial government organ. → 48:10.

Le **Moniteur Universel** Paris, 1811 to June 1901 under this title. Daily. —Founded 1789 as the *Gazette Nationale; ou Le Moniteur Universel.* It was an official government organ till 1868 (except in 1814–1816); superseded by the *Journal Officielle de la République Française.* #E197.

Montagnards The members of "the Mountain" in the National Convention during the French Revolution, i.e., the Jacobins and further left. #M338. *See also* Jacobins.

Montalembert, Count Charles Forbes de (1810 to 1870) French (London-born) journalist and politician. At first associated with Lamennais in the Catholic social-reform movement, editor of *L'Avenir* (1830–1832), he capitulated to church and papal pressure to withdraw from liberal positions on religious liberty, etc., eventually becoming hostile to liberalism. E's article gives a cutting view of his cowardly politics and alleged liberalism as he moved away from Bonaparte's regime. → 58:45. #E634.

Montanari, Geminiano (1633 to 1687) Italian astronomer and mathematician, prof at Bologna and Padua; also author of two works on the economics of money. These were pubd posthumously, included in the Custodi collection: *Breve trattato del valore delle monete in tutti gli stati* and *La zecca in consulto di stato (Della moneta);* M (1851) studied the second one at least. → 51:64.

Montebello Town in N. Italy; scene of Austrian defeat by the French in 1859. #E68.

Monte Carlo Capital of Monaco. → 82:19, 23.

Montefiore, Leonard (1853 to 1879) English publicist; NUC lists only his posthumous *Essays and letters contributed to various periodicals* (1881). He was clearly on a friendly-visiting footing with M, but there is no info on how this came about. → 79:8.

Montenegro Principality in S.W. Europe, independent 1799+; now part of Yugoslavia. #M795.

Montesquieu, Baron de. Charles de **Secondat;** *full* Charles Louis de Secondat, Baron de **la Brède et de Montesquieu** (1689 to 1755) French political philosopher and man of letters, a leading figure of the Enlightenment. Orig a lawyer, he withdrew from practice to study and write. His chief work, *De l'esprit des lois* (1748), laid the basis for constitutional liberalism based on the separation of powers in the state, much under the influence of English institutions. Other works: *Lettres persanes* (1721); *Considérations sur les causes de la grandeur des romains et de leur décadence* (1734). M's notes on the *Esprit de lois* were made in 1843 and 1860. → 43:32; 49:7; 60:65. #M530.

Montgaillard, Comte de; *pseud. of* Maurice Jacques **Roques** (1761 to 1841) French political adventurer. A royalist secret agent during the French Revolution, he later ingratiated himself with Napoleon and the Restoration, inventing his title in 1794. Besides memoirs, he pubd a number of works on the recent history of France, incl *Histoire de France depuis 1825 jusqu'à 1830* (1839), and also revised works written by his equally larcenous brother, Guillaume Honoré Roques, who called himself the Abbé de Montgaillard (1772–1825), e.g., *Histoire de France depuis la fin du règne de Louis XVI jusqu'à 1825* (1825–1833). → 43:33.

Montmartre Paris hill and city district. → 71:15.

Montreal; Fr. Montréal (Quebec) Largest city, and French-speaking center, of Canada. → 88:30.

Moore, George An English engraver; all available info is in the *Chronicle.* → 74:4.

Moore, Richard (1810 to 1878) English woodcarver, later a successful businessman in the trade. A radical in politics, he was active in the Chartist movement; treasurer (1848) of the People's Charter Union; also a supporter of other reform causes. In the movement, he was a moderate, opposed to force like Lovett. —He pubd a number of pamphlets on currency problems (1822–1838), esp *Treatise on paper and gold money* (2nd edn, 1832)—prob read by M (1850). → 50:50.

Moore, Samuel (1838 to 1911) English lawyer; M&E's friend and translator. A former territorial army officer, Moore orig had a small factory in Manchester, which went backrupt; he turned to studying law (c.1879), was called to the bar (1882), practiced in Manchester and Liverpool. By c.1863 he had become a close friend of M&E (E first); became active in the Manchester IWMA; acted as legal adviser to M&E. He began studying *Capital* on its publ, and was tapped by E as translator as early as the 1870s; trained for the task under E's tutelage, and began working on it by 1883, later (1884+) aided by Aveling. The pubd trans of Vol. 1 (1887) was signed by Moore and Aveling; Moore also did the standard English trans of the *Com Manifesto* (pubd 1888), likewise under the umbrella of E's editing. In June 1889 Moore left England to become chief justice in the territories of the Royal Niger Co. at Asaba (today Nigeria) for eight years. E named him one of his executors. Moore was also an amateur mathematician, geologist, and botanist. —Note: The life dates given above have been verified, says Kapp; MEW and other IML sources have given 1830–1912 and variations. → 67:17; 68:33; 73:31, 32; 82:33, 47; 83:18, 24, 26, 34, 38; 84:16, 25; 86:5, 11, 20, 34, 50; 87:19; 88:2, 13; 89:21; 92:61; 95:36, 37. #ME33; E692.

Moorish War See Morocco.

Mora, Francisco (1842 to 1924) Spanish socialist; shoemaker by trade. He was active in founding IWMA sections in Spain and Portugal; member of the Spanish Federal Council (1870–1872); an editor of *La Emancipación* (1871–1873); member of the New Madrid Federation (1872–1873); active in fighting Bakuninism; correspondent of M&E. In 1879 he was one of the organizers of the Spanish

SP; friend of J. Mesa. Author of *Historia del socialismo obrero español* (1902) → 71:3, 39; 72:13.

Morbihan (Fr.) N.W. département, in Brittany. → 49:31, 33.

More, Sir Thomas (1478 to 1535) English statesman and humanist writer; a lawyer by profession. First secular lord chancellor of England (1529–1532); executed by Henry VIII. —The *Chronicle* references are to Kautsky's book *Thomas More und seine Utopie* (1888; Eng. trans, 1927). More began writing his *Utopia* as envoy to Flanders; it was pubd in Latin in 1516 (posthumously in English trans, 1551). —Note: The Latin form Morus is usually used in German and some other languages. → 87:37; 91:24.

Moreau de Jonnès, Alexandre (1778 to 1870) French economist and statistician; orig an army officer. From 1834 he directed publ of *Statistique Générale de la France,* followed by other works of statistical compilation. M (1843) annotated his article in the *J. des Economistes* of 1842. → 45:50. #M575.

Morgan, Lewis Henry (1818 to 1881) American ethnologist; best known as a contributor to the development of social-evolutionary theory in anthropology. Orig a lawyer, he began investigating Indian culture, esp the Iroquois; decried the spoliation of the Indians; founded (1840) a society to study and aid Indian society. His chief work, *Ancient society* (1877), gave a systematic account of his view of social-historical origins. Other works: *League of the Ho-de-no-sau-nee, or Iroquois* (1851); *Houses and house life of the American aborigines* (1881); *Systems of consanguinity* (1870). Member of the NY state legislature (1861–1869). M discovered Morgan's work with delight, as an application of historical materialism to primitive history; E carried their joint appreciation further by highlighting Morgan in his #E573. While Morgan was once recognized as an outstanding anthropologist (he was elected pres of the American Assoc for the Advancement of Science, 1880), the later anti-evolutionary trend of this science has caused him to be downgraded to near the point of invisibility, not least of all because M&E's utilization of his work has caused it to be regarded as "Marxist" in some way. The legend that Morgan's work is simply "obsolete" (as distinct from requiring updating, like Darwin's own evolutionism) is equivalent to the belief that contemporary anti-evolutionism in anthropology is beyond debate; for some of the issues in this continuing controversy, see the work of Leslie A. White, beginning with the article and references in the *Inter-*

national *Encyclopedia of the Social Sciences*, under Morgan. → 80:3, 49; 81:7; 84:12, 21, 26. #M570; E573.

Morgenblatt für gebildete Leser Stuttgart, Tübingen, July 1, 1837, to 1865 under this title. Daily. —Literary journal. Founded 1807 as *M. für gebildete Stände*. → 40:2, 12, 15; 41:10, 15. #E188.5, E233, E454, E456, E550, E575, E651, E663, E674, E737, E774, E804.

Morley, John (1838 to 1923) English politician, biographer, and publicist; outstanding Liberal man of letters. As a politician: MP (1883–1908); Gladstone supporter; chief secy for Ireland (1886, 1892–1895); secy of state for India (1905–1910). As a biographer, his *Life of Gladstone* (1903) is best known. As a journalist: editor of the *Fortnightly Review* (1867–1882); editor of the *Pall Mall Gazette* (1880–1883). All the *Chronicle* references are to Morley as editor of the *Fortnightly Review*. → 68:44; 71:11; 75:13.

The **Morning Advertiser** London, 1794 to 1965. Daily. —In the 1850s–1860s, a Radical spokesman. → 52:47; 53:32, 34; 54:20; 71:34; 76:31. #ME31, ME58, ME510; M910, M913, M943.

Morning Post London, 1772 to 1937. Daily. —In 1937, absorbed by the *Daily Telegraph*. In the mid-18th century, organ of right-wing Whigs around Palmerston. #M532.

Morocco; Moorish War → 60:10, 19, 22. #E493, E494, E624.

Morozov, Nikolai Alexandrovich (1854 to 1946) Russian revolutionist. Son of a landowner by a serf, he became by age 19 a Narodnik activist and journalist, proponent of individual terror; an editor of *Zemlya i Volya*, later of *Narodnaya Volya*; in the mid-1870s, on the staff of *Rabotnik*. He worked abroad for some years; in Dec 1880, made the acquaintance of M in London. Shortly afterward he was arrested on the Russian frontier; freed by the Revolution of 1905, after which he turned to scientific pursuits and later to historical writings; after 1918, director of a science institute, and eventually a well-behaved scientific administrator and scholar. → 80:45.

Morris, William (1834 to 1896) English poet, artist-craftsman, and socialist. Morris became a socialist over the period 1878–1882; joined Hyndman's Democratic Federation (Jan 1883); became the leader (with Eleanor M et al.) of the anti-Hyndman opposition and its split to form the Socialist League (1884); editor of *Commonweal*. By this time Morris had evolved a long way toward Marxism, but with antiparliamentary peculiarities; however, he always opposed the anarchists, who finally took over the Socialist League and ran it into the ground; Morris returned to the SDF. —His chief socialist work was *Socialism, its growth and outcome*, with E. B. Bax (1894); his best-known short piece, *The dream of John Ball;* see the collection of his *Political writings* (1973). His famous *News from nowhere* (1892) depicted an advanced stateless communistic society (not anarchism) as a critique of Edward Bellamy's regimented vision of utopia. E. P. Thompson's *WM* (1955) supersedes all other writings on Morris's socialism. → 84:55, 59; 86:16, 36; 87:26; 94:15.

Morrison, William Hampson (fl. first half of 19th century) English economist. M (1851) read his *Observations on the system of metallic currency adopted in this country* (2nd edn, 1837). → 51:61.

Morse, Arthur English writer on economics. His essay "Agriculture and the Corn Law" was one of the *Three prize essays on agriculture and the Corn Law* (1842), read by M (1845). → 45:52. #M575.

Mortimer, Thomas (1730 to 1810) English diplomatic official and writer. He was vice-consul in the Low Countries (1762–1768); then returned to England to devote himself to letters. He was a voluminous writer, esp on economic subjects: e.g., *Elements of commerce* (1772), which was transd into German; *General commercial dictionary* (1810) and other such works; *Every man his own broker* (1761); also a *New history of England* (1764–(1766). His largest work was *The British Plutarch* (1762), biographical sketches. → 51:62.

Morton, John Chalmers (1821 to 1888) English agronomist. An early member of the Royal Agricultural Society, he was editor of the *Agricultural Digest* (1844–1888), prof at Edinburgh (1854+). His works included a *Handbook of farm labour* (1861) and other handbooks. M (1851) studied his *On the nature and property of soils* (1838); M (1868) excerpted his *Cyclopaedia of agriculture* (1855). → 51:64; 68:72.

Moscow (Russ.) → 77:3; 80:22, 26; 83:12. —Moscow University: → 60:30.

Moselle (Ger. Mosel) River and district The river flows from France into Germany, joins the Rhine at Coblenz, passing Trier. → 42:33; 43:4, 6; 62:51; 95:25, 29, 33. #M41, M965, M966.

Most, Johann (Joseph) (1846 to 1906) German radical journalist and agitator, best known for his later anarchist period in America. Son of a petty official, he worked as a bookbinder as a youth, then operated as journalist and agitator in a number of German cities, also Zurich and Vienna, as editor of S-D papers. Member of the SDWP (1871+); elected to the Reichstag (1874), defeated four years later; editor of the *Berliner Freie Presse*

(1876–1878), then expelled from Berlin. During this period he was known as Dühring's chief S-D disciple; for his abridgment of *Capital*, see ST/51. Most then emigrated to London; pubd *Freiheit* (1879+) as an émigré organ, with virulent attacks on the German party and its leaders; he was expelled by the 1880 party congress for "slanders." When his *Freiheit* praised the assassination attempt on Alexander II (Mar 1881), the English government sentenced him to prison; he fled to America (1882); reestablished *Freiheit* in NY; and entered on his best-known career as an anarchist specializing in wild rhetoric. Among his writings: *Die socialen Bewegungen in alten Rom und der Cäsarismus* (1878); *Der Kleinbürger und die Socialdemokratie* (1876); *Die Lösung der sociale Frage* (1876); *Die Anarchie (1888); The social monster* (1890). There is a full-length biography in German by fellow anarchist Rudolf Rocker, *JM* (1924). → 73:2; 75:29; 76:12, 13, 18; 77:26, 47; 78:10, 30, 34; 79:3, 10, 24, 33; 80:12, 14, 29, 39; 81:13, 14, 20, 28; 83:12, 20; 84:49.

Motley, John Lothrop (1814 to 1877) American historian. Secy of the U.S. Legation at St. Petersburg (1841). He specialized in Dutch history, with the well-known works *The rise of the Dutch republic* (1856) and *History of the United Netherlands* (1860–1868). —*MEW Daten* lists Motley as part of M's reading on Anglo-Russian relations (1856–1857); but I do not know of any writings by Motley directly on this subject; his book *Peter the Great* was pubd in 1877. → 56:18.

Motteler, Emilie Wife of Julius *Motteler. → 92:61.

Motteler, Julius (1838 to 1907) German Social-Democratic administrator. Orig a clothing worker, he became foreman and bookkeeper in an Augsburg cloth factory. His socialist career followed Bebel's from Verband Deutscher Arbeitervereine (1863) to the Saxon People's party (1866) to membership in the IWMA, finally taking part in founding the SDWP (1869). Reichstag deputy (1874–1878, 1903–1907). In 1874 he took over business management of the Leipzig co-op printshop and book distribution of the Eisenacher party. On passage of the Anti-Socialist Law, Bebel brought him (Nov 1879) to Zurich as business manager of the *Sozialdemokrat*, to organize its smuggling into Germany. In this capacity Motteler became famous in the movement as the "rote Feldpostmeister" (Red Postmaster) who ensured the illegal distribution of the paper. He followed the *Sozialdemokrat* staff to London (1888); when the law fell, he was not allowed back into Germany like the others till 1901, after which he was active for the party in Leipzig. Politically, a supporter of

Bebel. —*Note:* Some sources give his life dates as 1836–1908. → 88:27; 92:21, 61.

Mottershead, Thomas G. (c.1826 to 1884) English trade-unionist; silk weaver. A former Chartist, he became active in the IWMA relatively late, after the Basel (1869) congress; member of the GC (1869–1872); corr secy for Denmark (1871–1872). In the breakup after the Hague Congress, he was a leader of the reform wing seeking to take over the British Federal Council; ran for Parliament (1874) but was defeated. In the 1870s he was also an Exec member of the Land and Labour League, and secy of the Labour Representative League. → 69:65; 71:24; 72:3, 49.

Le **Mouvement Socialiste;** Revue de critique sociale, littéraire et artistique   Paris, Jan 1899 to June 1914. Semimonthly. Pub'r: Hubert Lagardelle. —One of the leading socialist journals of its period. #M464; E429.

Movimento Operaio Milan, Oct 1849 to Nov/Dec 1856. #E528.

M'Pherson, J. This name is alphabetized as if spelled MacPherson, q.v.

Müffling, *Baron* Friedrich Karl Ferdinand von (1775 to 1851) Prussian field marshal; Blücher's quartermaster-gen (1813–1814); chief of the gen staff (1821); specialist in cartography. He wrote works on military science and history under the nom de guerre C. von W. (i.e., Carl von Weiss): all on the modern period except for his *Ueber die Römerstrassen am rechten Ufer des Nieder-Rheins* (1834). → 57:26.

Mülheim (Ger.) Rhine town near Cologne, today part of that city. → 49:9.

Müller, Eduard (1804 to 1875) German teacher, art historian. Prof in a Liegnitz college, and its director (1853+). His chief works were *Geschichte der Theorie der Kunst bei den Alten* (1834–1837) and *Die Idee der Aesthetik* (1840). → 57:19.

Müller, Hans (b. 1867) German Social-Democratic journalist; a leader of the "Jungen" faction in the 1890s. One of the university-educated writers in the S-D party, he was an editor of the Magdeburg *Volksstimme* (a "Jungen" stronghold); but after attacks on the "corruption" of the party's Reichstag Fraction he was ousted, with the help of Bebel. He pubd a polemic *Der Klassenkampf in der deutschen Sozialdemokratie* (1892), arguing that the "Jungen" intellectuals represented the proletariat. Moving to Switzerland, he took out Swiss citizenship, moved right, and became active as a proponent of the moderate consumers' co-op movement. → 92:53, 55.

Müller, Tobias; *called* Tobie (1795 to 1875) Swiss army officer—captain, later colonel—who served in the army of Naples (1825+); helped suppress the 1848 revolution in Naples, likewise the Roman Republic in

1849. As early as 1831 he had served the military cause of reaction in his hometown, Freiburg. #E348, E499.

Müller-Tellering, Eduard von; *full* Paul Eduard; *for short* **Tellering** (b. c.1808) German journalist; orig a lawyer. He held a legal post in Coblenz till 1846, when he quit law and set out to travel. In the 1848 revolution he became the Vienna correspondent of M's *NRZ* by July D; M met him on visiting Vienna in Aug-Sep 1848. He was never a member of the CL. Tellering was expelled from Vienna at the year's end; in autumn 1849 he edited H. Becker's *Westdeutsche Ztg* (Cologne), and ended up publishing a denunciatory pamphlet against Becker. (As E later wrote, he was known as a "first-class brawler.") Emigrating to London, he embroiled M&E in a personal quarrel, and heaved another denunciatory pamphlet, *Vorgeschmack in die künftige Diktatur von M und E* (Cologne, 1850), prob the first anti-Semitic attack against M. Tellering then emigrated to the U.S. (1852), where he immediately gained a soupçon of notoriety by claiming that M's (really E's) *NYDT* articles on Germany (#E699) were plagiarized from him; then oblivion closes in. → 49:3; 50:12; 52:22.

Münster (Ger.) City in Westphalia, north of Dortmund. → 40:10.

Münzer, Thomas; *also spelled* **Müntzer** (c.1489/90 to 1525) German revolutionary leader in the Reformation period; preacher of Zwickau influenced by Hussite and Taborite ideas. Leader of the peasant-plebeian insurrection, linking the peasants' revolution with the social movement of miners and town workers; captured in the battle of Frankenhausen, tortured, and executed. He preached a utopian-equalitarian communal society in mystic form; a "true democrat insofar as was possible at the time" (E). His executioners' systematic slanders still figure as "history." The *Chronicle* refers to Kautsky's history, *Der Kommunismus in der deutschen Reformation*

(Eng. trans, *Communism in Central Europe at the time of the Reformation*), pubd as part of his *Von Plato bis zu den Wiedertäufern*, 1895); see Chap. 4 of this book; also #E579. → 95:31.

Mulhall, Michael George (1836 to 1900) British (Dublin-born) statistician. He emigrated (1858) to Buenos Aires, where he founded an English daily; wrote a *Handbook of the River Plata* (1869). From 1878 he devoted himself to statistics in England: *Dictionary of statistics* (1883); *History of prices* (1885); *Industries and wealth of nations* (1896). His Oct 1882 article was titled "Egyptian finance." → 82:39.

Mun, Thomas (1571 to 1641) English mercantilist economist. He amassed a fortune trading in Italy and the Levant; a director of the E. India Co., which he defended in his *Discourse of trade from England into the East Indies* (1621) and *Discourse on England's treasure by foreign trade* (1664). → 53:54.

Mundell, Alexander (fl.1790 to 1846) British writer on economics. Among his longer published works were: *Comparative view of the industrial situation of Gr Brit from 1775* (1832); *Reasons for a revision of our fiscal code* (1828); *The influence of interest and prejudice upon proceedings in Parliament stated* (1825). → 50:50.

Munich; Ger. München German city, capital of Bavaria. → 91:33; 92:43; 93:42.

Murphy, John Nicholas Irish publicist. His book *Ireland, industrial, political and social* (1870) was much used by E for his mss on Irish history, esp #E353D. Murphy also pubd a book on the papacy (1883) and on British convents (1873). → 70:8.

Muşoiu, Panait (1864 to 1944) Roumanian socialist; one of the editors of the paper *Munca*, and a contributor to other Roumanian socialist organs. He transd the *Com Manifesto* into Roumanian (pubd 1892), also #E759 (pubd 1891). → 94:15.

N

Nachalo; Organ russkikh sotsialistov St. Petersburg, Mar-May 1878 (four numbers). Irreg. —Illegal; issued by pro-Bakuninist intellectuals. → 78:12, 25.

Nădejde, Ioan (or Ion); Westernized Joseph (1854 to 1928) Roumanian journalist and politician; an early socialist. During the 1880s he transd M&E writings, and corresponded with E, on behalf of his organ *Contemporanul*, pubd 1881–1890 in Jassy. In the 1890s he was editor of *Lumea Nova*, and a member of the Exec of the S-D party (founded 1893). Coming out for liquidation of the socialist organization into the governing Liberal party—to be

"more effective"—he quit the party (1899) and, in a few years, was one of the most effective politicians in fighting the workers' movement. → 88:1.

Namur *See* Faubourg de Namur (Brussels).

Nantes (Fr.) Industrial city near the west coast, its port being Saint-Nazaire. → 94:35, 39, 43.

Napier, Sir Charles (1786 to 1860) English naval commander. In Portuguese service (1834) he was made Count Cape St. Vincent for a naval victory. Commander of the British fleet in the Baltic (Feb 1854+); removed by year's end for failure to storm Kronstadt;

created admiral (1858). He was elected MP (Feb 1855) and remained in the house till his death. #M452, M470.

Naples; *Ital.* Napoli Chief city of S. Italy. → 48:35; 55:26; 61:30; 71:28; 77:32. #E32, E637.

Napoleon I; b. Napoléon **Bonaparte** (1769 to 1821) End-product of the French Revolution: first consul (1799–1804); emperor of the French (1804–1814, 1815). —*Note:* In this work, the name Napoleon refers to Napoleon I; the name Bonaparte usually refers to Louis Napoleon *Bonaparte, who became Napoleon III. → 40:16; 51:55. #E370.

Narodnaya Volya [People's will] Russian Populist (Narodnik) organization formed in 1879 when *Zemlya i Volya split over the issue of terrorism. One wing, led by Plekhanov, formed the Chorny Peredel (Black Redistribution) group; the proterrorist Narodniks founded the group Narodnaya Volya, with an organ of the same name (1879–1885), linking the terrorist strategy to the political struggle for constitutionalism. Influential during the 1860–1880s, it was later absorbed into the S-R movement. → 80:39, 40, 45; 81: 13, 20; 80:13.

Narodnaya Volya [People's will] Paris, Oct 1879 to Oct 1885 (12 nos.). Irreg. — Illegal organ of the Narodnik group of the same name. #ME37.

Narodniks Russian Populists, advocates (c.1860–1895) of the view that Russia could bypass capitalism by developing the Russian village-communal system (*obshchina*) into the starting point of socialism; hence a type of peasant socialism, though it had a liberal wing as well as a terrorist one. → 75:11, 14, 17; 78:40; 80:26, 45; 90:18; 92:22; 93:10, 46.

Narodnoye Delo [People's cause] Geneva, Sep 1, 1868, to Aug/Sep 1870. Semimonthly. Ed by Bakunin, N. Zhukovsky (for no. 1, 1868); N. Utin (from no. 2/3); A. Trusov. — First, in magazine format, then newspaper (Apr 1870+). Anti-Bakuninist under Utin and after; organ of the IWMA Russian section in Geneva (Apr 1870+). → 71:7. #M343.

Nassau Region of S.W. Germany, formerly a duchy. → 48:33.

Le **National** Paris, 1830 to 1851. Daily. —Founded by Thiers, F. A. M. Mignet, A. Carrel; moderate-republican in the 1840s. #E659, E723, E771.

National Assembly See Frankfurt National Assembly.

National Labor Union (U.S.) First effort at national TU organization (1866), under Ira Stewart and W. *Sylvis. It was succeeded by the *Knights of Labor. → 66:44; 69:30, 49, 55; 70:36. #M7.

The **National Reformer** (with varying subtitles) London, Apr 14, 1860, to Oct 1, 1893.

Weekly. Ed by Ch. Bradlaugh (and Annie Besant). —Organ of the National Secular Society. → 72:5. #M834.

National Standard NY, July 30, 1870, to Dec 23, 1872, under this title; previously *National Anti-Slavery Standard* (1840 to Apr 1870), *Standard* (May–July 1870). Weekly. Director: Aaron B. Powell. —Pubd by the American Anti-Slavery Assoc as a "temperance and literary journal." Friendly to the IWMA, pubd some of its materials. #M521.

National-Zeitung Berlin, Apr 1, 1848, to 1915 under this title. Daily. —In the 1840s–1850s, liberal, under editor A. Rutenberg; later, an organ of the National Liberals. → 60:1, 7, 12, 13, 23, 34, 54; 61:15; 71:40. #M80, M454, M617.

Nationalverein (Ger.) First all-German political party, founded Sep 1859 in Frankfurt after preliminary conferences: for constitutionalism and liberal reforms, under Prussian hegemony; peaked 1862, dissolved 1868. → 60:46; 62:52, 57; 67:12.

Naut, Stephan Adolf German radical. A businessman of Cologne, he became business manager and responsible pubr of M's NRZ in 1848–1849. In 1850 he helped M extend the distribution of the *NRZ-Revue* in Germany. A revolutionary Democrat, he was possibly also a CL member. → 50:10, 18; 52:33, 36; 54:33, 53.

Ne Nashi Anarchistic group encountered in Siberia by *Lopatin. → 75:11.

Nechayev, Sergei Gennadyevich (1847 to 1882) Russian anarchist; the very model of the amoral terrorist and "revolutionary" swindler. Son of a house painter, he took part in the St. Petersburg student movement (1860s); collaborated with Tkachev on a revolutionary program (1868); and went to Geneva (1869) to collaborate with Bakunin. He and Bakunin jointly worked out the *Revolutionary catechism* and other manifestos, glorifying ruthless terrorism, Machiavellian amoralism in the worst sense, brigandage, and destruction for its own sake. Bakunin adopted N. as his protégé and partner, who then returned to Russia for three months. There he committed the notorious murder of his student comrade I. I. Ivanov (Nov 1869); returned to Switzerland (Jan 1870); resumed his alliance with Bakunin (who knew about the Ivanov murder). But when N. began to apply the same swindling tactics to Bakunin that both advocated for everyone else, Bakunin—only at this point—broke with his protégé. N. was arrested in Zurich in 1872 and handed over to Russia; after a noted trial, he was sentenced to 20 years for the Ivanov murder; died in prison. —N. was the original of the terrorist in Dostoyevsky's novel *The possessed.* For his relations with Bakunin, the indispensable documentation is in Michael Confino, *Violence dans la violence* (1973), esp the late-found letter by Bakunin to N. of June 2, 1870. → 69:57; 70:19; 71:5, 37, 52; 72:27, 42, 49, 65; 73:6; 75:35. #ME33, ME150; M224.

Necker, Jacques (1732 to 1804) French (Geneva-born, of Germanic descent) financier and financial statesman. A banker in Paris, he became director of the Treasury (1776) and director of finance (1777) till his retirement in 1781; recalled 1788, virtually premier of France; recommended calling the States General and proposed reforms; dismissed by the king—this sparking the assault on the Bastille. He was recalled again, but resigned Sep 1790, and retired to devote himself to writing. M (1859–1862) studied his chief works: *De l'administration des finances de la France* (1784); *sur la législation et le commerce des grains* (1775). → 59:78. #M575.

Negroes (U.S. blacks) → 62:56; 77:24; 78:39.

Népszava Budapest, 1872+. Weekly. — Socialist organ; continuation of *Munkás-Heti-Krónika* (for which, see *Arbeiter-Wochen-Chronik);* organ of the Hungarian S-D party (1890+). #E832, E845.

Neruchev, M. V. Russian writer. M (1877) read his *Russkoye zemlevladeniye i zemledeliye.* → 77:48.

Nesselrode, *Count* Karl Robert (or *Russ.* Karl Vasilyevich) von (1780 to 1862) Russian politician and diplomat; of German descent. Foreign affairs min (1816–1856); state councillor (1821+); chancellor (1844+). He guided Russian foreign policy for four decades, along the conservative lines of the Holy Alliance and counterrevolutionary intervention wherever possible (as in 1848–1849). #ME150.

Nestler & Melle Hamburg pub'r. → 86:24.

Netherlands → 35:9; 38:2, 8; 43:10, 11; 47:4, 35, 38, 39; 64:12; 69:40, 60; 70:24, 62; 71:24, 30, 56; 72:3, 24, 31, 41, 51, 65; 80:19; 81:6; 82:15; 84:14; 86:12. #M12; E32. *See also* Dutch language.

Neu-England-Zeitung Boston, 1846 to 1853. Weekly. —Pubd by German émigrés as a democratic organ; Weydemeyer was a contributor. → 53:11, 15. #M762.

Neuchâtel (Switz.) City (and canton) in the Jura Mts., west of Bern. → 48:75; 56:42.

Neue Badische Landeszeitung Mannheim (Ger.), 1867 to 1933. Daily. —Liberal paper. → 68:5. #E694.

Neue Berliner Zeitung Berlin, June to Oct 1848. Daily. —Conservative-monarchist. #ME98.

Neue Deutsche Zeitung; Organ der Demokratie Darmstadt, then Frankfurt (Apr 2, 1849+). July 1, 1848, to Dec 14, 1850. Daily.

Ed by O. Lüning, J. Weydemeyer. —Left Democratic in outlook; *Lüning leaned toward "True Socialism." In Oct 1849 it merged with Robert Blum's *Deutsche Reichszeitung,* taking on its editor, Georg Günther. → 49:33; 50:22; #ME11, ME33, ME164, ME165; M163A, M853.

Neue Freie Presse Vienna, Sep 1, 1864, to Jan 31, 1939. Ed (in 1870–1871) by Max Friedländer. Founded by Michael Etienne, Max Friedländer. —Liberal. → 69:50; 71:30, 34. #M175, M176, M926; E765.

Die **Neue Gesellschaft;** Monatsschrift für Sozialwissenschaft Zurich, Oct 1877 to Mar 1880. Monthly. Pub'r/editor: Franz Wiede. —Social-reform in outlook. → 77:25.

Neue Kölnische Zeitung für Bürger, Bauern und Soldaten [New Cologne Gazette for citizens, peasants, and soldiers] Cologne, 1848 to 1849. Pub'r: F. Anneke, F. Beust. — Revolutionary-democratic in outlook, this paper was an ally of M's *NRZ,* specif directed esp toward the peasant population of the region and the soldiers of the garrison. → 48:60, 66. #M853.

Neue Oder-Zeitung Breslau, Mar/Apr 1849 to Nov 1855. Daily. Pub'r: Max Friedländer. Ed by Moritz Elsner. —Radical-liberal in outlook, this was founded out of the Catholic opposition paper *Allgemeine Oder-Zeitung,* which had appeared 1846. M contributed more articles to this paper, after the *NYDT,* than to any other not edited by himself. → 54:1, 50; 55:1, 3, 9, 10, 13, 14, 16, 18–21, 23–25, 30, 35, 39, 43, 47; 61:26. *See* the checklist of articles pubd in the *NOZ* in the *Register,* Vol. 2. The following indexes other references: #ME187; M83.5, M444; E32, E57, E102, E251, E253, E267, E274, E302, E338, E340, E341, E422, E500, E509, E510, E629, E681, E736, E741, E773, E914.

Neue Preussische Zeitung; *also called* **Kreuz-Zeitung** Berlin, June 1848+. Daily. —Founded under the direction of Hermann Wagener; organ of the conservatives (1850–1858); Bismarck's mouthpiece after he came to power. Its unofficial title was due to the iron cross on its masthead, with the motto "Forward with God for King and Fatherland." → 50:20. #M437, M538.

Neue Rheinische Zeitung; Organ der Demokratie [New Rhenish Gazette; organ of the Democracy] Cologne (Ger.), June 1, 1848, to May 19, 1849. Daily. Ed by Karl Marx. —The daily newspaper established by M&E, together with the CL cadre in Cologne, on their return to Germany following the outbreak of revolution in 1848. M was editor-in-chief and undisputed political leader of the *NRZ* tendency; E was his hard-working associate member of the ed bd. The paper's name recalled the *Rheinische Ztg* which M had edited in the same city

(1842–1843). For M&E, the NRZ was not merely a paper but the revolutionary political center which constituted the organizational side of his strategy for revolution, in effect replacing the CL itself. The NRZ was subtitled *Organ der Demokratie*, which meant not "Organ of democracy," but "Organ of The Democracy," that is, the revolutionary Democratic front of proletariat + peasantry + petty-bourgeoisie which (in M's strategy) was counterposed to the twin ruling classes temporarily sharing power in the revolution, that is, the crown-cum-bureaucracy and the bourgeoisie. (See *Democratic Assoc for more on this). —The paper developed a Europe-wide reputation, and boasted in print of being the organ of "the European Democracy," not merely the German. It even claimed a wider distribution than any other German paper of the time. This was in line with M's aim of making it not merely a local voice but the spokesman of the left wing of the revolution on the broadest possible scale. —The paper appeared on June 1 (actually off the press the preceding evening). This was a month sooner than the original plan. It was financed by selling shares of stock, advertisements, contributions, and loans, as well as subscriptions and sales, and in a pinch, by M's personal money (which he lost). The format was a four-page blanket size, with occasional supplements (*Beilagen*) and extra edns. The original ed bd was comprised of Bürgers, Dronke, Weerth (in charge of the daily feuilleton), F. Wolff, and W. Wolff, besides M&E. Bürgers was dropped in Aug, and Freiligrath was added in Oct. —The Prussian government harassed the paper in various ways, esp by instituting lawsuits on the charge of "slandering" the officials who were engaged in harassing it. Its publ was suspended between Sep 27 and Oct 12, 1848. As the revolution declined, the regime took heart to decree M's expulsion from the country, thus effectively closing down the paper. The last issue was printed in red ink; the front page featured a farewell poem by Freiligrath; Weerth's last feuilleton was a "Proclamation to the women," whom he credited above the men; an edit statement (#ME186) warned against a putsch. E later (cf. #E469) vaunted the NRZ as a model of effective revolutionary journalism. → 48:1, 29–85 passim; 49:1–26 passim; 50:12; 51:46; 52:39; 53:32; 54:53; 58:31; 60:20; 61:5; 62:46; 81:8; 83:24; 84:13, 16, 19; 85:26; 94:2, 42; 95:5. #ME104, ME186; M125, M139, M266, M328, M450–M451, M718, M855, M870, M883, M946; E265, E395.5, E469, E871. — Note: For the list of M&E articles in NRZ, see *M–E Verzeichnis*, Vol. 1; but MECW (not yet indexed) augmented and revised this list—see MECW 7–9.

Neue Rheinische Zeitung (Cologne, in 1874)   For Blos's unrealized plan to issue a new NRZ, see → 74:29.

Neue Rheinische Zeitung, politisch-ökonomische Revue [New Rhenish Gazette, politico-economic review]   London and Hamburg, Jan-Oct 1850. Monthly [in theory]. Ed by Karl Marx. —Magazine pubd under M's editorship for six numbers (actually five, the sixth being a double number); pubd in London; printed in Hamburg. It offered some of M&E's most important works of the period, esp overviews of the recent revolution. — Dating and actual time of publ never jibed. Here is a summary: No. 1, dated Jan, pubd Mar c.8, in 2500 copies; No. 2, dated Feb, pubd Mar c.22, in 2000 copies; No. 3, dated Mar, pubd Apr c.11, in 2000 copies; No. 4, dated Apr, pubd May c.20, size of edn not known; No. 5/6 (double no.), dated May-Dec, pubd Nov 29, edn not known. → 49:36, 40, 43; 50:1, 2, 4–6, 10, 12, 14, 16, 18, 22, 28, 29, 33, 36, 37, 39, 41, 46; 51:6, 46; 69:21; 71:22; 84:12; 85:4; 93:19; 94:42. #ME11, ME33.

Die Neue Welt   Leipzig (till 1883); Stuttgart, Hamburg, 1876 to 1887; perhaps to 1919? Weekly. Ed by W. Liebknecht; then Bruno Geiser (till 1887). —Socialist publ; illustrated Sunday supplement to a number of socialist dailies. → 76:22; 84:37. #E918.

Die Neue Zeit   London, June 1858 to Apr 1859. Pub'r: Edgar Bauer. —Pubd for the German left emigration in England; a "little German sheet in London" (M). → 58:32, 51; 59:12, 34. #M911.

Die Neue Zeit   Stuttgart, 1883 to 1923. Monthly (till Oct 1890), then weekly. Ed by K. Kautsky (till Oct 1917)) —Theoretical organ of the German S-D party; in the era of the Second Int'l, the most prestigious forum of Marxist theory. → 82:45, 53; 83:40; 84:21, 26, 37, 48; 85:4, 9, 22, 24, 39; 86:19, 24, 25; 87:15, 48; 88:19, 25, 26, 30; 89:1, 9; 90:17–19, 26, 34, 50; 91:6, 11, 12, 17, 23, 26, 34, 46, 50, 55, 57; 92:5, 11, 18, 31, 35, 39, 44, 47, 49, 60, 65, 68; 93:16; 94:6, 27, 29, 30, 36, 43, 46; 95:16, 24. #M172, M186, M207, M345, M365, M455; E177, E198, E242, E284, E285, E301, E374, E392–E394, E428, E429, E457, E548, E554, E556, E574, E576, E578, E608, E655, E705, E757, E762, E781, E791.

Neue Zeitschrift   Cologne. —Planned communist magazine prepared by H. Becker in spring 1851, but never realized due to the government arrests leading to the Cologne Communist trial. → 51:20, 25, 27.

Neuer Social-Demokrat   Berlin, July 2, 1871, to Sep 29, 1876. Thrice weekly. — Organ of the Lassallean GGWA to replace the suspended *Social-Demokrat*, after Schweitzer's departure. With the Lassallean-Eisenacher unity of 1875, it was subtitled "Organ

COMPLETE TABLES OF CONTENTS OF THE NRZ-*Revue*

This list gives the actual contents; variations from the Contents (*Inhalt*) pubd in each issue are footnoted. Titles are given in English; original titles and related information are available through the *Register #*, which is given in brackets for all M/E pieces. Contributions by others than M/E are explained in the footnotes. For unlisted editorial notes, see #ME54.

No. 1, dated January 1850

Announcement [#ME54A].
M: Class struggles in France[1] [#M148]. Chap. I.
E: German campaign for a Reich constitution [#E328]. Chaps. I and II.
Austrian and Prussian parties in Baden. By K. Blind.[2]
Note[3] [#ME54B].

No. 2, dated February 1850

M: Class struggles in France[4] [#M148]. Chap. II.
E: German campaign for a Reich constitution [#E328]. Chap. III.
Literature [Cf #ME143]: I. Review of book by Daumer [#ME137]; II. Review of book by L. Simon [#ME142]; III. Review of book by Guizot [#ME138].
Review [of Jan-Feb 1850], by M&E [#ME134].

No. 3, dated March 1850

M: Class struggles in France[5] [#M148]. Chap. III.
E: German campaign for a Reich constitution [#E328]. Chap. IV.

No. 4, dated April 1850

Jambes. By Louis Ménard.[6]
E: The English ten hours bill [#E246].
Literature [cf. #ME144]: I. Review of Carlyle [#ME139]; II. Review of A. Chenu, L. de la Hodde [#ME141]; III. Review of Girardin [#ME140].
Review [of Mar-Apr 1850], by M&E [#ME135].
Miscellany:[7] M: Louis Napoleon and

Fould [#M489]; ME: Gottfried Kinkel [#ME69]; Supplementary material "from the Reich."[8]
Editor's note on Didier [#ME54D].

No. 5/6, dated May to October 1850

E: Peasant war in Germany (complete) [#E579].
Section III of the *Communist Manifesto*[9] [cf. #ME33].
Tailoring in London, or The conflict between big and small capital. Signed/ J. G. Eccarius.[10] With editor's note [#ME53].

[1]Titled "1818–1849" in the Contents list of the number; inside, "1848 bis 1849" [1848 to 1849].
[2]"Oesterreichische und preussische Parteien in Baden," signed only "Blind." (*See* Karl *Blind.*)
[3]For details, see the *Register* entry, #ME54B.
[4]In this number, the title is "1848–1849" inside as well as in the Contents list.
[5]In this number, ditto.
[6]Poem; longish, 26 quatrains. *See* *Ménard.* The poem has a subtitle in the Contents list of the issue: "Ecrits après les massacres de Juin 1848." Inside, it is preceded by a brief ed note introducing Ménard as author of the book *Prologue d'une révolution.*
[7]This heading: "Vermischtes."
[8]"Nachträgliches 'aus dem Reich.' " This piece is introduced by the following sentence: "From a letter by our friend W. Wolff, we give the following extracts on the late Reich regentship of Herr Vogt:". (*See* Karl *Vogt.*) The letter is signed "M. M." (according to St/53.5)—perhaps a misprint for W.W.
[9]The title is that of Section III: "Socialistische und kommunistische Literatur." Upon it is hung an ed note referring to the *Manifesto* (see #ME54D).
[10]"Die Schneiderei in London / oder / der Kampf des grossen und des kleinen Capitals."

des Sozialistischen Arbeiterpartei Deutschlands," and, by agreement, continued for a year after the unification itself. → 73:23, 27; 75:12. #E380, E543.

Neuenahr (Ger.) Town in the N. Rhineland. → 77:20, 29, 33, 34.

Neumay(e)r, Ludwig Austrian socialistic journalist. A member of the IWMA in the Vienna area, he was a delegate to the Basel

congress (1869); editor of the *Wiener-Neustädter Wochenblatt* (1869+), collaborator on the *Volkswille* (1870+); He pubd *Die Gleichheit* (1870+); it carried a "Manifesto to the agricultural population" for which N. was tried, and acquitted (1870). → 70:12.

Neustadt (Ger.) Industrial city in the S. part of the Rhineland-Palatinate. → 49:30; 62:12, 47.

Nevolin, Konstantin Alexeyevich (1806 to 1855) Russian law historian. Prof at Kiev (1835+), at St. Petersburg (1843+). His chief work was *Entsiklopediya zakunovyedyeniya* (1839–1840), an encyclopedia of jurisprudence with historical material. Also author of works on the history of Russian civil law (1851) and on the formation of government administration in Russia (1844). → 73:37.

Nevsky Prospekt Principal avenue of St. Petersburg (Russ.). → 76:10.

New American Cyclopaedia Ed by C. A. Dana, George Ripley. NY, D. Appleton & Co., 1858–1863. 16 vols. —In its time this popular U.S. encyclopedia was rivaled only by the *Encyclopaedia Americana*. Dana invited M to contribute in consequence of the latter's articles in the NYDT, of which Dana was managing editor. —M&E's articles were pubd in Vols. 1–5, 7, 9, 12, with the following publ dates: Vol. 1, 1858 on t.p., 1857 copyright, actually pubd Dec 31, 1857; Vols. 2–3, 1858; Vols. 4, 5, 7, 1859; Vol. 9, 1860; Vol. 12, 1861. For a detailed account of M&E's relationship to and work for the NAC, see the intro to ST/ME4. For M&E's articles in NAC, see the checklist in the *Register*. Following is the *Chronicle* index. → 57:1, 3, 14, 18, 19, 24, 26, 28, 31, 33, 38, 41, 46, 51, 52; 58: 2, 5, 10, 15, 19, 23, 27; 59:3, 20, 27, 39, 45, 55, 57, 61; 60:4, 49, 56; 61:1, 11.

New Caledonia; Fr. Nouvelle Calédonie French-controlled island in the S.W. Pacific. → 71:48.

New Madrid Federation (of the IWMA) It was established by supporters of the GC/IWMA to counteract the Bakuninists. → 72:42.

The **New Moral World** and Gazette of the Rational Society Leeds, London, Manchester, 1834 to 1845. Weekly. Founder: Robert Owen. —Leading Owenite organ. E was a contributor, 1843–1845. → 43:24, 27, 31; 44:2, 5, 7, 39, 47; 45:25, 27. #E182–E183, E296, E622, E623, E649, E808.

New Orleans (Louisiana) #M292.

New Testament (Bible) → 37:5.5; 41:3; 42:2; 83:31, 35; 92:42; 93:26. #M956; E787.5.

New York (U.S.) → 52:4, 25; 54:5, 45; 57:4, 8; 58:13; 67:22; 68:5; 69:33; 70:36, 51, 55, 59; 71:16, 21, 28, 49, 56; 72:41, 48, 49, 52, 55, 65; 73:1, 39; 83:12; 86:35, 47, 48; 87:25, 30, 40; 88:9, 28, 30; 90:4; 91:44. #M521; E445, E480, E671, E780. —For the NY Gen Council of the IWMA, see *IWMA.

New York Daily Tribune NY, 1841 to 1924. Daily. Founder: Horace Greeley. Managing editor: C. A. Dana (1849–1862). —M was recruited as a contributor by *Dana. Esp in the 1840s–1850s, this paper was the most leftish-liberal daily in the U.S.; till the mid-1850s, left wing of the Whigs, later of the new Republicans; it even ran a column on Fourierism by Albert Brisbane. Its weekly edn (not the NY daily edn) had the largest newspaper circulation in the country. Started in Sep 1841 out of Greeley's weekly *New Yorker*, the *Weekly Tribune* reached a record-breaking 200,000–250,000. Later, Greeley also started a *Semi-Weekly Tribune* (Tuesdays and Fridays) with more stress on literary affairs. The three versions—daily (the NYDT proper), semiweekly, weekly—carried the same editorials and selected articles. Some of M&E's articles were used in the *Weekly Tribune* or *Semi-Weekly Tribune* in whole or part: the facts and dates of this republication process are noted, for the first time, in *MECW* (not in *MEW*). In 1924 the paper was merged into the NY *Herald-Tribune*. —*Note:* The paper's masthead hyphenated *New-York*; I do not follow this style. The word "Daily" was deemphasized, hence led to the short form NY *Tribune*. —For M&E articles in the NYDT, see the Checklist in the *Register*. The following *Register* index takes note of other references. → 51:2, 4, 38, 46, 51, 57; 52:1, 10, 15, 18, 22, 29, 33, 36, 38, 43, 44, 47, 49, 52, 54; 53:1, 5, 8–11, 14, 15, 17, 19, 22, 23, 26, 30, 35, 37, 39–41, 44, 46, 55; 54:1–5, 7, 8, 12, 13, 15, 19, 24, 27, 28, 32, 37, 40, 42, 45, 49; 55:1, 3, 4, 9, 10, 13, 14, 16, 17, 19, 20, 24, 31, 36, 40, 41, 44, 46, 49; 56:1–3, 6, 7, 12, 15, 16, 21, 24, 28, 32, 34, 36, 41, 42; 57:1–4, 7, 8, 11, 15, 18, 20, 23, 25, 29, 34, 39, 42, 47, 51, 52; 58:1, 2, 6, 11, 16, 19, 23, 27, 32, 35, 38, 42, 45, 49; 59:3, 11, 15, 19, 26, 34, 39, 41, 45, 52, 55, 57, 58, 61, 67; 75; 60:4, 8, 10, 19, 22, 26, 31, 36, 40, 43, 48, 49, 52, 55; 61:1, 6, 7, 9, 11, 40, 44, 47, 49, 51, 55; 62:1, 11, 14; 65:32; 76:11; 77:17; 95:8. #ME8, ME9, ME40, ME107, ME108, ME160, ME187; M114, M135, M200, M272, M274, M275, M277, M282, M289, M297, M309, M311, M321, M346.5, M357, M435, M474, M485, M539, M540, M544, M547, M626, M628, M630, M638, M648, M684, M702, M740, M770, M780, M798, M800, M803, M823, M954, M975; E6, E47, E57, E65, E67, E70, E71, E102, E116, E117, E191, E251, E279, E303, E305, E338, E340, E341, E422, E509, E510, E523, E546, E546.5, E568, E583, E699, E711, E716, E717, E736, E773, E907.

New York Evening Post See Evening Post.

New York Herald NY, May 1835 to 1924. Daily. Founder: James Gordon Bennett. — Orig liberal; an organ of the Republican party. → 52:31; 71:33, 36, 42; 81:49. #M416, M897.

New York Times NY, Sep 18, 1851+. Daily. Founder: H. J. Raymond, editor till his death in 1869. → 57:4.

New York World NY, 1860 to 1931. Daily. —Pubd by Manton Marble (1869–

1875); its later reputation came with pub'r Jos. Pulitzer, 1883. → 71:36, 53. #M417, M829.

New Zealand → 71:24; 72:13.

New-Yorker Staatszeitung NY, 1834+. Weekly, then daily (1844+). —Founded as a liberal German émigré organ; later a voice of the Democratic party (mid-1850s+). → 51:16, 35.

New Yorker Volkszeitung NY, 1878 to 1932. Daily. Ed by H. Schlüter (c.1890+). — German-language socialist organ; in its day it had the largest circulation of any U.S. socialist publ. → 83:11, 16; 84:5; 86:29; 87:22; 88:30; 90:20. #E174, E389, E562, E778, E860.

Newcastle (upon Tyne) City in the north of England. → 71:39; 83:4; 90:10; 91:48. #M160.5.

Newcastle Daily Chronicle Newcastle-upon-Tyne (Eng.), 1862 to 1922 under this title; founded 1858. Daily. Ed by Joseph Cowen. —Though far from London, this became a much admired gen newspaper. → 90:10, 14. #E335.

Newman, Francis William (1805 to 1897) English scholar and man of letters. Prof of classical literature in Manchester (1840+); of Latin, U. of London (1846–1869). He was best known for his writings on religion; became a Unitarian by 1879 (he was the brother of Cardinal Newman). He wrote also on a number of areas of research, incl philology, mathematics, social problems, etc. He was radical-liberal in politics: friend of Mazzini and Kossuth; advocate of church–state separation; social-reformer; vegetarian; antisocialist. M (1851) read his *Four lectures on the contrasts of ancient and modern history* (1847); M (1853) studied his *Lectures on polit eco* (1851). → 51:70; 53:50, 52.

Newman, Samuel Philips (1797 to 1842) American philosopher and educationist. His most popular book was *A practical system of rhetoric* (1827). M (1851) excerpted his *Elements of polit eco* (1835), a schoolbook compilation. → 51:68.

Newton, Sir Isaac (1643 to 1727) English physicist, astronomer, and mathematician; founder of classical physics. The *Chronicle* refers to his work on calculus, i.e., invention of differential and integral calculus (1665–1666). → 82:47.

Newton (-le-Willows) (Eng.) Town near Manchester. → 60:44; 61:36. #E483, E685.

Niagara Falls Falls on the Niagara River, between the U.S. and Canada. → 88:30.

Nibelungen or (Eng.) **Nibelungs** operas Richard *Wagner's tetralogy *Der Ring des Nibelungen* ("Ring operas"), based on the old German epic *Nibelungenlied.* → 82:18. #E528.5.

Nice; *Ital.* Nizza City on the French Rivi-

era: ceded to France by Sardinia (1796); restored to Sardinia (1814); again ceded to France (1860). → 60:18, 19; 82:19. #E723, E725.

Nicholas I (1796 to 1855) Czar of Russia, 1825+. #E200.

Nicolovius, Georg Heinrich Franz Prussian judiciary official; in 1848–1849, chief prosecutor of the Rhineland court of appeals in Cologne. → 49:13.

Niebuhr, Barthold Georg (1776 to 1831) German (Copenhagen-born) historian. In politics, N. served first the Danish diplomatic service, then the Prussian (ambassador to Rome, 1816–1823); pro-Russian in tendency, right-wing liberal. Prof at Bonn (1823–1831). He was a pioneer in modern historiographic method, applied to the history of antiquity; highly valued as such by M, who studied (1855) his chief work, *Römische Geschichte* (1811–1832). Author of *Griechische Heroengeschichte* (1842); creator of the *Corpus scriptorum Historiae Byzantinae.* → 55:6.

Niel, Adolphe (1802 to 1869) French gen. Head of the army engineers corps in the Baltic (1854); ditto in the Crimea (1855). He was later created marshal of France (1859); min of war (1867–1869). #ME131.

Nieuwenhuis, Domela; *full* Ferdinand Domela (1846 to 1919) Dutch socialist. Orig a Lutheran pastor (1870–1879), he left the church, founded the socialist weekly *Recht voor Allen* (1879). He played a leading part in developing the Social-Democratic movement in the Netherlands; was elected to parliament for a term (1888–1891); disappointed in legislating social reform, he turned to anarchism (1890s). He authored a number of propaganda brochures, also a Dutch abridgment of *Capital.* → 80:19; 81:4, 6, 9, 11, 59; 83:17; 86:12; 90:23; 91:24, 44.

Niger (River) Great river of West Africa; rises in Guinea, flows to the Atlantic in Nigeria. → 89:21.

Nijmegen (Neth.) Town near the German border and the Rhine. → 35:9.

Nikitina, Varvara Nikolayevna; *née* **Gendre** (1842 to 1884) Russian publicist. She lived in Italy (late 1860s+); later in France, contributing to the French press. → 83:19.

Nikolsburg (Aust.) Town in S. Moravia, near Brünn (Brno); now in Czechoslovakia as Mikulov. → 66:30.

The **Nineteenth Century** London, Mar 1877 to 1900 under this title; then *The Nineteenth Century and After* (1901+), then *The Twentieth Century* (1951+). Monthly. Pub'r/ editor: James Knowles (till 1908). —Liberal magazine. → 78:25; 82:39; 83:18.

Nineteenth Army (of Austria) #E525.

Nobiling, Karl (Eduard) (1848 to 1878) German would-be assassin of Wilhelm I, who was only badly wounded (June 2, 1878); N. committed suicide in Sep. Dr. Nobiling was said to be an anarchist, but there is no proof of his connection with any radical group, least of all the Social-Democrats. → 78:19. See *Anti-Socialist Law.

Nobre França (or **Nobre-França**), José Correia   Portuguese socialist pioneer; a leading organizer of the IWMA in the country. He helped to found the first sections in Lisbon; corresponded with M&E (1872–1873); secy of the Lisbon section (1872); opponent of the Bakuninists. He pubd a number of writings, notably *A philologia perante a historia* (1890–1891). → 72:13, 36, 38.

Nokov, Stoyan (1872 to 1959)   Bulgarian socialist. An émigré in Geneva (1889–1894), he was one of the founders and leaders of the Bulgarian S-D student organization in Switzerland. In 1894 he returned to Bulgaria and worked as a village teacher. Later, a member of the Bulgarian CP. → 93:32. #E835.

Nonne, Heinrich   Prussian police agent. A student and language teacher in Paris, he was exposed in Sep 1884 as a spy operating in the French movement for the Prussian authorities. → 84:15.

Norddeutsche Allgemeine Zeitung   Berlin, 1861 to 1918. Daily. Pub'r/editor: A. Brass (till 1872); then E. F. Pindter. —Conservative; in the 1860s–1880s, a spokesman of the Bismarck regime. → 63:13, 19; 78:19; 82:42.

Norddeutsche Freie Presse   Hamburg-Altona (Ger.), Apr 1, 1849, to beginning of 1851. Daily. Ed by Th. Olshausen. —Previously pubd as *Schleswig-Holsteinische Ztg.* Left-Democratic; supported refugee aid for the German émigrés in London. #ME157C, ME157D; M163B.

Nordkapp; *Eng.* North Cape (Norway)   Northernmost point in Europe. → 90:30.

Nordstern (with varying subtitles)   Hamburg, Jan 1, 1860, to Mar 10, 1866. Weekly. Ed by Karl Bruhn. —Lassallean in tendency, 1863+. "Organ of the S-D Party" (Apr 1865+); ditto "and the GGWA" (Sep 1865+); pubd IWMA reports, 1865–1866. #M900.

Norfolk, *Duke of.* Henry Charles **Howard** (1791 to 1856)   English politician. Whig MP (1829–1841), first Catholic in the House of Commons since the Reformation; master of the horse (1846–1852); lord steward (1853–1854). #M873.

Norman, George Warde (1793 to 1882)   English economist and capitalist. A timber dealer, he was a director of the Bank of England (1821–1872, with gaps) and of an insurance company; defended Peel's Bank Charter Act of 1844. Member of the Political Economy Club, he pubd a number of writings on economic questions, incl: *Examination of some prevailing opinions, as to the*

pressure of taxation (1850); *Remarks upon some prevalent errors with respect to currency and banking* (1833, 1838); *Letter to Charles Wood . . . on money* (1841); *Remarks on the incidence of import duties* (1860). → 51:61.

Norse language   See Old Norse language.

The North (U.S.)   See Civil War (U.S.).

North, Sir Dudley (1641 to 1691)   English merchant who amassed a fortune—as treasurer of the Turkey Co. in Constantinople (1662–1680)—then became a Tory politician, and commissioner of the customs and of the treasury under Charles II and James II. He is best known as author of a tract *Discourses upon trade* (1691) which anticipated laissez-faire and free-trade doctrines. M (1845) read the tract *Considerations upon the East-India trade* (1701) which was attributed to North but is now considered of dubious authorship. → 45:51.

North America   See United States.

North American Review   Boston, May 1815 to 1940. Monthly. → 82:55.

North German Reichstag   Parliament of the N. German Confederation (1867–1871). → 67:14, 33; 68:16; 69:25; 70:28, 36, 40. #E341.5.

North of England Socialist Federation   Socialist organization founded (Apr 30, 1887) in Northumberland during a great miners' strike; initiated by J. L. *Mahon and other Socialist League members; short-lived. → 87:27; 88:3. #E788.

Northern Italian Federation *Ital.* Federazione dell'Alta Italia   Its second congress was held in Milan, Feb 17–18, 1877. → 77:6.

Northern Star   Leeds, 1837–1844; London, 1844–1852. Founded/ed by Feargus *O'Connor (to 1844); then by *Harney. Chartist organ; left wing. —MEW had E beginning his contributions only in 1845, but MECW 3 identifies a number of articles by E beginning in 1843; the first article E sent to the NS alone was #E618. → 43:24, 27, 31; 44:2, 7, 15, 17, 21; 45:38, 41; 46:10, 18, 21, 26, 29, 30, 41; 47:5, 13, 15, 23, 27, 40, 49, 54, 57; 48:6, 14, 17; 49:44; 50:22. #ME4, ME104, ME122; M57, M833, M888; E8, E20, E74, E145, E212, E261, E273, E291, E318, E336, E339, E420, E441, E466, E514–E515, E517–E518, E577, E582, E618, E622, E623, E641, E642, E656–E658, E723, E750, E768, E771, E772, E825, E887, E889, E924.

Northumberland   County in N. of England, on the Scottish border. → 87:27.

Norway   Ceded to Sweden by Denmark (1814) in a personal union with the Swedish crown; independent (1905). → 90:27, 30, 31.

Notes to the People   London, 1851 to 1852. Weekly. Founded/ed by Ernest Jones. —Left

Chartist organ. M&E collaborated with Jones on the editorial work. → 51:2, 19, 25, 28, 39; 52:3, 10, 15, 18. #M180, M425; E653.

Nothjung, Peter (1821 to 1866) German socialist worker (tailor). A member of the Cologne CL in 1848, he was active as a leader of the WA (Exec member), in the Cologne militia (platoon leader), member of the Comm of Public Safety in Sep. He took part in the Elberfeld uprising (May 1849). In 1851 he was arrested in Germany while acting as CL emissary; in the Cologne Communist trial of 1852 he was sentenced to six years. Though

Lassalle later appointed him GGWA plenipotentiary in Breslau, he was not active, broken by his prison term. → 49:11; 50:45; 57:48; 60:13, 15, 21.

Nottingham Town (and county) in north-central England. → 46:29; 72:37.

Nückel, Dr. Member of the Cologne city council in 1848–1850; it is M's article that refers to him as Dr. (No further info.) #M624.

Nuremberg; Ger. Nürnberg (Ger.) City in south-central Bavaria. → 68:48–50; 69:17, 41; 76:24.

O

Oberrheinische Courier —No info found. #M987.

Oberwinder, Heinrich (1846 to 1914) German-born journalist, active in Austria and Germany, with a checkered career as socialist, police agent, and reactionary leader. At first a Lassallean, he took part in founding the Eisenacher party (1869), though still a Lassalle admirer. In Vienna, where he edited a couple of papers in the early 1870s, he was leader of the right wing of Vienna socialism; defeated by the leftists, he returned to Germany (1874). While it is not clear when he became a police agent, he was later (1887) exposed as such by the *Sozialdemokrat* (in 1894, again, by *Vorwärts*). In Germany he became a leader and editor of the Christian Social party of Stöcker, a founder of the chauvinist Navy League, a spokesman of the extreme reactionary right in German politics. → 87:49.

Oborski, Ludwik; *Westernized* Louis (1787 to 1873) Polish revolutionist; army colonel. He took part in the Polish uprising of 1830–1831; emigrated to London (1834). In the 1840s he became a leading member of the Fraternal Democrats; a divisional commander of the Baden-Palatinate revolutionary army (1849). Later (1865–1867) he was a member of the IWMA/GC, and chairman of the London organization of Polish émigrés. → 65:53; 66:6.

O'Brien, James; *called* Bronterre (1804 to 1864) Irish-born Chartist leader, active in England. Son of a small businessman, trained for the law, settled in London (1830+), he became a radical journalist (*Poor Man's Guardian*, *Bronterre's National Reformer*) in the 1830s and a more or less leftist leader of the Chartist movement (esp 1838–1841). His translation of *Buonarroti's History of Babeuf's conspiracy for equality* (1836) was important in the movement —He adopted Bronterre as a pen name and came to be called by it as if a given name. There is a biography by Alfred

Plummer, *Bronterre* (1971); the birth date above is based on Plummer; other sources give 1802 or 1805. → 58:8.

O'Brien, Murray His two articles in the *Fortnightly Review*—read by M—were: "Irish rents, improvements and landlords" (Oct 1880); "Experiments in peasant proprietorship" (Nov 1880). → 80:42.

O'Brien, Richard Barry (1847 to 1918) Irish writer on history and biography; a lawyer by profession (in Dublin, 1874; in London, 1875+). He was a voluminous writer. M (1880) read his book *The parliamentary history of the Irish land question, from 1829 to 1869* (1880). Before M's death, O'Brien also pubd *The Irish land question and English public opinion* (new edn, 1881). → 80:51.

Ochsenbein, Johann Ulrich (1811 to 1890) Swiss politician and army officer; orig a lawyer. Editor of *Jeune Suisse*; his radical politics got him dismissed from the Gen Staff. In 1848 he was one of the framers of the new constitution; pres of the National Council. But in 1849 he broke with the Radical party; voted to expel all German refugees. Later, failing of reelection to the Council (1854), he entered French military service to organize a foreign legion for Crimea. #E499.

O'Clery, Patrick Keyes; *called* **The O'Clery** (1849 to 1913) Irish radical politician; lawyer by profession. Educated in Dublin, he practiced at the bar in London (1874+). He was MP for Wexford (Ire.) (1874–1880); pubd *The history of the Italian revolution ... 1796–1849* (1875). → 77:9, 16.

O'Connor, Arthur (1763 to 1852) Irish nationalist leader. Orig a landed proprietor, advocate of agrarian reform; lawyer by profession. Member of the Irish Parliament (1791–1795); a leader of the United Irishmen (1796–1798); editor of its organ, *Press*; arrested on the eve of the 1798 uprising, released to emigrate to France (1803) where Napoleon treated him as a repr of the Irish movement with the title of gen. Uncle of the Chartist,

Feargus O'Connor. —Among his pamphlets, which M (1869) might have read, were: *Monopoly the cause of all evil* (1848); *State of Ireland* (1798); *The measures of a ministry to prevent a revolution are the certain means of bringing it on* (1794). → 69:75.

O'Connor, Feargus (Edward) (1794 to 1855) Chartist leader; Irish-born, active mainly in England. Orig a lawyer; MP (1832–1835), but forced out. He became the leading spokesman of the "physical force" wing of the Chartist movement; powerful crowd orator; tended to dictatorial control; founder and editor of the *Northern Star* (1837–1852). Imprisoned for seditious libel (1840); launched (1845) his land colonization scheme, which had to be abandoned (1848) in a scandal. MP again (1847+); his erratic behavior turned into insanity (1852). → 46:13, 29; 48:5; 49:16; 55:39; 89:37. #ME4; M312, M588; E275.

Odda· (Norway) Village at the head of the S. branch of the *Hardanger Fjord. → 90:30.

Odermann, Carl Gustav (1815 to 1904) German educator; author of many textbooks on commercial subjects. For M's reference, see F. E. *Feller. → 69:13.

Odessa (Russ.) City in the S. Ukraine, on the Black Sea. → 83:16. #M89.

Odger, George (1820 to 1877) English trade-unionist. After joining the shoemakers' union in London, he was active in the 1850s in promoting TU amalgamation; a founder of the London Trades Council, and its secy (1862–1872); a member of the so-called Junta (group of TU leaders). He took an active part in a number of labor-led enterprises: TUC Parliamentary Comm (1872); Reform League; Labour Representation League; a founder of the Land and Labour League, and of the 1867 International League of Peace and Liberty. A participant in the founding meeting of the IWMA, he was a member of its GC (1864–1871) and pres (1864–1867); he broke with the movement after the Paris Commune, and subseqly carried on a campaign of denigration against the IWMA and the Commune. However, he was unable to break into rewarding politics; five times he was defeated for MP running on a lib-lab radical platform. → 64:26; 65:36; 66:17, 36, 43; 67:13, 32; 68:54, 61; 69:65; 71:2, 9, 28, 35, 40.

O'Dónnell, Leopoldo; *full* **O'Dónnell y Jorris**, *Duque de Tetuán, Conde de Lucena* (1809 to 1867) Spanish military man and politician (of Irish descent). At first a Progresista, he went over to the right-wing Moderado party; fought against Espartero (1843); governor of Cuba (1843–1848); later (1854–1856) war min under Espartero, whom he overthrew (1856); prime min at various times in 1856–1866. → 54:32. #M962.

O'Donovan Rossa, *Mrs.* Wife of the Irish Fenian leader, Jeremiah O'Donovan R. (1831–1915), who was sentenced to life in 1865, amnestied in 1870, then emigrated to the U.S. In 1865–1866 she organized a collection to support the families of Irish political prisoners, publicized by the GC/IWMA. —A letter by M (Feb 13, 1866) refers to her as "Roses [sic] O'Donovan"; other sources give no first name. → 67:18.

Österreichischer Arbeiter-Kalender Vienna, Wiener Neustadt, Brünn, 1874 to 1930. Socialist yearbook. → 87:31.

Offenbach (Ger.) City in Hesse, near Frankfurt. → 49:30.

Ohio (U.S.) → 79:35.

Old Norse language → 59:70.

Oldrini, Alessandro Italian socialist; an émigré in France (1870s+); expelled from France 1882. —So according to *MEW*. Maitron's *DBMOF* lists an A. Oldrini who as a refugee in London was one of the signers of the Blanquist manifesto *Aux communeux* (1874); a collaborator with G. Maroteau's *La Montagne* (1871). → 82:39.

Olmsted, Frederick Law (1822 to 1903) American landscape architect; best known as designer of Central Park (NY) and other parks, as city planner and national park advocate. His first fame came for books on the South and its slaveholding society; in the 1850s he pubd a number of books on his travels, esp in the South; contributor to *Putnam's Monthly*. He met M on his 1856 tour of Europe to examine its parks. → 56:34.

Olshausen, Theodor (1802 to 1869) German politician and publicist. Before 1848 he was active in Kiel as a lawyer, city official, liberal newspaper pubr; campaigned for separation of Schleswig-Holstein from Denmark. After participation in the 1848 fighting as a liberal democrat, and after publishing a paper in Hamburg, he emigrated (1851) to America under Danish pressure. He pubd German-American papers in NY and St. Louis (1851–1865); also books on Mississippi history, the Mormons, etc. He returned to Europe (1865) and settled in Zurich. M (1853) read him on Danish history, *Das dänische Königsgesetz* (1838). → 53:55.

Omar [I] or Omar (or Umar) ibn-al-Khattab (c.581 to 644) Caliph (634–644); converted to Islam by 618, he extended the Muslim empire with conquests. —The tale of his burning of the Alexandria library is now considered apocryphal; the library's destruction was prob started under the Romans and completed under Christian rule, after which the Christian writer Bar-Hebraeus blamed it on the Arabs. → 94:31.

Opdyke, George (1805 to 1880) American businessman and politician. Through a number of business enterprises, incl a clothing company and pharmaceuticals, he became a millionaire by 1853; army contractor (Civil War); banker (1869+). In politics, he began as an abolitionist, and became an active Republican; in the NY state legislature (1859); NYC mayor (1862–1863). He pubd a number of economic writings. M (1853) studied his first book, directed against J. S. Mill, *A treatise on polit eco* (1851). → 53:50, 52.

Oppenheim, Dagobert (1809 to 1889) German liberal; in 1842, closely involved with managing the RZ in Cologne. He took over as editor after M left. Of the Oppenheim banking family, he was at this time a junior lawyer, sympathetic to Young Hegelianism; later, a banker himself, removed from all political activity. → 42:22; 43:6.

Oppenheim, Heinrich Bernhard (1819 to 1880) German politician and publicist. He pubd a number of works on political science in the 1840s; in 1848, was editor of *Die Reform* (Berlin); emigrated (1849–1850); later a National Liberal. He pubd *Deutsche Jahrbücher* (1862–1864); Reichstag deputy (1874–1877); author of *Der Katheder-Sozialismus* (1872)— he is credited with coining this term. → 35:8.

Oppenheim, Max German businessman; owner of a dye and mineral oil factory with branches in Prague and Dresden. Brother of Mrs. *Kugelmann; friend of M since 1874, M's first stay in Carlsbad. At least in 1876, he was living in Prague. → 74:31; 75:21, 32; 76:26; 91:16.

Opportunist party (Fr.) Popular name for the French middle-of-the-road liberals in the last decades of the 19th century; to the right of the Radical party (left-liberals); in E's view, repr of the French bourgeoisie's main body. → 85:34.

Orges, Hermann (1821 to 1874) German publicist. Editor of the Augsburg *Allgemeine Ztg* (1854–1864). → 59:60.

Oriental despotism State form associated with what M called the "Asiatic mode of production." → 53:23.

Oriol, Henri French pub'r. An employee in the firm of Maurice *Lachâtre, he married Lachâtre's daughter and, from the beginning of the 1880s, became the owner of the Lachâtre publishing concern. He was an active member of the French WP (Guesdists), and pubd much party literature. → 85:3.

Orleanists That wing of French monarchism which supported the restoration of the Orleanist pretenders, stemming from *Louis Philippe (whose father was Duke of Orleans). → 52:35.

Orléans dynasty The Orléans family represented a younger branch of the Bourbons, originating from Philippe, Duke of Orléans (1640–1701), brother of Louis XIV. King *Louis Philippe had come from the Bourbon–

Orleans house, whose followers were called Orleanists. At the time of M's article, the Orleanist pretender to the throne was the Count of Paris. #M481.

Orlov (or **Orloff**), Alexei Federovich, *Count* (1825+), *Prince* (1856+) (1787 to 1862) Russian military man and diplomat. After rising to lieutenant-gen, he represented Russia in the treaty of Adrianople (1829); at Unkiar-Skelessi (1833) with Turkey; at the Paris Congress of 1856. #M86, M190.

Ormuzd (or **Ormazd**) In the Zoroastrian religion, the chief spirit of Good, also called Ahura Mazdah, as against the spirits of Evil headed by Ahriman. → 83:21.

Orsini, Cesare   Italian   revolutionist; brother of Felice Orsini. Cesare was a political émigré in England and the U.S. Orig a Mazzinian, he joined the IWMA and propagandized for its ideas abroad. —*Note:* The reference in the GC Minutes (Dec 4, 1866) to Orsini as a GC member is prob an error; certainly there is no record of his election or functioning as such. → 66:18.

Orsini, Felice (1819 to 1858) Italian nationalist-republican revolutionary, who, on Jan 14, 1858, attempted to assassinate Napoleon III, who, he decided, was the chief obstacle to Italian independence. His bombs killed 10 and wounded 150, but not the emperor; executed March 13. He had been a follower of Mazzini since before 1848; broke with him in 1857. → 58:8. #M622.

Ortes, Giammaria (1713 to 1790) Italian economist and social thinker; also a physician, philosopher, poet, etc. A Venetian monk till age 30, he left the monastery to study. His views were hostile to modern bourgeois relations and money economy; stressed the maldistribution of wealth as an evil. M (1859) studied his chief work, *Della economia nazionale,* which with some other writings is part of the Custodi set. → 59:77.

Osiander, Heinrich Friedrich (1782 to 1846) German writer on polit eco. A businessman in Holland through the 1820s, he began publishing on business issues (1828), esp in defense of free trade; then returned home to Stuttgart for study and writing. His books tended to sharp polemics. In latter years he esp fought against List's protectionism, as in his *Enttäuschung des Publikums über die Interessen des Handels, der Industrie und der Landwirtschaft* (1842). M (1844) read this work, also his *Über den Handelsverkehr der Völker* (1840). → 44:48.

Ostend; Flem. Oostende Seaport and watering place in N.W. Belgium. → 42:32; 46:31, 35; 47:20, 30, 45; 50:34; 68:53; 75:40.

Ostrau (Ger.) Silesian industrial city; now in Czechoslovakia as Ostrava. → 51:44.

Oswald, Ernst Prussian officer (army lieutenant); in 1860 he served under Garibaldi in southern Italy. At the end of 1861 he emigrated to the U.S. —Note: KMC spells his name Osswald; I here follow MEW. → 61:41.

Oswald, Eugen (1826 to 1912) German liberal journalist. In the 1848–1849 revolution he took part in the Baden-Palatinate uprising as a battalion commander and member of the Revolutionary Provisional Government of the Palatinate; he met E at this time, and remained friendly in emigration. In England he worked as a language teacher and journalist; taught French at the U. of London; ended as a teacher in the Royal Navy School, Greenwich. He was a friend also of Liebknecht during the latter's English sojourn; helped M's work for relief to Communard refugees. In the 1880s he was part of E's circle of personal friends. → 70:40, 45; 71:23; 75:48.

Oswald, Friedrich A pen name used by Friedrich Engels: first for #E330, pubd Nov 1839, and last for #E299, pubd in 1843. He signed it to 30 pubd pieces in one form or another. #E224, E233, E248, E256, E299, E330, E368, E370, E400, E404, E414, E454, E456, E467, E491, E524, E536, E550, E586, E651, E663, E674, E677, E683, E684, E721, E727, E737, E743, E774, E804, E897. See also S. *Oswald, and, for other pen names, F. *Engels.

Oswald, S. A pen name used once by Friedrich Engels, in a short piece (1839), then changed to Friedrich *Oswald. #E300.

Otechestvenniye Zapiski St. Petersburg, 1818–1819; ser. 2: 1820–1830; ser. 3: 1839–1884. Ed by V. G. Belinsky (till 1846); N. A. Nekrasov, Saltykov-Shchedrin (1868–1877). —Literary-political journal of radical-progressive outlook. After 1877, a spokesman for the Narodniks, till suppressed by the Russian government. → 77:9, 40, 41; 84:20, 29; 85:30; 86:2; 87:28. #M464.

Otto, Karl Christian (1817 to 1873) Danish-born left democrat. He took part in the 1848–1849 revolutionary movements in Schleswig-Holstein and Thuringia. In 1854 he was forced to emigrate, and met M on his way to the U.S. —Note: KMC calls him Dr. Ottomar Otto; M refers to him only as Dr. Otto; above identification is from MEW 28. → 54:29.

Otto, Karl Wunibald (b. 1809/1810) German chemist. He was active by 1845 in a Cologne workers' assoc; in 1848–1849 he was a member of the CL and of the Cologne WA; in 1850, treasurer of the reorganized CL in Cologne. A defendant in the Cologne Communist trial of 1852, he was sentenced to five years. —Note: The French edn of the M&E Correspondance (Eds. Sociales), t. 1–2, identifies this man with another person named Otto (see MEW 27 index) who emigrated to Amer-

ica and was an editor of the Deutsche Schnell-post (NY) in 1851. This is at best dubious, as of this writing. → 49:19.

Oudh Historic region of north-central India; annexed by the British (1856); now part of Uttar Pradesh. #M37, M279.

Overstone, Lord. Samuel Jones **Loyd** (1796 to 1883) British banker. Son of a Welsh parson turned banker, Loyd (who was created Baron Overstone of Overstone and Fotheringay in 1860) became one of the richest men in the country. Liberal MP (1819–1826); from 1833 on, he frequently testified before government bodies as an expert on banking and finance; his views influenced the adoption of the Bank Act of 1844 and the development of the joint-stock banking system. His writings advocated the "currency principle," i.a. in Reflections on the state of the currency (1837); his statements before parliamentary banking commsns were pubd as pamphlets. In Capital, Vol. 3, M pays much attention to his views and claims. → 51:61.

Owen, Robert (1771 to 1858) Great British (Welsh-born) pioneer of socialism and cooperativism; together with Saint-Simon and Fourier, one of the triumvirate standing at the source of modern socialism. For M&E's views, see the remarks under Fourier; also see, e.g., the Chronicle entry under 71:24. —Owen began as a self-made, successful cotton manufacturer in Manchester. Moving to New Lanark, Scotland (1800), he reconstructed the mills and town into a model industrial community. Since profits increased despite great benefits to the workers, the New Lanark experiment became world-famous. However, Owen's attempts to establish model ("utopian") communities elsewhere, as in New Harmony, Indiana, were unsuccessful. Also, he developed nonconformist views on religion, marriage, and other sensitive subjects, and was unable to gain governmental and capitalist support to recast the social system. For a while he turned to an alliance with the young TU movement, but he was basically hostile to working-class organization per se and looked to his own benevolent dictatorship as the mainspring of change. His chief contribution was made through the activity and influence of the Owenite movement he inaugurated, not his own. —There are a number of biographies, but it would be more important to have a good overall book on the movement of Owenism. A contribution is made by J. F. C. Harrison, Quest for the new moral world (1969). —Owen pubd many books. M's notebooks for 1845–1846 include notes on some of these: The book of the new moral world (1836–1844); A new view of society (1813); Six lectures delivered in Manchester (1837); Lectures on the marriages of the priesthood of the old immoral world (1840); Essays on the formation of the human character (1812). M's 1851 notebook includes notes on: Observations on the effect of the manufacturing system (1815). At other times, M must have read Owen's autobiography, The life of Robert Owen, by himself (1857–1858); The revolution in the mind and practice of the human race (1849); Report to the County of Lanark (1821); Lectures on the rational system of society (1841); and others. → 43:2; 46:52; 51:67; 71:24, 57; 77:30, 44. #M575.

Owenites Followers or supporters of the ideas of Robert *Owen. See also the Owenite organ *New Moral World. → 43:2; 64:31; 67:37.

Oxford (Eng.) University city 52 miles N. of London. → 72:64; 92:62; 93:48, 56.

P

Palatinate; Ger. Pfalz; i.e., the Lower or Rhine Palatinate Former German state, incl Trier, Mainz, Coblenz, Heidelberg. → 49:1, 27, 29, 30, 32. #E701.

Palermo (It.) Chief city and seaport of Sicily, N. coast. → 95:35.

The **Pall Mall Gazette** London, Feb 7, 1865, to Feb 5, 1921, under this title. Daily. Ed by F. Greenwood (in 1870–1871 at least). → 70:40, 41, 45, 50, 57, 61, 66; 71:7, 13, 19, 30, 34. #M318, M465, M466, M597, M902; E42, E531.

Palladino, Carmelo (1842 to 1896) Italian anarchist; a lawyer by profession. A leader of Bakunin's Alliance of the Socialist Democracy, as well as of the Naples IWMA, he helped to found anarchist groups in Italy. He remained an active Bakuninist at least through the 1870s. → 71:59.

Palma (de Mallorca) (Spain) Chief city of the island of Majorca, in the Balearics. → 71:3, 16.

Palmerston, Viscount. Henry John **Temple** (1784 to 1865) British politician. He entered Parliament (1807) as a Tory; secy of war (1809–1828). He broke with the Tories on parliamentary reform, and joined the Whig cabinet as foreign min (1830–1841). In opposition (1841–1846) during Peel's administration; foreign min again under Lord John Russell (1846–1851), friendly to Bonaparte's coup d'état; home secy (1852–1855); prime min (1855–1858), prosecuting the Crimean War; prime min again (1859–1865) sympathetic to the South in the U.S. Civil War, and suppressed the Sepoy Rebellion. —M's staunch conviction that Palmerston worked in favor of Russia's interests in foreign policy is viewed with virtually unanimous disfavor as his personal obsession; editorial annotations in IML works usually sidestep the question; but see the intros by Lester Hutchinson to ST/M97. → 53:1, 10, 39, 40, 42, 44–47; 54:2, 5, 9, 16, 20, 29, 34; 55:9, 13, 19, 21, 47, 49; 56:4, 9; 57:53; 60:24. #ME110, ME111; M229, M234, M258, M277, M389, M474, M480, M488, M533, M626–M630, M789.

Panama Canal scandal While the company established (1879) by F. de Lesseps to build the canal had collapsed in 1888, with widespread ruin of investors, it became known (Nov 1892) that the true state of the company had been concealed by bribery and corruption that extended into the highest reaches of government officials and parliamentary leaders; a scapegoat was found and the affair eventually hushed up. → 92:58, 63, 64; 93:4, 5, 8, 12. #E560.

Paniel, Karl Friedrich Wilhelm (1803 to 1856) German Protestant theologian. Pastor in Bremen, he represented the rationalist trend in Lutheranism. → 41:10. #E774.

Panizzi, Sir Anthony (1797 to 1879) Italian-born director of the BM Library, who did a great job of reorganizing its operation, as chief librarian (1856–1866). Orig a lawyer, he took part as a Mazzini sympathizer in a Modena uprising (1821); fled to Switzerland, then (1823) to England; prof of Italian in London. He joined the BM staff (1831); keeper of printed books (1837); knighted (1869). P. maintained his early interest in Italian national struggles, incl Garibaldi's. → 52:25.

Paoletti, Ferdinando (1717 to 1801 or 1803) Italian economist. A priest, teaching in a seminary near Florence, he was concerned with agricultural questions, more or less on the basis of Physiocrat theory. Author of Pensieri sopra l'agricoltura (1769). M (1859–1862 Notebooks) read his work I veri mezzi di render felici le società (1772) in the Custodi collection. → 59:78.

Papritz, Eugenie; Russ. Evgeniya Eduardovna (1854 to 1919) Russian singer. She researched and collected folk songs; belonged (1882–1884) to the illegal Society of Translators and Publishers (Moscow); transd some writings by M&E. She lived in emigration for many years (1884–1896); wife of the revolutionary Narodnik A. L. Linyov. → 84:35.

Pardigon, François (b. 1827) French Blanquist. After taking part in the June 1848 uprising in Paris, he emigrated to England, and became a leader of the London Blanquist group (early 1850s); pubd a pamphlet on the June Days (1850). → 50:19.

Paris (Fr.) Selected references: —M&E's moves to/from, residence in, visits to: →

43:1, 21–23, 26; 44:1, 29, 30, 35; 45:9, 12; 46:29, 36, 40, 44; 47:5, 26, 42, 45, 56; 48:1, 7, 16, 17, 19, 24, 28, 68; 49:1, 29, 31–33; 69:46; 81:40, 43; 82:14, 34. —Mrs. M in Paris area: → 56:33; 62:61; 69:35; 81:40, 43. — Laura Lafargue in: → 69:9, 23, 46; 81:43; 86:38; 91:47. —Lassalle in: → 55:33. —In IWMA affairs (see also *France): → 64:26; 65:9, 13, 23; 67:10; 70:17, 25, 39, 44, 49, 50, 52; 71:14, 48, 56. —Movement activities in: → 43:1, 26; 44:1, 27; 46:1, 29, 36, 40, 44, 47; 47:8, 42, 43, 45, 52, 56; 48:7, 13, 14, 19, 20, 22, 24–27, 40–42; 49:14, 29, 33; 50:7, 23; 51:39, 42, 50; 52:27; 56:6; 62:61; 66:5, 21, 23; 70:49; 71:9; 82:14, 34, 40; 83:12, 46; 84:28; 86:22; 87:11, 19, 20, 34; 88:38; 89:3, 4, 17, 23, 24; 90:11, 21; 92:64; 93:44; 94:16, 33. See also *France, *Paris Commune, *Treaty of Paris; also *Lafargue, etc.

Paris Commune The revolutionary government established in the capital on the basis of the assumption of power by the Central Comm of the National Guard and the election, which it sponsored, of a new repr assembly (the Commune itself, in the narrow sense); Mar 18 to May 28, 1871. It was overthrown militarily by the *Versailles government's forces, with extensive massacres, beyond military necessity, of Communard fighters and supporters. In M's view, the first workers' government ever established.   → 70:64; 71:1, 15, 20–23, 28–30, 33, 34, 40, 41, 48, 62; 72:13, 14; 73:17; 76:6, 27; 77:1, 6; 81:9, 13; 83:12; 84:5, 19; 86:15; 87:19; 91:5, 17, 18; 92:13; 93:13, 20; 94:16; 95:10, 27. #ME174, M143, M572–M574, M755; E4, E343, E344, E383, E432, E527, E621, E660, E848, E859, E887. —Communards (refugees, etc):→ 71:1, 28, 33–35, 41, 46, 51, 56, 59, 62, 64; 72:1, 5, 8, 13, 14, 28; 73:17; 74:4, 24; 75:7; 80:23; 90:31.

Paris-Journal Paris, 1868 to 1874. Daily. Pub'r: Henri de Pène. —Reactionary organ; Bonapartist; then supporter of Thiers government. It fomented hatred of the IWMA and Paris Commune. → 71:15.

Parish, Henry Headley (d. 1875) Author of The diplomatic history of the monarchy of Greece (1838), read by M (1854). → 54:26, 55; 57:16.

Parkinson, Richard (1797 to 1858) English clergyman. Ordained 1823, he became canon of Manchester. His writings were biographical sketches, poems, and religious essays and sermons—except for the work read by M (1846), viz., On the present conditions of the labouring poor in Manchester (1841), a pamphlet. → 46:52. #M575.

Parma City in Emilia, N. Italy, S.E. of Milan. → 72:35. #E822.

Parti Ouvrier (Fr.) See French Workers Party.

Patlayevsky, Innokenti I. (1839 to 1883)

Russian prof of financial law. M (1875) studied his Deneshnyi rynok v Rossii ot 1700 do 1762g. → 75:42.

Patow, Baron Erasmus (Robert) von (1804 to 1890) Prussian politician and administrative official. By 1845 he had risen to director, Foreign Affairs ministry. At first a moderate liberal, he joined the Camphausen cabinet in 1848 (min of trade, Apr-June); later opposed constitutionalism; min of finance (1858–1862); elected (1866) to the Chamber of Deputies; and became a state official in Hesse. #ME113.

La Patrie Paris, 1841 to 1871. Daily. —In 1850 it represented the united royalist camp (Party of Order); then Bonapartist. → 51:10.

Pattberg, Chr. American socialist; no further info. (The item is from ST/17, p. 254.) → 83:12.

Patton, Robert (1742 to 1812) Author of Principles of Asiatic monarchies (1801), read by M (1853). He entered the army of the E India Co., and eventually became governor of St. Helena. → 53:54.

Paul, Eden and Cedar #ME33.

Pauli, Philipp (Viktor) (1836 to after 1916) German chemist, who ran a chemical plant in Rheinau near Mannheim (1871–1880); friend of *Schorlemmer and of M&E. → 75:40.

Paya, Charles Jean Baptiste (1813 to 1865) French writer and journalist. Orig a printer, he became editor of the Toulouse Emancipation, as a left-democratic opponent of the Louis Philippe regime. He was arrested and jailed in 1849. → 49:4.

Peace and Freedom Congress (and League) An Organizing Comm of distinguished liberals, incl J. S. Mill, John Bright, V. Hugo, Garibaldi, L. Blanc, Herzen, et al., sponsored the first congress (Geneva, Sep 9+, 1867), for a "free democracy" and a United States of Europe, etc. A League of Peace and Freedom (Ligue Internationale de la Paix et de la Liberté) was established, with a CC; and a second congress was held (Bern, Sep 21+, 1868). The congresses being failures, the movement never got off the ground and died peacefully; but for its continuing magazine, see *Les Etats-Unis d'Europe. → 67:28, 29, 32, 37, 42; 68:69; 71:56.

Peasant (or Peasants') **War** Uprisings of German peasants, artisans, miners, and poor townsmen (1524–1526); sparked by the Reformation and its conflicts; aided by some dissenting nobles, while Luther called on the nobility to massacre the rebels. In Thuringia the movement was led by Th. *Münzer on a vaguely communistic basis. → 50:29, 37; 84:57. #E282.

Pease, Edward R., full Edward Reynolds (1857 to 1955) English Fabian socialist. Of a rich Yorkshire family, orig a Radical and Positivist, he tried an unsuccessful career as a London stockbroker, then turned his hand to cabinetmaking as more suitable to socialists. He was one of the founders of the Fabian Society (1883), its secy (1886); went off to the U.S. (1888) but soon returned to England; named gen secy of the Fabian Society (1890–1914), then honorary secy till 1939. Author of *History of the Fabian Society* (1916; 2nd edn, 1925) and some Fabian tracts. → 86:4.

Pecchio, *Count* Giuseppe; *Fr.* Joseph Pecchio (1785 to 1835) Italian economist and writer. He was active in the movement against Austria (1821); fled, eventually coming to England, where he taught and pubd, and made a rich marriage (1828). His chief works were *Saggio storico sull'amministrazione finanziaria dell'ex-regno d'Italia* (1830) and a book which M (1845) read in its French edn, *Histoire de l'économie politique en Italie* (1830; in Ital., 1829). → 45:50. #M575.

Pecqueur, Constantin (1801 to 1887) French socialist. After associating with the Saint-Simonians and then the Fourierists, he went his own way with a collectivist theory of state ownership plus Christian social reform, leavened by a pacifistic approach. In 1848 L. Blanc named him to the Luxembourg Commission, where he worked with Considérant. After Bonaparte's coup of 1851, he retired from public life. —M (1844) studied his *Théorie nouvelle d'économie social et politique* (1842). He also wrote: *Traité des améliorations matérielles* (1839); *La République de Dieu* (1844); *Salut de peuple* (1849–1850); *Catéchisme socialiste* (1849). → 44:48.

Peel, Sir Robert (1788 to 1850) English politician; moderate Tory. A cotton manufacturer, he entered Parliament (1809); held minor cabinet posts (1810–1818); home secy (1828–1830), establishing the first London police force ("Peelers," "Bobbies") in 1829; prime min (1834–1835, 1841). He carried through the Bank Act of 1844. The "Peelites"—supporters of Peel in repealing the Corn Laws (1846) against Disraeli's Tories—acted as a sort of third party till 1859, then absorbed by the Liberals. → 68:64. #M114, M963.

Pei-ho River River in N.E. China (Hopeh province). #M802.5.

Pelletier, Claude (1816 to 1880) French socialistic radical, active in the American IWMA. A Lyons typesetter, then tavern-keeper, he was briefly in Paris in 1848, then was elected from Lyons to the Constituent and Legislative Assemblies (1848–1851); exiled after Bonaparte's coup; went to the U.S. There he prospered with an artificial-flower factory, and continued his socialistic propaganda of a neo-Jacobin type; contributed (1871–1873) to

Le Socialiste (U.S. IWMA organ), and pubd writings with his socialist ideas, incl a utopia titled *Atercratie* (1873); played a leading part in the IWMA French sections. —*Note:* The above death date is from *DBMOF; MEW* et al. say 1881.) → 68:49; 72:11.

Pélissier, Aimable Jean Jacques (1794 to 1864) French gen. Serving through the conquest of Algeria (1830s–1850s), he was promoted for suffocating an entire Arab tribe in the interest of French civilization; *très aimable*. He supported Bonaparte's coup (1851); commanded the French army in the Crimea, created marshal of France and Duke of Malakoff (1855–1856); ambassador to London (1858–1859); governor of Algeria (1860–1864). #ME131; M649.

Peloponnesian War Decisive conflict between Athens and Sparta (431–404 B.C.), ending in Athens' defeat. → 61:23. #E351.5.

Pennsylvania (U.S.) → 79:35.

The **Penny 'Bee-Hive** London, Feb 19 to June 4, 1870. —See the *Bee-Hive*, which titled itself so for these few months. #M752.5.

O **Pensamento Social** Lisbon, Feb 1, 1872, to Apr 5, 1873. Weekly. Ed by J. Fontana, Anthero (or Authero?). —Socialist journal; organ of IWMA sections, pubd GC documents. → 72:13.

Pensiero ed Azione London, 1858 to 1859; Lugano, Genoa, 1860. Semimonthly. Ed by Mazzini. —Organ of Italian nationalist-republican movement. → 59:41.

The **People** NY, 1891 to 1893. Weekly. —Organ of the SLP. #E757.

The **People's Paper** London, May 30, 1852, to Sep 4, 1858. Weekly. Pub'r/editor: Ernest Jones. —Left Chartist organ. M&E helped Jones with the editorial work, as well as by contributing. → 52:20, 31, 35, 43, 54; 53:1, 11, 15, 34, 39, 44, 47; 54:13, 15, 24, 41; 56:1, 12, 16, 17, 21, 24, 42. #ME31; M90, M138, M189, M247, M271, M272, M308, M309, M320, M332, M380, M438, M468, M474, M547, M626, M758, M807, M808, M821.5, M827, M913, M943; E258, E682, E713.

People's Party *See* South German People's Party.

People's Will *See* Narodnaya Volya.

Perczel, Mór; *Ger.* Moritz (1811 to 1899) Hungarian gen and politician. After service in the Engineering Corps, he went into politics; was elected to the Diet (1840), reelected (1844, 1847); a leader of the democratic movement (1848). In 1848 he broke with the Batthyány cabinet over its lack of energy; organized a partisan corps to fight the Croat troops; fought through 1848–1849. After accusing Kossuth of softness he was stripped of command, but continued partisan warfare. After the defeat he fled to Turkey; moved to England (1851), settled in Jersey. → 52:7.

Péreire, Isaac (1806 to 1880) French banker and broker; founder of the Crédit Mobilier with his brother (Jacob) Emile (1800–1875). The family's orig name was Pereira. The brothers were converted to Saint-Simonism (1825) by their cousin Olinde Rodrigues; edited Le Globe, lectured on polit eco (1831). Writing for Le Temps et al., they introduced stock exchange reports. Subseqly they were involved in financing railway construction, and in 1852, under Napoleon III, founded the Crédit Mobilier. —M (1845) read Isaac P.'s Leçons sur l'industrie et les finances (1832). → 45:50. #M575.

Perret, Henri Swiss socialist; an engraver. A leader of the IWMA in Switzerland, he was at first a member of Bakunin's Alliance (1868–1869); secy of the Romance Swiss Federal Comm (1868–1873); member of the ed bd of L'Egalité; delegate to all IWMA congresses. He broke with the Bakuninists (1869), but at The Hague (1872) took a conciliatory attitude. → 70:44; 73:36.

Persia Officially renamed Iran in 1935; with varying borders. → 57:4, 8, 25. #M36, M651, M652, M973; E583, E635.

Persian language → 53:18.

Pertz, Georg Heinrich (1795 to 1876) German historian. A moderate conservative, he was early an archivist, then an editor, in Hanover; Berlin chief librarian; editor of the massive Monumenta Germaniae Historica (1823–1874); author of histories and biographies. E (1870) studied his Leben des Feldmarschalls Grafen Neithardt von Gneisenau (1864–1869). → 70:58.

Peter I; called Peter the Great (1672 to 1725) Czar of Russia, 1682+. → 56:8.

Peter the Hermit; pseud. of Edmond Loutil (b. 1863) The book read by M on publ was his The brigands in Egypt; solution of the international crisis; letters to an Englishman (1882), transd from the French. Loutil, who used the pen name Pierre L'Ermite also in French, was primarily a novelist; his 1955 autobiography was subtitled Souvenirs d'un vieux curé de Paris. → 82:56.

Petersen, Niels (Lorenzo) (1814 to 1894) Danish socialist, active also in other countries. A journeyman furrier, he was first active in Switzerland as a follower of Weitling; then joined the CL as an émigré in Paris. Later, he was a contributor to Das Volk (1859). In 1870 he was in the German section of the IWMA in Paris; also worked to found an IWMA section in Copenhagen. In the 1880s he was active in the Social-Democratic party of Denmark as a left-wing leader (with G. *Trier). In 1889 the party leadership

expelled this left wing, against E's remonstrances. → 93:35.

Petrarch; Angl. form of Francesco Petrarca (1304 to 1374) Italian poet and man of letters; best known for his Canzoniere, lyrics of highly spiritualized passion addressed to "Laura," a respectable French lady of Avignon. → 83:36.

Petrovskoe Academy (Moscow) → 83:12.

Petsch, Albert German pub'r/bookdealer in London, who pubd M's Herr Vogt. → 59:72; 60:45.

Petty, Sir William (1623 to 1687) English economist and statistician; in M's view, "Founder of modern polit eco, one of the most brilliant and most original economic researchers," representing the labor theory of value in its classical bourgeois form. A doctor by profession, he was a physician to the British army in Ireland. As surveyor-gen of Ireland, he pioneered large-scale surveying there; also a founder of the Royal Society. As an economist (his third hat), he pubd a number of important works, incl the first book on vital statistics (1662). M (1845) studied his Political arithmetick (1690) and "An essay concerning the multiplication of mankind" in his Several essays in political arithmetick (1699). M (1859) studied his Treatise of taxes and contributions (1679). → 45:51; 55:5; 59:76; 63:14. #M575.

Peuchet, Jacques (1758 to 1830) French administrative official and archivist; orig a lawyer. As a youth he contributed to Diderot's Encyclopédie and at first supported the French Revolution, then went over to the royalists and was jailed by 1792. By 1795 he was head of the bureau on émigré affairs, but lost power. In 1805 he became archivist of the Justice ministry; newspaper censor (1814); archivist of the police prefecture (1815+). — M's article has a brief biographical sketch of him; see MECW 4:598. The book M reviewed was his Mémoires tirés des Archives de la Police de Paris, pour servir à l'histoire de la morale et de la police (1838). He also pubd i.a. Dictionnaire universel de la géographie commerçante (1799–1800), Statistique élémentaire de la France (1807). → 45:3, 45; 46:7. #M653.

Pfänder, Carl (1818 to 1876) German socialist; a miniature painter by profession. An émigré in London (1845+), he was a leading member of the League of the Just and GWEA, then of the CL; temporary treasurer of the S-D Refugee Comm (1850); member of the GC/IWMA (1864–1867, 1870–1872). A longtime friend and coworker of M&E. → 49:36; 50:7, 34, 45; 51:1; 52:9; 59:34; 64:36; 70:3; 75:18; 76:8; 88:8. #ME52, ME64, ME179.

Pfister, Johann Christian von (1772 to 1835) German historian, from the Württemberg area. As a student of theology at Tübingen, he was close to Schelling. He became a tutor there (1800); then went to Vienna (1803) to work with his model, Johannes von Müller. His chief work was *Geschichte von Schwaben* (1803–1817); also authored *Geschichte der Teutschen* (1829–1835). → 43:32.

Pfuel, Ernst (Heinrich Adolf) von; *surname also written* **Pfuël** *to show pronunciation* (1779 to 1866) Prussian gen and politician. Military governor of Neuchâtel (1832–1848); in March 1848, governor of Berlin; in Apr-May, suppressed the Posen uprising; in Sep-Oct, prime min and war min. He was then considered part of the reactionary military camarilla; but having lost the king's confidence, he retired (end of 1848) to his Randau estate. Later (1854) he moved back to Berlin; elected (1858) to the Prussia Chamber of Deputies as a Liberal. In his last years he moved leftish (as M reported in 1861); e.g., he supported Garibaldi's movement in Italy. → 48:63, 64, 76; 61:15. #M654.

Phear, Sir John Budd (1825 to 1905) English jurist in India. His first field was mathematics, in which he became a lecturer and textbook writer. After becoming a lawyer (1847), he was named a judge in Bengal (1864). There he studied native social life; pres, Asiatic Society of Bengal (1870–1871); pres, Bengal Social Science Assoc. He left Bengal (1876); was knighted, and named chief justice in Ceylon (1877). Returning to England (1879) he engaged in local Liberal politics, and wrote books, esp the work studied by M: *The Aryan village in India and Ceylon* (1880), which had been preceded by *The Hindoo joint family* (Calcutta, 1867), a lecture. → 81:18, 45. #M571.

Philadelphia (Penna.) → 53:31; 75:25, 28.

Philips, Antoinette; *called* Nannette (c.1837 to 1885) M's cousin; daughter of Lion Philips. She was a member of the Dutch section of the IWMA; corresponded with M. → 63:41; 66:2.

Philips, August (d. 1895) M's cousin; son of Lion Philips. Lawyer in Amsterdam. → 62:51, 55; 64:7; 72:7.

Philips family → 65:27, 28; 66:41. See *also* Lion Philips.

Philips, Jacques M's cousin; son of Lion Philips. Lawyer in Rotterdam. → 61:20; 64:7.

Philips, Karl M's cousin; son of Lion Philips. Businessman in Aachen. → 69:56.

Philips, Lion (Benjamin) (1794 to 1866) M's Dutch uncle; he married Sophie Pressburg, sister of M's mother. An affluent businessman and banker in Zaltbommel, Neth., he acted as executor for M's mother. He converted from Judaism only in middle age, in

the 1840s. —*Note:* The present-day Philips business empire was founded by a grandson. → 61:14, 15; 62:45; 63:41; 64:5, 11, 14, 25; 66:55. See *also* Philips family.

Phillips, Wendell (1811 to 1884) American radical publicist. Of a rich Boston family; orig a lawyer; joined the Abolitionist movement (1837) and became a full-time agitator against slavery; famous orator; succeeded William L. Garrison as pres of the Anti-Slavery Society (1865–1870). In 1870 he ran for governor of Massachusetts on a labor ticket; joined the IWMA (1871); defended the Paris Commune, advocated woman suffrage, penal reform, regulation of corporations, Irish independence, labor rights, the eight-hour day, and other good things. → 71:39; 81:17. #M1.

Physiocrats The first school of polit eco, developed in 17th- and 18th-century France, by F. *Quesnay, Mercier de la Rivière et al.; orig called the *Economistes*. "The true fathers of modern polit eco," in M's view, who analyzed feudal relations from the viewpoint of a bourgeois production system just beginning to break out of the feudal order. See #M877, vol. 1, Ch. 2, and #E23, Ch. 10 (by M). → 60:66; 62:6; 79:20; 95:26.

Pianori, Giovanni (1827 to 1855) Italian nationalist revolutionary; a follower of Garibaldi. After taking part in the 1848 revolution in Italy, he emigrated to Piedmont, then to France. In April 1855 he made an unsuccessful attempt to assassinate Napoleon III in Paris; executed. #M656.

Piedmont; *Ital.* Piemonte Province of N.W. Italy; capital, Turin. It was ruled, from the 15th century, by the dukes of Savoy, who became kings of Sardinia (1720); annexed to France (1798–1814); after uniting with Sardinia, it became the center for Italian unification. → 56:21; 59:4, 14, 17. #M808; E214.

Pieper, Wilhelm (b. c.1826 to *after* 1890) German journalist and philologist. A member of the CL in Germany, he took part in the revolution of 1848–1849, then emigrated. As an émigré in London in the 1850s, he was close to M&E. He later returned to Germany, joined the Nationalverein in Bremen; in the 1890s, lived in Freiburg i. Br. → 51:1, 8, 10, 14, 45, 47, 50, 52; 52:33, 36, 54; 53:1, 25; 54:23, 41; 56:10, 25, 26; 57:53; 58:44; 62:57; 64:8. #M635.

Pigott, Richard (1828? to 1889) Irish journalist. Long a Fenian supporter, he was pub'r/editor of the *Irishman* (1865–1879), suffered imprisonment (1867), etc. Then in 1886 he sold out: sold an Irish anti-home-rule group forged papers incriminating Parnell; confessed the forgery; fled to Madrid, committed suicide. → 70:20.

Pindter, Emil F. (d. 1897) Prussian journalist and privy councillor. An editor (1865+) and editor-in-chief (1872+) of the Bismarck organ *Norddeutsche Allgemeine Ztg.* → 82:42, 46. #E361.

Pinto, Isaac (de) (1715 to 1787) Dutch merchant and financier, of Portuguese descent; resident for periods in France and London. His wealth and wide interests gave him a place as government adviser on economic and financial affairs. He pubd a number of works in French, incl *Traité de la circulation et du crédit* (1771)—read by M (1845). His *Apologie pour la nation juive* (1762) was an outcome of his concern for the position of the Jews. → 45:50.

Pio, Louis; *full* Louis Albert François (1841 to 1894) Danish socialist. Son of a French émigré; ex-army lieutenant; postal worker. Stirred by the Paris Commune, he became a pioneer socialist propagandist in Denmark; main organizer of the Danish section of the IWMA (1871); founder/editor of *Socialisten* (1871–1872). He was jailed (1872–1875); then established a S-D party (1876); visited M, corresponded with E. Under police pressure, he emigrated to the U.S. (1877) with two other leading activists, collapsing the Danish beginnings. Pio continued to carry on socialist propaganda (Lassallean in tendency) in the U.S.; died in Chicago. → 72:15, 20, 21; 75:48; 76:15.

Der Pionier NY; Boston (1859+). 1854 to 1879. Weekly. Ed by Karl Heinzen. —Organ of liberal German émigrés. Merged into the *Freidenker.* → 62:27; 72:26.

"Pissmarck" M's little joke about Bismarck. → 65:7.

Pius IX Giovanni Maria **Mastai-Ferretti** (1792 to 1878) Pope, 1846+. At first a reformer, he fled the 1848 Rome insurrection and was restored only by French bayonets, whereupon he turned into a bitter reactionary and turned the face of the Catholic church toward die-hard antimodernism. His pontificate produced the dogma of the Immaculate Conception (1854); the Syllabus, condemning modern science, tolerance, and other devilish inventions of modern civilization (1864); the dogma of papal infallibility (1869); various denunciations of socialism; and loss of the papacy's temporal power to Italy (1870). → 71:34. #E732.

Plaine Ste-Gudule District of Brussels → 46:21.

Platen, August. *Count* von **Platen Hallermund** or **Hallermünde** (1796 to 1835) German neoclassicist poet and man of letters, a great lyricist. Liberal in politics. Toward the end of his life (1826+) he lived in Italy. Author of: *Ghaselen* (1821); *Sonette aus Venedig* (1825); *Die Abbassiden* (1834). #E586.

Plato (427? to 347 B.C.) Greek philosopher of objective idealism. His *Dialogues* purport to present Socrates' teachings. P. was often taken, esp by early socialists, to be a herald of socialism, because of the mistaken notion that his dialogue *The Republic* advocates or pictures a communistic form of society; in fact, it sketches a society essentially property-holding in its ruling class which, however, is politically managed by an elite bureaucracy called the Guardians; the "communistic" elements in Plato's utopian vision, such as the "community of women," apply only to this elite. In general, Plato glorified the subordination of individual to state and the suppression of democratic control; the dialogue *The Laws* is less explicit. The best discussion of Plato from a Marxist standpoint is A. D. Winspear's *The genesis of Plato's thought* (1940). → 60:65; 95:21, 31.

Plattsburgh (NY state) City on the shore of Lake Champlain. → 88:30.

La Plebe Lodi, Milan, July 4, 1868, to Oct 29, 1875 (in Lodi); Nov 1, 1875, to Nov 1, 1883 (in Milan). Varying periodicity; in 1871, thrice weekly. Ed by E. Bignami. —At first, a left-republican organ; in 1871–1873, organ of IWMA sections, generally supporting the GC; favorable to the building an independent workers party in 1879. —Note: *MEW* 35 lists a monthly magazine put out by Bignami with the title *La Plebe, Revista Socialista,* Milan, 1881–1882. → 71:63; 72:23, 56, 60, 61, 65, 67; 73:6, 27, 33; 77:6; 78:4; 79:16; 82:52, 53. #M224; E29, E381, E436, E448–E451, E538, E567, E751, E809, E813, E829.

Plekhanov, Georgi Valentinovich (1856 to 1918) Russian pioneer Marxist. Of a petty gentry family, he became a revolutionist (c.1875) and joined the Narodnik group Zemlya i Volya; a Bakunin follower at this point, he fled abroad (1876–1877) to Paris and Berlin; returned as a Narodnik propagandist. In 1879 the organization was divided on the question of terrorism, with P. opposed to it; a split took place, with P.'s group Chernyi Peredel (General Redivision) opposed to the Narodnaya Volya. P. emigrated to Geneva (Jan 1880); in the course of study (1880–1882) he became a Marxist; played the leading role in founding the first Marxist group, Emancipation of Labor group (1883–1903). His first Marxist writing was his intro to his trans of the *Com Manifesto* (1882); his first essay was *Socialism and the political struggle* (1883); next, his influential polemic *Our differences* (1885). For the next decade, the Emancipation of Labor group represented Russian Marxism and was the embryo of the future S-D movement. In the early years of the 1900s he was an editor, with Lenin, of *Iskra* and *Zarya;* in 1903, after the second congress of the Russian Social-Democrats, which resulted in the Bolshevik-Menshevik split, P. (after some tergiversation) joined the Mensheviks, whom he led for the next decade. In World War I he became a prowar supporter of the Allied side, supporting czarist Russia in the conflict; after it, an opponent of the Bolshevik revolution and regime. —Best-known works: *Fundamental problems of Marxism* (1908); *Essays in historical materialism* (two essays, 1897–1898); *The development of the monist view of history* (1895); *Anarchism and socialism* (1894). —There is an English biography by S. H. Baron, *Plekhanov* (1963). Progress Pub. (Moscow) has pubd a five-volume collection of his *Selected philosophical works* (incl political-theoretical works). → 82:8; 84:16; 91:57; 93:16, 22, 24; 94:22, 42, 50, 51; 95:12, 14, 15. #ME33, ME37; E756.

Pleyel, *Colonel* According to *MEW*, a Hungarian officer who took part in the 1848 revolution in his country and later (1852) emigrated to the U.S. → 52:41.

Plutarch (46? to 120?) Greek writer. His best-known work is his *Lives*, actually *Parallel lives*, which presents biographies of eminent Greeks and Romans in related pairs. Plutarch's essay on Lycurgus played a role in the early socialist movement in enforcing the myth of Sparta as a socialist/communist society. #M239.

Po River Great river of northern Italy. #E587.

Podolinsky, Sergei Andreyevich (1850 to 1891) Ukrainian scholar; a socialist and Darwinist. Emigré (1871+) in Austria, France, and (1880+) Switzerland. He helped distribute socialist literature in the Ukrainian language, incl propaganda for M's economics; was personally acquainted with M&E, and corresponded with them. —P.'s article was titled "Il socialismo e l'unità delle forze fisiche," in *La Plebe,* 1881, Anno XIV, n.s., Nr. 3/4; reprinted in *NZ,* Jg. 1, 1883, p. 413, as "Menschliche Arbeit und Einheit der Kraft." → 82:53.

Poland; the Poles The three partitions—among Russia, Prussia, Austria—took place in 1772, 1793, 1795; united Poland established in 1918. → 48:37, 38, 52, 55; 49:17; 54:9; 56;38; 57:38; 63:10, 12, 18, 21, 31, 34, 37; 64:40, 44, 45; 65:5; 66:4, 6, 9, 19, 23, 24; 67:4, 8; 68:37; 69:49; 70:17; 71:51; 72:3; 74:19; 75:44; 77:9; 80:46; 84:3, 40; 90:1, 31, 44; 91:10; 92:1, 11, 20, 24; 93:4; 94:1. #ME185; M301, M360, M506, M665, M666, M695, M825, M828, M833; E20, E205, E283, E383, E512, E592, E615, E660, E699, E767, E768, E769, E915. —Commemorations: → 47:45, 46, 49, 52, 54; 48:10, 21; 65:19, 25, 29, 53; 66:6, 50, 53; 67:4; 75:7, 14, 44; 76:2; 80:39. —Polish émigrés: → 45:3; 48:58, 79, 85; 51:10; 53:32;

55:35; 63:10, 31; 66:24, 50; 71:56; 72:20; 74:19; 92:11.

Polyakov, Nikolai Petrovich (1843 to 1905) Russian leftist pub'r; pubd the first Russian edn of *Capital* in 1872. His publishing house lasted 1865–1873 despite government harassment, which finally forced dissolution. P. was close to Narodnik supporters of Chernyshevsky and the Tchaikovsky circle. → 68:52.

Polyarnaya Svezda London, 1855 to 1862; 1869 (8 vols. altogether). Yearbook for literature and politics. Pub'r: Herzen. → 55:20.

Polynices In Greek myth, son of Oedipus; a character in Aeschylus' *Seven against Thebes*—heroes who made war on *Eteocles. #E745.

Poor, Henry Varnum (1812 to 1905) American economist. Editor of the *American Railroad J.* (1849–1862); author of *The money question* (1896) and other works. With his son, he produced a series of *Poor's manuals,* business directories and handbooks. M (1878) read his *Money and its laws* (1877). → 78:48.

Poor Law inspectors (Eng.) → 70:26.

Il Popolino Turin, Apr 15 to Oct 6, 1872. Weekly. —Official organ of the Society for the Emancipation of the Proletariat in Turin. #E809.

Poppe, Johann Heinrich Moritz von (1776 to 1854) German mathematician and historian of technology. Prof at Tübingen (1818–1843) and Stuttgart. He pubd voluminously in the field of technological history. M (1851) read his *Lehrbuch der allgemeinen Technologie* (1809), *Die Physik vorzüglich in Anwendung auf Künste, Manufaktur . . .* (1830), *Geschichte der Mathematik* (1828), *Geschichte der Technologie* (1807–1811), Bd. 1. → 51:71.

Le Populaire Paris, Sep 1, 1833, to Oct 4, 1835; Mar 14, 1841, to 1851. Daily. Founder: E. Cabet —Organ of Cabet's "Icarian" movement; not to be confused with the socialist organ of a later year. → 48:27.

Populists (Russ.) See Narodniks.

Port Hope (Can.) Town on Lake Ontario. → 88:30.

Porte de Louvain (Brussels) → 45:26.

Porter, George Richardson (1792 to 1852) English statistician. Orig a sugar broker, he failed in business and turned to writing books on economics. He established the statistical department of the Bd of Trade (1834) and promoted the founding of the Statistical Society, becoming its vice-pres and treasurer (1841). In politics, a liberal and Free-Trader. His chief work was *The progress of the nation in its various social and economical relations* (1836–1843); also pubd a trans of Bastiat (1846) and *A manual of statistics* (1849). #M575.

Porto Alegre (Brazil)   Seaport city, near the south end. → 77:37.

Porto Maurizio (It.)   Seaport near the French Riviera; now part of the city of Imperia. → 72:49.

Portugal and Portuguese affairs → 72:13, 14, 36, 38, 53, 60; 73:33; 75:5.   #E32, E671, E751.5, E817, E922.

Posen; *Pol.* Poznań   Polish city, center of German controlled Poland (1815–1914). → 48:55; 69:49.   #E513, E594.

Positivists   *See* Comtism.

Possibilists (Fr.)   Reformist social-democratic tendency in the early French socialist movement, equivalent to the right wing, long led by Paul *Brousse, hence also called Broussists. They broke away from the Guesdists in the 1880s, in the name of advocating only what is practicable and "possible" (revolutionary goals being "impossible"). → 82:5, 34, 40, 43; 83:21, 46; 88:38; 89:3, 7, 12, 23, 24, 29; 90:37, 42, 49, 51; 91:8, 23.   #E598.

Possony, S. T.   #ME33.

Post (London)   *See* Morning Post.

Potter, Alonzo (1800 to 1865)   American clergyman; Episcopal bishop (1845+). Prof of philosophy and polit eco at Union College; its vice-pres (1838–1845). Author of *Religious philosophy* (1872).   —M (1859–1862 notebooks) read his *Political economy* (1840). → 59:78.

Pottier, Eugène (Edme) (1816 to 1887)   French socialist poet and song-writer; author of the anthem "The International(e)." A patternmaker, he organized a TU in his field; fought on the barricades in Feb and June 1848. He joined the IWMA (1870); became a member of the CC/NG; was elected a member of the Paris Commune, where he served in various posts, incl the Exec of the Artists Federation. Afterward he took refuge in England; went to the U.S. (1873–1880), where he worked as patternmaker and teacher; returned to France poor and part-paralyzed. In America he had written three narrative poems, at least one in English, "The workingmen of America to the workingmen of France" (1876). In France, he joined the French WP (Guesdists); pubd *Quel est le fou?* (1884); *Chants révolutionnaires* (1887). In 1871 he wrote "L'Internationale" a month after the Versaillese massacre of the Communards, while he was being hunted in Paris. See the sketch on him in *DBMOF*, which highlights his tribute to Blanqui, self-applicable: "Against a heartless class that'd hound him,/ He fought for people who lacked bread;/ Living, he owned four walls around him,/ And owned four planks of pine when dead." → 89:35.

Potts, Robert (1805 to 1885)   English mathematician. His reputation was first based on

his popular edn of Euclid's *Elements* (1845), which went through many edns; also pubd *Elementary arithmetic* (1876), *Elementary algebra* (1879). → 78:1.

Pozzo di Borgo, *Count* Carlo Andrea (1764 to 1842)   Corsican-born diplomat in Russia's service. He fled Corsica as an enemy of Napoleon, an enmity which remained his chief passion; entered Russian service (1804); envoy, then ambassador in Paris (1814–1835); made a count of France (1818); ambassador in London (1835–1839); then retired.   #M639.

Pradt, *Abbé* Dominique de; *full* Dominique Georges Frédéric **(Dufour) de Riom de Prolhiac de Fourt de Pradt** (1759 to 1837)   French prelate and diplomat. His family name was orig Dufour. A member of the States-General (1789); émigré (1791–1799); Napoleon's personal chaplain (1800). He negotiated the Treaty of Bayonne dethroning the Bourbons in Spain, and became archbishop of Malines (1808); supported the Restoration in France. His writings on Spain included *Mémoires historiques sur la révolution d'Espagne* (1816); *De la révolution actuelle de l'Espagne, et de ses suites* (1820). → 54:57.

Prague; *Czech.* Praha   Capital of Bohemia, in the Hapsburg Empire; now (1918+) capital of Czechoslovakia. → 75:32; 76:26; 93:42.   #ME65; E599.   —Treaty of Prague: → 66:30.

Pravitelstvenni Vestnik   St. Petersburg, 1855 to 1918. → 71:37; 73:6.

Prendergast, John Patrick (1808 to 1893)   Irish (Dublin-born) historian. He became a lawyer (1830), and acted for many years as an estate administrator, which experience made him an advocate of tenants' rights and sympathetic to land-reform schemes. In politics, a Liberal and nationalist, but not a Home Ruler; opponent of Parnell. His chief works were *The history of the Cromwellian settlement of Ireland* (1863) (studied by M 1869, in the 1865 edn) and *Ireland from the Restoration to the Revolution* (1887). → 69:75; 70:8.

Prescott, William Hickling (1796 to 1859)   American historian; author of a number of important works on Spain and Spanish America, essentially political and military history. M (1851) read his *History of the conquest of Mexico* (1843), *History of the conquest of Peru* (1847). → 51:68, 69.

Die **Presse**   Vienna, 1848 to 1896. Daily. Pub'r: August Zang. Ed bd: incl Max Friedländer (1860s).   —Liberal paper; anti-Bonapartist. Pubd a number of articles contributed by M.   → 57:53; 58:13; 59:21, 28, 40; 61:1, 17, 25, 32, 39, 43, 47, 49, 50, 54, 57; 62:1, 2, 9, 10, 15, 23, 25, 26, 32, 33, 36, 41, 42, 49, 53, 54, 58, 60; 63:9; 71:30.   #ME8; M1, M26, M27, M31, M45, M98, M146, M183, M192, M199, M202, M214, M242, M243, M264, M270, M280,

M288, M290, M292, M326, M336, M341, M386, M411, M413, M482, M505, M600, M602, M606, M615, M620, M691, M693, M791, M809, M812, M865, M871, M872, M938, M941, M942, M988, M993; E15.

La **Presse** Paris, 1836 to 1866. Daily. Pub'r/editor: Emile de Girardin (1836–1857). —This paper is famous in the history of journalism for inaugurating the cheap, mass press; see *Girardin. Oppositionist under Louis Philippe, it supported liberal republicanism in 1848–1849, briefly Bonapartist, then critical of Bonaparte. → 49:31; 52:36; 92:63. #M894.

Preussischer Staats-Anzeiger; *in full* Königlich etc. Berlin, May 1848 to 1871 under these name-forms; founded in Jan 1819 as *Allgemeine Preussische Staats-Ztg.* Daily. Official organ of the Prussian government. → 65:54.

Price, Richard (1723 to 1791) British (Welsh-born) publicist; economics writer, nonconformist clergyman. He pubd works on moral and political philosophy, America (favoring the Revolution), France (ditto); friend of Ben Franklin and Priestley. In economics, he advocated reduction of the national debt. M (1851) studied his *Appeal to the public, on the subject of the national debt* (2nd edn, 1772; 1st, 1771); *Observations on reversionary payments* (1772; pubd 1771). → 51:68.

Príncipe (y Vidaud), Miguel Agustín (1811 to 1863) Spanish writer. Prof of literature and history at Saragossa; later, curator of the National Library, Madrid, and other posts; a founder of the Spanish Institute. A progressive, he authored a number of works on Spanish history and literature. —The book read by M (1854) was, in point of fact, a collective work: *Espartero. Su pasado, su presente, su porvenir, por la redacción de El Espectador* (1848), hence Príncipe was a coauthor. → 54:55.

Prinz, Wilhelm; *full* Johann Wilhelm German radical. In the 1848–1849 revolution he was active in the Cologne WA as a close supporter of *Gottschalk and bitter enemy of M's group. When Gottschalk ran the WA, P. was a secy and pres of one of the branches. In Oct 1848 he took over editorship of the WA organ without authorization, until (Feb 1849) the WA established its own paper against his. P. followed Gottschalk in splitting from the WA, trying to build a rival organization, and making scurrilous attacks on M and the NRZ group. → 49:6, 9.

Le **Progrès** Le Locle (Switz.), Dec 18, 1868, to Apr 2, 1870. Irreg., then semimonthly, then (Nov 1869+) weekly. Ed by J. Guillaume. —Bakuninist organ; opposed to the IWMA/GC. Superseded by *La Solidarité.* → 69:70.

Progress London, 1883 to 1887. Monthly.

Director: G. W. Fode. Ed by E. Aveling (1884). —Socialist journal for a number of years. #E93.

Progressive Party; Progressivists (Fortschrittspartei) (Ger.) Left-liberal party, founded June 1861 in Prussia; in 1884 it merged with another liberal group to form the Freisinnige Vereinigung (Liberal Society). → 65:8.

Progressives (Eng.) The label used by the Fabian-Liberal coalition that controlled the London County Council. → 95:18.

"Proletarian Positivists" (Paris) A group of French *Comtists ("Prolétaires Positivistes") that applied for affiliation to the IWMA as a branch. → 70:17.

Il **Proletario Italiano** Turin, July 1871 to Sep 14, 1871. Semiweekly. Ed by Carlo Terzaghi. —Organ of the IWMA sections in Turin. When Terzaghi was ousted, he founded *Il Proletario* (1873–1874). → 71:59. #E831.

Propertius, Sextus (c.50 to c.16 B.C.) Roman elegiac poet of Maecenas' circle, writing chiefly amatory poems (to "Cynthia"). → 36:5.

Protot, Eugène; *full* Louis Charles Eugène (1839 to 1921) French Blanquist; lawyer by profession; journalist. He was elected to the Paris Commune, holding various posts. Afterward he was a refugee in a number of different cities; after the 1880 amnesty, he returned to France but was not reinstated as lawyer; in the Boulanger crisis, a Boulangeo-Blanquist, following Granger. An inveterate slanderer: in the 1889 Marseilles election, running against Guesde, he accused him of being a paid agent of Germany, for which he got a court sentence. His 1892 pamphlet *Chauvins et réacteurs* was a rather mindlessly scurrilous blast against the German Social-Democrats and M. → 92:52.

Proudhon, Pierre Joseph (1809 to 1865) French radical writer; "father of anarchism." Raised semirurally, so that his world would always be that of peasants and artisans, P. acquired some schooling but was otherwise self-educated, by dint of wide reading. At age 19 he became a compositor (later, a proofreader); came to Paris (c.1839). His first success was his book *Qu'est-ce que la propriété?* (1840); his answer (property is theft), borrowed from *Brissot, became famous. His chief work came in 1846: *Système des contradictions économique ou Philosophie de la misère.* (M's reply, *Misère de la philosophie* [#M681] took off from the subtitle.) The outbreak of the 1848 revolution dismayed P., but he plunged into the turmoil with his organs, *Représentant du Peuple* and its successors, and was widely regarded as a revolutionary extremist. Actually, what he wanted to do was, in peace and quiet, set up a mutual-credit bank (his own social utopia), and he did so in 1849; it failed instantly. He greeted Bonaparte's rise to power, expecting reform from above by a benevolent despot (as he also, at other times, looked to the czar or Prince Napoleon), but he reversed this line when Bonaparte scorned his prescriptions. His attacks on the church and other respectabilities in his De la justice dans la révolution et dans l'église (1858) forced him to flee to Brussels for many years. —P.'s admirers (who are the ones that write books about him) call his thought merely unsystematic, contradictory, and sprawling; others consider him one of the most muddleheaded thinkers in history. However, it is customary to regard him as an apostle of Liberty, since he said so himself, indeed the father of anarchist libertarianism. But like many anarchists, his demands for Freedom did not mean democratic freedom, which he denounced as "authoritarian," since a majority imposes on a minority; hence the enlightened minority must impose its freedom-loving nostrums on the majority. It is becoming more widely understood (esp since the publ of P's Carnets, notebooks) that he had a detailed plan in mind for imposing control over all society by a very small band of "good" libertarians; overtly planned to suppress dissent against his libertarian dominion; was a pathological hater of women's rights (and women); called for the physical extermination of Jews en masse; hated trade unions and strikes so viciously that he supported government strikebreaking with guns—this only scratches the surface. (See the unrefuted—but ignored—scholarly analysis by J. S. Schapiro, in an essay in Liberalism and the challenge of fascism.) —It must be understood that contemporaries did not think of P. as an "anarchist"; this came later. M was mainly concerned with P.'s economics (as in #M681) and, second, with his social nostrums (which no one is interested in today). P.'s followers did not call themselves anarchists but "mutualists" (after the mutual-credit bank scheme); the Proudhonist tendency which for years kept the IWMA a sect in France was the staunchest opponent in the movement of any socialistic program planks, and appeared as champions of small propertyholding against strikes, unions, and the wage-worker threat to small entrepreneurs (petty-bourgeoisie). In 1871 the top leadership of the Proudhonists (*Tolain et al.) went over bodily to the Versaillese reaction against the Paris Commune, and in the subseq period Proudhonism faded out of existence. —M's gen analysis of P. (besides #M681) is best found in two long letters (virtual articles): to Annenkov (Dec 28, 1846) and to Schweitzer (Jan 24, 1865). The chief biography of P. in English is an anar-choid apologia by George Woodcock (1956). Since Schapiro did not yet know of P.'s Carnets, his analysis can be usefully supplemented by Hal Draper's report on these notebooks in New Politics (NY), winter 1969. — M's reading covered P.'s books as they came out. Besides the titles already mentioned, I should list: Gratuité du crédit (Bastiat-Proudhon debate) (1850); Idée générale de la révolution au XIXe siècle (1851); Manuel du spéculateur à la Bourse (1857). → 42:26; 43:2; 44:22; 46:1, 20, 40, 48, 49; 47:2, 6, 9, 16, 22, 24; 48:52, 75, 82; 51:37, 46, 51, 52, 56, 71; 52:4; 57:5; 65:7, 17; 69:14; 72:30; 81:33; 84:12, 33; 91:20; 92:47. #ME121; M593, M681; E196, E639.

Proudhonists Followers of the views put forward by P. J. *Proudhon. His supporters usually called themselves Mutualists (not anarchists); dominated the French section of the IWMA in its early years. → 46:44; 57:5. —Proudhonists in the IWMA: → 66:9, 26, 43, 46; 68:48, 49; 69:1, 36, 40; 70:25.

Provinciale Overijsselsche en Zwolsche Courant Zwolle (Neth.), Apr 1845+. #M835.

Prussian Assembly See Berlin Prussian Assembly.

Przedświt; Czasopismo socyjalistyczne Geneva, then London, then Cracow, 1880 to 1914 or 1918. Weekly. Ed by A. Debski. — Polish socialist organ. Official organ of the Komitet Robotniczego Partii soc.-Rew. Proletariat. → 92:11. #E578, E615.

Public Opinion London, Oct 5, 1861, to June 22, 1951. Weekly. —Liberal journal. → 71:39, 40. #M899.

Püttmann, Hermann (1811 to 1894) German pub'r and journalist, from Elberfeld; with some reputation as a Rhenish poet. In the mid-1840s he held liberal views tending to "True Socialism." He collaborated on the Kölnische Ztg (1840+); became its feuilleton editor (1842), and its editor (May 1843 till autumn) after Hermes, using some RZ writers incl Hess. He pubd the Rheinische Jahrbücher für gesellschaftlicher Reform (1845–1846), Prometheus, and the Deutsches Bürgerbuch for 1845 and 1846. In 1850 he emigrated to Australia, and died in Melbourne. → 45:9, 19.

Puggé, Eduard (1802 to 1836) German lawyer, prof of law at Bonn; disciple of Savigny. Editor of the Rheinisches Museum für Jurisprudenz (1827–1829, 1833–1835). → 35:5; 36:5.

Pulszky, Ferencz (Aurel); Ger. Franz (1814 to 1897) Hungarian politician and writer; Polish born. After the 1848 revolution, he toured England and the U.S. with Kossuth (cf. his White, red and black, 1852); contributed to the NYDT on foreign affairs, using the by-line A.P.C. (1850s). He joined the Garibaldi expedition (1862), then returned to Hungary after the 1867 amnesty. There he became a member of the Diet (1867–1876, 1884–1897); director of the National Museum. #M485, M844.

Purves, George, pseud. of Simon Gray (fl. 19th century) English writer on economics. An official in the War Office, he wrote under both names, works signed Purves being used to boost Gray's productions. His earliest, *Happiness of states* (1815), written 1804, was an attack on the Physiocrats and Adam Smith. M (1851) read *Gray versus Malthus* by "Purves" (1818). → 51:69.

Pushkin, Alexander Sergeyevich (1799 to 1837) The greatest Russian poet. Author of: *Evgeni Onegin* (1832); *Boris Godunov* (1831); *Pique Dame* (1834); *Russlan and Ludmilla* (1820); etc. → 51:49; 83:36.

Putnam's (NY) A publishing house, founded by G. P. Putnam. → 56:34. # E32.

Putnam's Monthly Magazine NY, 1853 to 1857 under this title; founded in 1853 as *Putnam's Magazine.* Monthly. → 55:1, 26, 37, 41, 49; 56:1, 8, 34, 41; #E32, E720.

Puttkamer, Elisabeth von Niece of Bismarck, on his wife's side. —It is a strange fact that although her name appears clearly in the indicated letter by M, her name is omitted from the index of all books containing this letter pubd by the Moscow publishing houses, whether in German, French, or English. → 67:14.

Pyat, Félix; *full* Aimé Félix (1810 to 1889) French publicist and writer. In the 1830s, a lawyer, journalist, writer of melodramas. In 1848–1849, a deputy; he fled after the bungled putsch of June 1849, to Switzerland, then Brussels, and, after Bonaparte's coup, to England. In London, a group of *Pyatistes* formed the group Commune Révolutionnaire, which, after the formation of the IWMA, turned itself into the London "French section," and sought to build a rival international under Pyat's aegis. He returned to France after Bonaparte's fall (1870); founded *Le Vengeur* (Feb 1871); elected to the Assembly, but resigned to become a member of the Paris Commune, where he was on the Commsn of Public Safety. After the Commune, he took refuge again in London; returned after the 1880 amnesty with a whirl of political activity in alliance with the Blanquists. —Pyat's politics were vaguely neo-Jacobin republicanism hazed over with a propensity for wild-swinging r-r-revolutionary rhetoric unrelated to real action. He was widely, but not unanimously, regarded as an unprincipled maneuverer—"sincere only in his self-idolatry" (Lissagaray). As for M, it was a toss-up between contempt and hostility. → 44:9; 50:19; 60:12; 68:37, 55. #M548.5.

Pyrenees Mts. Range along the French-Spanish border. → 71:32, 39, 43, 49, 53; 91:59.

Q

Quarck, Max (Ernst) (1860 to 1930) German Social-Democratic publicist; lawyer by profession, fired from government employ as a leftist (1886). He then edited S-D papers in Vienna and Frankfurt; Reichstag deputy (1912+); supporter of S-D right wing. He sometimes used the name Freiwald Thüringer. Author of *Die Arbeiterschutzgebung im deutschen Reich* (1886); *Die Arbeiterverbrüderung 1848/49* (1900). → 83:47.

Queenstown (Ireland) Seaport in Cork harbor, S. coast; so named 1849–1922; now Cóbh. → 88:28.

Quelch, Harry (1858 to 1913) English socialist; typesetter by trade. He came to London (1872), interested in social reform; joined the SDF early (1881); began writing for *Justice*, its organ (1884); editor (1886); full-time editor (1892+). Q. was also active in the TU movement (the "New Unionism"), incl in the dock strike of 1889; secy of the South Side Protection League. He followed Hyndman not only through the vicissitudes of the SDF but also (1911) the British SP. —Q. was a key figure in policing the SDF for Hyndman's dictatorship and enforcing its essentially sectist char-

acter on the basis of left-socialist politics; thus in 1908 it was Q. who led the opposition to the SDF's reaffiliation to the Labour party, and won. → 95:27.

Quesnay, François (1694 to 1774) French economist; founder of the Physiocrats' school. Trained in medicine, he became the king's physician (1744) and his brain trust. He devoted himself (1756+) chiefly to economic studies, along with an immediate circle including J. C. M. V. de Gournay, Nicolas Baudeau, P. P. Mercier de la Rivière, etc. His *Tableau economique* was one of the landmarks in the development of polit eco—"a very brilliant insight, indisputably the most brilliant" up to then (M). —M (1846) studied his *Le droit naturel* (1846 edn) and his "Analyse de tableau économique" as pubd in the collective volume *Physiocrates*, ed by Daire. M (1863) studied his essay "Fermiers" in the Daire volume; also studied Q. in 1860. → 46:52; 60:65; 62:30; 63:27; 77:30; 95:26. #M575.

Quételet, Adolphe; *full* Lambert Adolphe Jacques (1796 to 1874) Belgian statistician; also astronomer–director of the then new

royal observatory (1828). Supervisor of statistics for Belgium (1830+): developed census-taking techniques, and used his statistical research to formulate a theory of the "average man." M (1851) studied an English trans (1842) of his chief work, *Sur l'homme et le développement de ses facultés* (1835). →
51:68, 71.

Qui Vive! London, Oct-Dec 1871. Daily. Ed by E. *Vermersch. —French-language organ of the so-called French Section of 1871, not recognized by the GC/IWMA, and hostile

to it. Vermersch continued with his *Vermersch-Journal.* #M224.

Quintana, Manuel José (1772 to 1857) Spanish poet and man of letters, also politician; lawyer by profession. He was active in the Spanish revolution of 1808–1814, then jailed (1814–1820); during the revolution of 1820–1823, a Moderado deputy; briefly min of education. His best-known poems were patriotic odes; also wrote tragedies, and *Vidas de Españoles celebres* (1807–1834); the first Spanish laureate. #E559.

R

Raciborski, Adam (1809 to 1871) Polish physician, émigré in France after the Polish uprising of 1830–1831. → 83:8.

Rackow, Heinrich; *Angl.* Henry (d. 1916) German socialist. In Berlin, a bookdealer; member of the GGWA, dispatcher of the *Neue Social-Demokrat.* Expelled from Berlin (1878), emigrated to London, where he was a businessman; also a member of the GWEA (Com WEA). → 81:46.

Racowitza, *Count* Yanko von; *also spelled* **Rakowitza, Racowiță;** *Ger. first name* Janko (d. 1865) Roumanian (Walachian) nobleman who fatally wounded Lassalle in a duel. → 64:22.

Radetzky, Joseph (Wenzel). *Count* **Radetzky von Radetz** (1766 to 1858) Austrian gen. Rising through the army ranks (1785+), he became chief of the gen staff (1809–1812); chief of staff to Prince Schwarzenberg (1813–1815) in the war against Napoleon. After a threat of rustication, he was saved by the beginning of unrest in Italy for him to suppress: he took command of the Austrian army in Italy (1834), was created field marshal (1836), and in 1848–1849 enjoyed the triumph of defeating the national-revolutionary forces in Italy, then as governor of Lombardy-Venetia (1849–1857) keeping the Hapsburgs' heel firmly planted on the Italians. #M77; E348, E478.

Radevormwald (Ger.) Industrial city of the northern Rhineland, near Düsseldorf. → 69:31.

Radford, Ernest (William) (1857 to 1919) English socialist; lawyer by profession; his pubd writings are books of poetry. Radford was a member of the Socialist League, then active in the Hammersmith Socialist Society, with William Morris. He was acquainted with the M family through Caroline ("Dollie") Maitland, whom he married in 1883; both were close friends of Eleanor M, all active in the amateur theater group, the Dogberry Club. → 83:12.

The **Radical** London, Dec 14, 1880, to July

1882. Weekly. —Left-liberal journal. → 82:6.

Radical Clubs (London) Clubs on the left wing of the Liberals, esp in the East End. Eleanor M and Aveling campaigned among them to break them from the Liberals and form an independent workers party. → 81:20; 87:2, 5, 17, 23, 26; 88:9.

Radical party (Eng.) The more leftist wing of the Liberals, in a loose sense; not an organized political party. #M150.

Radical Party (Fr.) French left-liberal tendency; not "radical" in any socialist sense. → 86:8, 22; 93:8.

Der **Radikale** Vienna, June 16 to Oct 26, 1848. Daily. Pub'r: A. J. Becher. —Liberal-democratic and republican organ. It merged (Aug 15) with the *Österreichisch-deutsche Ztg.* #M832.

Radimský, August (1862 to 1929) Czech Social-Democrat. An editor of the Vienna *Arbeiter-Ztg* (1891–1897), he translated the *Com Manifesto* into Czech. He was also a collaborator with the Czech socialist organ in Vienna, *Dělické Listy,* which pubd the trans (before its pamphlet publ) in its issues of Jan-Apr 1893. → 93:19.

Rae, John (1845 to 1915) British economist and sociological writer. His best-known work was *Contemporary socialism* (1884), which had five edns up to 1912. Also author of *Eight hours for work* (1894) and a life of Adam Smith (1895). → 81:52, 60.

Raffles, Sir Thomas Stamford (Bingley) (1781 to 1826) English colonial official in the Far East. Starting as a clerk in India House, he became a British "empire builder" best known for establishing Singapore as satrapy of the E. India Co. Governor of Java (1811–1816); lieutenant-governor of Benkulen in Sumatra (1818–1823). Also a naturalist and ethnologist, he was the founding pres of the London Zoological Society. —M (1853) studied his *History of Java* (1817). → 53:54.

Raguet, Condy (1784 to 1842) American economist. Founder of *Free Trade Advocate* and J. of Political Economy (1829); owner of the Philadelphia Gazette (1835+). Author of The principles of free trade (1835). M (1851) studied his Treatise on currency and banking (1839). → 51:63.

Rakovsky, Christian; Bulgarian Khristian Georgievich; or Krastju Georgiev (1873 to 1941?) Bulgarian socialist, later Communist. Of Roumanian descent, he became a Roumanian citizen (1913). —He got an M.D. degree in France; joined a S-D group of Bulgarian students in Geneva (1890s); delegate to the Int'l Socialist Congress of 1893; collaborated with both Lenin's and Trotsky's organ; organized the Roumanian SP. After the 1917 Russian Revolution he was a leader of the Bolshevik party; Ukraine premier during the civil war; Soviet diplomat (1924–1927); expelled as a Trotskyist (1927), readmitted (1934), jailed in the Stalin purges; it is believed he died in prison in 1941. → 95:27.

Ramboz, Monsieur (pseud.) → 49:33.

Ramm, Hermann German Social-Democratic journalist. He became a member of the ed bd of Volksstaat (1875–1876), later of Vorwärts (1877+). → 74:36.

Ramsay, Sir George (1800 to 1871) English writer on philosophy and other subjects. He was a voluminous writer, with a number of works also on psychology (love, emotions, instinct); A disquisition on government (1837) and Political discourses (1838); but it seems to be agreed that he produced nothing of special significance. In economics, he pubd his Essay on the distribution of wealth (1836), which was studied by M (1851). It highlighted the distinction between interest and profit, and is said to have sniffed on the track of M's distinction between constant and variable capital. → 51:66.

Ramsgate (Eng.) Port and resort on the N. Sea coast above Dover. → 58:37; 62:44; 64:21, 29; 68:45; 70:46; 71:50; 72:40; 73:39, 42; 74:18, 30; 75:30; 76:13, 17, 23, 25; 77:29; 79:31, 33, 35–37; 80:27, 28, 35. #M418.

Randall, F. B. #ME33.

Ranke, Johannes (1836 to 1916) German physiologist and anthropologist; prof at Munich (1889+), also museum curator. His chief work was Grundzüge der Physiologie des Menschen (1868), which was what M prob read in 1876. Also author of Der Mensch (1887). → 76:9.

Ranke, Leopold von (1795 to 1886) German historian; prof at Berlin (1825 to 1871) He was a leader and pioneer in scholarly historiography based on a conservative, antidemocratic ideology which viewed monarchism and the Prussian state as manifestations of the Divine Will. —M (1843) studied his Deutsche Geschichte im Zeitalter der Refor-

mation, Bd. 2 (1839–1840); also the periodical Historisch-politische Zeitschrift which he edited (1832–1836), Bd. 1. If M (1854) read him on Slavic history, this may refer to his Die serbische Revolution (1829, later expanded), or to his treatments of relations with East Europe in his many books on German history. → 43:32; 54:52.

Rappoport, Charles (Léon) (1865 to 1941) Russian-born socialist active in France. Orig a Narodnik, he was a student in Bern (to 1887); active in Berlin (to 1895); moved to Paris; became a French citizen (1899), active esp as a leftwinger, Marxist writer, member (to 1905) of the Fédération des Socialistes Révolutionnaires; thereafter, of the united SP. In World War I he supported the minority opposed to Union Sacrée; then supported the Bolshevik revolution, joined the CP (1920) and was an Exec member till 1922; quit the CP in 1938 and joined the SP. —He pubd a long list of writings, many of them pamphlets; among his books were La philosophie de l'histoire comme science de l'évolution (1903); La révolution mondiale (1921). → 93:46.

Rasch, Gustav (Heinrich) (1825 to 1878) German socialistic publicist; lawyer by profession. After taking part in the 1848–1849 revolution in Berlin, he emigrated to Switzerland and France. After 1870 he was a member of the Eisenacher SDWP and (1875+) of the united S-D party. —Following his Zwölf Streiter book (see Chron. ref), he pubd a number of books about various countries of Europe. → 67:24.

La **Rassegna** Agraria, Industriale, Commerciale, Letteraria, Politica, Artistica. For short, La Rassegna [The review] Naples, 1892+. Semiweekly. → 95:7.

Rastatt (Ger.) City in the former state of Baden, near Karlsruhe. → 49:30.

Raumer, Friedrich von; full Friedrich Ludwig Georg (1781 to 1873) German historian. Prof at Breslau and Berlin; a liberal. In 1848, a deputy to the Frankfurt National Assembly (right center), he became the Reich ambassador to Paris. M's article concerns R. in this post, when R. announced his agreement with the recent statement issued by Berlin and Halle professors expressing their "servile" abasement before the government (so described in #ME67). #M371.

Ravé, Henri French (Alsatian-born) journalist. He translated writings by E into French, in particular #E573, also Bebel's Woman and socialism. → 91:18, 24.

Raveaux, Franz (1810 to 1851)' German radical Democrat, of French descent; tobacco dealer in Cologne. He took part in the Belgian revolution of 1830 and the Carlist war of 1834–1836. From the early 1840s (at least

1844) he was active in the Cologne Democratic movement as a leading figure; not a communist, though he collaborated with the Cologne communists. In the 1848 revolution he was a member of the Frankfurt National Assembly; ambassador of the imperial government to Switzerland; in 1849, member of the Baden provisional government that was born of the South German uprising; after its defeat, he emigrated to Switzerland, then to Belgium. #E652.

Ravenstone, Piercy (d. c.1830) English writer on economics. Basing himself on Ricardo, like the "Ricardian socialists," he was sympathetic to the aspirations of smallholders and artisans. He pubd two works: *A few doubts as to the correctness of some opinions generally entertained on the subjects of population and polit eco* (1821), hostile to Malthus; and *Thoughts on the funding system and its effects* (1824), which M studied in his 1851 notebook and analyzed in #M877. —Since no personal info about him is known, there is speculation that the name was merely a pseudonym. → 51:66.

Razin, Stenka; *properly* Stepan Timofeyevich (d. 1671) Russian Cossack, leader of the propertyless Cossacks of the Don region. In 1666 he took the head of a popular Cossack army combining serfs and peasants of the Volga region with elements of brigandage; in 1670 he led an open rebellion against the czarist government (the greatest peasant uprising in Russia in the 17th century) with the aim of establishing a Cossack republic based on equality. After initial victories, defeated by the czarist troops, he fled to the Don, and was betrayed to the government by the propertied Cossacks; tortured; executed in Moscow; thereafter celebrated in song and story. → 77:48; 79:51.

Das Recht auf Arbeit Munich, 1884 to 1891. Weekly. #E537.

Reclus, Elie; *properly* Jean Pierre Michel, *called* Elie (1827 to 1904) French ethnologist and anarchist publicist. He and his brother Elisée (see next), sons of a Protestant pastor, were trained for the ministry, but soon quit. Elie became a Fourierist; after the Bonaparte coup of 1851, fled to London; returned to France (1855) and lived as a writer. He took part in founding a People's Bank (1863); editor of *L'Association*, co-op organ (1864), and other left publications in this decade; joined Bakunin's Alliance (1865) with Elisée. During the Paris Commune he was named director of the Bibliothèque Nationale; afterward, took refuge in Italy, Zurich, London; except for some left journalism, not very active politically. After the Université Libre de Bruxelles opened (1894), he gave courses in ethnography and origins of religion. Author of: *Les primitifs* (1885) in collaboration with his brother Elisée; *La Commune au jour le jour.* → 62:62; 64:35.

Reclus, Elisée; *full* Jean Jacques Elisée (1830 to 1905) French geographer and anarchist theoretician; the more important of the two Reclus brothers; *see* Elie R. for family background. He studied geography under Ritter (Berlin); then law in Paris; turned to anarchism by 1851. After Bonaparte's coup, he traveled in Europe extensively; returned to France (1857); active in the co-op movement, and worked for the co-op organ *L'Association* (1864+). In 1868 he joined Bakunin's faction in the Bern Peace Congress, then Bakunin's Alliance for boring from within the IWMA. Captured in 1870, he spent the Paris Commune period a prisoner. Afterward, in exile in Switzerland, he worked in the Jura Federation with his friend J. *Guillaume, and contributed to the Bakuninist press. He returned to France (1890); then (1894) to Brussels, at the Université Libre. —His high reputation as a geographic scholar was independent of his anarchist career. Beginning in the 1870s in Swiss exile, he began producing his multivolume work *La nouvelle géographie universelle* (1876–1894); also *La terre* (1868–1869). Political writings include *Evolution et révolution* (1860); *L'Evolution, la révolution et l'idéal anarchique* (1897). In 1882 he launched an "Anti-Marriage Movement." → 68:23; 69:42, 49.

Red Catechism A manifesto written (1849 or 1850) by Moses *Hess, "Rother Katechismus für das deutsche Volk." M not only had nothing to do with it, but did not even know its author. → 52:39, 45.

Red Republican London, June 22 to Nov 30, 1850. Weekly. Pub'r/editor: G. J. Harney. —Left Chartist organ; pubd articles by M's associates, also the first trans of the *Com Manifesto.* Superseded by (name changed to) *The Friend of the People.* → 50:40; 51:16. #ME33.

Reden, Baron Friedrich Wilhelm (Otto Ludwig) von (1804 to 1857) German statistician. In the 1848–1849 revolution he was a member of the Frankfurt assembly's left wing. M (1850) read his *Vergleichende Kultur-Statistik der Gebiets- und Bevölkerungsverhältnisse der Gross-Staaten Europas* (1848). He later pubd many more books on international statistics. → 50:50.

Redgrave, Alexander (1818 to 1894) English factory inspector, until 1878. His reports *The factory and workshop act, 1878* (1878) and *Textile factories . . .* (1879) were highly regarded. → 79:53.

Reeves, William Dobson (c.1827 to 1907)

English pub'r and bookdealer. → *87*:46; *89*:6.

Die **Reform** Hamburg, 1848 to 1892. Daily. —Liberal paper. → *59*:65; *60*:20. #M592, M631, M651, M784, M852, M863, M974, M983, M985; E252, E798.

Die **Reform** NY, Mar 5, 1853, to Apr 26, 1854. Weekly, then semiweekly, then (Oct 1853+) daily. Ed by G. T. Kellner. —Organ of the Amerikanische Arbeiterbund. Weydemeyer was an editor; it reprinted M–E articles from the *NYDT*; pubd contributions by Cluss (often written with M's help). It turned right, under Kellner's pressure, shortly before expiring. → *53*:1, 14, 24, 42, 45; *54*:21, 25.

Reform Club (London) → *70*:3.

Reformation The movement of religious-nationalist rebellion in 16th-century Europe leading to the separation of Protestantism from the Catholic church, led by Luther (Ger.), Zwingli (Switz.), Calvin (Fr. and Switz.), Knox (Scot.). → *85*:21.

La **Réforme** Paris, July 29, 1843, to Jan 11, 1850. Daily. Founder: Ledru-Rollin. Ed by F. Flocon et al. —In the pre-1848 period this paper represented the left wing of the liberal-radical opposition, together with a number of Louis Blanc–type socialists. E contributed from autumn 1847 to spring 1848. → *47*:5, 42, 49, 54, 57; *48*:5, 6, 19–22; *49*:44. #M633, M650, M730, M820, M833, M892, M895; E8, E20, E136–E140, E148, E151, E656, E659, E723, E746, E768, E771.

La **Réforme Sociale** Brussels. —This weekly, planned by Glaser de Willebrord, did not come into being. —*Note:* There were other publications of this name, in France. → *75*:13.

Regis, Vitale; *pseud.* Etienne Péchard Italian leftist. He took part in the Paris Commune; in London emigration, he was a member of the IWMA's Sezione Operaia Italiana and of the IWMA/GC (1871–1872). He traveled to Italy and Switzerland as a GC emissary (early 1872), and took part in the Spanish revolutionary events of 1873. → *71*:62; *72*:10, 15.

Regnaud Presumably a French émigré or Communard refugee in London. The entry "Regnaud (London)" is from M's notebook listing persons receiving copies of the French edn of *Capital*. Maitron's *DBMOF* lists no one of this name in the appropriate volume, and no likely candidate with the name Regnault. → *75*:48.

Regnault, Elias; *full* Elias Georges Soulange Oliva (1801 to 1868) French history writer and publicist; lawyer by profession. After the 1848 revolution he became head of a bureau in the Interior Ministry, then the Finance Ministry; after which he returned to his writing. He produced a number of popular

histories—of Ireland (1846), of England (1846), etc. M (1857 and in 1859–1862 notebooks) studied his *Histoire politique et sociale de principautés danubiennes* (1855). M (1865) read his *La question européenne* (1863). → *57*:6; *65*:39.

Reichensperger [I], August (1808 to 1895) German lawyer and judiciary official; liberal monarchist Catholic politician. In 1848–1849, deputy to the Prussian National Assembly and Frankfurt Assembly (right wing); pres of the Rhineland court of justice, in Cologne and Trier; named (1849) appellate judge, Cologne. Later he was a founder/leader of the Catholic group in the Reichstag and the Center party; also pubd works on art and architecture. — *Note:* The [I] in his name was sometimes added to distinguish him from another Reichsperger [II], for whom see *MECW* 7 Index. #ME128.

Reichhelm German émigré in NY; co-owner of the *New Yorker Staatszeitung;* his name comes from M's letters, which make clear that R. is a political acquaintance. Possibly this is the Julius Reichhelm who in 1848–1849 was an active member of the Cologne movement, working closely with the NRZ group. → *51*:35.

Reichstag Lower chamber of the parliament of Germany (1871–1945). → *71*:16, 22; *72*:44; *73*:8; *74*:5; *76*:4; *77*:2, 6; *78*:32, 37; *79*:41; *82*:4; *83*:5, 32; *84*:27, 37, 49, 52; *85*:43; *86*:3, 16, 17; *87*:10; *88*:7; *90*:7, 10; *91*:11; *92*:66; *93*:7, 29; *94*:18; *95*:3. #M179; E645. *See also* Social-Democratic Party (Germany), Reichstag Fraction, North German Reichstag.

Reid, Robert British journalist. A correspondent of British and American papers in Paris in 1871, he sympathized with the Commune. → *71*:28, 33, 39.

Reiff, Wilhelm Joseph (b. c.1824) German radical. In the 1848–1849 revolution, a member of the CL, active in the Cologne WA. In emigration, secy of the GWEA (London); in 1850, expelled from the CL (*see* M to E, May 8, 1860) but nevertheless arraigned in the Cologne Communist trial and sentenced to five years. → *49*:6.

Reimarus, Hermann Samuel (1694 to 1768) German theologian and *philosophe* of the Enlightenment. Prof at Hamburg; he developed a deist-rationalist view of a "natural" religion, hostile to revealed religion, viewing primitive Christianity as a communistic rebellion. → *37*:8.

Reinhardt, Richard (1829 to 1898) German poet; émigré in Paris; Heine's secy during 1849–1855. R. carried on much correspondence with M, with Heine's knowledge and approval, and was personally friendly with the M family. In the 1850s M regarded him as one of the best of his "party" (tendency) on the continent. During the Paris Commune he provided M with information. → 49:29, 44; 51:33, 48, 55; 52:7, 27, 41; 56:11, 33, 36; 62:35; 71:6, 23.

Reitbahn (Cologne) → 48:60.

Reitemeier, Johann Friedrich (1755 to 1839) German legal scholar and historian. In his last decades he was harassed by the conservative authorities because of his views. M (1850) read his *Geschichte des Bergbaues und Hüttenwesens bey den alten Völkern* (1785); M (1879) studied his *Geschichte und Zustand der Sklaverey und Leibeigenschaft in Griechenland* (1789). Also author of *Encyclopädie und Geschichte der Rechte in Deutschland* (1785). → 50:50; 79:53.

Rempel, Rudolph (1815 to 1868) German businessman in Bielefeld; a radical sympathetic with M's activities. In the mid-1840s, a "True Socialist"; in 1846 M hoped (vainly) he would ensure the publ of the *German ideology*. In 1848 he was active in the Demo Assoc in Bielefeld and nationally; in 1849 joined the CL. In 1850, still in Bielefeld, he contributed to the S-D Refugee Aid Comm of London; editor of *Der Volksfreund* (1848–1850). Later, a Progressist in Germany. → 49:21.

Renan, Ernest; *full* Joseph Ernest (1823 to 1892) French historian. He renounced the priesthood to study religion as history; became a leading scholar in Semitic studies; prof of Hebrew (1862+). His best-known work, *Vie de Jésus* (1863)—which M studied in early 1864—was one of a series on the *Histoire des origines du Christianisme* (8 vols.). —Political views: antidemocratic and antisocialist. → 64:5; 92:42.

Renard, Joseph Engelbert (1802 to 1863) German bookdealer/pub'r in Cologne. He acted as the legally responsible editor-pub'r of the RZ in 1842–1843. #M456.

Die Republik der Arbeiter NY, 1850 to Apr 1855. Monthly, then weekly. Pub'r/editor: W. Weitling. → 51:15; 54:21.

Reshid Pasha, Mustafa Mehmet (1802 to 1858) Turkish government leader. He was grand vizier in 1837–1838 and from 1846 to the early part of the Crimean War; foreign min at various times. #M750.

Reuters (press agency) → 91:56.

Revelation, Book of (Bible) → 83:31, 35. #E93.

Revista Socială Iaşi (Jassy) (Roumania), 1884 to 1887. Ed by I. Nădejde, C. Dobrogeanu-Gherea. —Socialist organ. → 87:13.

La Revolución Social Palma (Spain), 1871 (3 issues). —Replacing *L'Obrero*, which had been banned, this was likewise. → 71:3.

Die Revolution NY, Jan 6, 13, 1852 (2 nos. only); then May, June 1852 (2 more nos., irreg. periodicity). Pub'r/editor: J. Weydemeyer. — Weydemeyer orig planned it as a weekly. The

May 1852 issue contained M's *18th Brumaire* (#M267). → 51:56; 52:4, 7, 9, 12, 18, 22. #ME136; M267; E241.

Revolutionäre Zentralisation A radical group of German émigrés centered in Switzerland in 1850. → 50:15, 19, 25, 30.

La Revue des Deux Mondes Paris, 1831 to 1944; preceded (1829–1830) by a run under the same name. Semimonthly. Founder: F. Buloz. —Prestigious literary-political magazine. → 51:71; 76:32.

La Revue Socialiste Lyons, Jan 20 to Sep 5, 1880; Paris, 1885 to 1914. Monthly. Founder/editor: B. Malon; then G. Renard (1894–1898); later J. Jaurès et al. —Reformsocialist organ; later oriented toward tradeunionism. → 80:8, 13, 16; 90:49. #M994; E759.

Rey, Joseph Louis (1779 to 1820) French writer on economics. —M (1878) read his work *Des erreurs de la Banque de France* (1866). He also pubd a work on government policy on banks and credit, *Réponses aux 42 questions . . .* (1865). → 78:51.

Reynolds, George William MacArthur (1814 to 1879) English socialist journalist and reformer. Son of a naval officer, at first a military cadet, he turned to literature (novelwriting, criticism) by 1835; editor of the *London J.* (c.1846). In 1846 he launched *Reynolds's Miscellany*, which lasted 23 years. From 1848 he supported the Chartists; then moved to acceptance of socialism; supported Bronterre O'Brien, esp against E. Jones; helped found the National Reform League. Afterward he devoted himself entirely to journalism. In 1850 he launched *Reynolds's Weekly Newspaper* (preceded by *Reynolds's Political Instructor*). Its long career as a very popular socialistic organ was his main interest; his own novels and plays were usually first pubd serially; he did not write any political works of significance. → 58:8.

Reynolds's Newspaper London, 1850+; founded as *Reynolds's Weekly Newspaper*. Weekly. Pub'r: G. W. M. Reynolds. —Supported the Chartists; defended the Paris Commune; socialistic in outlook; later an organ esp of the cooperative movement. #M5, M834.

Rheims; *now usually* Reims (Fr.) City, N.E. of Paris → 81:57.

Rhein- und Mosell-Zeitung Coblenz (Ger.), 1831 to 1850. Daily. —Catholic paper. #M124, M233, M781, M782, M866, M957.

Rheinau (Ger.) Suburb of *Mannheim. → 75:40.

Rheinische Jahrbücher zur gesellschaftlichen Reform Darmstadt, Aug 1845; BelleVue (near Constanz), end of 1846—only these two vols. pubd. Pub'r/editor: H. Püttmann.

—Generally "True Socialist" in tendency; contained contributions by E. → 45:9, 19, 34; 46:4. #E277, E770.

Rheinische Zeitung für Politik, Handel und Gewerbe. [Rhenish Gazette for politics, commerce and business] Cologne, Jan 1, 1842, to Mar 31, 1843. Daily. Ed by G. Höfken; Rutenberg; then (Oct 15, 1842, to Mar 17, 1843) Marx. —Founded by a group of liberal Rhineland business and professional men (Camphausen, Mevissen, D. Oppenheim et al.); turned to the left wing of the Democracy under M's editorship; banned by the Prussian government. → 41:16; 42:1, 2, 4, 11, 12, 14, 15, 18, 20–23, 25–27, 29, 30, 32, 33, 36; 43:1, 4–6, 8, 9, 14; 44:9; 51:11; 95:25, 29. #M38, M41, M64, M65, M72, M123, M124, M165, M166, M187, M188, M216–M218, M233, M249, M265, M265C, M352, M431, M448, M456, M473, M477, M507, M541, M585, M594, M601, M667–M669, M687, M722, M731, M741, M742, M781, M782, M866, M869, M957, M965; E77, E132, E170, E186, E224, E237, E247, E379, E453, E467, E526, E549, E577.5, E591, E597, E703.

Rheinische Zeitung Cologne, 1892 to 1933 under this title; previously *Kölner Arbeiterzeitung* (1888+). Ed by Karl Hirsch (1894–1895). —Organ of the S-D party for the Upper Rhine province. → 95:29.

Rheinische Zeitung Düsseldorf (till 1866), Cologne, 1863 to 1874. Daily. —Unlike the other *RZ's*, a bourgeois paper. → 67:12, 38. #M688; E695.

Rheinischer Beobachter Cologne, 1844 to beginning of 1848. Daily. —Conservative; subsidized by the Prussian government. #M167.

Rheinländer, Georg Friedrich Orig a member of the League of Outcasts (Paris, mid-1830s), he was, after the 1848–1849 revolution, an émigré in London; businessman (by 1860); very friendly relations with M. In 1861 he joined the London organization of the German Nationalverein by agreement with M, and kept M informed about the liberals' doings; fades out of M's correspondence by the end of 1862. → 60:12, 20.

Rhenish Diet See Rhineland Diet.

Rhenish government See Rhineland.

Rhine River; Ger. Rhein → 38:8; 62:51; 69:56. #E587, E725.

Rhineland (Ger.) Here used to denote the region roughly equivalent to the former Rhine Province. → 42:22; 44:35; 48:51, 53; 49:24; 50:5; 53:31, 45; 56:6, 14; 64:17. #ME109; M40, M47–M49, M456, M687; E632, E702, E703, E925.

Rhineland Diet [legislative assembly] → 42:11, 14, 17, 26. #M216–M218, M477.

Ribbentrop, Adolph Prussian court official in Trier and Saarbrücken; émigré in Paris

(1837+). In 1847 he asked the king for permission to return. → 44:9.

Ricardian socialists Writers who drew socialistic (that is, anticapitalist) conclusions from Ricardo's polit eco; preeminently William *Thompson, also *Bray, *Gray, *Hodgskin, et al. → 45:31; 81:33; 86:45.

Ricardo, David (1772 to 1823) British political economist; in M's view, greatest master of classical economics. Born of a Dutch-Jewish family (converted to Anglicanism at age 21), he made a fortune as a stockbroker before turning 30; retired from business and, as a landed gentleman, devoted himself to study and writing, except for a late stint as MP (1819–1823). His first notable writings were: a polemical tract *The high price of bullion*... (1809–1810); *Reply to Mr. Bosanquet's practical observations* (1811); *On protection to agriculture* (1822); and an anti-Malthus polemic *An essay on the influence of a low price of corn on the profits of stock* (1815)—all read by M (1851). His chief work was *[On the] Principles of political economy and taxation* (1817), which M (1844) first studied in a French version of 1835 (MEGA I, 3), later in great detail in English. —Even more than Adam Smith, R. provided the basis for M's work by establishing much of the conceptual framework and the problems which M started with; if in basic respects M departed from R.'s analyses and conclusions, it is still true that they provided his point of departure. M had immense admiration for R. as a scientific thinker who aimed at "reaching a consistent and comprehensive theoretical view of the abstract, general foundations of the bourgeois system" (#M877:1). R. was the last great representative of "the period in which the class struggle was as yet undeveloped." Unlike his epigones, he "consciously makes the antagonism of class interests, of wages and profits, of profits and rent, the starting point of his investigations, naively taking this antagonism for a social law of nature" (#M130). Bourgeois polit eco could not go beyond this. What R. did was establish that "The basis, the starting point for the physiology of the bourgeois system ... is the determination of *value by labor time.*" This, together with his follow-up, was his "great historical significance for science." M then emphasizes that Carey consequently denounced R. as the father of communism, the progenitor of class hostilities (#M877:2). — In fact, though R. himself never evinced even ordinary liberal prolabor sympathies, he was followed, before M, by a number of socialists who drew anticapitalist conclusions from his economic theory; see preceding entry, *Ricardian socialists. Indeed, today a new investigation of R.'s analyses by Piero Sraffa (editor of R.'s *Works and Correspondence*, 1951) has given rise to a new cross-fertilization of Marxism and a neo-Ricardianism, in a movement to strengthen the scientific foundations of the labor theory of value. → 43:2; 44:48; 50:47, 51; 51:7, 12, 17, 22, 63, 64, 67; 62:30, 40, 50; 72:68; 73:16. #M361, M575, M580–M583.

Richard, Albert (Marie) (1846 to 1918 or 1925) French radical publicist. Leading activist in the Lyons IWMA; joined the Bakuninist faction (1868). But in the 1870 Lyons uprising he acted as a moderate; during the 1871 events in Lyons and Paris he acted as peacemaker with the government rather than as a revolutionary participant; but fled to England. Then, with G. Blanc, he adopted Bonaparte as revolutionary savior to replace Bakunin; pubd a pamphlet *L'Empire et la France nouvelle* (1872), denounced by his ex-friends; also another Bonapartist manifesto (1873). Later he claimed return to socialist views (reformist); came out in support of a Boulanger dictatorship; became a leading figure in the *Allemane group (1880s–1890s), his writings still imbued with antipolitical "libertarianism." In 1901 he edited a paper on behalf of a Radical who needed socialist votes; opposed the socialist unification of 1905; and by 1907 was again attacking all socialists in sight. In 1917–1918 he was violently opposed to the Russian Revolution. → 70:10, 18; 72:8.

Richmond (Eng.) Suburban area, W.S.W. of London, now part of Greater London. → 92:6.

Richter, Eugen (1838 to 1906) German liberal politician. In N. German Reichstag (1867+); German Reichstag (1871+); Progressivist and, later, Liberal leader; then leader of the People's party. Opponent of Bismarck and his state-socialistic measures; supporter of free trade ("Manchesterism"); antisocialist; inside his own movement, a thorough authoritarian. Founder/editor of the *Freisinnige Ztg* (1885). Author of an attack on the S-D party, *Sozialdemokratische Zukunftsbilder* (1891), which Mehring answered with *Herrn Eugen Richters Bilder aus der Gegenwart* (1892). → 92:18.

Riedel, Richard (1804 to 1878) German émigré worker in Brussels, in M's pre-1848 circle. Member of the WA and Demo Assoc; member of the Exec of the WA; treasurer of the Demo Assoc (this last according to Bertrand). —Note: The life dates above are given only by Somerhausen, who is not always accurate. → 47:28.

Rienzi, Cola di; *also* **Rienzo;** *real name* Niccolo **Gabrini** (1313 to 1354) Italian political leader. Son of a tavernkeeper, he made himself the "tribune" of the people of Rome;

in 1347, led a revolt against the autocratic government and emerged as a popular dictator. But his arbitrary conduct and expansionist ambitions alienated the people and the papacy; he was expelled from Rome (1348); returned (1354) and reassumed power; murdered in a riot. —He was the hero of an opera by Wagner and a novel by Bulwer-Lytton; E's libretto does not present him as its hero. → 40:18; 41:3. #E149.

La **Riforma** Lucca (It.), Nov 1847 to beginning of 1850. —Left-democratic paper. #E920.

Riley, William Harrison (b. 1835) English journalist. Orig a clothing worker in Manchester, he spent a few years in America; came to London in 1871; launched the *International Herald* (Mar 1872 to Oct 1873) first as a fortnightly, then as a weekly organ of the British section of IWMA. Member of the British Federal Council (1872–1873). But after R. failed in founding an Owen-type colony, the paper collapsed; R. moved to Sheffield, pubd *The Socialist*. In the IWMA and its British section, R. supported the GC against the reformist group led by Hales, even after the Hague Congress (after some wavering). His views were mainly O'Brienite-Chartist, not definitely socialist, but influenced in policy by M. After 1873 he did not participate in the working-class movement. —Author of pamphlets (1873): *Strikes, their cause and remedy;* and *British slavery . . .* → 72:8, 66; 73:24.

Rimini (It.) Adriatic seaport, in Emilia. → 72:42. #E809.

Rings, L. W. German communist émigré in London in the early 1850s; member of the CL, supporter of M. In the Cologne Communist trial of 1852, the forged CL minutes were allegedly written in his and Liebknecht's handwriting. —In 1844–1845 there was a "Rings" active in the Cologne workers' movement; perhaps the same. → 51:1.

Rio de Janeiro (Brazil) → 74:23.

Ripley, George (1802 to 1880) American journalist and literary critic. Orig a Unitarian clergyman of the Boston Transcendental group (who developed Swedenborgian views), he was a founder of Brook Farm (1841) with his first wife, Sophia W. (Dana) Ripley. Converted to Fourierism by Brisbane, he was pres of the American Fourierist congress (1844); editor of *The Harbinger* with C. A. Dana (1845–1849); became literary critic of the *NYDT* under Dana's editorship (1849–1880); a founder and literary editor of *Harper's* (1850); editor of the *NAC* with Dana (1858–1863). → 57:14.

Ripley, Roswell Sabine (1823 to 1887) American army officer (brigadier-gen., 1861+); fought in the war with Mexico (1846–1848). As a military writer, his chief work was *The war with Mexico* (1849). → 54:48.

La **Riscossa Socialista** Palermo (Sicily), 1894 to 1895. Weekly. —Pubd by the Sicilian Socialist party; ed by M. Colnago. —The preceding info comes from *MEW*, which, however, gives its name sometimes as simply *La Riscossa*; other info lacking. → 94:36. #E346.

Rissé, Joseph (b. 1843) German singer, in Hanover; authored *Franz Schubert und seine Lieder* (1872–1873). *MEW* 32 Index asserts that he pubd his collection of Irish folk songs in 1870, but NUC et al. do not list it. → 70:41. #E528.

Ritter, Karl (1779 to 1859) German geographer; prof at Berlin (1820+). A founder of modern scientific geography, he wrote on relations between geography and history; deeply religious viewpoint. Major work: *Die Erdkunde im Verhältnis zur Natur und zur Geschichte des Menschen* (1817–1818). → 38:7.

Robert, Fritz   Swiss teacher, from La Chaux-de-Fonds. A follower of Bakunin, he was a delegate to the IWMA congresses of 1868–1869; on the ed bd of the Bakuninist weekly *Solidarité* (Neuchâtel-Geneva, 1871). → 69:54.

Robespierre, Maximilien de; *full* Maximilien François Marie Isidore (1758 to 1794) Leader of the Jacobins (the "Mountain") in the Great French Revolution; in 1793–1794, head of the revolutionary government. Overthrown on the 9th Thermidor (July 27, 1794); guillotined. → 50:15.

Robin, Paul; *full* Paul Charles Louis Jean (1837 to 1912) French Bakuninist. A schoolteacher, he first joined the IWMA in Brussels; as secy of the Belgian Federal Council (1869) he signed a pro-Bakunin statement. In 1870 he moved to Geneva where he joined Bakunin in his Alliance work of boring the IWMA from within; then to Paris, finally to London. In London he was given financial help by M, and became a member of the GC, not despite but because of his known Bakuninism, and was expected to present Bakunin's cause in the open. But Robin compromised himself at the London Conference of 1871 in a series of acts; refused to take part in discussing the Alliance after demanding it be taken up; failed to show up at a hearing called on his charges, etc.; expelled for "discreditable conduct." Subseqly he became a teacher at a British military school and the U. of London; wrote for the Bakuninist press. He returned to France after the 1880 amnesty: orphanage director; editor of an education journal; founded the Ligue de Régéneration Humaine (1896+), advocating neo-Malthusianism. → 70:25, 55; 71:33, 35, 47, 48.

Robinson   The name "Robinson (London)" appears on M's list of people to whom he sent

the French edn of *Capital*; not identified. Perhaps this is the A. F. Robinson to whom E was writing in May 1889. → 75:48.

Rochat, Charles (Michel) (b. 1844) French radical, active in the IWMA; commercial employee. His activity began in 1869; became a member of the Paris Federal Council (1870); active also in republican clubs. During the Paris Commune he was an artillery captain, and secy to the Exec Commsn. A refugee in London, he joined the GC (1871–1872); at the London Conference, was its French secy; GC's corr secy for Holland (1871–1872); opponent of Bakuninism. Unable to find a job in England, he moved to Belgium, worked in a factory, and continued to take part in the labor movement. → 71:35; 72:21, 54.

Rodbertus, Johann Karl; *also* Rodbertus-Jagetzow (1805 to 1875) Prussian economist and landowner. In the 1848 revolution he was a deputy in the Prussian National Assembly, and briefly entered the cabinet. As an economist, he developed a type of promonarchist state-socialism-from-above (antidemocratic, anti–class-struggle, anti–S-D) embodied in his work, *Sociale Briefe an von Kirchmann* (1850–1851); M borrowed this book from Lassalle (1861) and wrote him about it (June 16, 1862). Lassalle corresponded with R. and felt an affinity for his "socialism." About 1884 a drive began by a wing of the German Social-Democracy, led by Carl A. Schramm, to substitute this Junker-conservative state-socialist for M as the theoretician of the movement; the rise of Katheder-socialism also added to R's reputation. E wrote two analyses of the once-popular charge that M had plagiarized from R. —*Note:* R. started using the hyphenated Rodbertus-Jagetzow after buying his estate at Jagetzow in Pomerania (1836). → 61:17; 62:29, 30; 84:13, 33, 40, 47, 53; 85:4, 18, 23, 29; 86:3. #E608.

Rodenback, Charles; *pseud.* Monterossi Dutch left journalist. *KMC* (which makes more than one error on his name) says, "French, later Dutch, journalist." A leading member of the Hague IWMA; editor of *De Vrijheid* (The Hague); former editor of *Toekomst*; correspondent for *Le Rappel* (Paris) and *De Werker* (Antwerp). —His name is also found spelled Rodenbach. → 71:18.

Rodenberg, Julius (1831 to 1914) German man of letters and publicist. Orig name: Isaak Levy; brother of Bertha *Markheim, née Levy. Author of novels, poetry, travel sketches; editor of *Der Salon* (Berlin) founder/editor of the *Deutsche Rundschau* (1874+). → 54:27.

Roebuck, John Arthur (1801 to 1879) English politician; b. Madras, educated in Canada; came to England 1824. Lawyer; Radical MP (1832+ and 1849–1879). In 1855 he carried a motion to investigate the conduct of the Crimean War; chaired a commsn of inquiry on the state of the army. #ME91, ME395, ME470.

Röser (or **Roeser**), Peter Gerhard (1814 to 1865) German worker (cigarmaker) from Cologne. In the 1848–1849 revolution he was vice-pres, then pres, of the Cologne WA, and pub'r of its organ. In 1850 he was vice-pres of the cigarmakers' union; joined the CL, and became a member of its CC. In 1852 he was one of the defendants in the Cologne Communist trial; sentenced to six years. He broke in prison (end of 1853) and told the police everything he could about the CL. In 1865 he joined the Lassalleans and became a furious opponent of M. → 48:71; 49:6, 11; 50:5, 7, 22, 34, 40; 57:48. #ME2.

Roesgen von Floss, Philipp von   Dutch journalist, socialist; engineering worker by trade. He contributed to the monthly De Rotterdamse Lantaarn (1868–1869); worked on the staff of Het Volk (Rotterdam) in 1870. —Note: A periodical reference work gives his name as Ph. Roesgen van Floss. → 70:17.

Rösing, Johannes (b. 1791) German businessman, in Bremen. Active as a radicaldemocrat (1830s–1840s); led the Demo Assoc in Bremen (1848–1849). → 49:20.

Rössler, Constantin (1820 to 1896)   German political publicist. An editor of the Leipzig Grenzboten (1848); prof of philosophy at Jena (1857–1860); then free-lance journalist. He was long the director (1877–1892) of the semiofficial Bismarckian press agency, the Literary Bureau; then legation counsellor in the Foreign Office (1892–1894). A strong supporter of Bismarck, he fell out with him in his last years over abandonment of the Kulturkampf. Chief academic work: Allgemeine Staatslehre (1857). M (1863) read his Sendschreiben an den "Politiker der Zukunft vom preussischen Standpunkte" (1858). → 63:12.

Rogers, Thorold; full James Edwin Thorold (1823 to 1890)   English economic historian. Prof at King's College, London (1859–1890). Left Liberal MP (1880+); he supported free trade, cooperatives, and Gladstone on Irish home rule. Chief work: History of agriculture and prices (1866–1902); also Six centuries of work and wages (1884); The economic interpretation of history (1888); Industrial history of England (1892). → 67:5; 92:4, 47.

Roland, Madame, i.e., Jeanne Manon Roland, née **Phlipon** (1754 to 1793) French political organizer. A leader of the Girondists in the French Revolution; her husband, Jean Marie Roland de La Platière (1734–1793), was the most influential leader of this tendency. Her Paris salon was Girondist headquarters (1791–1793); guillotined. M (1844) read her Appel à l'impartiale postérité par la citoyenne Roland (1794). → 43:33.

La **Roma del Popolo**   Rome, Feb 9, 1871, to Mar 21, 1872. Weekly. —Organ of left Mazzinists; hostile to the IWMA and the Paris Commune. → 71:63. #E829.

Rome, ancient → 55:6; 57:26; 61:13; 79:52, 54; #M251; E542.

Rome, modern (It.) → 49:9; 71:56, 64; 72:3, 41, 42; 91:12, 15; 92:17. #ME116.

Ronna, Antoine (1830 to 1902) Italian engineer and agronomist; London-born. Prof of industrial chemistry in France. Author of Les industries agricoles (1869). M (1880) read his Essai sur l'agriculture des Etats-Unis d'Amérique (1880). → 80:51.

Roscher, Wilhelm; full Wilhelm Georg Friedrich (1817 to 1894) German economist; a founder of the older "historical school" of polit eco in Germany. Chief work: System der Volkswirthschaft (5 vols., 1854–1894), whose Vol. 1 is Grundlagen der Nationalökonomie (1854), which M (1859–1862) annotated. M (1861–1862) also studied his Ansichten der Volkswirtschaft aus dem geschichtlichen Standpunkt (1861). He also wrote Geschichte der Nationalökonomie in Deutschland (1874). → 61:17.

Rosenkranz, Karl; full Johann Karl Friedrich (1805 to 1879)   German philosopher and literary critic. Prof at Königsberg (1833–1879); he represented the Hegelian center. M (1841) excerpted his Geschichte der Kantschen Philosophie (1840). Other works: Enzyklopedie der theologischen Wissenschaften (1831); Die Wissenschaft der logischen Idee (1858–1859); Handbuch einer allgemeinen Geschichte der Poesie (1832–1833). → 41:7. #M79.

Rosher, Percy (White)   English accountant, later unsuccessful small businessman, who in 1881 married Mary Ellen *Burns. → 95:37.

Rossi, Count Pellegrino (Luigi Edoardo) (1787 to 1848)   Italian politician and diplomat, lawyer, economist; active in, and citizen of, three countries incl Switzerland and France. As this indicates, he had a checkered career (ending up by getting assassinated), part of which was a stint as prof of law at Bologna (1812+) and prof of polit eco at the Collège de France (1833–1840). M (1845) studied his Cours d'économie politique (1840–1841). Other writings: Mélanges d'économie politique (1857); Traité de droit pénal (1829). → 45:50. #M575.

Rota, Pietro (1805 to 1890)   Italian economist. M (1878) read his Storia delle banche (1874) and Principi di scienza bancaria (2nd edn, 1873). → 78:38, 48.

Rothacker, Wilhelm (1828 to 1859)   German journalist, later an émigré in America. A radical-democrat, he took part in the Baden uprising in 1849; was briefly a member of the CL. He emigrated to the U.S. at the beginning of the 1850s; became editor of the Turnzeitung of Iowa and the *Menschenrechte* of Cincinnati, where he died young, after becoming a Kinkel supporter. → 50:31, 43; 51:15.

Rothschild family (Frankfurt) The great banking family, which now had branches in Vienna, London, Naples, and Paris, had been founded by Mayer Amschel (1743–1812) in the 18th century. In 1851 the Frankfurt house was headed by a son, Amschel (1773–1855). —Note: The *Grundrisse* editors (p. 1090) state erron. that Pieper was going to the London Rothschilds. → 51:45.

Rotterdam (Neth.) N. Sea port. → 38:8; 61:18, 20; 64:7; 93:42.

Roubaix (Fr.) N. city, near Lille. → 84:24.

Rouen (Fr.) N. city, N.W. of Paris. → 69:4; 70:55.

Roumania; *also spelled* Romania, Rumania Officially constituted 1861, with full independence in 1878; declared a kingdom in 1881; formed chiefly out of the *Danubian Principalities (Moldavia, Wallachia) plus Transylvania and part of Bessarabia. → 87:13, 50; 88:1; 92:1; 94:15.

Roumanian language → 87:13, 50; 93:32.

Rousseau, Jean Jacques (1712 to 1778) French (Geneva-born) philosopher and writer, the leading figure among the *philosophes* of the Enlightenment. His ideas directly conditioned the makers of the French Revolution. M (1843) excerpted his chief ideological work, *Du contrat social* (1762) in an edn of 1782. The other work by R. of special importance to socialists was his *Discours sur l'origine de l'inegalité des hommes* (1754). Other writings: *Julie, ou la Nouvelle Héloïse* (1761); *Emile* (1762); *Confessions* (1781, 1788). → 43:32.

Równość Geneva, 1879 to 1881. Monthly. —Polish-language organ of socialist émigrés. → 80:46.

Rowsell, Francis W. (c.1837/38 to 1885) KMC lists his book *The Domesday Book of Bengal* (1879), read by M the same year; but I can find bibliographic record only of his *Recollections of a retrieving officer* (1885)— no other info. → 79:53.

Roy, Joseph French writer and translator, best known for his trans of M's *Capital,* Vol. 1, a trans which in fact was heavily corrected and revised by M. Roy also pubd translations of Feuerbach. —Info about Roy himself seems to be nil. → 72:2, 7, 12; 73:2, 29; 82:30. #M129.

Royal British Bank #M686.

Royal Imperial Army (of Austria) #E482.

Rozan, Philomène French trade-union leader, the woman pres of the Lyons Society of Silk Winders (*ovalistes*); leader of the group of *ovaliste* strikers who declared for joining the IWMA. When their joining was announced at the GC (Aug 10, 1869), M moved that Pres

Rozan "receive special credentials"—prob credentials to attend the next congress (though she did not go). → 69:47.

Rozwadowski, Joséf (b. 1846) Polish revolutionist. He took part in the Polish uprising of 1863–1864; in the Paris Commune, chief of staff under Gen. Wróblewski; afterward, emigrated to England. In 1872, member of the IWMA/GC. → 72:20.

Ruding, Rev. Rogers (1751 to 1820) English numismatist; vicar at Maldon; member of the Society of Antiquaries. He pubd works on the money system of antiquity, esp *The annals of the coinage of Britain and its dependencies* (1817–1819); it is this book that M (1850) prob read. → 50:50.

Rudorff, Adolf (August) Friedrich (1803 to 1873) German jurist; prof of law at Berlin (1829+); disciple and biographer of Savigny. Editor of the *Zeitschrift für geschichtliche Rechtswissenschaft* (1815–1850); editor of the *Zeitschrift für Rechtsgeschichte* (1861–1878). Author of *Römische Rechtsgeschichte* (1857–1859). → 38:12.

Rüstow, Friedrich Wilhelm (1821 to 1878) German military writer. His 1850 book *Der deutsche Militärstaat vor und während der Revolution* got him condemned; took refuge in Switzerland. He served in the Swiss army; then (1860) with Garibaldi as colonel and chief of staff in the Two Sicilies campaign; returned to Zurich. R. supported the Lassallean movement in the 1860s, but sympathized with M&E's break with Schweitzer in 1865. E read his works on military history and strategy, incl: *Heerwesen und Kriegführung C. Julius Cäsars* (1855); *Geschichte der Infanterie* (1857–1858); *Demokratische Studien* (1861); *Der Krieg von 1866 in Deutschland und Italien* (1866). → 57:31; 62:35.

Rütten, Joseph Jakob (1805 to 1878) German pub'r; co-owner of the firm Literarische Anstalt Rütten & Loening in Frankfurt. → 44:40. *See also* *Löwenthal, Z.

Ruge, Arnold (1802 to 1880) German writer on philosophical and sociopolitical issues. Early active in the student Burschenschaft, he got a long prison sentence (1826), released in 1830. Prominent Young Hegelian and radical-democrat; edited various left journals; prof at Halle (1823+); a founder of the *Hallische Jahrbücher* (1838) and its continuation *Deutsche Jahrbücher* (1840–1843). In 1843–1844 he was a founder/editor, with M, of the *DFJ*; broke (permanently) with M in 1844. In the 1848 revolution he was a member of the Frankfurt National Assembly (left wing); afterward, an émigré in London, a founder of the C.C. of European Democracy with Ledru, Mazzini, etc. He settled in Brighton as teacher and writer (1850+); by 1866 he became a vigorous supporter of Bismarck, and ended his days, with a pension, as the chancellor's publicist. He pubd no noteworthy books. → 42:6, 8, 11, 20, 30; 43:1, 4, 7, 11, 12, 18, 20, 21, 26, 28, 30; 44:1, 8, 23, 25, 40; 51:5, 9, 31, 36; 53:32; 57:9; 66:30; 69:6; 90:49. #ME66, ME146, ME162; M64, M203, M471.

Ruhr region; Ger. Ruhrgebiet (Ger.)   Valley of the Ruhr River; industrial and mining area of the N. Rhineland-Palatinate. → 72:35; 89:18, 20. #M930; E490.

Rumohr, Karl Friedrich (Ludwig Felix) von (1785 to 1843)   German art historian, authority on Italian antiquities; also pubd poetry and fiction. M (1842) studied his *Italienische Forschungen* (1827–1831). #M93.

Rumpf, E.   German worker (tailor); a member of the CL, he first emigrated to Switzerland after the 1848–1849 revolution; then (1851) to London, where he was a supporter of M. In 1853 he became insane and went into an asylum. → 51:36.

Runkel, Martin (b. 1807)   German conservative publicist and journalist. Editor of the *Elberfelder Ztg* (1839–1843). #E572.

Rusanov, Nikolai Sergeyevich (b. 1859) Russian Narodnik; member of the Exec of Narodnaya Volya; an organizer of the Socialist-Revolutionary party. He emigrated (1882); became a friend of Lavrov, with whom he pubd *Vestnik Narodnoi Voli* and established a group in the early 1890s. He contributed to Narodnik and S-R publications and became known as a S-R theoretician. He returned to Russia in 1905–1908, again in 1917, still S-R. → 92:22.

Russell, Lord John (1792 to 1878)   English politician; Whig leader. MP (1813+); Whig leader in Commons (1834+). He entered the cabinet as home secy (1835); prime min (1846–1852). After moving in and out of the cabinet for a period—foreign min (1852–1853, 1859–1865)—he again became prime min (1865–1866). He supported Corn Law repeal and other Whig reform measures.   —R. pubd a number of historical and biographical works. M (1843) studied a German edn of his *Essay on the history of the English government and constitution, from the reign of Henry VII to the present time* (1821; enlarged edn, 1823).   → 55:30, 35. #ME147; M192, M486, M487, M494, M789–M791.

Russia and Russians   —For the Russian Marxists, see *Plekhanov, *Zasulich. For contacts with Russian émigrés, see, *Annenkov, *Bakunin, L., *Hartmann, *Lavrov, *Lopatin, *Nechayev, *Kravchinsky, G. M., *Tolstoy, *Tomanovskaya. For correspondents, see *Gorbunova, above all *Danielson. See also *Poland, *Urquhart. —For other Russian émigrés and visitors: → 44:9; 68:62; 71:56; 80:45; 81:5; 92:22; 93:11, 22, 46. —For M's

reading and study on: → 56:8, 18; 57:6; 63:10, 12; 65:39; 68:59; 69:64; 70:67; 71:6; 73:3, 16, 21, 26, 30, 37, 41; 74:40; 75:3, 22, 34, 42, 45; 76:14; 77:1, 5, 48; 79:14, 17, 28, 39, 42, 44, 51; 80:31, 45; 81:2, 3, 5, 45, 63; 82:1, 48, 55; 84:7, 16; 95:20. —For E's reading and study on: → 51:49; 53:16, 28; 54:52; 77:1, 19; 78:40; 85:38; 88:4; 90:26; 92:1; 94:10. —Correspondence about: → 53:9; 54:8, 16, 20; 58:21; 59:66, 72; 60:8; 63:10; 64:18; 65:39; 66:9; 67:29; 70:17, 48, 54; 71:6; 75:11, 37; 76:30, 36; 77:9, 35; 78:6; 79:14, 19, 29; 80:6, 26, 31, 39, 40; 81:10, 13, 20; 83:40; 84:20, 35; 85:16, 38, 43; 86:6; 87:20; 88:1, 6; 90:7; 91:45, 52; 92:16, 29, 48, 64; 93:10, 26, 46; 94:44; 95:12. —Polit activity on Russian affairs: → 54:46; 63:7; 65:54; 74:19; 76:33; 77:13, 16; 81:20; 85:4. —*Capital* in Russian: → 60:47; 68:52, 59; 70:63; 71:26, 31, 60; 72:2, 18, 22, 29, 45, 68; 78:39; 80:39, 40; 82:52; 83:47; 85:6, 23, 29; 86:5; 94:6, 17; 95:20. —Other Russian editions of M&E: → 69:57; 70:29; 82:8, 13, 17, 21, 25, 29; 83:47; 84:20, 26, 35; 90:35; 94:25. —Russian sections, IWMA: → 70:17; 71:51, 54. —IWMA/GC and Congress mentions: → 68:37; 70:50, 59; 71:47, 51. —Miscellaneous: → 72:8; 76:24; 83:12; 90:2; 91:10; 92:60; 93:40. —M & E's writings on: → 44:17; 48:52; 49:17; 53:1, 30, 40, 47; 54:4, 5, 7, 9, 19, 23, 28, 32, 42; 55:41, 49; 56:2; 57:6, 20, 38; 58:42, 45; 59:11, 50, 55; 60:43, 52; 62:10; 63:12; 64:18; 67:29; 68:64; 69:32; 74:19; 75:24; 77:1, 6, 9, 13, 40, 41; 79:16; 81:13, 20; 84:29; 86:2; 87:28; 89:39; 90:9, 13, 17, 26; 94:5.

Russian language   → 50:49; 51:49; 52:16; 53:16; 69:64; 70:6; 71:6; 73:3; 83:36.   *See also* Slavic languages.

Rutenberg, Adolf (1808 to 1869)   German publicist. First a teacher in a Berlin academy (to 1840); Young Hegelian in vieiwpoint; close friend of M. He became editor of *RZ* in Feb 1842, succeeded by M in Oct; member of the Berlin "Doctors' Club." In 1848 he was editor of the *National-Ztg*; later, editor of the *Preussische Staatsanzeiger*; National Liberal (1866+).   → 37:9; 42:4.

Rutson, Albert Osliff   Private secy in 1871 to Henry Austin Bruce (1815–1895), who was home secy (1869–1873) under Gladstone. It was, of course, the home secy who was interesting himself in IWMA affairs. → 71:36.

Ryazanov, David; *pseud. of* David Borisovich **Goldendach** (1870 to 1938)   Russian Marxist scholar and researcher; founder of the Marx-Engels Institute (Moscow), now the *In-stitute of Marxism–Leninism; editor of many Marxist texts and journals. He was liquidated in the Stalin purges, and is still a "nonperson" officially. #ME33, ME80.

Ryde (Eng.)   Town on the Isle of *Wight. → 57:32; 74:27; 91:36, 63; 92:21, 37, 43, 51.

S

Sabatier French revolutionary émigré in London. —*MEW* says he was a Blanquist (grounds unknown, for it does not even know his first name); but he cannot be identified for certain even in *DBMOF*. Perhaps he was Jean Jacques (Léopold Alfred) Sabatier (b. 1824), a socialist ex-student of the Polytechnique, who fled France after Bonaparte's coup—but, says *DBMOF*, to Belgium; it does not say he was a Blanquist. → 52:7.

Sadler, Michael Thomas (1780 to 1835) English social reformer and politician. MP (1829–1832). His activities included advocacy of a poor law, opposition to child labor, etc.; opponent of Malthusianism. Unsuccessful in politics, he settled in Belfast as a businessman. M (1845) studied his book *The law of population,* Vol. 1 (1830). Also author of *Ireland: Its evils and their remedies* (1828). → 45:51. #M575.

Sadowa. Village in Austrian Bohemia; now in Czechoslovakia. *See* *Königgrätz for battle. → 66:30.

Sächsische   Arbeiter-Zeitung. Dresden, 1890 to 1908. Daily. —S-D organ; dominated by the "Jungen" faction in 1890. → 91:11. #M207; E667.

Saedt, Otto Joseph Arnold (1816 to 1886) German official, in the Prussian court system. He was state prosecutor in Cologne (1848+); chief prosecutor in the Cologne Communist trial of 1852. Later, a high court official (Geheimer Oberjustizrat). #E719.

Šafařík, Pavel Josef; *Ger.* **Schaffarik,** Paul Joseph (1795 to 1861) Czechoslovak scholar— philologist, historian, etc. Prof at Prague (1848+). He was on the liberal wing of the Czech and Slovak national movement; an Austroslavist, whose works stimulated Pan-Slavism. E studied his *Geschichte der slawischen Sprache und Literatur* (1826). → 54:52.

Sagra, Ramón de la; *full* **Sagra y Périz,** Ramón Dionisio de la (1798 to 1871) Spanish naturalist and economist. Prof of botany at Havana (1823–1835); pubd a statistical survey of Cuba (1842–1861). Influenced by Proudhon, and inspired to economic liberalism by a trip to the U.S., he became something of a liberal reformer, adopting (c.1844) Colins' ideas and an antidemocratic type of collectivism. Toward the end he reverted to traditional Catholicism. Author of *Le problème de l'organisation du travail* (1848); *Opuscules socialistes* (1849); *Le mal et le remède* (1859), et al. M (1845) read an article by him in the *J. des Economistes* (1842). → 45:50. #M575.

Saint-Antoine *See* Faubourg Saint-Antoine (Paris).

Saint-Arnaud, Jacques Leroy de; *full* Armand Jacques Achille Leroy (1801 to 1854) French gen. He took part in the conquest of Algeria as Foreign Legion officer (1830s–1840s). A dissolute adventurer, he was adopted by Bonaparte as a fit tool for the military organization of his coup d'état of 1851; rewarded by being made marshal of France (1852). As war min (1851–1854) he slaughtered oppositionists as requested. French commander in the Crimea (1854); died of cholera. → 54:28; 56:24, 34, 36, 41; 57:24. #ME160; M734; E720.

St. Aubin (Eng.) Town on Jersey (Channel Is.), S. shore. → 79:31.

Saint-Etienne Industrial city in S. France, below Lyons. → 82:40.

Saint Gall; *Ger.* St. Gallen City in N.E. Switzerland, below Lake Constance. → 92:43.

St. Germain *See* Faubourg St. Germain (Paris).

Saint Helena British island in the S. Atlantic; Napoleon's last place of exile. #E721.

Saint Helier (Eng.) Chief city of isle of Jersey. → 57:45; 79:31.

Saint-Imier (Switz.) Industrial city, N.W. of Bern, near Biel. → 72:60.

St. James's Hall (London)   → 63:13.

Saint-Josse-ten-Noode (Belg.) Suburb of Brussels. → 45:26.

St. Lawrence River (Can.) Seaway flowing out of Lake Ontario to the Atlantic. → 88:30.

St. Louis (Missouri) → 66:38; 67:15; 77:31; 86:18.

St. Martin's Hall (London) → 64:26, 31; 65:25, 51, 63; 66:6.

St. Pancras Foreign Affairs Committee Urquhartite propaganda group in this northern metropolitan borough of London. → 65:54.

Saint-Paul, Wilhelm (c.1815 to 1852) Prussian army officer, he became an official in the Interior Ministry; in 1843, appointed as special censor to oversee the *RZ*. → 43:6.

St. Petersburg Capital of Russia, 1712–1914; renamed Petrograd in 1914–1917; renamed Leningrad in 1924+. → 67:37; 68:58; 72:18; 74:37; 77:46; 81:20; 94:25. #M692; E518.

Saint-Simon, *Count* Claude Henri (de Rouvroy) de (1760 to 1825) French pioneer socialistic thinker: one of the three great innovators of socialism (with Owen and Fourier). Although he was a seminal source of socialistic ideas at the start of the movement, his own writings do not propose social solutions that are socialist in a modern sense; his main contribution to the mix of ideas was stress on scientific social planning (from above, hierarchically, by a power elite); nor was he a "utopian" despite his common classification as a utopian socialist. It was only in his last work Le nouveau Christianisme (1825) that he stressed the working class (as a source of recruitment only); and this orientation gave rise to the Saint-Simonian "school" or "religion" (i.e., sect), led by Bazard and Enfantin after his death. Other works: Lettres d'un habitant de Genève (1802); Du système industriel (1821); Catéchisme des industriels (1823–1824); L'Industrie (1816–1818). The most comprehensive work in English on S-S. is F. E. Manuel's The new world of Saint-Simon (1956); on the Saint-Simonian movement, the unsuperseded work is S. Charléty's Histoire de Saint-Simonisme (1896). → 43:2.

Sainte-Beuve, Charles Augustin (1804 to 1869) French literary critic and man of letters. Critic for Le Globe (1824+), later for other journals; prof at Liège (1848–1849), at Paris (1857+). He pubd poetry, a novel, a historical work on 17th-century France, but was mainly known for his collections of literary criticism. He was the most prominent intellectual supporting the Bonaparte regime; also friend of Proudhon. E (1873) read his Chateaubriand et son groupe littéraire sous l'Empire (1861). → 73:54.

Salomons, Sir David (1797 to 1873) English banker. Offspring of a rich merchant family, he was a founder of the London and Westminster Bank (1832). He was influential as an economic adviser to government, and pubd a few tracts for the times (which M's reading of 1851 prob included), viz., A defence of the joint-stock banks (1837), The monetary difficulties of America (1837), Reflections on the recent pressure on the money market (1840). From 1831 on, he was involved in tests of whether a Jew could hold office, and helped establish a number of precedents; his election to Parliament (1851) was one test, though Jewish MPs were not admitted till 1858; and in 1858 Alderman Salomons was elected lord mayor of London, a first. → 51:61.

Saltykov, Mikhail Evgrafovich; pseud. N. **Shchedrin;** called M. E. **Saltykov-Shchedrin** (1826 to 1889) Russian writer of satirical novels and sketches of Russian society. Of an old aristocratic family, he was early banished (1848–1855) for radical writings. On returning to St. Petersburg, he entered government service (1856–1862) to further the ongoing reform movement (abolition of serfdom); retired (1862) to write; also to edit Sovremennik (1863–1864) and Otechestvenniye Zapiski (1868–1884). Chief works: Istoria odnavo goroda [History of a town] (1869–1870); Gos-

poda Golovyovy [The Golovyov family] (1876). → 53:53; 73:16; 80:45; 87:12.

Salzburg City, in N.W. part of present-day Austria, near the Bavarian border. → 93:42.

Samarin, Yuri Fedorovich (1819 to 1876) Russian publicist and historian. A leading Slavophile writer and theorist, he viewed the peasant commune as the source (with the czarist autocracy) of a regeneration of Russian society. In government service (1844–1852) he helped to draft the statutes on the abolition of serfdom. His writings also dealt with church and religious controversies, tax reform, national separatism (which he opposed), and the history of the Baltic region, Jesuits, etc. —For the book by Samarin and Dmitriev, see the latter name. → 75:34, 37.

Samwer, Karl (Friedrich Lucian) (1819 to 1882) German (Schleswig-Holstein) politician and government official. A lawyer in Kiel, he took part in nationalist agitation in Holstein against Danish rule; active in 1848 as a politician; in autumn, became a bureau head in the Foreign Affairs ministry of Prussia; at this time he worked with Droysen on their joint book (see J. G. *Droysen). Prof of law at Kiel (1851–1852); later an official in Coburg-Gotha. → 53:55.

Sand, George; pseud. of Aurore (Amandine Lucie) **Dupin;** mar. name Baronne **Dudevant** (1804 to 1876) French novelist. Once extremely popular, she wrote dozens of novels, many on social themes, now remembered (but not read) mainly for her positive views on women's right to an independent life, on sexual semiliberation, and to a much more limited extent on women's rights more generally; but her reputation as a feminist is exaggerated. She was hostile to the conscious women's movements of her day, to political rights for women, and to any generalized feminism. —She began (c.1836) to concern herself with the workers' lot, and eventually (by the 1840s) considered herself a sort of socialist; in the 1848 revolution she lined up with Ledru-Rollin against the left. The best short treatment of her sociopolitical side is Edith Thomas, George Sand (in French, 1959); English-language biographies tend toward soap opera. → 48:46, 50. #M71.

Sanial, Lucien #M143.

Saragossa; Span. Zaragoza City in N.E. Spain. → 72:13, 21, 24, 27. #E531, E722, E820, E863.

Sardinia; Ital. Sardegna (It.) See *Piedmont. → 56:21. #M554, M806–M808; E32.

Sarpi Italian émigré in Paris. No further info, outside of this mention in Alfred Meissner's memoirs. → 49:4.

Sauva, Arsène; full Toussaint Mathieu Arsène (1839 to at least 1884) French socialist; tailor. A follower of Cabet, he joined an Icarian colony in the U.S. (1850s–1860s); served in the Union Army in the Civil War. Returning to France (by 1867), he was active in the IWMA and a tailors' co-op; took part in the Paris Commune. Afterward, back in the U.S., his tailor shop was an IWMA hangout in NY; attended the Hague Congress (1872) as a U.S. delegate, supporting U.S. Section 12 and the Bakuninists. Back in NY, he became secy-treasurer of the French-language sections in NY. In c.1876 he moved to an Icarian community in Iowa, where he was secy-treasurer (1881–1884). → 72:49.

Savigny, Friedrich Karl von (1779 to 1861) German jurist and law historian. Head of the reactionary Historical School of Law, his theory of law as the emanation of the *Volksgeist* justified the retention of outlived traditional law maintaining the status quo. Prof at Berlin (1810–1842); Prussian min for legislative revision (1842–1848). Chief works: *Das Recht des Besitzes* (1806), read by M (1837); *Geschichte des römischen Rechts im Mittelalter* (1815–1831). M (1843) excerpted his articles pubd in Ranke's *Historisch-politische Zeitschrift*. → 36:12; 37:8; 43:32.

Savoy Region of S.E. France and N.W. Italy, ceded to France 1860; see *Piedmont. → 60:18, 19. #E724, E725.

Savoye, Henri Charles Joseph; Ger. Heinrich Karl Joseph (1802 to 1869) German liberal democrat; orig a Palatinate lawyer, he emigrated (1832) to France, where he tutored in German. Supporter of Ledru-Rollin; member of the Legislative Assembly (1849–1851); exiled after Bonaparte's 1851 coup. → 50:23.

Saxony; Ger. Sachsen   Former state in central Germany, incl Leipzig, Dresden; now in DDR mostly. → 66:26; 67:33; 68:61; 69:10, 11; 72:3, 44; 81:56; 87:10; 90:39.   #E673.

Say, Jean Baptiste (1767 to 1832) French economist. As systematizer and popularizer of Adam Smith's work, he also further adapted it to the needs of the liberal bourgeoisie. His original contributions included "Say's Law" (supply creates its own demand, hence general glut is impossible). —M (1844) studied his *Traité d'économie politique* (1817; orig, 1803); *Cours complet d'économie politique pratique* (1840; orig, 1828–1830) (*MEGA* I, 3). → 43:2, 29; 44:48.   #M575.

Say, Louis Auguste (1774 to 1840)   Brother of J. B. *Say, he ran a sugar refinery in Nantes and Paris. Also author of economic writings in which he criticized his brother's views. —M (1845) studied his *Principales causes de la richesse* (1818). → 45:50.

Sazanov, Nikolai Ivanovich (1815 to 1862) Russian leftist publicist; one of the first Russian émigrés in the West; long a friend and associate of Herzen. He settled in Paris (late 1830s); associated with the European left emigration; took part in the 1848 revolution; rejected the Russian government's demand he return (1850) and was declared expelled; also chose exile even after 1858 when he got permission to return. —He corresponded with M, whom he had met in Paris (1849), but remained a liberal. → 49:29, 44; 50:19; 51:42; 56:11; 60:28, 30.

Scandinavia → 90:27. #E32. *See also* individual countries.

Schabelitz, Jakob (Lucas) (1827 to 1899) Swiss pub'r/bookdealer, in Basel. In 1846–1848 he was editor of the *Deutsche Londoner Ztg*; either a member of, or at least close to, the CL; friendly relations with M&E in the late 1840s and early 1850s. —His first name is sometimes given gallicized as Jacques. → 51:6, 36; 52:9, 47, 50; 53:5, 11.   #M762.

Schaper, Justus Wilhelm Eduard von (1792 to 1868)   Prussian government official. Provincial governor in Trier (1837–1842); governor of the Rhine province (1842–1845); governor of Westphalia (1845–1846). #M456.

Schapper, Karl (1812 to 1870) German early communist leader; the chief figure among the artisan-communist émigrés with whom M&E merged (1847) to form the CL; member, CC/CL. Son of a poor rural parson, he studied forestry at the U. of Giessen; was active in the student movement; jailed for a conspiratorial putsch (1833), exiled. A revolutionary republican in politics, he took part in a Mazzinian putsch in Savoy (1834), a Young Germany conspiracy in Switzerland, and was expelled from the latter country (1836). After some traveling revolutionism, he settled in Paris, became a typesetter by trade, and also a socialist-communist; joined the League of the Outcast, absorbing the secret-society ideology of Blanqui's Society of the Seasons; took part in the putsch of May 1839. After a jail term, he was expelled from France, moved to London. There (1840–1848), the *League of the Just— formed in Paris after a split in the Outcast— set up the *GWEA (Feb 1840) as a legal front organization. The League itself came under the influence of Owen and Cabet, later Weitling, but became dissatisfied with all utopian ideas. By 1847 S. took a leading part in effecting a merger with M&E's group in Brussels, forming the CL. With the outbreak of the 1848 revolution, S. went to Cologne; worked actively as part of M's NRZ group, with his own focus on the WA (pres, Feb-May 1849), also a member of the Rhenish Democratic exec; worked as a NRZ proofreader. Afterward, in the 1850 split in the CL, Schapper chose the line of instant-revolutionism, which in practice meant a policy of alliance with the liberal-democratic emigration, in this joining with Willich. (See the *Willich–Schapper group.) When this group dissolved (1852), S. began to move back toward M, and (1856) repented his former position; he was fully reconciled with M, and remained his friend till his death. He was mainly active in the GWEA, but was elected (1865) to the GC/IWMA. He died from a virulent TB attack. → 43:14; 45:32; 46:11, 20, 29, 42, 45; 47:1; 48:19, 20, 22, 25, 29, 39, 49, 53, 54, 62, 64, 65, 71, 79–81; 49:6, 8, 9, 11, 19, 22; 51:14; 56:14; 58:28; 59:34; 60:12; 61:14; 65:29; 70:27, 32. #ME16, ME47, ME63, ME87; M836.5; E229, E433.

Schelling, Friedrich Wilhelm (Joseph) von (1775 to 1854)   German philosopher of "transcendental idealism." At first tending to liberalism, after 1810 he became the exponent of a mystical "philosophy of revelation." In 1841 the Prussian king called him to the U. of Berlin to strengthen the reactionary opposition to Hegelianism; this is what spurred the young E to write a series of polemics against him, beginning with #E727. At this time, his chief works were: *System des transzendentalen Idealismus* (1800); *Philosophie und Religion* (1804); *Philosophische Untersuchungen über das Wesen der meschlichen Freiheit* (1809). → 41:21, 23; 42:2, 9, 15; 43:22. #E726–728.

Scheu, Heinrich (1845 to 1926)   Austrian Social-Democrat. Orig a woodcarving artist; later, teacher in a Zurich applied-arts school and art critic. He was a member of the IWMA; delegate to the Hague Congress (1872); for a time, lived in Germany and Switzerland; edited *Volkswille* (Vienna), which hailed the Paris Commune; maintained close relations with Leo Frankel. In 1875 he emigrated to England; visited with M&E. —He should not be confused with his brother Andreas Scheu (1844–1927), who became prominent in the British socialist movement. → 71:15.

Scheveningen   Seaside resort in S.W. Netherlands, near The Hague; now part of that city. → 72:51.

Schill, Karl; *pseud. of* Karl *Schapper. #E229.

Schiller, Friedrich von; *full* Johann Christoph Friedrich (1759 to 1805)   German poet, dramatist, and man of letters; usually regarded as, next to Goethe, the leading figure of German classical literature. The *Chronicle* loci actually refer to the 1859 Schiller Festival in England and its outcome. → 59:63, 70. See *Schiller Institute.

Schiller Institute (Manchester)   This *Schiller-Anstalt* was founded by the German community of the city in Nov 1859, on the occasion of the centenary of the poet's birth, and as the outcome of a Schiller Festival. It was planned as a gen German cultural center, not as a society merely concerned with Schiller. London too had had a Schiller Festival, dominated by Kinkel's followers and Karl Blind, and M had nothing to do with it. Factional dissension among the emigration negated the plan to establish a Schiller Institute in the capital; only Manchester and Bradford ended up with such a society. Despite the fact that the first pres of the Manchester institute was *Siebel, E's attitude at first was distant and scoffing. It is not known when he actually joined (maybe from the first, anyway). For the first indication of his membership, see → 61:24. By Nov 1864 E was chairman (or pres) of the bd of directors; perhaps recently elected. In 1867–1868 this work became heavier because the institute was erecting a new HQ building. In Sep 1868, when E was out of town, the bd of directors decided to invite Karl Vogt to give a lecture. In the resulting dispute, E resigned both from the chairmanship and from the bd. He returned to the bd Apr 1870 (until he moved to London) but was not as active as before. → 59:70; 61:24; 64:21, 43; 65:21, 27; 66:19; 67:21; 68:9, 53, 60; 70:30.   #E143, E438, E815.

Schily, Victor or Viktor (1810 or 1815? to 1875)   German radical, from Trier; later active in France; lawyer by profession. He took part (early 1840s) in a Trier discussion group. In the 1848 revolution he was a leader in the Demo Assoc, Trier; elected a secy of the Rhenish Demo Congress in Cologne; participated (1849) in the Baden-Palatinate uprising; joined the CL in this period; emigrated first to Switzerland, then to Paris. There he became an active member of IWMA; worked with M and the GC to strengthen the Paris organization; delegate to the London Conference (1865). → 48:55; 55:28; 56:11, 33; 60:12, 20, 37; 61:30, 49; 62:20, 25, 27, 52, 62; 64:35; 65:7, 9, 13, 23, 29, 32; 67:31; 68:23; 71:20. #M576.5.

Schimmelpfennig (von der Oye), Alexander (1824 to 1865)   Prussian army officer, from Baden; leftist. In the 1848–1849 revolution he fought in Schleswig-Holstein, with Willich in the Baden-Palatinate uprising, with Kossuth in Hungary; then emigrated to England, where he joined the Willich–Schapper group. Later he went to the U.S.; lived in Washington (1858); fought for the North in the Civil War, as a colonel. → 54:21.

Schippel, Max (1859 to 1928)   German Social-Democratic journalist and politician. As a student (1877–1884), much influenced by Rodbertus; joined the S-D party (1886); on the ed staff of various Berlin S-D papers (1886+); regular contributor to the NZ. He supported the "Berlin Opposition" and the "Jungen" faction (late 1880s–1890), antiparliamentary in tendency. Reichstag deputy (1890–1907); turned to extreme right (1893+)

and became a Revisionist, in the openly pro-imperialist wing. → 84:37.

Schlechtendahl, Gustav Adolf (1840 to 1912) E's nephew; husband of a daughter (Elise Boelling) of E's sister Hedwig; active in the Evangelical church in Barmen. He spoke at E's funeral, briefly, on behalf of the Wuppertal relatives. → 95:37.

Schlegel, August Wilhelm von (1767 to 1845) German man of letters: literary historian, translator, poet; esp known for his trans of Shakespeare; a leader of the Romantic movement. Prof at Bonn (1818–1845); founder/editor of *Athenaeum* (with his brother, Friedrich). Esp influential was his *Vorlesungen über dramatische Kunst und Literatur* (1809–1811). → 35:5; 36:5.

Schleiden, Matthias Jakob (1804 to 1881) German biologist; a pioneer in founding the theory of the cell. Prof at Jena and Dorpat. He pubd a basic paper on cell theory, "Beiträge zur Phytogenesis," in *Archiv für Anatomie,* 1838—studied by M (1864). M (1876) studied his *Physiologie der Pflanzen und Tiere* (1850). → 64:48; 76:9.

Schleswig-Holstein Two former duchies, long held by the Danish kings in personal union, though the population was predominantly German (except in northern Schleswig). From 1848 to 1866 this area was the arena of German-Danish conflict, war, diplomatic maneuvers, and nationalist strivings, also between Prussia and Austria, until Prussia annexed it as a province (1866). Schleswig forms the southern part of Jutland, separated from Holstein by the Eider River; Holstein includes Kiel, Lübeck, etc. → 48:35; 63:42; 64:9, 11, 13, 18, 20, 23, 29, 43; 65:7; 72:20. #E434, E699, E784.

Schlöffel, Gustav Adolf (1828? to 1849) German student revolutionary. A leftist propagandist at Heidelberg, he had just moved to Berlin U. when the 1848 revolution broke out; became a leading militant advocating a revolutionary course, an organizer of the Volksverein unter den Zelten, a founder/contributor to *Volksfreund.* He was arrested; escaped; joined the Hungarian revolutionary army; then (1849) took part in the Baden-Palatinate uprising; killed at Waghäusel. In 1849 he was for a while correspondent of the NRZ. —*Note: MEW* confuses him with his father, Friedrich Wilhelm S. (1800–1870), Silesian manufacturer, left Demo deputy to the Frankfurt National Assembly. → 49:16.

Schlossberg (in Carlsbad) → 74:31.

Schlosser, Friedrich Christoph (1776 to 1861) German liberal historian. Prof at Heidelberg (1817+). M used his multivolume work *Weltgeschichte für das deutsche Volk* (1843–1856) for an extensive chronology of world events. → 57:26. #M141.

Schlüter, Anna Wife of Hermann *Schlüter. → 93:47.

Schlüter, Hermann (d. 1919) German socialist, later active in America. In the 1880s he was director of the Social-Democratic party's printshop and publishing agency in Zurich emigration; first organizer of the party archives; a pillar of the business-management side of the party's work. When the staff was expelled by Switzerland (Apr 1888), he emigrated (1889) to the U.S. There he was active in the socialist movement; editor of the *New Yorker Volkszeitung;* corresponded with E. He pubd a number of still valuable works, esp *Lincoln, labor and slavery* (1913); *Die Anfänge der deutschen Arbeiterbewegung in Amerika* (1907); *Die Internationale in Amerika* (190?); *Die Chartisten-Bewegung* (1915–1916). → 84:53; 85:1, 4, 21, 24, 26, 36; 86:26, 33, 46, 48, 53; 87:16, 32, 48; 88:11, 23, 27; 90:5, 6; 91:9, 11, 15, 28, 32; 92:15; 93:47; 94:29, 50; 95:4.

Schmalhausen, Caroline; *called* Lina; *mar.* Smith M's niece; daughter of his sister Sophie (*see* Sophie *Marx). In 1895, when Eleanor M heard from her, she was widowed and living at The Hague. —*Note: KMC* gives her first name as Bertha. → 65:21.

Schmalhausen, Wilhelm Robert (1817 to 1862) Dutch lawyer. M's brother-in-law; married (1842) to M's sister Sophie (*see* Sophie *Marx). An officer of the provincial court at Maastricht. → 42:19; 47:38, 47.

Schmerling, Anton von (1805 to 1893) Austrian liberal politician; lawyer. In the 1848 revolution: interior min; became prime min (Sep) to quell the Frankfurt uprising. Austrian justice min (1849–1851); as prime min (1860–1865), he failed in his program of liberal Germanization of the empire, and transferred over to the judiciary. → 61:32, 39.

Schmidt, Conrad (1863 to 1932) German Social-Democratic writer. As an economics student in England, he came to know E; later corresponded. Editor of the *Vossische Ztg* (Berlin); commercial editor of the *Züricher Post;* for a while (late 1880s) he supported the "Jungen" faction in the S-D party. He devoted himself to theoretical studies; pubd *Die Durchschnittsprofitrate auf Grundlage der Marxschen Wertgesetze* (1889); ed bd, *Vorwärts;* editor of the *Berliner Volks-Tribüne.* At first favorable to M's theory, he later went over to Revisionism; in *Sozialistische Monatshefte,* ran a social sciences department (1908–1930). His sister was the artist Käthe Kollwitz. → 87:44; 89:5; 90:23, 33, 43; 91:4, 38, 57; 92:4, 10, 35, 46, 47; 95:20, 26.

Schmidt, Ernst Alexander (1801 to 1857) German historian; author esp of school textbooks, incl a popular world history. M (1843) studied his *Geschichte von Frankreich*, Bd. 1 (1835–1848). → 43:32.

Schmidt, Julian; *full* Heinrich Julian (1818 to 1886) German journalist and literary historian. Copublisher, *Grenzboten* (1848+); editor of the *Berliner Allgemeine Ztg* (1861+). At first a moderate liberal, he became a supporter of Bismarck (1866+); rewarded by a pension from the kaiser (1878). —The polemic by *Lassalle was directed against his *Geschichte der deutschen Nationalliteratur* (4th edn., 1858; orig, 1853). Other works: *Geschichte des geistigen Lebens in Deutschland* (1861–1863); *Geschichte der französischen Literatur seit der Revolution* (1857). → 62:31.

Schmidt, L. W. NY pub'r; this name appeared on the orig (German) edn of *Capital*, Vol. 1, underneath the name of the German pub'r. → 68:5.

Schmidt-Dähnhardt, Marie (Wilhelmine); *also called* **Stirner-Schmidt**; *née* **Dähnhardt** (1818 to 1902) Wife of Max *Stirner, whose real name was J. C. Schmidt; her maiden name was Marie W. Dähnhardt; hence various combinations of these three names were used. → 51:59.

Schmitz, Richard (1834 to 1893) German physician in Neuenahr (1863+), where he treated M. → 77:33.

Schnapphahnski Derisive nickname for Prince Felix Maria von Lichnowski (1814–1848), a Silesian landowner and reactionary Prussian officer; in 1848, a member of the Frankfurt National Assembly (right wing); killed during the Sep uprising in Frankfurt. In 1838 he had become a brigadier-gen in the army of Carlos in Spain; returned to Germany after the defeat of the Carlists, and pubd his memoirs on the war. The nickname was hung on him by Heine in *Atta Troll* (a *Schnapphahn* is a highwayman) and was picked up by Weerth for his satirical feuilleton in *NRZ*. → 48:69.

Schneider [II], Karl German lawyer, in Cologne. In the 1848–1849 revolution he was the leading Left Democrat (noncommunist) collaborating with M's *NRZ* group in the political struggle; chairman, Cologne Demo Assoc; member, Rhenish district comm of the Democrats, and the Cologne Comm of Public Safety. In 1849 he acted as M&E's defense counsel in the trial of the NRZ. In 1852 he was the chief defense counsel in the Cologne Communist trial. —Note: The "II" was not part of the name, nor equivalent to "Jr."; it was used to distinguish people of the same surname operating in the same milieu. → 48:79–81; 49:8; 52:39, 45; 61:18. #M47, M848.

Schoelcher, Victor (1804 to 1893) French publicist and politician; left republican, anti-slavery agitator. After a career as a liberal journalist, he was elected (1848–1849) to the Constituent and Legislative Assemblies, and brought the abolition of slavery in French territory to successful fruition. Exiled after Bonaparte's 1851 coup, he emigrated to England. In 1871 he was a deputy to the National Assembly in Versailles, from where he tried to persuade the Paris Commune to capitulate to Thiers. In 1875 he was made senator for life. → 44:9.

Schöler (or Eng. **Schoeler**), Caroline; *called* Lina (1819 to 1891) German schoolteacher, from Cologne; sympathizer of the Cologne Communist group. She was orig Edgar von Westphalen's fiancée, but never married. She moved to England (1855) for a teaching job, bringing M further info on the Cologne Communist trial of 1852; became a good friend of the M family, at times their guest, sometimes lending them money, etc. E met her much later (1887). → 55:50; 81:36.

Schönbein, Christian Friedrich (1799 to 1868) German (Swabian-born) chemist; prof at Basel; known esp for discoveries re ozone and guncotton; prolific writer. M reportedly read him in connection with studies on agrochemistry, but S. did not have prominent publications specific to that area; his correspondence with Liebig (whom M greatly admired) was pubd 1900. → 65:61; 66:12.

Schoenlank (or **Schönlank**), Bruno (1859 to 1901) German Social-Democratic journalist and publicist. He came out for the party during the Anti-Socialist Law (1883); edited various S-D papers; an editor of *Vorwärts* (1891–1893); editor of the *Leipziger Volkszeitung* (1894+); Reichstag deputy (1893–1901); opponent of Bernstein Revisionism. Author of *Sociale Kämpfe vor 300 Jahren* (1894) and, with Kautsky, *Grundsätze und Forderungen der Sozialdemokratie* (1892). —The book in question (see Chron. ref.) was his work *Die Fürther Quecksilber-Spiegelbelegen und ihre Arbeiter* (1888), which first appeared in NZ, Jg. 5, 1887. → 87:36.

Scholl French worker; member of the Lyons section of the IWMA, he was in 1872 an émigré in London who joined the French branch there and was won by A. *Richard and G. *Blanc to their pro-Bonapartist plans. — Maitron's *DBMOF* believes this man was Jean Marie Scholl (b. 1829), a tailoring cutter from Lyons. → 72:41.

Schorlemmer, Carl (1834 to 1892) German-born chemist, active in England. In youth, he fought in the Baden uprising of 1849; came to England in 1858; became a research chemist of European reputation; held the first English university chair for organic chemistry (Manchester, 1874+); naturalized British (1879); author of many treatises and texts. E related that S. was already a communist when he met him in Manchester (1860s);

thereafter a dues-paying member of the German S-D movement, close personal friend of E, also M; accompanied E on trips to the U.S. and Norway. Nicknamed Jollymeier by E and the M family. → 63:4; 68:3; 73:31, 32; 75:48; 76:8, 25; 77:33; 79:32; 83:7, 12; 84:62; 86:28; 88:28; 90:30, 48; 91:25, 36; 92:28, 30, 34. #E125.

Schott, Sigmund (1818 to 1895) German liberal writer. By profession a lawyer, he became active as a writer on current affairs, from a strongly liberal standpoint; a founder of the Nationalverein (1859). He later (1887+) devoted himself to his profession and to belletristic writing incl poetry. → 77:45; 78:12.

Schoyen, A. R. #E433.

Schramm, Carl August (1830 to 1905) German social-reformer. An official in a Berlin insurance house in the 1870s, he became, as a member of the S-D party, a collaborator with Höchberg's journalistic enterprises: an editor of the *Jahrbuch für Sozialwissenschaft und Sozialpolitik;* contributor to *Zukunft* (1877–1878); one of the authors of the "Zurich trio" article (→ 79:38). He also pubd *Grundzüge der National-Oekonomie* (1876). He became a leader of the right-wing state-socialistic faction in the party which sought to have M replaced by *Rodbertus as mentor in economics (1884–1886). Besides articles, he pubd *Rodbertus, Marx, Lassalle* (1885) to glorify the first and third against the second. He quit the party in 1886. —*Caution:* He should not be confused with Konrad (or Conrad) Schramm, esp since NUC knows him only as "C. A. Schramm." → 75:21; 79:2; 82:4; 84:147; 86:3.

Schramm, Konrad (1822 to 1858) German communist. Son of a Krefeld businessman, he went to America (1846); became a U.S. citizen and businessman. With the 1848 revolution, he returned to Germany; as a left Democrat, active in the Schleswig-Holstein movement against Denmark; founded *Kieler Demokratische Wochenblatt,* influenced by the *NRZ;* active in the Kiel Demo Assoc. In 1849, headed for the Baden uprising, arrested in Cologne; escaped to London; here (if not before) he joined the CL and GWEA; became business manager of M's *NRZ-Revue* (1850), also a close friend of M&E; contributed to the German press and Harney's organs. In the 1850 split in the CL, he sided with M. Arrested in Paris (1851); then returned to London, unable to get a job; decided to move to the U.S. (1852)—Philadelphia. But after some collaboration with Cluss and Weydemeyer, his health worsened; returned to England (1857). → 49:20, 40, 43; 50:4, 5, 30, 34; 51:1, 10, 14, 31, 50; 52:20; 57:37, 45, 52; 58:9. #ME11; E433.

Schramm, Rudolph (1813 to 1882) German liberal publicist; brother of Konrad *Schramm. In 1848 he was a left deputy in the Prussian assembly; after the revolution (1849) he emigrated to England. By the 1860s he was a Bismarck supporter. Author of *Die Internationale vor dem Reichstage und die sociale Frage* (1878). → 50:5, 7, 16; 58:9; 72:48.

Schuberth, Julius (Ferdinand Georg) (1804 to 1875) German pub'r; owner of Schuberth & Co. (1826+). He was for a time close to the CL; in 1850 pubd the *NRZ-Revue.* —He also wrote a number of reference works on music. → 49:40, 43; 50:4, 6, 41; 51:6, 11.

Schücking, Levin (1814 to 1883) German novelist and journalist; a friend of E's in youth. On the staff of the Augsburg *AZ* (1843), then the *KZ* (1845–1852). Novels include: *Ein Sohn des Volkes* (1849); *Der Bauernfürst* (1851). → 40:10.

Schütz, Jakob Friedrich (1813 to 1877) German left Democrat in the 1848–1849 revolution. In Cologne (1848) he was involved in the WA's educational work; took part in the Baden-Palatinate uprising, and became the repr of the Baden Provisional Government in Paris (1849); later emigrated to Switzerland, England, and the U.S. → 49:29.

Schüz, Karl (or Carl) Wolfgang Christoph (1811 to 1875) German economist, at Tübingen; a founder of the so-called historical school of polit eco. M (1844) studied his *Grundsätze der National-Oeconomie* (1843). → 44:48.

Schulz (later **Schulz-Bodmer**), Wilhelm (1797 to 1860) German writer and left-liberal publicist. Orig an army officer (1811–1813), he studied law, then went into journalism. Jailed for advocacy of constitutional democracy, he escaped to Alsace; privatdocent at Zurich, as a Swiss citizen, up to the early 1840s. In this period he pubd a number of works, incl his chief writing on polit eco, *Die Bewegung der Produktion* (1843), which M (1844) studied. In 1848 he sat with the left wing in the Frankfurt assembly. Bodmer was the name of his second wife; he hyphenated it to his own. → 44:48.

Schulze-Delitzsch, Hermann; *full* Franz Hermann; *orig* Schulze (1808 to 1883) German liberal politician and social reformer, advocate of cooperatives; lawyer by profession. Deputy in various Prussian assemblies from 1848+, finally Reichstag (1881–1883). The type of co-op he encouraged tended to be a petty tradesman's or artisan's credit assoc, not the Rochdale type; his theory of economic self-help for workers (incl co-ops and "people's banks") was intended to steer them away from revolution. His reply to *Lassalle was *Die Abschaffung des geschäftlichen Risico durch Herrn Ferdinand Lassalle* (1866). Also

author of *Die arbeitenden Klassen und das Assoziationswesen in Deutschland* (1858).
—*Note:* In 1848 he added his birthplace, Delitzsch, to his name. → 63:36; 64:13.

Schumacher, Georg (b. 1844) German Social-Democrat, later liberal. He was a tanner in Cologne and London (1860–1875); went into journalism, editor of the *Kölner Freie Presse* (1876–1878); became a businessman in Solingen dealing in leather (1879+). As a S-D, Reichstag deputy (1884–1898); during the elections of 1898 he broke with the S-D party and went over to the liberals. → 85:39.

Schumacher, Hermann (c.1826 to 1904) German economist, of state-socialistic tendency. He pubd a biography of J. H. von Thünen (1868), also *J. H. von Thünen und Rodbertus* (1870); edited Thünen's *Der isolirte Staat* (3rd edn, 1875), which he sent to M; later, with Adolf Wagner, edited Rodbertus' "literarische Nachlass" (1878–1899). (He also used the surname Schumacher-Zarchlin.) → 75:26, 33.

Schumla See Shumla.

Schuster, Theodor German left publicist. First a privatdocent in Göttingen, disciple of Sismondi, he became, in Paris emigration, a founder of the League of Outcasts (1834) and the leader of its socialistic wing (which founded the League of the Just). In the 1840s he moved to liberalism and support of "peaceful progress," in Germany, but (1850s) gave material aid to German émigrés, working as a physician in Paris. —*New Mega* gives his birth date as c.1807. NUC lists a Theodor Schuster (b. 1808) as a translator and author of German-French dictionaries; perhaps the same man. → 50:16.

Schwanbeck, Eugen Alexis (1821 to 1850) German journalist. Member of the ed staff, *KZ* (1847–1849). #E923.

Schwann, Theodor (1810 to 1882) German physiologist and naturalist. Prof at Louvain (1838+) and Liège (1848+). With *Schleiden he is best known as the founder of the cell theory in biology. His most influential work—studied by M (1864)—was his *Mikroskopische Untersuchungen über die Übereinstimmung in der Struktur und dem Wachstum der Thiere und Pflanzen* (1839). → 64:48.

Schweigert, Ludwig Austrian officer; ex-captain under Garibaldi; in the early 1860s, organizer of Landwehr units in Germany. Politically a Nationalverein member; he was referred to M by Lassalle. → 62:35.

Schweitzer, Johann (or Jean) Baptist von (1833 to 1875) German socialist, Lassallean leader. Of an aristocratic Catholic family of Frankfurt; Jesuit-educated; lawyer. At first anti-Prussian and pro-Austrian in sympathy, he turned to workers for support. As the result of an arrest on a morals charge (homosexual offense in a public park), he faced ostracism from polite bourgeois society. He joined Lassalle's new GGWA; founder/editor of its organ, *Social-Demokrat* (Berlin, 1866–1871); after Lassalle's death, became pres of the GGWA (1867). Elected to the N. German Reichstag (first socialist deputy, 1867). He had accepted Lassalle's pro-Prussian orientation, and turned to a form of left-handed support to Bismarck; on this terrain, he warred with Bebel and Liebknecht in Germany and M&E abroad. Voted for war credits in the Franco-Prussian War (1870). His dictatorial regime in the GGWA and his pro-Bismarck policy undermined his influence; withdrew from politics, and was expelled (1872), to become a writer of successful comedies for the theater. —Author of *Der Kapitalgewinn und der Arbeitslohn* (1867); *Lucinde, oder Kapital und Arbeit* (1864), a novel dedicated to Lassalle. —The standard biography is by Gustav Mayer, *Johann Baptist von Schweitzer und die Sozialdemokratie* (1909). → 64:27; 65:2, 7, 14, 15, 18, 24; 68:2, 5, 13, 28, 35, 39, 43, 48, 50, 56, 64, 70; 69:2, 19, 25, 26, 41, 70; 70:55; 90:32. #M593.

Schweizer Handels-Courier Biel (Switz.), 1853 to 1909. Daily. Pub'r: Ernst Schüler. — In the 1850s–1860s, associated with Karl Vogt; pro-Bonapartist. → 59:44.

Schweizerische National-Zeitung Basel, 1842 to 1858. Daily. Pub'r: J. C. Schabelitz. Ed by J. Schabelitz, Jr. (1849). —In 1849–1850 it expressed a leftist outlook, supported aid for the London émigrés. → 52:9. #ME11.

Schweizerischer Republikaner Zurich, 1830 to 1851. Weekly. —Radical outlook. #E447.

Schwerin, Count Maximilian Heinrich Karl von (1804 to 1872) Prussian politician; prominent among the nobles in the Prussian bureaucracy. In 1848, a member of the Frankfurt National Assembly (right wing); min of cultural affairs (Mar–June). Interior min (1859–1862). Later, a National Liberal. → 61:49.

Schwitzguébel, Adhémar (1844 to 1895) Swiss Bakuninist leader, in the Jura Federation of the IWMA; engraver or watchmaker (sources differ). At the Hague Congress (1872), his expulsion was proposed along with that of Bakunin and Guillaume, but it was voted down. However, he went with the split-off anarchist rump of the IWMA and was a delegate to its congresses at St. Imier (1872) and Geneva (1873), remaining active in the Jura through the 1880s. —*Caution:* His name is misspelled very often. → 72:49, 56.

Science & Society NY, Oct 1936+. Monthly. —Marxist magazine. #ME87.

Scotland → 54:28; 55:34; 59:59; 77:36; 80:32; 81:35; 91:49; 94:29, 44. #M60.

Scott, Sir Walter (1771 to 1832) Great

Scottish novelist and poet. —M's reference to reading Scott prob referred to his novels, but M's letter did not specify. → 66:11.

Scrope, George Poulett; *full* George Julius Poulett; *orig name* **Thomson** (1797 to 1876) English geologist, also economist. He was distinguished as a geologist; but we are concerned with his writings on polit eco, in which he defended free trade, advocated a reformed poor law, criticized Malthus and the gold standard. Liberal MP (1833–1868). Author of *Principles of polit eco* (1833)—studied by M (1851). → 51:66.

Sebaldt, von Prussian government official. In 1848, a provincial counsellor and mayor of Trier. #ME189.

Sebastopol See Sevastopol.

Second International Common name of the int'l socialist organization, a loose alliance of national parties, founded (July 14, 1889) in Paris; other int'l congresses held during E's lifetime were in 1891 (Brussels) and 1893 (Zurich). → 89:23.

Section 12 of the IWMA (NY) → 71:56, 62; 72:1, 8, 13, 26, 49.

The **Secular Chronicle** Birmingham, 1872 to 1879. —An organ of the *Free Thought, or Secularist, movement. → 78:29. #M520.

Sedan City in N.E. France, in the Ardennes, on the Meuse River. The decisive battle of the Franco-Prussian War was fought nearby on Sep 2, 1870. → 70:45.

Sefeloge, Maximilian Joseph (1820 to 1859) Prussian noncommissioned officer. On May 22, 1850, he made an assassination attempt against King Friedrich Wilhelm IV; he was adjudged insane, died in an asylum → 50:20.

Ségur, Vicomte Joseph Alexandre (Pierre) de (1756 to 1805) French writer. At the outbreak of the 1789 revolution, he quit the army for a literary career; wrote *Réflexions sur l'armée* (1789), also plays and poetry, collected in his *Comédies, chansons et proverbes* (1802). M (1852) read his *Les femmes, leur condition et leur influence* (1803), which is "covered with Hegelian-Young-German sauce" (M). — While his books are signed J. A. de Ségur, NUC lists him as Alexandre Joseph Pierre de Ségur. → 52:56, 58.

Ségur, Count Philippe Paul de (1780 to 1873) French military man and historian; nephew of the preceding. He rose to gen under Napoleon; retired (1818–1830); was created a peer (1831), and retired again after 1848. His chief work was *Histoire de Napoléon et de la Grande Armée pendant l'année 1812* (1824); also author of *Histoire de Russie et de Pierre le Grand* (1829), which was studied by M (1856). → 56:18. #M141.

Seiler, Sebastian (c.1810 *or* 1815 to c.1890) German socialist, also active in America. A journalist and publicist, he was first a supporter of Weitling in France and Switzerland. In Brussels emigration he became a member of M's CCC (1846) and then the CL. In 1848–1849 he took part in the Baden uprising, then sent NRZ correspondence from Paris; later an émigré in London (early 1850s). He moved to NY (1856); as a journalist and teacher in America, he pubd a German weekly in New Orleans, expounding "funny money" schemes, and supported the American socialist movement. → 46:11; 49:29, 33, 36; 51:1; 54:31. #ME28.

Seine River River of N. France, flowing through Paris, to the English Channel. #E301.

Semevsky, Vasily Ivanovich (1848 to 1916) Russian historian, Narodnik in ideology. Prof at St. Petersburg; barred from teaching (1884) because of his opinions. His works esp covered the history of the Russian peasantry. M (1882) studied his *Krestyane v tsarstvovaniye imperatritsei Ekaterini II* (Vol. 1, 1881)—first comprehensive treatment of peasant conditions under Catherine II. → 82:55.

Sempere (y Guarinos), Juan (1754 to 1830) Spanish legal scholar and historian. Named to the Supreme Court by Joseph Bonaparte, he had to emigrate after the fall of the regime; later amnestied, and returned. His chief works were *Histoire des Cortes d'Espagne; Ensayo de una biblioteca de los mejores escritores del reinado de Carlos III (1785–89);* and a work which M read (1851), viz., *Considérations sur les causes de la grandeur et de la décadence de la monarchie espagnole* (1826). → 51:69.

Senior, Nassau William (1790 to 1864) English economist. Orig a lawyer, he turned to economics (1821), and became prof of polit eco at Oxford (1825–1830, 1847–1852). He was famed esp for his abstinence theory of profit. M regarded him as the "official economic spokesman of the bourgeoisie" and an apologist for capitalism. He pubd one book written as such, first pubd in the *Encyclopaedia Metropolitana*, the book title being *Outline of the science of polit eco* (1836); M (1845) studied it in a French trans and also in its encycopedia form; also, M (1850–1851) studied several of his lecture collections. → 45:50, 51; 50:50; 51:67. #M575.

Sepoy Rebellion (1857–1858). Revolt of the Bengalese soldiers (sepoys) of the E. India Co., capturing much of northern India; suppressed by the British with bloody atrocities. #M579.

Seraing Industrial city in E. Belgium, near Liège. → 69:25, 65; 72:27.

Serbia; *formerly* Servia Former Balkan kingdom; capital, Belgrade; now part of Yugoslavia. → 76:30; 82:9; 85:38. #E312, E712.

Serbian language → 63:22.

Sergeyevich, Vasily Ivanovich (1832 to 1910) Russian historian of law. Prof at St. Petersburg and Moscow; member of the State Council. His works dealt with Old Russian land ownership and serfdom; his chief work was a collection on Antiquities of Russian Law (1890–1903). M read his *Veche i knyaz* (1867). → 73:37.

Serno-Solovyevich, Alexander Alexandrovich; *for short called* Serno (1838 to 1869) Russian revolutionary. At first a Narodnik, adherent of Zemlya i Volya and a follower of Chernyshevsky, he went abroad (1862); in 1867, broke with Herzen in a pamphlet criticizing the latter's career. In Geneva he became an active supporter of the IWMA and of the local workers' movement (e.g., the building workers' strike); came into conflict with M. —He suffered from mental illness; committed suicide when a clever doctor told him he was going mad. —His brother, Nikolai A. (1834–1866), played a more prominent role in the strictly Narodnik movement. → 68:62, 69.

Serra, Antonio (b. late 16th century; d. early 17th century) Italian economist; an early repr of mercantilism. Little is known except that he was educated in Sicily; imprisoned for involvement in the Campanella conspiracy, or perhaps as a forger. M (1851) read his work *Breve trattato delle cause che possono far abbondare li regni d'oro e d'argento* (1613) in the Custodi collection. → 51:64.

Serraillier, Auguste (Daniel) (1840 to *after* 1876) French-born socialist active in England; shoemaker (lastmaker). His father, who had been a revolutionary activist in the Var département, settled in London, date unknown; Auguste's life before the IWMA is not known. He became a member of the GC (Oct 1869); corr secy for Belgium (Jan 1870+); later also corr secy for Holland and Spain. With the fall of Bonaparte's empire, he was sent to Paris as GC emissary (Sep 1870), to reorganize and rebuild the French sections; defeated in the election for the National Assembly (Feb 1871); returned to London, reported to the GC. With the outbreak of the Paris Commune, he returned to Paris (Mar 29); was elected a member of the Commune (Apr); worked on the Labor Commsn; supported the Minority against the Commsn of Public Safety. Afterward, returned to London. Delegate to the London Conference (1851); corr secy for France; delegate to the Hague Congress (1872), where he supported M. In 1873–1874 he was a member of the British Federal Council, still a close coworker of M&E. Sometime in 1874 he faded out of the movement. Maitron's *DBMOF* says only: "In 1874 S. had some hassles about finances with Lafargue and one day he stopped visiting M." (!) In a letter of Jan 1877, Mrs. Jenny M mentioned S. as one of the Frenchmen they "no longer see." — *Note:* His name ranks second among those in socialist history that are most frequently misspelled. → 70:3, 49, 50, 55; 71:9, 15, 20, 33, 34, 56; 72:41; 73:27, 36, 39, 43. #M753; E819.

Serraillier, Eugénie; *called* Jennie Wife of Auguste S. → 70:49; 71:15, 20.

Sevastopol; *formerly* Sebastopol (Russ.) Black Sea port, on the Crimean Peninsula. → 54:42. #ME77, ME151, ME152, ME187; M39, M60; E46, E65, E267, E302, E303, E546.5, E568, E720, E736, E740, E741, E741.5.

Seven Weeks War See Austro-Prussian War.

Seven Years War (1756 to 1763) A complex of wars fought on three continents to decide the imperial pecking order in terms of colonial domination and European spheres of influence; with Prussia, Britain, Hanover ranged against France, Austria, Russia, Saxony, Sweden, and, at the end, Spain; scorecard signed at the Treaty of Paris (Feb 10, 1763). → 54:44.

Severny Vestnik St. Petersburg, 1885 to 1898. Monthly. —Liberal Narodnik literary-political magazine; in the late 1880s, pubd articles by Western socialists; later (1891+) organ of Russian symbolism. → 85:30. #E837.

Severtsev, A. (*or perhaps* **Severtsov?**) The reference in the *Chronicle* is from *MEW Daten*; otherwise, no further info is available. → 73:26.

Seward, William Henry (1801 to 1872) American politician; lawyer. A leader of the Republican party right wing; governor of NY (1839–1843); senator (1849–1861); candidate for pres (1860); secy of state (1861–1869). #M606.

Sexton, George English physician; socialist. In 1872 he was active in the Manchester section of the IWMA, and became a GC member (May–Aug), also a delegate to the Hague Congress, where he supported the GC against Bakunin. In the British Federal Council, he opposed the lib-lab wing. At first a Freethinker (Secularist, atheist), he later turned spiritualist, in the Besant pattern. The NUC lists many post-1872 titles on secularism and spiritualism—I presume, by the same man. → 72:20.

Shakespeare, William (1564 to 1616) The M family's Shakespearophilia (or -mania) was thoroughgoing; E's was not far behind. It should be remembered that Germany was the country where Shakespeare was almost as much a national figure as in Britain or America. M's father-in-law, *Westphalen, read English fluently and was a Shakespeare admirer in both languages. M's Bonn prof, A. W. von Schlegel, was Germany's greatest translator of Shakespeare's plays. References to and quotes from Shakespeare characters abound in M&E's writings, perhaps exceeded by references to Heine. Eleanor M related that Shakespeare "was the Bible of our house, seldom out of our hands or mouths. By the time I was six I knew scene upon scene of Shakespeare by heart." → 73:59.

Shaw, George Bernard (1856 to 1950) Dublin-born British writer, now known mainly as a playwright. At the time of E's death, Shaw had had three minor plays produced: *Widowers' Houses* (1892), *The Philanderer* (1893), *Arms and the Man* (1894); but he was better known to the literate public as a reviewer of literature, music, and art— Wagnerite in music, Ibsenite in drama. He also pubd some mediocre novels in periodicals. He joined the Fabian Society in 1884, and besides writing tracts for it, edited its *Fabian essays* (1889), with two essays by himself. With the Webbs, he directed the society along the course of a militantly middle-class group of self-conscious elitists working out the theory and practice of a bureaucratic collectivist version of social-democracy. He had not yet invented the myth that he had studied *Capital* and understood its contents. → 92:35, 44, 57; 93:13.

Shaw, Robert (d. 1869) British trade-unionist; housepainter. He took part in the 1864 founding meeting of the IWMA, and became an active promoter, esp in local TUs: member of the GC (1864–1869); treasurer of the GC (1867–1868); corr secy for America (1867–1869). → 68:31, 68; 69:70; 70:3. #M587.

Sheffield Free Press Sheffield (Eng.), 1851 to 1857. Ed by Isaac Ironside. —Pubd by the Urquhartites of the local Foreign Affairs Comm; see Free Press (London). → 55:47; 56:4, 21, 23, 26, 30. #M308, M426, M764, M908.5.

Shelley, Percy Bysshe (1792 to 1822) Great poet of English romanticism, and young E's premier poetic hero, as a champion of Freedom. In 1839–1840 E tried unsuccessfully to find a pub'r for a volume of Shelley translations done jointly with two friends (Schücking, Püttmann); E had translated at least S.'s "Sensitive Plant," prob other pieces, none extant. Shelley's name recurs in E's early articles (e.g., #E414, E447, E171). The NZ article by Eleanor M and Aveling showed E's continued interest in Shelley; it also stressed that M too thought highly of the poet (though there is no mention of him in M's extant writings or letters); e.g., it quotes M on the difference between Byron and Shelley, much to the advantage of the latter. The book by Eleanor M and Aveling, *Shelley's socialism* (1888), fails to prove its title. → 88:25.

Shigaku Zasshi (Tokyo) *See* Zeitschrift für Geschichtswissenschaft.

Shipton, George (1839 to 1911) English trade-unionist and journalist. Founding secy of the Amalgamated Society of Housepainters and Decorators; secy of the London Trades Council (1871/72–1896); editor of the *Labour Standard* (1881–1885). Long a reformist, in the 1890s he went on the attack against the "New Unionism" on behalf of the old. → 81:42, 51.

Shmuilov, Vladimir Yakovlevich; Ger. Schmuilow (b. 1864) Russian socialist. Emigré in Germany after 1887, he took part in the German movement; ed board member of a S-D paper in Dresden (1892–1893). He was connected with Plekhanov's Emancipation of Labor group, and involved in sending its publications into Russia; lived in England in the 1890s. → 93:11.

Shternberg, Lev Yakovlevich; *Westernized* Sternberg (1861 to 1927) Russian ethnographer. Exiled for revolutionary activity (1889–1897), he investigated native society in Sakhalin and Kamchatka; his report on the Gilyaks was pubd in *Russkiye Vyedemosti* (Oct 1892). Later (1918+), prof at Leningrad. → 92:60.

Shumla; *Bulgarian* Shumen; *now* Kolarovgrad Town in Bulgaria, near the Black Sea coast at Varna. #M963.

Siberia Russia in Asia. → 75:11; 77:3.

Sicily (It.) → 60:31, 36; 93:44; 94:36; 95:35, 37. #M409, M817; E321, E346.

Sickingen, Franz von (1481 to 1523) German knight. In the Reformation, the military and political leader of the Knights' War (uprising) against the ecclesiastical princes (1522–1523) under the ideological influence of *Hutten; defeated by the alliance of the archbishop of Trier and the rulers of Hesse and the Palatinate. He is a figure romanticized by later writers, incl Goethe. → 59:23, 29, 37, 47.

Siebel, Carl (1836 to 1868) German poet and novelist; businessman in Barmen, like his father; a distant cousin of E. He lived in Manchester (1859–1860) on business; married (early 1861) and moved back to the Wuppertal. In 1856 he had pubd a long poem on Jesus of Nazareth; in 1860 a novel *Religion und Liebe*; also contributed to periodicals. Friendly with M&E, he helped to publicize their writings, esp *Capital*, and get needed info, etc. → 60:13, 23, 24, 63; 61:3, 17, 18, 53; 62:47; 64:46; 65:7, 15. #E349.

Siegburg (Ger.) Rhineland city, near Cologne. → 69:56.

Siegel, August (1856 to 1936) German

Social-Democrat; miner; TU organizer. Active in the TU movement (1880s), he was one of the organizers of the German TUs in 1890. He then emigrated (1891) to Scotland; took part in the miners' TU struggles there. Delegate to British and int'l congresses of mineworkers. → 92:12.

Siegfried; *also called* Sigurd Folk hero of German and Scandinavian mythology, embodiment of all virtues; prominent in the Nibelungenlied. → 40:16, 18. #E357, E743.

Silesia; *Ger.* Schlesien; and the Silesians Region of east-central Europe, watered by the Oder River; specif, Prussian Silesia—the area of E. Germany seized by Prussia from Austria (1742), now mostly in Poland (1945+). → 44:1, 18, 23; 46:34; 49:15; 51:46; 70:3. #E318, E649.

Silistra or **Silistria** Town in N.E. Bulgaria, on the Danube. #E742.

Simon, John (1816 to 1904) English physician, pioneer in public health and sanitation and in the study of industrial diseases; founder (with Edwin Chadwick) of the modern public health movement. He began (1848) as London's medical officer; chief medical officer for England (1855–1876). → 81:45.

Simon, Ludwig (1810 to 1872) German leftist; called "Simon of Trier"; lawyer by profession. In 1848 he was a deputy to the Frankfurt assembly (left wing); took part in the Baden uprising of 1849; emigrated to Switzerland, later to Paris (1866) and Montreux. In 1870 he protested against Alsace-Lorraine annexation. Author of *Aus dem Exil* (1855). → 50:4. #ME142.

Simpson, Sir James (1792 to 1868) British gen. For the British army in the Crimean war, chief of staff (Feb-June 1855), commander-in-chief (June-Nov). #ME131; M349.

Singer, Paul (1844 to 1911) German Social-Democrat; prominent as chairman of the party. Of a Jewish businessman's family, orphaned, he became a draper's clerk, and later (with a brother) established the Singer ladies' coat factory (1869). At first a supporter of J. Jacoby's left liberals, he joined the S-D party in the early 1870s—secretly until 1878 when the Anti-Socialist Law was imposed; made large financial contributions. Elected to the Berlin city government (1883), he emerged as an outstanding administrator; elected to the Reichstag (1884+); member of the party CC (1887+), its chairman (1890+); also presidium member at int'l congresses; member (1890) of the Int'l Socialist Bureau, Brussels. S. was not a public figure but a capable administrator and organizer, who in politics followed Bebel's lead; despite his notable practicality, he opposed Revisionism to the end. → 78:41; 80:44; 82:20; 84:27, 58; 85:17;

86:55; 88:7; 89:29; 90:47; 91:11, 22, 33; 92:26, 27, 29; 93:20.

Sino-Japanese War, First After jointly suppressing the Korean revolt of 1894, Chinese and Japanese forces fought it out for hegemony over Korea, Taiwan, and other disputed areas, ending in victory for Japan (treaty of Shiminoseki, 1895) → 94:35.

Sismondi, Léonard Simonde de; *full* Jean Charles Léonard (1773 to 1842) Swiss economist and historian; his family (named Simonde) came from Pisa via Dauphiné to Geneva. He lectured in history and economics, esp the history of literature, influenced by Mme de Staël and her circle, and emphasizing social and economic influences. His outlook was orig liberal and antidemocratic, expounding Adam Smith in economics; but his *Nouveaux principes d'économie politique* (1819) turned against liberal economics, criticized capitalism, argued for the reality of crises (on an underconsumptionist theory), and heralded a state-socialistic ideology. —M read this work in 1844; in 1845, his *Etudes sur l'économie politique* (1837); in 1852, his *De la littérature du Midi de l'Europe* (1813); in 1860, his *De la richesse commerciale* (1803). → 44:49; 45:50; 52:56, 57; 60:66. #M575.

Skaldin, V.; *pseud. of* Fyodor Pavlovich **Yelenev** (or **Elenev**) (1827 to 1902) Russian publicist. At first a liberal, he was secy (1859–1861) of the preparatory commsn for the 1861 reform; contributor to *Otechestvenniye Zapiski*. His chief work, *V zakholusti i v shtolitse* [In the sticks and in the capital] was pubd serially in 1867–1869, as a book in 1870, under the Skaldin name; influential. From the 1870s he turned toward extreme reaction. → 73:37; 81:5.

Skarbek, Count Fryderyk (Florjan); *Fr.* Frédéric; *Ger.* Friedrich (1792 to 1866) Leading Polish economist of his day; prof at Warsaw (1818–1831); mainly a follower of Adam Smith. He studied eco in Paris; on his return to Poland, active in administrative posts; also pubd history, sociology, and humorous novels depicting Polish society. M (1844) studied his *Théories des richesses sociales* (1829) (MEGA I, 3). → 43:29; 44:48. #M575.

Skeptical philosophy (Greek) → 39:9.

Skrebitzky, Alexander Ilyich (1827 to 1915) Russian historian; ophthalmologist (M.D.) by profession; degree in law (1849), in medicine (1859). A liberal, his chief historical work was *Krestyanskoe delo v tsarstvovaniye imperatora Aleksandra II* [Peasant affairs during the reign of Alexander II] (1862–1868)—studied by M, whose notes of 1882 were pubd in *Arkhiv Marksa i Engel'sa*, Vol. 12. → 73:16; 81:5; 82:55.

Slade, Sir Adolphus (1804 to 1877) English naval officer. After rising in the navy and publishing travel books—*Turkey, Greece and Malta* (1837), *Travels in Germany and Russia* (1840), etc.—he was loaned (1849–1866) to Turkey, whose navy he reorganized, as Admiral Mushaver Pasha. In the British navy he became rear admiral (1866), vice admiral (1873). M (1877) read his *Turkey and the Crimean War* (1867). → 77:5.

Slavic languages → 51:49; 53:16; 54:52. See also Russian language.

Slavonia Historic region of E. Croatia (now in Yugoslavia); not to be confused with Slovenia; and Slavonian does not mean the same as Slavonic (which = Slavic). #E507.

Slavonic Section of the IWMA (Zurich) → 71:51.

Slavs; Slavic peoples → 51:49; 53:6, 51; 55:1; 56:3, 8, 13; 65:39; 68:59; 76:18; 81:13; 82:9; 93:42. #ME174; E337.5, E763, E919. —Slavophiles: → 75:37.

Sleptsov, Vasily Alexeyevich (1836 to 1878) Russian writer and publicist; of a noble family. Serving as a government official (1857–1862), he was influenced by Chernyshevsky's socialistic ideas; founded a living commune in St. Petersburg (1863), came under police surveillance (by 1866). His radical writing began by the late 1850s; pubd in *Sovremennik, Otecheski Zapiski;* an editor of *Znaniye.* He chiefly wrote socially conscious fiction, also acted and directed. → 70:54.

Slovakia and the Slovaks This region, part of Hungary till 1918, then joined the Czech lands to form modern Czechoslovakia. #E199, E752.

Slovo St. Petersburg, 1878 to Apr 1881. Monthly. —Liberal magazine of literature and popular science. → 77:46; 79:17; 81:5.

Smith, Adam (1723 to 1790) British (Scottish) political economist; the founder of classical economics as a science, and its chief figure before Ricardo. His is perhaps the greatest reputation founded on a single book: *The wealth of nations;* in full *An inquiry into the nature and causes of the wealth of nations* (1776). —S. became prof of moral philosophy at Glasgow (1752–1763), after a year as prof of logic; here he pubd his *Theory of moral sentiments* (1759), which gave him his first reputation. He resigned to travel on the continent as a young duke's tutor (1764–1766); then retired to his birthplace, Kirkcaldy, to think and write for ten years, after which *The wealth of nations* gave him great fame, also a post as a commissioner of customs in Edinburgh (1778+). The book was directed against the then-dominant orthodoxy of mercantilism, and encouraged belief in the beneficence of an economic system founded on individual self-interest, where the "invisi-

ble hand" of the market led the capitalist "to promote an end which was no part of his intention." —M(1844) studied a French trans of 1802; later (1851+), the English original, also *Adam Smith on money theory,* ed by McCulloch (1836). → 43:2, 29; 44:48; 46:52; 51:63; 60:65; 62:8; 68:27. #M575.

Social-Democratic Aid Committee for German Refugees → 49:40; 50:12, 16, 23, 26, 30, 34. #ME68, ME157, ME164, ME179; M695.

Social Democratic Federation (Brit.) Formed at a conference (Mar 19, 1881) in London as the Democratic Federation, with a program not mentioning socialism, under the influence of H. M. *Hyndman, this organization gradually became overtly socialist, adopted the name Social Democratic Federation (Aug 1884), and eventually boasted of being "Marxist"—prob the worst blow delivered against Marxism in England. It changed its name to Social Democratic party in 1907. M&E viewed the SDF as a hopeless sect. → 83:33; 84:1, 55, 59; 85:11, 44; 86:7, 13, 32, 46; 87:26; 89:12; 90:20; 91:10, 27, 31; 92:14, 39, 57; 93:2, 13; 94:18, 22, 31, 44; 95:18, 36. #E388, E841.

Social-Democratic Party (Aust.) The first united socialist party in Austria was founded at a conference in Hainfeld held Dec 30, 1888, to Jan 1, 1889, under the leadership of V. *Adler. → 91:34, 37, 40; 92:9, 26, 31, 44; 93:16, 42; 94:16, 19, 29, 49; 95:4. #E849.

Social-Democratic Party (Ger.); Sozialdemokratische Partei Deutschlands Under this entry, the united party formed at the Gotha congress of 1875, merging the so-called Eisenachers (*Social-Democratic Workers party) with the Lassallean organization (*General German Workers Assoc). Actually it adopted this name-form at its Halle Congress of 1890. There is some confusion over the initials SDP (initials of the English name, without "Germany") and SPD (initials of the German name, with "Germany"), esp since the latter is often used in English—but not in the present work. Here, called the S-D party. → 75:20; 76:21; 77:2, 6, 24, 28, 31, 37; 78:9, 37; 79:2, 16, 24, 33, 38, 47, 49; 80:14, 18, 39; 81:1, 17; 82:28; 83:23; 84:49, 54; 85:13, 21, 24, 27; 86:3, 33, 41, 43; 89:7, 12, 15; 90:10, 19, 32, 37, 42, 47; 91:1, 7, 11–13, 22, 33, 50, 52, 61; 92:18, 52, 53; 93:29; 94:29, 48, 49; 95:3, 11, 16, 24. #ME29, ME33; M207; E198, E335, E387, E392, E393, E764, E765.—Reichstag Fraction: → 79:3, 24, 41, 45; 80:14; 82:4, 11; 83:23; 84:23; 85:13; 90:32; 91:11; 92:11; 93:12; 94:48. #E341.5.

Social-Democratic Party (Hung.) Founded at a congress in Budapest, Dec 7–8, 1890, which adopted the Hainfeld Congress program of the Austrian party; the leading figure was *Frankel. → 76:29; 93:4; 94:23. #E832, E844, E845.

Social-Democratic Refugee Committee
See Social-Democratic Aid Committee for
German Refugees.

Social-Democratic Workers Party (Ger.);
called Eisenachers; Ger. Sozialdemokratische
Arbeiterpartei In a congress held Aug 7–9,
1869, at Eisenach, the Bebel–Liebknecht–led
organization *Union of German Workers Assocs, augmented by a substantial dissident
minority of the Lassallean *GGWA, established a new socialist party, rival to the
Lassalleans, the SDWP. Its first Exec was often
called the "Brunswick Exec," since it consisted of leaders resident in or near this city.
→ 69:2, 41, 47, 48, 59, 60, 62, 66, 70; 70:1, 3,
18, 19, 28, 31, 36, 44, 45, 48, 50, 59, 60, 62, 65;
71:3, 5, 16, 58; 72:3, 9, 24, 33; 73:1, 6; 74:5, 8,
32, 36, 38, 39; 75:2, 12; 90:51; 91:23. #ME88,
ME184; M172, M597, M928.

Der **Social-Demokrat** Berlin, Dec 15,
1864, to Apr 26, 1871. First thrice weekly,
then daily (July 1, 1865+), then thrice weekly
(Apr 1, 1866+). Ed by J. B. von Hofstetten, J. B.
von Schweitzer, W. Hasselmann. —Official
organ of the Lassallean GGWA under
Schweitzer, after which it was continued by
the *Neuer Social-Demokrat. —Caution:
This title is often misspelled and confused
with the *Sozialdemokrat, even in otherwise
reliable sources. → 64:38, 45, 46; 65:7, 8,
14–18, 24; 66:7; 67:47; 68:5, 13, 48.
#ME166, ME182; M397, M593, M707, M861,
M929; E349, E644, E673.

Le **Socialisme** Paris, Nov 17, 1907, to Dec
28, 1912. Founder/editor: J. Guesde. —
Marxist theoretical organ. #M828.

Socialist-Democrats (of Pol.) → 72:3.

Socialist Labor Party (U.S.) The first socialistic party in the country, founded first as
the Working Men's party at a Philadelphia
congress (July 19–22, 1876), renamed at its
Dec 1877 congress in Newark. It was heavily
dominated by German-American émigrés,
mostly Lassalleans or somewhat Marxified
Lassalleans. Though later often called "De
Leonist," note that *De Leon did not become
prominent till c.1891. Virtually from its start,
M&E were extremely hostile to the sectism
and Lassallean policies of the SLP, and E
thought it would be a good thing if it liquidated itself. → 83:12; 86:10, 36, 37, 47; 87:1,
4, 14, 22, 25, 30, 38, 40; 89:37; 90:6; 91:9, 15,
31; 92:7; 94:22, 29, 44. #ME33.

Socialist League (Brit.) Organization
formed (Dec 1884) by a minority of the *Social
Democratic Federation which revolted against
*Hyndman's sectist and bureaucratic policies,
led by William *Morris, incl Eleanor M. In
1889 it was captured by its anarchist wing;
Morris, Eleanor M, et al. withdrew. It lasted
till 1892. → 84:59; 86:16, 32, 36; 87:26, 27;
90:20.

Socialist Party of Italian Workingmen; Ital.
Partito Socialista dei Lavoratori Italiani
Founded 1892 at Genoa, this organization
took the above name in 1893 (changed in 1895
to Italian Socialist party); the Imola congress
was its third. → 94:36. #E868.

El **Socialista** Madrid, 1885+. Daily, later
weekly. Founder/editor: P. Iglesias. —Organ
of the Spanish socialist party. → 87:20;
93:24. #E867.

Le **Socialiste** Paris, 1885 to 1915 with
suspensions. Weekly. Founder/editor: J.
Guesde. —Organ of the Guesdist party,
eventually the French SP. → 85:30, 34, 40;
86:15, 17, 48; 87:11, 19, 29; 90:49; 91:18, 44;
92:13, 22; 93:21, 25, 41; 94:16. #ME33; E13,
E106, E166, E174, E185, E290, E343, E344,
E390, E395, E432, E435, E446, E474, E593,
E830, E858, E859.

Le **Socialiste** NY, Oct 1871 to May 1873.
Weekly. —Organ of the French sections of
the IWMA in the U.S. It supported the Section
12 faction, and broke with the IWMA after the
Hague Congress. → 72:19.

Socialisten Copenhagen, July 1871 to May
9, 1874. Weekly, then (Apr 2, 1872+) daily. Ed
by H. Brix, L. Pio, et al. —Danish socialist
organ. Continued by the Social-Demokraten.
→ 71:48.

Sociální Demokrat Prague. Ed by Josef
Krapka. Czech-language organ of the Austrian
socialists. —Date info not found. #E824.

Société de la Ligue des Peuples → 50:40.

**Société des Proscrits Démocrates Socia-
listes** Group of Blanquist émigrés in London. → 50:15.

**Société Universelle des Communistes Ré-
volutionnaires** A united-front organization,
which was to include the CL (Germans),
Blanquist émigrés (French), and Harney's
wing of left Chartism, on the basis of a
programmatic statement signed i.a. by M&E. It
never actually got off paper, and the plan was
abandoned by M&E a few months later. →
50:15, 38. #ME80.

Society of Free Thinkers (Geneva) This
was the free trans at the GC of the name of the
Geneva society, Société du Sou pour l'Affran-
chissement de la Pensée et de l'Individu,
which at its Aug 15, 1868, meeting had
expressed sympathy with the IWMA. →
68:42.

Sohm, Rudolf (1841 to 1917) German jurist; prof of law at Göttingen (1870), Freiburg i.
Br., Strassburg, and Leipzig (1887+). An
authority on Roman, Germanic, and canon
law, he was a voluminous writer; a founder of
the National-Soziale Verein (1896); a drafter
of the German civil code. M (1881) studied his
Fränkisches Recht und römisches Recht
(1880). → 81:64.

Soho District of London south of Oxford

Street, known for foreign restaurants, lively lifestyles, picturesque poverty, and other un-English activities. → 50:21, 48; 55:12; 64:31.

Le Soir Paris, 1867+. Daily —Republican outlook. → 72:51. #M896.

Sokolovsky, Pavel Alexandrovich (1847 to 1906) Russian economist and historian. Liberal Narodnik; St. Petersburg librarian (1876+); secy of the St. Petersburg branch of a rural savings and loan assoc and editor of its publ (1890+). He focused on the history of the peasant communes and agricultural credit. M (1877–1878) studied his "Ocherk istorii selskoi obshchiny na Severe Rossii" in Znaniye, No. 1, 1877. → 77:48; 78:47.

Solferino Village in N. Italy (Lombardy); battle site in 1859. #E66, E69.

La Solidarité Neuchâtel, Apr 11 to Sep 3, 1870; Geneva, Mar 28 to May 12, 1871. Weekly in Neuchâtel; irreg. in Geneva. Ed by J. Guillaume. —Bakuninist; organ of the Jura Swiss sections of the IWMA dominated by the Bakuninist faction. It continued Le Progrès (Le Locle). #M752.

Solingen (Ger.) Industrial city in the Ruhr, near Düsseldorf. → 49:14, 24, 25; 50:22; 53:45; 56:6, 14; 64:17; 67:42; 69:26, 31, 36, 72; 70:13; 71:17.

Solís y Ribadeneira, Antonio de (1610 to 1686) Spanish historian, dramatist, and poet. He was private secy to Philip IV (1654+); historiographer of the Indies (1665); ordained a priest (1667). His chief work was Historia de la conquista de Méjico (1684), which M (1854) read in an 1884 edn. *Note:* Surname element also spelled Rivadeneyra, etc. → 54:48.

Solly, Edward (pubd 1812 to 1855) English economist, identified by NUC in lieu of life dates as E.S. "of Curzon Street, London." His publications were short pamphlets, incl some in German, or perhaps transd into German (1816). M (1850) read his The present distress in relation to the theory of money (1830). He also pubd Considerations on polit eco (Stockholm, 1812), On the mutual relations of trade and manufacturers (1855), etc. → 50:51.

Sombart, Werner (1863 to 1941) German economist and economic historian. Prof at Breslau (1890+), at Berlin (1906–1931). At first a quasiliberal, heavily influenced by M, early identified with a wing of Katheder-socialism, he later turned toward profascism and the Nazi movement. Chief works: Der moderne Kapitalismus (in various versions, beginning 1902, 1916–1927); Sozialismus und soziale Bewegung im 19. Jahrhundert (1896), later titled Der proletarische Sozialismus (1924);l Die Juden und das Wirtschaftsleben (1911); in his profascist incarnation, Deutscher Sozialismus (1934). → 95:20, 26.

Somers, Robert (1822 to 1891) British (Scottish-born) journalist and writer on economic affairs. As a journalist and editor in Edinburgh and Glasgow, he became a recognized authority on monetary and commercial matters; editor of the North British Daily Mail (Glasgow, 1849–1859); editor of the Morning Journal (1859–1870); pubd also on education and banking; wrote The Southern States of America (1871) after travels there. M (1851) read his Letters from the Highlands (1848) on the 1847 famine. → 51:67, 68.

Songeon French leftist. In 1848 he had participated in the Paris secret societies, took part in the revolution, then emigrated to London. In the 1880s, when M met him, he was pres of the Paris city council. (So according to MEW index; no other info found.) → 82:34.

Sonnemann, Leopold (1831 to 1909) German journalist and politician. Of a Jewish business and banking family, he established the Frankfurter Ztg (1859+) as one of the most influential organs of liberalism, constitutionalism, and moderate social reform. Reichstag deputy (1871–1884 with a gap); a founder of the Nationalverein; member of the Exec of the Verband Deutscher Arbeitervereine and the People's party, through which he sought to keep the workers' movement as a tail to liberalism. → 75:31.

Sonvilier (Switz.) Jura town, between La Chaux-de-Fonds and St-Imier. → 71:56, 64; 72:4. #E179.

Sophocles (496? to 406 B.C.) One of the great Greek dramatists of antiquity, author of Oedipus Rex, Electra, Antigone, et al. → 35:2.

Sorge, Adolph Son of F. A. *Sorge. → 81:29; 83:28.

Sorge, Friedrich Adolph (1828 to 1906) German-born socialist active in America; M's chief coworker in the U.S. Born in Saxony; music teacher by profession; he fought in the Baden uprising (1849); emigrated first to Switzerland, where he joined the Geneva workers' movement and came to know Hess, J. P. Becker, et al.; moved to the U.S. (1852). Here he joined the Communist Club of NY (1858); later the IWMA; helped to found Section 1 (1867); also worked to establish the Social party of NY (1868) and, after its dissolution, the Allgemeine Deutsche Arbeiterverein (1869) which began as Labor Union 5 of the National Labor Union. Increasingly active in the IWMA, he was a founder of the N. American CC of the assoc (1870), as well as leader of Section 1. After the transference of the GC/IWMA to NY, he became its gen secy (1872) and carried on its affairs till his resignation (1874). He transferred his activity to organizing socialist groups, the Working Men's party (1876), and the SLP. He pubd a number of articles in the NZ. → 52:12; 67:22; 68:34, 37, 49; 70:24, 32, 59, 62; 71:21, 28, 35, 46; 72:8, 14, 26, 41, 48, 51, 53, 55; 73:6; 74:28; 76:6, 7; 77:17, 31; 78:23; 79:35, 47; 80:37, 39; 81:23, 29; 83:19; 84:15, 45; 86:29, 33; 87:25, 38; 90:19, 20; 91:9; 94:25, 29. #ME6, ME29; M994; E185, E778. —In the following, Sorge is mentioned only as the addressee of a letter → 70:48; 71:59; 72:19, 31, 60, 65; 73:7, 11, 17, 36, 43; 74:29, 33; 76:10–12, 18; 77:35, 37, 39; 78:34; 79:38; 80:2; 81:33, 52, 58, 60, 61; 82:24; 83:11, 26–28; 84:3, 21, 22, 57, 59, 60; 85:22, 23; 86:7, 16, 18, 20, 36, 46, 47; 87:1, 16, 20, 22, 26, 27, 30, 40, 41; 88:1, 6, 27, 28, 40; 89:5, 17, 19, 22, 23, 36, 37; 90:6, 10, 17, 32, 37, 42; 91:6, 11, 13, 14, 17, 19, 22–24, 33, 35, 43, 44, 48, 50, 52, 53, 56; 92:1, 7, 29, 38, 63; 93:2, 13, 14, 24, 27, 49, 53, 54; 94:4, 9, 14, 15, 17, 22, 43, 44, 48, 50; 95:4.

Sotsial-Demokrat Sevlievo (Bulgaria), 1892 to 1893. Quarterly —Marxist literary journal in Bulgaria → 93:32. #E835.

Sotsial-Demokrat London, Geneva, Feb 1890 to 1892 (four nos. only). Ed by Plekhanov, Zasulich, Axelrod. —Pubd by the Emancipation of Labor group (first Russian Marxist formation). → 89:39; 90:9, 13, 17, 35. #E284.

Soulié, Frédéric (1800 to 1847) French novelist and dramatist. A republican, opponent of the Restoration, he took part in the 1830 revolution. His plays were very successful on the Paris stage. Among the novels that M may have read, incl historical novels, were: Le lionne; La Comtesse de Monrion; Le Comte de Toulouse; Si jeunesse savait, si vieillesse pouvait. A tomb was erected to him in 1875 in Père Lachaise cemetery → 83:6.

South Africa, Republic of; formerly Union of. → 54:1, 14.

South America → 55:48. See also individual countries.

South German People's Party More properly, the Saxon People's party (Volkspartei) and the German People's party, liberal tendencies with labor wings attached, bound by anti-Prussianism. → 68:22, 50; 69:41; 84:23.

Southport (Eng.) Resort town on the Irish Sea, N. of Liverpool. → 73:32.

Sovremennik St. Petersburg, 1836 to 1866. Monthly (1843+). Founder: Pushkin. Ed by Nekrasov, Panayev (1847+). —In the 1860s, it stood on the left; literary and sociopolitical content. → 73:26.

Der **Sozialdemokrat** Zurich (Hottingen-Zurich), Sep 1879 to Sep 1888; London, Oct 1888 to Sep 27, 1890. Ed by Vollmar (1879–1880; E. Bernstein (1881+). —Central organ of the German Social-Democratic party, distributed illegally in Germany under the Anti-

Socialist Law, thereafter superseded by *Vorwärts. It was adopted as official party organ at the Wyden congress (1880). The redaction moved to London after being expelled from Switzerland —Caution: Not to be confused with Der *Social-Demokrat. → 79:2, 24, 33, 38, 41, 49; 80:12, 14, 29, 39, 44; 81:1, 8, 15, 19, 44, 59; 82:4, 9, 11, 17, 21, 28, 38–42, 46, 50; 83:2, 5, 7, 12, 16, 17, 22, 25, 27, 29, 32, 39; 84:4, 16, 17, 19, 23, 52; 85:4, 11, 13, 22, 34, 36, 40; 86:3, 17, 43, 52, 54; 87:7, 19, 28, 42, 49; 88:2, 27, 37; 89:12, 19, 26, 31; 90:10, 14, 18, 39. #ME37; M226, M464; M929; E2, E105, E174, E272, E317, E319, E326, E327, E359, E361, E387–E389, E391, E398, E399, E401, E446, E468, E469, E547, E551, E557, E593, E600, E613, E667, E886, E917.

Der **Sozialdemokrat** Berlin, Feb 1894 to Dec 16, 1895. Weekly. Ed by Max Schippel. —Pubd by the S-D party of Germany, as a weekly supplement to the daily Vorwärts. → 94:30.

Sozialdemokratische Monatsschrift Vienna, 1889 to 1890. Monthly. —Social-Democratic organ. #E272.

Der **Sozialist** NY, Jan 3, 1885 to Nov 19, 1892. Weekly. Ed by J. Dietzgen (till 1888), then H. Schlüter. —German-language organ of the SLP; continued by Vorwärts (NY, 1892–1894). → 87:19. #E401, E446, E593.

Der **Sozialistische Akademiker** Berlin, 1895 to 1896. Ed by Heinz Starkenburg. —Superseded by Sozialistische Monatshefte (the Revisionist organ). → 94:7.

Sozialpolitisches Centralblatt Berlin, Jan 1892 to Mar 1895. Weekly. Pub'r: Heinrich Braun —Social-Democratic journal on socioeconomic conditions; continued by Soziale Praxis (1895–1910). → 95:21.

Spain and Spanish affairs —Events in Spain: → 54:1; 61:49; 68:51. —M&E's studies on: → 54:2, 26, 38, 44, 55, 57; 55:26; 68:51; 76:38; 92:1; 94:1. —Writings on: → 54:37, 40, 42, 45, 49; 56:32; 57:25; 61:49; 68:61; 73:44; 93:21, 24. —Correspondence on: → 73:13; 74:28; 87:20; 92:44; 93:21; 94:14, 29, 31, 32, 39. —Trans into Spanish: → 72:23, 58, 61; 73:20; 87:20; 91:20, 40. —In IWMA affairs:→ 68:68; 69:17; 71:1, 3, 10, 21, 24, 39, 46, 47, 51, 59, 62, 64; 72: 3, 8, 10, 13–15, 21, 24, 27, 31, 36, 42, 49, 55, 56, 60, 65; 73:6, 17, 33, 36. —M's daughters in Spain: → 71:32, 43; 72:40. —Miscellaneous:→ 83:12. See also *Madrid, *Iglesias, etc.

Spanish Armada The fleet that sailed against England in 1588. → 57:28, 41. #ME12.

Spanish language → 40:2; 54:22; 83:36.

Spartacus (d. 71 B.C.) Thracian-born gladiator, leader of the greatest slave revolt of ancient Rome (73–71 B.C.), called the "Third Servile War" or Gladiators' War. See F. A.

Ridley, *Spartacus* (1944). The well-known film, like the novel by H. Fast from which it was made, is quite unedifying on the meaning of the movement. → 61:13.

The **Spectator** London, July 5, 1828+. Weekly. —Orig liberal, later conservative —*Note:* Addison and Steele's literary daily of this name had appeared 1711–1712, 1714. → 50:22, 25; 71:30. #ME31, ME123, ME178; E826.

Spencer, Herbert (1820 to 1903) English sociological philosopher. Beginning as an engineer and journalist, he devoted himself to developing an all-embracing system of society and nature, in which modern evolutionary science is related to social theory ("survival of the fittest" leading to social-Darwinism), esp in three works, *Social statics* (1850); *Principles of sociology* (1876–1896); *The man versus the state* (1884). His conclusion, that state interference in capitalism is to be reduced to the minimum, meant the unrestricted and unregulated rule of capital in economic life, without welfare measures, etc.; thus he became the joint patron saint of bourgeois anarchism and extreme right-wing politics. —M (1853) read his *Theory of population* (1852); *Social statics*. → 53:50, 52; 73:45, 48; 75:48; 94:37.

Speyer (Ger.) City on the Rhine, in the southern part of the Palatinate. → 49:27.

Speyer, Carl (1845 to *after* 1880) German worker (cabinetmaker) active in England and America. In the 1860s he was secy of the London GWEA; member of the GC/IWMA in London and later in the U.S.; delegate to the Hague Congress (1872). He succeeded Sorge as gen secy in America (1874) and made the last report on dissolution (1876). Subseqly he was active in forming the Working Men's party, which became the SLP, and the International Labor Union (1878+), becoming the latter's secy (1880). → 68:64; 69:71; 71:59; 72:41. #M864.

Spier, Samuel (1838 to 1903) German Social-Democrat; schoolteacher, from Wolfenbüttel. Orig a member of the GGWA (1867–1869), he joined the Eisenacher SDWP at its congress (1869), and was elected vice-pres of its Exec (the "Brunswick" party exec), till 1870. Arrested (1870) with this Exec, he was held till Mar 1871; defendant in the treason trial of 1871, received a 14-month sentence. → 69:59.

Spilthoorn, Charles Louis (1804 to 1872) Belgian revolutionary democrat; lawyer, from Ghent. He played a leading role in Flanders during the Belgian 1830 revolution. In 1847 he was on the Exec of the Demo Assoc, and founder of its Ghent branch. Despite his absence from the country in Mar 1848 (having gone to Paris for the assoc), he was arrested on

his return for involvement in the Risquons-Tout émeute, condemned to death, pardoned, released (Jan 1855) after almost nine years imprisonment, and banished on condition of emigration to America. He returned to Belgium (1870) and to his Brussels law practice. → 55:7.

Spinoza, Baruch (or Benedict) (1632 to 1677) Dutch philosopher, of Iberian-Jewish descent; lens grinder by trade. Exponent of a pantheist interpretation of religion. —M (1841) studied his *Tractatus theologico-politicus* (1670) in a German translation, and his letters, *Epistolae,* in his *Opera* (1802 edn). → 41:7. #M79.

Splingard, Roch Belgian Bakuninist, active in the IWMA; lawyer by profession. Delegate to the Hague Congress (1872), where he was a member of the comm of inquiry into the Bakuninist Alliance. (His brother Pierre was more active in the Belgian movement.) —*Note:* His first name is also encountered as *Roche*—either erroneous or gallicized. → 72:49.

Splügen (*Ital.* Spluga) **Pass** Alpine pass between Splügen (Switz.) and Chiavenna (It.). → 41:11.

Spree River (Ger.) River that rises in the Saxon mountains and flows through Berlin. #M837.

Spurzheim, Johann Gaspar; *orig* Johann Christoph; *also called* Johann Friedrich Kaspar (1776 to 1832) German physician; a founder of the pseudoscience of phrenology. A collaborator with Franz J. Gall in Vienna (till 1813), he subseqly lectured and pubd many books (in French and English as well as German) to spread the doctrine in Europe and America. M (1864) read his *Anatomie et physiologie du système nerveux en général et du cerveau en particulier* (1810–1820). → 64:48.

The **Standard** London, 1827+. —Under this title, it appeared as an evening paper till 1857, then came out as a morning daily with an evening edn (see *Evening Standard*). Conservative. → 61:4; 71:30, 34; 75:13; 77:6. #M914, M915.

Starkenburg, Heinz German Social-Democrat; a collaborator with the NZ; editor of *Der sozialistische Adademiker* (1894–1895). For E's letter of Jan 25, 1894, on historical method, formerly called a letter to Starkenburg, see W. *Borgius. → 94:7.

Stechan, Gottlieb Ludwig (c.1814 to 1875) German worker (cabinetmaker), from Hanover, active in the 1848 revolution in Berlin. He became editor of the cigarmakers' journal *Concordia;* ran the *Deutsche Arbeiterhalle* in Hanover; became a member of the CL. In the CL he went with the Willich-Schapper group in the Sep 1850 split, but by Nov 1851 rejoined M. He headed the London GWEA (1852+). → 52:3.

Stefanoni, Luigi (1842 to 1905) Italian leftist publicist. In the 1870s, a leading exponent of Rationalism (Free Thought, atheism); Garibaldian; editor of the weekly *Il Libero Pensiero* (Florence), *Giornale dei Razionalisti*, pres of the free-thought society in Florence. A translator of Feuerbach, Büchner, Herzen, etc., he combined Rationalism with socialism. He supported Garibaldi's call (1872) for a leftist congress; active in forming the Fasci Operai in Tuscany. → 72:10, 21, 27. #M616; E810.

Steffen, Wilhelm A Prussian army officer (lieutenant), he was a defense witness in the Cologne Communist trial of 1852. He emigrated to England (Jan 1853), made M's acquaintance, and saw him often until he moved to Chester (Aug); then corresponded; S. did various services as requested. He moved to the U.S. in 1862; fought in the Civil War for the North. → 53:4, 43; 54:41; 55:41; 62:27, 46.

Steffens, Henrik (1773 to 1845) Norwegian-born philosopher, active in Germany. Prof at Berlin (1832+). A follower of Schelling, he sought to buttress an idealist philosophy of nature with modern science. Works incl *Beiträge zur innern Naturgeschichte der Erde* (1801); *Grundzüge der philosophische Naturwissenschaft* (1806); *Anthropologie* (1824). → 36:12.

Stegemann, Richard German economist, of Tübingen. He pubd *Karl Marx, über die Landwirthschaft* (1886), offprinted from a journal. —It is not clear whether this is the Richard Stegemann (b. 1856) who is listed in the NUC for publications (on factories) in 1905–1907 and as late as 1939. → 85:12, 20.

Stein, Julius (1813 to 1889; *death date sometimes given as* 1883) German liberal journalist; orig an assistant schoolmaster in Breslau. In 1848, deputy in the Prussian assembly (left wing), chairman of the Democratic Club in Berlin; in 1849, deputy to the Prussian Second Chamber; after the 1849 uprising he was tried but acquitted. In the 1850s, editor/pub'r of the NOZ. After moving right, he became editor of the *Breslauer Ztg* (1862+). → 54:50, 60:13; 61:26. #ME167.

Stein, Lorenz von (1815 to 1890) German political scientist and social philosopher. He went to Paris (1841) to study law and as a correspondent; came to know L. Blanc, Cabet, etc.; pubd one of the first books on French socialism: *Der Socialismus und Communismus des heutigen Frankreichs* (1842; 2nd edn, 1848), which in its last edn of 1850 was revised and titled *Die Geschichte der socialen Bewegung in Frankreich von 1789 bis auf unsere Tage.* Prof of philosophy and law at Kiel; prof at Vienna (1855+). Strongly influ-

enced by Hegel, S. developed something of an economic and class view of history and a view of the proletariat as a capitalist product; advocated a "social monarchy" to institute social reforms from above. —M (1853) studied his *System der Staatswissenschaft* (1852). The influence of S.'s book on M is problematic; there is no record of whether M read it on publ; M&E's later comments on it were mainly contemptuous, emphasizing, for example, that S. copied from Louis Reybaud's pioneer work. If M had a debt to Stein (as is often claimed), he did not appear to be conscious of it. → 53:51.

Steinthal German-born merchant in Manchester; head of the commercial firm that employed G. *Weerth. → 52:39.

Stephann, *Dr.* German-born physician in Algiers (1880s). He treated M in 1882 (Feb M to Apr D). → 82:15, 19.

Stephens, Joseph Rayner (1805 to 1879) English Chartist preacher. A Methodist clergyman, he was dismissed for protesting oppression of the poor; preached in working-class chapels around Ashton; famed for eloquence. Though he urged forcible resistance in inflammatory speeches, his views were more Tory-Democrat than radical. In 1838 he was arrested; broke; recanted; talked small at his trial (Aug 1839); was nevertheless sentenced to 18 months, which he served in comfort. He then remained a preacher in the Lancaster area, though now called a "renegade parson." → 86:26.

Stepney, Cowell; *full* William Frederick Cowell (1820 to 1872) English socialist. A maverick aristocrat (nephew of Lord Carnarvon), he supported a number of leftist activities, incl the Reform League and the League for Peace and Freedom as well as the IWMA. He was a member of the GC/IWMA (1867–1872), its treasurer (1868–1870), delegate to conferences (1868–1871), and member of the British Federal Council. He pubd a magazine *The Social Economist* (1868–1869). M had a high opinion of his heart and dedication to the working-class cause, but a low opinion of his head. → 68:49; 70:3.

Steuart, Sir James (Denham) (1712 to 1780) Scottish economist; one of the last exponents of mercantilism. Orig a lawyer, he spent years on the continent after the Jacobite revolt in Scotland. Returning (1763), he worked on his chief opus, *Inquiry into the principles of political oeconomy* (1767). Overshadowed by Adam Smith, his reputation was later revived by German scholars. —M (1851, 1859–1862) studied his opus. → 51:64; 55:5.

Stewart, Dugald (1753 to 1828) Scottish philosopher. Prof of mathematics at Edinburgh (1772+); lectured on moral philosophy

(1778–1779), prof of same (1785+). Eminent as a philosopher during his lifetime, he was soon forgotten, along with his writings, such as *Outlines of moral philosophy* (1793), etc. Since moral philosophy included polit eco, he gave a course of lectures in that subject in 1800, mainly following Adam Smith. M (1859–1862) read his *Lectures on polit eco*, Vol. 1 (1855). → 59:78.

Stieber, Wilhelm (Johann C. E.) (1818 to 1882) German police official; entered Prussian police service (1844). Lawyer by profession (1848+), he became a police assessor (1849), police counsel, *Polizeirat* (1851); head of the Security Police in Berlin (1852–1860) under Police Pres K. L. F. von Hinckeldey. In 1852 S. helped to organize the Cologne Communist trial, in which he was the prosecution's chief witness. Later his methods came under attack (1857); he was tried, acquitted, but forced to retire. He worked as a czarist agent (1861–1865); then was recalled to political-police work by Bismarck; during the war of 1866 and of 1870–1871 he headed the Prussian military police and espionage services. He was separated from the police in 1873, but was instrumental in preparing the (later) outlawry of the S-D party. —The notorious "red scare" book by Wermuth and Stieber, *Die Communisten-Verschwörungen des neunzehnten Jahrhunderts*, was pubd in two parts—Part 1, 1853; Part 2, 1854. The coauthor was his friend Karl Georg Ludwig Wermuth, Hanover police director. → 48:85; 52:39; 53:14; 59:72; 60:29. #M890.

Stimme des Volkes Chicago, 1860. Daily. Ed by J. Weydemeyer (resigned Aug A). — German-language workers' organ, pubd by the Chicagoer Arbeiterverein. → 60:24, 29, 35, 38, 42.

Stimmen der Zeit Gotha (Ger.), 1858 to 1862. Monthly. Pub'r: Adolph Kolatschek. → 61:46.

Stirling, Patrick James (1809 to 1891) Scottish lawyer, who wrote on polit eco, having studied the subject under Thomas Chalmers. His chief product in this field was *The philosophy of trade* (1846), read by M (1851). Subseqly he also pubd *The Australian and Californian gold discoveries* (1853); also translated Bastiat. → 51:62.

Stirner, Max; *pseud.* of Johann Caspar **Schmidt** (1806 to 1856) German writer; anarchist forerunner. Teacher in a Berlin girls' school, S. associated with the Young Hegelian circle at the university. Out of its discussions, he developed (1843–1844) his oddly written book *Der Einzige und sein Eigenthum* (transd as *The ego and its own*), pubd autumn 1844 but dated 1845. Here he moved from bourgeois liberal individualism to herald the future individual anarchism in which no authority outside of the individual ego is recognized; overtly antisocialist and anticommunist. He wrote nothing else of significance; later, lived on translating and hack writing.
—His book aroused interest for a few years up to the 1848 revolution, then was completely forgotten, until near the end of the century when it was exhumed by the poet-anarchist *Mackay as a herald of anarchist ideas. — For S.'s wife, see *Schmidt-Dähnhardt. → 44:26, 42, 44; 45:9, 36; 51:59; 89:33. #ME66.

Stirnerism → 66:26; 91:12.

Stoic philosophy School of Greek thought founded by Zeno, c. 308 B.C. → 39:9.

Stolberg, Count Christian zu (1748 to 1821) German poet and translator. Author of *Gedichte aus dem Griechischen* (1782); translations of Sophocles (1787); etc. His poetical and theatrical writings were pubd in *Gesammelte Werke* (1820–1825) jointly with those of his brother, Friedrich Leopold (1750–1819). → 59:25.

Storch, Heinrich Friedrich von; *Russ.* Andrei Karlovich Storch; *Fr.* Henri Storch (1766 to 1835) Russian, or German-Russian, economist and statistician; he was born in Riga of German parents. He studied in Germany; entered Russian governmental service (1788–1789); prof at a St. Petersburg academy (1803+); vice-pres of the Academy of Sciences (1830+). He mainly popularized Adam Smith in his chief work *Cours d'économie politique* (1815), which M (1845) read in its 1823 edn; M also read his *Considérations sur la nature du revenu national* (1824). → 45:50. #M575.

Stralau (Ger.) Suburb of Berlin, to the S.E. → 37:6.

Strasbourg (Fr.); *Ger.* Strassburg Chief city of Alsace: seized by France 1681; captured by Germany (1870; ceded to Germany, 1871); returned to France (1919). → 43:11; 93:40.

Stratford de Redcliffe, Viscount. Sir Stratford **Canning** (1786 to 1880) British diplomat. Advanced in the diplomatic service through the favor of his cousin George Canning, he acted as an envoy to Constantinople for many years (1810–1812, 1825–1828, 1841–1858); also envoy to Switzerland (1814–1818) and the U.S. (1820–1824). MP (1828–1841); raised to the peerage (1852), he sat in the House of Lords. Author of *The Eastern question* (1881). #M407.

Strauss, David Friedrich (1808 to 1874) German philosopher and theological writer. An early Young Hegelian, his work *Das Leben Jesu* (1835–1836), showing the mythical content of biblical history, caused a storm which kept him out of professorships at Zurich and Tübingen. This book marked a revolution in the critical study of the Bible (as well as in young E's thinking). He also pubd *Die christ-*

liche Glaubenslehre (1840–1841); later, other theological and biographical works. But S. himself had no revolutionary leanings; the 1848 revolution left him far behind as a conservative liberal, pro-monarchist, antisocialist; by 1866–1870, a chauvinist supporter of Bismarckism as a National Liberal. → 38:2. #M493.

Streit, Feodor (1820 to 1904) German bookdealer/pub'r in Coburg; lawyer; active also as a political journalist. He took part in the 1848–1849 revolution as a supporter of G. *Struve; pubd the *Allgemeine Deutsche Arbeiterzeitung* (Coburg, 1863–1866) as a means of keeping the workers' movement subordinated to liberalism; a founder of the Nationalverein. → 52:33, 36.

Strohn, Wilhelm German communist; member of the CL and friend of M&E. In the 1850s–1860s he lived as an émigré in Bradford (Eng.). → 49:20, 31; 55:33; 56:35; 64:15; 65:11, 20; 69:71.

Struik, Dirk J. #ME33.

Struve, Gustav (von) (1805 to 1870) German liberal-republican publicist; lawyer by profession. Editor of the *Mannheimer Tageblatt* (suppressed); with Friedrich Hecker, pubd *Deutscher Zuschauer* (1847–1848). In the revolutionary period he gained fame as a (rather putschist-inclined) leader of the Baden uprising of 1848 and of the Baden-Palatinate movement of 1849; after which he emigrated successively to France, England, and the U.S. In the U.S. he was active as a radical journalist; fought in the Union Army; returned to Germany (1862). → 49:40; 50:5, 16, 19; 67:24.

Struve, Peter Berngardovich (von) (1870 to 1944) Russian politician and publicist; orig a lawyer. In the 1890s, an exponent of "legal Marxism" (some Marxist theory without any revolutionary conclusions); he made a pioneering Marxist contribution to the debate with the Narodniks (1894); editor of *Novoe Slovo, Nachalo;* attended the International Socialist Congress (1896); drafted the manifesto of the Russian Social-Democrats (1898). By the turn of the century he abandoned socialism; became a leader of the Cadet party; editor of *Osvobozhdeniye* (1902–1905); evolved to the right wing; after the 1917 revolution, joined the Whites under Denikin and Wrangel. → 93:46; 94:44.

Stumpf, Paul (1826 to 1912) German worker (mechanic), from Mainz; later, he ran a prosperous plumbing business. He was a good friend of M&E; member of the Brussels GWEA (1847) and the CL (1847–1852); took part in the 1848–1849 revolution in Mainz. After the establishment of the IWMA, he resumed correspondence with M, founded a section in Mainz, was a delegate to the Lausanne Congress (1867); joined the SDWP (1869) and its successor parties; a friend also of Liebknecht. → 48:33; 66:30; 69:56.

Stupp, Heinrich Joseph (1793 to 1870) German official; court councillor in Cologne. In 1848 he was elected to the Prussian National Assembly (right wing, clerical). Later, mayor of Cologne (early 1850s). — N.B.: See the entries in the NUC for publications by one *Hermann* Joseph Stupp (d. 1870), who was apparently also a *Justizrat* in Cologne. #ME168.

Stuttgart Chief city of the former state of Württemberg, in S.W. Germany, on the Neckar River. → 48:48; 90:19; 92:43. #E674, E793.

Sue, Eugène; *orig name* Marie Joseph (1804 to 1857) French social novelist. At first a wealthy playboy (trained as a physician); wrote royalist-conservative novels. After squandering his fortune, he turned his novels to the new theme of the Paris under-mass, the lumpen-class, with a best-seller *Les mystères de Paris* (1843–1844), which is dissected at length in #ME76. S. then studied Fourierism, which is presented in his *Le Juif errant* (1844–1845), *Martin l'enfant trouvé* (1847). In 1848, defeated for the Constituent Assembly; elected to the Legislative Assembly (1850) on a socialistic welfare-reform platform. He opposed Bonaparte's coup of 1851, went into exile, and died forgotten. —For a biographical sketch, see Pierre Chaunu, *Eugène Sue et la Seconde République* (1948). → 44:22, 26.

Suez Canal Ship canal in Egypt, constructed 1859–1869. → 59:67.

Sumarokov, Alexander Petrovich (1718 to 1777) Russian writer; versatile author of poetry, drama, fables, epigrams, etc., incl the drama *The false Demetrius* and the classical tragedy *Khorev* (1747). Director of the first permanent theater in St. Petersburg (1756–1761). → 51:49.

The **Sun** London, 1792/1793 to 1875 under this title. Daily. —Liberal. → 50:22; 51:54. #ME122.

The **Sun** NY, 1833+. Daily. Ed by C. A. Dana (1868–1875); John Swinton (1875–1883). —As editor of the *Sun,* Dana introduced a brand of personal journalism on the road to Hearstian yellow journalism (Dana's term), and progressively moved right as a champion of Captains of Industry. *Swinton moved to socialism. → 68:5; 71:36, 39, 43, 49; 80:34, 39. #M418, M467.

Sunday League (Eng.) → 69:17.

Sundewitt (*Danish* Sundeved) Battle site (1848) in Schleswig-Holstein. #E213.

Susini, Etienne (1837 to 1908) French physician, Corsican-born, first active in Marseilles as medical student, intern, and socialist. Longtime disciple and friend of Blanqui, he took part in the Marseilles Commune movement of 1871; elected city councillor but forced out of the city (1881). In Paris he joined Eudes, friend and Blanquist leader. After his acquittal in 1886 (→ 86:44) he was active in socialist electoral contests in Paris, unsuccessfully. In later years, joined the SP; elected city councillor and mayor of a Corsican town (1904–1908). → 86:44.

Sutherland, *Duchess of* There were two duchesses involved in M's article: the current duchess, whose antislavery stance was the reason for recalling her family history, and the first Duchess of S., in whose time the clearing of the Scottish estates had taken place. The reprint of M's article in PP was introduced by a note which explained that "The Duchess of Sutherland here alluded to is the celebrated 'Countess-Duchess,' mother-in-law of the present Duchess." M headlined the duchess because of the news item he started from; actually, of course, the dukes of S. were equally involved. Following is an identification of all four figures. —George Granville Leveson-Gower, 2nd Marquis of Stafford (1758–1833), was a great Scottish landowner to begin with, and also inherited the estates of the Duke of Bridgewater. An MP in the 1770s–1790s, he was also England's envoy to revolutionary Paris (1790–1792), i.e., a royalist intriguer. He married (1785) Elizabeth, Countess of Sutherland (1765–1839), who had acquired, along with her title, almost all of Sutherlandshire (Scotland). This vast territory added to her husband's holdings made him a "leviathan of wealth" (as a contemporary said). He was created 1st Duke of Sutherland (1833), she becoming the first Duchess of S. (hence the popular tag "Countess-Duchess"). This noble couple inaugurated the policy of clearing the Sutherland estates of human tenants so that sheep might safely graze. Their son, George Granville Leveson-Gower (1786–1861), became the 2nd Duke of S., and in the fullness of time married Harriet Elizabeth Georgiana Howard (1806–1868), daughter of George Howard, 6th Earl of Carlisle. This Harriet—daughter-in-law of the "Countess-Duchess"—was the current Duchess of S. whose antislavery sentiments had caught M's notice. She was an intimate friend of Queen Victoria, among other distinctions. —N.B.: The name entries in MEW, MECW, etc., are inaccurate. → 53:8, 11, 22. #M271.

Svartisen glacier or ice field Norwegian glacier, on the Arctic Circle. → 90:30.

Swan Sonnenschein London publishing house, founded by William Swan Sonnenschein (1855–1931); issued many books on socialism. → 86:23; 87:6, 24; 91:55.

Sweden → 56:2; 63:31; 67:26.

Swedish language → 57:22.

Swinton, John (1829 to 1901) American radical journalist; Scottish-born. Orig trained as a printer, he entered journalism in NY; an ardent abolitionist, he was with John Brown's raid (1857). He worked for Greeley's *NYDT;* for the NY Times (managing editor during the Civil War); for Dana's Sun (1870+) and was its chief editorial writer (1875+). After the 1873 panic he focused on the labor movement; ran for mayor on the SLP ticket (1874); met M on a trip to Europe (1880). He quit the Sun in 1883 and invested all his money in a new weekly *John Swinton's Paper,* till funds were exhausted in 1887; he lost his eyesight in 1889. → 80:28, 34, 39; 81:23, 33; 83:12; 85:41. #M418.

Switzerland and Swiss affairs —M&E's moves to/from, trips, visits, etc.: → 41:11; 48:68, 75, 82; 49:1, 5, 32, 33, 35, 37–39; 65:49; 93:40. —Studies on:→ 56:42; 82:39. — Writings on: → 44:21; 47:49; 48:75, 82; 49:5; 53:19. —Correspondence on: → 91:16. — Movement activity in: → 50:15, 19, 25; 51:10, 27, 42; 53:11; 60:24; 78:3, 37; 84:42; 88:27; 94:33, 42. —In IWMA affairs (here esp, see *Geneva):→ 65:12, 29, 56, 62; 68:62, 68, 69; 69:4; 70:1, 4, 36, 39, 44, 49; 71:1, 2, 47, 51; 72:8, 10, 35; 73:23. —Miscellaneous:→ 59:8; 60: 20, 23; 62:12; 67:12; 82:19. See also *Bern, *Geneva, etc.

Sydow, Rudolf von Prussian diplomat; ambassador to Switzerland (1845–1848). #E237.

Sylvis, William H. (1828 to 1869) American labor leader; iron molder by trade. Entering the labor movement in a strike (1857), he became the founder of the national molders' union (1859), its treasurer (1860), pres (1863+), building it into the strongest union of the time. Cofounder of the National Labor Union; pres (1868+); first labor lobbyist in Washington. Eschewing pure-and-simple unionism, S. favored producers' co-ops and independent political action, supported Greenbackism vs. monopoly. Favorable to the IWMA, he sent A. C. Cameron as delegate to its 1869 congress. His sudden death was a blow to further progress along these lines. → 69:49.

Symons, Jelinger Cookson (1809 to 1860) English lawyer; liberal writer on various subjects, incl law, education. The Home Office commissioned him (1835) to investigate handloom weaving; he traversed Britain and Switzerland; and produced his *Arts and artizans at home and abroad* (1839)—which M read (1851). He later also inquired into mining in north England; member of the Children's Employment Commsn (1841); school inspector (1848–1860). His writings include *Outlines of popular eco* (1840). → 51:67.

Syria Ancient Asian country, near the E.

end of the Mediterranean, more extensive than contemporary Syria; controlled by the Turks in the 19th century. #M246.

Szabó, Imre (von) (1820 to 1865) Hungaraian revolutionist; army officer. He took part in the Hungarian revolution of 1848–1849; member of the first revolutionary government (Mar-Sep 1848); deputy to the State Assembly (1849). Afterward he emigrated to Paris, then London. His book *The state policy of modern Europe* (1857) was Urquhartite in viewpoint. → 60:35. #M305.5.

Szeliga; *pseud. of* **Zychlinsky,** Franz Szeliga Zychlin von (1816 to 1900) Prussian officer (lieutenant) who contributed, under his pen name, to the Young Hegelian press, *Allgemeine Literatur-Zeitung* and *Norddeutsche Blätter* of Bruno Bauer (1843–1845). → 44:26.

Szemere, Bertalan; *Ger.* Bartholomäus (1812 to 1869) Hungarian politician and publicist. In the 1848–1849 revolution, he was interior min in the Batthyány government; prime min (May-Sep 1849); opposed to Kossuth from the right. Afterward he emigrated to Turkey, subseqly to France and England; returned to Hungary in 1865. His brochure *Graf Ludwig Batthyány, Arthur Görgei, Ludwig Kossuth* (1853) made a stir on publ; also author of *La question hongroise* (1860). → 52:7, 12, 17, 20, 31, 51; 53:27; 59:58; 60:24, 35, 58. #M873.

Szerelmey, Miklós (1803 to 1875) Hungarian military engineer (colonel) and publicist. He took part in the July 1830 revolution in France, and in the 1848–1849 revolution in Hungary; émigré in England (1850+). — Note: Hungarian encyclopedias give his first name as above; *MEW* makes it N.; *KMC, Niklas.* → 52:12.

T

Taaffe, Count Eduard (Franz Joseph) von (1833 to 1895) Austrian conservative politician. Interior min (1867, 1870–1871, 1879); prime min (1868–1870, 1879–1893); his accession to power in 1879 marked the victory of his antiliberal coalition. After a career marked by antilabor measures and antinationaist repression, he suddenly (Oct 1893) introduced a bill to extend the suffrage, in order to ease social conflicts; but it was opposed from several sides and was quashed; T. resigned and retired from politics. → 93:44.

Tacitus, Cornelius (c.55 to c.117–120 A.D.) One of the great Roman historians. Though he attained the consulship (97 A.D.), he is important for his works on Roman history, of which the best known is prob *Germania* (with which #E542 is concerned, esp as compared with Caesar's account); also wrote *Historiae, Annales,* et al. #E542.

Tages-Chronik Bremen, 1849 to 1851. Daily. Ed by R. Dulon. —Liberal newspaper; Ruge contributed in 1851. —Renamed *Bremer Tages-Chronik* (Jan 1851+). #ME183.

Taiping (or T'ai P'ing) **rebellion** A revolt against the Manchu regime in China, initiated in 1848–1850 and suppressed in 1864–1865, led by a Christianized mystic named Hung Hsiu-ch'üan, and rallying large masses of poor, to found a new Taiping (great peace) regime. → 62:36.

Taylor, A. J. P. # ME33.

Taylor, Bayard (1825 to 1878) American man of letters, traveler, diplomat, journalist. Traveling correspondent for U.S. papers (1844–1846); joined the staff of the *NYDT* as its main foreign correspondent (1848+). He entered the U.S. diplomatic service (1862) on the staff of the embassy in Russia; became U.S. min to Germany and died in Berlin the same year. He pubd considerable poetry, incl a verse trans of Goethe's *Faust,* which he regarded as his chief work. → 57:42.

Taylor, James (1788 to 1863) English banker. After studying monetary problems in consequence of the bullion report of 1810, he became an active advocate of bimetallism; pubd a number of writings on money. M (1850) read his *A review of the money system of England* (1828). He also wrote *No trust, no trade* (1826), a defense of bankers, and *Polit eco illustrated by sacred history* (1852). → 50:50.

Taylor, Sedley (1834 to 1920) English academic; Fellow at Cambridge. His books were largely on music and sound, esp the scientific side; also pubd proposals for profit-sharing by workers; advocate of cooperatives. For his polemic with Eleanor M on the Brentano–Marx controversy, see Y. Kapp, *Eleanor Marx,* II, App. 1; however, he had no background in polit eco. #E375.

Taylor, W(illiam) Cooke (1800 to 1849) Irish writer, active in England esp on the staff of the *Athenaeum* (1829+). Whig in politics, free-trader in economics, he published a vast number of works on miscellaneous subjects, incl history and biography, not overburdened by scholarship. M (1851) read his *Natural history of society in the barbarous and civilized state* (1840). → 51:64.

Tchaikovsky, Nikolai Vasilyevich (1850 to 1926) Russian populist. As a student at St. Petersburg, he was a founder of what came to be known as the "Tchaikovsky circle" of left Narodniks (1869+), though not really its leader. He emigrated (1874) to a utopian community in Kansas; later returned, took part in the S-R revival at the beginning of the century. He headed the anti-Soviet government at Archangel; left for Paris (1919); and died in exile. → 81:13.

Techow, Gustav (Adolf) (1813 to 1893) German leftist military man active in the 1848–1849 revolution. A lieutenant in the Prussian army, he took part in the 1848 storming of the arsenal in Berlin; in 1849, became chief of staff of the Palatinate revolutionary army. After the defeat of the Baden-Palatinate uprising, he emigrated to London. In 1850 he was connected with the Revolutionäre Zentralisation group (which discussed unity with the CL). In 1852 he moved to Australia. → 50:25, 30; 51:42.

Tedeschi, J. M. A leader of the Portuguese section of IWMA, supporting the GC and working with Lafargue in his Lisbon organizing work (1872). —A Lafargue letter referred to "somebody called Tedeschi, or Quintal" (ST/E9, p. 469), later to "Tedeschy" (p. 490); ST/27, p. 423, 685, also spells it both ways; ST/21, 5:543, adds to the fun by spelling it Tedeschj. The initials "J. M." appear only in the index to ST/27. —Note: A Portuguese encyclopedia lists a João Maria Tedeschi (b. 1844), but there is no evident connection. → 72:13.

Tedesco (or **Tédesco**), Victor (André) (1821 to 1897) Belgian communist in the 1840s; of Luxemburgian origin, mostly active in Liège; lawyer by profession. A founder (1847) of the Brussels Demo Assoc; also a member of the CL, with close relations with M&E. Though in Mar 1848 he went to Paris on behalf of the Demo Assoc, he was charged with involvement in the Risquons-Tout riot, sentenced to death; sentence was commuted, he was released 1854, after which he became a liberal in politics. → 47:45.

Der **Telegraph** Vienna. —No info available. → 68:15.

Telegraph für Deutschland Frankfurt, 1837; Hamburg, 1838 to 1848. Founder: Karl Gutzkow. —Literary journal, representing Young Germany (to the early 1840s) in the period when young E contributed. → 39:2, 5, 6, 8, 10, 11; 40:2, 4, 5, 7, 12–14, 16, 18; 41:3, 6, 10, 23; 45:48. #E248, E256, E263, E300, E330, E354, E368, E370, E400, E404, E414, E452, E536, E586, E677, E683, E721, E727, E743, E881.

Ténot, Eugène; full Pierre Paul Eugène (1839 to 1890) French journalist and publicist. Republican; editor of Le Siècle. The two books that interested M&E were his La province en décembre 1851 (1865) and Paris en décembre 1851 (1868). After Bonaparte's fall, he was editor of the Bordeaux republican

organ Gironde; deputy (1881–1885); author of a number of works on France's fortifications and military defense situation. → 68:71.

Terrail, Gabriel; full Dieudonné Gabriel Jean; pseud. Mermeix (1859 to 1930) French journalist and publicist. Boulangist, he was elected deputy in 1889; subseqly he wrote an exposé, Les coulisses de Boulangisme (1890). Among many books on current affairs, he had pubd La France socialiste (1886), which contained i.a. Laura (M) Lafargue's revised trans of the Com Manifesto. → 86:2. #ME33.

Terry, Ellen; full Alice Ellen or Ellen Alicia (1847 or 1848 to 1928) The greatest English stage actress of the day (1863–1925), esp famed for Shakespearean roles with Henry Irving. She became Dame Ellen in 1925; also lectured on Shakespeare. → 81:39.

Terzaghi, Carlo (b. c.1845) Italian political adventurer; lawyer by profession. An organizer of the Federazione Operaia of Turin, and its secy (1871); editor of Il Proletario Italiano. He juggled with support of Bakunin, the IWMA/GC, even Mazzini, as an indefatigable intriguer; was expelled from the Turin IWMA (Feb 1872) and suspected of being a police agent; but he still remained active for the Bakuninists and intrigued with the GC, until V. Regis' reports caused E to break off relations. In 1873 the Bakuninists expelled him as a police spy; he established a new paper La Discussione, and formed a small sect of his own. → 72:53.

Tessier du Mothay, Marie Edmond French socialist; participant in the 1848 revolution and the June 1849 demonstration. In the 1850s he was an émigré in London, belonging to the Blanquist group. According to KMC, orig a chemist. —There are many spelling variants of this name. New Mega III, 3 (index, p. 1518) gives his name as Tessier de Mothé, with same given names as above; but in the text (letter by Seiler, p. 509), his name is written Tessier du Mothey. DBMOF lists a Tessié du Motay (no given name) who is identified only as secy of the 1845 general assembly of shareholders in the Fourierist Démocratie Pacifique. → 51:10.

Texas (U.S.) Orig part of Mexico; created independent Republic of Texas (1836–1845); annexed to the U.S. in 1845. → 65:36; 93:17.

Theiss River German name of the *Tisza.

Theisz, Albert (Frédéric Félix) (1839 to 1881) French Proudhonist; bronze engraver (self-employed in his shop). First joined IWMA in 1865, dropped out, active in his trade's strikes and in the Paris TU movement; rejoined the IWMA (Feb 1870). He was elected to the Paris Commune, where his main job was direction of the postal service; fought in Bloody Week. Afterward, an émigré in England, he at first supported the "French

Section of 1871" against the GC, but, influenced by reading *Capital*, he moved away from Proudhonism. Member of the GC and its treasurer (1871–1872); helped to establish the Cercle d'Etudes Sociales in London. On returning to France after the 1880 amnesty, he collaborated with Rochefort's *L'Intransigeant* and with the Alliance Socialiste Républicaine. → 71:39, 48, 51; 75:48. #M755.

Thessaly Region of ancient and modern Greece; ceded by the Ottoman Empire in 1881. → 54:26.

Thieblin, Nicolas Leon (1834 to 1888) Anglo-American journalist. Born in Italy, educated at a St. Petersburg military academy, he served in the Crimean War, then became a journalist in London, where he wrote esp for the *Pall Mall Gazette*; had friendly relations with M. Later (1874) he moved to New York, where he was i.a. a special correspondent for the *NY Herald* in Spain. He also pubd books (1870, 1874) under the pen name Azamat-Batuki. → 70:40, 41; 71:62; 72:54; 73:52.

Thierry, Augustin; *full* Jacques Nicolas Augustin (1795 to 1856) French liberal historian, and admirer of the rising bourgeoisie. Chief works: *Conquête de l'Angleterre par les Normands* (1825); *Récits des temps mérovingiens* (1840). M (1854) studied his *Essai sur l'histoire de la formation et des progrès du Tiers Etat* (2nd edn, 1853). → 54:35, 55.

Thiers, Adolphe; *full* Marie Joseph Louis Adolphe (1797 to 1877) French politician and historian; lawyer by profession. Under the Restoration, a liberal oppositionist; supporter of Louis Philippe, cabinet min for part of his reign; premier (1836, 1840). A moderate and Orleanist, he was in the liberal opposition under Bonaparte. During the siege (1870) he acted as negotiator between Paris and Bismarck. In Feb 1871, pres of the Third Republic; organized the suppression of the Paris Commune; retired from politics (1873). Chief works (which with time became more conservative and pro-Napoleon): *Histoire de la Révolution française* (1823–1827); *Histoire du Consulat et de l'Empire* (1845–1862). → 48:42, 52; 71:28; 73:28; 77:6. #ME93, ME121; M879; E527.

Thiersch, Friedrich Wilhelm (1784 to 1860) German classical scholar and educationist. Prof at Munich (1826–1860). An ardent supporter of Greek independence, he visited Greece (1832), wrote a Greek grammar, translations, and a work in French, *De l'état actuel de la Grèce et de moyens d'arriver à sa restauration* (1833), studied by M in 1857. → 57:16.

Thirty Years War (1618–1648) European war, chiefly devastating Germany, fought between German Protestant and Catholic princes and by various European powers versus the Holy Roman Empire and Hapsburgs. #M141.

Thomas, Antoine Léonard (1732 to 1785) French writer; a repr of the 18th-century Enlightenment; member of the French Academy (1766+). He was esp known for his Academy eulogies; cf. his *Essai sur les éloges* (1773). M (1852) read his *Essai sur le caractère, les moeurs, et l'esprit des femmes dans les différens siècles* (1772–1773). → 52:58.

Thompson, Benjamin; *later Count* **Rumford** (1753 to 1814) American-born adventurer, scientist, and inventor. He fled the American Revolution; obtained a government post in England; as a result of inventions, became a Fellow of the Royal Society (1779). He went to Strassburg (1783); was made Count Rumford by George III; entered Bavarian service (1784) as war min and police min. After an interlude in England (1795+), he went to Ireland (1796) where he worked on improving hospitals and workers' housing. Back to Munich (1802); to Paris (1805), where he married Lavoisier's widow; became a member of the Institut de France. His research played an important part in developing the modern theory of heat. — M (1859–1862) studied his *Essays, political, economical, philosophical* (1796–1802). → 59:78.

Thompson, William (1775 to 1833) Irish socialist pioneer, active in England. Born to a rich Protestant landowning family, he studied Saint-Simonian ideas on the continent, and became known at home as a "Red Republican" reformer. At first a supporter of utilitarianism, he stayed with Bentham (1822–1823), then remained in London. He now became a supporter of Owen's socialistic ideas, but not of Owen's appeals to the rich and mighty. He pubd the greatest product of Ricardian socialism, *An inquiry into the principles of the distribution of wealth* (1824), which made him the leading theoretician of the Owenite movement. In collaboration with Anna Wheeler (one of the first female socialist militants) he wrote *Appeal of one half of the human race, women* [etc.] (1825)—the first statement in favor of unconditional equal rights for women (far beyond Mary Wollstonecraft), the first linking of feminism with socialism, and also the first fusion of the socialist idea with that of consistent and complete democracy. This is one of the greatest works in socialist history, and the oblivion to which it has been consigned speaks volumes. In 1827 T. pubd *Labor rewarded* [etc.], a criticism of Hodgskin; this was the first work linking socialism to a favorable view of trade-unionism as well as to democracy in the state. Inside the Owenite movement, T. moved to oppose Owen's dictatorial control; if he had lived, the history of early socialism might have been different. It remains to add that T. was also a pioneer in championing Catholic emancipation, Rationalism, and sexual realism, and in denouncing priests, lawyers, doctors, and educators as dolts. Although he was the greatest exponent of socialist democracy in the early 19th century, by M's time all of his works had been relegated to oblivion except the 1824 economic tome, which M studied in 1845. —See Richard Pankhurst, WT (1954). → 45:51; 86:45. #M575.

Thorne, Will; *full* William James (1857 to 1946) English socialist and trade-unionist. Son of brickyard workers, a worker from age 6 on, he came to London (1881) and worked in the gas works. He joined the SDF (1884), became an active propagandist; life-long socialist, though later right-wing. He was one of the founding organizers and gen secy (1889) of the Gasworkers and Gen Labourers' union, hence one of the first leaders of the "New Unions" of the period. Long a member of the TUC's GC and Parliamentary Comm; MP for West Ham (1906–1945); member of its town council (1891–1946), mayor (1917–1918). In 1916 he went with Hyndman's prowar National Socialist party. —He was long a close friend of Eleanor M, and spoke at her funeral. → 90:47.

Thornton, Henry (1760 to 1815) English banker. Born to great wealth, he became a banker; a founder of the Sierra Leone Co., long its chairman. As a philanthropist he financed the evangelical movement, aided welfare institutions. Independent Whiggish MP (1782–1815): active on committees as an authority on finance; with Wilberforce, fought against slavery. His chief work on economics, praised by J. S. Mill, was his *Enquiry into the nature and effects of the paper credit of Gr Brit* (1802)— read by M (1851). → 54:51.

Thornton, William Thomas (1813 to 1880) English writer on economic affairs. At the E. India Co. he was a clerk (1836+), then public works secy for the India Office (1858–1880). In eco, he was a follower of J. S. Mill. M (1851) read his first work, *Over-population and its remedy* (1845), the remedy being colonization of Irish wastes. He also pubd *A plea for peasant proprietors* (1848); *On labour* (1869). → 51:69.

Thucydides (fifth century B.C.) Greek historian. An Athenian, commander of an expedition during the Peloponnesian War, he went into exile (423–403 B.C.) and wrote his *History of the Peloponnesian War*—which M studied in a Latin edition (1859–1862 notebooks). → 61:13, 23.

Thünen, Johann Heinrich von (1783 to 1850) German economist, esp concerned with agricultural questions and rent theory; a landed estate owner in Mecklenburg. His views were regarded as socialistic by some, having an affinity with state-socialist approaches à la Rodbertus, plus sympathy for profit-sharing and social measures for workers. His chief work was *Der isolirte Staat in Beziehung auf Landwirthschaft und Nationalökonomie* (1826–1863), studied by M (1868). → 68:72; 75:26, 33.

Thuringia; *Ger.* Thüringen   Former state in central Germany (now DDR); chief cities include Weimar, Jena, Gotha, Eisenach. → 62:51.

Thusis   Village in eastern Switzerland, middle of Graubünden canton. → 93:40.

Tibaldi, Paolo (1825 to 1901)   Italian leftist; an optical worker. After fighting with Garibaldi, he emigrated to Paris (1850). There he was arrested (June 13, 1857) on unproved allegations that he was plotting Bonaparte's assassination; deported to the Cayenne penal colony; amnestied (1870); returned to Paris, and took part in the Paris Commune. An émigré in England, he joined the IWMA; pubd memoirs *Da Roma a Caienna* (1888). → 71:34; 72:16.

Ticino; *Fr. and Ger.* Tessin   The Italian-speaking canton of Switzerland, neighboring Italy. #E276, E348, E476.

"Tidmann, Herr" (song)   #E349.

TIme (with varying subtitles)   London, Apr 1879 to 1891. Monthly. Ed by Edmund Yates; then E. M. A. Williams; then E. B. Bax (1890–1891). —Semisocialistic in content. Absorbed by *Munsey's Magazine.* → 90:17, 26. #E284.

The Times   London, Jan 1, 1788+ under this title; founded 1785 as *Daily Universal Register.* Daily. —Leading English newspaper; conservative. → 44:5; 50:19; 51:14, 54; 52:3; 54:23; 61:4, 39; 67:32, 35; 68:48, 54; 71:15, 20, 30, 41, 51; 72:41; 73:6; 83:12. #ME85, ME179–ME181; M54, M325, M434, M480, M481, M821.5, M859, M916–M919, M931, M952; E336, E808, E827, E828.

Tisza River; *Ger.* Theiss   River flowing from the W. Ukraine through Hungary and Yugoslavia, into the Danube. #E427.

Tkachev, Peter (or Pyotr) Nikitich (1844 to 1885 old style or 1886 new style)   Russian revolutionary; Narodnik ideologist of Blanquist tendency; lawyer by training; journalist. Active in the St. Petersburg student movement (to 1868), he collaborated with Nechayev. After arrests, he went abroad (1873); collaborated with Lavrov in Switzerland, then broke with him (1873–1874); pubd *Nabat* (1875–1881) in which he developed his views on putschism-from-above. In Paris, he contributed to Blanqui's organ; spent his last years as a mental patient, died insane. → 75:10, 11, 14, 17.

To-Day London, May 1883 to June 1889. Monthly. Ed by H. M. Hyndman (1884–1886). —Socialistic. Superseded by *International Review*. → 84:6, 46; 85:37. #E360.

Tölcke, Karl Wilhelm (1817 to 1893) German Lassallean socialist; lawyer by profession. He joined the Lassallean GGWA (1864); gained attention as a good speaker and organizer; and after B. Becker's resignation as pres, T. was elected to the post (Nov 1865 to 1866). He remained an Exec member till 1874; after 1875 he remained a member, not a leader, of the united party; ran a legal aid bureau in Dortmund. → 74:36.

Tönnies, Ferdinand (1855 to 1936) German sociologist. Prof at Kiel (1881–1933). His chief work, *Gemeinschaft und Gesellschaft* (1887), is very important in academic sociological circles; his analyses are largely based on a classification of will in society. T. was close to the Katheder-socialists, and may have considered himself a sort of Fabian. —In 1895 T. sent two of his articles to E: "Neuere Philosophie der Geschichte: Hegel, Marx, Comte" (*Archiv für Geschichte der Philosophie*, 1894) and "Pestalozzi als Sozialpädagog" (*Sozialpolitisches Centralblatt*, 1894). → 95:6.

Tolain, Henri (Louis) (1828 to 1897) French Proudhonist; a founding leader of the IWMA in France; bronze engraver by trade, self-employed from 1860. Active in workers' mutual-aid societies (1850s); assistant secy of the workers' delegation to the London Universal Exposition (1861–1862); took part in discussions in London on int'l workers' cooperation (Aug 1862); ran unsuccessfully as a workers' candidate in the gen elections, and with *Lefort drafted the Manifesto of the Sixty (1863); took part in a London meeting for Polish insurgents. In Sep 1864 he was the leading French repr at the St. Martin's Hall meeting where the IWMA was founded; became leader of the movement in France (with Fribourg and Limousin). The IWMA thus became at first a Proudhonist group in France, defending petty-bourgeois property against collectivization, hostile to strikes, etc. By 1868–1869 the French government's arrests and persecution of the IWMA leaders shifted the balance away from the Tolain wing to workers like Varlin; Tolain himself was prosecuted twice. After the fall of the Empire, in Feb 1871 he was elected to the National Assembly; on the outbreak of the Paris Commune, he stayed with the Assembly in Versailles and denounced the Commune; the French section expelled him as a traitor. His subseq career (elected senator, 1876+) was with the so-called Opportunist party (right liberals); in 1890 the French government named him its delegate to an international congress on labor protection. → 64:35; 65:7, 9, 13, 19, 23; 70:40; 71:14, 20. #E678.

Tolstoy, Grigory Mikhailovich (1808 to 1871) Russian landowner, from Kazan. A liberal, he helped the Narodniks, e.g., in financing *Sovremennik*. In the 1840s he became acquainted with M&E in Paris. → 44:9, 35; 46:11, 39, 43.

Tomanovskaya, Elisaveta Lukinichna; *née* **Kusheleva;** *pseud.* Elisabeth (or Elise) **Dmitriyeva** (or **Dmitriev, Dmitrieff**); *erron. called* **Tomanovsky** (1851 to 1910) Russian revolutionary, active also in France. Illegitimate child of a noble ex-officer, Luka Kushelev; educated in St. Petersburg, she absorbed radical and feminist ideas. In order to go abroad, she entered a pro-forma *mariage blanc* with a Col. Tomanovsky (or Toumanovsky), whose name thereafter was her legal name. She went abroad (autumn 1868), first to Switzerland, where she helped form the Russian IWMA section in Geneva and combated the Bakuninists; then to London (summer 1870), where she became a close friend of the M family. On the outbreak of the Paris Commune, she went to Paris (partly on behalf of M's need for information); in the Commune she was active on the Exec of the Union des Femmes, for which she drafted a plan for socialist production and for the organization of working-women; during Bloody Week she fought with the Women's Battalion. Afterward, having escaped to Switzerland, she returned to Russia (Oct 1871). There she married Ivan Davydovsky (1874); in 1876–1877 he was under arrest and due for Siberia; Utin alerted M, who wrote urgently to Russian friends to provide a lawyer and aid. When Davydovsky was deported, she went with him, and (according to most accounts) died in Siberia. However, the *Great Soviet Encyclopedia* states that from 1905 she lived in Moscow. → 70:64; 71:6, 15, 23; 77:3.

Tonkin Former French protectorate in N. Indochina; capital, Hanoi; now in N. Vietnam. → 83:40.

Tooke, Thomas (1774 to 1858) English economist. Born near St. Petersburg (son of an English clergyman), he first worked there and became a repr of a Russian firm in London. He was a zealous champion of free trade; "the last English economist of any value," thought M. Chief work: *History of prices ... 1793–1856* (1836–1857), of which Vol. 5–6 was by Tooke and William Newmarch (1820–1882), an English economist and statistician; studied by M in 1845, 1857. Other works: *An inquiry into the currency principle* (1844), studied by M in 1851; and *Considerations on the state of the currency* (1826). → 45:51; 50:50; 51:63; 54:51; 57:10; 68:27. #M575.

Toreno, *conde de.* José Maria **Queipo de**

Llano Ruiz de Saravía (or **Sarabia**) (1786 to 1843) Spanish liberal politician and historian. He took part in the revolution of 1808+; Cortes deputy (1811–1814, 1820–1823); finance min and prime min (1834). He was in emigration during the periods 1814–1820, 1823–1832, 1835+. His chief work was *Historia del levantamiento, guerra y revolución de España* (1835+)—read by M (1854). → 54:57.

Tories (Brit.) Here this term is used for either the historic Tory party or its continuation (1830s+), the Conservative party; in gen, the conservative party which through most of the 19th century was based on landed property in alliance with bourgeois elements, as against the Whigs and (later) the Liberals. → 56:8; 81:20; 85:44; 86:7; 92:32; 93:9; 94:9, 14. #M150, M272, M532.

Toronto (Can.) Capital of Ontario province. → 88:30.

Torrens, Robert (1780 to 1864) British (Irish-born) military man and economist. He was an army officer, attaining colonel, till 1835–1837; then retired. Liberal MP (1831–1835). From 1808 on, he pubd on economic matters, as a Ricardian; advocate of Corn Law repeal, and of the colonization of southern Australia. M (1851) read a number of his works: *On the operation of the Bank Charter Act of 1844* (1847); *Essay on money and paper currency* (1812); *Essay on the production of wealth* (1821); *On wages and combinations* (1834). M (1859–1862) also read his *Letter to the Rt. Hon. Sir Robert Peel* (1843) and *Principles and practical operation of Sir Robert Peel's bill* (1848). → 50:50; 51:63, 64, 66.

Tottenham Street (London) #E818.

Townsend, Joseph (1739 to 1816) English Methodist clergyman; known to his contemporaries mainly as a geologist. His chief economic work (studied by M in 1851) was *A dissertation on the poor laws* (1786), which anticipated Malthus' theory of population. Treating the poor as inferior animals thoughtfully provided by God for manual toil, this holy man denounced all public relief of poverty. → 51:68, 69.

Trades Union Congress (Brit.) National federation of TUs. #E841.

Trafalgar Square (London) With the Nelson monument, National Gallery, etc. → 86:7.

Tralee Atlantic seaport, S.W. Ireland. → 56:22.

Transylvania Region of historic Roumania: in the 19th century, a principality in the Hapsburg Empire; incorporated into Hungary (1867); later restored to Roumania. #E309, E715.

Traube, Moritz (1826 to 1894) German chemist and physiologist. He is best known

for his experiments (1864–1867) on the making of artificial cells in the laboratory and on semipermeable membranes. → 75:26.

Treaty of Paris (1856) Ended the *Crimean War. → 70:50, 59; 71:14.

Treitschke, Heinrich (Gotthard) von (1834 to 1896) German historian. Prof at Kiel, Heidelberg, and Berlin (1874+); editor of the *Preussische Jahrbücher* (1866–1889); official historiographer of the Prussian state (1886+). He was a strong supporter of Prussianism, Hohenzollerns, Bismarck, colonialism, etc., and a virulent enemy of the labor movement, Catholics, Jews, socialists, democrats, British, Poles, etc. His chief work was *Deutsche Geschichte im 19. Jahrhundert* (1879–1894). → 77:28.

Trémaux, Pierre (b. 1818) French naturalist. His chief work was *Origine et transformations de l'homme et des autres êtres* (1865)—read by M (1866). → 66:40.

Trendelenburg, Friedrich Adolf (1802 to 1872) German philosopher. Prof at Berlin (1833+). An idealist on the Platonic model, he was known esp for a commentary on Aristotle and opposition to Hegel. Chief works: *Logische Untersuchungen* (1840); *Naturrecht auf dem Grunde der Ethik* (1860). → 39:9; 40:4.

Trent Affair On Nov 8, 1861, a U.S. warship stopped the British packet Trent in the Bahama Channel and forcibly removed two Confederate envoys being carried to Europe, after which they were interned in the U.S. In the face of British threats, they were released in Jan 1682. → 61:49, 54, 57. #M183, M691, M941.

Treviranus, Georg Gottfried (1788 to 1868) Bremen pastor, at whose house E lived (1838–1841) while an apprentice. T. was an orthodoxer, editor of a church periodical, *Bremer Kirchenbote*. → 38:10.

La Tribuna Rome, 1883 to ? —Liberal. No other info available. → 92:11.

Trier; Fr. Trèves (Ger.) Rhineland city, on the Moselle River, near the Luxembourg border. M's birthplace. → 18:1; 23:1; 27:1; 30:1; 35:2–4, 8; 36:2, 4, 9; 37:17; 38:6; 41:9, 14; 42:4, 13, 19; 43:10; 44:20, 34; 45:30, 35, 39, 42; 46:9; 47:10; 49:28; 51:18; 53:25; 54:36, 39; 56:22, 29, 33; 61:18; 62:45, 46; 63:40, 41. #ME142; M885, M886.

Trier, Gerson (1851 to 1918) Danish left socialist; teacher by profession. He joined the Danish Social-Democrats (1888), and led a left wing against the reformist leadership; later, a member of the party's CC (1901). Antiwar during World War I, he split (1916) in protest against coalition-government policy; a founder of the Socialist Workers party (1918). He translated M&E's writings, and corresponded with E. → 89:37; 92:40.

Trier'sche Zeitung Trier (Ger.), 1815 to 1919 under this title; founded 1757. Daily. —Liberal (1842+), esp under the influence of H. Bettziech; tended to "True Socialism" (mid-1840s) under the influence of K. Grün. It reprinted some M articles from RZ in 1842–1843. → 46:5; 47:16; 59:14. #M847.

Trioen, Louis François Bernard M (1845) read his work *Essais sur les abus de l'agiotage* (Brussels, 1834). → 45:50. #M575.

Tromsö Chief seaport in the far N. of Norway, on a coastal island. → 90:30.

Trondheim Seaport, largest city of central Norway. → 90:30.

Trotsky, Leon #ME33.

Trübner, Nikolaus; Angl. Nicholas (1817 to 1884) German-born pub'r in London. Apprenticed to a bookseller in Heidelberg, he moved to London in W. Longman's employ (1843). Self-educated, he became a competent scholar, philologist, and Orientalist. Around his publishing enterprise, Trübner & Co. (in partnership with David Nutt), he gathered distinguished scholars; helped struggling scholars; and pubd learned books at risk, notably Trübner's Oriental Series, *Trübner's American and Oriental Record,* numerous catalogs, etc. But he was not sympathetic to the left; his firm, thought Engels, "specially represents Bismarckism in the London Book Trade" (letter, May 28, 1887). → 56:12, 19, 23.

Truelove, Edward (1809 to 1899) London pub'r and printer. A former Owenite and Chartist, member of the Reform League and the National Sunday League, active also as a Secularist, he often pubd radical and progressive materials. In 1858 he was arraigned for publishing a pamphlet favorable to *Orsini's attentat against Bonaparte. → 71:57.

Tucker, E. London pub'r. He pubd Urquhartite material i.a. His *Tucker's Political Fly-Sheets,* a pamphlet series (1855) to which M contributed, comprised Vol. 1, nos. 1–9, and Vol. 2, no. 1, "edited by E. Tucker." → 53:45, 47; 54:5, 9, 34, 47; 55:21.

Tucker, Josiah (1712 to 1799) British (Welsh-born) economist and clergyman. Dean of Gloucester (1758+). His first economic tract was pubd in 1749; his *Elements of commerce and theory of taxes* (1755) was one of the first comprehensive treatises. He was also a prolific pamphleteer, in particular in championing separation from the American colonies and agitating against war for the sake of trade; e.g., in *The case of going to war* [etc.] (1763) and *The true interest of Gr Brit* [etc.] (1774). Also author of *Important questions on commerce* (1755), transd by Turgot. → 60:66.

Tuckett, John Debell (d. 1864) English writer on public affairs; Quaker of Looe (Cornwall). His chief work—read by M

(1851)—was *A history of the past and present state of the labouring population* (1846). → 51:65, 66.

Tübingen (Ger.) City in the Swabian region, near Stuttgart. #E674.

Türr, Stephan or Stefan; Hung. István (1825 to 1908) Hungarian military man and politician. He served in the Austrian army first, then went over to the Italian forces against Austria (1849); also served with the British and the Turks. He followed Garibaldi into Sicily (1860) as a gen; then joined the Piedmontese army, becoming governor of Naples; returned to Hungary in 1867. → 50:19.

Tufnell, Edward Carleton (1806 to 1886) His *Character, object and effects of trades' unions* (1834)—read by M (1851)—came out as the result of Tufnell's membership in the parliamentary Commsn to Investigate Factory Labor of 1833. Later (1867) he was on the Commsn on Employment of Children, Young Persons, and Women in Agriculture, whose reports were pubd in 1868–1870. → 51:71.

Tuileries (Paris) Former palace, royal residence; destroyed by fire (1871) except for the gardens. #M818.

Tunisia N. African republic today. Under Turkish beys (1591+); in the 19th century, arena of French-Italian rivalry; made a French "protectorate" in 1881; independent (1956+). → 83:40.

Turati, Filippo (1857 to 1932) Italian socialist leader. A socialist from 1883, he changed *Cuore e Critica* to *Critica Sociale* (1890) and, as editor, made it the foremost socialist theoretical organ in the country; editor also of *Lotta di Classe* (1898+). A founding leader of the SP (1892+); deputy to Parliament (1896+); jailed (1898–1899). He became the leader of the party's reformist wing by the end of the century; but as a pacifist opposed the Libyan war (1911) and World War I (1915); however, supported "defense of the fatherland" by 1917. He resisted the revolutionary upsurge of 1919–1920; fled fascism (1926); died in Paris exile. → 91:19, 42; 92:11; 93:4, 19, 31; 94:4, 12, 30, 31, 33, 41, 48; 95:34. #ME33; E319, E614, E669.

Turgot, Anne Robert Jacques. Baron **de l'Aulne** (1727 to 1781) French economist and politician. Of a bourgeois family, influenced by the Physiocrats, he made an unsuccessful attempt in the 1770s, as the king's min and comptroller-gen of finance (1774–1776), to reform the economic system by abolishing feudal elements (e.g., corvées) and liberating bourgeois economic forces, plus stringent economizing. Chief work: *Réflexions sur la formation et la distribution des richesses* (written in 1766)—studied by M in his 1859–1862 notebooks—was a pioneer exposition of polit eco. Other works: *Lettres sur la tolérance*

(1753–1754); *Mémoire sur les prêts à intérêt* (1769). → 60:65; 68:27.

Turin; *Ital.* Torino Industrial city of N.W. Italy (Piedmont), on the Po. → 72:3, 4, 31, 36, 42, 53. #ME188; E839.

Turkey Formerly called the Ottoman Empire (extending far beyond Turkey proper) or Turkish Empire; Republic of Turkey proclaimed after World War I. → 53:1, 10, 15, 35, 40, 44, 46; 54:19; 56:12; 67:29; 68:68; 76:36; 77:1, 5, 13, 19, 35; 78:6, 40; 94:44. #ME25; M12, M250, M294, M358, M407, M479, M501, M801, M824, M873, M950–M954, M959, M989, M990; E32, E498, E595, E626–E628, E654, E716, E874, E874.5, E916.

Die **Turn-Zeitung** NY, Nov 15, 1851, to Apr 16, 1861. Monthly; later semimonthly.
—Socialistic and liberal in outlook; pubd by German émigrés. → 52:4, 17, 49. #E241, E579.

Twiss, Sir Travers (1809 to 1897) English lawyer; admitted to the bar (1840+); prof of civil law at Oxford (1855–1870); drafted the Congo's constitution for Belgium (1884). He was best known for his writings on interna-tional law, of which he was prof in London (1852–1855); pubd *The law of nations* (1861–1863). The writings by him which M read (1851) were prob his minor publications on polit eco, such as his *View of the progress of polit eco in Europe since the 16th century* (1847), also lectures *On money, On machin-ery, etc.* (1843–1845). → 51:63.

Tylor, Sir Edward Burnett (1832 to 1917) English anthropologist; the leading British pioneer in this field; prof at Oxford (1896–1909). His writings dealt esp with primitive religion: *Primitive culture* (1871); *Anthropol-ogy* (1881). M (1881) studied his *Researches into the early history of mankind* (1865). → 81:64.

Tyndall, John (1820 to 1893) British (Irish-born) physicist; prof at the Royal Insti-tution (1853+), its superintendent (1867+). Besides his own research on light, sound, heat, etc., he was well known as a popular-izer and popular lecturer on science, in such books as *Lessons in electricity* (1876); *On sound* (1867); *The forms of water* (1872); etc. —E read the 2nd edn (1865) of his book on heat, pubd in 1863. → 66:10.

U

Uetliberg (Switz.) Mountain with a sum-mit view (reached by rail) overlooking the Zurich area. → 93:40.

Ulmer, Johann German communist émi-gré, in London (1850+). Member of the CL; in the 1850 split he supported M, and functioned as a M supporter in the GWEA. → 51:36.

Union of German Workers Associations; *Ger.* Verband Deutscher Arbeitervereine A loose federation of local workers' clubs, founded at Frankfurt in June 1863, esp strong around Leipzig (Saxony), led by the young *Bebel, whose conversion to socialism started when Liebknecht settled in Leipzig in 1865. This workers' movement was allied with the Saxon People's party and German People's party, in a liberal-labor coalition considerably based on anti-Prussianism. It adopted a social-ist program in 1868–1869, and dissolved into the new *SDWP in 1869. → 68:49, 50, 56, 61, 64, 70; 69:2, 25, 26, 41, 48.

United Labor Party (NY) A labor-based party constituted in the summer of 1886 to run Henry George for NYC mayor; in the election of Nov 2 he obtained 31% of the vote. In Aug 1887 it held a conference in Syracuse to nominate George for NY governor, this time excluding SLP support; it petered out soon after. → 87:40.

United States —For correspondence about the U.S., *see* esp *Cluss, *Cuno, S. *Meyer, *Sorge, *Weydemeyer, *Wischnewetzky; *also* see *Bolte, W. *Burns, A.*Cahan, *Dana, Henry *George, *Hourwich, *Kamm, *Kriege, L. *Lewis, Abr. *Lincoln, *Lingenau, H. D. *Lloyd, J. T. *McEnnis. See *NYDT and other U.S. periodicals. See organizations: *AFL, *Knights of Labor, *Labor Reform Assoc, *National Labor Union, *SLP. See *Civil War (U.S.), *NY. —For the IWMA in the U.S., *see* subheadings under *IWMA, also *Section 12, and *Sorge, S. *Meyer; also the following miscellaneous entries: → 68:68; 69:30; 70:3, 39, 49, 59, 62; 71:3, 16, 35, 56, 57, 62; 72:20, 24–26, 35, 39, 41, 49. —General U.S. social-polit problems and affairs: → 47:46; 57:43; 58:13; 60:8; 68:40, 42, 68; 69:30; 70:32; 71:4, 33, 39, 47; 74:21; 75:5; 76:12; 77:24; 78:39; 79:19; 80:37; 81:10, 31, 32, 37, 51, 63, 64; 82:21; 83:8; 84:1, 5, 45; 86:9, 25, 32, 47, 51; 87:5; 91:23, 28; 92:7, 15, 60. —American socialist movement after 1872, its problems and defects: → 77:24; 79:43; 81:51; 82:12; 84:45; 86:9, 18, 25, 47, 51; 87:4, 25, 38, 40; 90:6; 91:9, 15, 35, 53; 92:7, 15; 93:53; 94:29, 44; 95:4. —M's possible emigration to the U.S.: → 45:39; 50:31; 66:41. —Other rela-tions with U.S. leftists; see above; miscella-neous entries: → 51:6; 53:20; 55:33, 48; 57:37; 84:49. —Emigrants and travelers going to the U.S.: → 50:5; 61:41; 64:17; 65:25; 67:37; 69:32; 72:51; 80:11, 40; 81:17, 28, 32, 51; 82:5; 84:15; 86:3, 13, 35, 37, 38; 87:1, 5, 8. —E's American tour: → 88:28, 30. —German-

American press: → 51:15, 32, 54; 54:21; 57:45; 59:1, 43, 68; 64:39; 67:27; 81:4; 93:6; 94:1.

Universal Federalist Council → 72:20, 24. #M857.

Universal Republican League → 72:3.

University of . . . See name of city; e.g., Jena, University of.

Unkiar Skelessi; now Hunkyar Iskelesi (Turkey) Village on the Bosphorus where a Russo-Turkish treaty of mutual assistance was signed on July 8, 1833. → 54:9.

Unsere Zeit Leipzig, 1857 to 1891. Monthly (1865+). Pub'r: Brockhaus. —Liberal magazine of literature and politics. → 62:22.

Unter dem Banner des Marxismus Vienna, Mar 1925 to Nov 1935. —German edn of the IML's theoretical organ. #M368, M970.

Ure, Andrew (1778 to 1857) Scottish chemist; popular-science writer, lecturer, and encyclopedist. Prof of chemistry at Glasgow (1804–1830); director of Glasgow Observatory (1809+); later practiced in London as a commercial chemist (1830–1857) and chemist of the Bd of Customs (1834+). He pubd reference works on chemistry, geology, etc., incl a *Dictionary of arts, manufactures and mines* (1839) which M studied (1851) in a German trans, *Technisches Wörterbuch* (1843–1844). But M's main interest was in Ure's sole work on polit eco theory, *Philosophy of manufactures* (1835), a defense of the factory system and free trade, which M first read (1845) in French trans. Ure also pubd *The cotton manufacturers of Gr Brit* (1836). → 45:50; 51:71. #M575.

Urquhart, David (1805 to 1877) British (Scottish) diplomat, politician, and publicist. He fought in the Greek war of independence (1827–1828); entered British diplomatic service, first on the embassy staff in Turkey (1831); led a mission to Constantinople (1833), recalled; embassy secy in Constantinople (1835), recalled (1837). MP (1847–1852); virulent opponent of Palmerston's foreign policy. As the leading Russophobe and Turkophile in Britain, he developed the view that Palmerston was acting as a Russian agent; and organized a movement of "Urquhartite" groups, called Foreign Affairs Comms, throughout the country, incl within the Chartist movement as well as the Tories. Besides publishing denunciations of Russia in his *Turkey and its resources* (1833) and other books, he founded *The Portfolio* (1835); also founded the *Sheffield Free Press* and (1855) the *Free Press* of London, which was renamed the *Diplomatic Review* (1866). Other books: *The crisis* (1840); *Familiar words as affecting England and the English* (1856); *The Lebanon* (1860). A minor accom-

plishment was his introduction of Turkish baths into England. —M recognized only one point of agreement with U.: opposition to Palmerston's foreign policy as pro-Russian in effect; otherwise M&E rejected his general views and, privately and publicly (in the *NYDT*), characterized them as reactionary, backward-looking nonsense, and explained that U. was a crazy, crackpot, medievalizing, pro-Turk idealizer of Islam. M met him only once (Feb 1854), and reported to E that he was a "complete monomaniac," thought revolutionists were all Russian agents, and had fits when contradicted. But while openly publishing his negative opinions of U. several times, M also defended the idea of limited joint propaganda action with his groups on the common area of foreign policy (letter to Lassalle, June c.2, 1860). → 53:1, 10, 15, 41, 42, 45, 54; 54:4, 8, 20, 28, 29; 55:47, 49; 56:4, 26; 57:16; 60:12, 35; 72:54. #M212.5, M426, M959.

Urquhartites Supporters of *Urquhart, esp in the Foreign Affairs Comms founded by him. → 53:32; 54:1, 20; 56:1, 4, 17, 21, 23, 26, 30, 36; 57:1, 7, 12, 16; 58:18; 59:34, 35; 60:7; 65:54; 69:32. See also Free Press; Sheffield Free Press.

Ursulines Religious order of nuns founded (1525) for education and care of sick and needy people; patron saint, St. Ursula; at peak in the 18th century. #E885.

Utin, Nikolai Isaakovich; Fr. **Outine** (1845 to 1883) Russian revolutionary. Son of a banker, he became active in the student movement; joined the Zemlya i Volya (member of its CC); emigrated (1863) first to England, then to Switzerland. In the 1860s he was a leading figure among the so-called Young Emigration in disputes with Herzen, within the Narodnik movement; ed bd of *Narodnaya Delo* (1868–1870). He was one of the founders of the Russian section of the IWMA in Geneva (1870); an editor of *Egalité* (1870–1871); delegate to the London Conference (1871). In Geneva he was a leader in the fight against Bakunin and his Alliance operation; he was M's main source of info in exposing the content of Bakunin's Russian writings, relation to Nechayev, etc., though never a Marxist in any sense. After the collapse of the IWMA he returned to Russia (1877), quit the revolutionary movement, and eventually became a wealthy government contractor. → 71:35, 62; 72:8, 9, 42; 73:51, 52; 76:26; 77:3, 7. #ME6, ME7A, ME133.

Utina, Natalia Yeronimovna; *Westernized* Natalie Hieronimovna **Utin;** *née* **Korsini** Russian writer; wife of N. I. *Utin. She was a contributor to *Vestnik Yevropy* and other journals. → 77:7.

Utješenović, Ognjeslav Matthias; *also*

called **Utiešenović-Ostrožinski** *or spelled* **Utieshenovich-Ostrozhinski** (1817 to 1890) Croatian writer and poet. M (1876) read his work *Die Hauskommunionen der Südslawen* (1859). → 76:40.

Uttenhoven, *Captain* von (d. 1849) Prussian army officer. In 1849 he commanded a company attacking barricades during the Elberfeld uprising in May, and was shot there. → 49:14.

V

Vahlteich, Julius; *full* Karl Julius (1839 to 1915) German socialist. Shoemaker by trade, he learned of Weitling's ideas and French socialism while a traveling journeyman; settled in his native Leipzig (1861–1862) where he helped establish a WEA to promote workers' political action and universal suffrage. The left wing of this movement decided on a workers' congress, and contacted Lassalle, thus leading to the formation of the GGWA (1863), with V. as first secy. But he dissented from Lassalle's dictatorship; resigned as secy (1864), and, though still loyal to the organization, was expelled. V. then became a supporter of the Bebel–Liebknecht tendency; founded an IWMA section in Dresden (1867); helped found the Eisenacher SDWP (1869). Editor of a Crimmitschau daily (1871); editor of the *Chemnitzer Ztg* (1872). Deputy to the N. German Reichstag and German Reichstag (1871–1874, 1874–1876, 1878–1881). After the imposition of the Anti-Socialist Law, he emigrated to the U.S. (1881), where he remained an active socialist, as shoemaker, photographer, and (1906+) editor of German-American socialist papers in NY and Chicago. Author of a critique of Lassalle, *FL und die Anfänge der deutschen Arbeiterbewegung* (1905). → 63:39; 76:29; 83:12.

Vaillant, Edouard (1840 to 1915) French socialist; longtime leader of the Blanquist tendency. Science student in France and also (1866–1870) in Germany; in Vienna, he associated with J. Most and A. Scheu. Back in France (Sep 1870) he worked closely with the IWMA and helped Blanqui. He was elected to the Paris Commune, where he functioned on the Exec, Education Commsn, and *Journal Officiel.* In London emigration, his M.D. degree and family money avoided hardships; a leader of the Blanquist refugees, he also came to know M, read *Capital,* became a member of the GC, and, in the London Conference (1871) and Hague Congress (1872), championed political action and opposed Bakunin; but he was alienated by removing the GC to NY; helped draft Blanquist propaganda pamphlets. Back in France after the 1880 amnesty, he wrote for Blanquist papers and helped form the Comité Révolutionnaire Central with co-leaders Eudes and Granger; active in electoral work; elected (1884) to the Paris city council. After Eudes' death (1888) and Granger's split (1889), V. became the undisputed leader of the Blanquist group, which moved to convergence with a semi-Marxist social-democracy; became the Parti Socialiste Révolutionnaire (1898); and entered into the 1905 unified SP, in which V. was one of the top triumvirate. The outbreak of World War I reanimated the traditional Blanquist national chauvinism in addition to social-democratic social-patriotism, and when he died in 1915 there were government eulogies over his coffin. → 71:39, 47; 72:35, 49, 54; 90:48; 92:13; 94:4; 95:10, 16–19, 24.

Valais; *Ger.* Wallis Alpine canton in S.W. Switzerland; mostly French-speaking. #E145, E732.

Valdenaire, Victor (1791 to 1859) Ger. landowner; Trier liberal. In 1848 he was a deputy to the Prussian assembly (left wing). → 56:40. #ME189; E155.

Vandenhouten, Alphonse Belgian socialist; painter by trade, from Charleroi. A founder of the IWMA in Belgium (1865), member of its Federal Council, and its corr secy. —*Caution:* The historian L. Bertrand spells his name four different ways, incl Van den Houte. → 67:16.

Vanderlint, Jacob (d. 1740) English writer on economics, who in 1734 pubd a pamphlet *Money answers all things* (studied by M, 1859) which gained notoriety in the 19th century because it opposed restrictions on business and advocated wage cuts. Little is known of him otherwise. → 59:77.

Vandervelde, Emile (1866 to 1938) Belgian socialist; lawyer by profession. A founder of the Belgian Labor party; long a leader of the reformist wing of the Second International, and its chairman (1900+). He entered Parliament (1894), served in many cabinets (1918+). Author of a number of social-democratic tracts, often pitched in Marxist phraseology, incl *Le collectivisme et l'évolution industrielle* (1900), *Le socialisme contre l'état* (1918). → 94:39.

Vanity Fair London, 1868 to 1928. Weekly. —Conservative. → 77:9, 13; 82:55.

Van Patten, Philip American socialist. A former member of the Knights of Labor (1881+), he became secy of the Workingmen's party of America (1876+) and of the SLP

(1879+); sympathized with Lassallean social-ism; one of the few native Americans active in the leadership of the movement. In Mar 1883, as the result of J. Most's lying claims (at a Marx memorial meeting in NY) of having M's support, Van P. wrote a letter of inquiry to E; but without waiting for E's reply, he suddenly (Apr 22) walked off into oblivion leaving a note which explained that he felt the German-American socialist leaders did not care whether Americans understood their ideas or not. He found a federal government job, and later became a merchant in Hot Springs, Arkansas. → 83:20. #E551.

Varenholz, Karl (1858 to 1930) German-born member of the British SDF in 1884–1885. → 85:11.

Varlin, Eugène; *full* Louis Eugène (1839 to 1871) French socialist: trade-unionist (book-binder), IWMA leader, Communard. Of a peasant family, he was active in his TU society (1857+); member of the delegation of French workers to London (1862); active in bookbinders' strikes (1864, 1865), and formed a new union excluding employers and allowing equality for women workers. He joined the IWMA (1865); attended the London Conference that year; came to know M; delegate to the Geneva Congress (1866); again active in a strike wave (1869), harassed by government arrests and persecution. Besides, he was active in forming co-ops; contributed to the left press. Varlin tried to orient the French IWMA toward socialist political action, breaking with the Proudhonist tendency in this respect as in others; in fact, although only age 32 at death, he was the French leader who pointed the way out of the sterility to which the IWMA was condemned in France by the Tolain–Fribourg leadership. He was elected to the Paris Commune, in which he was active in several posts; during Bloody Week he took a leading part in the barricade fighting; was captured by the Versailles forces; it took three volleys by a firing squad to kill him, after which the lieutenant in command stole his watch. → 71:23.

Varna; *now called* Stalin Bulgarian Black Sea port. #M323.

Varnhagen von Ense, Karl August (1785 to 1858) German man of letters; liberal. After a career in the Prussian military and diplomatic service, he devoted himself to writing, esp literary criticism and biographies (e.g., *Biographische Denkmaler,* 1824–1830); collaborated with Chamisso on the *Musenalmanach* (1804+). In 1814 he married Rahel Antonie Friederike Levin (1771–1833), who for many years sponsored an important salon frequented by leading writers. After his death, his niece Ludmilla Assing edited his correspondence and his *Tagebücher* (diaries,

1861–1870)—which M referred to in 1862. → 62:21.

Vasilchikov, *Prince* Alexander Ilarionovich (1818 to 1881) Russian publicist, representing a liberal-landlord view among the nobility. He favored zemstvo (local government) development, producers' co-ops for the peasantry, and the development of the *obshchina* (village community) to save Russia from capitalism and revolution. Chief works: *Zemlevladeniye i zemledeliye v Rossii i drugikh yevropeyskikh gossudarstvakh* (1876), which M studied in 1877, and *O samoupravleniyi* (1869–1871). → 77:48.

Vatke, Wilhelm; *full* Johann Karl Wilhelm (1806 to 1882) German Protestant theologian. Hegelian; prof at Berlin (1837+); a founder of modern Hexateuch criticism. Chief work: *Die Religion des alten Testaments* (1835–1836). M (1842) wanted to review his book *Die menschliche Freiheit in ihrem Verhältnis zur Sünde* [etc.] (1841). → 42:6.

Vaud; *Ger.* Waadt Swiss canton, the westernmost except Geneva; French-speaking; capital, Lausanne. → 49:32.

Vaughan, Robert (1795 to 1868) British clergyman (born in W. England, of Welsh descent), Congregationalist. Prof of history in London (1834+), he pubd writings esp on the Stuart and Commonwealth periods and on religious history, esp after retiring from religious labors (1857). M (1851) read his *The age of great cities* (1843). → 51:69.

Vehse, Eduard; *full* Karl Eduard (1802 to 1870) German historian. He was first an archivist in Dresden (1825–1838); traveled in the U.S. (1839); in 1851 pubd the first vol. of his chief work, *Geschichte der deutschen Höfe seit der Reformation* (1851–1860), for which he was harassed by the Prussian authorities after he settled in Berlin (1853). He retired to near Basel (1856), later to Italy and Saxony. —G. *Weerth was an acquaintance. → 52:27, 48.

Veltheim, Werner von (1817 to 1855) German relative of Mrs. Jenny M; landowner in Ostrau-Stumsdorf near Halle. He was the son of Franz von Veltheim (a former inspector-gen of mines), the brother of Ludwig von Westphalen's *first* wife Lisette (1778–1807), whereas Jenny was the product of Ludwig's second marriage. Werner had been a student chum of Edgar von *Westphalen, and through Edgar had met M in 1839. → 51:44.

Venedey, Jakob (1805 to 1871) German liberal publicist and politician. Born in Cologne, later active in Heidelberg, he fled arrest in Germany, and in the Paris emigration helped found the Deutscher Volksverein, later (1834) a more radical group, the League of the Outcast (Bund der Geächteten), whose organ

V. edited with a tax-the-rich platform. In 1836 the communist wing of this league (T. Schuster, Ewerbeck, et al.) split and established the League of the Just (which later became the CL), leaving Venedey behind. In 1848 he was a deputy in the Pre-Parliament and in the Frankfurt National Assembly, where he endorsed the government's suppression of revolutionary strivings; afterward, a liberal. → 48:28.

Venice; *Ital.* Venezia Chief city of the province of Venetia (*Ital.* Veneto): included in Napoleon's Kingdom of Italy (1805); seized by Austria (1815); revolted (1848–1849); ceded to Italy (1866). → 83:4.

Ventnor (Eng.) City and resort, Isle of Wight (S. shore). → 81:59; 82:3, 39, 49, 54; 83:3, 6.

Verband Deutscher Arbeitervereine See Union of German Workers Associations.

Verein für Arbeiter und Arbeitgeber (Cologne) As the name indicates (Assoc for Workers and Employers), this was the most rightish of the three Cologne groups involved in the Democratic movement (1848–1849). #M40.

Vereinbarung-Policy (Germany, 1848) See the note appended to #E154. —A number of titles of articles by M/E in the NRZ of 1848 are affected by a translation problem which is a confusing element in all English versions. These are titles containing the word *Vereinbarungs-* (the combining form of compounds). *Vereinbarung* literally means agreement; in the *Register* it is translated conciliationist, e.g., "conciliationist assembly." *MECW* uses the literal form: "agreement assembly"; other translators have used a variety of forms, often much worse, and sometimes flatly wrong. — Here is the problem. M&E's policy in the NRZ was to urge the Frankfurt assembly to declare itself the sovereign power, as against the power of the crown; but the assembly chose the line of seeking an agreement, a deal, a *Vereinbarung*, with the crown in the hope that the crown would share state power with the bourgeois constitutionalists. To highlight this fundamental difference, the NRZ adopted a verbal expedient to keep harping on the issue: *Vereinbarung* was made a pejorative prefix for various things about the assembly. It was tagged a *Vereinbarung*-Assembly; its debates were called *Vereinbarung*-debates; its sessions, *Vereinbarung*-sessions; etc. That is, the assembly sought conciliation with the crown rather than its overthrow; and this issue was the focal problem of the entire revolution.

Veritas A pseud. used by E. #827.

La Vérité Paris, Oct 6, 1870, to Sep 3, 1871. Daily. —Radical paper, not socialist. → 71:40. #M896.

Verlet, Henry (or Henri); *real name* (Louis Joseph) Henri **Place** (1847 to 1902) French Blanquist journalist; orig a typographical worker. In 1870 he was edit secy of *Libre Pensée;* on P. Lafargue's recommendation, the GC/IWMA voted him credentials as a Paris organizer; he helped found a Paris section in Apr. In the Paris Commune he fought as an army officer; captured; imprisoned till 1879. After the amnesty he again became active in the Blanquist group; in 1889 went with the "Boulangeo-Blanquist" split led by *Granger, but returned (1896) to Vaillant's party. → 70:24.

Vermersch, Eugène; *full* Eugène Marie Joseph (1845 to 1878) French radical ranter. Son of a Lille police sergeant, he became a journalist in Paris; pubd verse; worked on Vallès' *Le Cri du Peuple.* Just before the Paris Commune he founded *Le Père Duchêne* (stealing the 1793 name), which produced much revenue and a reputation as a "filthy sheet" of yellow journalism yelling for blood and mass killings, filled with slanders. Afterward he took refuge in various countries, finally England; joined the "French Section of 1871," and founded *Qui Vive!*, the *Vermersch Journal*, and *Union Démocratique* (all in 1871–1872); left England (1874) for various countries, eventually coming back to London (1875); half insane, he died three years later. —V. acted out in print (not in action) the very model of the mindless, wild-eyed, foaming-at-the-mouth "revolutionist," tossing off irresponsible invocations to bloodletting and crime—a model which may very well have been the conception of a Lille police sergeant. M&E's comments on this "arch-scum" were uninhibited. —His name is often misspelled Vermesch. → 71:46.

Vermorel, Auguste (Jean Marie) (1841 to 1871) French left journalist and publicist. A Proudhonist in general orientation, he worked during the 1860s on the staff of the *Presse, Liberté,* and other papers; in 1866–1867, edited *Courrier Français.* Harassed and imprisoned for his attacks on the government, he was eventually released by the fall of the Empire (Sep 1870). Elected to the Paris Commune, he fought in its defense, was wounded on the barricades, was captured, and died in prison. Author of *Les hommes de 1848* (1869), also of a number of novels; edited the works of Mirabeau, Marat, et al. → 67:29; 69:22.

Verri, Count Pietro (1728 to 1797) Italian economist; an early critic of the Physiocrats. After publishing *Elementi di commercio* (1760), he worked for the Austrian government in Milan; copublished a liberal organ, the *Caffè.* He was regarded as the leading economist of the century; an advocate of laissez-faire. His chief work was *Meditazioni sulla economia politica* (1771), which M

(1859) excerpted from the Custodi collection. → 59:77.

Versailles (Fr.) City near Paris; site of Louis XIV's palace. The government being moved there in response to the Paris Commune, "Versailles" in 1871 connotes this government and its "Versaillese" forces. → 71:20, 23.

Vésinier, Pierre (1824 to 1902) French left republican. An anti-Bonapartist émigré after 1851, he lived in Belgium and Switzerland by writing pornographic fiction; returned to France after 1859 and was active with Blanquist elements. During the 1860s he was expelled from one or another country at intervals. He joined the IWMA in 1865 in London, and helped found the London French section, soon getting into a venomous dispute by attacking the IWMA in France; in 1868 he was secy of this section when it was expelled. After the fall of the Empire he was active in Paris, with Pyat's papers, and with the Garibaldians. Elected to the Paris Commune, he was for a time editor of its *Journal Officiel.* Afterward, a refugee in London, he wrote for *Vermersch's press, and helped found the "French Section of 1871," which, cast out by the GC, sought to form a rival International. His journal *La Fédération* came to be regarded as a police enterprise by the French Refugee Society, which expelled him. Returning to France after the amnesty, he eventually joined the Guesdist party (1883), which survived this blow. In 1892 he pubd a work on the Commune, haled into court as libelous. —V. was widely seen by fellow Communards as one of the most unpleasant characters in the movement, a bitter Quasimodo twisted in mind and body. → 65:62; 66:5, 9, 17; 68:55, 61; 72:53.

Vestnik Barodnoi Voli; Messager de la volonté du peuple   Geneva, 1883 to 1886. —Emigré Narodnik journal.   #M464.

Vestnik Yevropy   St. Petersburg, 1866 to Jan/Apr 1919. Monthly. —Liberal journal, political and literary. → 80:31.

Vevey; Ger. Vivis (Switz.) City in Vaud canton, N.E. shore of Lake Geneva. → 49:32, 33, 35; 82:30,34; 83:27, 28.   #E812.

Vickery, Samuel   British socialist. As secy of the IWMA's British Federal Council (Dec 1872 to May 1873), he actively supported M&E against the lib-lab wing, and corresponded with E; chairman of the congress (1873) of the British Federation in Manchester. → 73:11, 23.

Vico, Giovanni Battista or Giambattista (1668 to 1744) Italian social thinker and historian. Prof at Naples (1697+); historiographer to the King of Naples (1734+). His ideas on establishing laws of social development in history were put forward in his *De universi iuris uno principio et fine uno* (1720) and in

Principi di una scienza nuova d'intorno alla comune natura delle nazioni (1725; revised, 1730, 1744). → 62:21.

Victoria, *Princess; full* Victoria Adelaide Mary Louisa; *later* Empress of Germany, *called (Angl.)* Empress Frederick (1840 to 1901) The oldest child of Queen Victoria and Prince Albert, princess royal of Gr Brit, she married (1858) Prince Friedrich Wilhelm of Prussia, who later became emperor (kaiser) as Friedrich III three months before his death (1888). She was the mother of Kaiser Wilhelm II, whose politics she detested; she remained a British liberal to the last, hostile to Bismarck, friendly with German liberals like Bamberger. After her husband's death, she was generally known in England as Empress Frederick. → 58:13; 79:8, 13.   #M184.

Victoria, *Queen; full* Alexandrina Victoria (1819 to 1901)   Queen of the United Kingdom of Gr Brit and Ireland (1837+) and Empress of India (1876+); of the house of Hanover. She married Prince Albert of Saxe-Coburg-Gotha (1819–1861) in 1840.   #E887.

Vidal, Francois (1812 to 1872) French socialist writer; lawyer by profession. In the 1830s he was strongly influenced by the Saint-Simonians and Fourier, whose teachings he combined with Blanc, Buchez, and Pecqueur; contributed to the *Démocratie Pacifique*; chief work: *De la répartition des richesses* (1846); advocated consumers co-ops and productive associations financed by capitalists and the state. In 1848 Blanc appointed him secy of the ill-fated Luxemburg Commsn, for which he pubd an eclectic plan. Author of *Vivre en travaillant* (1848); *Le travail affranchi* (1849). In 1850 he won election as a socialist to the Legislative Assembly. After Bonaparte's Dec 1851 coup, he retired from public life to practice law in the Gironde. → 51:71.

Vidil, Jules   French Blanquist; former army oficer. In the London emigration of the 1850s, he was a leader of the French Blanquist organization, and supported the Willich–Schapper faction against M in 1850. → 50:15; 51:14.   #ME80, ME171.

Vienna; Ger. Wien   Capital city of Austria. → 48:57, 58, 71, 72, 76, 77, 79, 82; 49:3; 50:12; 54:28; 57:53; 58:13; 61:1, 17, 50, 54; 62:9; 68:15, 37, 42; 69:35, 47, 50, 60; 70:59; 71:10, 16, 30; 76:6; 80:11; 90:14, 46; 91:6, 27, 34, 54; 92:43; 93:21, 40, 42; 94:1; 95:5, 32, 33.   #ME190; M43, M329, M373, M445, M449, M559, M563, M643, M777, M831, M832, M961–M964; E363, E537, E699, E765, E795, E813.5, E888.

Vienna, University of → 84:19.

Viereck, Louis (1851 to 1922) German social-reform pub'r and publicist. As a Social-Democrat during the Anti-Socialist Law, he sought to turn the party rightward, and to this end founded over a dozen right-wing S-D papers (1882–1889); e.g., his *Das Recht auf Arbeit* endorsed Bismarck's social program; his chain pubd C. A. *Schramm's pro-Rodbertus and anti-M campaign. He entered the Reichstag (1884), was defeated (1887); by this time, also, the police had suppressed most of his papers in blind ingratitude. The party congress (Oct 1887) expelled him from party posts for organizational indiscipline; he quit the S-D party, and emigrated (1890) to the U.S. → 81:4, 17, 32; 83:7.

Villafranca di Verona Town in N.E. Italy, near Verona; Austro-French treaty signed here in 1859. #M940.

Villegardelle, François (1810 to 1856) French socialist writer. Orig a Fourierist and collaborator with *La Phalange;* later a communist, i.e., advocate of communal property; strongly influenced by Buonarroti, whom he pubd in excerpts. He produced edns of Morelly and Campanella; author of *Besoins des communes* (1835); *Accord des intérêts* (1836). M (1845) read his *Histoire des idées sociales avant la Révolution française* (1846). → 45:50. #M575.

Villeneuve-Bargemont, Alban de; *full* Jean Paul Alban, *vicomte* de Villeneuve-Bargemont (1784 to 1850) French economist and administrator. Administrative official (prefect) under Napoleon and the Restoration; deputy (1840+). His works differed from other conservative royalists in concern with workers' conditions and an interest in industrialization. His chief work, read by M (1845), was *Economie politique chrétienne* (1834), which looked to curbing the excesses of capitalism and heralded social-catholicism. Also author of *Histoire de l'économie politique* (1839). → 45:50. #M575.

Villières A French émigré in London in 1852. Maitron's *DBMOF* lists a refugee of this name who, in 1853, belonged to F. Pyat's "Commune Révolutionnaire" group. → 52:7.

Virginia (U.S.) → 62:26.

Vischer, Friedrich Theodor (1807 to 1887) German philosopher; prof at Tübingen, later Zurich (1855+), then Stuttgart (1866+). He sought to apply the Hegelian dialectic to art in a large work on *Aesthetik* (1846–1857). He took part in the 1848 revolution; later moved away from Hegelianism; also wrote satirical novels, literary criticism, and poetry. → 57:19.

Vivanti, Anna Sister of Paul Lindau; no other info. → 72:16.

Vivis (Switz.) *See* Vevey.

Vlissingen; *Angl.* Flushing Seaport and resort in S.W. Netherlands. → 76:25.

Voden, Alexei Mikhailovich (1870 to 1939) Russian man of letters; translator. He

took part in Social-Democratic circles in the 1890s. → 93:22.

Vögele, August German typesetter working in London. In 1859 he worked in F. Hollinger's printshop; helped M on the Vogt affair. → 59:56, 60, 65; 60:12, 14.

Vogler, Carl Georg (b. c.1820) German émigré, pub'r-bookdealer in Brussels. He pubd M's #681. → 47:18; 48:31, 47, 74.

Vogt, August (c.1830 to c.1883) German communist worker (shoemaker). Member of the CL; supporter of M; took part in the 1848–1849 revolution. In the 1860s he was a member of the GGWA, belonging to the anti-Lassallean opposition; with S. Meyer, he urged M (1865) to become pres; helped form the Berlin section of the IWMA (1866). Then (May 1867) he emigrated to the U.S. There he joined the Communist Club of NY; was active in the IWMA in America; sent German correspondence on the movement to the GC and M. → 65:57; 68:49; 70:26.

Vogt, Johann Gustav (1843 to *after* 1912) German philosopher, of materialist tendency; author of a number of works on science and philosophy, e.g., *Die Kraft* (1878), *Das Empfindungsprinzip und das Protoplasma auf Grund eines einheitlichen Substanzbegriffes* (1891). → 91:39.

Vogt, Karl (Christoph) (1817 to 1895) German naturalist (zoologist and geologist), also politician. His main reputation was as a Darwinian scientist—prof at Giessen (1847+), at Geneva (1852+)—who advocated a form of mechanical materialism, and also wrote popularizing works on scientific subjects. In 1848 he was a liberal member of the Pre-Parliament and the Frankfurt National Assembly; in June 1849, named one of the five Reich regents. In the 1850s–1860s he pubd on European politics (*Studien zur gegenwärtigen Lage Europas*, 1859), advocating a pro-Bonaparte attitude; enemy of socialism. Under the Paris Commune, government records revealed that he received payment as a propagandist from the Bonaparte regime. —His slanderous attack on M appeared in his book *Mein Prozess gegen die Allgemeine Zeitung* (1859). → 50:18; 59: 2, 6–9, 31, 35, 44, 49, 53, 56, 60, 65, 66, 71; 60:1, 5, 7, 9, 12, 13, 15–17, 20, 23, 28, 34, 37, 39, 41, 45, 51, 54, 61; 61:3, 21, 46; 67:37; 68:53; 71:22, 25. #M372, M592, M617; E383, E571. *See also* *Dâ-Dâ Vogt.

Das **Volk** London, May 7 to Aug 20, 1859. Weekly. Founder: E. Biskamp. —German-language organ of the London GWEA. M began contributing with No. 2, and in July virtually took over the editorship of the paper. → 59:3, 8, 34, 35, 43, 44, 46, 50, 51, 54, 55, 59. #M181, M296, M321, M342, M419, M590.5, M675, M725, M837; E56, E69, E115, E134, E257, E397, E587, E687.

Het **Volk** Rotterdam. Pub'r: P. von Roesgen von Floss. —No more info is available. → 70:17.

Volkhovsky, Felix Vadimovich (1846 to 1914) Russian revolutionary. Of a noble family, he became a collaborator with Lopatin (1867+), was repeatedly arrested, led a group in Odessa (1873); arrested and banished (1874), escaped (1889), and went first to America, then to London (1890). There, a friend of Stepniak, he was a leader in the Russian émigré society and its fund-raising activities; in the early 1900s, a Socialist-Revolutionary. → 92:61.

Volks-Kalender Brunswick (Ger.), 1874 to 1878. Yearbook. Pub'r/editor: W. Bracke — Social-Democratic. #E406.

Der **Volks-Tribun** NY, Jan 5 to Dec 31, 1846. Weekly. Ed by H. Kriege. —Kriege here expounded his own peculiar brand of mystical pop-radicalism, as a disciple of Weitling. #ME28.

Volks-Zeitung Berlin, 1853 to 1889. Daily. —Liberal oppositional organ. → 59:65. #M592, M617, M852.

Der **Volksfreund** Brünn (now Brno), 1881+. —German-language organ of the Austrian socialists in this Moravian (now Czechoslovakian) center. → 91:59. #M831, M880; E838.

Der **Volksstaat** Leipzig, Oct 2, 1869, to Sep 29, 1876. Semiweekly; then (July 2, 1873+) thrice weekly. Ed by W. Liebknecht. —At the founding congress of the German SDWP ("Eisenachers"), the *Demokratisches Wochenblatt was renamed Volksstaat and made the central organ. It came to an end a year after the 1875 unification congress, when the party congress (again at Gotha, Aug 23, 1876) voted to merge Volksstaat and the Lassallean Neuer Social-Demokrat into a single central organ named *Vorwärts. — Volksstaat pubd IWMA documents and statements; E began writing for it May 1871, most often in 1874–1875; M pubd only his replies to Brentano (#M739, M740) in 1872. → 69:66; 70:19, 21, 28, 29, 33, 36, 40, 45, 48, 52, 57; 71:5, 15, 21, 22, 25, 28, 29, 41, 57, 58, 61; 72:3, 4, 8, 23, 24, 27, 30, 33–35, 39, 47, 51, 52, 56, 62, 67; 73:8, 9, 12, 14, 23, 27, 33, 36, 38, 44, 49, 51; 74:2, 7–10, 13, 15, 19, 22, 24, 26, 29, 36, 37, 39; 75:8, 10, 12, 14, 17, 36; 76:4, 7, 13, 21, 30. #ME88, ME133, ME184; M143, M224, M268, M347, M478, M521, M696, M737, M738, M745, M751, M752.5, M756, M762, M763, M813, M898, M920, M927, M930; E4, E59, E66, E111.5, E179, E195, E245, E283, E307, E358, E371, E380, E382, E383, E539, E543, E555, E569, E571, E579, E580, E592, E621, E645, E660–E662, E678, E679, E689, E730, E744, E754, E820.

Der **Volkswille** Vienna, Jan 30, 1870, to June 27, 1874. Weekly; then (Oct 2, 1872+) semiweekly. Ed by A. Scheu, Heinrich Oberwinder, et al. —S-D organ; it pubd documents of the IWMA. Continuation of Die Volksstimme. #E358.

Vollmar, Georg (Heinrich) von (1850 to 1922) German Social-Democrat; right-wing leader in Bavaria. Of an old aristocratic family, his army career was ended when he was permanently crippled in the Franco-Prussian War; turned to studies; contributed to the liberal press; joined the Social-Democracy (1872); editor of the Dresdener Volksbote (1877). During the Anti-Socialist Law, an émigré; in Zurich, he became the first editor of the Sozialdemokrat (till succeeded by Bernstein in 1880). During the 1880s he stressed ultraleft antiparliamentarism, the use of force, etc., as against Bebel's policy of "revolutionary parliamentarism"; left-wing leader at the 1883 party congress. Elected to the Saxon Diet (1883–1889) he devoted himself to practical parliamentary work. He returned to Munich; was elected to the Reichstag (1890); became the recognized leader of the Bavarian party; moved right, and developed a program of extreme reformism, anticipating (or pioneering) the later Revisionism, esp with regard to vote-catching among big farmers. The 1903 party congress condemned his policies, he lost in the party debate, and faded into the background. Reichstag deputy (1890–1918). Author of Der isolierte soziale Staat (1880); Über die nächsten Aufgaben der deutschen Social Demokratie (1891). → 79:2, 33, 38, 41; 82:44; 84:43; 91:33; 92:33, 55; 94:39, 43, 48. #E444.

Volunteer Corps (Eng.) Movement, initiated in May 1859 by the British war secy, for voluntary paramilitary bodies of civilians, within the framework of an 1804 army act in response to a war scare (invasion by Napoleon III). → 60:3, 40, 44, 50, 53, 57; 61:16, 19, 29; 62:43, 58.

The **Volunteer Journal** for Lancashire and Cheshire Manchester, 1860 to 1862. Weekly. Pub'r: W. H. Smith & Sons. Ed by Capt. Isaac Hall. —Organ of the *Volunteer Corps movement. → 60:3, 44, 50, 53, 57, 64; 61:1, 7, 12, 16, 19, 24, 29, 36, 52, 58; 62:1, 16, 43. #E11, E99, E153, E249, E293, E297, E355, E431, E483, E563, E685, E686, E704, E890–E893, E896, E901, E909.

Der **Vorbote** Geneva, Jan 1866 to Dec 1871. Monthly. Ed by J. P. Becker. —German-language organ in Switzerland of the IWMA; subtitled (Jan 1867+) "Central organ of the German-speaking sections of the IWMA." Becker wanted to make it the organ of German-speaking sections in all countries, e.g., Austria, U.S., etc. → 65:62; 66:6, 9; 67:12, 37; 70:45; 71:29. #M318, M325,

M397, M707, M743, M744, M747, M751, M813, M826.

Vorontsev, Vasily Pavlovich (1847 to 1918) Russian liberal-Narodnik economist; physician by profession; journalist (pseud.: V. V.). After contributing to Lavrov's *Vpered,* he broke with the Narodniks on violence but was regarded as their theoretician on economic questions. Chief works: *Sudbi kapitalizma v Rossii* (1882); *Krestyanskaya obshchina* (1892). → 82:48.

Vorwärts Berlin, Jan 1, 1891 to 1933; revived 1946. Daily. Ed by W. Liebknecht (till 1900). —Central organ of the Social-Democratic party. Beginning Jan 1, 1891, the *Berliner Volksblatt* changed its name to *Vorwärts* with *B.V.* as the subtitle. → 90:42; 91:1, 11, 17, 29, 33, 44, 50; 92:18, 29, 32, 34, 60; 93:4, 12, 19, 24, 40, 55; 94:5, 6, 12, 43, 46; 95:3, 6, 16, 24, 25. #E17, E106, E118, E125, E166, E385, E393, E395, E444, E560, E561, E759, E764, E765, E806, E845, E852.

Vorwärts Leipzig, Oct 1876 to Oct 1878. Thrice weekly. Ed by W. Liebknecht, W. Hasenclever. —Organ of the S-D party after the 1875 unification; it was issued a year after the unity congress, replacing both the *Volksstaat* and the *Neuer Social-Demokrat.* It ceased when the Anti-Socialist Law came in, replaced by the illegal *Sozialdemokrat.* → 77:4, 10, 15, 18, 23, 27, 46; 78:16, 35, 37. #M207, M370, M739; E23, E373, E533.

Vorwärts! Paris, Jan 2 to Dec 28, 1844, and one number in Jan 1845. Semiweekly. Pub'r: Alexis Reynaud. Ed by H. Börnstein; Bernays for a period (July 1 to Sep 12). —German-language émigré organ; M became active in its edit work Sep+. Suppressed under Prussian pressure; a planned monthly, *Vorwärts! Pariser deutsche Monatsschrift,* did not come into being. —See Jacques Grandjonc, *Marx et les communistes allemands à Paris 1844* (Paris, 1974); transd and rev as *"Vorwärts!" 1844. Marx und die Deutschen Kommunisten in Paris* (Berlin, 1974). → 44:22, 23, 25, 29, 32, 36, 40, 44, 45; 45:8. #M203, M383; E167, E168.

Voss or **Vossevangen** (Norway) Village, a tourist center, inland from Bergen. → 90:30.

Vossische Zeitung See Königlich priv. Berl. Ztg.

Vperyod! Vorwärts! En avant! Zurich, 1873; London, 1874 to 1877. Irreg periodicity. Ed by Lavrov (1873–1876); V. N. Smirnov, N. G. Kulyabko-Koretzky (1877). —An organ of the moderate wing of revolutionary Narodniks in emigration. There were five numbers in all: Nos. 1–2 issued in Zurich (1873); No. 3 in 1874, No. 4 in 1876, No. 5 in 1877. Between Nos. 3 and 5 Lavrov pubd a semimonthly *Vperyod! Dvuchnedelnoye obozreniye* (London; Jan 1, 1875, to Dec 31, 1876). → 74:14; 75:11, 44; 76:24, 30. #E767.

De **Vrijheid** The Hague, 1871, Nos. 1–18. —Subtitled "Organ of the people." → 71:18.

W

Wachsmuth, Wilhelm; *full* Ernst Wilhelm Gottlieb (1784 to 1866) German historian. Prof at Kiel (1820+), at Leipzig (1825+). He authored many works on European history and culture, classical antiquity, etc. M (1843) studied his *Geschichte Frankreichs im Revolutionszeitalter,* Vols. 1–2 (1840–1844); M (1852) studied his *Allgemeine Culturgeschichte* (1850–1852); M(1853), his *Europäische Sittengeschichte* (1831–1839). → 43:32; 52:56, 58; 53:51.

Wachter, Karl German revolutionary democrat in Cologne; lawyer by profession. In the early 1840s he frequented RZ circles. In the 1848–1849 revolution he was active in the Demo Assoc and worked with M's NRZ group, though not a communist; a captain in the militia, member of the city Comm of Public Safety. → 48:62, 65.

Wade, John (1788 to 1875) English journalist and writer of popularizations. A contributor to many periodicals, he was on the *Spectator* staff (1828–1858); pensioned by Palmerston (1862). His best-known work was *The black book, or Corruption unmasked* (1820–1823); also pubd a popular *British history* (1839), *Women, past and present* (1859), and a book about banking (1826), etc. M (1845) read his *History of the middle and working classes,* 3rd edn (1835; orig. 1833). → 45:52. #M575.

Der **Wächter am Rhein** Cologne, 1848 to May 1849. Pub'r/editor: Carl Cramer. —Alongside M's NRZ, this paper supported the right (liberal) wing of the Demo Assoc movement. #M748; E670.

Der **Wähler** —No info available. → 93:19. #E17, E118, E473.

Wagener, Hermann; *full* Friedrich Wilhelm Hermann (1815 to 1889) German conservative party publicist, journalist, and politician; lawyer by training. Close to Bismarck, he was a leading ideologist of the adaptation of Prussian Junkerdom to capitalist society; influenced in views by Rodbertus and Bismarckian "state-socialism"; a bridge between the conservatives and the Katheder-socialists or Lassalle. He founded the conservative organ *Neue Preussische Ztg* (*Kreuzzeitung*); its editor (1848–1854). Reichstag deputy

(1867–1873); also helped establish other conservative periodicals and organizations. He was ruined (1873) by a business scandal. → 82:50.

Wagner, Adolf; *full* Adolf Heinrich Gotthilf (1835 to 1917) German economist; a leading Katheder-socialist. Prof in various universities, finally at Berlin (1870+). His main economic work was on banking and public finance; *Finanzwissenschaft* (1877–1901). A supporter of Bismarck's policies and of the Christian Social party, he was a founder of the Verein für Sozialpolitik (Katheder-socialist center); member of the Prussian Diet (1882–1885). Works: *Die Abschaffung des privaten Grundeigenthum* (1870); *Der Staat und die Versicherungswesen* (1881); *Die Strömungen in der Sozialpolitik und der Katheder- und Staatssozialismus* (1912). M commented on his *Allgemeine und theoretische Volkswirtschaftslehre* (Bd. I of his *Lehrbuch der politischen Ökonomie*), 2nd edn (1879). → 79:5, 30; 80:1, 42. #M578.

Wagner, Richard (1813 to 1883) German composer and music dramatist, famous esp for operas. He took part in the Dresden uprising of 1849; fled abroad; eventually received a pardon for political offenses. W. was not only a virulent anti-Semite and bitter racist, but applied his systematic racism also to music and musical theory. For an anti-Wagnerite overview of his politics, see Peter Viereck, *Metapolitics* (1961). → 49:24; 56:10; 82:18.

Der **Wahrer Jacob** Stuttgart. 1884 to 1932. Monthly, later semimonthly. —Illustrated S-D magazine of humor and satire. #ME35.

Wakefield, Edward Gibbon (1796 to 1862) English writer on colonial policy and economics. Imprisoned for fraud, he studied colonial affairs, and with this training became a prominent executor of imperial policy and a British "empire builder." A founder of the South Australian Assoc, the New Zealand Land Co., and other humanitarian enterprises; he entered New Zealand politics (1852) but suffered a breakdown (1854). His writings on colonialism include: *A view of the art of colonization* (1849), studied by M (1851); *An account of Ireland* (1812), studied by M (1869). M also studied his edn of Adam Smith with his own commentary (1843). → 51:68, 69; 69:75; 70:8.

Waldemar, *Prince* Friedrich Wilhelm (1817 to 1849) Prince of Prussia; brother of King Friedrich Wilhelm III. Trained as an army officer, he was known as a traveler (trip to India, 1844–1846). On March 9, 1848, he was named cavalry commandant at Münster, where he died, Feb 17, 1849. → 49:14.

Waldenburg (Ger.) Industrial city of Silesia; now in Poland as Walbrzych. → 69:72; 70:3.

Waldersee, *Count* Friedrich Gustav von (1795 to 1864) Prussian lieutenant-gen; writer on military subjects. He entered military service (1812); war min (1854–1858). — The book ascribed to Waldersee in #E896, *Die französische Armee auf dem Exercirplatze und im Felde* (2nd edn, 1861), pubd anonymously, is cataloged (NUC, BM) without any author attribution. In a letter (Oct 1, 1860) E discussed Waldersee's *Die Methode zur kriegsgemässen Ausbildung der Infanterie und ihrer Führer im Felddienste* (1860). — Caution: There is confusion in bibliographies and catalogs between this man and Count Franz Georg von Waldersee (1763–1823), a writer and poet. → 61:29. #E896.

Wales and the Welsh → 65:46; 66:20.

Wales, *Prince of* In 1872 the prince was known as Albert Edward (1841–1910), eldest son of Queen Victoria; he came to the throne in 1901 as Edward VII, after he had been Prince of Wales for 60 years. The Thanksgiving celebration held on Feb 27, 1872 (at St. Paul's), was due to the fact that he had been ill with typhoid since the previous Nov, and his life had been despaired of. → 72:8.

Walesrode, Ludwig (Reinhold) (1810 to 1889) German liberal publicist and journalist; a friend of Johann Jacoby. He was jailed for his work *Unterthänige Reden* (1843) and again after 1849. Pub'r of *Demokratische Studien* (1860–1861). #E467.

Walker, Amasa (1799 to 1875) American economist. Businessman till 1840, prof at Harvard et al., congressman (1862–1863), he was an Abolitionist and a Free Soiler. His popular textbook, *The science of wealth* (1866), was written with his son, Francis Amasa (1840–1897), who later became M.I.T. pres. He also wrote *The nature and uses of money and mixed currency* (1857). → 78:38.

Wallachia or Walachia → 56:2. #M301, M407, M561, M788. See Danubian Principalities, Moldavia, Roumania.

Wallau, Karl (1823 to 1877) German printshop worker, from Mainz. In Brussels emigration in the late 1840s, he was a member of the CL, working with M; also worked as a typesetter for the *DBZ*; pres of the Brussels GWEA (1847). In 1848, in Paris with M, he was sent by the CL back to Mainz, where he built and headed the WA; member of the CC/CL. Later, mayor of Mainz. → 47:28; 48:22, 27, 28.

Walter, Ferdinand (1794 to 1879) German jurist; prof of law at Bonn (1821+), a popular lecturer there. Conservative deputy to the Prussian assembly in 1848, also in the legislatures of 1849–1850. His *Lehrbuch des Kirchenrechts aller christlichen Confessionen* had its 5th edn in 1831 and its 14th in 1871. → 35:5; 36:5.

Walther von der Vogelweide (1170? to

1230?) Leading lyric poet in Middle High German; perhaps born in the Austrian Tyrol. He largely lived as a wandering singer in European courts. His "Sprüche" (maxims, epigrams) were often political, championing independence and unity, etc. E refers to his love song "Unter den Linden." → 90:8.

War Office (Brit.) #E909.

Warnebold, Ernst German lawyer, in Hanover; active in politics. A supporter of Bismarck, W. was first a Progressivist, then a National Liberal. → 67:12.

Warsaw; *Pol.* Warszawa; *Ger.* Warschau Capital of Poland and of Solidarność. During the 19th century, chief city of Russian Poland. #M794.

Washburne, Elihu Benjamin (1816 to 1887) American politician. Republican congressman (1853–1869); supporter of Pres Grant. U.S. ambassador to Paris (1869–1877), the only envoy remaining in the city during the Paris Commune—to protect foreigners against the diabolical Communards, as he explained in his book *Recollections of a minister to France* (1887). → 71:33. #M521.

Washington (District of Columbia) → 51:45; 63:7; 71:4. #M988.

Waterloo or Waterloo-with-Seaforth (Eng.) Northern suburb of Liverpool, a bathing resort. → 57:32.

Watteau, Louis (b. 1824) French Blanquist; physician by profession. As a military doctor in Lille, he took part (1851–1853) in a garrison plot and in a secret insurrectionary society; arrested with others, he got five years (1854+). In Belle-Ile prison he became a friend of Blanqui. Subseqly he settled in Brussels; founded the weekly *Le Bien-être Social* (1856+). Blanqui was his guest on a couple of occasions; collaborated on the ed bd of *Candide* (1865) with other Blanquists. In Nov 1868 he broke politically with Blanqui; reasons not given by the *DBMOF*, which, by the way, says his pseudonym was Dr. Dunol, and does not mention the one known to M, viz., Denonville. → 61:15, 26, 30, 41, 49; 66:22.

Watts, Hunter; *full* John Hunter (d. 1924) English socialist. A leading supporter of Hyndman in the SDF, he replaced Morris as treasurer after the Socialist League split; delegate to the Int'l Socialist Congress of 1891. He stayed with Hyndman in the formation of the British Socialist party and (as a war supporter in 1914) of the National Socialist party. He was also an early member of the Fabian Society. → 94:18.

Watts, John (1818 to 1887) English social reformer, later liberal. A self-educated son of a ribbon weaver, he became an Owenite traveling lecturer; conducted a school in Manchester

(1841–1844). In 1844 he abandoned Owenism and went into business to seek his fortune. As a respectable philanthropist, he took part in promoting education and libraries, and was an active supporter of the co-op movement; also pubd tracts against strikes ("the workman's bane") and *The catechism of wages and capital* (1867). M (1845) read his early radical tract *The facts and fictions of political economists* (1842). → 45:50. #M575.

Wayland, Francis (1796 to 1865) American educator; clergyman; pres of Brown U. (1827–1855). In the Dorr Rebellion of 1842 he was a Law and Order leader. M (1859) studied his *Elements of polit eco* (1843; 1st edn, 1837). He usually wrote pop-philosophical books (like *Elements of moral science,* 1835) and biography. → 59:76.

Webb, Sidney (James) (1859 to 1947) English socialist; a leader of the Fabian Society. Civil-service clerk in the War Office and Colonial Office (1878–1891); barrister (1885+). Member of the London County Council (1892–1910); MP (1922–1929); colonial secy in the Ramsay MacDonald cabinet, and created Baron Passfield (1929). He was best known for a number of books mostly in collaboration with his wife, née Beatrice Potter (1858–1943; Mar. 1892): e.g., *History of trade unionism* (1894) and a number of Fabian tracts. → 90:5; 93:13; 95:18.

Weber, *Counselor* Prussian counselor-at-law (*Justizrat*) in Berlin. He carried on M's suit against the *National Ztg.* —His first name, which is never mentioned in M's correspondence, appears to have defied historical research. → 60:13, 20, 23, 24, 37, 41, 51, 54. #M454.

Weber, Georg (1816 to 1891) German radical Democrat; physician by profession, from Kiel. In the 1840s he was active in the Democratic movement, and prob regarded himself as a sympathizer with M's communism (though apparently not a CL member). An émigré in Paris in 1844, he contributed to *Vorwärts!*—often on polit eco—and was a friend of M and Ewerbeck. He returned to Kiel (Oct-Nov 1844); corresponded actively with the League of the Just people in Paris and London, and in 1846 with M's CCC in Brussels. After taking part in the 1848–1849 revolution, he emigrated to the U.S. (1854); returned to Kiel (1861). → 44:22; 46:24, 29; 74:23.

Weber, Joseph Valentin (1814 to 1895) German worker (watchmaker), from Neustadt (in the Palatinate). In the 1849 Baden campaign he was on the staff of Willich's free corps; took refuge in Switzerland; joined the CL; émigré in London (1850+). In London he was for many years active in the leadership of the GWEA. → 61:56.

Weber, Wilhelm German worker (watchmaker) from the Palatinate; son of Joseph Valentin *Weber. A Lassallean, he emigrated to America (1864), and was pres of the Allgemeine Deutsche Arbeiterverein in NY (1866). According to a letter by M (1867), Countess *Hatzfeldt had paid him to kill Lassalle's slayer, Count von Racowitza, but he got cold feet and took off for the U.S., with the money. → 62:12, 47.

Wedde, Johannes (1843 to 1890) German Social-Democratic publicist and pub'r; also a writer (poems, translations from Latin, etc.) under the pen name Silvanus. Active in Hamburg, he began as a private-school teacher (1867–1879). He entered the Social-Democracy in 1872; founded the Hamburg S-D *Bürgerzeitung* (banned 1887) and the *Hamburger Echo.* In 1888 he was delegate to the Int'l Socialist Congress (Paris). He died shortly before his election to the Reichstag. → 77:26.

Weerth, Georg (Ludwig) (1822 to 1856) German revolutionary poet and writer. A commercial employee in the Rhineland, he moved to Bradford, Eng. (1843), for a German textile firm; became close friends with E in Manchester. In 1845 he stayed in Brussels for a while, them moved there (1846), close to M&E. He had been writing since 1843; now (1847) *DBZ* began publishing his poems and sketches. An active member of the CL and the Demo Assoc in Brussels. With the outbreak of the 1848 revolution, he went to Paris with M&E, later to Cologne, where as a member of the NRZ ed bd he edited its feuilleton (feature) section, which gained considerable popularity. Afterward he did commercial traveling, also working for the CL's behalf; in the 1850 CL split he sided with M. For some years he continued commercial traveling to Caribbean, Central and S. American countries as well as Europe; contracted a fatal case of yellow fever in Havana in Nov 1855. —E's judgment on his literary work, even long afterward, was very high: "the first and most important poet of the German proletariat." A 5-vol. edn of his works was pubd in 1956. → 43:31; 45:30; 46:21; 47:14; 48:26, 33, 34, 69; 49:28, 29; 51:19, 20, 23, 32, 46, 53, 56; 52:7, 35, 39, 42, 48, 49; 55:48; 56:33, 34; 83:25, 29. #E327.

Weerth, Karl (b. 1812) Brother of Georg Weerth; a secondary-school teacher in Detmold, in the field of natural science. In July 1851 Karl was visiting with his brother in London, and July CD, went on to Paris. → 51:33.

Wegmann, Adolph (b. c.1852) German worker, émigré in England; member of the Foreign Section of the IWMA in Manchester, in 1872. By June 1874 when W. wrote to E, he had emigrated to Rio de Janeiro. —KMC calls him Theodor Wegmann. → 72:66; 74:23.

Weiden (Ger.) Industrial city in N. Bavaria → 76:24.

Weill, Alexandre; orig Abraham (1811 to 1899) Alsatian-born writer, active in France after ten years' education in Germany and involvement there with the Young Germany movement. Returning to France, he lived in Paris, in close contact with German émigré circles and as correspondent for German papers, e.g., *Telegraph für Deutschland.* During the 1840s he collaborated on the *Démocratie Pacifique, La Presse,* and with L. Blanc. He pubd a study on the German peasants' war (1847); later came out in defense of constitutional monarchy; under Bonaparte, wrote belles lettres; pubd also writings on Jewish questions. → 44:22.

Weiss, Guido (1822 to 1899) German liberal journalist. He took part in the 1848–1849 revolution in Germany; in the 1860s, was a supporter of the Progressivist party and its more liberal wing. Editor of the *Berliner Reform* (1863–1866); editor of *Zukunft* (1867–1871); pub'r of the weekly *Die Wage* (1873–1879). → 67:47; 75:31, 48.

Weiss, Johannes German medical student in Berlin in the mid-1880s; friend of Conrad Schmidt. He subseqly emigrated to S. America. → 87:44.

Der **Weisse Adler** Zurich, Feb 1864 to June 1865. Thrice weekly. —Liberal journal. → 65:29. #M185.

Weitling, Wilhelm (Christian) (1808 to 1871) German pioneer socialist; early propagandist for a utopian "communism." Son of a French officer and German maidservant, he became a tailor; as a journeyman, traveled much, and lived in Paris (1835–1841), absorbing French socialist ideas, which he adapted. He joined the League of the Outcast (see *Venedey), entered the League of the Just (1837), and became its first important theoretician; pubd *Die Menschheit, wie sie ist und wie sie sein soll* (1839); moved to Switzerland, worked in Geneva, and founded communistic groups; pubd a journal, *Hilferuf der deutschen Jugend* (1841–1842), then *Die Junge Generation* (1842–1843). Chief work: *Garantien der Harmonie und Freiheit* (1842), developing his messianic approach, views on the use of the lumpen-class, etc.; also *Das Evangelium der armen Sünder* (1843), appealing to primitive Christianity; a book of prison poetry, *Kerkerpoesien* (1844). His next sojourn was in London, for one and a half years, during which he made no contact with the English workers' movement; in discussions with the German émigrés and communist workers, he persuaded them that he was no longer of interest. In early 1846 he quit London for Brussels; on March 30 he engaged in a sharp discussion with M's circle of the CCC, and briefly participated in the CCC work. Later in the year he went to Bremen, perhaps Paris, and by the beginning of 1847 was in NY, where he founded a group, also in Philadelphia. With the news of the 1848 revolution, he returned to Germany. In Berlin, he pubd a short-lived journal, *Urwähler*; failed to gain any influence in the Berlin workers' movement (led by Born) or in the Demo Assoc. In Nov he moved on to Hamburg for a short stay. By the end of 1849 he was back in the U.S. There he pubd the *Republik der Arbeiter* for five years. His attempt to establish a utopian community "Communia" failed, generating much hostility against his dictatorial control. Increasingly W. became a peaceful reformer, pro-imperialist, anti-Semitic, antilabor, antifeminist, pro-Bonapartist, a supporter of the Democratic party and Tammany, advocate of a blue-shirted storm-troop-like formation, a scurrilous journalist, and inventor of crackpot astronomical theories. → 43:2; 44:38; 46:1, 11, 15, 24, 46, 49, 55; 51:15; 54:21; 88:35. #M748.

Welcker, Friedrich Gottlieb (1784 to 1868) German classical scholar and archeologist, specializing in Greek art and literature. Prof at Giessen (1809+), Göttingen (1816+), Bonn (1819–1861). Brother of the liberal politician K. T. Welcker. By 1835 when M took his course, he had mainly pubd scholarly edns of Greek writers. → 35:5.

De **Werker** Antwerp, Oct 18, 1868, to May 31, 1914. Weekly; later, daily. Ed by P. Coenen (1860s). —Subtitled "Organ of the Flemish sections of IWMA"; later, organ of the Belgian socialist party. Founded as the organ of the Volksverbond, Antwerp WA. → 71:15, 16, 21. #M922.

Werner, Ernst German worker (bookbinder); TU organizer. Founding pres of the Int'l Union of Bookbinders (1869); delegate to the Eisenach congress founding the SDWP; member of the Leipzig section of the IWMA. → 69:26, 31, 36, 48, 60.

Weser-Zeitung Bremen, 1844 to 1930. Weekly. —Liberal paper. → 50:25. #ME183, ME433.

Wesseling or **Wesslingen** (Ger.) Town on the Rhine, south of Cologne. (The form Wesslingen, strangely enough, was used by the NRZ in 1848 but has not been found elsewhere; perhaps a local variant.) → 48:61, 71.

West, *Sir* Edward (1782 to 1828) English jurist; writer on economics. A lawyer (1814+), he was knighted (1822), and became chief justice in Bombay (1823). His economic writings anticipated Ricardo's theory of rent, as in his *Essay on the application of capital to land* (1815). M (1851) read his *The price of corn and wages of labour* (1826). → 51:67.

West, William American social-reformer. A founder of the reform group New Democ-

racy (1869); a clerk in Victoria Woodhull's bank. He was a leader of Woodhull's Section 12 of the IWMA; member of the CC of the N. American Federation; advocate of demoting the "labor question" from the top concern of the movement, denouncing "foreign" control (i.e., by the GC); he led the Nov 1871 split in the organization along these lines. → 72:49.

West Indies Collectively, the archipelagic islands in the Caribbean. → 52:48; 55:48.

Westdeutsche Zeitung Cologne, May 25, 1849, to July 21, 1850. Daily. Pub'r/editor: H. Becker. —Semisocialistic; supported refugee aid for the London émigrés; suppressed by the Prussian press law of June 1850. → 49:28; 50:12. #ME11, ME68, ME157A, ME157C; M163A, M163D, M853.

Westermarck, Edward Alexander (1862 to 1939) Finnish anthropologist and sociologist. Prof at the U. of London (1907–1930), at Turku, Finland (1830–1935). Best known for his early work *History of human marriage* (1891); a virulent opponent of L. H. Morgan's views; champion of the thesis that humans have always been monogamous. Also author of *The origin and development of the moral ideas* (1906–1908); *Christianity and morals* (1939). → 93:30.

Weston, John English socialist; handrail maker and carpenter, later a manufacturer; long a socialist propagandist and organizer. He was an early Owenite; active in O'Brien's National Reform League; treasurer (1869) of the Land and Labour League; active in the Land Tenure Reform Assoc founded by J. S. Mill (1870). —He participated in the founding meeting of the IWMA (1864) and was a member (1864–1872) of the GC, where he still represented the old socialist ideas of Owenism. → 64:31; 65:33, 35, 38, 41; 72:20, 24.

Westphalen, Caroline von; *full* Amalie Juliane Caroline; *née* **Heubel** (1776 or 1780 to 1856) Mother of M's wife Jenny; born in Salzwedel. Second wife of Ludwig von Westphalen; married in 1812. Her father, Julius Christoph Heubel, a minor government official, came from a Thuringian bourgeois family; he married a cousin of the same family name, Sophie Friederieke Heubel. —Her birth date is given as 1776 by L. von Schwerin-Krosigk, as 1780 by the *New Mega* index. → 40:9; 43:13; 44:20, 34; 45:23, 30; 46:9, 11; 49:29; 54:36; 56:22, 29, 35.

Westphalen, Edgar von; *full* Gerhard Julius Oscar Ludwig Edgar (1819 to 1890) Brother of M's wife, Jenny; full brother (son of Caroline); closest to Jenny in the family. He went to school with M; attended the U. of Berlin, studying law. In 1845 he became engaged (*see* C. *Schöler), and in 1846 went to live in Brussels, where, under M's influence, he became a member of the CCC and considered himself a communist. In 1847 he emigrated to Texas to seek his fortune; returned broke, went back in 1849 and yet again in 1851, this time as a farmer with some success. But he was dogged by yellow fever, and returned to Germany (1865) sick and penniless; lived with the M family for a half year; then moved to Berlin, where he got a minor judiciary job (no doubt through his half-brother Ferdinand) till 1879; in Berlin he pubd a book of poems. After 1879 he lived as a pensioner; died after a long illness in Kreuzberg. His friends considered him rather weak and shiftless, though intelligent. → 65:36; 74:32. #ME28, ME129.

Westphalen, Ferdinand von; *full* Ferdinand Otto Wilhelm Henning (1799 to 1876) Half-brother of M's wife, Jenny; son of Ludwig von W.'s first wife, Lisette. Albeit the reactionary wing of the family, he had much brotherly affection for Jenny. —He was not brought up in Trier like Jenny: when his parents moved there (1816) he remained at school in Salzwedel, then went to the U. of Berlin. From 1819 on, he moved through a series of government posts in the Prussian civil bureaucracy; he was stationed in Trier during two periods: 1820–1822, 1838–1843 (hence also in a period when he could oppose Jenny's marriage—but this is speculative). In 1850–1858 he became interior min in Manteuffel's cabinet of reaction. A leading liberal's verdict on him, obviously biased, was: a mediocreminded pedant-bureaucrat. → 51:36.

Westphalen, Heinrich Georg von (1768 to 1855 [*MEW*] or 1765 to 1853 [Schwerin-Krosigk]) Uncle of M's wife, Jenny; older brother of Ludwig von W. A lawyer by profession, he held an assessor's post in Brunswick, but because of his health, quit, lived in retirement (to a ripe old age) on an income from his parents, and did independent scholarly research on the Seven Years War. → 55:42; 56:22.

Westphalen, *Baron* Ludwig von; *full* Johann Ludwig (1770 to 1842) Father of M's wife, Jenny. Of an old Brunswick family of government officials, he was the son of Philipp von W. (1724–1792; from 1764, Ritter von W.), who during the Seven Years War had been private secy to Duke Ferdinand of Brunswick. His mother was Jeanie Wishart (1742–1811), daughter of an Edinburgh clergyman of an old Scottish family descended from Campbells and Argylls. Ludwig studied law at Göttingen; became assessor in the Ducal Chamber at Brunswick (1794); married (1798) Lisette von Veltheim (1778–1807), and went to live on an estate just purchased in Mecklenburg. After Lisette died, he was named (1808) gen secy to the Royal Westphalian prefecture in Halberstadt, and then (1809) to a similar post in

Salzwedel, which was under French rule till 1813. In 1812 he married again (*see* Caroline von *W.). After the French left (1814–1816) he was Prussian district pres in Salzwedel. But as the Restoration reaction deepened, he was considered too liberal, hence was transferred to the newly Prussianized Rhineland, where liberal officials were needed; he became state councillor in Trier (1816). Reactionary Berlin's hostility toward its Trier official made his situation unpleasant, and he tried (1830+) to get retired on a pension, finally succeeding (1834); retired as privy councillor. He died after being bedridden by illness for months. —*Note:* Jenny's table of relatives was complicated by the fact that her father had married twice. The sons of his first marriage were her half-brothers, e.g., Ferdinand von *W., the eldest. → 40:9; 42:4, 7.

Das **Westphälische Dampfboot** Bielefeld (Ger.), Jan 1845 to Dec 1846; Paderborn, Jan 1847 to Mar 1848. Monthly. Ed by Otto Lüning. —Under Lüning, it reflected "True Socialist" views. → 47:25, 29, 34, 40; #ME66; E792.

Westphalia; *Ger.* Westfalen Prussian province in west-central Germany, incl the Ruhr, Münster, Bielefeld, etc. → 40:10; 46:17; 49:19.

Westphalia, Peace of #M141.

Weydemeyer, Joseph (1818 to 1866) German propagandist of Marxism, in Germany and America. Son of a Prussian official in Münster, he entered on an army career. As an artillery lieutenant in Minden (1842) he came to know the RZ group in Cologne; discussed social issues with them and with fellow officers (*Anneke, *Willich, *Korff, *Beust) in a study circle; quit the army for journalism; joined the staff of the *Trier'sche Ztg* (1844), which was then influenced by Grün's "True Socialism"; read #ME76 and #E171; visited M in Paris (1844); co-edited the *Westphälische Dampfboot* (1845) with O. Lüning. He visited M in Brussels (1846), was definitely converted to M's communism, and took part in CCC work; joined the CL (1847) and worked on organizing it in Cologne and the Rhineland. With the outbreak of the 1848 revolution, he was active in Hamm, which he represented at the first Demo congress; with Lüning, accepted to edit the *NDZ* (Darmstadt) as a Left Demo organ (July +), and continued in this post till the paper was banned (Dec 1850). During 1849–1851 he remained active in the CL and in touch with M; then, unable to work in Germany, he emigrated to the U.S. (Nov 1851). In NY he launched the journal *Die Revolution* (two issues). During the 1850s he formed the Proletarian League of NY on Marxist lines; was active in the German-American labor movement, esp in a NY strike wave (1853); with G. T. Kellner, helped establish *Die Reform* till it died (Apr 1854); did free-lance writing and lecturing; moved to Milwaukee for a job as notary and surveyor, and worked in the movement there and in Chicago. Returning to NY, he continued TU work; joined the Communist Club of NY (1857+). The Civil War impelled him into the Union Army, in which he rose to colonel (1865). After the war he was a county surveyor in St. Louis; wrote for the German-American press there; died in a cholera epidemic. Throughout he remained a correspondent and disciple of M, according to his lights. — There is an English-language study, Karl Obermann's *Joseph W., Pioneer of American socialism* (1947). → 46:11, 17, 19, 27, 46; 47:25; 48:26; 49:27, 28, 31, 33, 35, 43; 50:16, 18, 34, 39, 43, 48; 51:2, 20, 27, 29, 35, 42, 45, 46, 50, 56; 52:4, 5, 7, 9, 10, 12, 15, 17, 18, 22, 25, 31, 43, 49; 53:1, 4, 14, 19, 20, 24, 43; 58:25, 31; 59:13, 14, 36; 60:24, 29, 35, 38, 42; 64:35, 39, 40; 65:25; 66:38; 67:15; 75:11; 77:17, 47; 78:34. #ME11; M212.5, M267, M429, M836, M969; E241.

Whigs (Brit.) Historic party of the landed gentry and big bourgeoisie, considered progressive (as compared with the *Tories) because it oriented toward channeling bourgeois development into channels least hurtful to the old landed ruling class; it is generally regarded as later debouching into the Liberal party's right wing. → 55:30; 56:8. #M272, M532.

The **Whitehall Review** London, 1876 to 1929. Weekly. —Conservative. → 77:6; 78:41.

Wicksteed, Philip Henry (1844 to 1927) English Christian socialist and advocate of marginal-utility economic theory. He was chiefly known as a popular teacher and lecturer (on Dante, economics, etc.) and as a Unitarian theological writer; minister in a London Unitarian chapel (1874–1897). He was first a disciple of Henry George (1880), active in the English Single Tax movement incl the Land Reform Union (founded 1883). Converted to marginalism by Jevons' writings, he became its propagandist by the mid-1880s; pubd *The alphabet of economic science* (1888) and esp *The common sense of polit eco* (1910). In 1884–1885 he was engaged in a public polemic with G. B. Shaw, who was then pretending to defend Marx's economics; W. became the Fabians' mentor in economic theory. As a moderate Christian socialist, he pubd sermons, *Our prayers and politics* (1885), and founded the London Labour Church (1892), later the Unitarian Free Christian Union for Social Science (1906). → 84:46.

Wiede, Franz (b. c.1857) German (Swed-ish-born) socialistic journalist, active in Swiss emigration, as pub'r/editor of the *Neue Gesellschaft* (Zurich, 1877–1880), also a coeditor of Höchberg's *Zukunft*. → 77:25.

Wiehe, Johann Friedrich German typesetter, working in F. Hollinger's London printshop. → 59:65; 60:12, 14.

Wiener Zeitung Vienna, 1780 to 1931. Daily. —Government organ. #M832.

Wierzejski, J. Polish émigré in France; a friend of *Wróblewski in Nice. → 91:15.

Wiesbaden (Ger.) City, capital of Hesse, on the Rhine near Mainz. → 69:56; 94:15.

Wiesen, F. German socialist in America; a contributor to the paper *Volks-Anwalt* (Cincinnati). He wrote to E from Texas. → 93:17.

Wigan (Eng.) Industrial town of Lancashire, near Manchester. #M651.

Wigand, Otto (1795 to 1870) German liberal pub'r/bookdealer in Leipzig; known for publishing works by radical authors, e.g., E's first book (#E171). He pubd *Wigand's Vierteljahrsschrift* (1844–1845), *Wigand's Conversations-Lexikon* (1846–1852), *Jahrbücher für Wissenschaft und Kunst* (1854–1856). → 52:14; 67:12; 92:23.

Wigand's Vierteljahrsschrift Leipzig, 1844 to 1845 (8 vols.). Quarterly. Pub'r: Otto Wigand. —Philosophic spokesman for Young Hegelians. → 45:36. #ME129.

Wight, Isle of (Eng.) Island, just off the S. coast near Southhampton. *See* Ryde, Ventnor.

Wilhelm I (1797 to 1888) King of Prussia, 1861–1888; German emperor (kaiser), 1871–1888. As prince of Prussia (1840+) he had become, in 1848, leader of the reactionary court camarilla; in 1849, commander of the troops that crushed the Baden-Palatinate uprising (hence the "Kartätschenprinz," prince of grapeshot); when King Friedrich Wilhelm IV became insane, he was made regent (1858–1861). His reign was the era of Bismarckian blood and iron, Prussianization of the German empire, wars and militarism, antisocialist witch-hunts, rise of anti-Semitism and racism, and the actualization of the Prussian-German stereotype which became a stink in the nostrils of world civilization. → 61:4; 78:15, 19; 88:11.

Wilhelm II (1859 to 1941) King of Prussia and Emperor (Kaiser) of Germany, 1888–1918. This is the kaiser of the Triple Alliance and the First World War, driven out by the Revolution of 1918; formally abdicated in 1919. → 95:16.

Wilhelmi, Franz German radical; participant in the 1848–1849 revolution; émigré in London, then moved to the U.S. He later fought in the Civil War in the Union Army. → 51:6.

Wilkinson English patriot, proprietor of

St. George's Hall in London, who refused to permit the International to hold a Paris Commune meeting on his premises. → 72:13.

Wilkinson, Henry (1793 to 1861) English gunsmith. Author of *Engines of war: or . . . observations on ancient and modern warlike machines and implements* (1841), which was prob the work read by M (1857). → 57:26.

Wilks, Washington (1825? to 1864) English radical publicist; an editor of the London *Morning Star.* His books dealt mainly with current affairs and biography: besides *Palmerston in three epochs* (1854), he pubd *The half-century: its history . . .* (1852), *Turk, Greek, and Russian* (1853), et al. → 53:54; 54:20.

Willich, August (1810 to 1878) German radical. A lieutenant or captain in the Prussian army, he gave up his army career on acquiring left-wing republican views (1846). In 1847–1848 he was influenced by the CL in Cologne; perhaps joined by 1847, certainly by 1849. In the 1848 revolution he served with Hecker's forces in Baden; in 1849, led a partisan corps in the Baden-Palatinate uprising—E joined it as adjutant. Afterward W. took refuge in Switzerland, then England. Now or previously he learned carpentry as a trade to earn a living. In the CL, joined by Schapper, he represented the viewpoint of impatient adventuristic putschism; after the CL split of Sep 1850, the *Willich–Schapper group operated till about 1852. He emigrated to the U.S. (1853); worked in the Brooklyn Navy Yard as a carpenter; later became a surveyor. He contributed to the German-American press; editor of the *Deutsche Republikaner* (Cincinnati, 1858–1861). In the Civil War he rose to brigadier-gen; wounded. After the war, he was elected auditor of Hamilton County, Ohio; did badly in the post and left under a cloud; died in Ohio. → 49:1, 30, 32, 39, 40; 50:15, 20, 22, 25, 30, 34, 45; 51:5, 10, 14; 52:9; 53:20, 43; 54:5, 9, 21; 62:26, 46. #ME80, ME89, ME122, ME123, ME164, ME179; E676.

Willich–Schapper group Faction of the *Communist League, under the leadership of *Willich and *Schapper, which in the split of Sep 1850 came out with a majority of the League membership (though not of its CC), and proceeded to constitute itself as the CL. → 50:34, 40, 45; 51:10, 36, 42, 54; 52:3, 27, 39. #M836.5.

Willigen, P. van der   Shortly before M sent him the French edn of *Capital*, W. had sent M a pamphlet (unidentified) that he had just pubd in Amsterdam, asking for an opinion. W. was staying in London at the time but presumably was a Dutchman; no further info. → 72:54.

Willis, Robert (1800 to 1875)   Prof of ap-

plied mechanics at Cambridge (1837 to death), he was a scholar in allied technological fields; pubd *Principles of mechanism* (1841); lectured at the School of Mines; pres (1862) of the British Assoc. He also did notable work in architecture and archeology, on the side interfacing with his specialty, producing *Remarks on the architecture of the Middle Ages* (1835) and other works. He came to M's notice by giving a special course of lectures for working-men in London (1854–1867). → 63:5.

Willisen, Baron Karl Wilhelm von (1790 to 1879)   Prussian gen and military theoretician. Royal commissioner in Posen (1848); commander of the Schleswig-Holstein army in the war against Denmark (1850). Author of *Der italienische Feldzug des Jahres 1848* (1849); *Theorie des grossen Krieges angewendet auf den russisch-polnischen Feldzug von 1831* (1840). → 52:2.

Wilmart, Raymond or Raimond; *pseud.* **Wilmot**   Belgian radical, active in France. *DBMOF* says he was a commercial employee of Belgian nationality; elsewhere it seems to be assumed he was French; reported to have taken part in the Paris Commune. —At the Hague Congress of 1872 he was a delegate from Bordeaux; combated the Bakuninists. Right after, he wrote E from Madrid, about arrangements to go to Buenos Aires for employment, though he would like to stay in Spain. He seems to have read and admired *Capital.* In 1873 he emigrated to Argentina. *KMC* (only) identifies him as a prof of law there. —*MEW* erroneously gives his name as Vilmart. → 71:59; 73:33.

Wilson, J. Havelock; *full* Joseph Havelock; *usually* Havelock **Wilson** (1858 or 1859 to 1929)   English labor leader (seamen). He led in founding (1887) the National Amalgamated Sailors' and Firemen's Union, and remained its pres till rigor mortis set in. He was a prominent case of pure-and-simple tradeunionism, antisocialist, hostile to the Labour party, to political action, and to militant struggle. In World War I he was more of a jingo than Lloyd George; in 1917, more anti-Soviet than Churchill. In his last years his union was widely regarded as "little more than a company union" (Pelling). —In 1892 the three seats E refers to were contested by trade-unionists as independents; W. soon made his peace with the Liberals; he dropped even Liberal politics when defeated in 1922. —*Caution:* MEW and other IML indexes are confused and erroneous on this man, apparently mixing him up with the miners' leader John Wilson. → 92:32.

Wilson, John (1785 to 1854)   Scottish writer and publicist, best known for verse and essays written under the pen name Christopher North, esp the rambling *Noctes Ambrosianae*

(1822–1835). In *Blackwood's*, launched as a Tory organ, Wilson became the house Whig-killer, often with vicious swingeing polemics; for which service to humanity he was rewarded with the post of prof of *moral* philosophy at Edinburgh (1820–1851), despite a notable absence of formal (or other) qualifications. Since moral philosophy included polit eco, Wilson pubd a work in that field, *Some illustrations of Mr. M'Culloch's principles of polit eco* (1826), by "Mordecai Mullion . . . secy to Christopher North." M (1859–1862) read even this thing, as he swept through the literature. → *59:78.*

Wimbledon (Eng.) Residential suburb of London, now part of Greater London. The Rifle Assoc met here, 1860–1888. #E99.

Windham, Sir Charles Ash (1810 to 1870) English gen. He took part in the Crimean War (1854–1856) with success. Elected MP as a Liberal (1857), his political career was cut short the same year when he was posted to India to put down the Indian Mutiny; commanded British troops in Lahore (1857–1861); returned to England (1861); commander in Canada (1867–1870). #E215.

Windischgrätz, Prince Alfred zu; *full* Alfred Candidus Ferdinand; *also spelled* **Windisch-Graetz** (1787 to 1862) Austrian field marshal. Military governor of Bohemia (1840–1848). In the revolution of 1848–1849, a leader of the counterrevolution: suppressed the Prague and Vienna uprisings (1848); headed the suppression of the revolutionary army in Hungary (1849); but defeated at Gödöllö, he was cashiered, proving that brutality is not enough, even for generals. Subseqly, fobbed off with minor posts, he rarely appeared in public life. → *48:72;* #E315, E919.

Wirth, Max (or Maximilian) (1822 to 1900) German economist and statistician. In 1848 he was editor of the liberal *Westfälische Ztg* (Paderborn); banished from Paderborn, he went to Frankfurt, where he and his brother founded (1856) a magazine dealing with economics, free trade, etc., *Der Arbeitgeber*. Later (1864–1873) he was director of the Swiss statistics bureau in Bern. Author of *Grundzüge der National-Oekonomie* (1856–1859), *Geschichte der Handelskrisen* (1858). —His father, Johann Georg August Wirth (1798–1848), was a liberal historian and publicist whose chief work was *Geschichte der Deutschen* (1842–1845), which M (1858) read in its 1846 edn. → *61:56.*

Wischnewetzky, Florence Kelley (1859 to 1932) American socialist and social-reformer; in later years, longtime (1899+) gen secy of the National Consumers League. — Her father, William D. Kelley, a Philadelphia judge and congressman, though conservative, was an early supporter of women's suffrage; she was a lifelong feminist. Educated at Cornell, then at the U. of Zurich, where she met European socialists, she was married abroad (1884) to a Polish-Russian physician, Lazar Wischnewetzky (or Wisnieweski?), who returned to the U.S. with her (1886). In Zurich, in contact with the émigré headquarters of the German Social-Democratic party, she arranged to translate Engels' book #E171 (pubd in 1887; soon after, she translated #M836). —Back in the U.S., she belonged to the SLP (which expelled her for a while for criticizing the leadership), later to the SP and the Intercollegiate Socialist Society (which became the League for Industrial Democracy); she was also a founder of the NAACP; long a vice-pres of the National Woman Suffrage Assoc. —In the late 1880s she began campaigning against child labor, for protective legislation. From Dec 1891 to 1899 she lived and worked at Hull House (Chicago), with Jane Addams, campaigning for labor legislation in alliance with the TUs; on passage of a pioneering state labor law, she was named by Governor Altgeld as chief inspector of factories (1893–1897). In 1899 she was invited to head the National Consumers League (focused on organizing boycott power to enforce better working conditions for store employees in the absence of TU protection); and this was the center of her best-known career. The biography *Impatient crusader* by Josephine Goldmark (1953) is detailed only about this phase; otherwise, see D. R. Blumberg's biography, *FK* (1966). During the 1920s she actively fought the type of Equal Rights Amendment proposed by the Woman's party, one of whose aims was to destroy protective laws for women workers. In 1905 she pubd a book *Some ethical gains through legislation.* —Note: After her divorce in 1891 she used the name "Mrs. Florence Kelley," but during the period of her correspondence with E (1885 to Jan 1889) she used Wischnewetzky. → *84:63; 85:4, 7; 86:4, 9, 10, 25, 33, 34, 51; 87:1, 4, 22, 25, 30, 38, 40, 48; 88:17, 19; 91:55; 92:20.* #M836.

Wiss, C. German liberal journalist, a Young Hegelian; physician by profession. An émigré in London, he moved to the U.S. (beginning of the 1850s), where he was a supporter of Kinkel, contributed to Weitling's *Republik der Arbeiter.* —KMC calls him E. Wiss. → *54:21.*

Woking (Eng.) Town in Surrey, S.W. of London. → *95:37.*

Wolf For various names, see the alternative spelling Wolff.

Wolf, Julius (1862 to 1937) German economist; editor of the *Zeitschrift für Socialwissenschaft* (1898+). Author of *Sozialismus* und kapitalistische Gesellschaftsordnung (1892). His article on M was "Das Rätsel der Durchschnittsprofitrate bei M," in *Jahrbücher für Nationalökonomie und Statistik*, 3. Folge, Bd. 2, 1891. → 92:4, 10.

Wolff, Ferdinand; *sometimes spelled* **Wolf;** *called* der rote Wolff *or* der Rote (Red) (1812 to 1895) German communist journalist, from Cologne. Member of the CCC in Brussels (1846), of the CL in Cologne (1847+). In the revolution of 1848–1849 he was active on the ed bd of the NRZ with M. After the revolution, an émigré in Paris and London; in the 1850 CL split, sided with M; later, withdrew from political activity. → 40:30, 65; 49:29, 31; 50:5; 51:1, 45, 56; 93:48, 56.

Wolff, Luigi Italian Mazzinian republican. An army major, he was an adjutant of Garibaldi, later secy to Mazzini, who lived in England in 1860–1866. W. was a member of the Associazione di Mutuo Progresso in London, took part in the founding meeting of the IWMA; was a member of its GC (1864–1865) seeking to Mazzini-ize its politics. Documents later pubd by the Paris Commune showed him to be in the pay of the Bonaparte regime. — Note: His name is spelled Wolf in some sources; perhaps he used this form in England. → 64:31; 66:17, 18, 21; 71:34.

Wolff, Wilhelm; *full* Johann Friedrich Wilhelm; *nickname* Lupus *or* lupus (1809 to 1864) Son of a Silesian peasant still under serf conditions, he began working his way through Breslau U., with great privations. There, atheist in views, active in the student movement, he collided with the authorities; arrested (1834), jailed (1835), sentenced (1836) to eight years; released (1838). Unable to finish at the univ., he worked as a private tutor; read socialist literature; contributed to the liberal-leftist press. The Silesian weavers' rising (1844) radicalized him and interested him in communism; he read the DFJ and Paris *Vorwärts!*; had to flee Silesia, and eventually came to London; joined the GWEA. In 1846 he came to Brussels; met M&E; joined the CCC's work; and henceforth was a close coworker and friend of M&E. He wrote for the DBZ; was active in the CL (1847+), and in the Demo Assoc. With the outbreak of the 1848 revolution he went with M&E to Paris and thence to Germany. Preceding M&E, he made an organizational tour of a number of German cities, to his native Silesia, arriving in Breslau (Apr 13). There he was active in the Democratic movement, in the May elections (getting elected alternate deputy to the Frankfurt National Assembly), contributed to the left press; then he moved to Cologne, to collaborate directly with M&E on the NRZ. When arrest warrants were issued (Oct) he fled to Dürkheim but returned illegally to Cologne

and worked through the winter. In Mar 1849 he launched a famous series of articles in the NRZ on the "Silesian milliard" (cf. #E918). When the NRZ ended, he left Cologne for the Frankfurt Assembly, took his alternate's seat, and made (May 26) prob the first communist speech in any parliament. Afterward he went to Baden, and after the end of the uprising there, to Switzerland (July 1849). He lived in Zurich by private tutoring; corresponded with M&E; worked to distribute the NRZ-Revue; joined the reform group Revolutionäre Zentralisation and reported to M; finally the Swiss government expelled him (Mar 1851), and he went to London (June). While active in CL affairs with M&E, he suffered from poverty, and planned to go to America for work; but friends found employment for him in the Manchester area, where he moved (Sep 1853). Working as a language teacher, until his death he was E's constant companion and conscience, thus participating in whatever M&E were involved with; traveled occasionally (to Germany, 1861); but suffered much from illness. His will left his library and some money to M. The first volume of *Capital* was dedicated by M to him: "To my unforgettable friend . . . intrepid, faithful, noble protagonist of the proletariat." → 46:16, 34; 47:20, 28; 48:17, 20, 22, 28, 29, 33, 62, 65; 49:11, 15, 19, 37; 50:15, 18, 19, 34; 51:1, 5, 19, 27, 32, 36, 46, 53, 54, 56; 52:22, 39, 47; 53:25, 38, 42; 54:9; 55:41; 56:33; 57:17; 58:13, 28; 59:34, 46; 60:12, 13, 46, 51; 61:26, 35; 62:31, 47; 64:14, 15; 67:24; 76:1, 19, 22, 34; 85:26, 36; 86:24. #ME28, ME31, ME47, ME54B, ME58, ME87; M584; E229, E395.5, E558, E918. *See also* *Heide.

Wollmann, Madame Cousin of F. Fleckles; wife of a paint manufacturer in Paris. The copy of the French *Capital* that M sent her went to her in Carlsbad. It seems that M had met her years before (in Carlsbad?) and thought her "a very interesting lady." The following year (1876) Wollmann lost all his money and also hers in stock speculation, and they retired to Germany. → 75:48.

Wood, Sir Charles; *later* Viscount Halifax (1800 to 1885) English politician; Whig. Chancellor of the Exchequer (1846–1852); pres of the Bd of Control for India (1852–1855); first lord of the Admiralty (1855–1858); secy of state for India (1859–1866); lord privy seal (1870–1874). #M798.

Woodhull, Victoria; *née* **Claflin** (1838 to 1927) American adventurer, briefly a social-reformer and feminist. With her sister, Tennessee C. Claflin (1846–1923), she organized the notorious Section 12 of the IWMA in America as a catchall repository of various faddists and crackpots (spiritualists, funny-money schemers, Free Love prophets, professional atheists, occultists, necromancers, Universal Language saviors, magi of Universology, Pantarchy, etc.) along with advocates of important liberal-progressive reforms like labor laws, women's rights, cooperatives, etc. Her main motivation was an early, persistent ambition to become the first female pres of the U.S. To this end the National Society of Spiritualists, of which she was pres, was more important to her than the IWMA, which she sought to capture as she had done the Spiritualists. For a couple of years, no more, she adopted socialistic-tinged views, while her Section 12 was explicitly antilabor, anti-class-struggle, anticommunist, and mainly a wrecking element within the serious sections of the International. Since she had herself nominated for pres in 1872 by a fabricated "Equal Rights party," feminist writers, seeking a colorful heroine, have made the mistake of glorifying an unscrupulous woman who quickly became an apostate, was transparently motivated by personal ambition, and never furthered the real movement for women's suffrage and equal rights that already existed. Before reaching out to take over the International in America, she had grown up (out of a lumpen-family background which was a genuine snake pit) into an expert spiritualistic faker, evangelistic fraud, medicine-show snake-oil seller, inveterate liar, probable blackmailer, who hit it rich when Cornelius Vanderbilt's money financed the sisters' establishment as stockbrokers (whose broker activity consisted of cashing in on Vanderbilt's market tips) and also financed their *Woodhull & Claflin's Weekly* as their organ of publicity (1870–1876). Her radical-feminist phase, as well as her IWMA connection, was a matter of a brief year or two in a long life mainly devoted to skullduggery. She soon repudiated all progressive beliefs (but not her spiritualism and occultism) as a respectable county matron married to a rich English banker, J. B. Martin. Her vivid, forceful personality and hearty contempt for convention (the latter being her chief claim to sympathy even today) have engendered a number of biographies, of which the most serious one, Emanie Sachs' *The terrible siren* (1928), devotes only a handful of lines to the IWMA connection, mostly garbled. *See* S. Bernstein, *The First International in America* (1962), and #M30. → 72:8, 14, 26.

Woodhull & Claflin's Weekly NY, May 14, 1870, to June 10, 1876, with suspensions in 1872. Weekly. Founded/ed by Victoria Woodhull and T. Claflin. —The weekly, partly representing Woodhull's brief radical period, became the spokesman of the Section 12 faction in the IWMA. → 71:49, 53, 66; 72:19. #ME33; M417, M521, M756, M921.

Worcell, Stanisław (Gabriel) (1799 to 1857) Polish revolutionary. He took part in the Polish uprising of 1830–1831; then went to England. There he was active as a leader of the Democratic wing of the emigration; a founder (1835) of the Polish Democratic Society; friend of Herzen and Mazzini. → 53:32.

Workers Association (Cologne and Rhineland); *Ger.* Arbeiterverein The Cologne WA had several branches during the 1848–1849 revolutionary days, working with the WA in Rhenish cities. It worked in political alliance with the *Democratic Associations; and M&E's circle was active in both. → 48:29, 33, 36, 39, 49, 56, 60, 62, 64, 65, 71, 77, 79, 84, 85; 49:2, 6, 7, 9, 18, 19, 22. #M40, M830.

Workers Association of Ferrara; *Ital.* Società dei Lavoratori Ferraresi #E869.

Workers Associations (in other places) Esp in 1848–1849 Arbeitervereine were organized all over Germany and in foreign cities with substantial German worker émigré populations. For London and Brussels, see the *German Workers Educational Assoc. → 48:19, 27–29, 33, 58, 71, 75, 82; 49:6, 19. #M449, M831; E843.

Workers Party (Fr.) *See* French Workers Party.

Working Men's Union (NY) → 69:30.

Workingmen's (or Working Men's) **International Association** *See* IWMA.

Workman's Advocate London, Sep 9, 1865, to Feb 3, 1866. Weekly. Ed by J. G. Eccarius (Jan 1866+). —Trade-union journal; official organ of the IWMA/GC (Sep 1865+). M was a member of the ed bd. It continued the *Miner and Workman's Advocate* (1863–1865), and was itself reorganized and renamed *The Commonwealth* in Feb 1866. → 65:2, 46, 51, 63; 66:13.

Workman's Times Huddersfield; later London, Manchester. Aug 1890 to Sep 1894. Weekly. Ed by Jos. Burgess. —It absorbed the *Birmingham Workman's Times,* then (1892) the *Trade-Unionist.* → 93:13, 49.

Workmen's Advocate NY, 1885 to Mar 1891. Weekly. Ed by D. De Leon. —Organ of the SLP; superseded by the *People.* → 90:20.

Worringen (Ger.) Town on the Rhine, north of Cologne, now part of that city. → 48:56, 64, 65, 71. #ME124.

Worthing (Eng.) Seaside resort on the Channel, near Brighton. → 84:44.

Wrangel, Count Friedrich Heinrich Ernst von (1784 to 1877) Prussian gen. In 1848 he commanded the troops used to suppress the Prussian assembly in Nov, and to intimidate the popular movement. Created field marshal (1856) and count (1864), he died in bed in Berlin. → 48:76.

Wright, Carroll (Davidson) (1840 to 1909) American economist and statistician. Orig a lawyer and state senator, he was head of the Massachusetts Bureau of Statistics of Labor (1873–1885) and the first U.S. commissioner of labor (1885–1905). He was the outstanding figure in the organization of U.S. labor statistics, before rusticating as pres of Clark College. Author of *The factory system of the U.S.* (1880); *The industrial evolution of the U.S.* (1887). → 79:35.

Wróblewski, Walery (Antoni) (1836 or 1841 to 1908) Polish left-democratic revolutionist. Of a small gentry family, he was orig a pianist and forestry student; worked in Byelorussia while propagandizing for radical-nationalist ideas. He was one of the leaders of the Polish uprising of 1863–1864; wounded; emigrated to Paris, where he gave piano and music lessons. In the Paris Commune, he became a leading general of its forces. An émigré in London, he was a member of the IWMA/GC and corr secy for Poland (1871–1872); active in combating the Bakuninists; well acquainted with M&E. He headed (1872) the Polish democratic society Lud Polski, advocating an alliance of Polish and Russian revolutionaries. He returned to France by 1885; lived in Nice and the Paris area in great poverty and need. After the 1905 Russian revolution, he temporarily returned to Poland; died near Chartres at the home of his friend Dr. Gierzynski; buried in Père Lachaise cemetery. → 71:64; 72:3; 74:19; 75:7, 44, 48; 76:2; 90:31; 91:15; 95:10. #E767.

Wuppertal (Ger.) Valley of the Wupper River; E was born here in Barmen and went to school in Elberfeld. In 1929 these two industrial towns, plus some smaller ones, were merged into the city called Wuppertal. → 39:5, 6, 8; 46:24; 48:32; 49:25. #ME86; E452, E572.

X

Xenophon (c.434–430 B.C. to c.355 B.C. or after) Greek soldier, historian, writer. His best-known work, *Anabasis,* described the retreat of the Ten Thousand from Persia to the Black Sea; *Memorabilia* and *Symposium* are sources on Socrates, of whom he was a disciple; *Oeconomics* dealt with household management; *Cyropaedia* (studied by M in his 1859–1862 notebooks) was an account of the education of Cyrus the Great. M (1844) studied a German edn of his works. → 44:48.

Y

Yanson, Yuli Eduardovich (1835 to 1893) Russian economic statistician. Prof at St. Petersburg (1865–1893); head of the St. Petersburg bureau of statistics (1881+); director of the city census (1881, 1890). He pubd a number of works on theory and history of statistics, e.g., *Teoriya statistiki* (1885); the book M studied in 1881 was possibly *Opit statisticheskago izsledovaniya o krestyanskikh nadelakh i platezhakh* (1877), on the decay of the post-Reform peasant economy. → 81:5.

Yiddish language → 90:4. #E615.5.

York (and Albany), *Duke of.* Frederick Augustus (1763 to 1827) Second son of George III, king of England. Field marshal (1795+); army commander-in-chief (1798–1809, 1811–1827). In 1809 he was removed because of financial diddling; it seems his mistress had trafficked in military appointments. Aside from this temporary embarrassment, his military career was not brilliant, esp against the French Revolutionary armies. M enjoyed this story. #M380.

Yorkshire County in N. England, incl York, Leeds, Sheffield, etc. → 69:35; 80:27; 81:41. *See also* Bolton Abbey, Bridlington Quay.

Young, Arthur (1741 to 1820) English agriculturalist and writer. After a stint of managing a farm, he wrote it up in *Course of experimental agriculture* (1770); edited *Annals of agriculture* (1784–1809); his writings on scientific agronomy had wide influence. But he was best known for books on his travels through the British Isles with sociopolitical observations: *Political arithmetic* (studied by M, 1860); *A tour in Ireland* (studied by M, 1969). → 69:75.

Young Germany The designation, promoted by a ban against their writings issued by the German government (Dec 1835), of a number of writers who expressed aspirations for a more liberalized Germany, united and progressive, esp Ludolf Wienbarg, Karl Gutzkow, Theodor Mundt, Ludwig Börne, and, in the public consciousness, Heine. They did not constitute a group or a movement, or in fact anything but a tendency in thought hostile to the status quo. → 38:2; 39:2, 5; 40:2; 41:3.

Young Hegelians Left-wing followers of *Hegel, who drew radical conclusions from the Master's thought, whether only radical-religious (D. F. Strauss), or radical-philosophical (Feuerbach), or radical-conservative

(B. Bauer), or radical-liberal (A. Ruge), or radical-political (Marx). It was a more or less unorganized tendency in the late 1830s and early 1840s in Germany. → 37:6; 39:1; 41:1, 18, 23; 42:17; 81:52; 89:33. See also Doctors Club; The Free.

Z

Zabel, Friedrich (1802 to 1875) German liberal journalist. Editor of the Berlin *National-Ztg* (1848–1875); member of National-verein. → 60:7, 23, 34; 61:15.

Zabicki, Antoni; *Ger. and Angl.* Anton (c.1810 to 1889) Polish national-revolutionary; typesetter by trade. After the 1830–1831 Polish uprising, he went abroad; in 1848–1849, took part in the Hungarian revolution; afterward, an émigré in England (1851+). He was a leader of the Polish Democratic Society in London; pub'r (1863+) of the organ *Głos Wolny;* secy of the Polish National Comm. He joined the IWMA: member of the GC and corr secy for Poland (1866–1871). → 71:51.

Zaltbommel or Zalt(-)Bommel Town in central Netherlands; the largest nearby city is 's Hertogenbosch. → 61:14, 15, 18; 62:45, 46; 63:41; 64:5, 7, 11, 25; 65:25, 27, 28. #M170.

Zasulich, Vera Ivanovna; *Ger. spelling* **Sassulitsch** (c.1849–1852 to 1919) Russian revolutionary; early Marxist. Of a gentry family, she worked as a schoolteacher; became a Narodnik activist in her late teens; came to St. Petersburg (1868); arrested (1869), released (1871), and exiled; went underground (1875), then moved back to the capital (1877). On Jan 24, 1878, she shot and wounded the St. Petersburg governor Trepov (for ordering the flogging of a political prisoner); acquitted (Apr 1), she emigrated; returned to Russia (1879) aligned with the Black Redistribution group; emigrated again to Switzerland (1880) and worked with Lavrov on aid to prisoners in Russia. By 1883 she joined the early Marxist group Emancipation of Labor; began translating M&E's writings; corresponded with E for the group; pubd a history of the International (1888). An editor of *Iskra* and *Zarya* (1900+), she was early affected by Bernsteinian Revisionism; at the S-D party congress (1903), she sided with the Mensheviks; returned to Russia (1905) permanently; in 1917, supported Plekhanov's group, always hostile to the Bolsheviks. While esteemed for her idealism and integrity, she never played any role as a political thinker or leader. — Her birth date is variously given as 1849, 1851, or 1852. → 81:10, 13; 83:43, 47; 84:20; 85:16; 86:15; 90:17, 18; 93:24, 40; 94:51; 95:10, 14, 15, 24, 37. #M464, M469; E756.

Zedlitz-Neukirch, Baron Konstantin von (b. 1813) Prussian government official. In 1860–1861, Berlin police chief. → 61:15, 17. #M457.

Zeitschrift für Geschichtswissenschaft; German title of Shigaku Zasshi Tokyo, Dec 15, 1889+. #M51, M889.

Zeitung des Arbeiter-Vereines zu Köln See Freiheit, Brüderlichkeit, Arbeit.

Zeitung für den deutschen Adel; also called Adelszeitung Leipzig, then Altenburg, 1840 to 1844 or 1846. Pub'r: Ludwig Alvensleben (till 1842). Ed by Friedrich Fouqué (1840–1842). —Spokesman of the feudalistic nobility. #E677.

Zeitung für Norddeutschland Hanover, 1848 to 1872. Daily —Liberal paper. #M186.

Zemlya i Volya [Land and Freedom] Russian Populist (Narodnik) organization founded in St. Petersburg (1876), took this name in 1878, issued an illegal organ of the same name (1878–1879). Orig looking to a peasant revolution aided by factory workers, it turned toward individual terrorism, and split. → 80:45. See Narodnaya Volya.

Zerffi, Gustav or George Gustavus (1821 to 1892) Hungarian journalist and writer; later active in England. He took part in the revolution of 1848–1849 in Hungary; émigré in Paris (1852), in London (1853+). He was acquainted with M in the early 1850s; later followed Kinkel. KMC alleges that he was an Austrian secret agent. —In later years in London, he pubd prolifically (1871+) on a variety of cultural subjects, esp art history, signing George Gustavus Z. According to KMC, he was in fact an "art historian." Note: Without explanation, MEW states: "real name, Hirsch," and KMC adds "(Piali)" after the name Zerffi. → 52:31, 35, 36, 43, 51; 53:7, 27.

Zetkin, Clara (or Klara); née Eissner (1857 to 1933) German socialist and communist leader—organizer, writer, journalist, etc. She was long the leading figure in what was the most powerful women's movement ever established: the German and (pre-1914) Int'l Socialist women's movement; and she was also a leader of the left wing in the German S-D party and the Socialist Int'l, along with her friend Luxemburg. —Child of a village schoolmaster, she joined the Social-Democrats (1878); left Germany (1882); taught school in various countries; in Paris, joined Ossip *Zetkin. With the rise of the German women's movement, she became its leading organizer and spokesman: editor of *Gleichheit* (1891–1917); active in the International's congresses (1889+); opponent of Bernstein Revisionism. Antiwar in 1914, she joined the Independents (1917), and helped found the Spartacus group, then the CP of Germany (1918); subseqly, member of the Comintern Exec (1921+) and of its Women's Secretariat (1924+). Reichstag deputy (1920–1923). Although a dissident in the Comintern leadership (1921), she did not break with it; lived mainly in Russia in her last decade. → 95:6.

Zetkin, Ossip (1852 to 1889) Russian Marxist revolutionary, from Odessa. Expelled (1874) from Russia for revolutionary activity, he thereafter took part in the German and French movements. He met Clara (see *Zetkin) as a fellow student in Leipzig, where he was active in a group of Russian émigrés and students. Expelled from that city (1881), he went to Paris; joined by Clara (1882); they lived together, without being formally married; had two sons. He suffered from illness for a long time before his death. → 87:11.

Zhukovsky, Vasily Andreyevich (1783 to 1852) Russian poet. Best known were his ballads and his translations (Homer, European literature, etc.); also wrote patriotic odes, including the then national anthem. Tutor of the future Alexander II (1818+). —For other Zhukovskys, see the next entry. → 51:49.

Zhukovsky, Yuli Galaktionovich (1822 to 1907) Russian economist and publicist. Director of the state bank; a senator. During the 1860s he contributed to *Sovremennik* on economic and legal questions; de facto editor of *Narodnaya Letopis* (1865). In M's view, a supporter of "vulgar bourgeois economics." Zh. was the author of an article "KM i ego kniga o kapitalie" [KM and his book on capital] in *Vestnik Yevropy* (Sep 1877) which virulently attacked Marxism and led to much debate. —Note: Not to be confused with the Bakuninist, Nikolai Ivanovich Zhukovsky (1833–1895). → 77:40; 82:19.

Ziber, Nikolai Ivanovich; *Ger. spelling* Nikolaus **Sieber** (1844 to 1888) Russian-Swiss liberal economist. Russian-born son of a Swiss immigrant, orig trained as a lawyer, he followed a stint (1873–1875) as prof of polit eco

at Kiev by settling in Switzerland. In London (1881) he became acquainted with M&E. — He was among the earliest academics in Russia to popularize M's economic work. He contributed articles (1876–1878) to *Znaniye* and *Slovo* expounding M's *Capital*. In 1885 he expanded his 1871 dissertation by publishing his main work, dealing with *David Ricardo and KM and their socioeconomic research.* Although he defended M's economic theory, he did not accept, or understand, M's socialpolitical views; he has been called Russia's first "legal Marxist." —*Caution:* The German transliteration of his name, Sieber, is often found in English, taken over from (erroneous) English edns of *Capital.* → 72:68; 73:16; 74:14; 81:5.

Ziegenhainer German émigré in London. → 51:36.

Znaniye St. Petersburg, 1870 to 1877. Monthly. —Progressive outlook. → 70:54; 74:14.

De **Zuid-Afrikaan;** The Zuid Afrikaan Cape Town (South Africa), 1830 to 1930. — Pubd in English and Afrikaans. → 53:47; 54:5, 14. #M979.

Di **Zukunft** NY, Jan 1892+. Ed by Abr. Cahan. —Yiddish-language socialist organ. → 90:4. #E615.5.

Die **Zukunft** Berlin, 1867 to 1871. Founded/ed by Johann Jacoby. —Liberal journal; organ of the Deutsche Volkspartei. → 67:31, 38, 47; 70:19. #M657; E405, E673, E696.

Die **Zukunft** Berlin, Oct 1877 to Nov 1878. Semimonthly. Pub'r: Karl Höchberg. —Reformist-socialist. → 77:26, 37; 79:33.

Zurich; *Ger.* Zürich In N.E.-central Switzerland, it is the chief city, in population and commerce, of the German-speaking region. → 41:11; 43:4; 50:15; 51:5, 19; 65:62; 69:10; 71:51; 72:3; 74:14, 40; 79:2, 33, 38; 80:12; 81:4; 82:51; 83:29, 31; 84:31, 34, 38, 52, 53; 85:1, 22, 36, 46; 87:19, 32; 88:27; 92:43, 44, 56; 93:20, 40, 42. #E166. —Zurichers: → #ME29.

Zweiffel Prussian official, chief prosecutor in Cologne; in 1848, deputy to the Prussian constituent assembly (right wing). → 48:45, 80.

Supplementary Index

This indexes the names of persons mentioned in the course of Glossary entries. Note: it includes persons only, not periodicals or organizations. The names of Marx and Engels themselves are not indexed. Entries in the Supplementary Index below which are also Glossary entries are marked with an asterisk. Some of these Supplementary entries are *alternative* names given in the text: pseudonyms, real names, some family names. And some (note!) are incorrect forms, as explained in the Glossary. Names like Bonaparte, Louis Philippe, etc., are not indexed when they are used primarily as the label of a historical period, rather than as a reference to the person. And "See" references are not indexed.

Besides its function as a finding device, this Supplementary Index also provides the full names (where available) of persons who are referred to in the text only by surname or by surname plus initials. However, for asterisked entries the entry in the Glossary may have fuller information.

The reference is to the page number followed by a letter (a, b, c, or d) which designates one of the quarters of the page. The first column on a page is divided into a top half (a) and a bottom half (b); the second column likewise divides into (c) and (d). Thus, each page is to be viewed as divided into four equal parts:

a	c
b	d

For example: a reference to 136c is to the top half of the second column on page 136.

A

B

C

D

E

F

G

H

L

N

O

P

Q

R

S

T

U

V

W

Y

Z